# The Routledge Handbook of Language Learning and Technology

The exponential growth and development of modern technologies in all sectors has made it increasingly difficult for students, teachers and teacher educators to know which technologies to employ and how best to take advantage of them.

*The Routledge Handbook of Language Learning and Technology* brings together experts in a number of key areas of development and change, and opens the field of language learning by exploring the pedagogical importance of technological innovation. The handbook is structured around six themes:

- historical and conceptual contexts
- core issues
- interactive and collaborative technologies for language learning
- corpora and data-driven learning
- gaming and language learning
- purpose designed language learning resources.

Led by fundamental concepts, theories and frameworks from language learning and teaching research rather than by specific technologies, this handbook is the essential reference for all teachers, researchers and advanced students of Language Learning, Language Teacher Education, TESOL and Applied Linguistics.

**Fiona Farr** is senior lecturer in TESOL at the University of Limerick. She is author of *The Discourse of Teaching Practice Feedback* (2011) and *Practice in TESOL* (2015).

**Liam Murray** lectures in French and language technologies at the University of Limerick. He is the co-editor of *Quality Issues in ICT Integration: Third Level Disciplines and Learning Contexts* (with T. Hourigan and E. Riordan, 2011).

# Routledge Handbooks in Applied Linguistics

*Routledge Handbooks in Applied Linguistics* provide comprehensive overviews of the key topics in applied linguistics. All entries for the handbooks are specially commissioned and written by leading scholars in the field. Clear, accessible and carefully edited *Routledge Handbooks in Applied Linguistics* are the ideal resource for both advanced undergraduates and postgraduate students.

**The Routledge Handbook of English for Academic Purposes**
Edited by Ken Hyland and Philip Shaw

**The Routledge Handbook of Language and Digital Communication**
Edited by Alexandra Georgakopoulou and Tereza Spilioti

**The Routledge Handbook of Literacy Studies**
Edited by Jennifer Rowsell and Kate Pahl

**The Routledge Handbook of Interpreting**
Edited by Holly Mikkelson and Renée Jourdenais

**The Routledge Handbook of Hispanic Applied Linguistics**
Edited by Manel Lacorte

**The Routledge Handbook of Educational Linguistics**
Edited by Martha Bigelow and Johanna Ennser-Kananen

**The Routledge Handbook of Forensic Linguistics**
Edited by Malcolm Coulthard and Alison Johnson

**The Routledge Handbook of Corpus Linguistics**
Edited by Anne O'Keeffe and Mike McCarthy

**The Routledge Handbook of World Englishes**
Edited by Andy Kirkpatrick

**The Routledge Handbook of Applied Linguistics**
Edited by James Simpson

**The Routledge Handbook of Discourse Analysis**
Edited by James Paul Gee and Michael Handford

**The Routledge Handbook of Second Language Acquisition**
Edited by Susan Gass and Alison Mackey

**The Routledge Handbook of Language and Intercultural Communication**
Edited by Jane Jackson

**The Routledge Handbook of Language Testing**
Edited by Glenn Fulcher and Fred Davidson

**The Routledge Handbook of Multilingualism**
Edited by Marilyn Martin-Jones, Adrian Blackledge and Angela Creese

**The Routledge Handbook of Translation Studies**
Edited by Carmen Millán-Varela and Francesca Bartrina

**The Routledge Handbook of Language and Health Communication**
Edited by Heidi E. Hamilton and Wen-ying Sylvia Chou

**The Routledge Handbook of Language and Professional Communication**
Edited by Stephen Bremner and Vijay Bhatia

# The Routledge Handbook of Language Learning and Technology

*Edited by Fiona Farr and Liam Murray*

First published 2016
by Routledge

2 Park Square, Milton Park, Abingdon, Oxfordshire OX14 4RN
52 Vanderbilt Avenue, New York, NY 10017

*Routledge is an imprint of the Taylor & Francis Group, an informa business*

First issued in paperback 2020

Copyright © 2016 Fiona Farr and Liam Murray

The right of Fiona Farr and Liam Murray to be identified as the authors of the editorial material, and of the authors for their individual chapters, has been asserted in accordance with sections 77 and 78 of the Copyright, Designs and Patents Act 1988.

All rights reserved. No part of this book may be reprinted or reproduced or utilised in any form or by any electronic, mechanical, or other means, now known or hereafter invented, including photocopying and recording, or in any information storage or retrieval system, without permission in writing from the publishers.

Notice:
Product or corporate names may be trademarks or registered trademarks, and are used only for identification and explanation without intent to infringe.

*British Library Cataloguing-in-Publication Data*
A catalogue record for this book is available from the British Library

*Library of Congress Cataloging-in-Publication Data*
Names: Farr, Fiona, 1971- editor. | Murray, Liam.
Title: The Routledge Handbook of language learning and technology / edited by
   Fiona Farr and Liam Murray.
Description: Milton Park, Abingdon, Oxon ; New York, NY : Routledge, [2016] | Series:
   Routledge Handbooks in Applied Linguistics | Includes bibliographical references and index.
Identifiers: LCCN 2015039257 | ISBN 9780415837873 (hbk) | ISBN 9781315657899 (ebk)
Subjects: LCSH: Language and languages—Study and teaching—Technological innovations. |
   Language and languages—Study and teaching—Data processing. | Web-based instruction. |
   Curriculum development—Technological innovations. | Educational technology.
Classification: LCC P53.855 .R68 2016 | DDC 418.0078—dc23
LC record available at http://lccn.loc.gov/2015039257

ISBN: 978-0-415-83787-3 (hbk)
ISBN: 978-0-367-52897-3 (pbk)

Typeset in Bembo
by Apex CoVantage, LLC

# Contents

| | |
|---|---|
| *List of figures* | *xi* |
| *List of tables* | *xiii* |
| *Acknowledgements* | *xiv* |
| *Permissions* | *xv* |
| *List of acronyms* | *xvi* |
| *List of contributors* | *xix* |

Introduction: Language learning and technology   1
*Fiona Farr and Liam Murray*

## PART I
## Historical and conceptual contexts   7

1  Language learning and technology: Past, present and future   9
   *Deborah Healey*

2  Theory in computer-assisted language learning research and practice   24
   *Philip Hubbard and Mike Levy*

3  Towards an 'ecological' CALL theory: Theoretical perspectives and their instantiation in CALL research and practice   39
   *Françoise Blin*

Contents

**PART II**
# Core issues                                                                55

4  Technology standards for language teacher preparation                      57
   *Greg Kessler*

5  Researching participatory literacy and positioning
   in online learning communities                                             71
   *Mirjam Hauck, Rebecca Galley and Sylvia Warnecke*

6  Language materials development in a digital age                            88
   *Gary Motteram*

7  Researching in language learning and technology                           101
   *Mike Levy*

8  Literacies, technology and language teaching                              115
   *Gavin Dudeney and Nicky Hockly*

9  Evaluation in CALL: Tools, interactions, outcomes                         127
   *Catherine Caws and Trude Heift*

10 Language testing and technology                                           141
   *James Dean Brown*

11 From age and gender to identity in technology-mediated
   language learning                                                         160
   *Elisabeth (Hayes) Gee and Yoonhee N. Lee*

12 Culture, language learning and technology                                 173
   *Robert Godwin-Jones*

13 Language learning and technology in varied technology contexts            185
   *Hyun Gyung Lee and Joy Egbert*

14 Limitations and boundaries in language learning and technology            197
   *Richard Kern and Dave Malinowski*

15 Teacher education and technology                                          210
   *Elizabeth Hanson-Smith*

16 Sustainable CALL development                                              223
   *Françoise Blin, Juha Jalkanen and Peppi Taalas*

## PART III
## Interactive and collaborative technologies for language learning          239

17  Telecollaboration and language learning                                  241
    *Francesca Helm and Sarah Guth*

18  Social networking and language learning                                  255
    *Lara Lomicka and Gillian Lord*

19  Computer supported collaborative writing
    and language learning                                                    269
    *Muriel Grosbois*

20  Interactive whiteboards and language learning                            281
    *Euline Cutrim Schmid*

21  Mobile language learning                                                 296
    *Glenn Stockwell*

22  Virtual worlds and language learning: An analysis of research            308
    *Mark Peterson*

23  Online and blended language learning                                     320
    *Pete Sharma and Kevin Westbrook*

## PART IV
## Corpora and data-driven learning                                          335

24  Introduction to data-driven learning                                     337
    *Martin Warren*

25  Spoken language corpora and pedagogical applications                     348
    *Andrew Caines, Michael McCarthy and Anne O'Keeffe*

26  Written language corpora and pedagogical applications                    362
    *Angela Chambers*

27  Learner corpora and pedagogical applications                             376
    *Fanny Meunier*

28  Corpus types and uses                                                    388
    *Bróna Murphy and Elaine Riordan*

Contents

29  Designing and building corpora for language learning  404
    Randi Reppen

## PART V
## Gaming and language learning  413

30  Metaphors for digital games and language learning  415
    Jonathon Reinhardt and Steven Thorne

31  Mini-games for language learning  431
    Frederik Cornillie and Piet Desmet

32  Gaming and young language learners  446
    Pia Sundqvist

## PART VI
## Purpose designed language learning resources  459

33  CALL tools for lexico-grammatical acquisition  461
    Li Li

34  CALL tools for reading and writing  478
    Hsien-Chin Liou

35  CALL tools for listening and speaking  491
    Úna Clancy and Liam Murray

36  Multimodality and CALL  509
    Nicolas Guichon and Cathy Cohen

37  Intelligent CALL and written language  522
    Cornelia Tschichold and Mathias Schulze

38  Translation and technology: The case of translation
    games for language learning  536
    Pierrette Bouillon, Cristiana Cervini and Manny Rayner

Index  550

# Figures

| | | |
|---|---|---|
| 1.1 | Interaction from *London Adventure* | 10 |
| 1.2 | Entrance to SchMOOze University | 16 |
| 3.1 | Illustration of Bronfenbrenner's (1979) nested ecosystems | 43 |
| 3.2 | Representation of a CALL activity system | 45 |
| 3.3 | Nested affordances in CALL ecosystems | 49 |
| 5.1 | Glogster poster 1, Malgorzata – Tuesday, 17 January 2012, 06:44 PM | 74 |
| 5.2 | Glogster poster 2, Maria – Monday, 23 January 2012, 12:58 AM | 75 |
| 5.3 | Community Indicators Framework by Galley et al. (2011) | 82 |
| 5.4 | Revised CIF | 84 |
| 6.1 | A sociocultural representation of a teacher's materials creation domain, showing its complexity | 93 |
| 9.1 | Life cycle of the tool development and implementation | 130 |
| 14.1 | Kaleidoscope analogy | 202 |
| 15.1 | Communities of practice in relationship to networks, communities and groups | 218 |
| 16.1 | Two models for sustainable development | 224 |
| 16.2 | SpeakApps sustainability roadmap | 230 |
| 16.3 | The four pillars of sustainable CALL | 235 |
| 17.1 | The UNICollaboration platform homepage | 251 |
| 19.1 | Abstract of text produced as a result of collaborative practice | 270 |
| 19.2 | Chat exchange preparing for common text (displayed in Figure 19.1) | 272 |
| 19.3 | Chat excerpt about attention to form | 273 |
| 20.1 | Classroom interactive display penetration | 283 |
| 23.1 | Blended learning: Synchronous and asynchronous communication | 321 |
| 26.1 | Verbs following *thesis* in Lextutor | 365 |
| 26.2 | Phrases including *thesis* in Lextutor | 365 |
| 26.3 | The use of *we* in statements of purpose | 367 |
| 26.4 | *Permettre* in *Le Monde* in 1998 | 368 |
| 26.5 | The use of *nous* (*we, us*) in single-authored research articles in French | 370 |
| 29.1 | WordSmith 6.0 plot showing position of *however* in texts | 409 |
| 29.2 | Examples from the KWIC of *however* using WordSmith 6.0 | 409 |
| 31.1 | Mini-game *Article Wolf*, providing focused practice of English articles in the meaningful context of a story | 437 |
| 31.2 | Mini-game *Johnny Grammar's Word Challenge*, providing practice of vocabulary and grammar with time pressure | 438 |

# Figures

| | | |
|---|---|---|
| 33.1 | A screenshot of Vsee used to provide immediate corrective feedback, with short transcription of included text | 471 |
| 33.2 | Concordance for *suggest* | 472 |
| 35.1 | Common audio icon | 502 |
| 35.2 | Common audio icon with IPA transcription and spell options | 502 |
| 35.3 | Audio icon option showing individual syllables | 503 |
| 38.1 | Screenshot of CALL-SLT interface for version used in experiments at University of Bologna | 541 |
| 38.2 | Screenshot of multimodal version of CALL-SLT | 542 |

# Tables

| | | |
|---|---|---|
| 1.1 | Roles of teacher, learner and technology | 15 |
| 4.1 | Basic and advanced skills for classroom teachers | 64 |
| 5.1 | Training programme overview | 73 |
| 5.2 | Swan's (2002) adaptation of the Social Presence template developed by Rourke et al. (1999) | 76 |
| 6.1 | Materials design flow chart | 92 |
| 7.1 | Summary of benefits and limitations of interactionist theory for CALL | 105 |
| 10.1 | Acronyms used in this chapter for current computer-based tests and testing systems | 142 |
| 10.2 | What we have learned about language testing and technology | 143 |
| 10.3 | Drawbacks of using computers in language testing | 147 |
| 10.4 | Benefits of using computers in language testing | 151 |
| 14.1 | Examples of technology both creating and transcending limits and boundaries | 201 |
| 16.1 | Examples of SpeakApps sustainability indicators | 231 |
| 17.1 | Framework for the goals of telecollaboration proposed by Helm and Guth (2010) | 244 |
| 18.1 | Representative SNS | 261 |
| 22.1 | Significant findings on the use of virtual worlds in CALL | 316 |
| 23.1 | Test results, general English courses, Level B2, January 2014 | 330 |
| 25.1 | Highly frequent second person interrogative zero auxiliary patterns in the spoken section of the BNC | 356 |
| 31.1 | Examples of DGBLL according to two dimensions | 435 |
| 31.2 | Linguistic-pedagogical attributes of mini-games | 436 |
| 31.3 | Game attributes of mini-games | 437 |
| 32.1 | Categorisation of *WoW* and *The Sims* according to three models | 453 |
| 36.1 | Modes and media in different temporalities | 510 |
| 36.2 | Semio-pedagogical competence | 518 |

# Acknowledgements

An undertaking on the scale of a 38-chapter volume is always going to be a very collaborative endeavour, as this one was. We are extremely grateful to a number of people for their support and involvement in the making of this handbook. First, a strong word of appreciation to all of the contributors and reviewers for their participation – working with such esteemed colleagues has been a pleasure, and we thank you for your patience during the process, and your patience with us as we worked through it. We would like to express our thanks to Louisa Semlyen, Rosemary Baron, Sophie Jaques, Laura Sandford and all of the team at Routledge, who were always available and incredibly responsive. Finally, we would like to acknowledge the support of friends and colleagues at the Centre for Teaching and Learning, and the School of Modern Languages and Applied Linguistics at the University of Limerick.

# Permissions

The publishers, editors and relevant authors would like to thank the following for permission to reproduce previously published material:

Figure 1.2: From SchMOOze University (http://schmooze.hunter.cuny.edu/)
Figure 15.1: From Vance Stevens (http://www.slideshare.net/vances/the-webheads-and-distributed-communities-of-practice)
Figure 20.1: From Futuresource Consulting
Figure 31.1: From Biscuit Software Ltd
Figure 31.2: From the British Council

Every effort has been made to contact copyright holders. Please advise the publisher of any errors or omissions, and these will be corrected in subsequent editions.

# Acronyms

| | |
|---|---|
| AES | automatic essay scoring |
| AI | artificial intelligence |
| ANC | American National Corpus |
| BASE | British Academic Spoken English Corpus |
| BAWE | British Academic Written English Corpus |
| BL | blended learning |
| BNC | British National Corpus |
| BoE | Bank of English |
| CALL | computer-assisted language learning |
| CALL-IS | Computer-Assisted Language Learning Interest Section of the TESOL professional organisation |
| CANBEC | Cambridge and Nottingham Business English Corpus |
| CANCODE | Cambridge and Nottingham Corpus of Discourse in English |
| CANELC | Cambridge and Nottingham E-Language Corpus |
| CCLE | Cambridge Corpus of Legal English |
| CCTFC | Contemporary Chinese Translated Fiction Corpus |
| CEEC | Corpus of Early English Correspondence |
| CEEM | Corpus of Early English Medical Writing |
| CEFR | Common European Framework of Reference |
| CMC | computer-mediated communication |
| COCA | Corpus of Contemporary American English |
| *CoD* | *Call of Duty* |
| COHA | Corpus of Historical American English |
| COIL | collaborative online international learning |
| COLT | Corpus of London Teenage English |
| CoP | community of practice |
| CORIS | Corpus di Italiano Scritto |
| COTS games | commercial-off-the-shelf games |
| *CS* | *Counter-Strike* |
| CSCW | computer supported collaborative writing |
| CSPAE | Corpus of Spoken Professional American English |
| EAP | English for academic purposes |
| EFL | English as a foreign language |
| ELDA | Evaluations and Language Resources Distribution Agency |
| ELFA | English as a Lingua Franca in Academic Settings Corpus |

| | |
|---|---|
| ELLiE Project | Early Language Learning in Europe Project |
| ELT | English language teaching |
| ENPC | English-Norwegian Parallel Corpus |
| ENSIC | English Native Speaker Interview Corpus |
| ESP | English for specific purposes |
| ESPC | English-Swedish Parallel Corpus |
| EVO | Electronic Village Online |
| F2F | face-to-face |
| FLOB | Freiberg London-Oslo/Bergen Corpus |
| FROWN | Freiberg Brown Corpus of American English |
| *GTA* | *Grand Theft Auto* |
| IATEFL | International Association of Teachers of English as a Foreign Language |
| ICALL | Intelligent CALL |
| ICC | intercultural communicative competence |
| ICE | International Corpus of English |
| ICFLE | Internet-mediated intercultural foreign language education |
| ICLE | International Corpus of Learner English |
| ICT | information and communications technologies |
| IM | instant messaging |
| ITS | intelligent tutoring systems |
| IWB | interactive whiteboard |
| L1 | first language |
| L2 | second and foreign language |
| LCMC | Lancaster Corpus of Mandarin Chinese |
| LEP | LearnEnglish Pathways |
| LINDSEI | Louvain International Database of Spoken English Interlanguage |
| LMS | learner management system |
| LOB | London-Oslo/Bergen Corpus |
| *LoL* | *League of Legends* |
| LTSIG | Learning Technology Special Interest Group of the IATEFL professional association |
| MALL | mobile-assisted language learning |
| MATESOL | Master of Arts in Teaching English to Speakers of Other Languages |
| MERLOT | Multimedia Educational Resource for Learning and Teaching Online, California State University System |
| MICASE | Michigan Corpus of Academic Spoken English |
| MICUSP | Michigan Corpus of Upper-level Student Papers |
| M-learning | mobile learning |
| MMORPG | massively multiplayer online role-playing game |
| MMO games | massively multiplayer online games |
| MOOC | massive open online course |
| NBLT | network-based language teaching |
| NLP | natural language processing |
| NNMC | Nottingham Multimodal Corpus |
| OER | open educational resource |
| OIE | online intercultural exchange |
| OL | online learning |

## Acronyms

| | |
|---|---|
| OLPC | one laptop per child |
| OMC | Oslo Multilingual Corpus |
| OPUS | Open Parallel Corpus |
| PC | personal computer |
| PLE | personal learning environment |
| PLN | personal learning network |
| RPG | role-playing game |
| RSS | really simple syndication |
| SACODEYL | System Aided Compilation and Open Distribution of European Youth Language |
| SBCSAE | Santa Barbara Corpus of Spoken American English |
| SCMC | synchronous communication chat |
| SEN | special educational needs |
| SLA | second language acquisition |
| SOLE | self-organised learning environment |
| SSI Model | Scale of Social Interaction Model |
| TEC | Translational English Corpus |
| TESOL | Teachers of English to Speakers of Other Languages professional association, or Teaching English to Speakers of Other Languages |
| TNC | Turkish National Corpus |
| VLE | virtual learning environment |
| VOICE | Vienna-Oxford International Corpus of English |
| VSL | Virtual Software Library, Diigo, sponsored by the TESOL CALL-IS |
| WiA | Webheads in Action |
| *WoW* | *World of Warcraft* |
| ZPD | zone of proximal development |

# Contributors

**Françoise Blin** is senior lecturer in the School of Applied Language and Intercultural Studies at Dublin City University (Ireland). She is co-editor of *ReCALL* and the current president of the European Association for Computer Assisted Language Learning (EUROCALL). Her more recent work focuses on the applications of ecological and activity theoretical approaches to CALL research, design and practice.

**Pierrette Bouillon** is ordinary professor and vice dean at Geneva University's Faculty of Translation and Interpretation. She has coordinated various projects in the fields of machine translation and speech technology (in particular the European project ACCEPT 'Automated Community Content Editing PorTal', 2011–2014 and the Swiss project CALL-SLT, 'A generic platform for CALL based on speech translation', 2009–2012) and has numerous publications in natural language processing.

**James Dean Brown** is professor in the Department of Second Language Studies at the University of Hawai'i at Mānoa and director of the National Foreign Languages Resource Center in Hawai'i. He has spoken and taught courses in places ranging from Brazil to Yugoslavia, and has published numerous articles and books on language testing, curriculum design, programme evaluation and research methods.

**Andrew Caines** is a postdoctoral researcher in the Institute for Research in Automated Language Teaching and Assessment at the University of Cambridge. He has published research on the effect of document length and the effect of topic on language features in learner corpora. His doctoral dissertation was on zero auxiliaries in spoken British English.

**Catherine Caws** is an associate professor of French applied linguistics at the University of Victoria, Canada. Her research focuses on the nature and effects of electronic learning environments on second language learners, in particular on task-tool-learner interactions.

**Cristiana Cervini** has a PhD in educational linguistics and teaches 'Foreign language teaching and learning' at the Lingue, Letterature e Culture Moderne (LILEC) Dep. (University of Bologna). Her present studies focus on assessment and evaluation and on CALL systems for hybrid and self-learning. She is currently in charge of the Système d'évaluation en Langues à visée formative (SELF) research and development actions in the frame of the Initiatives d'Excellence en Formations Innovantes (IDEFI) Innovalangues project (Langues pour Spécialistes d'Autres Disciplines, Grenoble 3).

Contributors

**Angela Chambers** is professor emerita of applied languages at the University of Limerick. Her research interests focus on the use of corpora in language learning, with particular reference to French. She has published extensively in this area, as well as creating two corpora in French, of journalistic discourse and research articles. These are available through the Oxford Text Archive.

**Úna Clancy** is currently a research fellow in the School of Modern Languages and Applied Linguistics at the University of Limerick, Ireland. Her research area is the acoustic aspect of spoken language and the bearing this has on early language acquisition, specifically during the prenatal period of development. She holds an MA in TESOL and has been teaching in the field since 2007.

**Cathy Cohen** obtained her PhD in linguistics in 2011. She has been an associate professor at the teacher training college at Lyon 1 University France since 2012, where she gives courses to trainee teachers on language pedagogy and bilingualism. She is a member of the ICAR research laboratory (*Interactions, Corpus, Apprentissages, Représentations*) and her research interests include language pedagogy, teacher education, computer-mediated communication and bilingual acquisition in children and young learners.

**Frederik Cornillie**, PhD, is a senior researcher in applied linguistics (computer-assisted language learning) at KU Leuven (University of Leuven) and iMinds, Belgium. His research is situated at the intersection of tutorial CALL, second language acquisition and digital games, and he takes a particular interest in corrective feedback, skill acquisition and individual differences. He was guest editor of the special issue of *ReCALL* on digital game-based language learning.

**Euline Cutrim Schmid** is full professor of TEFL and applied linguistics at the University of Education Schwäbisch Gmünd in Germany. She teaches at undergraduate and postgraduate levels on a variety of topics including: CALL, applied linguistics, and qualitative research methodologies.

**Piet Desmet** is full professor of French and applied linguistics and computer-assisted language learning at KU Leuven and KU Leuven KULAK, Belgium. He coordinates the iMinds research team ITEC (Interactive Technologies), focusing on domain-specific educational technology with a main interest in language learning and technology. He leads a range of research projects devoted amongst others to serious gaming and to the effectiveness of adaptive and personalised learning environments.

**Gavin Dudeney and Nicky Hockly** co-run the award-winning educational consultancy 'The Consultants-E' (http://www.theconsultants-e.com), specialising in teacher training in the application of technologies in the classroom. They have also co-written a number of books about technology in ELT.

**Joy Egbert** is professor of ESL and Education Technology at Washington State University, USA. She has published and presented widely in the areas of CALL, teacher education and education technology. Her interests are engagement and differentiation.

**Fiona Farr** is senior lecturer in TESOL at the University of Limerick. She has published in journals such as *ReCALL*, *TESOL Quarterly*, *Language Awareness*, *Language Teaching* and *Classroom*

*Discourse.* She is author of *The Discourse of Teaching Practice Feedback* (2011) and *Practice in TESOL* (2015). Her research interests include language teacher education, technology, reflective practice and applied corpus linguistics.

**Rebecca Galley** leads the learning design team in the Institute of Education Technology at the Open University, UK. She is interested in how collaborative spaces – face-to-face and online – can be used to promote innovation in learning and teaching, and lead to changes in pedagogical practice. Rebecca has been teaching since 1995 and her broader background is in professional development and training, and informal learning and assessment.

**Elisabeth (Hayes) Gee** is Delbert & Jewell Lewis Chair in Reading and Literacy and associate director, Center for Games and Impact at Mary Lou Fulton Teachers College, Arizona State University. Recent publications include *Language and Learning in a Digital Age* (with J. Gee, 2011) and *Learning in Game-Based Affinity Spaces* (co-edited with S. Duncan, 2012).

**Robert Godwin-Jones** is professor of world languages and international studies at Virginia Commonwealth University. His research is principally in applied linguistics, in the areas of language learning and technology, and intercultural communication. He has published four books, multiple articles and book chapters, and writes a regular column for *Language Learning & Technology* on emerging technologies.

**Muriel Grosbois** is an associate professor in applied linguistics at the School of Education of the University Paris–Sorbonne, France. She is head of the Centre for Digital Resources in Languages and Cultures. Her research and teaching focus on L2 learning in a technology-enhanced context.

**Nicolas Guichon** is a professor in language sciences at the University of Lyon 2 and belongs to the ICAR (*Interactions, Corpus, Apprentissages, Représentations*) research team. His research interests include teacher education in computer-assisted language learning (CALL), the study of online interaction and materials design.

**Sarah Guth** teaches English language at the University of Padova and is a consultant for the State University of New York (SUNY) COIL Center. She has extensive experience in telecollaborative practice and teacher training and has presented and published internationally. Her current research focuses on curricular internationalisation.

**Elizabeth Hanson-Smith** has been an educator of international teachers for over twenty-five years, working in China, Sri Lanka, Belize, Russia and Egypt, as well as providing online courses for the US Department of State and the University of Oregon. Formerly head of the California State University, Sacramento TESOL Program, she offers free ESL/EFL resources at her website: http://webpages.csus.edu/~hansonsm. Recent publications include *TESOL Technology Standards* (Alexandria, VA: TESOL, 2008).

**Mirjam Hauck** is a senior lecturer in the Faculty of Education and Language Studies at the Open University, UK. She has written numerous articles and book chapters on the use of technologies for the learning and teaching of languages and cultures covering aspects such as task design, tutor role and training, and digital literacy skills. She is the associate editor of the *CALL* journal and an editorial board member of *ReCALL*.

**Deborah Healey** teaches online and face-to-face teacher education courses at the University of Oregon's American English Institute and Gabon Oregon Center. She is a member of the board of directors of TESOL International. She writes and presents extensively internationally on appropriate use of technology in language teaching. Her doctorate is in computers in education.

**Trude Heift** is professor of linguistics at Simon Fraser University, Canada. Her main research areas combine aspects of SLA and ICALL with a focus on the design as well as the evaluation of CALL systems.

**Francesca Helm** is a researcher and English teacher at the Department of Political Science at the University of Padova, Italy. She has extensive experience in online education and telecollaboration. Her research focuses on language and intercultural learning, telecollaboration and most recently on internationalisation policy in higher education.

**Philip Hubbard** is senior lecturer in linguistics and director of English for foreign students at the Stanford University Language Center. His CALL work includes courseware authoring and publications in software development and evaluation, technology and listening, teacher education, learner training, research, and theory. He edited the four-volume series *Computer Assisted Language Learning: Critical Concepts in Linguistics* (Routledge, 2009) and was on the team of six that produced the TESOL Technology Standards (TESOL, 2008). He is an associate editor of *Language Learning & Technology* and *Computer Assisted Language Learning*, and serves on the editorial boards of the *CALICO Journal* and *ReCALL*.

**Juha Jalkanen,** MA, works as a lecturer at the University of Jyväskylä Language Centre in Finland. His research interests include organisational learning in educational contexts and co-design of language learning and teaching practices. His doctoral research addresses pedagogical development in technology-rich environments for language teaching and learning. He has experience with national and international research and development projects.

**Richard Kern** is professor of French and director of the Berkeley Language Center at the University of California, Berkeley. He teaches courses in French linguistics, applied linguistics and foreign language pedagogy. His research interests include second language acquisition, reading, writing and technology. He is associate editor of the journal *Language Learning & Technology*, recently released the book *Language, Literacy, and Technology* (Cambridge University Press, 2015) and is currently co-editing a book on screens and representations in videoconferencing.

**Greg Kessler** is director of the Language Resource Centre and associate professor of CALL at Ohio University. He is currently editor of the Action Research Column for the journal *Language Learning & Technology*. He co-authored the TESOL Technology Standards.

**Hyun Gyung Lee** is a postdoctoral researcher at Washington State University, where she earned her PhD in 2012. Her major research interests are L2 learner engagement, CALL, and ESL/EFL curriculum development. She has published and presented on these topics in a number of international forums.

**Yoonhee N. Lee** earned her PhD in curriculum and instruction in the language and literacy concentration and teaches at Arizona State University. Her research interests centre on improving the understanding, design and implementation of learning practices with technology in English Language Learning (ELL) education in and out of the classroom. She envisions technology will greatly enhance second language acquisition and ELL education.

**Mike Levy** is professor of second language studies and director of the Brisbane Universities Language Alliance (BULA) in the School of Languages and Comparative Cultural Studies at the University of Queensland, Brisbane, Australia. His research work includes studies on the distinctive role of technology in mediating language learning, mobile language learning, online cultures and culture as concept, teacher education and learner training. His publications include *WorldCALL* (Routledge, 2011), *CALL Dimensions* (with Glenn Stockwell, Routledge, 2006) and *Teacher Education in CALL* (with Philip Hubbard, Benjamins, 2006). He served as chair of the steering committee for the WorldCALL 2013 Conference (http://www.worldcall2013.org/).

**Li Li** is senior lecturer and director of the MEd in TESOL in the Graduate School of Education, University of Exeter. Her main research interests include new technologies in language education, language teacher cognitions, developing thinking skills and classroom interaction.

**Hsien-Chin Liou** is a professor in the Department of Foreign Languages and Literature, Feng Chia University (Taiwan ROC), and has conducted research on CALL over the past twenty-five years. Her interests include corpus applications, Web 2.0 technologies and CALL for writing, reading and vocabulary learning.

**Lara Lomicka** is professor of French at the University of South Carolina, where she currently serves as Graduate Director for Languages. She has received the Language Instruction Using Technology award from ACTFL/Cengage Publishers and was recently honoured as a Chevalier dans l'Ordre des Palmes académiques. Her research interests include teacher education, intercultural learning, social media, study abroad and CALL/MALL.

**Gillian Lord** is associate professor of Spanish and linguistics at the University of Florida, where she is also chair of the Department of Spanish and Portuguese Studies. Her research focuses on language teaching and learning in both the classroom and immersion settings, focusing primarily on the acquisition of foreign language sound systems as well as on the role of technology in language acquisition and education.

**Dave Malinowski** is language technology and research specialist with the Center for Language Study at Yale University. His research explores the effects and consequences of technology and place in mediating intercultural understanding and subjectivity in second language learning contexts. He holds a PhD in education from the University of California, Berkeley.

**Michael McCarthy** is emeritus professor of applied linguistics at the University of Nottingham, UK. He is author/editor and co-author/co-editor of more than 50 books, including *The Routledge Handbook of Corpus Linguistics* (Routledge, 2010), and more than 100 articles on language teaching and on vocabulary, grammar, spoken discourse and spoken corpus linguistics.

**Fanny Meunier** is a professor of English language, linguistics and didactics at the University of Louvain (UCL, Belgium). She has been involved in learner corpus research for over twenty years and her main research interest is the link between second language acquisition (SLA) studies and pedagogical applications. She is also actively involved in pre- and in-service teacher training.

**Gary Motteram** is a senior lecturer in education at the University of Manchester, UK. His latest book is *Innovations in Learning Technologies for ELT* (2013), produced for the British Council. You can find out more on his blog (http://garymotteram.net).

**Bróna Murphy** is lecturer in language education at the University of Edinburgh. Her principal research areas span corpus linguistics, spoken discourse and sociolinguistics. Her work involves looking at small specialised sociolinguistic-oriented corpora to explore functionally motivated linguistic variation across social groups.

**Liam Murray** lectures in French and language technologies at the University of Limerick. He is reviews editor of *ReCALL*. He has published in journals such as *AJET*, *System*, *Eludamos*, *Computer Game Culture*, *Classroom Discourse*, *Educational Media International*, *ReCALL* and *Learning, Media and Technology*.

**Anne O'Keeffe** is senior lecturer in applied linguistics at Mary Immaculate College, University of Limerick, Ireland. She is author of numerous publications on corpus linguistics, media discourse and language teaching. She has published six books and has co-edited *The Routledge Handbook of Corpus Linguistics* (Routledge, 2010).

**Mark Peterson** is associate professor at Kyoto University. He is author of *Computer Games and Language Learning* (2013). His current research investigates the use of network-based virtual worlds and digital games in foreign language education. His website is located at http://www.peterson.h.kyoto-u.ac.jp/.

**Manny Rayner** is a senior researcher at Geneva University's Faculty of Translation and Interpretation, and has previously held positions at SRI International, NASA Ames Research Center and two language technology start-ups. He has over one hundred refereed publications in human language technology and computational linguistics.

**Jonathon Reinhardt** is associate professor in the Department of English and faculty in the Second Language Acquisition and Teaching programme at the University of Arizona. He is director of the Games for Literacies Project at CERCLL, the university's National Foreign Language Resource Center. His research interests are in exploring the relationship between changes in sociocultural, educational and technological practice and the theory and practice of technology-enhanced second and foreign language pedagogy, focusing especially on emergent technologies like social media and digital gaming.

**Randi Reppen** is professor of applied linguistics and TESL at Northern Arizona University. She has a keen interest in using corpus research to inform language teaching and teaching materials. Randi is the author of *Using Corpora in the Language Classroom* (Cambridge, 2010) and the lead author of *Grammar and Beyond* (Cambridge, 2012), and co-editor of *The Cambridge Handbook of English Corpus Linguistics* (2015).

**Elaine Riordan** is a lecturer in TESOL at the University of Limerick, Ireland. Her research interests include language teacher education, corpus linguistics, new technologies for language teaching and learning, and computer-mediated communication (CMC).

**Mathias Schulze** is a professor of German (applied linguistics) at the University of Waterloo, Canada, the director of the Waterloo Centre for German Studies, and the editor of the *CALICO Journal* (together with Bryan Smith). He has published his research on Tutorial CALL (in particular Intelligent CALL) and online language learning in journal articles and books. For a number of years, he has been interested in the application of Complexity Theory to the study of second language development in CALL.

**Pete Sharma** is a lecturer in EAP (English for academic purposes). As an author, he has written extensively on technology in language teaching, including as co-author *Blended Learning* (Macmillan 2007), *Key Concepts in ELT: Blended Learning* for ELTJ (ELT Journal (OUP), 2010), and has edited the *CALL Review* (newsletter of the IATEFL Learning Technologies SIG). He has a master's degree in educational technology in ELT.

**Glenn Stockwell** is professor in applied linguistics at Waseda University, Tokyo, Japan. His research interests include mobile learning, motivation and technology, and technology integration in language learning. He has published two books and numerous book chapters and articles in the field of CALL. He is editor-in-chief of the *JALT CALL Journal*, associate editor of *Computer Assisted Language Learning* and *Language Learning & Technology*, and is on the editorial boards of *ReCALL*, *System* and the *CALICO Journal*.

**Pia Sundqvist** holds a PhD in English linguistics from Karlstad University, Sweden, where she is associate professor of English at the Faculty of Arts and Social Sciences. Her main research interests are informal language learning, L2 vocabulary acquisition and assessment.

**Peppi Taalas**, PhD, adjunct professor, works as the director of the University of Jyväskylä Language Centre, Finland. Her research is on educational and organisational change on policy and practice levels, including change in learning and teaching cultures in technology-rich settings. She has been in many national and international projects in the areas of knowledge society, teaching innovation and the future of education.

**Steven Thorne** is associate professor of second language acquisition in the Department of World Languages and Literatures at Portland State University (USA), with a secondary appointment in the Department of Applied Linguistics at the University of Groningen (Netherlands). He has a PhD from the University of California, Berkeley. His research utilises cultural-historical, usage-based, distributed and critical approaches to language development, often with a focus on human interactivity in technology-culture contexts.

**Cornelia Tschichold** is a senior lecturer at Swansea University. She has worked on grammar checking and on English multiword units in computational lexicography. Her current research interests include the acquisition of vocabulary and phraseology, computer-assisted language learning (CALL) in general and digital vocabulary trainers in particular, and learning words that are translation-ambiguous.

Contributors

**Sylvia Warnecke** is lecturer in German at the Department of Languages at the Open University, UK. In addition to teaching since 2003, she has designed blended learning teacher training and language courses. Her special interests are synchronous/asynchronous online facilitation, identity, participation, task design and tutor role. Her current research explores social presence as a central driving force in collaborative CALL and teaching.

**Martin Warren** is professor of English language studies in the English Department of the Hong Kong Polytechnic University and a member of its Research Centre for Professional Communication in English. He teaches and researches in the areas of corpus linguistics, discourse analysis, intercultural communication, lexical semantics, pragmatics and professional communication.

**Kevin Westbrook** is a lecturer in EAP (English for academic purposes) and director of training at Pete Sharma Associates Limited. His duties involve online materials writing, teacher training and consultancy in the area of learning technologies. He has a master's degree in applied linguistics for language teaching.

# Introduction
# Language learning and technology

*Fiona Farr and Liam Murray*

As Ray Clifford of the Defense Language Institute put it: 'Computers will not replace teachers. However, teachers who use computers will replace teachers who don't' (quoted in Healey et al. 2008: 2). Technology, in some form or another, has been with the language teaching profession for many years, and teachers have succeeded to various degrees in integrating general or specific tools into their pedagogical practices. Technology-enhanced practices have revolutionised the ways in which we learn and teach languages. In the space of the last thirty years, the field of language learning and technology research and application has branched out to many areas, for example, interactive and collaborative technologies, corpora and data-driven learning, computer gaming and tailor designed tools, to name but some. However, the rate and extent of technological development over the past ten to fifteen years have been making it increasingly difficult for students, teachers and teacher educators to know what technologies to employ and how best to employ them in a global society of ever new and enhanced modes of communication.

As a result of the expansion and progress in the area, it is timely to bring together experts in a number of key areas of development and change. The aim of this handbook is to help to open the field to novices, many of whom will be technology users and digitally literate but may not have considered the role that it can play in language learning. When undergraduates or postgraduates begin studying in this area, they are often daunted by what seems like an endless array of choices and applications. An added difficulty comes from the often ephemeral nature of some of the technologies. It can be difficult to tell where it all began, where it is going and what it means. This book provides a guide through the key areas that prospective or practising teachers might need. It is led by fundamental concepts, theories and frameworks from language learning and teaching research rather than by specific technologies, so that when the inevitable happens and some of the technologies are replaced over time, professionals will be left with the requisite attributes to continue to make well-informed choices in relation to integration in their future teaching.

Crucially, this volume is written with newcomers in mind. There are some excellent publications whose titles suggest that they are for the uninitiated, but many actually assume a certain level of background knowledge of the area. The handbook is guided by the principle that all chapters will be accessible to an undergraduate student who has a background in the study of language but who has no expertise in language learning and technology. It is in the advanced readership category, the primary intended audience being college and university students at undergraduate level on applied language/linguistics, education and TESOL (Teaching English to Speakers of Other Languages) programmes, and graduates (pre- or postexperience) studying on relevant master's and doctoral programmes, all of whom may need an introduction to the topics for both their taught courses and their research. It is also suitable for new professionals and those starting out on a PhD, who wish to use the book for self-study.

## The scope of this volume

The integration of technologies into language learning has a long and distinguished history. It has been known under various guises and acronyms, from CBT (computer-based training) to CALL (computer-assisted language learning), to name but two. In this current volume of the Routledge Handbook series, we aim to explore both established and emerging themes in the related fields of research and practice in six discrete yet interrelated parts.

### *Part I: Historical and conceptual contexts*

Part I of this volume provides an historical overview and a discussion of the main theoretical influences in the field. Chapter 1 offers an introduction to the handbook, highlighting many of the issues that will be explored in more detail in later chapters. In it, Healey reviews associated terminology and looks at the roles of the teacher, learner and technology from geographical and temporal perspectives. Chapter 2 by Hubbard and Levy continues the theory coverage in discussing the very concept of theory in CALL, and the huge range of theories that researchers and practitioners have drawn upon. Such is the range that the authors propose the term 'theory ensembles' to illustrate both the more common theoretical foundations – interactionist, sociocultural and constructivist – and the more pragmatic use of the theories by developers and teachers, before proposing future directions for theory. Chapter 3 by Blin concludes the conceptual context chapters by analysing a group of theories, frameworks and models making up an 'ecological toolkit' for technology and second language acquisition research. In addition to the three main theories (dynamic systems, ecological systems and cultural historical activity theory), the theory of affordances is also explored with explanatory examples provided throughout. Blin ends with a short discussion of the challenges of adopting an ecological viewpoint when undertaking CALL research and practice.

### *Part II: Core issues*

In such a wide and diversified field, Part II aims to investigate many of the core issues therein. In Chapter 4, Kessler looks at 'technology standards for language teacher preparation' and the growing expectations for student and in-service language teachers to be adequately proficient in pedagogical and technical knowledge and skills. He also explores established standards and the challenges of developing them in a context where technologies are consistently evolving over relatively short timescales. In Chapter 5, Hauck, Galley and Warnecke present the results from their TESOL-Electronic Village Online module *Tutoring with Web 2.0 Tools – Designing for Social Presence,* which was created for education professionals from different backgrounds in order to develop effective learner-centred online moderation skills with a specific focus on the role of Social Presence. Their results offer new understandings of the notion of online participation whilst highlighting the importance of factors such as learner identity, creative agency and participatory literacy. Motteram, in Chapter 6, investigates materials development in the digital age, with a practical focus on the range of available software and some advice for teachers wanting to build their own courseware.

The importance of research in language learning and technology is discussed in some detail in Chapter 7. Here, Levy outlines some of the challenges and obstacles facing researchers, both technical and theoretical, as well as appropriate research methodologies from experimental to ethnographic approaches. Literacies, technology and language teaching is the focus of Chapter 8 by Dudeney and Hockly. In their highly practical exploration of '21st century skills', they elaborate on traditional understandings of digital literacies to include an awareness of social practices in an expanded taxonomy directly relevant to the classroom. Chapter 9 provides an overview of the long tradition of evaluation to assess the pedagogical affordances of new technologies. Caws and Heift illustrate the various stages of evaluation through two distinct case studies which reveal three key factors: the evaluation of tools, interactions and outcomes.

Chapter 10 explores another long and established tradition in the field, that of language testing and technology. It examines the substantial literature and discusses some of the drawbacks and benefits of using computers in language testing. Brown also considers how technology is likely to direct language testing in the future. In Chapter 11, (Hayes) Gee and Lee look at age and gender issues in technology-mediated learning environments. They suggest that the significance of age and gender is also influenced by individual, situational, social and cultural variables, and argue for the importance of considering learner identities in a holistic way. Cultural variables are again the focus of a more detailed examination in Chapter 12, where Godwin-Jones outlines an approach where language learning incorporates elements of the target culture, including aspects of everyday life, behavioural norms, traditions and values from the outset. The affordances of the Web, online exchanges and computer-mediated communication to gain insights into other cultures and develop intercultural competence are identified.

In the midst of all of the discussions on technology integration, Lee and Egbert remind us in Chapter 13 that 'there are many ways in which a language learning context may be technology limited, and there are many causes for these limitations'. They suggest the use of the term 'technology-varied contexts' as being a more accurate reflection of the reality in some countries, where, nonetheless, they exemplify effective ways in which technology can be integrated in locally appropriate ways. Kern and Malinowski address the related theme of the limitations and boundaries of technology-enhanced teaching in Chapter 14. They argue that while technology can remove many limitations and boundaries, it can produce others and exemplify this through two vignette accounts. Teacher education contexts have been recognised as strong platforms for the promotion of change in the language classroom. In Chapter 15, Hanson-Smith presents an overview of some less than satisfactory accounts of practices in relation to the integration of technology-focused pedagogy and methodology into language teacher education programmes. She then provides a range of approaches, tools and online resources that can be used to enhance teachers' continuous professional development. Finally, the central issue of sustainability in a rapidly changing and uncertain knowledge society is the focus of Chapter 16 by Blin, Jalkanen and Taalas. They discuss the 'institutional model' and the 'CALL ecosystem model' as appropriate ways of integrating sustainability in CALL design and development.

## Part III: Interactive and collaborative technologies for language learning

Interactivity has been enhanced in unprecedented ways in online environments in the last decade and is therefore the underlying theme of the seven chapters in Part III, which begins with a discussion of telecollaboration in Chapter 17. Helm and Guth suggest that this involves going beyond mere language-based exchanges to include a strong intercultural communicative experience, as they present several models of telecollaboration. Practical considerations for implementing this approach are presented, as well as the many associated challenges around sustainability in higher education contexts. Social networking is the anchor for Chapter 18, in which Lomicka and Lord illustrate ways in which social community practices (social networks, media sharing, blogging, etc.) can be brought into the classroom in effective ways. In Chapter 19 Grosbois probes the potential of computer supported collaborative writing (CSCW) for language learning. Collectivity and individuality as dynamics in co-writing are examined, as well as the evolving nature of writing in a technologically rich environment. Chapter 20 sees Cutrim Schmid overview interactive whiteboards (IWBs) and their role as CALL enablers amidst some unease in relation to their inherent tendencies to coax towards teacher-centred pedagogies and cognitive overload. She draws on practice-informed accounts of how IWBs might be used with other interactive systems in congruence with contemporary language teaching methodologies.

The penetration and potential of mobile devices form the basis of the discussion in Chapter 21, in which Stockwell examines ways that they might be used in their own right rather than in ways which try to replicate computer-based activities. He takes the reader from a theoretical to a practical account of implementation, peppered with a discussion of key considerations. Chapter 22 enters the arena of virtual worlds and language learning. Here, Peterson critically traces the research which provides an account of the major studies in the field, revealing some positive findings but also a number of restrictions and difficulties. Online and blended language learning courses are investigated by Sharma and Westbrook in Chapter 23 and are exemplified through case study accounts, unearthing a number of associated practicalities.

## Part IV: Corpora and data-driven learning

Some practitioners and researchers in the broad field of language learning and technology question the level of successful integration of corpus-based approaches in language learning classrooms. While it is difficult to find relative published accounts to suggest that this is actually the case, even if it is, the profound influence that corpus linguistics has had in indirect ways on materials development and online reference tools makes it impossible to exclude in a volume such as this. Part IV begins with a pedagogical focus on Johns's data-driven learning approach as recounted by Warren in Chapter 24. This is followed by dual accounts of the learning potentials of both spoken and written corpora in the next two chapters. In Chapter 25, Caines, McCarthy and O'Keeffe highlight the importance of spoken language corpora to a fuller understanding of everyday casual conversation and other spoken genres, and go on to describe the relevance of large sampled corpora and smaller specialised corpora. Their chapter 'reviews key findings from research into spoken corpora and current pedagogical applications and discusses how spoken-corpus-informed pedagogy might be expanded and brought further into the domains of conventional classrooms and blended and online learning' (page 348 this volume). Chapter 26 puts a strong emphasis on how learners can benefit from corpus data to improve their writing skills, particularly academic writing. The notion of a pedagogical corpus is introduced and some potential uses are explored by Chambers, who expands the discussion to languages other than English.

In Chapter 27, Meunier examines the growing range and applications of learner corpora, which include grammar books, learners' dictionaries and writing aids, automatic assessment, annotation and rating, and pre- and in-service teacher training for nonnative teachers. Murphy and Riordan provide a very useful guide to the numerous types of corpora that are now available, how they might be usefully categorised and the ways in which they can be used for pedagogical purposes. Chapter 28 is therefore a good starting reference point for those new to the world of corpus databases and how they might be manipulated by the language teaching profession. Chapter 29, authored by Reppen, provides guidelines for those who may wish to design and build their own corpora, individually or in teams. Key considerations for corpus construction are presented for those interested in this endeavour for research or teaching purposes.

## *Part V: Gaming and language learning*

Games-based language learning (GBLL) represents a strong and emerging area of research and is explored in the three chapters contained in Part V. Chapter 30 by Reinhardt and Thorne echoes metaphors made in earlier chapters (tool and tutor; ecology) as a backdrop to their proposed metaphor of 'game as method', which they present and critically evaluate. This new metaphor illustrates several alignments between game design and L2 activity design including goal orientation, interaction or interactivity, feedback, context and motivation. Chapter 31 sees Cornillie and Desmet tracing the potential of mini-games for language learning purposes. This contribution introduces the concept, and discusses design and evaluation within an architecture of human cognition known as skill acquisition theory. Finally, Chapter 32 concentrates on younger game players, with a focus on learning English through playing digital games in and out of school. Sundqvist devotes a section to various game genres and also addresses the relevant question of gender.

## *Part VI: Purpose designed language learning resources*

This part of the handbook looks more specifically at the CALL tools and resources which have been developed to enhance and promote language learning, rather than those which have been repurposed with this goal in mind. Chapter 33 opens Part VI with a focus on how technology can support lexico-grammatical acquisition. Li takes a principled approach to overviewing the benefits, applications and key research perspectives in the area. Moving to a skills-based perspective, Liou focuses on reading and writing in Chapter 34, which illustrates the potentials of tools such as e-books, weblogs, wikis, Google Docs, corpus software, mobile devices, and automatic essay graders. Challenges associated with L2 acquisition factors like interaction, feedback and group dynamics in the L2 reading and writing processes, as well as technological design factors are also debated. Listening and speaking skills are central in Chapter 35 by Clancy and Murray. They set their chapter against a backdrop of a number of key historical and social circumstances including digital acoustics and the long-term use of audio in language pedagogy. They take an integrated approach to oral/aural skills outlining resources that are authentic and sociolinguistically relevant.

Guichon and Cohen consider the issues pertaining to multimodality, including the distinction between mode, modality and channel. They explore the potential of multimodality for second language comprehension and interaction and highlight the issue of cognitive load. Chapter 36 finishes with a look at multimodality from learners' and teachers' perspectives. The coverage of Intelligent CALL (iCALL) by Tschichold and Schulze in Chapter 37 encompasses a wide ranging discussion of themes such as automatic evaluation and assessment, corrective feedback in Tutorial CALL, computational parsers and grammars, and lexical glosses and electronic dictionaries. The final chapter in this part, and indeed in the handbook, traces the development and use of translation games. Bouillon, Cervini and Rayner organise Chapter 38 around a case study using CALL-SLT, a multilingual web-enabled spoken translation game system under development at Geneva University since 2009. They critically evaluate the system in terms of its application and effectiveness to assist students acquiring productive language skills.

## Reference

Healey, D., Hegelheimer, V., Hubbard, P., Ioannou-Georgiou, S., Kessler, G. and Ware, P. (2008) *TESOL Technology Standards Framework*, Alexandria, VA: TESOL.

# Part I
# Historical and conceptual contexts

# 1
# Language learning and technology
## Past, present and future

*Deborah Healey*

This chapter serves as the introduction to the handbook, touching on many of the issues that will be addressed in more depth in the rest of the book. The first section addresses what the field has been called – CAI, CALL, ICT, MALL, and more – and why a name is important. The next section looks at the varying roles of the teacher, learner, and technology in different parts of the world and over time. Few teachers now fear losing their jobs to a computer, but they may fear losing their jobs to those who know more about technology than they do. As learners are better able to access learning resources via technology, their role and that of the teacher will continue to change. The Internet has been a large force for change in language learning over time. The introduction of the Web created opportunities for a sea change in resource availability, especially with languages not spoken locally. With mobile devices, computing has become ubiquitous; the social web has emerged and become part of most people's lives. These two factors are creating another revolution in ways that people communicate with each other, and thus how we can learn languages. Finally, this chapter will take current trend lines and make some guesses as to what may come, given where we've been and where we are going now.

## What's in a name?

Names are important. A name not only describes a concept, it also shapes how we interpret the concept. The early names associated with language learning with technology, such as computer-aided instruction (CAI), show both an emphasis on the machine and a behaviouristic approach to learners. The machine taught and learners sat and pressed keys in response. The mainframe-based PLATO (Programmed Logic for Automated Teaching Operations) system was created in the 1960s at the University of Illinois and became more widespread by the 1970s. The very acronym – 'Programmed Logic' – indicates the underlying mindset. Learners worked through increasingly difficult activities, and their ability to complete an activity (and its multiple-choice test) would either allow them to move on or send them to review material. Faculty members worked on remote terminals to create content, often collaboratively. Initial language teaching programs were basic drills, but PLATO became much more robust over

Deborah Healey

time. Later implementations included audio and limited graphics. While the lessons were 'programmed', PLATO courseware came with curriculum.

## Microcomputers: Technology for the masses

The advent of microcomputers in the 1980s made it possible for more computer use in the classroom. Much was still CAI-like drill and practice and was sometimes called computer-assisted language instruction (CALI). However, some early teachers using computers suggested a change of nomenclature to aim at language learning specifically. Davies and Higgins (1982), among others, suggested the term 'CALL': computer-assisted or computer-aided language learning, and it became the preferred acronym.

Publishers in the US focused attention on recreating some of the early drills typical of PLATO systems. Some were sequenced so that they contained a curriculum. Many others were simple drills with a menu of possibilities. Where teachers took an active role in helping learners select material, more learning could take place. Language teachers also created simple drill-and-practice programs in BASIC, though rarely at the level and complexity of what was done with PLATO.

Outside the US, the British Council was actively producing software for language learning. There were some drills, but many programs were simulations, such as *London Adventure* or *Lemonade Stand*. Students playing *London Adventure* were told to purchase a set of items in London. They had to make the appropriate choices about how to interact with shopkeepers and others as they went from place to place. An inappropriate choice of language in interacting with a shopkeeper would result in the learners being unable to get what he or she was trying to find out or purchase. For example, Figure 1.1 shows an interaction from *London Adventure*.

These programs represented a focus on learning, not drilling. They also required teachers to take an active role in setting up groups and perhaps keeping score. The teacher and the learner were in charge, not the machine.

---

1  Excuse me, where is Trafalgar Square?
2  I want this postcard.
3  Excuse me. I like this postcard.
4  I'd like this postcard, please.
5  I'd like these postcards, please.

Depending on the user's selection, the following responses appear, one choice at a time:

1  'It's right outside the National Gallery', but no other action is forthcoming.
2  The assistant ignores you and serves another customer.
3  'Yes. It is nice', but no other action is forthcoming.
4  'That will be 25p, please', followed by the sale of the postcard.
5  'I'm sorry. You can't have them all'. No other action.

---

*Figure 1.1*   Interaction from *London Adventure*

## Growth in terminology

As more computer programs became available, writers and researchers suggested different acronyms: Computer-enhanced language learning (CELL), computer-assisted writing (CAW) for writing programs, computer applications in second language acquisition (CASLA), and technology-assisted or technology-enhanced language learning (TALL or TELL). The Computer-Assisted Language Instruction Consortium (CALICO) retained the computer-assisted language instruction (CALI) acronym. CALI is still used, but more often in non-English languages than for English language instruction. As practitioners and researchers looked for 'intelligent' CALL, the ICALL acronym appeared and is still used for a subset of CALL. Although different names were discussed, CALL remained the most widely used term. It became part of *CALL Digest* and the CALL Interest Section of TESOL in 1985; the publication *ReCALL* in 1989; *CALL Journal* in 1990; EuroCALL in 1993; and many others.

## Early Internet

In the 1980s, the Advanced Research Projects Agency Network (ARPANET) expanded from its exclusive consortium with the US Department of Defense and selected research universities, becoming the Internet. Initially, the Internet was difficult for teachers to use and lacked content. It was a time of text-based MUDs (Multi-User Dungeons, based on *Adventure* and *Dungeons & Dragons*) that shifted over time into MOOs (Multi-User, Object-Oriented) and Internet Relay Chat (IRC) rooms.

These text-based environments allowed learners to interact with others who were in the same virtual space ('rooms' or 'buildings' in a MOO, or the chat space in IRC). Some teachers used the MOO space for interacting with other teachers. Diversity University (DU MOO), for example, offered scheduled meetings for teachers to talk with each other about selected topics. These interactions were like Chat, where participants overlapped each other and conversations became disjointed when more than a handful of people participated. Still, this was now ICT: information and communications technology. That term became widely used not only in language teaching, but also across education. It is the term used in the UNESCO ICT Standards for Teachers (2008; see also Kessler, Chapter 4 this volume), which addresses education as a whole. One of the best-known current users of the term in language circles is the website ICT4LT: Information and Communications Technology for Language Teachers (Davies 2012).

A related term that arose early on was computer-mediated communication (CMC). CMC was considered a subset of CALL, with its emphasis on learners communicating with each other using the Internet. The *Journal of Computer-Mediated Communication* began publication in 1995 – evidence of interest by educators and academics. With work by Tim Berners-Lee and the development of the web browser Mosaic in 1992–93, the Internet became the World Wide Web, and CMC became more feasible and common. Interest in research on CMC in discourse analysis continues today, often examining the communication taking place in social media. A related area of research on CMC focuses on digital literacies: how people communicate effectively using digital media. Because of concerns that CMC did not cover the full extent of what learners do with computers, CALL retained its popularity as the overarching term, especially in English language teaching.

## *More than just computers*

The 21st century added Web 2.0 and new devices for language teachers and learners to use. As a result, discussions are ongoing about the most appropriate term to use to describe the new reality of learner/teacher-generated content, web-enabled devices, and mobile technology. The term TELL (technology-enhanced language learning) has reemerged. Terms with some reference to 'mobile' have also become more common, with mobile-assisted language learning (MALL; see also Stockwell, Chapter 21 this volume) the most frequent 'mobile' term used in material indexed by Google.

The new terms reflect the idea that 'computers' are not necessarily what language learners and teachers are using. New methods incorporate the creative potential of the so-called social web and the mobility of small devices. Still, not every learner uses mobile technology, so terminology that fully describes the range of what language teachers and learners do is still in flux. TESOL's Technology Standards Task Force retained the term CALL in its work, with the proviso that it referred to the full range of digital technology-enabled activities. The UK-based International Association of Teachers of English as a Foreign Language (IATEFL), however, uses the term 'learning technologies' in its Learning Technologies Special Interest Group. Perhaps that will become the overall term of choice, despite its broader focus than just language learning. We do need terminology to address technology use as mobile devices of various kinds become more common among language learners than computers.

## Technology, teacher and learner roles

Terminology has provided some insight into the roles of technology, the teacher, and the learner. CAI was computer-centred instruction. Computer-assisted language learning shifted focus to student learning rather than instruction. In exploring how teachers and learners use technology, it is important to keep in mind the different roles that each can play.

### *Role of technology*

Work in the 1980s by British researcher and theoretician John Higgins provided a dichotomy between a 'magister' and a 'pedagogue' role for computers. As he put it:

> For years people have been trying to turn the computer into a magister. They do this by making it carry the learning system know as Programmed Learning (PL). . . . PL in fact does not need a computer or any other machinery; it can be used just as effectively in paper form, and computers which are used exclusively for PL are sometimes known disparagingly as page-turners. The real magister is the person who wrote the materials and imagined the kind of conversation he might have with an imaginary student.
>
> Suppose, instead, that we try to make the machine into a pedagogue. Now we cannot write out the lessons in advance, because we do not know exactly how they will go, what the young master will demand. All we can do is supply the machine with a template to create certain kinds of activities, so that, when these are asked for, they are available. The computer becomes a task-setter, an opponent in a game, an environment, a conversational partner, a stooge or a tool.
>
> *(Higgins 1983: 4)*

The move to microcomputers opened a 'tool' use of computers for teachers and learners. Word processing became an option in the classroom. There are important caveats related to the type of writing instruction, language proficiency of the learner, and role of the teacher. Still, research continues to show an overall positive impact of word processing on second language writing. Benefits include better attitude towards writing, longer writing, greater willingness to edit and an end result of better writing in many cases (see e.g. Phinney 1989; Li and Cumming 2001; Pennington 2004). Other tools, such as spell-checkers, dictionaries, spreadsheets and authoring programs were also brought into the language classroom.

## *Taxonomies: Roles of technology*

Higgins's dichotomy of magister and pedagogue was further refined by Jones and Fortescue into three roles for computers: 'Knower of the Answer', 'Workhorse' and 'Stimulus' (Jones and Fortescue 1987). Another early book, *Something to Do on Tuesday* (Taylor and Perez 1989), built on Jones and Fortescue's taxonomy and used 'Knower of the Right Answer', 'Workhorse' and 'Stimulus' to describe roles of software programs for Apple IIe, Atari, Commodore 64 and MS-DOS computers.

Two current well-known taxonomies are from Warschauer (1996) and Bax (2003). The Warschauer model sets three stages: 'behaviouristic', 'communicative' and 'integrative'. The first stage, behaviouristic CALL, focused on drill and practice programs like PLATO and 1980s software. Instrumental CALL was the second stage, described as a computer-as-tool era. The post-Internet era is the integrative stage, where technology is integrated into classroom practice and language learning, not separate from it. Elements of earlier stages are still found in current uses of CALL.

The Bax model takes a somewhat different approach, with 'restricted', 'open' and 'integrated' CALL. Early use of technology in language teaching was not necessarily behaviouristic, but it was more limited in what it could do, thus the 'restricted' label. With the Internet and a pedagogy that does not focus on technology so much as use it for a purpose, we are currently in the open stage. Fully integrated CALL will emerge and become 'normalised' where there is no more 'CALL', just use of technology as a routine part of teaching, much like textbooks. As Bax writes:

> This concept is relevant to any kind of technological innovation and refers to the stage when the technology becomes invisible, embedded in everyday practice and hence 'normalised'. To take some commonplace examples, a wristwatch, a pen, shoes, writing – these are all technologies which have become normalised to the extent that we hardly even recognise them as technologies.
>
> *(Bax 2003: 23)*

## *Role of the teacher*

Identifying multiple roles for technology, however, does not fully address the dynamic in the classroom. The teacher and learner also have important roles to play. With PLATO, teachers were the designers and creators of language teaching programs. Carol Chapelle comments on PLATO:

> The PLATO project also contributed to the professional expertise in CALL. The courseware developed on that system, which supported audio (input to learners), graphics, and

flexible response analysis, was the product of language teachers' best judgement of what supplemental course materials should consist of the in the late 1970s.

*(Chapelle 2001: 6)*

The teacher was behind the scenes, and the computer was a tutor. Students were recipients, especially when the lessons were offered in a fixed sequence rather than allowing learners to choose what they would work on. Technology was viewed as a way to free the teacher to do more interesting things in class by shifting drills from classroom time to computer lab time.

Taking a look through CALL history, the shift of technology from mainframe PLATO systems to microcomputer systems in the 1980s opened up computer use in teaching to far more people. In the UK, the low-cost BBC Micro and Sinclair Spectrum enabled teachers to begin creating their own material using BASIC. The limitation was the very small screen and chiclet-like keyboard. In the US, Commodore's Vic-20 and C-64 models were lower-cost options than the Apple IIe. Teachers could create their own material using BASIC on any of those computers, but commercial publishers moved to the Apple IIe platform for early CALL material. It is important to note in this Internet-centred age that programs were platform-dependent; what ran on a BBC Micro had to be rewritten to be used on an Apple IIe, and so on. Teachers shared the programs they had written in BASIC, which allowed some interoperability across systems. However, the skill level and resources available to most teachers using BASIC, as well as the difference in computing power, resulted in programs less sophisticated than those created for PLATO.

A series of studies in the late 1980s and early 1990s focused on the role of the teacher. CALL practitioners had long recommended having students work in groups at the computer so that they would benefit from additional linguistic practice in their interactions with each other. Studies by Piper (1986) and Abraham and Liou (1990) demonstrated that just grouping learners did not automatically ensure communication and collaboration. The orientation of those engaged in a task on the computer often resulted in short utterances by those not at the keyboard ('There!' 'This one!' 'Yes!') and nothing from the person at the keyboard. The teacher's work in selecting the groups, establishing roles and setting tasks proved to be a key factor in the quality and quantity of talk at the computer. This should come as no surprise, since most group work by learners is dramatically affected by how the teacher sets up groups and establishes roles and tasks.

## *Role of the learner*

In a magister setting, the computer treats the learner as a passive recipient of the computer's (programmed) knowledge. The user may be able to type in his or her name and get customised feedback or have some choice about which lesson to practise. The learner has little control over the content. With the computer as pedagogue, the learner is the one making choices about how to use the information or tools provided by the computer.

When learners are using a word processor, they are as fully in control of the process as their linguistic and technical skills will allow. Learners using a simulation similarly rely on the computer to do tasks: to throw the virtual dice and give next steps. The computer does not teach; it assists learning or creates an environment in which learning can occur. Learners can become more autonomous in their language study with the use of computer tools that provide direct student access to resources.

Looking overall at the three components of teacher, learner and technology, we can set up some roles, as shown in Table 1.1.

*Table 1.1* Roles of teacher, learner and technology

|  | Teacher | Learner | Technology |  |
|---|---|---|---|---|
| Passive | Turn on the machine | Respond | Controller/Curriculum/Lessons | Visible |
| ↑↓ | Cheerleader | Respond/Use information | Controller/Provide information | ↑↓ |
|  | Facilitator: process and scaffolding | Use information | Facilitator: information and tools |  |
| Active | Creator/Evaluator | Creator | Resource/Tool | Hidden |

## Impact of the Internet

The advent of the Internet introduced a sea change in the use of technology in teaching, much like the shift from mainframes to microcomputers. The shift to microcomputers extended computer use to a wide audience. The early Internet dramatically broadened access to people and resources; Web 2.0 made even more possible.

ARPANET enabled PLATO developers to communicate with each other and share their work with an early version of email. With more computers in more places, ARPANET became the Internet – the global network of networks. Language teachers and learners could communicate with each other through email and then Internet Relay Chat (chat). This text-based chat was authentic communication, but it was also quite difficult and frustrating. Lag, the delay between when the user typed and when the text appeared, turned a conversation into a series of disjointed messages to other people. Multiple participants in a chat meant multiple overlapping, decontextualised messages. Teachers could set up small groups with focused tasks, which helped. Abbreviated writing was one way to try to respond to someone before the next message came in, potentially overlapping. The anonymity of chat sites also allowed 'flaming' behaviour, where a user responded to another with highly destructive comments, and sometimes setting off 'flame wars', with escalating nasty comments. Students needed to learn online etiquette – 'netiquette' – and that the best response to a disturbing comment was often to log out.

Data repositories in the pre-Web era were generally shared using the Gopher protocol, again text-based. To access data, users had to type commands that were not intuitive. Most language teachers did not even try to use Gopher given the limited resources it provided and the difficulty in getting to them. However, one gateway to a Gopher site was provided by SchMOOze University, a MOO (Multi-user, Object-Oriented dimension). MOOs allowed users who were in the same virtual space to type different commands and interact with each other. SchMOOze was the first MOO used specifically by language teachers and learners. The brainchild of Julie Falsetti, SchMOOze provided a textually interesting space that users could wander through, interact with different elements in the MOO (such as a virtual cook in the cafeteria) and chat with each other (Falsetti 1995). In SchMOOze and its Spanish counterpart, MundoHispano, users could move in different directions, type @WHO to see who was around, WAVE to others, READ information, and use other specialised commands created in the MOO interface. Learners could encounter people from countries around the world to interact with. Those who wanted to do more could learn the MOO commands to create their own spaces within the MOO. A number of language teachers and

```
<!--
Content-type: text/html
*************************************************************************
*                    Welcome to schMOOze University                     *
*                                                                       *
*    ==> To connect to an existing player type:   CONNECT NAME PASSWORD *
*    ==> To connect as a guest type:              CONNECT GUEST         *
*                                                                       *
*************************************************************************
*           all text is copyrighted by the various authors              *
*     TIME FLIES LIKE AN ARROW             FRUIT FLIES LIKE A BANANA    *
*                                 ***                                   *
*                          *              *                             *
*                     *                        *                        *
*                 *                                *                    *
*              *                                     *                  *
*           *                         (__)              *               *
*        *         *                  (oo)                 *     *
*      *        *              _____/                      *      *
*     *       *              /|                              *       *
*     *       *            /  |  |------  | |                *       *
*     *       *      *        |  |^^      | |                *       *
*     *       *                ^  ^        ^ ^               *       *
*  ***********                                            ***********

2 people are connected.
-->
```

*Figure 1.2* Entrance to SchMOOze University

learners became very involved with SchMOOze and MundoHispano. SchMOOze still exists, but its text-based interface, shown in Figure 1.2, is foreign to those who never used early microcomputers.

### The Web emerges

The Mosaic web browser and the HTTP protocol transformed the use of the Internet. The new graphical interface was more accessible to language learners than the text-only commands of the pre-Web Internet. Finally, teachers and learners who lacked technical skills could access resources online. Further developments in web browsers, such as Internet Explorer and Firefox, and an exponential growth in websites meant that 'authentic material' no longer had to be physically sent to a foreign language teacher, but could be accessed through the Web. That learners could also access native speakers and authentic material on their own allowed a previously unprecedented level of learner autonomy – and threats to teacher control of information. For example, if a learner disagreed with the teacher's decision that a sentence was grammatically correct, the student could submit the sentence to a website like Dave's ESL Café with friendly native speakers, many of them teachers, for their opinion. The expert opinion could often be returned within an hour of the query, no matter where in the world the learner was located.

Of greatest importance for language learning, the Internet enabled connections to others that could be sustained across time and space. Pen pal projects traditionally had a lengthy wait time between sending a message and getting the response via regular mail, making it possible to have only a few interactions during a semester. Keypal projects using email could have interactions on a daily or near-daily basis; the constraint was the time taken for the tasks set by the teacher, not transmission time. Small groups of learners could also interact via chat, with the same caveats listed earlier. Lag was shorter in later versions of chat, but overlapping conversations and truncated writing remained troublesome.

The growth of the Internet was fuelled by the sense that it was a free resource. Teachers and learners could go online, visit different websites and download a few resources, all for free. Commercialisation appeared as advertisements on websites – something to warn language learners about, but not a major problem. Along with commercial sites came open source resource providers, such as the online book repository Project Gutenberg and the open source Open Office productivity suite. The dark side appeared with viruses, email scams and hoaxes, and malicious websites that captured private information and sold it or used it to infect or control a computer. The sense that everything online was free resulted in widespread piracy of commercial and non-commercial material. Teachers were also guilty of illegal practices in this regard. Serious threats to safety emerged as well, with online predators trolling for children, especially in chat rooms.

## *Affordances: What the tool allows the user to do*

Teachers had to develop an extended skill set to deal with the new possibilities, both positive and negative, in the Internet world. Teachers and learners had easy access to graphics and audio, though video was often difficult with the early Web. Multimedia could be part of any lesson, and authentic material no longer meant weeks-old copies of *Le Monde* or salsa-stained menus from a Mexico City restaurant. Authoring programs made it easier to create multimedia. It was unnecessary to have a dedicated computer system and professional videographers to create video; programs that teachers and learners were able to use were available for a few hundred dollars, and later for free. The information revolution was in full swing, and many teachers struggled to catch up. The power of the teacher to be the centre of the classroom further eroded as tech-savvy learners became classroom resources, helping the teacher and other learners.

Distance education took on new meaning in the Internet era. Tandem learning sites such as the International Tandem Network were established to let users trade languages with each other (see Part III of this volume for an account of present-day activities). Teacher collaborations were facilitated by mailing lists such as the now-defunct International Email Classroom Connections list and websites such as the International Education and Resource Network (iEARN), as well as informal forums on websites such as Dave's ESL Café. More sites now exist for individual keypal exchanges and class exchanges, along with more information on setting up successful joint projects or exchanges for language learners (Robb 2001; Schueller 2007).

Fully online and hybrid classes that combined online and face-to-face elements also became practical with the expansion of the Internet. Teachers could set up websites, discussion groups, and mailing lists, and provide updated digital material in response to learner needs. The cost of delivering material was no longer based on physical distance, but on having a server capable of handling the expected number of students. Creating an effective course proved much more difficult than just uploading PDFs to a website, perhaps with links to video lectures. It called for a new way of imagining courses (Cahill and Catanzaro 1997; Neumeier 2005). The early Web did not provide many opportunities for learners to easily express themselves orally online. Hybrid courses often provided information online but gave students opportunities to enhance and demonstrate their skills in the face-to-face setting.

New research was needed to respond to the new possibilities afforded by the Internet and the Web. Computer-mediated communication spawned a range of studies. As with earlier research on the use of technology, these studies were based on specific technologies, which could change rapidly and dramatically, as well as pedagogy that was less likely to change (see also Levy, Chapter 7 this volume). A nongraphical interface has dramatically different affordances from a multimedia-rich environment, and new technologies have opened up new possibilities that simply did not exist before. Various authors have provided research reviews (e.g. Debski 2003; Ohlrogge and Lee 2008; Grgurović, Chapelle and Shelley 2013). Jung's extensive CALL Bibliography offers over 5,300 entries in the 2005 edition, many of them research-related (Jung 2005). New possibilities brought new challenges. The question of 'what works?' became even more complex.

## The social Web and ubiquitous computing

The Internet and the Web described in the previous section were primarily transmission ('pull') technologies, where users chose what to view, but they were passive viewers of content created by others. Web 2.0, also known as the social web, has turned the model around (see also Dudeney and Hockly, Chapter 8 this volume). Users create material for each other and can choose either to view (pull) information or to have it automatically sent to them (push). Creating a website requires no more skill than using a word processor. Creating and uploading a video is as simple as recording on a mobile phone and sending it to a video site like YouTube. Everyone is a content generator with the social web.

The populist element of the social web has not gone unnoticed by governments. Different governments block access to sites and content providers. Some Google tools were blocked in China starting in 2010. By 2012, many more Google tools were blocked, including Google Sites and Google-owned Blogger (Pepitone 2012). YouTube goes in and out of favour with various governments as well; for example, it was partially or completely blocked in China, Iran, Pakistan, Turkmenistan and Egypt in 2013 (ReelSEO 2013). Lack of access and uncertainty about access to such useful sites for language learning poses challenges for teachers and learners.

### Connectivity and mobility

People can also be constantly connected in the world of mobile devices, whether via wireless or via their phone. Computers, tablets and mobile phones can make phone calls; phones, tablets and computers can connect to the Internet and share information. Mobile devices allow teaching and guided learning to happen outside the classroom. Learners do not need to imagine what their neighbourhood looks like while sitting in class; they can walk out and take photos or videos, then bring them back to share. Mobile devices also allow learning to be highly personalised, if teachers and learners know how to take advantage of the opportunities the devices offer. Certainly, learners could memorise a dialogue asking for directions to the library, but they might as well record a real interaction with someone where they ask for and get directions to a place they want to go. The topic of mobile learning is interesting and serious enough that the online journal *ReCALL* in 2009 published the proceedings from the 2008 EuroCALL Conference on new technologies and mobile learning as a series of articles. Of particular interest are Kárpáti's keynote on Web 2.0 technologies (Kárpáti 2009) and Kukulska-Hulme's reflection on whether mobile learning will change language learning (Kukulska-Hulme 2009).

The use of mobile apps in language learning is expanding rapidly (see Stockwell, Chapter 21 this volume). Chinnery (2006) provides a look at a number of mobile applications and how to use them, and Bradin-Siskin (2009) offers a grouped list of mobile apps for language learning. Godwin-Jones offers an overview of where emerging technologies, including mobile apps, may be going in language learning. He mentions peer-to-peer networking, phrase books, travel guides, flashcard programs and programs that use the mobile device's location awareness to provide practice appropriate to that location (Godwin-Jones 2011). Mobile apps often encourage users to connect with their friends, which can provide a community of practice for language learning. Social media sites allow people to share information with friends and strangers easily and constantly. For language teachers and learners, a communication-rich context offers wonderful opportunities for meaningful interaction and motivated learning. The students who are growing up or have grown up with mobile devices take their ability to share information for granted. They are familiar with the social connections available, and many need little urging to take advantage of language learning opportunities via social sites. Research is developing on the use and effectiveness of social media in language teaching, such as that by Kabilan, Ahmad and Abidin (2010) (see also Lomicka and Lord, Chapter 18 this volume).

Connectivity also has its drawbacks. Websites have pop-up ads that appear, often on the margins of the site. The smaller screen size of mobile devices means that pop-up ads appear very prominently on the screen and can be much harder to ignore or dismiss. Encouraging learners to connect with each other or sign in with a common password (Facebook or Google, for example), also allows apps to gather even more data about their users – their friends, their circles, links they click on and more. Seemingly innocuous apps can ask for access to the contacts stored on a user's mobile device, providing a list of names, email addresses, phone numbers and other information to be exploited if the app is malicious. The flaming and flame wars of the early Internet have expanded in the mobile age into cyberbullying. Malicious posts can go viral and be spread across the Internet with very few clicks and sometimes disastrous results (Bullying Statistics 2009). There is even more need for lessons about safety and appropriate behaviour in this new world of always-on connectivity (see Dudeney and Hockly, Chapter 8 this volume).

## Gaming

Devices may be smaller, but the number of people interacting can be much larger. One interesting development has massively multiplayer online role-playing games (MMORPGs), online environments shared by a very large number of people. Games have long been a staple in language teaching (see Part V of this volume). Technology has enabled a wide variety of games over time, with early text-based simulations like *London Adventure* and *Lemonade Stand* and media-rich *A la rencontre de Philippe* on videodisc and multilingual versions of *Who is Oscar Lake?* on CD-ROM. Students now have access to the language teaching-oriented online game *Trace Effects* as well as to MMORPGs like *World of Warcraft* (*WoW*). *WoW* has 9.6 million users who subscribe to the service (Stickney 2013) and can interact with each other via voice or text, as well as through their avatars strictly within the game. However, the multiuser game *FarmVille*, part of Facebook, boasts some 40 million monthly users (Sarkar 2013). Players can work cooperatively to grow and harvest crops. Action tends to be asynchronous, even though users can cooperate. The multiplayer games give learners an authentic environment for communication. With the massive multiplayer games, however, it is more difficult for teachers to scaffold language use and ensure that beginning or intermediate learners can be at $i + 1$ when interacting.

With appropriate protection in mind, teachers can find new ways to use the combination of smaller, faster, always-on devices and language learning. Student and teacher creativity and communication with others are easier and more extensive than ever. Lower cost and increased accessibility have been boons to schools and to individuals, both teachers and learners. Even in low-resource environments, students may have feature phones that allow them to record audio and video. However, the teacher's role in guiding students remains an important one (see Reinhardt and Thorne, Chapter 30 this volume).

Deborah Healey

## Guessing what's to come

This review of language teaching with technology has covered several waves of technology use. In each, the move forward with technology has been accompanied by an initial step back to earlier implementations and pedagogy. The Intelligent CALL with audio and sophisticated error correction and feedback of late-stage PLATO was lost with the shift to microcomputers. Early microcomputer CALL programs of text-only grammar or vocabulary drills and feedback initially consisted at best of 'Nice work' or 'Keep trying', customised with the learner's name. Record keeping was a component of many of the programs, even early ones. Teachers were avid creators, but they were, in general, not very skilled programmers. Eventually, greater diversity emerged, and software began to be multimedia-enabled, with sophisticated error-correction in many cases and interesting and appropriate user interface elements. Software became more commercial, and commercial software had the benefit of using paid programmers and graphic designers, as well as teachers serving as curriculum consultants. Authoring programs even allowed students and teachers to make material that had the possibility of incorporating multimedia and being motivating to use.

With the advent of the Web, CALL implementations and pedagogy stepped back to early drill and practice, with even less intelligent feedback than in early Apple IIe programs: there was not even customisation with the user's name, and no record keeping at all. Quiz sites abounded, most without even a hint of level or curriculum. Teachers once again flocked to creating exercises with more enthusiasm than programming skill. Initially, only those with access to a web server and knowledge of HTML were able to create material and put it online, so most teachers and students were shut out of creating online material. Little by little, though, teachers began using the Web primarily as a communication tool rather than trying to turn it into drill and practice software. As the Web developed into Web 2.0, highly interactive sites allowed students to create and distribute content online easily. Learners could communicate via text, audio or video with teachers and each other, enabling a wide range of learner-centred form- and fluency-building activities. Users could have several programs open simultaneously on a large screen so that they could move seamlessly between a collaborative word processor such as Google Docs, a drawing program and an audio or video interaction on a program like Skype.

Mobile devices have created yet another step forward in technology with an accompanying step backward in tools and pedagogy. The screen size on many mobile devices, such as smartphones, is too small to allow looking at more than one open application at a time, and typing a long text can be laborious. Fortunately, not all of the advantages of the earlier era have been lost; there are still communication-centred apps that teachers and learners are using. Of note is Kathy Schrock's list of iPad apps organised by level of Bloom's Taxonomy that they support (Schrock 2012). Pedagogy is catching up again.

Each wave has left language teaching and learning better off than the previous wave. Teachers and learners do become proficient in the new affordances and better aware of the right tool for the job. But just what will that 'job' look like?

### *Predicting the future*

Vannevar Bush's 'As We May Think' (Bush 1945) visualised a world of data on virtual desktops, linked and manipulated. His vision of a 'memex' was not that far removed from the reality of large screens, extensive databases, and powerful computers today. Bush also imagined using speech to text to record ideas (common in many physician's offices today) and being able to photograph any object that appears in one's glasses (a simpler version of Google Glass).

The *Star Trek* television show in the late 1960s envisioned flip-up communicators and teleportation. There are mobile phones today that look a great deal like those communicators, but teleportation is still far from reality. The point is that the future, while it seems that it should be quite different from today's reality, is still built on the present. Certain trends are likely to continue: smaller, faster, more ubiquitous computing; more noncomputer devices that have networking and communication capability (in addition to today's cars and 'smart' household appliances); more information available to more people, more of the time in structured ways (the massive open online courses – MOOCs – that have a curriculum and enrol thousands in a course may not always be free, but they will likely continue to expand their reach, see Hanson-Smith, Chapter 15 this volume); easier access to experts and expert knowledge; better text-to-speech and speech-to-text; and better instant translations (Google Glass with Google Translate built in may provide instant translation of signs in a foreign language, for example).

In the foreseeable but not immediate future, it will be easier for people to get accurate translations of information in the news in a wide variety of languages, and to translate their own writing into other languages. The accuracy may depend on the content and genre, of course, and the result may need an added cultural gloss to be fully correct. It may no longer be necessary to spend time at an intensive language program in order to be prepared to get a degree from a foreign university if translations are good and information is in digital form online.

In the nearer future, self-directed language learners will have more tools at their command to create their own pathways to learning language. Those not skilled at learning language on their own will still want help in selecting appropriate resources from the vast array of information available; creating a path to learning that fits the learner's time, needs and learning style; understanding the role of culture within the language being learned; and becoming part of a supportive learning community. Providing those elements may be the future role of language teachers – human teachers, at least for now.

## Further reading

Davies, G. (2012) 'ICT4LT homepage', in G. Davies (ed), *Information and Communications Technology for Language Teachers* (ICT4LT), Slough, UK: Thames Valley University [Internet], available: http://www.ict4lt.org/en/en_home.htm (accessed 28 Apr 2013).
  This is an electronic text for teaching and learning about CALL. Chapters are updated fairly regularly.
Egbert, J. and Hanson-Smith, E. (2007) *CALL Environments*, 2nd edn, Alexandria, VA: TESOL.
  Each of the nine topics in this collection (Interaction, Authentic Audience, Authentic Task, Exposure and Production, Time and Feedback, Intentional Cognition, Atmosphere, Autonomy, and The Future) includes chapters on research, application, and critical issues, allowing a deeper look at those topics.
EuroCALL (2000) *The History of Computer Assisted Language Learning Web Exhibition* [Internet], available: http://www.eurocall-languages.org/resources/history_of_call.pdf (accessed 28 Apr 2013).
  While somewhat quirky, this provides an interesting perspective on CALL over time.
Levy, M. (1997) *Computer-Assisted Language Learning: Content and Conceptualization*, Oxford, UK: Clarendon Press.
  This is still one of the best overviews of theory and practice in CALL. Written by a single author, it has more coherence than edited volumes.
Thomas, M., Reinders, H. and Warschauer, M. (2013) *Contemporary Computer-Assisted Language Learning*, London, UK: Bloomsbury Academic.
  This recent collection includes chapters on social media and mobile devices, in addition to chapters on research and pedagogy.

## References

Abraham, R. and Liou, H.-C. (1990) 'Interaction generated by three computer programs: Analysis of function of spoken language', in P. Dunkel (ed), *Computer Assisted Language Learning and Testing*, Rowley, MA: Newbury: 85–109.

Bax, S. (2003) 'CALL – Past, present and future', *System*, 31(1): 13–28.

Bradin Siskin, C. (2009) *Language Learning Applications for Smartphones, or Small Can Be Beautiful* [online], available: http://www.edvista.com/claire/pres/smartphones/ (accessed 28 Apr 2013).

Bullying Statistics (2009) *Bullying and Suicide* [online], available: http://www.bullyingstatistics.org/content/bullying-and-suicide.html (accessed 28 Apr 2013).

Bush, V. (1945) 'As we may think', *The Atlantic*, July 1: 1–9.

Cahill, D. and Catanzaro, D. (1997) 'Teaching first-year Spanish on-line', *CALICO Journal*, 14(2–4): 97–113.

Chapelle, C.A. (2001) *Computer Applications in Second Language Acquisition: Foundations for Teaching, Testing and Research*, Cambridge, UK: Cambridge University Press.

Chinnery, G.M. (2006) 'Going to the MALL: Mobile assisted language learning', *Language Learning & Technology*, 10(1): 9–16.

Davies, G. (2012) *ICT4LT: Information and Communications Technology for Language Teachers* [online], available: http://www.ict4lt.org/ (accessed 28 Apr 2013).

Davies, G. and Higgins, J. (1982) *Computers, Language and Language Learning*, London, UK: CILT Publications.

Debski, R. (2003) 'Analysis of research in CALL (1980–2000) with a reflection on CALL as an academic discipline', *ReCALL*, 15(2): 177–188.

Falsetti, J. (1995) *What the Heck Is a MOO and What's the Story with All Those Cows?* [online], available: http://schmooze.hunter.cuny.edu/~eflmoo/MOOarticle.html (accessed 28 Apr 2013).

Godwin-Jones, R. (2011) 'Mobile apps for language learning', *Language Learning & Technology*, 15(2): 2–11.

Grgurović, M., Chapelle, C.A. and Shelley, M.C. (2013) 'A meta-analysis of effectiveness studies on computer technology-supported language learning', *ReCALL*, 25(2): 165–198.

Higgins, J. (1983) 'Can computers teach?' *CALICO Journal*, 1(2): 4–6.

Jones, C. and Fortescue, S. (1987) *Using Computers in the Language Classroom*, New York, NY: Longman.

Jung, O. (2005) 'An international bibliography of computer-assisted language learning: Sixth instalment' [sic]. *System*, 33: 135–185.

Kabilan, M.K., Ahmad, N. and Abidin, M.J.Z. (2010) 'Facebook: An online environment for learning of English in institutions of higher education?' *The Internet and Higher Education*, 13(4): 179–187.

Kárpáti, A. (2009) 'Web 2 technologies for Net Native language learners: A 'social CALL'', *ReCALL*, 21(2): 139–156.

Kukulska-Hulme, A. (2009) 'Will mobile learning change language learning?' *ReCALL*, 21(2): 157–165.

Li, J. and Cumming, A. (2001) 'Word processing and ESL writing: A longitudinal case study', *International Journal of English Studies*, 1: 127–152.

Neumeier, P. (2005) 'A closer look at blended learning – Parameters for designing a blended learning environment for language teaching and learning', *ReCALL*, 17(2): 163–178.

Ohlrogge, A. and Lee, H. (2008) 'Research on CALL and distance learning: A briefly annotated bibliography', in S. Goertler and P. Winke (eds), *Opening Doors Through Distance Language Education: Principles, Perspectives, and Practices*, San Marcos, TX: CALICO [online], available: https://calico.org/DistanceEd-Biblio.pdf (accessed 28 Apr 2013).

Pennington, M. (2004) 'Electronic media in second language writing: An overview of tools and research findings', in Sandra Fotos and Charles M. Browne (eds), *New Perspectives on CALL for Second Language Classrooms*, Mahwah, NJ: Lawrence Erlbaum Associates: 69–92.

Pepitone, J. (2012) 'Google blocked in China as government leaders meet', *CNN Money*, November 9 [online], available: http://money.cnn.com/2012/11/09/technology/google-china-blocked/index.html (accessed 28 Apr 2013).

Phinney, M. (1989) 'Computers, composition, and second language teaching', in M. Pennington (ed), *Teaching Languages with Computers: The State of the Art*, La Jolla, CA: Athelstan: 81–96.

Piper, A. (1986) 'Conversation and the computer: A study of the conversational spin-off generated among learners of English as a foreign language working in groups', *System*, 14(2): 187–198.

ReelSEO (2013) *YouTube Censorship: Countries That Restrict Access [Feb 2013]* [online], available: http://www.reelseo.com/youtube-censorship-countries-that-restrict-access-feb-2013/ (accessed 28 Apr 2013).

Robb, T. (2001) *Web Projects for the ESL/EFL Class: Famous Japanese Personages* [online], available: http://www.cc.kyoto-su.ac.jp/~trobb/projects.html (accessed 28 Apr 2013).
Sarkar, S. (2013) *FarmVille 2 Has 40 Million Monthly Active Users, Amid Other Staggering Numbers* [online], available: http://www.polygon.com/2013/1/4/3837236/farmville-2-infographic-40-million-monthly-active-users (accessed 28 Apr 2013).
Schrock, K. (2012) *Bloomin' Apps* [online], available: http://www.schrockguide.net/bloomin-apps.html (accessed 28 Apr 2013).
Schueller, J. (2007) 'One good turn deserves another: Sustaining an intercultural e-mail exchange', *Die Unterrichtspraxis/Teaching German*, 40(2): 183–196.
Stickney, A. (2013) *World of Warcraft Down to 9.6 Million Subscribers* [online], available: http://wow.joystiq.com/2013/02/07/world-of-warcraft-down-to-9-6-million-subscribers/ (accessed 28 Apr 2013).
Taylor, M. and Perez, L. (1989) *Something To Do on Monday*, Houston, TX: Athelstan.
UNESCO (2008) *ICT Competency Standards for Teachers: Competency Standards Modules.* Paris: UNESCO.
Warschauer, M. (1996) 'Computer-assisted language learning: An introduction', in S. Fotos (ed), *Multimedia Language Teaching*, Tokyo: Logos International: 3–20.

# 2
# Theory in computer-assisted language learning research and practice

*Philip Hubbard and Mike Levy*

Despite its brief history, computer-assisted language learning (CALL) has been informed by a wide variety of theories, and that variety appears to be growing. In the first section of this chapter, we describe the concept of theory in this field and discuss its role in illuminating what happens when humans interact with materials and one another through the mediation of digital devices, programs, networks and tools in the pursuit of language learning objectives. In the second section we provide detail concerning the enormous diversity of theories that have been used by CALL researchers and practitioners and offer a typology of theory use in CALL, ranging from theory borrowing to theory construction. The third section looks more closely at the role of theory in CALL research. We begin with a brief overview of three of the more prevalent theoretical foundations for CALL research: the interaction account, sociocultural theory and constructivism. We then include a short example of contrasting theoretical analyses, sociocultural and interactionist, on the same topic: synchronous computer-mediated communication. The fourth section considers the role of theory in CALL practice, emphasising the pragmatic use of theories by teachers and developers to inform their choices of design and implementation and the increasing role of collections of theories we label theory ensembles. The final section focuses on current trends in theory, highlighting examples of how theory is being utilised in the growing segment of digital gaming for language learning, and concludes by speculating on the direction of theory in CALL for the future.

## The place of theory in technology and language learning

In the late 1970s and early 1980s, language teachers with access to the new desktop 'microcomputers' and an urge to tinker began creating their own simple programs to support their students' learning. In time, a critical mass of these language teachers and their institutional support staff would converge at language teaching conferences and create an embryonic field, widely, though not universally, known as computer-assisted language learning (CALL). Over the past three decades, the overall field and individual parts of it have expanded dramatically, leading to a number of other appropriately descriptive terms and acronyms. However, given the number of professional organisations, conferences, books and journals that have incorporated the term *CALL*, for ease of exposition and continuity with previous work we use it throughout this chapter to refer to the field as a whole.

This chapter provides an introduction to CALL theory. Research, practice and theory can be said to constitute the three foundational pillars of any applied field. Indeed, the field of applied linguistics – or more specifically, second language acquisition (SLA), to which CALL is often said to belong (see e.g. Chapelle 1997) – is supported by the same three pillars. Given that close connection to SLA, it is useful to begin with a consideration of how theory is viewed there. Mitchell, Myles and Marsden (2013) characterise theory for SLA in broad though somewhat traditional scientific terms: 'a theory is a more or less abstract set of claims about the units that are significant within the phenomenon under study, the relationships that exist between them, and the processes that bring about change' (p. 2). They further note that 'theories may be embryonic and restricted in scope, or more elaborate, explicit, and comprehensive' (pp. 2–3). Finally, following a more or less standard rationalist position, they note that theories aim at explanations rather than just descriptions. However, other SLA scholars, such as Long (1990), acknowledge that not all theories incorporate explanations. For the purposes here, we also take into account more pragmatic conceptions of theory (Coyne 1997), the idea that theory and practice are intertwined in the pursuit of solutions that work. This is a position that is particularly in line with the needs of developers and teachers (Levy and Stockwell 2006), whose utilisation of theories we discuss later in the chapter.

Consequently, we use the term *CALL theory* to represent collectively the set of perspectives, theoretical models, frameworks and specific theories that:

1. offer generalisations to account for phenomena related to the use of digital technology in the pursuit of language learning objectives;
2. ground and sustain relevant research agendas;
3. inform effective CALL design and teaching practice (Hubbard 2009, 2012).

We acknowledge that this characterisation is not universal and that some may wish a broader or narrower scope. However, we believe that this is a useful starting point for the discussion that follows.

For readers new to the field, it may be surprising to discover that there is no established CALL theory or even set of CALL theories that have been developed internally by scholars in the field to uniquely characterise it. Instead, CALL is largely a consumer of theories from other sources, not only at the level of teaching and development (Levy and Stockwell 2006: 39) but arguably also in its research tradition. In the next section, we look at the range and most common disciplines from which theoretical sources are drawn and offer a typology of their use within the field based on how those sources are utilised.

## Theoretical sources in technology and language learning

Those who venture into a discussion of theory in the field of technology in language teaching and learning must tread carefully. Background and biases may lead one to expect more coherence and consistency than demonstrably exist. Although digital technology has only been a significant component of language teaching and learning for a few decades, the theoretical landscape captured by its researchers and practitioners is already wide-ranging. In a review of theory in a single specialist journal (the *CALICO Journal*) over the period 1983 to 2007, Hubbard (2008) extracted references to 113 distinct theories across 166 articles. With the exception of a small number of general labels (SLA theory, learning theory, linguistic theory, etc.), these were specific references (activity theory, item-response theory, speech-act theory, schema theory, cognitive theory of multimedia, etc.). Surprisingly, there were no clearly 'dominant' theories showing up with any consistency: in fact, none of the specific theories mentioned appeared in more than six articles, and 77 of the 113 appeared in just one.

That review identified four primary sources for the theories: (1) language learning–centred extensions of human-computer interaction or technology in education theories, (2) technology-centred extensions of second language acquisition theories, (3) learning theories from psychology and education and (4) linguistic theories. Interestingly, across twenty-five years of articles, it identified just one solid reference to a theory developed specifically for this field: Oller's (1996) technologically assisted language learning theory, along with one reference to generic 'CALL theory' and two to 'CMC [computer-mediated communication] theory'. Despite all the work in CALL-specific research and methodology, there appears little at the CALL-specific theory level.

The type and sheer quantity of sources reflect the complexity and diversity of the field up to that time. However, given the range of other published sources and the years that have passed since 2008, the number of theoretical sources incorporated in CALL works no doubt greatly exceeds the 113 from that study. As we show in the final section, the range of theoretical sources continues to grow as concepts from domains such as gaming (see Reinhardt and Thorne, Chapter 30 this volume) begin to take hold in language education.

In order to understand the role of theory in CALL, it is not enough to focus just on their number and the diversity of their sources. It is also important to see how these theories are co-opted, combined and potentially evolve as a result of being applied in an environment they were not originally conceived for. To address this issue, Hubbard (2009) introduced a framework for categorising the type of theoretical presence in CALL works. We next summarise that framework and expand it with two additional categories. The categories presented stand in contrast to *atheoretical* CALL (Hubbard 2009), a label that can be applied to studies that have no explicit theoretical connection.

## *Theory borrowing*

The simplest and most direct employment of theory in a CALL study is *theory borrowing*. This process consists of taking a theory from another domain such as linguistics, psychology, education, human-computer interaction and especially second language acquisition and plugging it in to the CALL environment without any changes. In fact, a significant subset of research in computer-mediated communication (CMC) fits into this category. The objective of many of such studies is to show that the CMC environment can be analysed as having features, such as the negotiation of meaning construct from the interactionist perspective, that are claimed to facilitate language acquisition. See for example the discussion of Fernández-Garcia and Martínez-Arbelaiz (2002) in the following section. In theory borrowing, a theory is used as a frame to test the environment, but the theoretical construct (i.e. negotiation of meaning) remains untouched.

## *Theory instantiation*

Related to theory borrowing is *theory instantiation*, a category absent from the original Hubbard (2009) framework. We introduce it here to accommodate studies that take general purpose or broad learning theories such as activity theory, ecological theory or the theory of affordances (see Blin, Chapter 3 this volume) and situate them in a language learning environment where the technology and language can both be *explicitly* recognised as elements for analysis. An

These understandings and widely differing interpretations of constructivism have carried over into the CALL area (Felix 2002). In a special issue of the *TESOL Journal* titled 'Constructing Meaning with Computers', the editors speak of cognitive and social constructivism (Healey and Klinghammer 2002). In essence, the cognitive constructivist describes the mind in terms of the individual; the social constructivist describes the mind as a distributed entity that extends beyond the bounds of the body into the social environment. Healey and Klinghammer also emphasised the centrality of the learner in the learning process and the importance of the teacher in creating motivating authentic activities that involve investigation, discussion, collaboration and negotiation. Each author in that special issue draws rather differently on the constructivist idea, often listing overlapping sets of principles that underpin the individual constructivist CALL learning environments they are creating.

*The role of theory in research*

Theory guides and shapes research in many ways, but perhaps one of its most important roles concerns its influence on the ways in which the researcher sees the problem. Through theory, the researcher is guided not only towards particular ways of formulating the research problem initially, but also towards ways of investigating it, through the choice of terminology and constructs, research method and procedure, data collection procedures and mechanisms of analysis and interpretation: each are both directly and indirectly suggested by theory. This role of theory in research is described eloquently by Neuman:

> Theory frames how we look at and think about a topic. It gives us concepts, provides basic assumptions, directs us to the important questions, and suggests ways for us to make sense of data. Theory enables us to connect a single study to the immense base of knowledge to which other researchers contribute. To use an analogy, theory helps a researcher see the forest instead of just a single tree.
>
> *(Neuman 2003: 65)*

In other words, the theory drives and shapes the whole research conceptualisation and process. It also sets the boundaries and largely governs points of focus, the concepts or constructs to be included and excluded, and of those included, those foregrounded and those that remain in the background.

An instructive way to appreciate the ways in which theory shapes the researcher's thinking is to look at two studies undertaken in similar settings, and with broadly equivalent participant profiles and data sets, but differing in their theoretical orientations. A suitable example in CALL drawn from Levy and Stockwell (2006) compares and contrasts two studies in an online chat environment. Fernández-García and Martínez-Arbelaiz (2002) used the interaction account to guide them; Darhower (2002), in contrast, looked at the interactional features of synchronous CMC chat from a sociocultural perspective. The two contrasting theoretical approaches illustrate well the choices that confront contemporary researchers when no single language learning theory is preeminent and when more than one theoretical account lends itself to the job of description and explanation. The different theories exert their influence in the way they encourage the researcher to structure and process the data in particular ways, and then to determine what mechanisms of analysis and interpretation are used to, in our case, provide a basis for an argument that says 'learning' has occurred.

Levy and Stockwell (2006) discuss essential differences between these two theoretical positions and their implications. Guided by the sociocultural approach, Darhower's study was driven by a concern with learners' levels of active participation in a community of practice. As such, it focused upon 'specific interactional features', notably 'intersubjectivity' and 'off-task discussion'. Intersubjectivity refers to the shared perspective experienced by participants: it is an interactional feature that needs to be maintained if effective communicative action is to continue. Within the sociocultural orientation, such interactional features are key because they speak to the learner's level of participation in the online community. The quality and degree of participation are essential in generating cognitive change (see earlier discussion).

Thus, Darhower is interested in the maintenance (or otherwise) of intersubjectivity and the ways learners participated and managed their interactions – for instance whether they chose to stay on-task or go off-task, and if they went off-task, what topics they chose to discuss. Sometimes conflicts occurred – also of interest to Darhower – when one learner wanted to stay on-task while the other did not. With his theoretical position, this movement between on-task and off-task work is fundamental to the way social cohesiveness is built up and maintained. Thus, off-task work is firmly in the frame and remains very much a feature of this study: essentially, it is treated equally with on-task work. As Darhower says: 'Sociocultural theory emphasizes that the locus of learning is . . . a product of social interaction with other individuals' (2002, 251); therefore constructs such as intersubjectivity and off-task discussion become central when sociocultural theory is employed to guide research.

In contrast, Fernández-Garcia and Martínez-Arbelaiz (2002) only refer to the term 'task' four times in their paper, and when it is used, it is referred to in its general sense as would be found in a dictionary. The authors show no interest in the possibility of off-task discussion: it is not a salient feature of their theoretical framework, and the tacit assumption is made that students remain on-task throughout the activity (whether true or not, we do not know). The construct of intersubjectivity is also not a concern. Instead, for Fernández-Garcia and Martínez-Arbelaiz (2002), the theory dictates that constructs such as 'negotiation of meaning' (interaction by two speakers aimed at mutual understanding) are central and, additionally, more technical interpretations of the idea of negotiation in language learning, such as 'negotiation of comprehensible input' (ensuring that a word, phrase, etc. is understood), 'negotiation routines' (patterned ways of interacting in the pursuit of meaning) and 'pragmatic negotiation' (interacting to understand the intended functional meaning rather than just the literal one). These terms derive directly from the particular theoretical orientation that drives the research study.

In both studies, the theoretical point of departure sets the field of view and the mechanisms of interpretation. The theory defines the key constructs, the data to be collected and the way in which the argument that learning has occurred will be made. Both use theory to support their rationale and justify their research, and both draw on theory to identify desired features in the chat room interaction. Darhower (2002) is looking for evidence of the intersubjectivity and social cohesiveness hypothesised in sociocultural theory to be important for language development and learning and the development of sociolinguistic competence. Fernández-Garcia and Martínez-Arbelaiz (2002), on the other hand, are looking elsewhere for evidence in their transcripts seeking signs of interactional modifications and modified learner output which are regarded as key indicators of learning in the IA. The two theoretical bases led the researchers in different directions.

## Theory in CALL practice

When theory is used for teaching and CALL, it is often used as a guide rather than as a prescription. Instead of drawing upon one theory exclusively, language teachers are more likely to draw on a number of theories simultaneously. Thus, there is a distinct difference between the way in which theory is used in teaching, and similarly in design and development, compared to the single theoretical framework of many research studies. Following the typology presented previously, this means that CALL theory in practice is more likely to be an *ensemble* or a *synthesis*.

This approach to the nature, use and application of theory for teaching and CALL is examined by Doughty and Long (2003) in their very useful discussion of task-based language teaching (TBLT). They describe TBLT as 'an embryonic theory of language teaching, not a theory of SLA' (p. 51). They continue:

> And whereas theories generally strive for parsimony, among other qualities – to identify what is *necessary* and *sufficient* to explain something – a theory of language teaching seeks to capture all those components, plus whatever else can be done to make language teaching *efficient*. Language education is a social service, after all, and providers and consumers alike are concerned with such bread-and-butter issues as rate of learning, not with what may or may not eventually be achieved through a minimalist approach motivated exclusively by theory of SLA.
>
> *(Doughty and Long 2003: 51)*

So TBLT, as a theory of teaching rather than of language acquisition, is informed by a number of theoretical sources that blend into one another. Doughty and Long (2003) use theory to derive ten methodological principles, or 'language teaching universals', for TBLT, and these in turn are converted to pedagogical procedures, according to contextual factors determined by the teacher, the learners and the learning context – the online environment in this case. Thus, the role of theory here is to provide a principled foundation, inasmuch as current research findings are able, for the methodological principles (see also González-Lloret 2003).

A good example of a more broadly defined set of guidelines that are drawn from a number of theories rather than a single one is that presented by Egbert et al. (2007). For their 'theoretical framework' (p. 4), they identify eight optimal *conditions* for CALL and use these conditions to organise the content of their book, e.g. (2) learners interact in the target language with an authentic audience, (6) learners are guided to attend mindfully to the learning process and (8) learner autonomy is supported. These eight conditions are drawn from a number of theoretical accounts and research studies which the authors argue are 'the most widely researched and supported in the literature and make up a general model of optimal environmental conditions' (Egbert et al. 2007: 4). Within our model, this could be considered a *theory synthesis*, though the sources are more varied and the connections less explicit than in Plass and Jones (2005).

This theoretical diversity stands in contrast to the seven *hypotheses* that derive directly from the interaction account, described by Chapelle (1998: 23–25), for example (1) the linguistic characteristics of target language input need to be made salient, (4) learners need to notice errors in their own output and (6) learners need to engage in target language interaction whose structure can be modified for negotiation of meaning.

For Chapelle, the IA is used to provide a set of explicit assumptions for CALL research and practice. Chapelle's list of hypotheses is narrower and more tightly focused on language interaction than the earlier list. Neither is necessarily better than the other, but they do speak to practice in rather different ways, one being broader and more encompassing, the other more finely targeted and focused. Both have a role to play. Perhaps most interestingly, although both claim to be guidelines for CALL, neither has any direct reference to technology in their core generalisations. They are borrowed from theory and research in SLA and transported into the CALL setting without incorporating any explicit role for technology.

Nevertheless, these two contrasting positions are helpful in understanding how theory can relate to practice. The position held by Egbert et al. reflects a trend in recent CALL articles to draw upon a number of theoretical perspectives simultaneously when developing a conceptual framework for online teaching and learning. Perhaps multiple theoretical perspectives are an acknowledgement that no single theory is preeminent in describing the processes of language learning; or it may indicate that no single theory is sufficiently powerful to provide a broad and principled set of guidelines for the many decisions that need to be made in creating online teaching and learning environments.

## Current trends and future directions

We would really like to end this chapter on a note of surety, where we could point to a particular theory or cluster of theories and say 'here is the best answer', or 'this one looks like the best bet for the future', but to do so would distort the reality of the matter. Scholars new to the field (and indeed some who are not so new) who are looking for the 'truth' that theories seem to promise, will not find it.

As noted previously, CALL projects are regularly influenced by multiple theoretical perspectives, what we have called theory ensembles. For example, Levy and Stockwell (2006: 134) noted the multiple theoretical sources for the *Lyceum* distance language learning environment, an audio-visual conferencing system developed by the Open University in the UK and used extensively for language learning purposes. They included the interactionist account, sociocultural theory, constructivism, situated learning and multimodality. Some of these theories and their proponents clash with one another in the research-centred SLA arena, yet in the pragmatic development of *Lyceum*, the different theoretical perspectives spoke to distinct elements and processes within the learning environment that was being created. Such learning environments are multifaceted and complex, so it should perhaps not be surprising to learn that multiple theoretical influences, even those that might on the surface appear incompatible, are referenced to inspire them.

To begin to understand how this trend of multiple theories is being realised, it is instructive to examine some recent examples closely. Consider the six research studies on digital gaming described in the *ReCALL* Special Issue, 'Digital Games for Language Learning – Challenges and Opportunities' (Cornillie, Thorne and Desmet 2012). Each study references multiple theories and each theory is called upon for different reasons. For instance, the first study (Cornillie et al. 2012) discusses the value of 'interweaving theory in the SLA and GBL (game-based learning) literatures' (p. 258). Their work points to the essential conundrum found at the centre of the design of all language learning games: 'between learning and playing'. It is this core problem that engages Cornillie and his research team as they aim to design corrective feedback such that learning is facilitated while, at the same time, the high levels of interactivity and engagement in gameplay are not interrupted. Managing both of these goals simultaneously is not straightforward. The circumstances call for a balance between instruction and play in designing corrective feedback (CF), and the study draws on the two theoretical bases accordingly. This project also includes a number of further theoretical sources, including the cognitive mediational paradigm (p. 260), 4-Component Instructional Design Model (p. 265), self-determination theory (p. 262) and flow theory (p. 262), the latter being highly relevant in the design of the game. Each theory is included to serve a particular purpose.

Two more studies in the special issue are worthy of deeper consideration. Both involve using the massively multiplayer online (MMO) game *World of Warcraft* (*WoW*). The first study, by Zheng, Newgarden and Young (2012), uses an ensemble of theories or pseudotheories to motivate the project, including communicative project theory, multimodal analysis, languaging, situated learning, values-realising theory and an ecological perspective, among others. A particular focus is on how L2 learners coordinate gameplay and manage 'multiple perspectives and dynamics in a given moment of action' (Zheng et al. 2012: 340). The complex nature of both the environment of the game and the activity give rise to the activation of a number of different theories employed for different purposes. The second study, by Rama et al. (2012), examined the affordances for second language learning in *WoW*. It used sociocultural theory as a central pillar in a blend with notions of 'affinity spaces' and goal-directed cooperative action. Here theory is used to help make observations about the gaming environment, especially on its affordances for language learning, forms of participation, and its effectiveness as an arena for building and sustaining relationships (intersubjectivity).

In these varied examples on the uses of sophisticated games for language learning we see many theories in play (excuse the pun). The context of the language learning game is not the same as the typical teacher-fronted face-to-face language classroom. Care needs to be taken, therefore, in using theories developed and tested on face-to-face settings in game-based learning environments. In fact, a broader principle applies here. The default position for the researcher should always be that the online learning environment is substantively different from – not the same as – the classroom setting. Interacting via a screen, often with several windows open at the same time, presents the teacher and learner with multiple options for simultaneous interaction (e.g. interaction via the chat window while listening to the teacher and looking at a shared whiteboard, as in a typical distance learning setting). Theories emerge in new combinations according to the affordances of these novel language learning environments. Therefore, as such settings emerge and evolve, and as 'gamification' increases in the CALL literature, we are likely to see more examples of this multitheoretical approach to research and development. Recent special issues of the *CALICO Journal* (30.2, 2013) on learner preparation and *Language Learning & Technology* (17.3, 2013) on mobile-assisted language learning (MALL) attest to the fact that gaming is just one of several emerging topics enriching the theoretical inputs to the field.

In this chapter, we have presented a working definition of CALL theory and shown that it draws on many sources and an expanded framework for classifying how theory is integrated into various CALL studies. As a part of reading and interpreting others' work in this field, we believe it is important to understand and identify the process through which theory is brought to bear on whatever research question or practical issue the study is addressing. More importantly, in bringing theoretical orientations and constructs into one's own work in CALL, it is essential to stop and reflect deeply on why those orientations and constructs are there. Theories should not be chosen lightly, or simply because they happen to be in vogue at the time. Ideally, theory should play a foundational role in the study and be fully integrated into its goals, constructs and design. Beyond the increasing use of theory ensembles in design/development and teaching, there is clearly a need for more central consideration of the role of the technology itself as something other than a neutral entity. As Chapter 3 (Blin, this volume) demonstrates, options such as activity theory that have a place within their frameworks for the technology are already showing promise for meeting this need. What will be interesting to see over time is what types of progress can be made in establishing useful theory ensembles and in increasing the instances of theory adaptation, synthesis, instantiation and perhaps construction. It is the theoretical innovation in these areas that will ensure the field remains dynamic and relevant.

To conclude this chapter, we would like to emphasise our position that the incorporation of technology in language teaching and learning, whether called CALL or something else, should continue to be influenced and guided by theory. The presence of theory provides the frame through which the complexity of the object under study can be coherently interpreted and the means to reach out beyond the single, context-specific research study. Whether theory in this field ever reaches the explanatory level aspired to in rationalist positions remains an open question, but it is clear that theory can play a role in illuminating teachers' and learners' experiences and in pointing the way towards more promising tasks, applications and environments.

## Further reading

Chapelle, C. (2001) *Computer Applications in Second Language Acquisition: Foundations for Teaching, Testing and Research*, Cambridge, MA: Cambridge University Press.
　Chapelle approaches CALL theory from the perspective of SLA and the interactionist approach. As far as theory is concerned, chapter 3 provides important foundational concepts and a particular elaboration that has been employed in subsequent research projects. Her distinction between judgemental and empirical evaluation is key, as are her five principles of evaluation that emphasise the importance of incorporating findings and SLA theory when conceptualising new research projects. Her six criteria for CALL task appropriateness are especially helpful for research aimed at task evaluation.

Egbert, J. and Petrie, G. (eds) (2005) *CALL Research Perspectives*, Mahwah, NJ: Lawrence Erlbaum Associates.
　In this edited volume, many of the current options for CALL theory are introduced, chapter by chapter. More recent perspectives are included such as flow theory and design-based research, as well as more established areas such as interactionist SLA theory and sociocultural perspectives. In addition, Part 1 addresses some important background issues, some of the questions and dilemmas that need to be addressed, and ways to identify criteria that help ensure theory application is effective.

Hubbard, P. (2008) 'Twenty-five years of theory in the CALICO Journal', *CALICO Journal*, 25(3): 387–399.
　This study of theory in CALL is useful for providing a look into how the term was incorporated into published studies in one CALL journal from the early 1980s through 2007. Based on a corpus of work comprising 166 articles where the term *theory* appears in the body of the text, the paper offers an analysis of the number and type of theories in use. The study is illuminating for the reader who wishes to explore and understand the particular ways in which theory was elaborated and applied in CALL during that quarter century.

Hubbard, P. (ed) (2009) *Computer Assisted Language Learning: Critical Concepts in Linguistics. Volume I: Foundations of CALL*, New York, NY: Routledge.
　The first part of Volume 1 in this four-volume series provides valuable points of departure for those wishing to orient themselves to the ways theory in CALL has been understood. Two chapters examine different roles for the computer (Higgins: magister/pedagogue; Levy: tutor/tool), and another discusses the broad phases through which it has progressed (Warschauer and Healey: behaviourist, communicative, integrative). The relationship between research and practice (Garrett) and the 'normalisation' concept (Bax) further illustrates some of the unique qualities of the field. The final contribution by Chapelle draws from theory and instructed SLA research to examine how theory is employed to elaborate and guide practice. Though the contributions are disparate, these six chapters provide a complementary and thought-provoking set of perspectives on theory and CALL.

Levy, M. and Stockwell, G. (2006) *CALL Dimensions: Options and Issues in Computer-Assisted Language Learning*, Mahwah, NJ: Lawrence Erlbaum.
　Chapter 5 in this volume presents a detailed overview of theory use in CALL. It pays particular attention to the qualities and features of CALL and theory use, especially in relation to closely associated fields such as second language acquisition (SLA). As a result, it not only considers research studies motivated by a single theoretical perspective (e.g. interactionist theory and sociocultural theory), but also studies and projects that use two or more theories in their design and development (e.g. Cornillie et al. with games). Continuing this exploration of the various roles theory can play, the chapter also considers how theory may be applied differently according to its role and function, as in theory for design, theory for teaching and theory for research. The discussion highlights some of the special qualities of CALL as far as theory application and use is concerned.

## References

Basharina, O. (2007) 'An activity theory perspective on student reported contradictions in international telecollaboration', *Language Learning & Technology*, 11(2): 36–58.
Bax, S. (2003) 'CALL – Past, present, and future', *System*, 31(1): 13–28.

Bax, S. (2011) 'Normalisation revisited: The effective use of technology in language education', *International Journal of Computer Assisted Language Learning and Teaching*, 1(2): 1–15.

Chapelle, C. (1997) 'CALL in the year 2000: Still in search of research paradigms?', *Language Learning & Technology*, 1(1): 19–43.

Chapelle, C. (1998) 'Multimedia CALL: Lessons to be learned from research on instructed SLA', *Language Learning & Technology*, 2(1): 22–34.

Chapelle, C. (2003) *English Language Learning & Technology: Lectures on Applied Linguistics in the Age of Information and Communication Technology*, Amsterdam, Netherlands: John Benjamins.

Chapelle, C. (2005) 'Interactionist SLA theory in CALL research', in J.L. Egbert and G.M. Petrie (eds), *CALL Research Perspectives*, Mahwah, NJ: Lawrence Erlbaum: 53–64.

Chapelle, C. (2009) 'The relationship between second language acquisition theory and computer-assisted language learning', *The Modern Language Journal*, 93: 741–753.

Colpaert, J. (2004) 'Editorial: Transdisciplinarity', *Computer Assisted Language Learning*, 17(5): 459–472.

Cornillie, F., Clarebout, G. and Desmet, P. (2012) 'Between learning and playing? Exploring learners' perceptions of corrective feedback in an immersive game for English pragmatics', *ReCALL*, 24(3): 257–278.

Cornillie, F., Thorne, S. L. and Desmet, P. (2012) 'Digital games for language learning: From hype to insight?' *ReCALL*, 24(3): 243–256.

Coyne, R. (1997) *Designing Information Technology in the Information Age: From Method to Metaphor*, Cambridge, MA: MIT Press.

Darhower, M. (2002) 'Interactional features of synchronous CMC in the intermediate L2 class: A sociocultural case study', *CALICO Journal*, 19(2): 249–277.

Donato, R. and McCormick, D. (1994) 'A sociocultural perspective on language learning strategies: The role of mediation', *The Modern Language Journal*, 78(4): 453–464.

Doughty, C.J. and Long, M.H. (2003) 'Optimal psycholinguistic environments for distance foreign language learning', *Language Learning & Technology*, 7(3): 50–80.

Egbert, J., Hanson-Smith, E. and Chao, C. (2007) 'Introduction: Foundations for teaching and learning', in J. Egbert and E. Hanson-Smith (eds), *CALL Environments: Research, Practice and Critical Issues*, 2nd edn, Alexandria, VA: TESOL: 1–14.

Felix, U. (2002) 'The web as a vehicle for constructivist approaches in language teaching', *ReCALL*, 14(1): 2–15.

Fernández-Garcia, M. and Martínez-Arbelaiz, A. (2002) 'Negotiation of meaning in non-native speaker non-native speaker synchronous discussions', *CALICO Journal*, 19(2): 279–294.

González-Lloret, M. (2003) 'Designing task based CALL to promote interaction: En Busca De Esmeraldas', *Language Learning & Technology*, 7(1): 86–104.

Healey, D. and Klinghammer, S.J. (2002) 'Constructing meaning with computers: Special issue', *TESOL Journal*, 11(3): 3.

Hubbard, P. (2008) 'Twenty-five years of theory in the CALICO Journal', *CALICO Journal*, 25(3): 387–399.

Hubbard, P. (2009) 'Developing CALL theory: A new frontier', in M. Thomas (ed), *New Frontiers in CALL: Negotiating Diversity*, Japan: JALT CALL SIG: 1–6.

Hubbard, P. (2012) 'Exploring the impact of technology implementations on theories and models of language learning', in J. Burston, D. Tsagari and F. Doa (eds), *Foreign Language Instructional Technology: Theory & Practice*, Nicosia, Cyprus: University of Cyprus Press: 6–19.

Hutchby, I. (2001) *Conversation and Technology: From the Telephone to the Internet*, Malden, MA: Blackwell.

Hutchby, I. and Barnett, S. (2005) 'Aspects of the sequential organisation of mobile phone conversation', *Discourse Studies*, 7(2): 147–171.

Hutchby, I. and Tanna, V. (2008) 'Aspects of sequential organisation in text message exchange', *Discourse and Communication*, 2(2): 143–164.

Lantolf, J. (1994) 'Introduction to the special issue', *Modern Language Journal*, 78: 418–420.

Lee, L. (2009) 'Promoting intercultural exchanges with blogs and podcasting: A study of Spanish-American telecollaboration', *Computer Assisted Language Learning*, 22(5): 425–443.

Levy, M. and Stockwell, G. (2006) *CALL Dimensions: Options and Issues in Computer-Assisted Language Learning*, Mahwah, NJ: Lawrence Erlbaum Associates.

Long, M. (1990) 'The least a second language theory needs to explain', *TESOL Quarterly*, 24(4): 649–666.

Long, M. (1996) 'The role of the linguistic environment in second language acquisition', in W.C. Ritchie and T.K. Bhatia (eds), *Handbook of Second Language Acquisition*, San Diego, CA: Academic Press: 413–468.

McDonell, W. (1992) 'Language and cognitive development through cooperative group work', in C. Kessler (ed), *Cooperative Language Learning*, London, UK: Prentice Hall: 51–64.

Mitchell, R., Myles, F. and Marsden, E. (2013) *Second Language Learning Theories*, 2nd edn, London, UK: Arnold.

Neuman, W. (2003) *Social Research Methods: Qualitative and Quantitative Approaches*, 5th edn, Boston, MA: Allyn and Bacon.

Oller, J. (1996) 'Toward a theory of technologically assisted language learning', *CALICO Journal*, 13(4): 19–43.

Peterson, M. (2012) 'EFL learner collaborative interaction in Second Life', *ReCALL*, 24(1): 20–39.

Phillips, D.C. (1995) 'The good, the bad, and the ugly: The many faces of constructivism', *Educational Researcher*, 24(7): 5–12.

Pica, T. (1991) 'Classroom interaction, participation and comprehension: Redefining relationships', *System*, 19(3): 437–452.

Plass, J. and Jones, L. (2005) 'Multimedia learning in second language acquisition', in R. Mayer (ed), *The Cambridge Handbook of Multimedia Learning*, Cambridge, MA: Cambridge University Press: 467–488.

Rama, P.S., Black, R.W., van Es, E. and Warschauer, M. (2012) 'Affordances for second language learning in *World of Warcraft*', *ReCALL*, 24(3): 322–338.

Smith, B. (2003) 'Computer-mediated negotiated interaction: An expanded model', *The Modern Language Journal*, 87: 38–57.

Varonis, E. and Gass, S. M. (1985) 'Non-native/non-native conversation: A model for the negotiation of meaning', *Applied Linguistics*, 6(1): 71–90.

Vygotsky, L. (1978) *Mind in Society*, Cambridge, MA: Harvard University Press.

Warschauer, M. (2005) 'Sociocultural perspectives on CALL', in J. Egbert and G. Petrie (eds), *CALL Research Perspectives*, Mahwah, NJ: Lawrence Erlbaum: 41–52.

White, C. (2005) 'Towards a learner-based theory of distance language learning: The concept of the learner-context interface', in B. Holmberg, M. Shelley and C. White (eds), *Distance Education and Languages: Evolution and Change*, Clevedon, UK: Multilingual Matters: 55–71.

Zheng, D., Newgarden, K. and Young, M.F. (2012) 'Multimodal analysis of language learning in *World of Warcraft* play: Languaging as values-realising', *ReCALL*, 24(3): 339–360.

# 3

# Towards an 'ecological' CALL theory

## Theoretical perspectives and their instantiation in CALL research and practice

*Françoise Blin*

### Towards ecological CALL: Preliminary definitions

Since the 1960s, the ecology metaphor, borrowed from the natural sciences, has underpinned theoretical developments in many independent fields, including applied linguistics and CALL. This chapter introduces a set of theories, frameworks and models that can be assembled to constitute an 'ecological toolkit' for CALL research and practice. The discipline of *ecology*, traditionally linked to biology and environmental science, is normally understood as the study of interactions between living organisms and their environment. An important concept in ecology is the notion of *ecosystem*, which consists of living organisms, nonliving components and all their interrelationships in a particular unit of space (adapted from the Merriam-Webster online dictionary), such as a forest or a pond. Building upon the aforementioned definitions, and drawing heavily on the work of van Lier (2004, 2008) and Lemke (2001, 2002, 2005) among others, I borrow from Hubbard and Levy (Chapter 2 this volume) and use the term *ecological CALL theory* to 'collectively represent the set of theoretical perspectives and models' that (1) place a strong focus on the context of language learning, language use and technology use as well as on the relationships between them; (2) explore language learning and language use across multiple timescales and spaces; (3) view the relationship between perception and action (i.e. affordances) as core to learning processes; and (4) seek to inform the design and deployment of a variety of *CALL ecosystems*, which I tentatively define as follows:

> *CALL ecosystems* consist of interacting components including language learners, teachers and other users of the target language, technological devices, applications and platforms, and multimodal material/semiotic artefacts and resources, all of which participate in a language learning/use activity, as well as the social processes and semiotic practices that characterise the way the human actors interact with one another and with other components of the system.

Following a brief discussion of the *ecological metaphor* (Kramsch 2002a) and of its contribution to second language acquisition (SLA) research, this chapter introduces the main tenets of three distinct theories that can be part of an ecological toolkit for investigating CALL ecosystems: dynamic systems theory (DST)/complexity theory (CT) (see e.g. Byrne 1998), Bronfenbrenner's (1979, 1993) ecological systems theory and Engeström's (1987) formulation of cultural historical activity theory (CHAT) and his theory of expansive learning. The temporal and spatial dimensions of CALL ecosystems are then briefly explored. Finally, the chapter concludes with an introduction to the theory of affordances, which has its roots in Gibson's (1979) seminal work on visual perception, and its instantiation in CALL research. Throughout the chapter, recent examples of instantiation of these theories in the context of CALL research are given. The chapter concludes with a brief discussion of the challenges faced by researchers seeking to adopt an ecological perspective on CALL research and practice.

## *The ecology metaphor in SLA*

Since the 1960s, the ecology metaphor, borrowed from the natural sciences, has underpinned theoretical developments in many independent fields, such as systems theory, developmental psychology and educational linguistics (Kramsch 2002b: 3). In relation to SLA, theories and approaches that are inspired by the ecology metaphor 'capture the *interconnectedness* of psychological, social, and environmental process in SLA' (Lam and Kramsch 2003: 144; see also Lafford 2009: 674). According to van Lier (2004, 2008), 'an ecological perspective on language learning sees language as part of larger meaning-making resources that include the body, cultural-historical artefacts, the physical surroundings, in short, all the affordances that the physical, social, and symbolic worlds have to offer' (van Lier 2008: 599). Language is viewed, not as a static system, nor as a code to be acquired, but as 'a *process* of creating, co-creating, sharing, and exchanging meanings across speakers, time, and space' (van Lier 2008: 599). In other words, language and language use are seen from a dialogical perspective (Bakhtin 1981; Linell 2009; Zheng and Newgarden 2011) – which gives primacy to 'interactions, activities and situations' (Linell 2009: 15) and focuses on the interdependence of a person with 'others' experiences, actions, thoughts and utterances' (Linell 2009: 11) – and 'communicative activity is always seen as contextualized, situated and embodied' (De Bot, Lowie, Thorne and Verspoor 2013: 202; see also Zheng and Newgarden 2011 for a more detailed discussion).

Van Lier (2004) and others (see e.g. De Bot et al. 2013) argue that 'ecology and sociocultural theory (SCT) share a number of important features' (van Lier 2004: 21) and can enrich each other (see also Hubbard and Levy, Chapter 2 this volume). More generally, ecological perspectives on language and language learning are said to transcend the cognitive-social debate (Larsen-Freeman 2002; Lafford 2009; Reinhardt 2012) that followed Firth and Wagner's (1997: 286) call for a better integration of 'both the *social* and *cognitive* dimensions of S/FL use and acquisition'. This cognitive-social debate continues to divide the SLA community, and by extension the CALL community. Chapelle (2009), noting the limited scope of drawing on any one SLA theory to inform CALL design and evaluation, advocates combining different SLA theoretical approaches into a meta-theory, such as a theory of complex systems. This takes into account 'the multiple factors working together' (Chapelle 2009: 748) under such a meta-theory.

## *Understanding complex systems in CALL*

A *complex system* is a set of interacting and interdependent components, which forms an integrated whole, bigger than its parts, closed or open (Larsen-Freeman and Cameron 2008), as well as self-organised and self-sustainable. Complex systems are dynamic and adaptive. They continuously change over time, through internal reorganisation and interaction with the environment in which they operate (Larsen-Freeman 2012; De Bot et al. 2013), often with unpredictable and unintended consequences, sometimes with a 'high risk for damage and harm' (Gee and Hayes 2011: 43). Complex systems are ubiquitous and have always existed (e.g. weather, national and global economies, the natural environment, etc.). Some have been created by humans; others have evolved as a result of human intervention (Gee and Hayes 2011: 72).

A number of different theories can be called upon to investigate complex CALL ecosystems with a view to better understand their dynamics. Three of these will be briefly introduced: dynamic systems theory (DST)/complexity theory (CT) (Byrne 1998), Bronfenbrenner's (1979) ecological systems theory and Engeström's (1987, 2001) cultural historical activity theory and his theory of expansive learning. Although they have their origins in different traditions, and despite some ontological differences, these theories are often seen as complementing each other (Stetsenko 2008) and share enough common features to be included in an 'ecological' toolkit for CALL research and practice. In particular, all three place a strong focus on the role of context in development, and on the interconnectedness of psychological, social and environmental processes in learning. Most importantly, each one is a theory of change 'that takes time as a core issue' (De Bot et al. 2013: 201), and is a powerful lens for understanding transformations and development across multiple spaces and timescales. Due to space constraints, only a broad overview of each theory, followed by some examples of instantiation in CALL, can be given here. The reader interested in finding out more about a particular theory is invited to consult the works indicated in the further reading and references sections at the end of this chapter.

## Dynamic systems theory/complexity theory

The terms dynamic systems theory (DST) and complexity theory (CT) are often used interchangeably and refer to a group of complexity science theories that describe the development over time of 'complex, dynamic, non-linear, self-organising, open, emergent, sometimes chaotic, and adaptive systems' (Larsen-Freeman and Cameron 2008: 4). A key property of chaotic systems is that despite their apparent randomness, they follow patterns and rules that may not be easily observable. Another key property is that a very small variation in the initial state of the system may trigger a disproportionate response and have a huge impact on its final state and on interacting systems (Smith 2007).

In the last decade, the potential applications of DST/CT to SLA research have generated strong interest (Larsen-Freeman 2002; Ellis and Larsen-Freeman 2006; Larsen-Freeman and Cameron 2008; De Bot et al. 2013). DST/CT is seen by some authors as the meta-theory called for by Chapelle (2009). For example, Larsen-Freeman (2002: 43) argues that 'a [chaos/complexity theory (C/CT)] perspective supports a social participation view of SLA [but] not to the exclusion of the psychological acquisitionist perspective'. De Bot et al. follow a similar line of argument and claim that:

> Dynamic Systems Theory (DST) can be seen as a comprehensive theory that can unify and make relevant a number of different *middle level* theories (Littlewood 2004) [...] provided of course that the middle level theories are commensurable with DST principles.
>
> *(De Bot et al. 2013: 216)*

Digital games, whether serious or recreational, are examples of complex and chaotic systems of relevance to CALL. For Gee and Hayes (2011), the massively multiplayer online (MMO) game *World of Warcraft* (*WoW*) is 'an example of popular culture giving rise to a complex system for people to play in, live in, and study' (p. 82). It includes 'game-generated texts, player-to-player communication and collaboration, and associated websites that support in-game play' (Thorne et al. 2012: 279), and thus potentially provides a site for language use and development. The interactions between the various internal and external components of the system are however so complex that the outcomes of actions carried out in *WoW* can be emergent and unpredictable, so much so that the game designers themselves 'do not fully understand its dynamics' (Gee and Hayes 2011: 82). Massive open online courses (MOOCs) (McAuley, Stewart, Siemens and Cormier 2010), based on connectivist principles (Siemens 2005) and heralded in the media as the future of higher education (for good or for ill), also constitute complex systems, characterised by openness, interconnectedness, collective emergence (deWaard et al. 2011: 99), as well as unpredictability and chaos. According to deWaard et al. (2011), 'chaos theory and the science of complexity can help us to understand and improve the process in which educational systems engage to transform themselves' (p. 112).

In relation to CALL more specifically, Schulze (2013) argues that 'viewing language learning as a complex dynamic system can give a new impetus to research in CALL and yield new insights into language learning' (p. 23), thanks to the relative ease with which longitudinal and complex datasets can be collected and analysed using 'methods, algorithms and mathematical models that have been developed in dynamic systems theory (DST) (Hirsch, Smale and Devaney 2004; Luenberger 1979)' (Schulze and Penner 2008: 433).

## Bronfenbrenner's ecological systems theory

Bronfenbrenner's (1979) ecological systems theory provides another useful theoretical framework to understand the complexity of the interconnectedness between psychological, social and environmental processes in learning and development. Bronfenbrenner (1979) emphasises the role of the immediate setting and larger social environment in human development. His nested ecosystems model represents the context in which development occurs as comprising four interacting nested levels, 'with bidirectional influences within and among systems' (Johnson 2010: 177) ; it is usually represented as concentric circles as illustrated in Figure 3.1. In this diagram, the learner is shown at the centre of the inner circle representing his/her immediate environment comprising of various settings 'with particular physical and material characteristics' (Bronfenbrenner 1979: 21).

The 'activities, roles, and interpersonal relations' experienced by the learner [in a given setting] constitute the elements of the *microsystem* (Bronfenbrenner 1979: 21). The *mesosystem* is a system of interacting microsystems containing the learner and includes, for example, the relations between different settings such as the workplace and college, peers and family, and so forth. The *exosystem* is broader again and includes at least one setting that does not contain the developing person but still influences processes within their immediate settings (e.g. the relation between the school and the educational system). Finally, the *macrosystem* consists of the overarching pattern of micro-, meso-, and exosystems, and provides the societal blueprints for these systems 'at the level of a the subculture or the culture as a whole' (Bronfenbrenner 1979: 25).

Bronfenbrenner's ecological systems theory informs a wealth of studies aiming to explore contextual factors affecting student achievement (Johnson 2008), the integration of technology

Towards an 'ecological' CALL theory

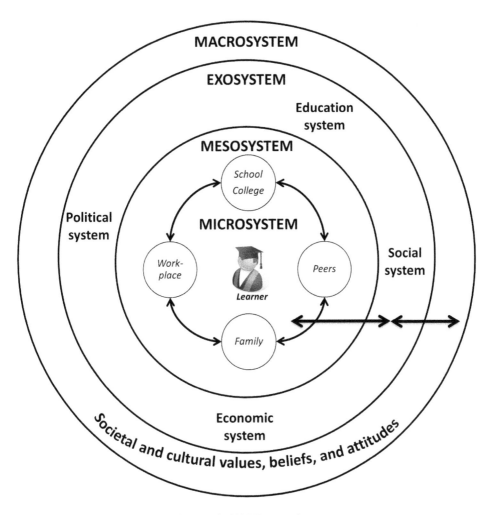

*Figure 3.1* Illustration of Bronfenbrenner's (1979) nested ecosystems

in education (Staples, Pugach and Himes 2005) and language education. In relation to the latter, Peng (2012) uses Bronfenbrenner's nested ecosystems model to investigate factors influencing willingness to communicate (WTC) in the EFL classroom in China. Her study provides a rich and contextualised understanding of WTC and shows that the willingness to communicate in the L2 classroom (microsystem) is 'nurtured by, and thus fluctuate[s] because of the interaction between factors internal and external to individual learners, and inside and beyond the classroom walls' (Peng 2012: 211). Van Lier (2003) explores the integration of technology in project-based language and teaching, and focuses on two language classrooms where computers are used during class. In this study, he used Bronfenbrenner's theory to analyse the interactional talk occurring in the classroom and to unravel the relationships and practices that 'have an impact on moment-to-moment interaction and meaning making in the setting' (van Lier 2008: 601).

Françoise Blin

## Cultural historical activity theory and the theory of expansive learning

The third and last theory to be introduced in this section is contemporary cultural-historical activity theory (CHAT) and the accompanying theory of expansive learning. CHAT draws upon two related but distinct traditions: Vygotsky's (1978) concept of mediated action and Leontiev's (1978) *first generation* activity theory (Engeström 2001). Leontiev proposed a tripartite hierarchical structure of human activity: collective activity, individual or group actions, and routinised operations. *Activities* are collective, oriented towards one or more *objects* and motivated by the need to transform these objects into desired outcomes. The term 'object' may refer to a physical need (e.g. hunger, material comforts), socially determined aspirations or perceived problems. This motive gives sense and direction to the *goal-oriented actions* that are carried out by the *subjects* (individuals or teams) of the activity. These actions are intentional, mediated by tools and carried out through a series of automated *operations* that are contingent on material conditions. For example, the action of consulting an online encyclopaedia to retrieve pertinent information depends on the type of device available to the individual and adequate access to the Internet in general and to the specific site in particular.

While Leontiev's work mainly focused on the activity, actions and operations of an individual, *second generation activity theory*, which was primarily developed by Engeström (1987, 2001), takes the whole activity systems as the unit of analysis. Engeström (2008) defines activities as object-oriented collective systems that have a complex mediational structure (Engeström 2008: 26), which now includes not only Leontiev's tool-mediated relationship between subject and object but also 'social mediators' (Engeström 2008: 27). In the case of a language learning activity supported by technology, *mediating tools* may include the technologies available to language learners, language (e.g. L1 and/or L2) and methods, as well as a broad range of material or digital artefacts generated by teachers, content-creators or users of the target language. *Social mediators* may consist of the *community* of language learners and language users participating in the activity, the horizontal and vertical *division of labour* within the community, as well as the implicit or explicit *rules* governing the actions carried out by the subjects of the activity. The mediational structure of an activity system is normally represented by a triangle highlighting the relationships between its constitutive elements. Figure 3.2 represents the simplified structure of a typical CALL activity system.

*Third generation activity theory* seeks 'to understand dialogue, multiple perspectives, and networks of interacting activity systems' (Engeström 2001: 135). The object of an activity is both ideal and material: for example, individual learners involved in the co-production of a digital artefact (e.g. PowerPoint presentation, websites, video clip, etc.) are likely to bring to the activity different ideas or representations of what this artefact may be or look like (Roth 2004). Activity systems are inherently dynamic and constitute unstable and multivoiced entities (Engeström 2001). They interact with other activity systems and evolve over time in response to internal and external contradictions (Engeström 2001). Contradictions are a source of change and development. They emerge within and between interacting activity systems and 'manifest themselves as problems, ruptures, breakdowns, clashes' (Kuutti 1996: 34), or as disturbances, which Engeström (2008) defines as 'actions that deviate from the expected course of normal procedure' (p. 27), such as, in the case of education, deviations from usual assessment practice or from instructions outlined in course documents.

As they respond to emerging contradictions, activity systems move through cycles of transformations, which can be *expansive*, leading to new forms of activity that are shaped by expanded objects and characterised by a new mediational structure (Engeström 2001). Expansive learning

# Towards an 'ecological' CALL theory

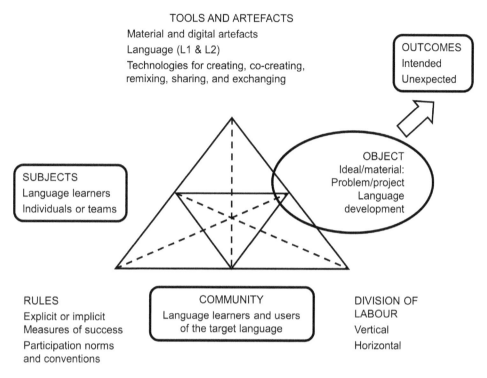

*Figure 3.2* Representation of a CALL activity system
Source: Based on Engeström (1987).

is normally triggered when 'individuals begin to question the existing order and logic of their activity' (Engeström and Sannino 2010: 5).

CHAT and the theory of expansive learning increasingly underpin studies in the field of educational research (Engeström and Sannino 2010), educational technology and CALL. Since the early 2000s in particular, CHAT has been instantiated to design and analyse CALL-related activities. *Single activity systems* constitute appropriate units of analysis to study 'intraclass' language learning activities (Blin 2012a). For example, Hadjistassou (2012) uses CHAT and the notion of contradiction to investigate online peer-reviewing activities. Her study examines the drafting of students' papers, topic exchanges and online feedback via a discussion board, with a view to identifying the conditions under which guidelines imposed from the outside, that is by the instructor, 'led to culturally perceived tensions among student-authors and student-reviewers' (Hadjistassou 2012: 368). Blin and Appel (2011) study the establishment and development of online collaborative writing practices among a group of EFL distance learners. Drawing on Engeström's (2008) work on teamwork in organisational settings, their analysis focuses on the goal-oriented actions carried out by students as they jointly revise their text, on the emergence of deviations from planned procedures, and highlights the pivotal role that artefacts used and created by students play in the process and outcomes of an online collaborative writing task. Their findings also reveal the emergence of different modes of interaction (i.e. coordination, cooperation and reflective communication), and suggest that while a cooperation mode of interaction afforded the development of language awareness and language use, the lack of transition to a reflective mode of communication constrained the attainment of learning outcomes.

Françoise Blin

In the case of intercultural telecollaboration activities involving two or more partners from different institutions and countries, *joint activity systems*, which partially share their object (Engeström 1987, 2001; Engeström and Sannino 2010) and possibly other elements, become the unit of analysis. At the beginning of the exchange, each activity system is characterised by a different mediational structure (Blin 2012a). As the joint activity unfolds, contradictions within and between the joint activity systems are likely to emerge (Thorne 2003, 2009; Basharina 2007). In response to these emerging contradictions, participants may soon move towards the construction of a new shared object, which in turn may lead to the mutual transformation of the initial activity systems mediational structures, in the form of a new division of labour or in the construction and adoption of new tools or rules.

Last but not least, CHAT and the theory of expansive learning are drawn upon to inform and investigate pedagogical and professional development (Ellis, Edwards and Smagorinsky 2010). For example, Blin (2010, 2012b) proposes a five-step activity theoretical design model that can be applied in a variety of CALL contexts and at different levels of granularity (e.g. entire course, module, unit of learning, 'small' task, etc.). The enactment of the design can then be analysed, emerging contradictions and their resolution (or nonresolution) can be identified, the object of the learning activity can be renegotiated by teachers and learners, and a new learning activity can emerge through a series of transformations. The latter may include, for example, the adoption of new technologies or new ways of using existing technologies, a new division of labour and collaborative practice or modified rules. The initial design thus serves a dual purpose: it is a blueprint not only for the learning activity that will unfold as the design is enacted, but also for continuing professional development, which may entail the teachers' reconceptualisation of their approach to language, language learning and language teaching in technology-rich language learning environments (Blin and Jalkanen forthcoming). Such an approach to professional development is reminiscent of some action research (AR) principles and methods (see Burns 2005). Indeed, CHAT and AR can be seen as complementary as explained by Orland-Barak and Becher:

> While AR *zooms into* the dynamic processes of participants' meaning making of their practice, as they engage in recursive cycles of reflection, CHAT *zooms out* to display connections and tensions within these processes, considering the wider social and cultural contexts that are grounded in the history of that particular professional practice.
> *(Orland-Barak and Becher 2011: 116)*

## Studying CALL ecosystems across multiple timescales and spaces

Combining the theories discussed in the previous section – despite some potential ontological incommensurabilities that may arise, mainly between CHAT and DST (De Bot et al. 2013) – can help us further illuminate particular learning and development processes as well as inform educational policies, curriculum and tool design, and teaching practice. For example, Johnson (2008) combines Bronfenbrenner's ecological systems theory and complexity theory in her study of student achievement, which she claims to be 'best understood as a developmental outcome that emerges as a result of interactions among layers within a complex system' (Johnson 2008: 1). In the domain of human-computer interaction (HCI), Gay and Hembrooke (2004: 1) use activity theory 'as an orienting framework for context-based design' and propose to integrate it with Bronfenbrenner's ecological model. In doing so, they emphasise the importance of analysing both the activity system under study at one particular level and 'its relations with activities at other contextual levels' (Gay and Hembrooke 2004: 9), whose changes 'need to be described and analysed by locating changes in the past, present, and future' (Gay and Hembrooke 2004: 10). The temporal and spatial dimensions of SLA have however been largely ignored by the SLA community in general (De Bot et al. 2013: 203), and by the CALL community in particular.

According to the three theories previously outlined, not only does the system under study operate at different levels of granularity, from the macro level to the micro level, it also operates on different timescales that can be aligned to Vygotsky's temporal domains, that is phylogenetic, sociocultural, ontogenetic and microgenetic (which concern, respectively, the development of a species, of society, of individuals, and the emergence of single mental processes or psychological acts), and 'mutually influence one another to a greater or lesser degree' (De Bot et al. 2013: 206). This is also reflected in Bronfenbrenner's (1993) *chronosystem model*, which allows researchers to take into account 'change or consistency over time not only in the characteristics of the person but also of the environment in which that person lives' (Bronfenbrenner 1993: 40). Similarly, according to CHAT, there are three hierarchical levels that constitute an activity interact across different timescales: activities are cyclical and long-term, actions are finite in duration, and operations involve real-time processes that include automatic and routinised behaviour (Blin and Appel 2011: 474–475). Finally, DST/CT also gives primacy to the interaction between nested levels and timescales. For example, De Bot et al. remind us that, when studying language development:

> a change in the retrievability of a lexical item at the millisecond scale may have an impact on the scale of seconds in language production, which in its turn may have an impact on storage on the scale of days, weeks, or even larger time scales.
>
> *(De Bot et al. 2013: 203)*

Lemke's (2000, 2005) *heterochrony* principle, where 'longer-term processes and shorter-term events [are] linked by a material object that functions in both cases semiotically as well as materially' (Lemke 2000: 281), provides a powerful lens to understand 'how processes that occur on short timescales become embedded in and potentially cumulative towards longer time-scale processes' (Lemke 2005: 112). In activity-theoretical terms, these *material-semiotic artefacts* connect the longer-term object-oriented activity and shorter-term individual goal-oriented actions (Blin and Appel 2011: 477). Material-semiotic artefacts abound in CALL ecosystems and include material objects (physical or digital) that are created and shared by language learners or users of the target language as part of a language learning activity. Some may be short-lived and temporary (e.g. Skype instant messages or voice exchanges that are not recorded); others may be more persistent, such as a Word or Google document, a multimodal artefact (e.g. comprising text, sound, images or video), a note or a scripted object created in Second Life (Blin, Nocchi and Fowley 2013). All these material-semiotic objects are part of a longer-term process than their initial creation or immediate use. They allow us to trace the nonlinear trajectory that language learners produce as they move across settings, genres, media and activities (Lemke 2005: 113). For example, Blin and Appel (2011) argue that chat transcripts, forum postings, wiki pages and shared documents used and created by language learners involved in a computer supported collaborative writing activity provide rich data not only on language use and development but also on the evolving social and communicative structure of the activity as it is negotiated and reconstructed by the participants as the activity unfolds across different timescales. Their findings show that the somewhat unpredictable individual and collective trajectories actually produced by students impact, positively as well as negatively, on the attainment of the intended learning outcomes.

Material-semiotic artefacts carry significant information not only across time but also across space (Lemke 2000: 21). Students have always engaged in language learning activities in varied places, in the classroom, at home, in the library and in many other physical places, linked by semiotic artefacts (e.g. material texts or graphical displays) and spatial resources (e.g. walls, doors, pathways) that separate or connect different spaces (Lemke 2005: 115). CALL ecosystems, however, bring a new spatial dimension to the learning environment: while the physical space is still the site of students' physical presence and that of the device that links them to the virtual learning environment, learners' actions, including language use, take place elsewhere, in a virtual space and in a different timescale. Bakhtin's (1981) *chronotope*, '[literally "time-space"], [ ... which] expresses the inseparability of space and time' (Bakhtin 1981: 84), is a useful notion that can help capture the spatiotemporal organisation of action in the overall language learning trajectory, which in turn provides significant insights into learning processes. It is particularly useful in the context of digital games and simulations taking place in virtual worlds such as Second Life. For example, Blin et al. (2013) demonstrate the emergence of learning chronotopes following a critical incident that occurred during an Italian session in Second Life and interrupted the flow of the simulation in unpredicted and unpredictable ways. Yet, each chronotope became the site for the emergence, perception and potential realisation of *affordances*, which is the last conceptual tool to be considered in this chapter. The next section will briefly examine the theory of affordances and its potential contribution to the construction of an ecological CALL theory.

## The theory of affordances

The term *affordance* was initially coined by Gibson (1979, 2013). Affordances are action possibilities offered by the environment to organisms: they are 'what [the environment] offers the animal, what it provides or furnishes, either for good or ill' (Gibson 2013: chap. 8, para. 2). For example, a chair affords sitting, and a ladder affords climbing. Possibilities for action in the environment are determined by both the objective properties of the environment and by the action capabilities of the animal: a chair affords sitting to an adult but not to an infant (Kaptelinin and Nardi 2012a: 968). According to Baerentsen and Trettvik (2002), affordances can only be realised 'in the interaction between organisms and objects in the environment', and are thus emergent properties of the material world (p. 52). In order to be realised, affordances need to be perceived by the observer, who must possess the required physical or mental capabilities to enact them. Adopting an activity-theoretical approach to HCI, Baerentsen and Trettvik (2002: 54) argue that the 'objective features' of the environment only become affordances when they are related to the actors' (or users') needs and activity: tools specifically designed for use in the construction industry are unlikely to provide affordances to a lawyer in the normal exercise of her profession.

A theory of affordances for CALL should not however be reduced to the technological dimension. Rather, it should relate the latter to educational and social affordances. Following Kirschner (2002), Lee (2009: 151) defines educational affordances 'as the relationships between the properties of an educational intervention and the characteristics of the learner that enable certain kinds of learning to take place'. Van Lier (2008: 598) emphasises the relationship between affordances and learning: 'while being active in the learning environment the learner detects properties in the environment that provide opportunities for further action and hence for learning'. This also relates to discussions on social (or communication) affordances as found in the literature associated with action-based and ecological approaches to language learning. Van Lier (2004: 95) introduces the concept of *language affordances*, which he defines as 'relations of possibility between language learners [that] can be acted upon to make further linguistic action possible' (actions performed by given utterances such as declaring, requesting, promising, assessing, etc.).

The features or 'objective characteristics' of CALL ecosystems offer educational, technological, social and language affordances. Some of these affordances have been consciously engineered by CALL designers; others will emerge as learners interact with digital objects, fellow students, teachers or other users of the target language. In their aforementioned study, Blin et al. (2013) examine the emergence and realisation of technological, educational and language affordances in the context of a simulation in Second Life, which is part of a larger CALL ecosystem. Educational affordances originate in the interactional and action-oriented approach to language learning that underpins the design of the simulation and of its component tasks as well as their integration in the broader language curriculum. Language affordances have their origin in the actions carried out in response to prescribed tasks by language learners, who avail of a rich 'semiotic budget' (van Lier 2000: 252), and by native speakers of the target language. These language affordances emerge in synchronous and asynchronous multimodal interactions between avatars, and between avatars and some scripted objects that have been placed in the environment and carry semiotic resources. As illustrated in Figure 3.3, educational and language affordances interact, on different timescales (e.g. macro and micro levels, respectively), and are connected by the technological affordances (e.g. at the meso level) offered by the virtual world, such as the possibility of displaying information attached to scripted objects, of moving within and across different places, of zooming on objects, entering text in the local chat or activating vocal communication (Blin et al. 2013). Failure to perceive and enact these technological affordances may constrain the realisation of longer-term educational affordances, which in turn may impact on the emergence of language affordances in unpredictable ways.

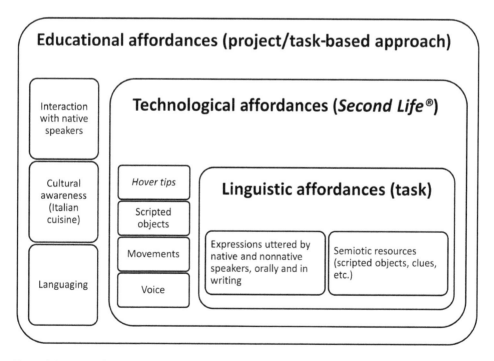

*Figure 3.3* Nested affordances in CALL ecosystems

Françoise Blin

## Future directions

This chapter introduced what I consider to be three essential pillars of an ecological CALL theory. First, it gave a brief overview of three theories that, on their own or combined, provide a powerful lens to analyse and understand complex CALL ecosystems. It then briefly examined how these theories link macro and micro levels of analysis and showed how the notions of heterochrony and chronotope can be used as conceptual tools to guide our explorations of CALL ecosystems across multiple timescales and spaces. Finally, it introduced some of the main tenets of the theory of affordances, which, by linking perception and action across different timescales and spaces, can contribute to the design of successful CALL ecosystem as well as providing the blueprint for their evaluation.

At the time of writing, ecological CALL is still in its infancy. Theoretical perspectives on the dynamics of CALL ecosystems, their temporal and spatial dimensions, and on the affordances that they provide need to be refined, expanded and instantiated through the design and in-depth study of new technology-rich settings for language learning and language use. Issues of ontological commensurability between the different theories and notions presented here also need to be further explored. In particular, the construction of an ecological CALL theory, or the instantiation of some of its components in CALL research, design and practice, entails a view of language, language learning and language use that is commensurable with the ecological principles that have been introduced here. Such a view requires a number of paradigm shifts that are already the focus of much debate and advances in the broader domain of applied linguistics as evidenced by the large body of work on languaging, meaning-making, agency and dialogism (Linell 2009). Together with technological advances – more specifically in the areas of cloud computing, augmented reality, and 3D graphical immersive environments, the ubiquity of mobile technologies and social media, and current trends in HCI – these paradigm shifts force us to rethink our approach to CALL research, design and practice.

## Further reading

Dooly, M.A.D. and O'Dowd, R. (eds) (2012) *Researching Online Foreign Language Interaction and Exchange Theories, Methods and Challenge*, Bern, Switzerland: Peter Lang.
    This edited volume provides an accessible introduction to theoretical approaches and methods that are particularly suited for researching foreign language interaction and exchange in online environments. Jonathon Reinhardt's contribution, 'Accommodating Divergent Frameworks in Analysis of Technology-Mediated L2 Interaction', provides a detailed account of the social-cognitive debate in SLA, and discusses the potential role of ecological approaches in the context of L2 interaction mediated by technology. The contribution by Blin, 'Introducing Cultural Historical Activity Theory for Researching CMC in Foreign Language Education', explicates the main tenets of CHAT principles and methods and illustrates how it can be applied in the context of CMC and foreign language education.

Kaptelinin, V. and Nardi, B. (2012) *Activity Theory in HCI: Fundamentals and Reflections*, San Rafael, CA: Morgan & Claypool Publishers.
    In this short book, Kaptelinin and Nardi revisit the fundamentals of activity theory and reflect on its contribution to HCI theoretical foundations. Following a concise introduction to the main principles of activity theory, three key HCI topics are discussed: agency, experience and activity-centric computing, which are particularly relevant to CALL from an ecological perspective. New trends of research are also discussed, including sustainable interaction design. The book reminds us of the importance of theory in domains, such as HCI research, which may be largely atheoretical.

Larsen-Freeman, D. and Cameron, L. (2008) *Complex Systems and Applied Linguistics*, Oxford, UK: Oxford University Press.
    The first three chapters of this book introduce and make accessible key concepts in complexity theory. The remaining chapters explore and discuss their usefulness and applicability to the study of language, second language acquisition, discourse analysis and language teaching. While the book does not directly

address issues relating to CALL, it nevertheless provides a robust grounding in the contribution that complexity theory can make to applied linguistics.

Van Lier, L. (2004) *The Ecology and Semiotics of Language Learning: A Sociocultural Perspective*, Boston, MA: Kluwer Academic Publishers.

Van Lier explores language education from an ecological and sociocultural perspective and provides a comprehensive overview of theoretical approaches that contribute to an ecological view of language and language learning. The theoretical discussions focus, inter alia, on theories of language, semiotics, emergence and affordances, and language learning pathways. The book is thought-provoking, but readers new to the field probably need to familiarise themselves with some of the topics listed earlier to fully appreciate it.

Yamagata-Lynch, L.C. (2010) *Activity Systems Analysis Methods: Understanding Complex Learning Environments*, New York; London: Springer.

This book describes how to study complex learning environments from a CHAT perspective, and more specifically, how to design and conduct trustworthy activity systems analyses. The first three chapters provide a comprehensive introduction to CHAT concepts and principles as well as a thorough discussion of its strengths and limitations. Chapters 4–6 will be of particular interest to graduate students or researchers wishing to conduct an activity system analysis. Chapter 4 provides numerous examples of activity systems analysis used for various purposes. Chapter 5 gives an overview of qualitative research methodologies as they can be applied to activity systems analysis. Chapter 6 provides an in-depth account of a comparative case study research using activity systems analysis. It must be noted, however, that the activity systems analysis explicated by Yamagata-Lynch is not interventionist, as is the case with the Change Laboratory methodology developed by Engeström and his team at the University of Helsinki.

## References

Baerentsen, K.B. and Trettvik, J. (2002) 'An activity theory approach to affordance', in *Proceedings of the Second Nordic Conference on Human-Computer Interaction*, 51–60, available: http://dl.acm.org/citation.cfm?id=572028 (accessed 30 Aug 2012).

Bakhtin, M.M. (1981) *Dialogic Imagination: Four Essays*, Austin, TX: University of Texas Press.

Basharina, O. (2007) 'An activity theory perspective on student-reported contradictions in international telecollaboration', *Language Learning & Technology*, 11(2): 82–103.

Blin, F. (2010) 'Designing cybertasks for learner autonomy: Towards an activity theoretical pedagogical model', in M.J. Luzón, M.N. Ruiz-Madrid and M.L. Villanueva (eds), *Digital Genres, New Literacies and Autonomy in Language Learning*, Newcastle upon Tyne, UK: Cambridge Scholars Publishing: 175–196.

Blin, F. (2012a) 'Introducing cultural historical activity theory of researching CMC in foreign language education', in M. Dooly and R. O'Dowd (eds), *Researching Online Foreign Language Interaction and Exchange*, Bern, Switzerland: Peter Lang: 79–106.

Blin, F. (2012b) 'Bologna and the 21st century language learner: integrating technology for learner autonomy', in J. Burston, D. Tsagari and F. Doa (eds), *Foreign Language Instructional Technology: Theory & Practice*, Nicosia: University of Nicosia Press: 60–77.

Blin, F. and Appel, C. (2011) 'Computer supported collaborative writing in practice: An activity theoretical study', *CALICO Journal*, 28(2): 473–497.

Blin, F. and Jalkanen, J. (forthcoming) 'Learning to design and designing for learning: Agency and languaging in digitally enhanced learning environments', *Apples – Journal of Applied Linguistics*, available: http://apples.jyu.fi

Blin, F., Nocchi, S. and Fowley, C. (2013) 'Mondes virtuels et apprentissage des langues: vers un cadre théorique émergent', *Recherches et applications*, 54: 94–107.

Bronfenbrenner, U. (1979) *The Ecology of Human Development: Experiments by Nature and Design*, Kindle edition, Cambridge, MA: Harvard University Press.

Bronfenbrenner, U. (1993) 'Ecological models of human development', in M. Gauvain and M. Cole (eds), *Readings on the Development of Children*, 2nd edn, New York, NY: Freeman: 37–43. Reprinted from the *International Encyclopedia of Education* (1994), Volume 3 (2nd edn.), Oxford, UK: Elsevier: 1643–1647.

Burns, A. (2005) 'Action research: An evolving paradigm?', *Language Teaching*, 38(2): 57–74.

Byrne, D. (1998) *Complexity Theory and the Social Sciences: An Introduction*, London, UK: Routledge.

Chapelle, C.A. (2009) 'The Relationship Between Second Language Acquisition Theory and Computer-Assisted Language Learning', *The Modern Language Journal*, 93(Focus issue): 741–753.

De Bot, K., Lowie, W., Thorne, S.L. and Verspoor, M. (2013) 'Dynamic Systems Theory as a comprehensive theory of second language development', in M. Mayo, M. Gutierrez-Mangado and M. Adrian (eds), *Contemporary Approaches to Second Language Acquisition*, Amsterdam, Netherlands: John Benjamins: 199–220.

deWaard, I., Abajian, S., Gallagher, M.S., Hogue, R., Keskin, N., Koutropoulos, A. et al. (2011) 'Using mLearning and MOOCs to understand chaos, emergence, and complexity in education', *International Review of Research in Open & Distance Learning*, 12(7): 94–115.

Dooly, M.A.D. and O'Dowd, R. (eds) (2012) *Researching Online Foreign Language Interaction and Exchange Theories, Methods and Challenge*, Bern, Switzerland: Peter Lang.

Ellis, N.C. and Larsen-Freeman, D. (2006) 'Language emergence: Implications for applied linguistics – Introduction to the special issue', *Applied Linguistics*, 27(4): 558–589.

Ellis, V., Edwards, A. and Smagorinsky, P. (eds) (2010) *Cultural-Historical Perspectives on Teacher Education and Development*, Oxon, London: Routledge.

Engeström, Y. (1987) *Learning by Expanding: An Activity-Theoretical Approach to Developmental Research*, Helsinki, Finland: Orienta-Konsultit Oy.

Engeström, Y. (2001) 'Expansive learning at work: Toward an activity theoretical reconceptualization', *Journal of Education and Work*, 14(1): 133–156.

Engeström, Y. (2008) *From Teams to Knots: Activity-Theoretical Studies of Collaboration and Learning at Work*, Cambridge, MA: Cambridge University Press.

Engeström, Y. and Sannino, A. (2010) 'Studies of expansive learning: Foundations, findings and future challenges', *Educational Research Review*, 5(1): 1–24.

Firth, A. and Wagner, J. (1997) 'On discourse, communication, and (some) fundamental concepts in SLA research', *The Modern Language Journal*, 81(3): 285–300.

Gay, G. and Hembrooke, H. (2004) *Activity-Centered Design: An Ecological Approach to Designing Smart Tools and Usable Systems*, Cambridge, MA: MIT Press.

Gee, J.P. and Hayes, E. (2011) *Language and Learning in the Digital Age*, Oxon, London: Routledge.

Gibson, J.J. (1979) *The Ecological Approach to Visual Perception*, New York, NY: Houghton Mifflin. Kindle Edition.

Gibson, J.J. (2013) *The Ecological Approach to Visual Perception*, New edition, New York, NY: Psychology Press.

Hadjistassou, S. (2012) 'An activity theory exegesis on conflict and contradictions in networked discussions and feedback exchanges', *CALICO Journal*, 29(2): 367–388.

Hirsch, M.W., Smale, S. and Devaney, R.L. (2004) *Differential Equations, Dynamical Systems, and an Introduction to Chaos*, 2nd edn, Amsterdam, Netherlands: Elsevier Academic Press.

Johnson, E.S. (2008) 'Ecological systems and complexity theory: Toward an alternative model of accountability in education', *Complicity: An International Journal of Complexity and Education*, 5(1), available: http://ejournals.library.ualberta.ca/index.php/complicity/article/viewArticle/8777 (accessed 15 Aug 2013).

Johnson, G.M. (2010) 'Internet use and child development: Validation of the ecological techno-subsystem', *Educational Technology & Society*, 13(1): 176–185.

Kaptelinin, V. and Nardi, B. (2012a) 'Affordances in HCI: Toward a mediated action perspective', in *Proceedings of the 2012 ACM Annual Conference on Human Factors in Computing Systems*: 967–976.

Kaptelinin, V. and Nardi, B. (2012b) *Activity Theory in HCI: Fundamentals and Reflections*, Kindle edition, San Rafael, CA: Morgan & Claypool Publishers.

Kirschner, P. (2002) 'Can we support CCSL? Educational, social and technological affordances for learning', in P. Kirschner (ed), *Three Worlds of CSCL: Can We Support CSCL?*, Heerlen: Open University of the Netherlands: 7–47.

Kramsch, C. (2002a) *Language Acquisition and Language Socialization: Ecological Perspectives*, London, UK: Continuum.

Kramsch, C. (2002b) 'Introduction: "How can we tell the dancer from the dance?"', in C. Kramsch (ed), *Language Acquisition and Language Socialization: Ecological Perspectives*, London, UK: Continuum: 1–30.

Kuutti, K. (1996) 'Activity theory as a potential framework for human-computer interaction research', in B.A. Nardi (ed), *Context and Consciousness: Activity Theory and Human-Computer Interaction*, Cambridge, MA: The MIT Press: 17–44.

Lafford, B.A. (2009) 'Toward an ecological CALL: Update to Garrett (1991)', *The Modern Language Journal*, 93(Focus issue): 673–696.

Lam, W.S.E. and Kramsch, C. (2003) 'The ecology of an SLA community in a computer-mediated environment', in J. Leather and J. Van Dam (eds), *Ecology of Language Acquisition*, Dordrecht: Kluwer Academic Publishers: 141–158.

Larsen-Freeman, D. (2002) 'Language acquisition and language use from a chaos/complexity theory perspective', in C. Kramsch (ed), *Language Acquisition and Language Socialization: Ecological Perspectives*, London, UK: Continuum: 33–46.
Larsen-Freeman, D. (2012) 'Complex, dynamic systems: A new transdisciplinary theme for applied linguistics?', *Language Teaching*, 45(2): 202–214.
Larsen-Freeman, D. and Cameron, L. (2008) *Complex Systems and Applied Linguistics*, Oxford: Oxford University Press.
Lee, M. (2009) 'How can 3D virtual worlds be used to support collaborative learning? An analysis of cases from the literature', *Journal of e-Learning and Knowledge Society*, 5(1), available: http://je-lks.org/ojs/index.php/Je-LKS_EN/article/view/300 (accessed 13 Jun 2013).
Lemke, J. (2002) 'Language development and identity: Multiple timescales in the social ecology of learning', in C. Kramsch (ed), *Language Acquisition and Language Socialization: Ecological Perspectives*, London, UK: Continuum: 68–87.
Lemke, J. (2005) 'Place, pace, and meaning: multimedia chronotopes', in S. Norris and R.H. Jones (eds), *Discourse in Action: Introducing Mediated Discourse Analysis*, Oxon: Routledge, Taylor and Francis: 110–121.
Lemke, J.L. (2000) 'Across the scales of time: Artifacts, activities, and meanings in ecosocial systems', *Mind, Culture & Activity*, 7(4): 273–290.
Lemke, J.L. (2001) 'The long and the short of it: Comments on multiple timescale studies of human activity', *Journal of the Learning Sciences*, 10(1): 17–26.
Leontiev, A.N. (1978) *Activity, Consciousness and Personality*, Englewood Cliffs, NJ: Prentice Hall.
Lewin, K. (1935) *A Dynamic Theory of Personality: Selected Papers*, New York, NY: Wiley.
Linell, P. (2009) *Rethinking Language, Mind, and World Dialogically: Interactional and Contextual Theories of Human Sense-making*, Charlotte, NC: Information Age Publishing.
Littlewood, W. (2004) 'Second language learning', in C. Elder and A. Davies (eds), *The Handbook of Applied Linguistics*, Oxford: Blackwell: 501–524.
Luenberger, D.G. (1979) *Introduction to Dynamic Systems: Theory, Models, and Applications*, New York, NY: Wiley.
McAuley, A., Stewart, B., Siemens, G. and Cormier, D. (2010) *The MOOC Model for Digital Practice* [online], available: https://oerknowledgecloud.org/sites/oerknowledgecloud.org/files/MOOC_Final_0.pdf (accessed 15 Aug 2013).
Merriam-Webster (2013) *Online Dictionary*, available: http://www.merriam-webster.com/
Orland-Barak, L. and Becher, A. (2011) 'Cycles of action through systems of activity: Examining an action research model through the lens of activity theory', *Mind, Culture, and Activity*, 18(2): 115–128.
Peng, J.-E. (2012) 'Towards an ecological understanding of willingness to communicate in EFL classrooms in China', *System*, 40(2): 203–213.
Reinhardt, J. (2012) 'Accommodating divergent frameworks in analysis of technology-mediated L2 interaction', in M.A.D. Dooly and R. O'Dowd (eds), *Researching Online Foreign Language Interaction and Exchange*, Bern, Switzerland: Peter Lang: 45–77.
Roth, W.-M. (2004) 'Introduction: "Activity theory and education: An introduction"', *Mind, Culture, and Activity*, 11(1): 1–8.
Schulze, M. (2013) 'Complexity science and CALL. Short paper presented at the symposium on data and elicitation methods in interaction-based research', in *Conference Proceedings*, Presented at the World-CALL 2013 Conference, Glasgow, Scotland, 23, available: https://dl.dropbox.com/s/p3853ngyb-94dazq/Short%20Papers.pdf
Schulze, M. and Penner, N. (2008) 'Construction grammar in ICALL', *Computer Assisted Language Learning*, 21(5): 427–440.
Siemens, G. (2005) 'Connectivism: A learning theory for the digital age', *International Journal of Instructional Technology & Distance Learning*, 2(1): 3–9.
Smith, L. (2007) *Chaos: A Very Short Introduction*, Oxford: Oxford University Press.
Staples, A., Pugach, M.C. and Himes, D. (2005) 'Rethinking the technology integration challenge: Cases from three urban elementary schools', *Journal of Research on Technology in Education*, 37(3): 285–311.
Stetsenko, A. (2008) 'From relational ontology to transformative activist stance on development and learning: expanding Vygotsky's (CHAT) project', *Cultural Studies of Science Education*, 3(2): 471–491.
Thorne, S. (2003) 'Artifacts and cultures-of-use in intercultural communication', *Language Learning & Technology*, 7(2): 38–67.
Thorne, S.L. (2009) '"Community", semiotic flows, and mediated contribution to activity', *Language Teaching*, 42(01): 81–94.

Thorne, S.L., Fischer, I. and Lu, X. (2012) 'The semiotic ecology and linguistic complexity of an online game world', *ReCALL*, 24(03): 279–301.

Van Lier, L. (2000) 'From input to affordance: Social-interactive learning from an ecological perspective', in J.P. Lantolf (ed), *Sociocultural Theory and Second Language Learning*, Oxford: Oxford University Press: 245–259.

Van Lier, L. (2003) 'A tale of two computer classrooms: The ecology of project-based language learning', in J.H. Leather and J. van Dam (eds), *The Ecology of Language Acquisition*, Dordrecht: Kluwer Academic: 49–64.

Van Lier, L. (2004) *The Ecology and Semiotics of Language Learning: A Sociocultural Perspective*, Dordrecht: Kluwer Academic Publishers.

Van Lier, L. (2008) 'Ecological-semiotic perspectives on educational linguistics', in B. Spolsky and F.M. Hult (eds), *The Handbook of Educational Linguistics*, Malden, MA: Blackwell: 596–604.

Vygotsky, L.S. (1978) *Mind in Society: The Development of Higher Psychological Processes*, Cambridge, MA: Harvard University Press.

Zheng, D. and Newgarden, K. (2011) 'Rethinking language learning: Virtual worlds as a catalyst for change', *International Journal of Learning and Media*, 3(2): 13–36.

# Part II
# Core issues

# 4
# Technology standards for language teacher preparation

*Greg Kessler*

This chapter addresses technology standards for language teachers. Recently there has been increased interest in preparing language teachers to use technology for instructional purposes. This interest has inspired exploration into the relationship between specific aspects of pedagogical and technical knowledge and skills that should be expected of professional language teachers. These expectations are discussed in this chapter through the lens of established standards. The author provides an overview of current standards as well as a discussion about the challenges of creating standards for technologies that are experiencing rapid evolution. He provides an overview of varied approaches that teacher preparation programmes have taken to incorporate these standards as well as contextualised examples of technologies being used effectively. Suggestions for the incorporation of emerging forms of media and technology are also discussed.

## Overview of standards in education

Competency-based instruction is becoming common across instructional contexts around the world. A growing concern for measuring academic achievements has driven this movement, and national and international professional organisations have developed many standards and competencies. Standards are benchmark expectations of competency that can be used in objective evaluation of teacher abilities. In response, teachers are eager to identify ways to align their instruction with these standards that have become commonplace in recent years. At the national level, these projects are often initiated as educational reform with the intention of creating measurable learning outcomes. Standards have also been established that address the use of instructional technology as well as the more specific area of technology within language teaching and learning.

### Technology-focused standards for education

Some educational standards projects have focused heavily on technology. These include the International Society for Technology in Education (ISTE) National Educational Technology Standards (NETS), and the Information and Communication Technologies Competency

Standards for Teachers (ICT-CST) released by UNESCO. Both of these projects approach the need for standards from a different perspective. The UNESCO ICT-CST standards are intended for use by ministries of education around the world to promote educational reform through the incorporation of ICT. They are organised around the three approaches of technology literacy, knowledge deepening and knowledge creation. Each of these approaches is supported by implementation guidelines categorised as policy, curriculum and assessment, pedagogy, ICT, organisation and administration, and teacher professional development. These standards are supported by a series of modules that serve as a reference for teachers in the use of ICT. (Versions of these documents can be found at http://cst.unesco-ci.org/sites/projects/cst/.) However, as these are intended to guide ministries of education, the scale of implementing these standards is likely to exceed the reach of most educational professionals.

The ISTE/NETS standards are likely more accessible for individual teachers. These standards provide guidelines for technology use for teachers across disciplines from prekindergarten to postsecondary school. The ISTE/NETS teacher standards include:

1.  Facilitate and inspire student learning and creativity

    Teachers use their knowledge of subject matter, teaching and learning, and technology to facilitate experiences that advance student learning, creativity and innovation in both face-to-face and virtual environments.

2.  Design and develop digital age learning experiences and assessments

    Teachers design, develop and evaluate authentic learning experiences and assessment incorporating contemporary tools and resources to maximise content learning in context and to develop the knowledge, skills and attitudes identified in the NETS-S*.

3.  Model digital age work and learning

    Teachers exhibit knowledge, skills and work processes representative of an innovative professional in a global and digital society.

4.  Promote and model digital citizenship and responsibility

    Teachers understand local and global societal issues and responsibilities in an evolving digital culture and exhibit legal and ethical behaviour in their professional practices.

5.  Engage in professional growth and leadership

    Teachers continuously improve their professional practice, model lifelong learning and exhibit leadership in their school and professional community by promoting and demonstrating the effective use of digital tools and resources.

*Note: NETS-S refers to the student standards.*

The ISTE/NETS standards (along with the accompanying performance indicators) are freely available online at http://www.iste.org/standards/nets-for-teachers.

This is a good example of standards that are clear and can be easily adopted by teachers. The ISTE/NETS standards also include a significant amount of support material to guide teachers. While both of the UNESCO ICT-CST and ISTE/NETS standards should certainly serve to guide all teachers in their reflections upon the use of technology, there are no discipline-specific recommendations. Each individual discipline is likely to have some unique circumstances that would justify establishing more targeted standards.

Another recent standards project in education is the European Higher Education Area (EHEA) set of competencies. These include benchmarks for technology standards within both their general competencies as well as those focused on specific disciplines. This European project is directed at higher education and was initiated by a desire to align economic prosperity with a unified multicultural and multilingual European community.

## Standards for language teachers

Many language teachers in the United States celebrated the release of the American Council of Teachers of Foreign Languages (ACTFL) *Standards for Foreign Language Learning in the 21st Century*. This first attempt to introduce standards into the foreign language teaching context has been recognised by many as a significant agent of change. The five goal areas (commonly referred to as the 5 Cs) are communication, cultures, connections, comparisons and communities. While these perspectives have been influential on the changing nature of the foreign language education landscape, many have acknowledged the inherent limitations that result from a lack of attention to appropriate technology preparation for teachers. In the intervening years, a number of scholars have offered suggestions for introducing a focus on technology.

While intended to be comprehensive, the ACTFL standards offer little specificity regarding the role of technology. These have become the cornerstone language standards for North America. Published in 1999, these standards are built around a core curriculum that weaves together language and culture that benefits from the incorporation of technology. However, there is little in the way of specific details describing how technology should be incorporated. In the intervening years, there have been numerous suggestions that a future version of these standards would incorporate technology in a significant way. For example a 2011 report by ACTFL, evaluating the first decade of their standards, acknowledged that the use of technology in teacher preparation was largely limited to accessing other instructional materials.

Recently, there have been other attempts to conduct research into the overall effectiveness of these standards. While many positive outcomes have been observed, the lack of attention to technology has been acknowledged. Glisan (2012) explored numerous studies directed towards evaluating the effectiveness of the ACTFL standards. Among the many observations made by the author is the acknowledgement that technology has 'yet to influence classroom practice in a significant way' (Glisan 2012: 518). While this claim is discouraging in light of the body of research that has been amassed over the past few decades about the potential for using technology in language teaching, it is reassuring that there is an awareness of the absence of technology. Furthermore, it is encouraging to note the ongoing research examining the effectiveness of standards projects in practice. Along with publications focusing on pedagogical implementation of standards, such investigations can only result in improved standards and practices throughout the profession.

ACTFL has also released a position statement that takes a bold stand on the integration of technology in foreign language education. The organisation has clearly recognised reliance upon technology as a potential threat to teacher facilitated instruction. The statement is publicly available on the ACTFL website and is presented here in its entirety.

**Position Statement**

The American Council on the Teaching of Foreign Languages (ACTFL) acknowledges and encourages using the potential of technology as a tool to support and enhance classroom-based language instruction. ACTFL also acknowledges the potential of well supervised and articulated distance learning programs to fill a need where classroom teachers are not available. However, because language is one of the most complex of all human activities and interactions ACTFL also recognises the pivotal role of a qualified language teacher to incorporate and manage the implementation of technology so that it effectively supports the language learning experience.

The use of technology should never be the goal in and of itself, but rather one tool for helping language learners to use the target language in culturally appropriate ways to accomplish authentic tasks. Further, all language learning opportunities whether provided through technology or in a traditional classroom setting, should be standards-based and help develop students' proficiency in the target language through interactive, meaningful, and cognitively engaging learning experiences, facilitated by a qualified language teacher.

Therefore, ACTFL strongly advises school and university administrators to place the responsibility for language instruction in the hands of qualified language teachers rather than solely in technology programs. Cost-cutting measures such as replacing teachers with software or online programs for language learning or launching new language programs using language software or other technologies will disadvantage language learners if learners will have significantly fewer opportunities to develop language proficiency under the necessary conditions of a dynamic environment and interaction with and guidance from a qualified language teacher.

*(http://www.actfl.org/news/position-statements/role-technology-language-learning)*

This position statement makes it clear that there are concerns in the profession about the role that technology ought to play in formal language education. This concern reflects the tension between informed and appropriate pedagogical integration and the commercially driven realm of technology that has been recognised by many as undermining academic integrity. These concerns underpin the need for technology-related standards that reinforce the importance of preparing language teaching professionals to make informed decisions about the integration of technology. Technology has long functioned in a precarious manner within language teaching programmes. While many have promoted the numerous benefits of thoughtfully incorporating technology-based solutions, others have perceived the introduction of technology as a threat. This threat perception is not an irrational response. After all, many industries have faced threats from technological developments, in some cases even leading to the eradication of industries. Throughout human history, previously reliable professions have disappeared with the introduction of new technologies. Our cities are no longer filled with blacksmiths, cobblers or alchemists. It is understandable that educators might be a bit apprehensive about technological intrusion; in some cases language teaching positions have actually been threatened by the introduction of technology. While language teachers have largely been unprepared for the technological advancements in communication that surround us, the potential is obvious to other stakeholders, including administrators and policy makers. The insufficient nature of teacher preparation for the use of technology in language teaching has resulted in some becoming increasingly reliant upon commercial software solutions. Unfortunately, much of the language learning software that is currently available is lacking. This is partly owing to the fact that most language teaching professionals lack the training to be able to properly evaluate and critique these offerings.

In fact, there have been some experiments with reducing teaching staff in favour of relying on commercially distributed technology-based language instructional systems. A small number of language teaching programmes have developed their own autonomous systems of instruction.

In some rare cases robots are being created as substitutes for language teachers (Lee et al. 2011). All of these alternative approaches are in their infancy and it would be premature to evaluate their effectiveness. However, most language teaching professionals anticipate that these attempts will fall far short of the expectations that we can assign to language teachers. Yet, these developments accompany a concern that they are not realistically preparing language learners for the expectations they will face in the increasingly multilingual world. Many have observed that fully automated language teaching technologies lack the critical aspects that a teacher can provide. Although natural language processing has offered much in developing learner models that can predict and anticipate, automated systems are as of yet unable to identify and respond to subtle linguistic nuances the same way a teacher can. Therefore, it is critical that teachers be prepared to utilise technology in meaningful and appropriate ways. Over the past few decades there have been numerous research-based observations about the specific technology needs of language teaching professionals. For the purpose of establishing a foundation for language teacher technology standards, the following is an overview of some of these observations.

## Language teacher technology preparation and standards

Many standards projects have resulted from concerns about teacher preparation. While the overwhelming consensus of research suggests that language learning benefits in varied ways from the inclusion of technology, there have been many concerns about the preparation that language teachers received in their educational programmes. Some have identified a dearth of computer-assisted language learning (CALL) focused content within language teacher preparation (Kessler 2006; Hubbard 2008; Healey et al. 2011). Further, there has been concern that what little preparation may occur is often inadequate or inappropriate for teachers' situational needs such that teachers are even unlikely to utilise technology in their own teaching after having been prepared to do so (Egbert, Paulus and Nakamichi 2002; Hegelheimer 2006; Peters 2006; Hubbard 2008; Dooly 2009).

In recent years, many have commented on the increasing role that technology should play across language learning and teaching contexts (Hubbard and Levy 2006; Slaouti and Motteram 2006; Hubbard 2008). While this observation often focuses on the supportive resources available to students or the institutional practices that benefit from technological integration, it is often concluded that teachers lack the skills or knowledge to support these initiatives. Consequently, there has been a growing recognition of the need to prepare teachers to integrate technology into their language instruction. Research over the past few decades has demonstrated numerous benefits in language learning that result from the use of technology. In addition to language learning and retention, improvements in attitude and motivation are often observed in CALL studies. Therefore, it is critical that teachers are prepared to use these technologies and make decisions about how they are integrated into their instruction. In order to make such decisions, teachers need to have a comprehensive understanding of CALL pedagogy and practices (Hubbard 2008; Healey et al. 2011). Numerous studies over the years have recognised that there is generally inconsistent and unpredictable awareness and use of technology among language teachers. Quite simply, it has become clear that the majority of language teachers are not aware of technology solutions even for their specific teaching contexts (Egbert et al. 2002; Kessler and Plakans 2008; Dooly and Sadler 2013). Some researchers have recognised that what little teachers do know about the use of technology tends to result from a significant reliance upon short-term professional development such as conference presentations, workshops or in-service training (Kessler 2010). This kind of training can lead to limited understanding. Further, this is a common weakness across language teacher preparation in the field that has resulted in a recent increase of pedagogy- and technology-focused courses in teacher preparation programmes.

Ideally, language teacher preparation should be aligned with related standards. However, it is unlikely that teacher preparation programmes and courses are revamped each time a professional organisation releases a new set of expectations. Consequently, dissemination of the expectations established by technology standards is likely to occur through a variety of professional contexts. Some may take place in formal academic settings, but it is most likely that dissemination of language technology standards will occur in more casual short-term professional development contexts such as workshops and in-service trainings or through communities of practice. Such short-term exposure can lead to a limited understanding or even misunderstanding. This concern can be heightened in an environment where technological innovation is in such a rapid state of change. Considering the various opportunities for exchanging feedback through today's digital communication tools, it should be no surprise that individuals may develop highly personalised preferences for one tool over another. However, establishing consistent technology integration throughout language programmes can be critical to successful implementation. CALL professionals need to carefully consider the benefits and challenges of any tools within this structural context and be aware of their own individual, and perhaps idiosyncratic, bias. The establishment of standards can help to avoid these pitfalls.

## Basics of CALL teacher preparation

While many scholars have argued for increased and improved technology teacher preparation, there has not been a consistent understanding of exactly what this should entail (Hubbard and Levy 2006). Not only is it not clear which technologies should be included or which pedagogical practices would best benefit from such integration, but the methods of preparation also vary greatly (Egbert 2006; Robb 2006; Slaouti and Motteram 2006). This presents a significant challenge to preparing teachers to use technology. Perhaps the greatest challenge in conducting CALL teacher preparation results from the diverse lineage of the field. With theoretical and methodological influences from across education, the social sciences, humanities and computer science, this field has cultivated a rich diversity of perspectives that can make teaching it complicated. For example, there is no single theory or approach to language teaching that is recognised by all CALL professionals. Although there is no universal consensus, there are some *general themes* that most scholars engaged in CALL teacher preparation address. These often include the ability to manage classroom activities and student records, the ability to provide feedback in appropriate and salient ways, the ability to disseminate materials in an organised and effective manner, the ability to coordinate digital communications, the ability to manage group projects and the ability to design and/or adapt learning materials for specific educational goals. Each of these areas holds potential for extensive description, but a brief illustration should serve our purposes here.

## Record keeping

Class management and record keeping is critical in organising educational experience. Keeping digital records that are at once organised and meaningful, yet also secure and confidential is not necessarily a simple thing. For example, if student progress is tracked electronically and available to students, it needs to be maintained. Such information must also be secure and reliable, requiring teachers to use technology in a manner that is consistent with their awareness of ethical obligations.

## Feedback

Feedback is critical for language learning improvement. Without feedback, students are likely to continue to repeat the same errors in perpetuity. Feedback involves linguistic nuances that can determine its effectiveness: too much feedback and a student can be overwhelmed, while too little can leave them unchallenged. Providing feedback digitally allows language teachers to enhance their message with media files when appropriate or to monitor student access of the feedback. It also allows multimodal feedback to be offered so that comments on a written work may be spoken in order to promote student's individual needs at any given moment. Individualising feedback through digital formats can provide students with the most salient and actionable opportunities.

## Individualised material

Managing the dissemination of learning materials in an organised and meaningful way can be challenging. By understanding how technology can be used to do this, teachers can create new efficiencies in their instructional practices. They can also be better prepared to individualise instruction so that each student has access to the material that is most suitable and salient at that precise point in her development. This ability to better target the delivery of material could focus upon an individual student's proficiency in order to support incremental improvements or topical interests in order to increase motivation. Determining when such decisions need to be made is an important ability for teachers in these technologically enhanced environments.

## Digital communications

Recently there has been an increase in attention to the potential of social media and the many collaborative web-based tools for language teaching. These tools have dramatically transformed communication throughout society, and it is reasonable to expect that teachers learn to harness these tools for language learning communication opportunities. After all, teachers and students are both already quite accustomed to using these tools in their personal lives. The potential of these tools is still in a state of evolution. With the unique opportunities that these tools offer for communication, collaboration and interaction, we should anticipate a variety of developments across language teaching contexts. Some of the considerations that need to be incorporated into teacher preparation around the use of social media include the implications of the social nature of communication. This social nature has been found by some to motivate students to participate and to strive to improve their language abilities. Others have found that the strong emphasis on social media provides unique and otherwise unavailable opportunities for students to interact with others in the target language. However, some social contexts may present a threat or compromise students' security in some manner. Understanding and planning for such circumstances is an important part of a teachers' repertoire of abilities.

As technology evolves and we encounter new tools and new accompanying pedagogical practices, the manner in which we interact with and manipulate these tools also changes. However, there are basic technology skills that we learn through practice that have proven to be transferable to these new contexts. Therefore, the necessary technical skills for teachers can be reduced to small sets of initial skills that are expanded upon when contextualised. How these skills are utilised in a pedagogical context is a more complicated issue. An example of recommendations for teacher skills from the CALL teacher preparation literature can be seen in Table 4.1. These are presented in the context of working with video, but other forms of media should be easily substituted.

These skills distil what could be a very complex and complicated set of abilities across curricular goals and varied forms of media into a very finite set of abilities. They are presented as a

Greg Kessler

*Table 4.1* Basic and advanced skills for classroom teachers

*Basic CALL skills for classroom teachers*

| Skill | Teacher action |
| --- | --- |
| Locate | Use Internet search engine to find relevant movie files |
| Evaluate | Watch videos to determine if the language level is appropriate, if the content is accurate, if the quality of video is acceptable, etc. |
| Select | Select the file that best meets pedagogical needs |
| Distribute | Determine the best means for distributing a video file to students, including web links, CDs, local files, etc. |
| Integrate | Construct a language lesson around the content of the video file that utilises the images, audio, and text in meaningful pedagogical ways |

*Advanced CALL skills for classroom teachers*

| Skill | Teacher action |
| --- | --- |
| Create | Create a video using a combination of personally created images, text, and voice recordings |
| Customise | Edit the movie file expanding the narration with a more challenging version for a higher-level class |
| Convert | Edit the movie file deleting the audio to utilise as a reading activity |
| Repurpose | Use the instructional materials, media, or technology in multiple contexts with relatively minor alterations |

Source: Kessler (2012: 4).

simple example within one media domain, yet they can serve as a foundation upon which more specific activities and tasks can be constructed.

There have been suggestions for preparing teachers across a hierarchy of CALL specificity (Hubbard and Levy 2006; Hubbard 2008). In this type of approach, the highest level of expertise would be arranged for CALL experts, those who are specifically engaged in the field of CALL, who conduct research in that area and who focus on the preparation of others. This would require extensive knowledge and ongoing training across the spectrum of tools, skills and language learning environments. The next level of professionals would be CALL specialists. These individuals would require expertise in tools and pedagogical solutions within a more specific domain such as a language skill area or specific type of learning context (e.g. refugee/immigrant learners, adult, higher education or intensive English language programmes). A foundational layer of skills would be required of all teachers regardless of their teaching context or other area of expertise. This base level of skills may largely reflect the expectations for students as well. In this sense, CALL teacher preparation would also help teachers to help their students meet the student technology standards.

Some have also approached CALL teacher preparation from a skills-based model. They argue that since many language teachers focus upon individual skills for different purposes through their instruction, perhaps their technology integration ought to be focused upon those skills as well. Certainly, it is easy to recognise that the ability to master word processing software and tools that support exchanging written forms of feedback would be crucial for teachers of writing. Similarly, it is obvious that teachers who work largely with listening and speaking ought to have advanced skills using audio software that supports recording, editing and providing auditory feedback. Likewise, teachers who devote extensive amounts of their time to teaching reading should be familiar with technology tools that support the promotion of reading skills such as skimming, scanning, annotating and contextualising. They should also be familiar with new forms of disseminating written works through technology that offer readers the opportunity to share their reflections with one another, store their notes in the cloud and participate in online social media groups where they can share their reading experiences. However, in an integrated skills approach to language teaching, which is commonly accepted as preferable these days, it is likely that all teachers need to have some degree of proficiency across these technologies and skill areas. In fact, some researchers have observed that students who are engaged in extensive writing may sometimes benefit more from auditory feedback rather than feedback that is written. Likewise, it may sometimes be necessary to provide digitally written feedback to student speech. Consequently, teachers are most likely to benefit from a comprehensive preparation that is guided by the kinds of objectives we can find in a set of standards. The establishment of technology-related standards is likely to increase, enhance and focus the CALL components of teacher preparation programmes. We can also expect that the creation of standards will help teachers avoid the ineffective, inefficient or inappropriate use of technology in instruction. These changes would be a welcome response to many calls for more attention to this area of teacher preparation. However, creating standards for technology use in language teaching can be extremely challenging.

## Challenges of establishing standards

While it cannot be assumed that any standards project is going to result in perfect solutions to the challenges that we face, establishing standards allows us to focus the conversation around these realities in actual classroom practice. All standards projects are likely to face a healthy amount of suspicion or scepticism. After all, standardising anything can be seen as controlling or stifling the creativity of those teachers involved. Language teachers have long relied upon their creative talents to design authentic, engaging and meaningful learning activities and environments. Thoughtfully designed standards ought to take this reality into account and undergird these talents rather than undermine them. Allowing flexibility for individual teachers as well as institutional and cultural differences should serve to strengthen technology standards for teachers. This flexibility can allow institutions to adopt and adapt the standards for their unique situational needs.

I believe this can lead to healthy discussions about the role of standards and the role of technology in language teacher preparation programmes. We have learned over the past two decades that there are many challenges associated with both the creation and implementation of standards (Glisan 2012). While it is obvious that establishing any set of standards for language teaching would present unique challenges, creating technology standards can be exceptionally difficult. Not only is it difficult to anticipate the access to professional development and technological resources that particular groups of teachers might have, it is nearly impossible to predict the technologies that will be used in coming years as well as how they will be used effectively in teaching. These challenges have been addressed in different ways through different standards projects. For example, the ISTE standards focus upon skills rather than specific technologies, while the TESOL Technology Standards promote localised interpretation to align with specific contexts.

There is no consensus regarding the tools and resources that teachers should be required to know. In fact, with the wide variety of tools available that could be used in language communication it is likely that no two teacher preparation programmes are preparing teachers to use the same tools. This likely diversity reinforces the use of the aforementioned basic skills. Regardless of the specific technologies, adhering to the body of knowledge that has been constructed around language teaching methodology and pedagogy should help to inform classroom practice. However, the affordances that some technologies bring to learning contexts are likely to require critical reflection upon established pedagogical practices since these practices have largely been developed in face-to-face and paper-based contexts. Not only is it important that we understand established pedagogy in order to alter it for these new contexts, but it is also important that we maintain focus upon our instructional goals.

While we live in a time of accelerated technological innovation, the dramatic force of technology is nothing new. Technology has influenced significant changes throughout human history. Many of these changes have been unpredicted and unpredictable. Many have specifically influenced the ways in which we communicate with one another. It is sensible that we prepare for such change as best we can, but there is no guarantee that our preparations will be suitable for future developments. Therefore, it is imperative that any established set of expectations such as language teacher technology standards be revisited on an ongoing basis. Such continual attention will help to keep our goals relevant to practice.

Furthermore, unlike other sets of standards, technology standards rely upon access to technology. The level of this access may not be obvious and can be difficult to identify or predict in many contexts. This can include basic infrastructure and hardware issues such as reliable networks, available computers or various peripheral devices. This can also include cultural and contextual expectations and policies. Of course, this also includes students and teachers who are prepared to interpret and work within the parameters of the standards. One goal of technology standards should be to promote greater access for educators.

## Technology standards contextualised in practice

One of the major obstacles that teachers and administrators face when implementing standards is relating the expectations to their local context. Therefore, it is probably most useful when standards include a variety of specific contextualised examples to aid users in this alignment. It is also beneficial that standards are designed in a manner that is flexible enough to allow them to be adapted for the wide range of language teaching contexts that exist.

There is an increasing body of publications intended to assist educators in their pursuit of understanding and addressing standards within their own teaching environments. Some of these have included specific practical pedagogical recommendations for technology-enhanced practices that support teachers in aligning their classroom practices with standards. For example, Kessler and Ware (2013) identified an array of studies that demonstrated the potential for supporting the competencies of the European Higher Education Area (EHEA) through collaborative practices. Including both telecollaborative and local collaborative practices, the authors offer a variety of practical activities gathered from previous research in language learning contexts that align with the standards. The authors conclude that addressing technology competencies should be considered a vehicle for accomplishing pedagogical goals rather than a goal in itself. Such pedagogically grounded recommendations are necessary for successful large-scale implementation of standards. Ideally, standards projects would include extensive contextualised examples to guide teachers in their use. One example of a language teaching technology standards project that provides such examples is the TESOL Technology Standards.

### *TESOL Technology Standards*

To date, the TESOL Technology Standards are the most comprehensive set of technology standards specifically designed for the unique needs of language teaching professionals around the world. They are explicitly intended for use across the breadth of English teaching contexts around the world. These standards are also designed to address the full range of language teaching contexts with a focus upon teacher technology knowledge and use. The goals and standards are as follows:

### *TESOL Technology Standards for Teachers*

*Goal 1*

Language teachers acquire and maintain foundational knowledge and skills in technology for professional purposes.

Standard 1: Language teachers demonstrate knowledge and skills in basic technological concepts and operational competence, meeting or exceeding TESOL technology standards for students in whatever situation they teach.

Standard 2: Language teachers demonstrate an understanding of a wide range of technology supports for language learning and options for using them in a given setting.

Standard 3: Language teachers actively strive to expand their skill and knowledge base to evaluate, adopt, and adapt emerging technologies throughout their careers.

Standard 4: Language teachers use technology in socially and culturally appropriate, legal, and ethical ways.

*Goal 2*

Language teachers integrate pedagogical knowledge and skills with technology to enhance language teaching and learning.

Standard 1: Language teachers demonstrate knowledge and skills in basic technological concepts and operational competence, meeting or exceeding TESOL technology standards for students in whatever situation in which they teach.

Standard 2: Language teachers demonstrate an understanding of a wide range of technology supports for language learning and options for using them in a given setting.

Standard 3: Language teachers actively strive to expand their skill and knowledge base to evaluate, adopt, and adapt emerging technologies throughout their careers.

Standard 4: Language teachers use technology in socially and culturally appropriate, legal, and ethical ways.

*Goal 3*

Language teachers apply technology in record keeping, feedback, and assessment.

Standard 1: Language teachers evaluate and implement relevant technology to aid in effective learner assessment.

Standard 2: Language teachers use technological resources to collect and analyse information in order to enhance language instruction and learning.

Standard 3: Language teachers evaluate the effectiveness of specific student uses of technology to enhance teaching and learning.

*Goal 4*

Language teachers use technology to improve communication, collaboration, and efficiency.

Standard 1: Language teachers use communication technologies to maintain effective contact and collaboration with peers, students, administration, and other stakeholders.

>Standard 2: Language teachers regularly reflect on the intersection of professional practice and technological developments so that they can make informed decisions regarding the use of technology to support language learning and communication.
>
>Standard 3: Language teachers apply technology to improve efficiency in preparing for class, grading, and maintaining records.
>
>*(TESOL Technology Standards Framework, Healey et al. 2008: 29–41)*

Each standard within this set includes performance indicators and vignettes that help to illustrate the intention of the goal and how it might be implemented in a specific teaching context with a specific activity and level of access to technology. Each vignette is presented across three potential technology access scenarios: low resource/low access, medium resource/medium access and high resource/high access. This diversity of examples allows teachers to identify their own circumstances more readily. Teachers are also supported by a 'can-do' checklist of specific abilities that can guide them in a self-evaluation. This checklist can also assist teachers in assessing the technology abilities of their students that are relevant to language learning.

The TESOL Technology Standards also include a concordance that compares this set of standards to other standards projects that are likely to impact language teaching professionals, including the ISTE NETS and UNESCO ICT-CST standards. Furthermore, there is a comprehensive section on programme evaluation, including an instrument for conducting such evaluations. This instrument is designed to be applicable to programmes across the globe and across the breadth of language teaching contexts. While these standards were published within the domain of the TESOL organisation, they are intended for use across languages. As such, they include the claim that the TESOL Technology Standards, 'provide the clearest and most consistent link to date between technology and the specific considerations relevant to the tasks and processes of second language learning' (Healey et al. 2011: 139). Numerous projects are underway to integrate CALL solutions in an attempt to address these standards. We are likely to learn about the success of these projects in the near future.

As this project is the first of its kind, it is reasonable to anticipate that future technology standards projects will reference and utilise the TESOL Technology Standards as a foundational document. We can certainly anticipate that other professional organisations, nonprofit organisations, national educational bodies and other groups will develop new sets of standards related to the use of technology in the teaching of language. As technology and related communication abilities continue to evolve along with pedagogical practice, we can look forward to more insight into how we can best prepare teachers to use these technologies in language instruction.

## Future directions

It is likely that as we develop a better understanding of the pedagogical practices that emerge in tandem with technological innovations, we will be in need of a completely new way of conceptualising the role of technology in classroom practices. Some have predicted such a paradigm shift and we can see initial evidence of this. As technology has becomes more centrally coordinated within language programmes and courses, we have witnessed a shift in understanding and appreciation for the potential it can offer. Bax (2003) described CALL as being 'normalised' over a decade ago. This conception of normalisation assumes that technology is so commonplace and familiar that it is barely noticeable. However, many other scholars have pointed out that the availability of technology resources and teacher preparation for their use have not yet reached a point where they can support such claims. If we do reach a point where technology is so integrated within education that it is transparent, technology standards would certainly require revisiting.

Rapid innovation presents a significant challenge in creating standards for preparing language teachers to use technology. There is no way to predict what tools we will use in the future or even how we will use these tools to communicate, but we can be certain we will continue to engage in communication through varied technological means. We will certainly continue to witness many advances in the area of communication technologies that present us with unforeseen teaching opportunities. We are likely to see an expansion of language and technology teacher preparation standards in the future. Not only should we expect to see a refocused attention to emerging technologies and communication practices that they can support, we are also likely to witness an increase in support for teachers working towards aligning standards with their classroom practices. Workshops, conferences and publications have already begun to fill this need. We can anticipate seeing more support for addressing standards across the language teaching spectrum. We should also anticipate seeing significant changes not only in the ways we teach and learn in technology enhanced environments, but also in the ways we prepare to participate as teachers and learners.

## Further reading

Chapelle, C. and Sauro S. (eds) (2016) *The Handbook of Technology in Second Language Teaching and Learning*, Oxford, UK: Wiley-Blackwell.
  This anticipated handbook includes contemporary and comprehensive entries from across a broad range of topics related to technology use in second language teaching and learning. There is a particular emphasis on language teacher technology use, assessment and research.
Hubbard, P. (ed) (2009) *Computer Assisted Language Learning: Critical Concepts in Linguistics*, Volumes I–IV, London; New York: Routledge.
  This collection presents foundational and highly cited articles from the field of CALL selected by a panel of experts. Many of these entries should be considered crucial for developing an understanding of the field.
Thomas, M., Reinders, H. and Warschauer, M. (2013) *Contemporary Computer-Assisted Language Learning*, London, UK: Bloomsbury Academic.
  This extensive recent collection addresses a thorough range of established topics across the CALL spectrum, including design, teacher preparation, evaluation and assessment. It also includes emerging topics such as social media as well as broad trends such as new literacy studies and constructivism.

## References

Bax, S. (2003) 'CALL – Past, present and future', *System*, 31: 13–28.
Dooly, M. (2009) 'New competencies in a new era? Examining the impact of a teacher training project', *ReCALL*, 21: 352–369.
Dooly, M. and Sadler, R. (2013) 'Filling in the gaps: Linking theory and practice through telecollaboration in teacher education', *ReCALL*, 25: 4–29.
Egbert, J. (2006) 'Learning in context: Situating language teacher learning in CALL', in P. Hubbard and M. Levy (eds), *CALL Teacher Education*, Philadelphia, PA: John Benjamins: 167–181.
Egbert, J., Paulus, T. and Nakamichi, Y. (2002) 'The impact of CALL instruction on classroom computer use: A foundation for rethinking technology in teacher education', *Language Learning and Technology*, 6(3): 108–126.
Glisan, E.W. (2012) 'National Standards: Research into practice', *Language Teaching*, 45(4): 515–526.
Healey, D., Hanson-Smith, E., Hubbard, P., Iannou-Georgiou, S., Kessler, G. and Ware, P. (2011) *TESOL Technology Standards: Description, Implementation, Integration*, Alexandria, VA: TESOL Publications.
Healey, D., Hegelheimer, V., Hubbard, P., Iannou-Georgiou, S., Kessler, G. and Ware, P. (2008) *TESOL Technology Standards Framework*, Alexandria, VA: TESOL Publications.
Hegelheimer, V. (2006) 'When the technology course is required', in P. Hubbard and M. Levy (eds), *Teacher Education in CALL*, Philadelphia, PA: John Benjamins: 117–133.

Hubbard, P. (2008) 'CALL and the future of language teacher education', *CALICO Journal*, 25(2): 175–188.

Hubbard, P. and Levy, M. (2006) 'The scope of CALL education', in P. Hubbard and M. Levy (eds), *Teacher Education in CALL*, Philadelphia, PA: John Benjamins: 3–20.

Kessler, G. (2006) 'Assessing CALL teacher training: What are we doing and what could we do better?', in P. Hubbard and M. Levy (eds), *Teacher Education in CALL*, Amsterdam, Netherlands: John Benjamins: 23–42.

Kessler, G. (2010) 'When they talk about CALL: Discourse in a required CALL class', *CALICO Journal*, 27(2): 376–392.

Kessler, G. (2012) 'Language teacher training in technology', in C.A. Chapelle (ed), *The Encyclopedia of Applied Linguistics*, Oxford: Wiley-Blackwell.

Kessler, G. and Plakans, L. (2008) 'Does teachers' confidence with CALL equal innovative and integrated use?', *Computer Assisted Language Learning*, 21(3): 269–282.

Kessler, G. and Ware, P. (2013) 'Addressing the language classroom standards of the European higher education area through the use of technology', in M.L. Pérez Cañado (ed), *Competency-Based Language Teaching in Higher Education*, Amsterdam, Netherlands: John Benjamins, 93–105.

Lee, S., Hyungjong, N., Jonghon, L., Kyungsong, L., Geunbae, G., Seongdae, S., et al. (2011) 'On the effectiveness of robot-assisted language learning', *ReCALL*, 23(01): 25–58.

Peters, M. (2006) 'Developing computer competencies for pre-service language teachers: Is one course enough?', in P. Hubbard and M. Levy (eds), *Teacher Education in CALL*, Philadelphia, PA: John Benjamins: 153–165.

Robb, T. (2006) 'Helping teachers to help themselves', in P. Hubbard and M. Levy (eds), *Teacher Education in CALL*, Amsterdam, Netherlands: John Benjamins: 335–347.

Slaouti, D. and Motteram, G. (2006) 'Reconstructing practice: Language teacher education and ICT', in P. Hubbard and M. Levy (eds), *Teacher Education in CALL*, Amsterdam, Netherlands: John Benjamins: 81–97.

# 5

# Researching participatory literacy and positioning in online learning communities

*Mirjam Hauck, Rebecca Galley and Sylvia Warnecke*

As discussed in earlier chapters, the potential of Web 2.0 tools and social networking environments for enhanced peer interaction is being recognised across the education sector. Many institutions are moving their blended and online learning provision from a 'computer-as-tutor' approach towards models which foster knowledge co-construction and sharing in socially networked learning communities. Yet, many education professionals find that they do not have the skills required to help their students to fully benefit from this paradigm shift.

The TESOL–Electronic Village Online (EVO) 2012 module *Tutoring with Web 2.0 Tools – Designing for Social Presence* provides the backdrop for this contribution. The module was designed to develop effective learner-centred online moderation skills, with a focus on the role of Social Presence (SP). Although hosted by the EVO, the programme was open to practitioners from all subject areas, and participants represented a multifaceted community in terms of educational, social and cultural backgrounds, online learning and teaching skills, and ICT literacy.

Drawing on examples from the participants' learning journey, we hypothesise that a group's capacity to send and read SP cues is a precondition for successful knowledge creation and sharing in online learning communities. Our findings provide new insights into the notion of online participation and challenge aspects of Garrison, Anderson and Archer's (2000) Community of Inquiry (CoI) model. In accordance with Morgan (2011) we highlight the need for a different way of conceptualising what happens in networked learning contexts, taking into account aspects such as learner identity, creative agency and participatory literacy.

## About this chapter

In January/February 2012, two of the authors of this chapter ran a five-week online training module titled *Tutoring with Web 2.0 Tools – Designing for Social Presence*. The aim of the module was to prepare tutors and teachers of English as an additional language and other subject areas for teaching in an online-only context. This was the third iteration of a training event originally designed and delivered at the British Open University for tutors of English for academic purposes course.

The first iteration of the training module provided the basis for a detailed analysis and evaluation of the developing dynamics among the teacher trainees, and later on between the trainees and their students (Hauck and Warnecke 2012). This study focused on Kehrwald's (2008) definition of SP, that is the ability of the individual to demonstrate his/her availability for and willingness to participate in interaction. The primary aim of the study was to explore 'how SP is developed, under what conditions and through what media, and which [SP] indicators are more prominent in a socially present online community' (Lomicka and Lord 2012: 213). We carried out a content analysis of the trainees' asynchronous interactions through the lens of the CoI framework (Garrison et al. 2000), and more specifically applied Swan's (2002) adaptation of the original coding template for SP (discussed in more detail later; see Table 5.2).

Garrison et al. (2000) see SP as distinct from Cognitive and Teaching Presence. However, our study concluded that there was a case for a fundamental reconsideration of this three-dimensional approach. In line with Morgan's (2011) critique of the CoI, we argued that it 'does not consider the complexities of the community's global and local contexts, the potential multi-linguistic demands of the teaching and learning contexts, and how power, agency, and identities are negotiated in these multicultural contexts' (p. 2).

In this chapter we will provide a more detailed introduction to the notion of SP and its interrelationship with online participatory literacy. We will give a brief overview of the EVO training programme and participants before presenting our methodological approach to data gathering and evaluation, namely discourse-centred ethnography. Then we will dedicate the following section to a summary of our main findings and the presentation of a new framework, the Community Indicators Framework (CIF), which we argue is particularly well suited to capture the development of productive online learning communities as reflected in the participants' constant efforts to position and reposition themselves during the learning process. Towards the end of this chapter we outline some recommendations for further reading.

## Social Presence, computer-mediated communication and participatory literacy

SP and its role in mediated interactions including computer-mediated-communication (CMC) has been a research topic since the early 1970s. Initially, the SP concept emerged from the attempt to distinguish between mediated interactions (e.g. telephone) and nonmediated (face-to-face) interactions. SP was defined by Short, Williams and Christie (1976: 65) as 'the degree of salience of the other person in a mediated interaction and the consequent salience of the interpersonal interaction'. SP was seen as a characteristic of the affordances of the media, where the 'capacity to transmit information about facial expression, direction of looking, posture, dress and non-verbal vocal cues, all contribute to the SP of a communications medium' (Short et al. 1976: 65). Subsequently, SP was used to theorise communications media and became closely related to media richness theory (Daft and Lengel 1986). From this perspective, text-based CMC was conceived of as a 'lean' medium in comparison to face-to-face interaction (Spears, Lea and Postmes 2001: 605). However, the human capacity to adapt to lean media and to develop strategies to compensate for reduced cues was foregrounded by later theories of communications media (Walther 1992, 1994). Gunawardena (1995) for example, argued that although text-based CMC offered only low social contextual cues, participants' perception of the medium was primarily based on their sense of community, and consequently interactions among participants using lean mediums could be social, active and interactive. As a result SP began to be increasingly understood in terms of the quality of the communication among participants, rather than the technology used (for a more detailed overview see Satar 2010).

Bacon (1995) argues that 'sustained interaction between participants' is central to successful online learning. She observes that 'dialogue helps learners connect with their reality, thus promoting learning [. . .] the reader and the writer become each other's audience; their relationship is based on sharing the power, rather than one person controlling the other' (Bacon 1995: 195). This observation points to the notion that Kehrwald's definition of SP as the *availability for participation* and *willingness to participate* should be understood as two interdependent factors. Pegrum takes this notion further and suggests that participation 'is not optional: those who lack appropriate literacies barely exist in digital culture and are doomed to hover on the fringes of digital societies and digital economies' (2011: 9–10). Participatory literacy can be seen as belonging to a set of key skills – personal, network, participatory, cultural and intercultural literacy – that have a focus on the ability to connect, which Dudeney et al. (2013) have identified as crucial for full participation in a digitally networked world. Thus the ability to participate effectively, and through this demonstrate SP, can be seen as a precondition for learning in CMC contexts and also a fundamental e-literacy skill, as opposed to merely a facilitator for Cognitive Presence as suggested in the CoI framework.

Most published research deals with the SP construct from the researcher's or teacher-as-researcher's perspective. However, Kehrwald's (2008, 2010) case study belongs to a small number of investigations that approach SP from the learner's perspective. His case study explores four online postgraduate education courses from the learners' viewpoint using dialogic interviews and focus groups. He concludes that SP is a subjective quality which translates 'subjective projections of self [...] into technology mediated environments, subjective assessments of others' presence and assessments of the subject's relations with others' (Kehrwald 2010: 41). He sees SP as something that emerges organically, and attaches great importance to the learners' ability to send and read SP cues and the way in which these skills are learned collaboratively: 'through seeing and experiencing how others project themselves into the environment, how others interact with one another and how others react to their personal efforts to cultivate a Social Presence' (Kehrwald 2010: 47).

## The training module: *Tutoring With Web 2.0 Tools – Designing for Social Presence*

This module was presented during January/February 2012 as part of the annual training events organised by the EVO community which is part of TESOL. Table 5.1 provides an overview.

*Table 5.1* Training programme overview

| | |
|---|---|
| Aims | Engagement with a series of activities designed to highlight the relevance of SP in online learning and teaching contexts and to foster participants' development and use of participatory literacy skills. |
| Duration | 5 weeks |
| Approach to task design | The programme was inspired by<br>a. Hoven's (2006) 'experiential modelling approach' where the tools and processes the tutors are expected to use in their teaching are experienced beforehand from a learner's point of view;<br>b. Allwright's (2003) and Allwright and Hanks's (2009) understanding of 'exploratory practice' or inclusive practitioner research which foregrounds the learners' (tutors as learners) perspective. |
| Participants | Fifty-seven teachers and tutors of English and other subjects from around the world representing a mixed cohort of learners in terms of academic histories, linguistic backgrounds and range of e-literacy skills. For some the programme was their first experience with learning and teaching in an online-only context. |
| Venue | A dedicated Moodle site (http://moodle.click-lounge.eu/login/index.php) which is open to the public and can be accessed as soon as interested parties have set up their account. |

A relatively wide range of topics was covered from the exploration of the host site's functionalities and the sharing of icebreaker ideas early on in the programme, to an exploration of the challenges associated with motivation and participation halfway through (see Figures 5.1 and 5.2) and finishing with strategies for assessing forum contributions in online modules in week 5. Here we share a task example from week 3 which uses Salmon's (2002: 171) animal descriptors for learner behaviours online as a framework for discussion.

---

**Week 3 Task 1 – Patterns of participation: forum**

Dear all,

This week we will consider two key issues with regard to the tutor role in asynchronous communication: motivation and participation. We want to find out to what extent our work can tip the balance either in favour or against participation and whether what [participant] calls 'let students get on with it' is something we need to take on board and to communicate to our learners.

Now:

- Think about your own patterns of participation (either as a moderator or as a student). How often, when, why, how intensively do you participate?
- Then have a look at the attached document, which is a collation of common patterns of online participation as categorised by Salmon (2002: 171).
- Which one applies to you? Is there anything you have learned that you want to practise in order to help your group become / be / stay (inter)active?

---

*Figure 5.1*   Glogster poster 1, Malgorzata – Tuesday, 17 January 2012, 06:44 PM

Researching participatory literacy

*Figure 5.2* Glogster poster 2, Maria – Monday, 23 January 2012, 12:58 AM

The module was structured to provide opportunities for 'experiential modelling', immersing participants 'in the use of the technologies, while at the same time providing them with the freedom and framework within which to experience the practical application of the theory in their own learning' (Hoven 2007: n.p.). The module was also influenced by Allwright and Hanks's (2009) understanding of 'exploratory practice'. Exploratory research originated in the 1990s in an attempt to bridge the teacher-researcher gap. Allwright (2003) focuses on the social nature of teaching and the need for all participants to be aware of the processes involved. Similarly Allwright and Hanks draw our attention to the fact that language learning, teaching and research are social processes and call for learners to be seen, and see themselves, as 'key practitioners' alongside teachers; '"practitioner colleagues" with the teacher playing a collegial role in helping learners develop as researchers of their own practices and as practitioners of learning' (2009: 146).

## Methodology

In our first study (Hauck and Warnecke 2012), we followed the approach taken by Arnold and Ducate (2006) and other SP researchers by carrying out a content analysis of the trainees' asynchronous interactions in the forum through the lens of the CoI framework (Garrison et al. 2000), using Swan's (2002) adaptation of the original coding template for SP indicators (see Table 5.2). In common with most investigations of SP, the study took the perspective of the researcher or teacher-as-researcher. However, it was different insofar as we were also able to consider the learner's perspective, namely tutors as learners on a training programme.

In general, this categorisation of forum contributions according to Swan's SP indicators was found to be unhelpful, as most postings were found to contain a densely woven and rich mix of indicators. In addition, the mere occurrence of SP indicators did not, in itself, appear to convey the 'SP message' expressed in the participants' contributions. The study had hoped to explore how the participants developed an awareness of the interactions they were involved in, and thus an awareness of their own and others' SP and its impact on the interaction. However, we felt that the analysis based on indicators moved us away from an understanding of the 'storyline' through the postings in terms of emerging SP among participants.

In particular, we found that the CoI framework and the indicators template were not able to do justice to the constant shifting of roles, identities and patterns of participation that are characteristic of CMC-based interactions. Swan's indicators template has also met criticism in the literature, and some (e.g. Kim 2007) have rejected it outright, arguing that it is not an accurate representation of SP. Since Rourke, Anderson, Garrison and Archer's (1999) original template was developed several attempts have been made to distinguish new and different aspects of SP. These attempts acknowledge the influence of variables such as the affordances of the media, group dynamics and number of participants (Lomicka and Lord 2007), peer status and discourse markers (Satar 2007) and task type (Batstone et al. 2007). After some consideration, we decided to look at the contributions to the training forum from a broader perspective in line with Kehrwald's approach.

Our data collection and analysis methodology could be broadly described as discourse-centred online ethnography (Androutsopoulos 2008: 1), that is 'a combination of systematic observation of online activities and interviews with online actors'. It encompasses and extends Herring's Computer-Mediated Discourse Analysis framework (Herring 2004), using ethnographic insights 'as a backdrop to the selection, analysis, and interpretation of log data' (Androutsopoulos 2008: 3). There are broadly three dimensions to this kind of research: data analysis; observation; and interviews and surveys.

*Table 5.2* Swan's (2002) adaptation of the Social Presence template developed by Rourke et al. (1999)

| Affective | Interactive | Cohesive |
|---|---|---|
| Paralanguage | Greetings and salutations | Acknowledgement |
| Emotion | Vocatives | Agreement/disagreement |
| Value | Group reference | Approval |
| Humour | Social sharing | Invitation |
| Self-disclosure | Course reflection | Personal advice |

## Initial findings and discussion

In this section we will present participant interactions as rich narratives which include contextual and other supplementary information such as illustrations as appropriate. We hope that we have captured the complex nature of online interaction from an authentic learner perspective. The names of the participants are pseudonyms.

### Shifting roles and identities and varying patterns of participation

Shea and Bidjerano (2010) as well as Shea et al.'s (2012) revised CoI model introduce the notion of Learner Presence as a distinct element and suggest that nearly all components and relationships interact with and influence each other. Our investigation takes this notion further with a shift in focus onto the relevance of participation in successful online learner communities as a first step towards the required interaction. To illustrate our observations, we have selected data from five of our participants who are representative of the diversity of the group that worked together online.

The chosen extracts relate to tasks 1 and 2 in week 3. Both tasks focus on the theme of 'participation' and triggered a high volume of reflective comments. They highlight the broad range of factors that are perceived to influence participation. Importantly, many participants' statements confirm Shea et al.'s claim that 'learners and instructors do not perform identical roles and thus must engage in different behaviours to succeed' (2012: 93). The following forum contributions are representative to that effect:

> My situation changes depending on whether I'm a moderator or a participant. [...] Related with my other studies, I think I'm mostly a wolf or a squirrel for the forums that I'm a participant of; I don't have much time to contribute especially at the beginning and end of the semesters, but I think I'm mostly an elephant for the forums that I moderate.
> *(Huseyin – Sunday, 15 January 2012, 08:34 AM)*

> As a student, I have found that the role played by online tutors can make a huge difference in the learning that occurs in discussion forums. [...] However, in other contexts I've also observed that the type of tutor behaviour (more than the frequency) makes a huge difference.
> *(Lara – Monday, 16 January 2012, 08:27 AM)*

> When I have had time I have been visiting every day, so perhaps I have elephant tendencies. Although with time constraints [...] I am more mousey! I have been dipping in and out and enjoying reading all the posts and discussions at my leisure without forcing myself to respond ... I will aim to become more dolphin like as the course progresses! When I moderate a course I block off time daily and keep on top of it and am most definitely an elephant. It's interesting to think about different types of participation and how we can all display several of the characteristics and still enjoy a good learning experience.
> *(Anne – Tuesday, 17 January 2012, 06:39 AM)*

The task initiated a lively exchange about motivational factors underlying participation in online groups along with reflections about the changing nature of participation according to assigned roles, personal circumstances and/or institutional settings:

> I think, many times as a student, I have behaved as an elephant. I think it is because I am a responsible student who likes to do her homework! I've noticed I just do what the instructors ask me to do, no more, no less, so perhaps I have the tendency of a squirrel and a mouse, too.
>
> *(Maria – Thursday, 19 January 2012, 07:18 PM)*

> The most important factor affecting my contribution [...] online [...] is the size of the group. The smaller the group the more I contribute, perhaps because I remember who the participants are and what they said before in their comments. I could say that in a smaller group I am a dolphin. However, things are different if the group is bigger [...] I think I turn into a mouse or an elephant because I try to read my peers' comments and then try to remember what they said before [...]. It makes me really confused and I don't participate as fully as I could.
>
> *(Anabel – Tuesday, 17 January 2012, 03:10 AM)*

Participants were then asked to use the Web 2.0 interactive poster website Glogster to produce visual representations of their actual online participation, and that to which they aspired:

---

### Week 3 Task 2 – My animal Glogster

Following on from task 1 we now ask you to look at your online participation patterns from a more playful and creative angle.

- Please make a note of the animals from Salmon's (2002) list you could identify with.
- Brainstorm ideas and associations with these animals, i.e. music, images, poems etc.
- Then go to www.glogster.com and create a poster that represents the associations you have with the 'your' animals. What does your 'online creature' look like?
- Please have a look at this one we produced as a suggestion . . . we are sure you will be more creative than we were, but it is a start. (Please note: Feel free to use any other Web 2.0 tool that you consider appropriate for this task.)
- Please post the link to your Glogster (or any other media you created) in the appropriate thread in the week 2 forum. (click *reply* at the very bottom of all contributions only!)

Enjoy!

---

Both these examples not only emphasise the participants' realisations of their changing participation patterns and shifting roles, but they also are poignant visible representations of identity formation and the coexistence of a number of online identities. The frequent use of arrows highlights the process nature of what happens in online communities.

A further aspect this chapter seeks to emphasise is the need to distinguish between participatory literacy as a prerequisite for SP and SP itself, and we suggest that what we can actually train for in teacher education is participatory literacy as defined by Pegrum (2009), that is 'digital communicative literacy, which provides a foundation for online interactions, [...] and which facilitates the collaborative processes at the core of participatory literacy'. The following extracts bring this into focus:

> This is a very interesting task as we are required to observe ourselves in this session and of course also observe you, the moderators, and how we interact with you and each other.
> *(Tomek – Monday, 16 January 2012, 03:26 PM)*

> I suppose a bit of lurking is healthy, as long as teacher/participant are happy with it. [...] I am very glad of the opportunity to do this course and get the student-side experience as it's a very different view and funny how easy it is for me to assume student characteristics!
> *(Anna - Friday, 20 January 2012, 08:43 AM)*

The next quote demonstrates how participants feel, and the approaches they might adopt, if they have not fully developed their participatory literacy. It shows how this limitation might lead to a breakdown of communication, or even stop participation entirely:

> First emotion: I feel unable to cope with all these interesting and intelligent posts. Regarding the content as well as regarding the amount of posts. [...] Given a certain number of participants it is difficult for me to follow each and every entry [...] I realise that I tend to concentrate on the replies of the tutors, trying to extract, whether the referred post is worth reading. Doesn't give much clues on the content either. As I don't read the posts in detail or don't have time to think them over (seeing that there are plenty more waiting), I don't react to the posts often, which leads to the fact that the online coaches are the only ones to react to the posts. Is that what I call collaborative learning? Reminds me more of old fashioned teaching: pupils fulfilling the chores and the teacher giving their 'placet'. Now the reaction is that I don't write a post at all, or maybe a funny one or a very critical one, just to avoid repeating thoughts that have been posted already. Isn't that a pity?
> *(Claudia – Monday, 23 January 2012, 03:45 AM)*

Participatory literacy may be achieved by systematically raising awareness for SP cues such as the cohesive SP indicator 'invitation' in 'Isn't that a pity?' Such an approach corroborates Kehrwald's (2010: 47) conceptualisation of SP as the ability to send and read SP cues, and his assertion that these skills are best acquired collaboratively 'through seeing and experiencing how others project themselves into the environment, how others interact with one another and how others react to their personal efforts to cultivate a Social Presence'.

## Hierarchy versus process

We argue that the key to developing a skill such as participatory literacy is continuous meaningful reflection on the learning/interaction process, and consideration of this process as an 'organic' one. The task performances described earlier move the participants well beyond the self as a 'static entity' in online interactions. The examples reflect the ongoing process of identity formation depending on ever-changing contextual circumstances on the one hand, and insights gained from newly acquired or preexisting theoretical knowledge on the other. The following statement underlines a participant's acknowledgement of these processes:

> [One aspect that is crucial in online courses] is the opportunity to develop personally or professionally. I would suggest focusing on social aspects to keep motivation up.
> *(Tomek – Thursday, 26 January 2012, 11:10 AM)*

In the same vein, the hierarchical division of the elements of the CoI model is challenged by participants' experiences:

> In an online course I think student-student interaction is key [...] I think peer exchanges really enrich online courses and really help to engage, motivate and inspire learners and help them to think outside the box and [...] this rich student-student interaction can promote analysis and syntheses in response to others views, opinions and knowledge. Besides that the connections formed through these interactions provide support in many ways not just academically and make the online learning environment a fun place to be.
> 
> *(Anne – Friday, 20 January 2012, 09:27 AM)*

What these participant contributions highlight, in terms of those involved taking on different responsibilities and functions, is corroborated by Comas-Quinn, de los Arcos and Mardomingo:

> We argue that our attempt to promote interaction through our VLE model has resulted in a contested space where traditional hierarchies and relationships between tutors and learners are in a state of flux and where new hierarchies and relationships are constantly being forged. [. . .] tutors are no longer the only 'experts' that learners have access to, whilst learners can more easily adopt the roles of content-creators and peer-supporters.
> 
> *(Comas-Quinn et al. 2012: 129)*

## *The impact of experiential modelling and exploratory practice*

The extracts quoted earlier also hint at the added value of experiential modelling and exploratory practice in terms of cultivating a SP. Such modelling can be carried out by moderator/teachers and participants alike:

> Observing you and [other trainer] I see you letting us get on with the tasks and observing while we get on with it, yet responding when there are questions and clarification is needed. This is energy-saving for the moderators and allows the participants time to engage with the tasks and each other. This has been a learning experience for me.
> 
> *(Tomek – Thursday, 2 February 2012, 09:45 PM)*

> Every post commented on gave a sense of inclusion in the group and left more food for thought. I thought that you both did a very good job of making the group knit together and your comments were valuable. The measure of how successful this is will be seen in the f2f component of my blended course. The bonding of the group will also be a success.
> 
> *(Caroline – Tuesday, 7 February 2012, 10:18 PM)*

The remarks suggest a direct link between experiential modelling and SP. The ways in which others position and reposition themselves in an online learning community offer a model which one can adopt and follow. To this effect the moderator-colleagues who ran the training intentionally positioned themselves in a variety of ways, which in turn gave them the opportunity to shift roles, if not identity. As a result the shifting between the perspectives of the teacher, the learner and the researcher became the centre of attention and could be discussed by the group.

## Defining participation/positioning

The discussion about the division of labour, roles and participation patterns in online learning and teaching has shown that participation is more often than not measured and defined by a visible 'presence'. Yet, as the following quotes illustrate, there are problems attached to such a conceptualisation:

> It's interesting to think about different types of participation and how we can all display several of the characteristics and still enjoy a good learning experience.
> *(Anne – Tuesday, 17 January 2012, 06:39 AM)*

> Otherwise, I am very active reader and writer on forums. I like to give some additional help to fellow learners, as well as new ideas to teachers. Usually, I look for some new ideas, resources, links about the current topic in others' posts. In regular circumstances, I visit forums every day and if I find something to add, I do it. My posts vary from short to middle long. Comparing to the given table, my type would be an Elephant, sometimes a Rabbit, but nowadays I tends to act like a Mouse. Anyway, striving to be a Dolphin.
> *(Malgorzata – Tuesday, 17 January 2012, 06:41 PM)*

> I am amused at how I slot back into the role of student and become a little more hesitant than I would as in my role as a teacher!
> *(Anne – Thursday, 26 January 2012, 06:12 AM)*

This study maintains that participation as a concept is too limiting a description of what happens in online communities and ought to be replaced by Davies and Harre's (1990) notion of 'positioning' as an attempt at describing how we relate ourselves to our contexts and environments; the notion of positioning is closely linked to identity formation. Linehan and McCarthy establish that positioning as a process of negotiation 'is a useful way to characterise the shifting responsibilities and interactive involvements of members in a community' (2000: 441). What are being negotiated are all participants' (learners' and teachers') expectations, conceptualisations of their own as well as others' identity and realisations of changes to these. The following extract supports Morgan's view that the 'dynamics of positioning and identity are already at play at the entry stages of an online teaching context' (2011: 4):

> I also feel that I post more reluctantly when I am a participant of a course, especially at the beginning until I 'get to know' the tutors and the other participants. Being a moderator/teacher of a course gives me more confidence. Funny, isn't it?
> *(Anabel – Thursday, 26 January 2012, 07:56 PM)*

## Supporting and guiding online learning communities

As discussed earlier, several attempts have been made to distinguish new and different aspects of SP which acknowledge the influence of a number of variables. Yet we do not feel that these attempts have successfully represented the fluid nature of these online learning spaces, and the dynamic identities of participants – tutors and learners alike. Galley, Conole and Alevizou's (2011; Galley, Conole and Panagiota 2012) Community Indicators Framework (CIF) emerged out of a series of attempts to more systematically position transactions and emerging patterns of activity on a social networking site for educators called Cloudworks in order to provide guidance for communities using the site. The framework attempts to account for aspects such as identity, creative agency and participatory literacy. In our view it provides a more effective way of representing the development of the democratic, learner-centred, and identity building processes online which the new electronic media facilitate (Warschauer 1999), and provides a useful framework for supporting and guiding online learning communities.

Galley et al. (2012) gathered empirical evidence from the site, and related it to the literature from a range of disciplines concerned with professional and learning communities. They included literature relating to distance learning communities – including Garrison et al. (2000) – and studies into CMC, self-organising communities on the web, and wider research about the nature of learning organisations and continuous professional development. The framework is built around four key aspects of community experience: *identity* – how individuals perceive the community and their place within it; *participation* – the ways in which individuals engage in activity; *cohesion* – the ties between individuals and the community as a whole; and *creative capability* – the ability and willingness of the community to create shared artefacts, and shared knowledge and understanding. Each of these aspects is seen as being dependent on the others, in that the absence of one is likely to significantly impact on the presence of the others.

It is noteworthy that the category of identity has found its way into the understanding of online communities, and the distinction between learner and teacher roles is entirely absent. Here work and play, private and professional, academic and informal spheres interweave. In contrast to the CoI framework, all elements are equally weighted and their impact on each other and on the nature of activity is seen to be fluid, depending on context and participants. Galley et al. (2011, 2012) take account of social hierarchies that emerge in communities online and see these as important in structuring interactions (see Figure 5.3). However, these are seen as being capable of evolving, and often of a temporary nature.

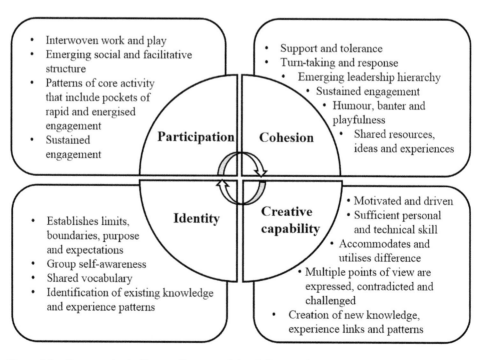

*Figure 5.3* Community Indicators Framework by Galley et al. (2011)

In this chapter, we suggest further development of the CIF framework through a reconceptualisation of participants' tasks and other performances as 'role' outlined in the 'emerging social and facilitative role structure' element in the participation category. We propose an understanding of participatory behaviours as 'positioning' in line with by Morgan (2011). This then moves us beyond Kehrwald's (2008) notion of 'projecting oneself' towards a notion of shifting patterns in the way we relate to others online, responsive to learning context. To that effect we draw on Davies and Harre's (1990) concept of 'positioning' as a way to describe how humans relate to their contexts and 'a dynamic alternative to the more static concept of role' (van Langenhove and Harre 1999: 14). Morgan, who explored this understanding in view of the teaching presence construct in CoIs, writes:

> In Linehan and McCarthy's (2000) view positioning 'is a useful way to characterise the shifting responsibilities and interactive involvements of members in a community' when looking at particular practices (p. 441). This notion seems particularly relevant to online teaching, where instructors arrive in the teaching context with at least some professional identity that has been constructed through experiences in other practices. At the same time, the members of the community (in this case the students) have some notion of the practice of learning and the positioning of themselves in relation to an instructor in that practice. Therefore, dynamics of positioning and identity are already at play at the entry stages of an online teaching context. [...] If we truly want to understand effective teaching presence, it is perhaps timely to focus on conditions and affordances that the context provides, and pay greater attention to the role of positioning.
>
> *(Morgan 2011: 4)*

Based on our findings from the TESOL module, we also maintain that the category of 'creative capability' should be replaced by 'creative agency' to highlight that creative skills and actions can be developed and turn into agency rather than defining these as more static qualities (see Figure 5.4). In Galley et al.'s (2011) model the arrows serve to represent movement through the categories towards creative productivity; however, we suggest that these arrows describe the participatory process from which SP develops and manifests itself. We argue for a reconsideration of the SP construct in the light of this framework as an overarching concept and as both the means *and* the end of communication and interaction in online communities, and the result of participatory literacy as understood by Pegrum (2009).

The question arises, how can the insights gained from this study contribute 'to equip educators with a state-of-the-art underpinning theoretical framework so that they are better placed to guide teaching and learning efforts, to convert hunches and intuition into demonstrable student gains' (Pegg, Reading and Williams 2007)? Morgan (2011: 1) suggests 'that a shift to understanding Teaching Presence within a sociocultural perspective has important implications for teaching and design'. The same, we propose, holds true for SP. We believe that Galley et al.'s (2011) CIF is useful as a framework for supporting and guiding developing communities, as it expresses the tensions and challenges which can emerge as these evolve. A critical approach to these tensions and challenges may help to manage and limit risk to the community as people debate, discuss and work to create new knowledge together openly and online. On the basis of our study we would argue that tasks designed to spark collaborative reflection on issues related to participation, motivation and SP seem particularly well suited to foster SP itself and should therefore be more systematically trialled and integrated into CMC-based teacher education, and learner preparation for online interaction. We can claim with some certainty that it was the participants' interpretation of tasks designed to trigger exchanges on motivation and participation that led to reflection, discussion and learning about

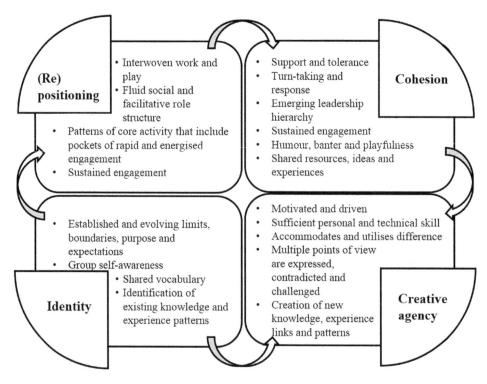

*Figure 5.4* Revised CIF

the relevance of SP in online communities and – at the same time – helped SP emerge among the trainees. By witnessing how others 'project themselves into the environment, how others interact with one another and how others react to their personal efforts to cultivate a Social Presence' (Kehrwald 2010: 47), participants acquired the skill to send, receive and interpret SP cues. They found out about the way roles and identities can shift through interaction, and were able to engage in the process of positioning and repositioning themselves, which in turn allowed them to revisit and reconceptualise their position in the online interactions and to accept – and even strategically use – the transient nature of their role to improve the creative agency of the learning community.

## Further reading

Allwright, D. and Hanks, J. (2009) *The Developing Language Learner: An Introduction to Exploratory Practice*, London, UK: Palgrave Macmillan.
   This publication promotes Exploratory Practice (EP) as a viable means of investigating and improving a deeper understanding of processes and interactions in the second language classroom, here understood as the context in which learning and teaching takes place also beyond the confines of brick and mortar institutions.
   EP is based on learners as 'developing practitioners', on involving learners and teachers in all aspects of the language learning process, which encapsulates the authors' motto of moving from global thinking to local practice – applying theoretical concepts wisely in specific teaching and learning contexts.
   The authors illustrate how EP can support practitioners in overcoming traditional notions of good reflective practice as identifying 'problems'. Instead they suggest that such 'problems' ought to be considered as 'puzzles' that spark enquiry. Yet, the volume also draws attention to possible ethical and

epistemological challenges of such investigations. The project examples present invaluable insights into good EP practice, particularly the participant narratives and rich descriptions of activities showcase meaningful collaboration with learners in order to enhance the quality of 'life' in the on- as well as offline classroom.

Higgins, C. (ed) (2011) *Identity Formation in Globalizing Contexts: Language Learning in the New Millennium*, Berlin: Mouton de Gruyter. Abridged from http://linguistlist.org/pubs/reviews/get-review.cfm?SubID=4550581, review by Damian J. Rivers, *The Linguist List*, International Linguistics Community Online.

Through qualitative methodologies including narrative analysis, case studies, and ethnographic research, this volume investigates the multitude of ways that globalisation in the new millennium influences language learning, transnational living, and the construction of dynamic identities. From a theoretical standpoint, the book explores how global flows of people, ideas and technology, as well as interconnected global 'scapes' continually construct new identity choices for language learners. It highlights how these identity options impact on language learning, language teaching and language use.

This volume focuses on three key aspects of globalisation: the blurring of ethno-national boundaries due to immigration and travelling, the rise of intercultural awareness and 'third spaces' (Bhabha 2004) through language learning and border crossing, and identity formation influenced by media and cyberspace.

The volume highlights how in the new millennium we are 'require[d] to take a deeper look at how identity is formed in relation to mobility and the transgression of modernist boundaries' (p. 2). However, it also illustrates in much interesting detail and case studies how these new identities do not necessarily erase or remove former traditional ones but create more fluid 'hybrid identities'.

Thomas, M., Reinders, H. and Warschauer, M. (eds) (2013) *Contemporary Computer-Assisted Language Learning*, London, UK: Bloomsbury.

*Contemporary Computer-Assisted Language Learning* explains key terms and concepts, synthesises the research literature and explores the implications of new and emerging technologies.

The three sections focus on 'the CALL context', 'CALL learning environments' and 'CALL in language education'. The link between the sections is the change that has been brought to language learning and teaching by digital technologies.

The volume includes chapters on design, teacher education, evaluation, teaching online and testing, as well as current trends like the immense increase in the use of social media. A glossary of terms to support those new to CALL as well as to allow those already engaged in the field to deepen their existing knowledge is also provided. (Text abridged from http://www.bloomsbury.com/uk/contemporary-computer-assisted-language-learning-9781441193629/.)

## Websites

Crowd-Learning (http://crowd-learning.org/): This website is an open initiative to explore the emerging concept of crowdlearning and how it can complement, add value and affect traditional learning structures and practices.

EDUCAUSE is a nonprofit association and the foremost community of IT leaders and professionals committed to advancing higher education. This project connects people seeking and providing information on all aspects of working in and with computer-assisted learning (http://www.educause.edu/).

NMC Project, Horizon Reports, for example for Higher Education (HE) to highlight trends that influence the learning and teaching in the future (http://www.nmc.org/horizon-project).

Sharples, M., McAndrew, P., Weller, M., Ferguson, R., FitzGerald, E., Hirst, T. and Gaved, M. (2013) *Innovating Pedagogy 2013. Exploring new forms of teaching, learning and assessment, to guide educators and policy makers*. Report published by the Open University, http://www.open.ac.uk/blogs/innovating/, specifically the chapter on crowdlearning (http://www.open.ac.uk/blogs/innovating/?page_id=40).

## References

Allwright, D. (2003) 'Exploratory practice: Rethinking practitioner research in language teaching', *Language Teaching Research*, 7(2): 113–141.

Allwright, D. and Hanks, J. (2009) *The Developing Language Learner: An Introduction to Exploratory Practice*, London, UK: Palgrave Macmillan.

Androutsopoulos, J. (2008) 'Potentials and limitations of discourse-centred online ethnography', *Language@ Internet*, 5(9), available: http://www.languageatinternet.de/articles/2008/1610/androutsopoulos.pdf/

Arnold, N. and Ducate, L. (2006) 'Future foreign language teachers' social and cognitive collaboration in an online environment', *Language Learning & Technology*, 10(1): 42–66.

Bacon, S. (1995) 'Coming to grips with the culture: Another use of dialogue journals in teacher education', *Foreign Language Annals*, 28: 193–207.

Batstone, C., Stickler, U., Duensing, A. and Heins, B. (2007) *Social Presence in Face-To-Face and Online Language Tutorials*. Presented at the BAAL-CUP Seminar: Spoken Online Learning Events: The need for a new paradigm in languages research and practice, Milton Keynes.

Bhabha, H.K. (2004) *The Location of Culture*, Oxon, UK: Routledge Classics.

Comas-Quinn, A., de los Arcos, B. and Mardomingo, R. (2012) 'Virtual learning environments (VLEs) for distance language learning: shifting tutor roles in a contested space for interaction', *Computer Assisted Language Learning Journal*, 25(2): 129–143.

Daft, R.L. and Lengel, R.H. (1986) 'Organizational information requirements, media richness and structural design', *Management Science*, 32(5): 554–571.

Davies, B. and Harre, R. (1990) 'Positioning: The discursive production of selves', *Journal for the Theory of Social Behaviour*, 20: 43–63.

Dudeney, G., Hockly, N. and Pegrum, M. (2013) *Digital Literacies*, Harlow, UK: Pearson.

Galley, R., Conole, G. and Alevizou, P. (2011) *Indicators of Community Table – Presentation Transcript*, available: http://www.slideshare.net/OULDI/indicators-of-community-table

Galley, R., Conole, G. and Panagiota, A. (2012) 'Community indicators: A framework for observing and supporting community activity on Cloudworks', *Interactive Learning Environments*, 22(3): 373–395.

Garrison, D.R., Anderson, T. and Archer, W. (2000) 'Critical inquiry in a text-based environment: Computer conferencing in higher education', *The Internet and Higher Education*, 2(2–3): 87–105.

Gunawardena, C.N. (1995) 'Social presence theory and implications for interaction and collaborative learning in computer conferences', *International Journal of Educational Telecommunications*, 1(2/3): 147–166.

Hauck, M. and Warnecke, S. (2012) 'Materials design in CALL: Social presence in online environments', in M. Thomas, H. Reinders and M. Warschauer (eds), *Contemporary Computer-Assisted Language Learning*. Contemporary Studies in Linguistics Series, London; New York: Continuum: 95–115.

Herring, S.C. (2004) 'Computer-mediated discourse analysis: An approach to researching online behavior', in S.A. Barab, R. Kling and J.H. Gray (eds), *Designing for Virtual Communities in the Service of Learning*, New York, NY: Cambridge University Press: 338–376.

Hoven, D. (2006) 'Designing for disruption: Remodelling a blended course in technology in (language) teacher education', in *Proceedings of the 23rd Annual Ascilite conference: Who's learning? Whose technology?* 3rd–6th December. Sydney: University of Sydney: 339–349.

Hoven, D. (2007) 'The affordances of technology for student teachers to shape their teacher education experience', in M.A. Kassen, R.Z. Lavine, K. Murphy-Judy and M. Peter (eds), *Preparing and Developing Technology-Proficient L2 Teachers*. CALICO Monograph Series, 6, San Marcos, Texas: CALICO: 133–162.

Kehrwald, B. (2008) 'Understanding social presence in text-based online learning environments', *Distance Education*, 29(1): 89–106.

Kehrwald, B.A. (2010) 'Being online: Social presence and subjectivity in online learning', *London Review of Education*, 8(1): 39–50.

Kim, E. (2007) 'Students' perception of social presence and its influence on their learning in an online environment: A case study', in E. Simonson (ed), *2007 Annual Proceedings* (Vol. 1), pp. 118–124. Presented at the annual convention of the association for educational communications and technology, Anaheim, CA: Nova Southeastern University.

Linehan, C. and McCarthy, J. (2000) 'Positioning in practice: Understanding participation in the social world', *Journal for the Theory of Social Behaviour*, 30(4): 435–453.

Lomicka, L. and Lord, G. (2007) 'Social presence in virtual communities of foreign language (FL) teachers', *System*, 35: 208–228.

Lomicka, L., and Lord, G. (2012). 'A tale of tweets: Analyzing microblogging among language learners', *System*, 40(1): 48–63.

Morgan, T. (2011) 'Online classroom or community-in-the-making? Instructor conceptualizations and teaching presence in international online contexts', *Journal of Distance Education*, 25(1): 1–15.

Pegg, J., Reading, C. and Williams, M. (2007) *Partnerships in ICT Learning Study: Report*, Canberra: Department of Science, Education and Training.

Pegrum, M. (2009) *From Blogs to Bombs: The Future of Digital Technologies in Education*, Perth: University of Western Australia Press.

Rourke, L., Anderson, T., Garrison, R. and Archer, W. (1999) 'Assessing social presence in asynchronous text-based computer conferencing', *Journal of Distance Education*, 14(2): 50–71.

Salmon, G. (2002) *E-tivities: The Key to Active Online Learning*. Sterling, VA: Stylus Publishing.

Satar, H.M. (2007) *The Effects of Computer Mediated Communication on Oral Language Development*. Unpublished MRes dissertation, The Open University, Milton Keynes.

Satar, H.M. (2010) *Social Presence in Online Multimodal Communication: A Framework to Analyse Online Interactions Between Language Learners*. Unpublished PhD thesis, The Open University, Milton Keynes.

Shea, P., and Bidjerano, T. (2010) 'Learning presence: Towards a theory of self-efficacy, self-regulation, and the development of a communities of inquiry in online and blended learning environments', *Computers & Education*, 55(4): 1721–1731.

Shea, P., Hayes, S., Uzuner Smith, S., Vickers, J., Bidjerano, T., Pickett, A. et al. (2012) 'Learning presence: Additional research on a new conceptual element within the Community of Inquiry (CoI) framework', *Internet and Higher Education*, 15: 89–95.

Short, J., Williams, E. and Christie, B. (1976) *The Social Psychology of Telecommunications*, London, UK: Wiley & Sons.

Spears, R., Lea, M. and Postmes, T. (2001) 'Social psychological theories of computer-mediated communication: Social pain or social gain', in W.P. Robinson and H. Giles (eds), *The New Handbook of Language and Social Psychology*, London, UK: John Wiley and Sons: 103–118.

Swan, K. (2002) 'Building communities in online courses: the importance of interaction', *Education, Communication and Information*, 2(1): 23–49.

Van Langenhove, L. and Harré, R. (1999) 'Introducing positioning theory', in R. Harré and L. van Langenhove (eds), *Positioning Theory: Moral Contexts of Intentional Action*, Oxford: Blackwell: 14–31.

Walther, J.B. (1992) 'Interpersonal effects in computer-mediated interaction: A relational perspective', *Communication Research*, 19(1): 52–90.

Walther, J.B. (1994) 'Anticipated ongoing interaction versus channel effects on relational communication in computer-mediated interaction', *Human Communication Research*, 20(4): 473–501.

Warschauer, M. (1999) *Electronic Literacies: Language, Culture, and Power in Online Education*, Mahwah, NJ: Lawrence Erlbaum Associates.

# 6
# Language materials development in a digital age

*Gary Motteram*

This chapter will explore language materials development in a world where digital technologies are rapidly replacing their analogue predecessors. The tablet computer is replacing the laptop and mobile phones have become available to almost everyone in the world who wants to have one. In some classrooms the tablet PC is already the only resource that is available, and is carried from home to classroom and back again (see Kern and Malinowski, Chapter 14 this volume).

After a short introduction looking at the nature of the digitally aware learner and the 'classrooms' they inhabit, this chapter will review some of the literature on materials development and evaluation in language learning, reminding us of the landscape of this domain. It will then turn to looking at the origins and developments in the field of digital courseware design in general and consider current thinking. It will also look at the extensive range of software that is available to modern-day teachers and their learners and make recommendations about how teachers might make choices in this ever-changing world. At the end of the chapter practical examples will show how a teacher wanting to build courseware might go about the task.

## The changing nature of the classroom and the learner

It is likely to be true for a considerable time that the typical space that primary and secondary school children learn in will be a physical classroom with four walls that they travel to every day; however, this is simply the case because of the way that societies manage the care of children. Despite this, in the modern era there have always been children who have not attended a typical school and in our digital age these numbers will continue to grow. This is because online tools and twenty-four-hour access to information make the need for physical spaces for learning less and less important. We will also find many more parts of the curriculum taught in virtual classrooms, or classrooms having virtual elements blended into their face-to-face activity. Many schools in the developed world might already have tools like interactive whiteboards; they might have a number of laptops available for use by a class. They also have access to wireless Internet, and as the time comes to upgrade their technology more schools are turning to tablet PCs. These tools will change and develop over time, but they all have the potential of enabling more contact with the world outside of the classroom and more flexibility. They allow teachers, if nothing else, to enhance lessons with up-to-date authentic texts, pictures and videos.

With older learners the landscape can be very different, and although many people still learn languages in classrooms, people have been learning in nontraditional classrooms and also studying on their own for many years. Take for example my own attempts to learn Spanish. I have tried to improve my Spanish each time I have visited Spain, in different ways according to the time periods when I was studying. My first attempt was when I was staying with some friends in northern Spain. I found a beginner's course on the bookshelf that came with a cassette of listening materials. I stayed in Spain about ten days and did a bit of studying most days. By the end of the stay I was able to do some basic ordering in a café and successfully buy train tickets.

In more recent years I have turned to the Internet as a source of study material. There is a very good basic BBC course, *Mi Vida Loca*, which has video and interactive exercises; you can study for twelve weeks and get a certificate; this is free, or what these days would be described as 'open source'. Latterly, I have also been exploring mobile apps (Godwin-Jones 2011; Steele 2012) to see what they have on offer. I can also make use of tools like Google Translate (http://translate.google.com) or Word Lens (https://play.google.com/store/apps/details?id=com.questvisual.wordlens), a phone app that will translate objects in the target environment while I travel, like a menu or a street sign (the app gets mixed reviews). I have the advantage that I can go to Spain on holiday so that I can actually use the language to try to make and negotiate meaning – 'languaging', as Swain (2000, 2006) would describe it. Swain argued that only by actually engaging in direct language activity and producing output that can be compared to the target utterances will learners develop higher level language skills. If I couldn't actually go to Spain, as an adult I could go online to a virtual world like Second Life and visit one of the many islands where there is a Spanish-speaking community. Another possibility might be to do some online lessons making use of a video conferencing tool like Skype.

I have described both my actual and possible activities in learning Spanish to give a flavour of the possible alternative 'classrooms' that exist where an adult learner could study a language. I have not mentioned other tools like virtual learning environments (VLEs), companies that offer online course environments or language wikis, for example, but these are also possibilities. I will return to tools later.

## Born digital

I, however, was not 'born digital' (Palfrey and Gasser 2008), and even though I make use of a lot of digital technologies in my personal and professional lives, I may well not use them in the same ways as people who have grown up surrounded by 'computers' from birth (I use scare quotes around 'computer', because I am referring to mobile tools like phones and tablets as well as traditional PCs and laptops). What it means to be born digital and the impact it has on what and how we learn is a very contested area currently with people on both sides of the argument making radical claims. One side of the argument is that the Internet is dumbing down learning and we approach knowledge in a more 'shallow' (Carr 2010) way than we should. Arguments here suggest that we might be going the opposite way to that advocated by theorists like Marton and Säljö (1984), who argued for a deep approach to learning processes. On the other side we have suggestions that tools like mobile phones are changing the actual nature of children's brains, rewiring them in effect, making learning a very different process to what it has been until recently, where there was an assumption that there is a 'knowledge base' that needs to be acquired; this is now sometimes questioned (Pogue 2013). With the increasing sophistication of mobile technologies and translation tools like Word Lens, it is entirely possible that in future we won't need to learn languages for the basic practices that I engage in while I am on holiday, because these can be managed by the tools themselves. We will input our needs and our tools will negotiate our requirements (Pegrum 2014).

However, we don't necessarily learn languages just to be able to do practical things with them; we learn them to get access to other cultures and develop intercultural understandings (Hua 2011). While this is still the case, we will want to learn to continue to design effective courseware, although it will be for a diverse set of spaces and will need to keep in mind the target audience for the materials.

## Course design for language learning

While this chapter is not going to talk specifically about 'blended learning' (see Tomlinson and Whittaker 2013), that is to say the bringing together of the face-to-face classroom with opportunities to interact online, it is likely that a lot of teachers are going to be looking at ways of enhancing or supplementing their regular classes with technology. However, to do this it is necessary for teachers to have some understanding both about how materials can be and are produced and the decisions that need to be taken when teachers want to create their own materials, rather than relying just on the textbook. Teachers will also want to be able to effectively evaluate materials that they plan to use and also materials that they create for themselves. One may want to argue that any use of materials in a class is a form of evaluation, because we teach a lesson and then reflect on how it went and how we might do it better. We look to adapt material to suit the needs of the particular group of learners that is in front of us. This section will therefore start with a brief overview of the evaluation of materials and then consider some of decisions and processes that need to be borne in mind when we come to the creation of any language learning materials.

When you search for materials development for language teaching on the Internet and look for recent references, most of them are about the world of technology in language learning, particularly about computer-assisted language learning (CALL). Other hits from recent publications in the more general area of English language teaching materials development include Tomlinson (2011, 2012), probably the most prolific writer; McDonough, Shaw and Masuhara (2012); McGrath (2002); and Harwood (2010). Most of these publications focus on what are termed 'published materials', which despite movements like Dogme (Meddings and Thornbury 2009) – that to a greater extent focuses on teaching without materials that are not available within the local context – are still the core of most lessons around the world, particularly in schools. Most of these texts look both at materials evaluation as well as development. Developing teachers' skills in evaluation will help them to view commercial materials more objectively, but also enable them to work on the development of their own skills in materials creation. Increasingly, although there may be a core textbook, teachers are increasingly encouraged to make use of various types of digital technologies to enhance what they are doing, and this is often linked to the process of checking the quality of this use through a set of standards (Barron et al. 2003) against which the use of technology in schools is measured.

Tomlinson, in his article (2012) on materials development, points out that there have been a lot of checklists of criteria created. However, he argues that 'evaluators need to develop their own principled criteria which take into consideration the context of the evaluation and their own beliefs' (Tomlinson 2012: 148). He advises evaluators to generate their criteria from 'a list of principled beliefs that they hold about how languages are most effectively acquired' (p. 148). A set of beliefs might be supported by an exploration of second language acquisition theories. Ellis (2005) summarises current beliefs about language learning as follows:

## Ellis's (2005) principles of instructed language learning

1. Instruction needs to ensure that learners develop both a rich repertoire of formulaic expressions and a rule-based competence
2. Instruction needs to ensure that learners focus predominantly on meaning
3. Instruction needs to ensure that learners also focus on form
4. Instruction needs to be predominantly directed at developing implicit knowledge of the L2 while not neglecting explicit knowledge
5. Instruction needs to take into account the learner's 'built-in syllabus'
6. Successful instructed language learning requires extensive L2 input
7. Successful instructed language learning also requires opportunities for output
8. The opportunity to interact in the L2 is central to developing L2 proficiency
9. Instruction needs to take account of individual differences in learners
10. In assessing learners' L2 proficiency it is important to examine free as well as controlled production.

Some of Ellis's principles work at a more global level, so here we would be looking at development over time; principles 1 and 6, for example, are of this type. However, focusing on meaning, while not ignoring form, avoiding too much language explanation and making sure that there is plenty of input but also opportunities to practise, can be a part of most lessons and is a good way of beginning to ask questions about any commercial materials we find ourselves using.

We then need to look at the specific context, and considering that we are looking at a variety of classroom types and the role that technology would play, we would need to take this into account, too. Context can vary enormously; it can range from a primary school in a rural village in the developing world with no electricity – and in some cases where teachers' knowledge of English is limited at best – to a highly technological college somewhere in the Middle East where there are no analogue resources, everything is taught via a tablet PC and the teachers are bilingual (see Kern and Malinowski, Chapter 14 this volume).

In a useful framework for materials writing, Jolly and Bolitho (2011) point out that there are inevitable choices that are made when materials are created, and that as a result teachers will need to accept some limitations. They say that course book creators make selections when it comes to language that they include, these selections are always going to have limits and a course book cannot possibly cover everything; they say that materials developers need to make sure that the tasks work in providing the right kind of practice:

> Part of a materials writer's task must be to provide clear exercises and activities that somehow meet the need for the language-learning work that has been initially recognised. Some would say that this is the core of materials writing.
> *(Jolly and Bolitho 2011: 109–110)*

The materials need to be designed to look attractive and be easy to follow. The authors reiterate the point that all material needs to be evaluated in the classroom and adjusted to make it work effectively. They produce a useful flow chart (Table 6.1) that starts off with the identification of need, which is a topic we will return to later.

Needs analysis is an area that is more often discussed when materials are being designed for an English for Specific Purposes (ESP) context. It was considered by Richards and Rogers (2001) to having been central to what they saw as the 'second phase' of the development of Communicative Language Teaching (CLT). Munby (1978) provided the most comprehensive

*Table 6.1* Materials design flow chart

| |
|---|
| IDENTIFICATION by teacher or learner(s) of a need to fulfil or a problem to solve by the creation of materials |
| ↓ |
| EXPLORATION of the area of need/problem in terms of what language, what meanings, what functions, what skills, etc. |
| ↓ |
| CONTEXTUAL REALISATION of the proposed new materials by finding of suitable ideas, contexts or texts with which to work |
| ↓ |
| PEDAGOGICAL REALISATION of materials by finding appropriate exercises and activities AND the writing of appropriate instructions for use |
| ↓ |
| PHYSICAL PRODUCTION of materials, involving consideration of layout, type size, visuals reproduction, tape length, etc. |
| USE in the classroom |

Source: Jolly and Bolitho (2011: 112).

early book on the topic, and West (1994) produced a survey article where he explored the different types of needs analysis in detail. One book that looks at this in detail is Long (2005). Essentially, needs analysis is a process whereby teachers, or in some cases learners, decide how the language course should be taught, what topics it should cover and the methodologies to be used in teaching. It should be the precursor to any course and would lead to the development of a syllabus and a number of activities linked to certain types of materials for each session to be taught. In the case of my Spanish course, my current needs are still very much linked to basic survival when on holiday, so the emphasis would be on language production with elements of listening – trying to understand the responses to questions asked, so if I ask for directions, I need to be able to understand the response. I may also need to understand some basic written signs to identify the type of shop I am interested in visiting. However, as I get beyond these basic needs, my needs as a learner are likely to change.

Having established the basis for the evaluation and design of ELT materials, I will turn to look at some of the principles we find in the more general digital world, as I believe we can see interesting similarities but also growing differences in the ways that materials design is thought about and which we could learn from more both in digital and nondigital language learning.

## Course design for the digital world

It is useful to look at general issues in course design for the digital world, because they do have a lot in common with language teaching materials design and have had a lot of influence in the design of CALL materials. Levy's (1997) early book on materials development shows the eclectic nature of the world of courseware development for language teaching. He showed how there were a number of influences in the development of the CALL field, and we find Conole (2013) doing something very similar for academics creating e-learning materials in higher education. She shows, like Levy, that digital materials development draws upon a complex mix of theory and practice, on fields as diverse as educational psychology, human-computer interaction and instructional design. What Conole (2013: 17–18) makes clear is that when it comes to any materials development, despite their disciplinary background, designers do need to be aware of relevant theory and practice and will also have personal beliefs about the teaching and learning. One might broadly divide these between the hard sciences, the social sciences and humanities, but there is also a division between subjects that are oriented towards developing certain skills and those that are oriented towards developing a particular knowledge base. Language learning is initially more about skills development in 'learning to read' rather than 'reading to learn', although it could be argued that the more quickly you start with the latter, the easier it is to get learners onside, seeing the values of a skill in a foreign language.

Conole (2013: 18) points out that despite subject background and the way that they explore materials development, 'it is important to take into account the contextual and in particular the human dimension, within which e-learning takes place'. She argues, as I have (Motteram 2013), that we should be taking a sociocultural perspective on materials design.

Figure 6.1 shows a sociocultural representation of a particular language teacher with some of the factors that need to be taken into account when we focus on course design. It uses a triangular representation for sociocultural theory that was created by Engeström (1987). In Activity Theory the different nodes, going clockwise from the top, represent the tools (mediating artefacts – see later), the object of the activity (outcome), what different roles people play in the environment (divisions of labour), the community, the constraints and affordances in the environment and the subject of the activity – the teacher and the learners, in our case. Tools here are web pages, Hot Potatoes exercises etc. The outcome for this lesson is the development of skills and knowledge of the UK. The rules in play are that the learners are supposed to engage with the extra materials the teacher provides or the tasks won't work. The wider community will impact on whether this is going to be possible, and the constraints may be that there is no technical infrastructure or that learners are not net savvy.

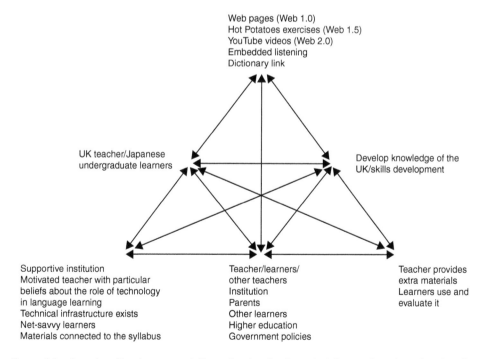

*Figure 6.1* A sociocultural representation of a teacher's materials creation domain, showing its complexity

Figure 6.1 represents the world of a teacher working in higher education in Japan and is abstracted from a case study from Slaouti, Motteram and Onat-Stelma (2008). If we start from the top of the triangle, we can see here that this teacher in Japan uses a lot of technology in his teaching (e.g. web pages and YouTube videos) and we can see in the bottom left-hand corner that he also has a supportive and well-equipped institution with learners having good Internet skills. His aim is to develop intercultural materials, to get his learners to both learn more about UK society, but also to engage with their own society in comparison. He is developing supplementary materials and trying to evaluate them; he has a strong belief in the values of technology in education. As we see at the bottom of the triangle in the community node, lots of people have a stake in the learning of this undergraduate group, including the institution itself and members of staff, parents and perhaps future employers, too. We can see here laid bare the complexity of the materials design process and all of the elements that teachers deal with almost instinctively when they begin to work on their own materials creation.

Conole (2013) calls her practice learning design, bringing into the field of materials development the concept of 'designing for learning', which Beetham (2008: 3) defines as 'a set of practices carried out by learning professionals ... defined as designing, planning and orchestrating learning activities which involve the use of technology, as part of a learning session or programme'.

Design for learning supersedes more traditional practices in the design of digital materials that is termed instructional design. Instructional design is broadly similar to ideas suggested by Tomlinson (2011), or Jolly and Bolitho (2011). The most well-known model of development is the ADDIE model (Morrison, Ross and Kalman 2013: 13) where ADDIE stands for:

Analyse
Design
Develop
Implement
Evaluate.

This is often interpreted as a linear development model with each stage being more or less completed before the next begins, but it is now much more like the rapid prototyping models found in computer programming. These models focus less on the different stages and more on getting ideas up and running, testing to see how well they work and then readjusting those ideas based on findings from the trials. Although instructional design has been criticised lately (see e.g. Roytek 2010), this model still forms the basis of many types of courseware development and is taught in many courses that train instructional designers.

Having explored the developments in thinking that have occurred in more general digital materials design, I am now going to turn my attention to the mediating artefacts themselves and give a quick overview of what might be possible.

## Typical tools for courseware development and choosing the right one for your needs

In a recent publication (Motteram 2013: 178), I refer to the tools that people are increasingly using in the design and development of courseware as technical cultural artefacts. I describe them as such because the digital tools that we are now using in the development of material both allow us to design for learning in the way that I have already discussed, but also impact our understanding of language development. Their nature as cultural artefacts provides opportunities for the continued development of our understanding of the field of language teaching.

The range of tools that we have available has exploded in recent years. This is partly as a result of the move in the digital world from what has been termed Web 1.0 to Web 2.0, or what is more commonly referred to as social media (see Lomicka and Lord, Chapter 18 this volume). It is also partly due to the development and proliferation of hardware that is both versatile and highly portable. A mobile smartphone is capable of a great many things that would have required several expensive and large and bulky pieces of equipment in earlier materials design. This opens up a large range of possibilities for the teacher (and the learner), but at the same time can be a daunting prospect mostly because there is so much choice and it is difficult to know where to start.

A useful way of categorising social media is what Poore refers to as 'the big four' (2013: 41): blogs, wikis, social networking and podcasting. We are all likely to recognise most of these, even if we are not sure how to use them in language teaching. A blog is essentially a diary, which is usually created by an individual and can be commented on by others. Teachers often use blogs to deliver material to their learners, or perhaps to get learners to post material that others comment on. A wiki is an interactive web page that anyone can contribute to; it has a 'memory' of the edits that have occurred. Wikis are commonly used for collaborative writing or project work. Social networking tools may include blogs and wikis, but the most commonly cited example is a tool like Facebook, which allows people to post and comment on a variety of materials and interact as a community, thus helping to develop the affective in language learning. Podcasts can be audio and/or video. Tools like YouTube and the TED Talks have revolutionised the range of available material for use in class and have also enabled more exciting video-based project work to be undertaken and displayed. If we use the big four in conjunction with a smartphone for capturing material (pictures, audio and video, plus potentially finding or creating text), we have a powerful starting place for the design of our materials. We have both ways of creating materials and places where they can be utilised and evaluated.

I will now go on to give some examples of courseware design using a selection of mediating artefacts, showing different contexts and types of students.

## Selecting and assembling suitable materials

Bringing all of the elements together that we have been talking about so far means that a typical teacher is likely to be engaged in a world where the needs of their learners are likely to feature some form of digital technology. What is increasingly likely is that a teacher will be looking to extend their teaching of a textbook with technology. This might mean that the teacher asks learners to look at something in advance, which is then used as the lead-in to a lesson. It might be that some of the supplementary activities are located on the Web in a virtual learning environment. It might be that a lesson is built around a reading app that is found on a tablet. Perhaps the learners will be asked to bring into the class examples of how they use English online to communicate with other English language users elsewhere in the world – via a digital game, for example. It may be that the teacher uses their own connections to bring in someone from outside of the classroom, perhaps by using a tool like Skype or Twitter.

Activity 1: Preparing in advance

The range of materials that are available on the Web that can be used to link to the existing course book is very extensive. They are attractive to learners because they are authentic and up to date. They can add realism to course book material and make good links between the classroom and the real world. Let us consider a course book lesson with the theme of travel. A typical lesson for a group of teenagers might focus on a trip that the group might take to an English-speaking country. Let's propose a group of Japanese learners in a secondary school are asked to plan a two-week visit to Australia. This activity is set two weeks before the main activity that the learners are going to do in class. The class is divided into smaller groups: each is given a particular topic, for example travel to and from Australia; possible places to visit; types of accommodation and costs; eating and drinking; or other activities. The planning in class will involve the different groups presenting their ideas and then as a class they will agree on itinerary, activities, types of accommodation and so forth. It will depend on the class and the level, but this work could be managed by the teacher by setting up a series of electronic worksheets with links to various websites and guide questions, somewhat like a web quest (Dodge 1995). If the learners have the necessary digital literacy (see Dudeney and Hockly, Chapter 8 this volume), they can manage this themselves. The electronic worksheets can be set up in various ways, such as on Google Docs, as part of a class wiki, or as more traditional web pages. From the preparation, the learners are expected to present ideas in class using tools like PowerPoint, KeyNote, or Google Presentation, after having sought guidance from each other and the teacher about language. Information and ideas can be added to a Google Map and shared with parents and friends.

This kind of activity is task-based learning. Towards the end of the task cycle, the group and the teacher could go back over the language that they have used and consider areas where they have had difficulties and then consider how these can be resolved. Following on from Ellis's (2005) principles, we see learners engaging in meaning-focused activity, but with some emphasis on form. We are developing implicit knowledge of language: the learners are engaged in exploring real language, interacting about it and then talking about what they have found with the larger group. Following Jolly and Bolitho (2011), the teacher has identified a problem – that the textbook needs to be made more relevant to digital natives – has found a suitable way of mediating the process using particular technologies, has designed and set up electronic worksheets, or has provided guided tasks to scaffold the process, if the learners are more advanced. With the help of a range of technological resources, the teacher has produced good-looking materials that can be tried out with one group and then adjusted for others.

## Activity 2: Extending classroom activity

*This activity is based on a lesson idea from Taslima Ivy (2013), reproduced with her kind permission and created as a part of her MA coursework.*

It has been argued for some time that writing should be seen as a process (Flower and Hayes 1980) and that technology can aid that process (Pennington 1996). As Web 2.0 has taken centre stage in language teaching and we have moved theoretically towards constructivism, the field of technology and writing has started to refer to collaborative writing with a particular emphasis on the use of wikis (Kessler and Bikowski 2010). There are many other options for promoting writing and other social media; in this example, Facebook is proposed. This use of technology extends the lesson. The extension is required because the actual lessons themselves focus on a discussion of writing, not the act of writing itself. Ivy (2013) identifies the problem as being one of a lack of writing practice. The learners are already making use of social media to communicate outside of the classroom; it is therefore a short step to design a lesson extension that encourages the learners to begin to make use of Facebook as a medium for writing practice. The journey is not as far for either the teacher or the learners and fits in with the sociocultural realities of this and many other contexts. The lesson is built around descriptive writing. The teacher uses a picture to stimulate student discussion about what they might say, and students work together in small groups to start a *mind map* giving them the basic structure. They are expected to describe a typical local dish as if it is going to appear on a poster as a part of an international food festival. Outside of the lesson in Facebook they begin to start writing and are prompted by the teacher to extend their ideas – to add new adjectives, for example. This lesson, which can be adapted for use in many other contexts and at different levels, is a useful starting point for materials design for teachers who are not so familiar with the process. This is more in the realm of the adaptation of materials, starting with what is already known and building additional material around it, making up for some of the constraints within the context.

Using the framework outlined by Jolly and Bolitho (2011), the lesson identifies a real need for these learners and explores this to make adaptions that fit in with the context. It takes a technology, a contextual realisation that is already being commonly used by the students for other tasks, and utilises this for effective delivery of this additional part of the lesson. The teacher makes a number of pedagogical decisions and produces additional materials – for example, a checklist for commenting on the online writing so that the students can be encouraged to move towards a more process approach to writing. Ivy (2013) also includes a rubric for assessment, with 15% of the total being apportioned to the online element of the materials. The learners are then encouraged to make judgements about what their colleagues have produced and in turn become more critical of their own output. In this case the 'physical production' is taken out of the teacher's hand because Facebook has a standard user interface. In fact, this is true for most uses of a digital technology for materials design. This is again a good starting point for beginner materials writers, because they have less to think about and can focus on issues that they are more familiar with.

From Ellis's (2005) perspective, the material focuses on getting learners to engage with meaning, but at the same time there is attention to form, there is input, and in doing this lesson Ivy is trying to make sure that the students are not just learning about the language. If we are to consider our sociocultural model here, then we can immediately see the desire of the teacher to make a difference in the learning outcomes of her students. She makes a pragmatic choice when it comes to the technology and gets around some of the institution constraints as a result. She doesn't stop teaching the expected classes and the community then doesn't react negatively over her decision-making. She is still taking an effective role as a teacher, but is supporting the learners with a particular need; she is also developing their own autonomous development and seeing a real value for writing.

### Activity 3: Bringing the outside in

One of the popular ways of enlivening classrooms and making them more relevant is promoting connections between classrooms in different parts of the world. We have seen this at various levels, and it has often been connected to intercultural development, initially in higher education. There are now good examples of this conducted at a primary and secondary level in Motteram (2013) where Pim (2013: 26–27) describes two case studies of the use of video conferencing: one to develop cultural understanding and spoken language skills and one used to develop reading skills with remote tutors. Stanley (2013: 48–50) describes how an Egyptian teacher invites a colleague she has met online to 'visit' her classroom and answer questions about the impact of climate change on her country.

In all of these cases the teachers again identify a particular issue: promoting reading skills or spoken language skills where the traditional context constrains what is possible. In the case of teachers trying to deal with effective reading practices for their learners, this use of technology supports the skills of the classroom teacher in an area that they find difficult because of their low-level language skills. For the Egyptian teacher, she is constrained by the facilities that are available in the school and can normally make little use of technology in her classes. This activity gives her the freedom to do something that the learners find motivating and that gets around the limits of what the school can offer. She provides her own laptop, but the school has a projector and an Internet connection. Appropriate tasks are created in each situation and then a range of different technologies can be utilised to support these lessons. The reading class might be supported by a blog of additional materials that are related to the books that are being read. In the second primary example, the students use a wiki to post descriptions of their daily lives. The Egyptian teacher ends up using blogs, Facebook and a virtual learning environment called Edmodo with her learners. In all these examples we see that these teachers are able to apply a number of Ellis's principles.

This chapter has shown that digital technologies can increasingly help teachers to design effective materials that meet the needs of language learners both in the traditional classroom and beyond. By designing for learning and starting with easily accessible and usable tools, which in many cases learners are likely to be accessing for their own uses, teachers can implement the Principles of Instructed Learning (Ellis 2005). As a result classes are going to be more effective and more targeted. The design for learning framework's holistic nature means that teachers can be more aware of the domain that they are trying to explore, but also use it as a way of articulating what they are trying to achieve to others. The mediating artefacts that have been discussed in the activities offer opportunities for teachers to provide effective and targeted material that are principled and fit for purpose.

## Further reading

Conole, G. (2013) *Designing for Learning in an Open World*, London, UK: Springer.
    This is a book outside of the field of English language teaching (ELT), but is a very interesting and useful overview of learning design in general. It covers many of the topics that you expect to find in a book on language teaching materials design, but takes a broader view. It also has useful guidance on getting teachers to think about and plan their materials development.

Motteram, G. (ed) (2013) *Innovations in Learning Technologies for English Language Teaching*, London, UK: The British Council.
    A useful book, edited by myself, showing a broad range of practice on the use of technology in language learning. It is divided into chapters rather differently than typical books in this area and focuses on different educational contexts. It explores both early years and adult education and also includes a chapter on classroom assessment. What will be particularly helpful for a teacher new to this area will be the case studies. The book is freely available online: https://www.escholar.manchester.ac.uk/uk-ac-man-scw:190410.

    Other similar and more detailed case studies can be found on the blog that was created as a part of the research project we conducted for Cambridge University Press: http://blogging.humanities.manchester.ac.uk/CUP/.

Poore, M. (2013) *Using Social Media in the Classroom: A Best Practice Guide*, London, UK: Sage.
    This is again not an ELT book, but more general in its coverage of the use of social media in teaching. I find this a good introductory overview, which usefully divides social media into four broad areas. Its classroom examples can be easily adapted to language teaching, but the text takes you a lot further than a recipe book by providing good additional literature for follow-up.

Stanley, G. (2013) *Language Learning with Technology*, Cambridge: Cambridge University Press.
    This is an ELT-focused book and contains a wealth of ideas for using a broad range of technologies in the language classroom. The book builds on his extensive classroom practice and is also firmly embedded within a practice-led framework. There are both plans for lessons as well as a list of suitable technologies that can be employed. This is a good starting point for anyone wishing to begin to use technologies for materials design.

## References

Barron, A.E., Kemker, K., Harmes, C. and Kalaydjian, K. (2003) 'Large-scale research study on technology in K–12 schools', *Journal of Research on Technology in Education*, 35(4): 489–507.

BBC Languages Spanish *Mi Vida Loca*, available: http://www.bbc.co.uk/languages/spanish/mividaloca/

Beetham, H. (2008) 'Review of the design for learning programme phase 2' (JISC Design for Learning programme report), available: http://www.jisc.ac.uk/elp_designlearn.html

Carr, N. (2010) *The Shallows*, New York, NY: W.W. Norton and Company Inc.

Conole, G. (2013) *Designing for Learning in an Open World*, London, UK: Springer.

Dodge, B. (1995) 'WebQuests: A technique for Internet-based learning', *Distance Educator*, 1(2): 10–13.

Ellis, R. (2005) 'Principles of instructed language learning', *System*, 33(2): 209–224.

Engeström, Y. (1987) *Learning by Expanding: An Activity-Theoretical Approach to Developmental Research*, Helsinki: Orienta-Konsultit.

Flower, L. and Hayes, J.R. (1980) 'A cognitive process theory of writing', *College Composition and Communication*, 32(4): 365–387.

Godwin-Jones, B. (2011) 'Emerging technologies: Mobile apps for language learning', *Language Learning and Technology*, 15(2): 2–11.

Harwood, N. (2010) *Materials in ELT: Theory and practice*, Cambridge: Cambridge University Press.

Hua, Z. (2011) *The Intercultural Reader*, London, UK: Taylor and Francis.

Ivy, T.I. (2013) 'Using Facebook to develop writing skills', unpublished assignment submitted for the MA course unit, *Language Learning and Technology* at the University of Manchester.

Jolly, D. and Bolitho, R. (2011) 'A framework for materials writing', in B. Tomlinson (ed), *Materials Development in Language Teaching*, 3rd edn, Cambridge: Cambridge University Press.

Kessler, G. and Bikowski, D. (2010) 'Developing collaborative autonomous language learning abilities in computer mediated language learning: Attention to meaning among students in wiki space', *Computer Assisted Language Learning*, 23: 41–58.

Levy, M (1997) *Computer-Assisted Language Learning*, Oxford: Clarendon.

Long, M. (ed) (2005) *Second Language Needs Analysis*, Cambridge: Cambridge University Press.

Marton, F. and Säljö, R. (1984) 'Approaches to learning', in F. Marton, D. Hounsell and N.J. Entwistle (eds), *The Experience of Learning*, Edinburgh: Scottish Academic Press: 39–58.

McDonough, J., Shaw, C. and Masuhara, H. (2012) *Materials and Methods in ELT: A Teacher's Guide*, 3rd edn, London, UK: Blackwell.

McGrath, I. (2002) *Materials Evaluation and Design for Language Teaching*, Edinburgh: Edinburgh University Press.

Meddings, L. and Thornbury, S. (2009) *Teaching Unplugged: Dogme in English Language Teaching*, Peaslake, UK: Delta.

Morrison, G.R., Ross, S.M. and Kalman, K. (2013) *Defining Effective Instruction*, 6th edn, Hoboken, NJ: John Wiley.

Motteram, G.F. (2013) *Innovations in Learning Technologies for English Language Teaching*, London, UK: The British Council.

Munby, J. (1978) *Communicative Syllabus Design*, Cambridge: Cambridge University Press.

Palfrey, J. and Gasser, U. (2008) *Born Digital*, Philadelphia, PA: Basic Books.

Pegrum, M (2014) *Mobile Learning: Languages, Literacies and Cultures*, London, UK: Palgrave Macmillan.

Pennington, M.C. (1996) 'Writing the natural way: On computer', *Computer Assisted Language Learning*, 9(2–3): 125–142.

Pim, C. (2013) 'Emerging technologies, emerging minds: digital innovations within the primary sector', in G. Motteram (ed), *Innovations in Learning Technologies for English Language Teaching*, London, UK: The British Council 15–42.

Pogue, R. (2013) 'Smartphones mean you will no longer have to memorize facts', *Scientific American*, 25th July, available: http://www.scientificamerican.com/article.cfm?id=smartphones-mean-no-longer-memorize-facts

Poore, M. (2013) *Using Social Media in the Classroom: A Best Practice Guide*, London, UK: Sage.

Richards, J.C. and Rogers, T.S. (2001) *Approaches and Methods in Language Teaching*, Cambridge: Cambridge University Press.

Roytek, M.A. (2010) 'Enhancing instructional design efficiency: Methodologies employed by instructional designers', *British Journal of Educational Technology*, 41(2): 170–180.

Slaouti, D., Motteram, G. and Onat-Stelma, Z. (2008) *The Case-Study Report*, Cambridge: Cambridge University Press.

Stanley, G. (2013) 'Integrating technology into secondary English language teaching', in G. Motteram (ed), *Innovations in Learning Technologies for English Language Teaching*, London, UK: The British Council, 43–66.

Steele, C. (2012) 'Fitting learning into life: Language students' perspectives on benefits of using mobile apps', in M. Brown, M. Hartnett and T. Stewart (eds), *Future Challenges, Sustainable Futures, Proceedings of Ascilite Wellington*, Wellington, NZ: Proceedings of Ascilite Conference 2012: 875–880.

Swain, M. (2000) 'The output hypothesis and beyond: Mediating acquisition through collaborative dialogue', in J.P. Lantolf (ed), *Sociocultural Theory and Second Language Learning*, Oxford: Oxford University Press, 97–144.

Swain, M. (2006) 'Language, agency and collaboration in advanced second language proficiency', in H. Byrnes (ed), *Advanced Language Learning: The Contribution of Halliday and Vygotsky*, London, UK: Continuum.

Tomlinson, B. (2011) *Materials Development in Language Teaching*, 2nd edn, Cambridge: Cambridge University Press.

Tomlinson, B. (2012) 'Materials development for language learning and teaching', *Language Teaching*, 45(2): 143–179.

Tomlinson, B. and Whittaker, C. (2013) *Blended Learning*, London, The British Council.

West, R. (1994) 'Needs analysis in language teaching', *Language Teaching*, 27(1): 1–19.

# 7
# Researching in language learning and technology

*Mike Levy*

While researching in the area of language learning and technology can be a most rewarding endeavour, it can also present some major challenges for the uninitiated. Most significant is the impact of the rate of technology innovation and change on any research plan. This is especially true for longer-term theory-oriented research studies such as those conducted at the doctoral level. A related obstacle concerns the ways in which our culture judges progress through ownership of the latest technologies. Thus, for example, a school may be considered deficient because it has not purchased the latest state-of-the-art technology; the same judgements are often made of an individual who has not purchased the 'coolest' smartphone. There are also technical challenges for researchers in the field. These include the many theories, models or frameworks that are adopted to guide research studies, such as those derived from education, second language acquisition, or newer areas like game-based learning. Similarly, the research methods employed are numerous including quantitative and qualitative methods, descriptive case studies, design projects, ethnographic and experimental studies. It can all be a little overwhelming.

This chapter aims to guide the reader through this terrain with a view to constructing robust, meaningful research studies. In doing so, it considers different kinds of research, from the more established to the more innovative. It looks at research studies that use theories of second language acquisition (SLA) as the driving force for research design. It considers research that examines features of social media where the ways in which participants communicate and interact is key. This extends to research on language learning games and virtual worlds. Further, the importance of research that is designed to influence educational change is considered, as in design-based research (DBR), for example, with its commitment to informing broader practice through involving teachers and stakeholders from the beginning of the study.

## Understanding the research landscape

The topic area that deals with researching the design and use of new technologies in language learning, commonly known as CALL (computer-assisted language learning), has now been in existence for more than thirty years. During this period, the quantity of research has expanded dramatically, as have the number of journals that specialise in this area and serve as outlets for new research.

For any novice researcher new to the field, perhaps the most important piece of advice one can give is to emphasise the importance of systematically and thoroughly reading past work before setting out on a new research project. To repeat the well-known adage, 'We stand on the shoulders of others'. Too often in CALL, we find authors whose articles do not sufficiently absorb the lessons of the past. These lessons include recognition of such problems in CALL research as comparative studies that aim to compare the online experience with FtF (face-to-face), or the so-called traditional classroom with its online equivalent. Comparisons may be made, but there are traps and pitfalls for the unwary (see Levy and Stockwell 2006: 147–148). Reading of past work also needs to be undertaken with a view to not only identifying gaps in the research that has been done, but also in locating weaknesses in previous studies, such as missing information about the background of participants, including language proficiency and computer proficiency, and superficial surveys which simply pick up novelty effects rather than long-term effects. Initially, this reading should be broad, then gradually refined and increasingly targeted so that it is purposeful, critical and relevant to the goals and parameters of the new research project that is envisioned.

In reading work from past years, and cognisant of the fact that the field now has a history, we can now not only make use of the methods and research findings from individual studies, but we also have access to a meta-level of analysis and discussion of CALL research. In other words there exists a collection of commentaries on what has been done, how it has been done and its merits and drawbacks. Articles and collections include the seminal article by Chapelle (1999) at the turn of the century, 'CALL in the Year 2000: Still in Search of Research Paradigms?' and Salaberry's (1999) insightful response to it. Though they are over a decade old, such articles remain important today. Further single articles of this nature highly relevant for today's researchers include: Levy (2000) with an overview; Felix (2005) on analysing recent CALL effectiveness research; Stockwell (2007) on technology choice; Hubbard (2005) on subject characteristics; Wang and Vásquez (2012) on researching Web 2.0 and second language learning; and Meskill and Quah (2013) on researching language learning and social media. In addition to the individual article or paper, we also have access to edited collections on CALL research such as *CALL Research Perspectives*, edited by Egbert and Petrie (2005). Such works should be compulsory reading for those newcomers contemplating research involving language learning and technology. But they must also be read critically. In other words, the reader's stance is not simply one of blind acceptance of what is said, but one of assessment and evaluation of the arguments and ideas presented. Of course, such should be the case with all reading that relates to a future research project. Collectively, these books and articles remain important because they provide a sense of the whole, and a valuable commentary on how the field is evolving as well as providing a useful distance from the technical details and concerns of individual studies.

Reading about past activity also encourages the newcomer to clarify their understanding of what researching in language and technology involves. Obviously, the technology side of the partnership has changed and evolved over time, and continues to do so. In the early days, the definition of a computer was relatively straightforward: a standalone technology that was, at best, 'connected' with other computers in a lab. More recently, in a section on defining CALL research, Egbert (2005: 4) says: 'CALL means learners learning language in any context with, through, and around computer technologies', and these technologies are 'not limited to desktop computers but include any form of electronic, chip-driven technology and the software that makes it run'. Thus, language learning mediated by a whole range of different devices is possible including mobile phones, landlines, desktops, tablets, laptops, digital cameras and so on; the software component includes applications from word processors to phone apps. Sometimes research will be designed to explore the influence of different technologies on the same task to see what effects there may be on language input/output, or duration or timing of use (e.g. Stockwell 2010). Different technologies exert different modifying effects or affordances (see Blin, Chapter 3 this volume) and are surrounded by different cultural practices that also influence how and when they are used. Also, research in the area often involves development as well. CALL research is not just about researching the use of existing commercial products repurposed for language learning (e.g. PowerPoint, *World of Warcraft*), but it may also involve the creation of new products (e.g. SpeakApps).

Research in language learning and technology may be conducted inside or outside the classroom in many different settings and contexts. The notion of mobile learning is relevant here, and the idea of mobility brings many settings and scenarios into play for the researcher (e.g. home, library, in transit). This line of thought also brings to light the role of the learners' own personalised technologies in learning, including use in the more conventional language classroom setting (an emerging area of interest). A focus on context can also be approached more broadly. Thus research may engage with many languages other than English, from major world languages to minority languages, although the vast majority of research studies still focus on the learning of English as a foreign or second language. Research does tend to be imagined differently according to the language and related opportunities and constraints. Inevitably, different priorities come into play depending on the language in focus and its role and status. Similarly, there has been work done on hegemonies in CALL (Lamy and Pegrum 2010) and CALL in limited technology contexts (see Egbert 2010). Egbert (2005: 4) says: 'CALL research currently does not address these differences in context well' (see also Chapelle 2005).

Given such variables as the number of technologies in use, the variety of potential settings and the rate at which technology is evolving, grasping a 'sense of the whole' is challenging and difficult to embrace. CALL is not one thing, but many things (e.g. Steel and Levy 2013). The span of CALL research is broad, and it tends to be underestimated. Sometimes writers try and associate it with earlier tutorial style, computer-student interactions, yet there is ample evidence that the term CALL is used broadly both in the titles and contents of the leading journals (e.g. *ReCALL, Computer Assisted Language Learning*) and in recent publications such as *Contemporary CALL* (Thomas, Reinders and Warschauer 2013). This breadth of activity spanning established and emerging technologies also militates against the easy emergence of an agreed, unitary research agenda. Both the number of theories in play and the number of technologies in use add layers of complexity for the researcher who is trying to conceptualise and clarify a new project. It is therefore quite natural for the researcher to impose restrictions on the field of view.

## The role of theory

CALL by its very nature is both interdisciplinary and a relatively new venue for serious research. As a result it has been subject to many influences theoretically, especially from variously related, older and more established disciplines (see Hubbard and Levy, Chapter 2 this volume). Theoretical influences in past and current work are apparent from areas such as: psychology, SLA, language learning pedagogy, education, media studies and, more recently, fields such as virtual worlds and game-based learning and design. The net result has been at times confusing as different theories vie for prominence and acceptance by those in the field (e.g. Zuengler and Miller 2006).

As theory is typically used as a point of departure in CALL research, the decision of which one to choose is critical. Egbert and Petrie (2005) discuss this issue in setting the scene for their book. In the preface, the editors identify ways in which the new volume is different:

> Other texts generally address only one theoretical foundation (e.g., interactionist) rather than providing an overview of ways to conceive of and conduct research on CALL. In contrast, the intent of *CALL Research Perspectives* is to compensate for this piecemeal approach and to help teachers and researchers understand the many complementary options that they have available for grounding and explaining their research questions. In devising this resource, we assume that all approaches to research have a place in the study of computer-enhanced language learning.
>
> *(Egbert and Petrie 2005: ix)*

According to Egbert and Petrie, 'complementary options' to research are acceptable and 'all approaches . . . have a place'. The book contains chapters featuring many different models, perspectives and theoretical frameworks (e.g. sociocultural, systemic functional, situated learning, design-based research and interactionist). This perspective on research has its parallels in the related field of SLA, particularly in the well-known work by Lantolf published in the journal *Language Learning* in 1996, 'SLA Theory Building: Letting All the Flowers Bloom!', which supported the idea of multiple approaches, or what others later referred to as theoretical pluralism. Not everyone agreed, however – notably Gregg who in 1993 and again in 2000 was very critical of this open-ended approach; Gregg (1993) suggests, rather less effusively, 'let a couple of flowers bloom'.

It also quickly becomes evident in the Egbert and Petrie book that positions shift. Thus on page 3, Egbert says, 'the research seems to be scattered across such a wide area that a specific picture of what CALL is and does has not emerged'. So on the one hand, all approaches have a place; on the other hand, research seems to be scattered over a wide area and this is a problem. In chapter 2, Huh and Hu add:

> Another problem is that there are no agreed-on standards for CALL research, making the topics addressed in the literature appear hodgepodge and making it difficult for CALL teachers to use the results in ways that improve their language teaching. Although leaders in the field have called for a research agenda, their pleas thus far remain unanswered.
>
> *(Huh and Hu 2005: 10)*

This position echoes Chapelle's (1999) earlier observation about still seeking research paradigms. In addition, and contrary to the position presented earlier, Huh and Hu (2005) insist upon grounding all CALL research in SLA and lay much of the blame for weaknesses in previous research on cases where SLA was not the point of departure. Nonetheless, many of the chapters in *CALL Research Perspectives* do not refer to SLA at all, or do so only in passing not as their foundation (e.g. Warschauer, 'Sociocultural perspectives on CALL'; Mohan and Luo, 'A systemic functional linguistics perspective on CALL'; Petrie, 'Visuality and CALL research'; Egbert, 'Flow as a model for CALL research'; Brander, 'Considering culture in CALL research'; Yang, 'Situated learning as a framework for CALL research'; Yutdhana, 'Design-based research in CALL'; and Raby, 'A user-centred ergonomic approach to CALL research'). In fact, each editor of the book contributes a chapter that does not mention SLA. Broader frameworks for CALL also include but are not limited to activity theory (Blin, Chapter 3 this volume), game-based learning (Cornillie, Clarebout and Desmet 2012) and ecological CALL (Lafford 2009).

In her chapter titled 'Interactionist SLA theory in CALL research', Chapelle (2005) provides a valuable overview of the benefits and limitations, especially pertaining to the leading theory of SLA in relation to CALL (Table 7.1).

*Table 7.1* Summary of benefits and limitations of interactionist theory for CALL

| Benefits | Limitations |
| --- | --- |
| Has a tradition of L2 classroom research that serves as a point of departure | Has tradition based on face-to-face interaction |
| Has cognitively based constructs that are transportable from classroom-based research to CALL | Doesn't provide constructs for looking at the complete context of CALL use |
| Makes specific hypotheses about how the cognitive processes by which vocabulary and syntax are acquired through interaction with external sources | Has focused less on acquisition of pragmatics, which is of great interest in CALL |
| Has proven to be productive as an evaluative perspective for developing CALL tasks and research questions | Has a narrow pragmatic focus, dealing primarily with linguistic functions associated with misunderstanding |

Source: Chapelle (2005: 61).

It is the problem of accommodating 'the complete context of CALL use' that generates the central problem or dilemma from the interactionist perspective. While this theory may not be equipped to incorporate critical contextual factors, other theories that are currently being applied in contemporary CALL bring context into the foreground. Yet elevating or foregrounding context can also result in a loss elsewhere, given that evaluating individual student learning per se tends to be forced into the background.

While theory is often the point of departure for research in language learning and technology, this is not necessarily the reality. Gaps in language curriculum or course textbook, learner needs, context-related opportunities and constraints, or investigations into new hardware or software may each provide the spark for a research project. The discussion provided by Levy (1997: 130–134) still has relevance because it demonstrates the range of possibilities, from the more abstract, such as a particular theoretical orientation, to those with more immediately applicable results, as in action research designed to address a specific language learning problem in the classroom. The variety of points of departure is further evidence of the practical concerns of the CALL researcher, who in many cases may be a language teacher using research to inform practice (see Levy and Stockwell, 2006, chap. 5; Hubbard and Levy, Chapter 2 this volume).

Thus far in this chapter we have discussed the importance of being familiar with the repertoire of CALL literature and building upon past work; the problem of definition; and the speed with which CALL is evolving and its effects, especially as a result of the introduction of new technologies and software. Although language learning research and pedagogy develop and evolve, they have not done so at the same rate. In light of this discussion, research in this area may be said to have a number of (highly) distinctive qualities:

- It can be implemented in a wide range of settings including school, university, home and many virtual settings;
- It can focus on in-class or out-of-class use and both formal or informal technological settings;
- It can focus on technology-rich or technology-poor contexts;
- It involves personalised technologies as well as institution supplied and supported technologies;
- It involves a set of participant skills and literacies (separate from language learning) associated with the operation and use of a variety of technologies;

- Points of departure for research can be derived from theory or practice;
- Many theories, models, frameworks, either singly or in combination, may be drawn upon to support not only research per se, but also research and development (on existing technologies and applications but also in the creation of new ones).

The next section focuses in more detail on three sample research studies involving new technologies and language learning (see also Levy and Stockwell 2006). The studies are used to help identify some of the distinctive features of CALL research as opposed to research in cognate areas such as SLA or educational technology. Due to limitations of space, the discussion will focus specifically on those special features of the studies noteworthy for CALL research (all the studies are listed in the references at the end of this chapter should the reader require a more comprehensive understanding of the study in focus). The idea here is to demonstrate through example the points made in the previous list and to expand upon these ideas with regard to identifying key considerations when planning research projects in the future.

## Exemplars

### Smith (2008)

This study has a number of features that are interesting for CALL research specifically. While there are many studies that examine the use of computer-mediated communication (CMC) between pairs of students – in this case Smith focuses upon the learning of German – the study is distinctive in its methods of data collection and analysis. Instead of only using a chat log file, this study extended the data collection procedures by also using and examining a video file of the screen capture of the whole interaction. Access to further data that resulted from this additional data collection instrument substantially changed the results and their interpretation and thereby altered the researchers' understandings of the phenomena in focus, in this case 'self-repair'. The additional data collection instrument allowed a missing element to be discovered, hence the homage to the detective genre in the title of the article: 'The case of the missing self-repair'. While the chat log file collected some of the examples of repair, it did not capture the *history* of the construction. With this additional data collection tool, what had been written and edited in the chat box before the participants' contribution was uploaded could be captured, enabling many more examples of repair to be exposed. It became clear that only collecting data in one dimension (the chat log) which had previously been the case (Tudini 2010), rather than two (chat log and video capture), had led to a severely diminished understanding of the construct in focus, that of self-repair. As Smith (2008: 85) says: 'Many CALL studies do not make use of existing technology in their data collection and analysis methods, which can severely limit the impact and relevance of their findings'.

Smith's study is firmly grounded in SLA research and theory with its examination of the role of self-repair in L2 development. However, rather than looking at self-repair in a face-to-face (FtF) setting, it is considered in a task-based synchronous computer-mediated communication (SCMC) setting. Smith says 'self-repair' is one of the core areas of current SLA theory, yet very few studies in CALL or CMC have looked at this construct. The majority of SLA studies instead look at such constructs as negotiation of meaning (NoM) between partners. Interestingly, Smith's findings not only increase our understanding of self-repair, but also potentially our understanding of NoM because in the CMC setting one construct inevitably involves the other. It is here that the CALL context makes itself felt and it is uniquely different from the FtF context, where much of our current understandings of NoM have been derived.

The FtF context does not require or impose a two-step process as far as output is concerned: it is the technological design itself that imposes this constraint upon the user in text chat. This makes the communication process in the CALL context different, and the researcher has to be very cautious in assuming findings in one context apply unequivocally/directly to the other.

This study demonstrates well the ways a comparative study might be conducted in CALL. The comparison here is not a broad-brush comparison between SCMC and FtF – the kind of comparison that has been criticised in CALL – but between the results generated from screen capture and hard copy transcript chat logs. This latter comparison is perfectly valid. This study also illustrates the immense value of using a data collection device or instrument that is capable of capturing a richer and more in-depth picture of the phenomena in focus. Tracking software, video capture and eye-tracking techniques are being used increasingly in CALL research studies for precisely this reason, that is to record a more complete picture of what students actually do at the computer (see Levy and Stockwell 2006: 153). Finally, this example shows perfectly how the researcher needs imagination and an ability to notice gaps. Here Smith spots something important that others had missed and then, like Sherlock Holmes, he is able to expound on 'the case of the missing self-repair'.

## *Cornillie, Clarebout and Desmet (2012)*

This example from Cornillie et al. (2012) appears in a special issue of *ReCALL* dedicated to digital games for language learning. Significantly, the project study involves research *and development*, not research only. This broader focus – research with development – reflects an often overlooked or undervalued dimension of CALL: its creative function as a design discipline. CALL is not merely the study of existing commercial applications. Cornillie and his colleagues 'create a fully immersive 3D avatar-based game using a game development kit' (2012: 264). This approach is reminiscent of the authoring programs in the early days of CALL, and echoes a time when practitioners and researchers did not simply use off-the-shelf commercial products already complete, but built their own content into program templates of various kinds.

Given that the focus in this study is on research in connection with the development of a game, it should not be surprising that a number of theories are invoked to motivate the project. SLA theory alone is insufficient: the deeper and broader context of game-based learning led the developers to seek theoretical guidance from other sources also. In this case, the learning environment is more complex and multidimensional and is not built around a simple jigsaw task or linear interactions. Planning and researching around learning interaction (e.g. Smith) is relatively straightforward compared with the factors that come into play and have to be managed when designing a language learning game. Thus, game-based learning (GBL) theory and flow theory provide additional perspectives and points of departure in the design of the game. This example again exhibits some of the special qualities of CALL research that are different and do not apply in more conventional FtF settings. Here the researcher/developer is thinking about the design of a technology-mediated learning environment, not the testing of an existing tool, as with Smith who was using the chat function in Blackboard to evaluate a task interaction.

This study also explicitly steps beyond SLA theory, though it still includes it 'by interweaving theory in the SLA and GBL (game-based learning) literatures' (Cornillie et al. 2012: 258). It argues for a balance between instruction and play in designing corrective feedback (CF) and draws on the two theoretical bases accordingly. Here, a trade-off is required in the design of CF because, in simple terms, implicit feedback helps play but not instruction, while explicit feedback helps instruction but can interfere with game play. This kind of trade-off is typical of the tensions that often arise in designing a learning environment rather than a learning interaction. These kinds of issues may simply not arise in the evaluation and testing of a learning interaction, as in the evaluation of the task, for example. Reference to the GBL literature is essential in the design of the game. Reliance on SLA theory alone is much more closely circumscribed and restrictive and would be insufficient to provide a basis or point of departure for an effective game (see also Hubbard and Levy, Chapter 2 this volume).

Clearly, an appreciation of the context plays a key role here. The context of the game is not the same as the typical teacher-fronted face-to-face language classroom. Care needs to be taken, therefore, in applying theories developed and tested in face-to-face settings to game-based learning environments. This project also invokes a number of further theoretical sources as well as SLA theory and game-based learning theory, including the cognitive meditational paradigm (Cornillie et al. 2012: 260), the 4-Component Instructional Design Model (p. 265), self-determination theory (p. 262) and flow (p. 262), the latter being highly relevant in the design of the game. As 'gamification' increases in the CALL literature, we are likely to see more examples of this multitheoretical approach to research and development.

## Chambers and Bax (2006)

We noted earlier that numerous technologies are being used to support language learning in many different settings and contexts. Parameters or factors surrounding the particularities of the context of use have sometimes been ignored or overlooked in research because of the CALL researchers' natural desire to focus on the more limited field of learning interactions. Accounting for significant contextual factors is critical to the long-term success of CALL, as discussed by Yutdhana (2005) regarding the complications of context. The bigger issues open the door to new horizons, more context-aware theoretical frameworks like Activity Theory, Ecological CALL, Complexity Theory, design-based research and so forth.

There are many ways of looking at contextual issues and many points of departure using theory or practice as a starting point. One way in is through the idea of normalisation, a path taken by Chambers and Bax (2006). As many readers will know, Bax introduced the idea of normalisation:

> when computers ... are used every day by language students and teachers as an integral part of every lesson, like a pen or a book ... without fear or inhibition and equally without an exaggerated respect for what they do. They will not be the centre of any lesson, but they will play a part in almost all.
>
> *(Bax 2003: 23)*

This particular qualitative research study seeks to explore two EFL settings to discuss obstacles to normalisation and ways of overcoming them. The approach brings to the forefront – as do others with a focus on context – the realities of the conditions surrounding the implementation of the technology used. They aim to identify key features that appear to impact upon normalisation, positively or negatively. Such studies are typically qualitative and longer term, so novelty effects are reduced and everyday working conditions are established and experienced. Contextual factors are at the forefront in such investigations and, as Chambers and Bax pointed out, 'factors differ from context to context' (2006: 466). Significant variables include physical as well as logical aspects of the setting (see Levy 1997). Physical aspects concern, for example, the location of the language laboratory and the organisation of the computers, tables and chairs in the classroom (ergonomics; Raby 2005). In this study, for example, on one site (Site 1), the computer laboratory was not in the same building; it was a five-minute walk from the college. The researchers concluded: 'This distance, though small, was perceived as contributing to the failure to integrate CALL fully as it was "a bit of a faff [problem] going all the way over there" (teacher B)' (Chambers and Bax 2006: 469–470). Location made a difference (pp. 468–469). Ignoring this kind of contextual problem in CALL research is problematic because language learning with technology in the real world requires access to the necessary technology; it is not simply a matter of a whether a learning interaction satisfies a particular language acquisition requirement.

The study goes on to cluster these kinds of contextual issues into four groups, with subgroups: (Chambers and Bax 2006: 469):

1   Logistics
    a   Location and access
    b   Layout
    c   Lack of time
2   Stakeholders' conceptions, knowledge and abilities
    a   Worries, expectations and misunderstandings
    b   Monitoring and evaluation
3   Syllabus and software integration
    a   Syllabus integration
    b   Software integration
4   Training, development and support
    a   Teacher development
    b   Dealing with technical problems

All items in the aforementioned groups could play a role or be a focal component of a research study, and because all elements relate directly to contextual factors, studies done in different parts of the world with different languages, cultures and settings are liable to lead to different conclusions on what is necessary for normalisation. Such issues need to be considered in any CALL research study that aims to take context into account.

In CALL research projects, an appreciation of the context of the study is becoming increasingly important and researchers want to build contextual factors into the design of the study. This orientation pays much more attention to the learning *environment* rather than a learning *interaction*. Theories associated with ecological CALL, affordances, Activity Theory, Complexity Theory and design-based research all in their different ways fit this broader orientation (see also Blin, Chapter 3 this volume). This broader orientation aims to acknowledge the 'C' in CALL (Levy and Harrington 2001). The 'computer' may be invoked in widely different ways through mobile personal technologies – from the mobile phone through tablets and laptops – to computers that are effectively immobile, as in desktops, library machines or a computer lab. Associated with all these technologies, but in widely differing ways, are financial costs, access issues, available support, training and so on. The dimensions increase further when we broaden the horizons to languages other than English, endangered languages, countries underserved technologically, and cultures widely different from those of the West who may perceive Internet access and security in very different ways (high-tech/low-tech contexts). Maintenance and sustainability of programs that involve technology are also issues that arise in the longer term and that are increasingly being considered by researchers. Online and distance education and language learning add yet another parameter.

Mike Levy

## Research designs and methods

There is no substitute for conscientious reading of past work, especially those meta-analyses of CALL research referred to in the introduction. Through this process, the researcher not only gains an understanding of *what* has been done, but also *how* it has been done. Thus, with focused reading, the researcher will also be able to gain insights, ideas and guidance on setting research questions, research design and methods, data collection and interpretation. This process also helps the budding researcher to identify topic areas of interest and theoretical or design frameworks that are compatible with the researcher's preferred approach. In many cases, these processes will occur through consultation and discussion with collaborators, possibly a supervisor or a more experienced colleague.

In gaining this initial orientation for CALL, it is important for the researcher to avoid the trap of the passing trend. Generally speaking, it is best to avoid a research project that is inescapably tied to a specific technology or application, but rather connects with the deeper ideas associated with learning goals, the pedagogical approach, or curricula innovation. In this process, of course, a particular technology may be implicated from the outset, but the technology itself is not the primary determinant in the initial conceptualisation of the research project. Another related pitfall is to focus on a particular product item. It is always advantageous to think about the generic type rather than the particular product (e.g. tablet computer rather than iPad, smartphone instead of iPhone), even if one particular brand appears to be a clear market leader at a given point in time. This is especially important for longitudinal research, or doctoral studies, that are likely to continue over a number of years.

Once the point of departure and/or theoretical orientation is set, typically a group of participants needs to be chosen. A key factor here is to recognise differences among language students as far as background knowledge and competence with technologies are concerned. Language students maybe familiar with one technology but not another and, as we know, numerous technologies are in use (Steel and Levy 2013). Students may be highly conversant with a technology for social purposes, but have no idea how to use it for learning purposes (Stockwell 2010, 2012). We know from authors such as Hubbard (2004) that learner training can make a significant difference to how students approach and use technologies for learning purposes. We also know from critiques of Prensky's term 'digital natives' (e.g. Bennett, Maton and Kervin 2008) that young people are far from homogeneous in their knowledge and competence with new technologies. They vary enormously in their individual knowledge, experience and capabilities, especially when the technology is being invoked for learning rather than social purposes or for play. Understanding learner background in relation to the technologies in use is critical. Not only does this kind of information need to be considered at the outset of a study when selecting participants, it is also very important that the information is included in the study report. This will ensure that other researchers, when assessing the findings, know whether the study deals with novice users or those well versed in the technologies and their use for learning.

In conducting research involving new technologies and language learning, a wide range of methods and techniques are being employed ranging from the traditional experimental design to more interpretive, ethnographic studies. Also in evidence are 'mixed methods' which aim to combine quantitative and qualitative data. This latter approach is 'defined as a procedure for collecting, analysing, and mixing quantitative and qualitative data at some stage of the research process within a single study in order to understand a research problem more completely' (Heigham and Croker 2009: 137). Heigham and Croker (2009) describe four basic mixed methods designs – explanatory, exploratory, triangulation and embedded – that vary according to the timing, sequencing, weighting and mixing of the quantitative and qualitative components. In

CALL, Jones (2003) provides a good example where qualitative followed quantitative (explanatory) in a study that examined the design of multimedia annotations for listening comprehension and vocabulary acquisition (see also Levy and Stockwell 2006: 173).

As far as data collection is concerned, we saw from the Smith study earlier that it was only by collecting data using video capture that he was able to spot the 'missing self-repair' in the chat boxes before the user's message was uploaded. Transcripts of the chat logs, which had been the common practice before Smith's study, completely missed this crucial data of learners' self-repair. Such work is indicative of the importance of (1) capturing as comprehensively as possible what students do at the computer (or with their technologies) and (2) utilising the available technological options for data capture to accomplish this task.

Data collection techniques include focus groups, video recordings (online and offline), observation and analysis of class and group activities using written and orally recorded utterances of teachers and students, written and verbal reports of various kinds as well as chat logs. In connection with researching language learning with social media, Meskill and Quah provide a valuable account of the possibilities of data collection techniques and methods:

> We have identified several notably more sophisticated methods of capturing data to help describe student interactions in social media spaces including focus groups, interviews, iterations of learner revisions, video records of face-to-face learner collaborations, digital records of learner content development, open-ended questionnaires, learner self-reports, questionnaires and transcripts of collaborative work.
>
> *(Meskill and Quah 2013: 51)*

Screen capture, eye-tracking software, keyboard tracking software and combinations of methods old and new are also being used to provide as rich a picture as possible of learner activity. What quickly becomes clear is that technological innovation not only brings new opportunities for language learning, but also new opportunities for research through providing new mechanisms and support for collecting data, analysing this material once collected, and generating results and conclusions.

While new opportunities for research continue to emerge, some considerations do not change and remain as important now as they ever were – perhaps more so – because new technologies penetrate into so many parts of our lives. It is crucial that strict ethical standards are maintained at all times. While always imperative, there are particular pitfalls and traps when working with new technology, such as favouring one group over another through privileging access to a state-of-the-art technology, inadvertently copying or releasing private information, or intruding into areas of the students' personal life through their technologies. The line between the public and the personal is easily crossed. In all research, it is imperative that the researcher reflects very carefully upon the ramifications of any action, especially concerning the collection or distribution of information electronically. Permission to carry out an investigation must always be sought at an early stage and the greatest care must be taken always to ensure study participants provide informed consent (see Merriam and Simpson 2000; Mackey and Gass 2005).

## Making a contribution through research

Theory is often used as a point of departure for researching new technologies in language learning, and we have noted there are now many theories from which to choose (see also Hubbard and Levy, Chapter 2 this volume). In some cases, it may not be so much a question about whether a theory is right or wrong, or has an application in a particular context, or even that it may potentially be of value someday, but whether the theory is capable of generating a research agenda with studies that can be replicated and with findings that are ultimately of broader value and applicability. Building a research agenda is important, and is not a trivial question. This is a field that has limited resources – the research that is done should count and be of value to the development of the field.

Throughout this paper, the importance of reading prior work in CALL has been emphasised repeatedly. With limited resources, it is increasingly important that we make our research count, both in contributing to the discipline and in making a real difference in the world. With the former, it is imperative to build upon past work. This may involve replication of a prior research study (Chun 2012; Smith and Schulze 2013) to validate prior findings as much as it may be a new study. We also need to make a difference in the world. By this, I mean we need to think carefully about research studies that fully incorporate contextual factors into their designs such that there may be a well-informed response to the complexities and realities of CALL in actual practice. These complexities of practice need to be accounted for because they often make a difference in terms of the initial levels of acceptance of CALL by teachers, students and administrators, and they help us better understand the necessary requirements for sustainability of use over time. They also help guard against CALL becoming overly dependent upon the 'lone operator', that is the knowledgeable and committed language teacher around whom CALL practice in a particular school tends to revolve – such that when this key individual leaves the institution CALL practice ceases too. CALL research should remain connected to understanding the use of new technologies in the midst of day-to-day concerns of teachers and students learning another language.

## Further reading

Chapelle, C. (2001) *Computer Applications in Second Language Acquisition: Foundations for Teaching, Testing and Research*, Cambridge: Cambridge University Press.
    Carol Chapelle has been a major contributor in the field for many years, especially from the perspective of SLA and the interactionist approach. This volume provides a valuable overview, but in particular, chapter 3 provides important foundational concepts for research. Her distinction between judgemental and empirical evaluation is key, as are her five principles of evaluation that emphasise the importance of incorporating findings and SLA theory when conceptualising new research projects. Her six criteria for CALL task appropriateness are especially helpful for research aimed at task evaluation.

Egbert, J.L. and Petrie, G.M. (eds) (2005) *CALL Research Perspectives*, Mahwah, NJ: Lawrence Erlbaum Associates.
    As with the other references in this section on further reading, this text is valuable in providing the potential researcher with an overview of the field, and many of the current options for CALL research are introduced. More recent perspectives are included such as design-based research and situated learning, as well as more established areas such as interactionist SLA theory and sociocultural perspectives. In addition, Part 1 addresses some important background issues, some of the questions and dilemmas that need to be addressed, and ways to identify criteria that help ensure research is effective.

Levy, M. and Stockwell, G. (2007) *CALL Dimensions: Options and Issues in Computer-Assisted Language Learning*, Mahwah, NJ: Lawrence Erlbaum.
    This volume presents a detailed overview of the field by looking at key dimensions such as theory, design and research. The research chapter describes many of the prevalent approaches to CALL research studies including survey research and comparative studies, and it discusses strengths and weaknesses. It then describes six 'exemplar' studies in detail. The studies are chosen to represent different kinds of research in the field with various research objectives, research designs, data collection techniques and methods. These include studies focusing upon CMC, intercultural learning, researching the students' use of feedback and help and optimising the design of annotations.

Thomas, M., Reinders, H., & Warschauer, M. (eds) (2013) *Contemporary Computer-Assisted Language Learning*, London, UK: Bloomsbury.

This publication provides a broad overview of contemporary work in new technologies and language learning. The volume is especially effective in providing a sense of the breadth of the field as it now stands, and thus provides a backdrop of topics around which research might be contemplated. Further, there are particular chapters that are highly relevant for research, notably the chapter by Meskill and Quah on researching language learning with social media. Their division of key techniques in the three principal areas – the online environment, the socio/affective dimension and pedagogy – is particularly helpful for the researcher when visualising options and opportunities for research on new technologies and language learning.

## References

Bax, S. (2003) 'CALL – Past, present, future', *System*, 31, 13–28.
Bennett, S., Maton, K. and Lisa Kervin, L. (2008) 'The 'digital natives' debate: A critical review of the evidence', *British Journal of Educational Technology*, 39(5): 775–786.
Chambers, A. and Bax, S. (2006) 'Making CALL work: Towards normalisation', *System*, 34, 465–479.
Chapelle, C. (1999) 'CALL in the year 2000: Still in search of research paradigms?', *Language Learning and Technology*, 1(1): 19–43.
Chapelle, C. (2005) 'Interactionist SLA theory in CALL research', in J.L. Egbert and G.M. Petrie (eds), *CALL Research Perspectives*, Mahwah, NJ: Lawrence Erlbaum Associates: 53–64.
Chun, D. (2012) 'Replication studies in CALL research', *CALICO Journal*, 29(4): 591–600.
Cornillie, F., Clarebout, G. and Desmet, P. (2012) 'Between learning and playing? Exploring learners' perceptions of corrective feedback in an immersive game for English pragmatics', *ReCALL*, 24(3): 257–278.
Egbert, J. (2005) 'Conducting research on CALL', in J.L. Egbert and G.M. Petrie (eds), *CALL Research Perspectives*, Mahwah, NJ: Lawrence Erlbaum Associates: 3–8.
Egbert, J. (2010) *CALL in Limited Technology Contexts*, CALICO Monograph Series, Volume 9, San Marcos, TX: CALICO.
Egbert, J.L. and Petrie, G.M. (eds) (2005) *CALL Research Perspectives*, Mahwah, NJ: Lawrence Erlbaum Associates.
Felix, U. (2005) 'Analyzing recent CALL effectiveness research? Towards a common agenda', *Computer Assisted Language Learning*, 18(1–2): 1–32.
Gregg, K. (1993) 'Taking explanation seriously; or, Let a Couple of Flowers Bloom', *Applied Linguistics*, 14(3): 276–294.
Gregg, K. (2000) 'A theory for every occasion: postmodernism and SLA', *Second Language Research*, 16(4): 383–399.
Heigham, J. and Croker, R.A. (2009) *Qualitative Research in Applied Linguistics: A Practical Introduction*, New York, NY: Palgrave, Macmillan.
Hubbard, P. (2004) 'Learner training for effective use of CALL', in S. Fotos and C.M. Browne (eds), *New Perspectives on CALL for Second Language Classrooms*, Mahwah, NJ: Lawrence Erlbaum Associates: 45–68.
Hubbard, P. (2005) 'A review of subject characteristics in CALL research', *Computer Assisted Language Learning*, 18(5): 351–368.
Huh, K. and Hu, W.-C. (2005) 'Criteria for effective CALL research', in J.L. Egbert and G.M. Petrie (eds), *CALL Research Perspectives*, Mahwah, NJ: Lawrence Erlbaum Associates: 9–24.
Jones, L.C. (2003) 'Supporting listening comprehension and vocabulary acquisition with multimedia annotations: The students' voice', *CALICO Journal*, 21(1): 41–65.
Lafford, B. (ed) (2009) 'Towards an ecological CALL: Update to Garrett (1991)', *The Modern Language Journal*, 93, 673–696.
Lamy, M.-N. and Pegrum, M. (eds) (2010) 'Hegemonies in CALL', *Language Learning and Technology*, 14(2): 111–112.
Lantolf, J.P. (1996) 'SLA theory building: "Letting All the Flowers Bloom!"', *Language Learning*, 46(4): 713–749.
Levy, M. (1997) *Computer-Assisted Language Learning: Context and Contextualisation*, Oxford: Oxford University Press.
Levy, M. (2000) 'Scope, goals and methods in CALL research: Questions of coherence and autonomy', *ReCALL*, 12(2): 170–195.
Levy, M. and Harrington, M. (2001) 'CALL begins with a "C": Interaction in computer-mediated language learning', *System*, 29(1): 15–26.

Levy, M. and Stockwell, G. (2006) *CALL Dimensions: Options and Issues in Computer-Assisted Language Learning*, Mahwah, NJ: Lawrence Erlbaum Associates.

Mackey, A. and Gass, S.M. (2005) *Second Language Research: Methodology and Design*, New York, NY: Routledge.

Merriam, S.B. and Simpson, E.L. (2000) *A Guide to Research for Educators and Trainers of Adults*, Malabar, FL: Krieger Publishing Company.

Meskill, C. and Quah, J. (2013) 'Researching language learning in the age of social media', in M. Thomas, H. Reinders and M. Warschauer (eds), *Contemporary Computer-Assisted Language Learning*, London, UK: Bloomsbury: 39–54.

Raby, F. (2005) 'A user-centred ergonomic approach to CALL research', in J.L. Egbert and G.M. Petrie (eds), *CALL Research Perspectives*, Mahwah, NJ: Lawrence Erlbaum Associates: 179–190.

Salaberry, R. (1999) 'CALL in the year 2000: Still developing the research agenda. A commentary on Carol Chapelle's CALL in the year 2000: Still in search of research paradigms?', *Language Learning and Technology*, 3(1): 104–107.

Smith, B. (2008) 'Methodological hurdles in capturing CMC data: The case of the missing self-repair', *Language Learning and Technology*, 12(1): 85–103.

Smith, B. and Schulze, M. (2013) '30 years of the CALICO Journal – Replicator, replicate, replicate', *CALICO Journal*, 30(1): i–iv.

SpeakApps. (2012) Open University of Catalonia, Barcelona, Spain, available: http://speakapps.eu/ (accessed 19 Dec 2013).

Steel, C. and Levy, M. (2013) 'Language students and their technologies: Charting the evolution 2006–2011', *ReCALL*, 25(3): 306–320.

Stockwell, G. (2007) 'A review of technology choice for teaching language skills and areas in the CALL literature', *ReCALL*, 19(2): 105–120.

Stockwell, G. (2010) 'Using mobile phones for vocabulary activities: Examining the effect of the platform', *Language Learning and Technology*, 14(2): 95–110.

Stockwell, G. (2012) *Computer-Assisted Language Learning: Diversity in Research and Practice*, Cambridge: Cambridge University Press.

Thomas, M., Reinders, H. and Warschauer, M. (eds) (2013) *Contemporary Computer-Assisted Language Learning*, London, UK: Bloomsbury.

Tudini, V. (2010) *Online Second Language Acquisition: Conversation Analysis of Online Chat*, London, UK: Continuum.

Wang, S. and Vásquez, C. (2012) 'Web 2.0 and second language learning: What does the research tell us?', *CALICO Journal*, 29(3): 412–430.

Yutdhana, S. (2005) 'Design based research in CALL', in J. Egbert and G.M. Petrie (eds), *CALL Research Perspectives*, Mahwah, NJ: Lawrence Erlbaum and Associates: 169–178.

Zuengler, J. and Miller, E.R. (2006) 'Cognitive and sociocultural perspectives: Two parallel SLA worlds?', *TESOL Quarterly*, 40(1): 35–58.

# 8
# Literacies, technology and language teaching

*Gavin Dudeney and Nicky Hockly*

In our increasingly connected society, new skills are needed. So-called 21st-century skills are making an appearance in curricula the world over as governments and educators recognise the need to educate children (and in many cases adults) in how to effectively navigate an increasingly digital world.

An umbrella term for these new skills and competences, 'digital literacies' and the concept of 'being digitally literate' refer to our ability to effectively make use of the technologies at our disposal. This includes not just 'technical' skills, but perhaps more importantly, an awareness of the social practices that surround the appropriate use of new technologies.

In this chapter we look at digital literacies and their application in the language classroom. Starting from a brief overview of the path to digital literacies, we then explore a taxonomy of these new literacies. Finally, we examine how we might best bring them into our practice through a number of practical classroom activities, using English language teaching as an example.

## The path to digital literacy

Today we have more access to technology than ever before: from gaming machines to mobile phones, fast Internet access at home, on the move and, increasingly, at school as new initiatives bring interactive whiteboards (IWBs), electronic content, netbooks and other technological tools into learning. From the mass implementation of IWBs in the UK to 'One Tablet per Child' projects in Thailand or Rwanda, there are increasing opportunities for the integration of technologies in educational contexts in both developed and developing countries. Today's learner – especially those in developed contexts – is more likely than ever to have access to technology both at home and at school and to be interacting with learning materials and other learners on a near-constant basis.

Coupled with this greater access to technology and information is a regularly asserted belief in the ability of people to know how to operate these technologies, and to use them safely, wisely and productively. It is widely held that people these days – especially young people – are very tech savvy. However, a closer inspection reveals this claim to be somewhat erroneous.

The source of much of this misunderstanding of how technology works and how it is used by younger people can be traced back to the early work of Prensky, who promoted the concept of a knowledge digital divide (as opposed to a financial one) by popularising the terms 'digital natives' – those born into a world already brimming with new technologies and connectivity – and 'digital immigrants' – those born before such times (Prensky 2001).

Much has been made of this distinction since that time. Prensky himself has gradually moved away from such a polemical age-based differential, and many commentators have been quick to elaborate that it is not necessarily the age of the user, but rather how much time and effort they put into using technology that leads to the biggest gap in skills between the more comfortable 'digital residents' and the less able 'digital visitors' (Le Cornu and White 2011).

The 'Net generation' (Tapscott 1999) consists of, it is often assumed, regular and skilled users of all the technologies that are available to them: from social networks through blogs, from wikis to podcasts, video tutorials and beyond. The assumption is that because we regularly see users glued to their mobile phone screens, they must – by extension – be competent users of *all* technologies. Our mistake, then, is in assuming that the mere presence of some technologies is enough to draw regular technology users to them, when in fact most current surveys of technology use point to a heavy dependence on mobile phone usage over any other medium (ONS Report 2011; see also Stockwell, Chapter 21 this volume). Rare is the learner who has worked out the edge that can be achieved by using various technology platforms in the service of their learning.

Indeed, many reports on youth technology use globally suggest a predominately social use of technologies. One such report carried out for the Channel 4 television station in the UK concluded:

> However, the research explodes this myth by showing that young people's immersion in these devices and the time spent on them is not due to an obsession with the technology per se, but largely due to the gadgets' ability to facilitate communication and to enhance young people's enjoyment of traditional pursuits. For most, the focus of their passion is not so much the device itself, but more about how it can help them connect, relax or have fun. The technology itself is 'invisible' to the young consumer.
>
> *('A Beta Life – Youth' 2009)*

This would seem to bear up earlier assertions by Prensky that digital natives often tend to refer to technologies in the form of verbs (that is to say in terms of what technologies can do, and what technologies can enable them to do), whilst digital immigrants tend to describe technologies through a predominant use of nouns. This also squares well with Bax's ideas around the concept of 'normalisation' (Bax 2003) whereby technologies reach their greatest level of utility when they become ubiquitous, commonplace, everyday objects – invisible save for the processes that they facilitate.

However, this level of comfort with certain technologies, this 'invisibility' does not necessarily carry over into any tangible or positive benefits in terms of their learning. As Sansone (2008) notes, natives are too often described as 'tech savvy' when what we really mean is that they are 'tech comfy': that is that they are comfortable with technology, but not necessarily in a good position to put it to work in service of their knowledge and learning. He argues that perhaps a part of a new educator role may be to assist in the transformation from practical, social use of technology to a more rigorous, pedagogical use.

## What are digital literacies?

We live, then, in an interconnected world (albeit a predominately social one) of always-on societies where new skills are gradually being identified and coming to the forefront in education. These 21st-century skills are starting to appear in curricula around the world as governments, education authorities and educators recognise a need to equip learners with new skills to complement the old. Whereas once the aim of traditional, formal education was to ensure that those leaving were sufficiently skilled in what, in the United Kingdom at least, were commonly called the three Rs (reading, 'riting and 'rithmetic), the focus is now gradually turning to the need to ensure that young people leave formal education equipped to deal with an increasingly connected world, and with a skill set that will allow them to prepare for new jobs and new ways of working.

In the United States one can read of the need to address 'new media literacies' and '21st-century skills' in education; in Australia there is much talk of 'digital literacy skills'; and in countries as far apart as Finland and Spain one can find increasingly frequent references to 'digital competences' (see Belshaw 2011). In most cases these literacies are set to play a fundamental part in the education of all young people as they progress through their formal education.

Whilst the terminology may vary on its journey around the globe, the concept remains the same: digital literacy, at its heart, refers to the concept of understanding – and making best use of – the current technology toolset available to each individual. This does not merely involve the acquisition of a set of discrete skills such as the ability to, for example, use a spreadsheet to take care of personal accounts but rather extends the use of technology into areas with which, perhaps, it is not traditionally associated. The new digitally literate individual knows how to accomplish goals, but also understands why these goals are important, and what relationship they have with the wider world around them. Knowing how to use Facebook is a skill; knowing how to use it to build a community of like-minded individuals and to use that community for professional and personal development is a literacy. Herein lies the difference.

That is not to say that skills are unimportant, but it is in the application of these skills, in the way they interconnect and interact, that true literacy is acquired. As such, digital literacies encompass a wide variety of skills and knowledge, from being able to install new software through to an understanding of online copyright options such as Creative Commons (http://creativecommons.org/), social networks, digital footprints and beyond.

How then do we break down and categorise these new literacies?

## A taxonomy of digital literacies

In recent years a variety of ways of classifying and describing digital literacies have been proposed. Dudeney, Hockly and Pegrum (2013) explore these new literacies in some detail, dividing them into four main areas: language, information, connections and (re)design.

### A focus on language

The following are key digital literacies that focus on communication via the language of text, image and multimedia:

> **Print literacy:** the ability to read and produce online text, such as blog entries, tweets, and emails. This is clearly related to traditional print literacy, but includes an awareness of online text genres. This requires some familiarity on the part of the teacher, particularly when working on writing skills. As email and synchronous chat overtake the use of more formal letter writing, an awareness of genre, register and appropriateness will become ever more important.
> **Texting literacy:** an awareness of the conventions of texting language, such as abbreviations, acronyms and symbols, and of knowing in what contexts to use or not use it.

Whilst print literacy is a familiar typology, texting literacy remains the domain of regular mobile phone users and is much maligned in educational circles for the purported detrimental effect it is having on literacy. In fact, as Crystal (2008) points out, 'typically less than ten per cent of the words in text messages are actually abbreviated in any way'.

*Hypertext literacy:* an understanding of how hyperlinks in online text work, and being able to produce texts with effective use of hyperlinking. Here we might include knowing how many hyperlinks to include in a text and why, what to link to, understanding the effects of overlinking (or underlinking) in a text and so on. Hypertext literacy also extends beyond the producer to the consumer, to issues of focus, concentration and multitasking. In an age where everything is linked to something else, hypertext literacy demands that we consider how people read online, and how to keep them focused on particular sources, resources and tasks.

*Visual media and multimedia literacy:* an understanding of how images and multimedia (audio, video) can be used to supplement, enhance, or even subvert or replace text communication. There is also an underlying need to produce multimodal messages ourselves, from sharing our photos on Facebook to creating video clips for YouTube. In the age of Web 2.0 we are no longer passive consumers who need to learn how to sit back and critique mass media (although this is still a key skill). We are now 'prosumers' (producers and consumers) of multimedia artefacts.

*Gaming literacy:* a macro literacy involving kinaesthetic and spatial skills, and the ability to navigate online worlds (e.g. Second Life; see Peterson, Chapter 22 this volume) or use game consoles such as the Wii. Although at first glance this literacy may seem unconnected to education, there is a growing interest in serious games for education. From flipped classroom-style game-based learning initiatives such as the Khan Academy (http://www.khanacademy.org/) through the rise of gamification in social learning to projects such as Mozilla's Open Badges project (http://openbadges.org), there is a growing recognition of the power of games and learning challenges to engage some groups of learners. For more on gaming in language learning, see Part V of this volume.

*Mobile literacy:* an understanding of how mobile technology is transforming our world, from issues of hyperconnectivity (always being connected to the Internet) to understanding how to use geolocation and augmented reality. As suggested earlier, mobile phones themselves are perceived as somewhat problematic in class, where issues of focus and concentration appear to clash with having connected devices in the hands of learners. This is exacerbated in the language class, where perceptions of a resultant erosion in the quality of language produced by learners are coupled with teacher anxiety that an overreliance on translation and phrasebook-style apps and resources may impact negatively on the independence of learners. Many of these concerns are a result of teachers simply misunderstanding how mobile devices are being used by learners, but they also arise from draconian policies that prohibit the use of such devices in school. Key to acquiring mobile literacy and integrating it into the classroom are school policies regarding acceptable mobile use, as well as negotiation between teachers and learners as to best practice in class.

*Code and technological literacy:* apart from basic technical skills (such as knowing how to use a word processing program, or how to send an attachment by email), a basic knowledge of HTML coding can help us understand how online tools and products are put together and, more importantly, enable us to make changes to these to overcome limitations. As Rushkoff (2010: 133) puts it: 'If we don't learn to program, we risk being programmed ourselves'. We are not talking here about becoming fully fledged computer programmers, but rather about developing an awareness of the basics. Some very basic coding skills can help one customise elements in one's blog, for example, or route around censorship (for good or bad). A renewed interest in computer programming and related code skills can be seen in many countries around the globe, including the United Kingdom, where initiatives such as the Raspberry Pi (http://www.raspberrypi.org) have brought cheap, programmable computers to schools across the country. Social networks such as CoderDojo (http://coderdojo.com/) have sprung up to fill the knowledge gaps in the teaching body, allowing young people to jointly develop these vital skills.

## A focus on information

The following are key digital literacies that focus on how we find information and resources, how we evaluate them and how we store them for later retrieval:

*Search literacy:* the ability to search for information effectively online. This includes an awareness of search engines beyond Google, including visual search engines, voice-driven search engines and specialised search engines concentrating on single resource types. Arguably the most basic and vital of the literacies, search literacy is increasingly important in an age where the production – and sharing – of online resources is spiralling out of control and data management is becoming increasingly challenging. Getting to what we are looking for is more of a challenge than it has ever been.

*Information literacy:* coupled with effective search literacy, information literacy is the ability to evaluate online sources of information for veracity and credibility. In this age of information overload, we also need to augment these two skills with filtering and attention literacy so as to know what to pay attention to and what not – and when. Information literacy requires a heightening of critical analysis of resources, an ability to judge and evaluate the utility of those resources and an ability to use them in the service of our learning.

*Tagging literacy:* knowing how to tag (or label) online content, how to create tag clouds and to contribute to 'folksonomies' (user-created banks of tags). As resources become more plentiful, there is an increased need to be able to classify, label, store and retrieve sites and information. Moving beyond simple bookmarking in browsers, tagging literacy moves classification systems online, into a more social space where scattered groups of users contribute to a group's knowledge and access to information by keeping a shared repository of relevant data.

## A focus on connections

These literacies come to the forefront in social networking spaces and other online media where personalisation occurs. They may include blogs and wikis, as well as social networks such as Facebook. In such spaces users not only write about themselves and their lives, but also participate in wide social groupings that transcend more closed groupings in terms of ethnicity, religion, geography and so forth. They include the following:

- ***Personal literacy:*** knowing how to create, project and curate our online identity. This includes an awareness of issues such as online safety or identity theft. Knowing what to share – and with whom – has huge implications not only for our personal lives, but also for our professional image and our career trajectory. What is amusing as a 16-year-old can be severely detrimental as a 25-year-old, and understanding the potential impact our digital footprints can leave behind is key to managing them. As Holman (2010) observes: 'I don't believe society understands what happens when everything is available, knowable and recorded by everyone all the time', predicting that in the near future young people may be obliged to change their identities to escape their digital pasts. If, as teachers, we encourage the use of social and creative platforms in our classrooms, then we have a duty of care to ensure that our learners are engaging with them safely and constructively.
- ***Network literacy:*** the ability to take part in online networks and to leverage these to help us filter and find information. For teachers, their PLN (personal learning network) – online professional contacts – can be useful as a means of tapping into ongoing professional development. Network literacy is about pure connections, about how people share and transfer information from one grouping to another. In many ways network literacy has obvious parallels in early communities of practice theory with its core and boundary members and their interactions inside and outside a given group.
- ***Participatory literacy:*** closely aligned to network literacy, participatory literacy involves contributing to and participating in online networks. This equates to something over and above merely reading professional development tweets on Twitter, but contributing your own tweets. It means not just reading blog posts, but leaving comments – or even writing your own blog. Participatory literacy is the lifeblood of the post Web 2.0 social era of distributed computing, where what you share is what you are. In this sense, many of the major implications of personal literacy also hold for this skill.
- ***Cultural and intercultural literacy:*** understanding digital artefacts from other cultures and interacting effectively and constructively with people from other cultures takes on even more importance in our global world, where intercultural contact via digital communication is increasingly possible and increasingly likely. Take, for example, Internet memes such as 'Keep calm and carry on' (see http://knowyourmeme.com/memes/keep-calm-and-carry-on, and Activity 5), or LOLcats (see http://knowyourmeme.com/memes/lolcats). Memes are ideas or concepts, often in the form of phrases, images and videos that spread via the Internet and can contain a humorous or even a subversive quality. Both understanding and contributing to a meme requires a certain amount of culturally specific knowledge. As learning projects become more globalised, and more exchange based, learning how to interact with other cultures is key – not only to the successful completion of a given project, but beyond it, with wider implications in the professional sphere.

## A focus on (re)design

Macro literacy refers to the ability to repurpose or change already-made content in order to create something new. Typically associated with multimedia expression, the sole literacy in this group is:

**Remix literacy:** this refers to the modern trend of 'remixing' pictures, videos and other media, to often striking effect. This may refer, for example, to the trend of making 'literal versions' of music videos (http://tinyurl.com/l397zp), through remixing music videos for political or satirical ends (http://preview.tinyurl.com/yffhgnb) to the doctoring of digital images afforded by sites such as Photofunia (http://www.photofunia.com). This literacy is also closely associated with Internet memes (http://en.wikipedia.org/wiki/Meme, and see the examples of memes earlier). In each instance, recognition of the remix that has taken place is crucial to an understanding of the media being viewed.

Elsewhere, Belshaw (2011) identifies eight essential elements of digital literacies:

1. *Cultural:* This refers to an understanding of the different digital contexts we may encounter online, from more traditional, structured environments such as school virtual learning environments (VLEs) to less organised spaces such as Facebook. As we move between these environments we are encouraged to change the way we interact and operate. In Web 1.0 terminology this might equate to the notion of netiquette, whilst in language learning terms we may think of notions such as register and genre, and a need to accommodate to different situations.
2. *Cognitive:* Here the focus is on cognitive ability and critical awareness, rather than on any kind of technology tools; the cognitive element is concerned with critical appraisal of media and media sources, with an aim to helping develop strategies for learners to 'see nuance where they have previously seen dichotomy' (Belshaw 2011: chap. 9).
3. *Constructive:* The constructive element refers to a more participatory and contributory approach to content, to the concept of creating something new (either original, or a remix of something already in existence). In this element there are clear pointers to related concepts of copyright, plagiarism, Creative Commons and other similar parameters.
4. *Communicative:* Clearly much of what we do online involves an element of communication, particularly as we move further into the production side and engage with the contributory aspects of networked environments. This element refers to our ability to interact and communicate successfully in these environments. For example, how one communicates via a microblogging site like Twitter is different to how one communicates via email, which is in turn different to how one communicates via traditional print forms such as letters or postcards.
5. *Confident:* This refers to a sense of confidence and well-being mediated by technologies; a confidence born of the ability to step backwards, to undo actions and try them again, a confidence that is inspired by working in safe environments where experimentation is encouraged, and where 'learning by doing' is the norm. It is, perhaps, the skill of using technology over being used by technology.
6. *Creative:* The creative element refers to understanding and defining new ways of learning and of acquiring knowledge and experience. It is closely allied with confident experimentation, and with learning to put new tools to work for us in order to achieve new aims and outcomes.
7. *Critical:* Here we need to consider the skill of evaluating, tagging and curating the resources that come our way and understanding them at a relatively deep and critical level. This element squares with Dudeney, Hockly and Pegrum's (2013) focus on information and an ability to manage the information flow and information overload.
8. *Civic:* As technologies afford better connections and communications, they also encourage civic action and the development of 'civil society' (Belshaw 2011), more engagement on a

societal level, and can encourage civil action below the usual layers of government and state. Such use of technologies is often perceived as disruptive or challenging by more traditional entities, though much of it tends to reside in the practice of 'slacktivism' whereby social change is attempted through online expressions of disapproval and protests.

In both Belshaw's and Dudeney, Hockly and Pegrum's explorations of digital literacies there is a clear emphasis on both the conceptual nature of much of the content (rather than a list of practical skills to be acquired), and also a clear suggestion that these change and evolve as we explore them. In these early days of digital literacy it is hard to see a complete picture. Indeed a complete picture may not be possible as new technology affordances and demands will inevitably change and transform the original concepts, leading to new skills and literacies that may take on greater importance as they become more apparent and better observed.

Clearly, then, this is a complicated mix of skills and elements to master, and teachers can play a part in helping learners acquire some of the necessary skills by integrating them into their classroom practice alongside the regular content they deal with. In this way they can make a difference in their learners' comfort level, helping them beyond the 'tech comfy' to the 'tech savvy' which will contribute to their life beyond school as they move into the professional workplace and (increasingly) knowledge-based economies.

## Digital literacies in the language classroom

What exactly are the implications for the language classroom? Quite apart from the emphasis put on lifelong learning and the acquisition of ICT skills in all areas of education in the UK, we are language teachers teaching the language of global communication – a communication that is becoming increasingly digitally mediated. If our learners are to fully embrace their 21st-century citizenship, they need linguistic *and* digital skills. We can promote these digital skills in parallel with teaching language. Indeed, one could argue that it is our duty to do so.

However, to date there is very little evidence of this happening in language classrooms. Although national primary and secondary curricula in many countries now feature elements of digital literacy–related skills, at the teaching end it is often a challenge for teachers to implement these alongside the existing elements and demands of any given course. The Technology, Pedagogic and Content Knowledge (TPACK) model proposed by Mishra and Koehler (2006) provides one way forward for teacher training courses wishing to help teachers develop their skills in this area.

For practising language teachers, Dudeney et al. (2013) propose the addition of a digital literacy layer to activities designed around learning technologies, advocating a dual approach whereby activities have both a language aim and a digital literacy aim. How does this work in practice? Here, five activities are described which illustrate this dual approach of enhancing both language and literacy at the same time. The first two activities focus on language, with an activity on hypertext literacy and one on multimedia literacy. The third activity focuses on information literacy, and the fourth on connections (personal and network literacy), with an emphasis on online safety. The final activity focuses on remix – arguably the most complex of the literacies to develop.

### Activity 1: Hypertext literacy – comparing texts

We increasingly read texts online, and this means reading 'hypertext' (text which includes hyperlinks, that is, links to other web pages). This activity explores the effects of reading and creating hyperlinked texts with learners. Hypertext literacy includes not just knowing when to ignore hyperlinks in a text so as not to lose the thread, but also knowing how many hyperlinks to include in one's own online texts, in the interests of readability and credibility.

Find two online texts of a similar length on the same topic (e.g. a news item): one text with few or no hyperlinks, and one text with many hyperlinks. Ask learners to read each text online and to follow any hyperlinks. Give a time limit for learners to read each text. Discuss which text was easier to read and why. It is usually more demanding to read a text with more hyperlinks because one is continually faced with split-second decisions about whether to follow a link or not, as well as assessing what that link might lead to, and what the implications are of this additional information. The activity can be extended by asking students in pairs to produce their own texts on a similar topic, and to decide exactly what elements to hyperlink, and why.

## Activity 2: Multimedia literacy – images and copyright

As we saw in Chapter 6 of this volume, an awareness of the constraints of copyright and the appropriate use of images from the Web under alternate licensing schemes such as Creative Commons, is fundamental if we and our learners are to be law-abiding digital citizens. Knowledge and appropriate use of copyright is an essential part of multimedia literacy; if learners are creating their own online content, they need to know what images they can legally reuse in their digital contributions and how to acknowledge sources. The activity described here aims to raise learners' awareness of this important issue.

Choose a topic/theme that you are currently working on with the class (e.g. animals). Ask learners to search with Google for images of a given animal, and to choose the three images they like the most. In pairs, they compare their images and explain their choices. Ask learners to then prepare a short blog entry about the animal/topic, which they will illustrate with an image. Ask learners to look again at their chosen images online and the copyright license for each. With a Google image search, the percentage of 'all rights reserved' copyright images will usually be high. In Google advanced search, show learners how they can filter their image search results to include only images that can be reused. Ensure that everyone is familiar with Creative Commons licensing. Ask learners to also search popular image banks such as Flickr (http://www.flickr.com), where there is a higher percentage of Creative Commons images. There are also Creative Commons images available at sites such as ELT Pics (http://www.eltpics.com/) or FreePhotoBank (http://www.freephotobank.org). Learners make a final choice of a (copyright-free) image with which to illustrate their blog post. Show learners how to attribute the source of Creative Commons images in their post, via a caption stating the author and hyperlinked back to the source.

## Activity 3: Information literacy – spoof websites

Knowing how to search for and evaluate information online is arguably one of the most important digital literacies. Information is increasingly accessed online, and learners will probably need to do this not only in their native language, but also in English. By carrying out the activity described here, we are providing our learners with fundamental digital skills that can be applied to searching for information in any language. This activity provides learners with the tools to analyse specific websites, but it also provides a good opportunity to discuss the importance of triangulating information by looking at more than one online source.

Ask learners to visit a spoof website, such as that dedicated to the Pacific Northwest tree octopus (http://zapatopi.net/treeoctopus), or choose one from a list of spoof sites (see http://goo.gl/f7YNk). Set a comprehension task on the website content without telling learners it is a spoof site. After completing the comprehension task, ask the class if they think this is all true. Analyse what makes your chosen spoof site look believable (layout, links to real websites, links to other research, informational style of language, the use of maps or images, etc.). Analyse the elements that show the site is a spoof (URL, questionable content, headers and footers, taglines, layout and font, etc.). In small groups, learners then examine pairs of spoof sites and real sites, using the elements described earlier (URL, font and layout, etc.) to decide which is the fake, and report back to the class.

*Activity 4: Personal and network literacy – online safety*

With the rise of social networks (see Lomicka and Lord, Chapter 18 this volume), how to stay safe online has become of particular importance to teenagers and younger learners who are learning to navigate and forge identities in this new social space. Inevitably there are negatives as well as positives in this, and the aim of this activity is to explore with learners a range of online scenarios which throw up particular challenges. Rather than banning the use of social networking sites, many educators now agree that it is of more benefit to equip learners with the skills and strategies to deal with uncomfortable situations online.

Ask the learners what social networking sites they belong to (e.g. Facebook, VKontakte, Badoo, Twitter), and what they use these sites for. Put the learners in pairs to brainstorm the pros and cons of belonging to social networks, and put these on the board. Put the learners into small groups of three or four, and hand out a set of cards with online scenarios – for example, cards describing cyberbullying, friends posting photos of you without permission, strangers contacting you requesting personal details, websites asking for mobile phone details and so forth. Discuss the scenarios and what learners would do in each, as whole-class feedback. You could tie the lesson in to language for giving advice. You can extend the lesson by getting students to produce online or paper-based e-safety posters.

*Activity 5: Remix literacy memes*

Remix literacy requires not just the ability to manipulate a range of media, but also an understanding of the cultural norms or themes that are often being teased out, played with or subverted. One of the simplest forms of remix, at least on a technical level, are image memes: images, often with captions, that spread among online users because they are catchy or fun. An example of an image meme that became fairly well known and has had a considerable shelf life is 'Keep calm and carry on', usually accompanied by the image of the crown of the Queen of England (for the background to this meme see: http://en.wikipedia.org/wiki/Keep_Calm_and_Carry_On). Variations on this meme have included 'Keep calm and evade the police', 'Keep calm and call Batman', 'Keep calm and ... arrghhhh', 'Keep calm and fake a British accent' ... An image meme can form the basis of a lesson introducing learners to both understanding and producing remixed images.

Show learners a remixed version of 'Keep calm and carry on' (there are several examples here: http://knowyourmeme.com/memes/keep-calm-and-carry-on). Ask them if they know this particular meme and any other examples of it. Explore more examples of this meme with the learners, unpicking the meanings behind them, and drawing attention to the style (crown image at the top, message in caps, etc.). Put the learners in pairs and ask them to create their own versions of the meme. They can do this on paper or via the meme generator site Keep calm-o-matic (http://www.keepcalm-o-matic.co.uk/). As an extension activity, put learners into pairs to choose and research other image memes online, and to then present one to the class, describing its background and showing examples.

Each of the five activities just described focuses on a different literacy, although there is often some overlap between literacies, with more than one coming into play at any one time. Remix literacy, for example, is a macro literacy that draws on a range of skills: critical thinking, cultural competence, visual and multimedia literacy, and even network and participatory literacy if remix artefacts are shared with a wider audience online.

Each activity also has a clear focus on language, and builds on communicative language teaching pedagogy: in many ways these are standard classroom activities, with an additional focus on digital literacy. The first activity on hypertext, for example, requires reading, discussion and writing. The second activity examining images and copyright requires discussion and writing. The third activity on spoof websites revolves around reading (website content), analysis and discussion. The fourth activity (online scenarios) is an extended speaking activity including language for asking for and giving advice, with some writing at the end if learners produce a poster. And finally, the fifth (remix) activity involves speaking, reading and some writing.

Thus introducing digital literacies into the language classroom does not imply a complete change in methodology or approach. Rather, we would argue that mainstream communicative language teaching of the sort most often advocated in course books, and practised in classrooms around the world, is particularly well suited to the dual approach we mentioned at the beginning of this chapter: that of developing our learners' language skills (and all that entails) at the same time as bringing digital literacies into our classrooms when there is a fit with the curriculum, or the current course book topic, or the language aim of the lesson.

## Digital literacies and the language teacher

In this chapter we have looked at the changing face of today's learners with particular reference to evolving digital literacies, and at ways in which teachers can address these literacies through the creative use of technologies in class. We discussed how teachers can integrate a range of free web-based tools into their current teaching practice. Integrating technology into teaching does not necessarily mean having to embrace an entirely new approach to pedagogy. Simple tools and websites can serve well as a first step to integrating technology into teaching, with the use of more complex tools that rely on user-generated content (such as blogs or wikis) being implemented with learners later on, once both parties have become accustomed to the presence of technology in the classroom context.

We believe that the digital literacies described in the chapter, such as print and texting literacies, collaborative and intercultural literacies, information and search literacies, and finally remix literacies – are fundamental skills needed by learners for the knowledge society of which we are all a part. We suggest that the teacher's role is to help learners acquire these literacies alongside English language skills, and that this can be done through the integration of a range of practical activities based on a range of technologies.

Finally, we would suggest that it is vital for teacher education programmes, both pre-service and in-service, to ensure that teachers are equipped with not just basic technical skills and a working knowledge of the key Web 2.0 technologies (see Lomicka and Lord, Chapter 18 this volume), but also with a clear idea of digital literacies: what they are, why they are important and how to make them operational in the language classroom. We hope that this chapter provides the reader with an idea of where and how to start with this process.

## Further reading

Dudeney, G., Hockly, N. and Pegrum, M. (2013) *Digital Literacies*, Harlow: Pearson.
  Provides a clear theoretical framework for conceptualising digital literacies and a rationale for integrating these into the English language classroom. Practical classroom activities are described, along with a consideration of how to integrate digital literacies into the syllabus and how to assess them.

Hockly, N. [with Clandfield, L.] (2010) *Teaching Online: Tools & Techniques*, Peaslake: Delta Publishing.
  A guide with practical activities to teaching English online. Includes a consideration of purely online and blended courses, possible course tools, and essential online teacher skills, as well as suggestions for teachers to further their professional development online via personal learning networks (PLNs).

Pegrum, M. (2009) *From Blogs to Bombs: The Future of Digital Technologies in Education*, Perth: UWA Publishing.
  A consideration of digital literacies and how they affect young people, education and society as a whole, through five complementary 'lenses': technological, pedagogical, social, sociopolitical and ecological. Future developments in education and society are suggested based on this thorough and informed analysis.

Stanley, G. (2013) *Language Learning with Technology: Ideas for Integrating Technology in the Classroom*, Cambridge: Cambridge University Press.
  Contains classroom activities with a range of technologies, including mobile technologies and social networking. Areas covered include the four skills: language work (grammar, pronunciation and vocabulary), and project work, assessment and evaluation.

## Websites

Digital literacy in higher education (http://dlinhe.ning.com/)
eLanguage (http://e-language.wikispaces.com/)
Future lab: Digital literacy across the curriculum (http://www2.futurelab.org.uk/resources/documents/handbooks/digital_literacy.pdf)
JISC: Developing digital literacies (http://www.jisc.ac.uk/developingdigitalliteracies)

## References

'A Beta Life – Youth'. (2009) Research report by OTX Research, commissioned by Channel 4, available: http://tinyurl.com/yza799c (no longer available online) (accessed 9 Dec 2014).

Bax, S. (2003) 'CALL – Past, present and future', *System*, 31: 13–28, available: http://tinyurl.com/yk6v6u6 (accessed 13 Apr 2015).

Belshaw, D. (2011) *What Is Digital Literacy? A Pragmatic Investigation*. Ed.D thesis, Durham University, available: http://neverendingthesis.com (accessed 13 Apr 2015).

Crystal, D. (2008) *On the Myth of Texting*, available: http://tinyurl.com/yhwb5dj (accessed 13 Apr 2015).

Dudeney, G., Hockly, N. and Pegrum, M. (2013) *Digital Literacies*, Harlow, UK: Pearson.

Holman, W.J. Jr. (2010) *Google and the Search for the Future*, available: http://tinyurl.com/2efmxne (accessed 13 Apr 2015).

Le Cornu, A. and White, D.S. (2011) 'Visitors and residents: A new typology for online engagement', *First Monday*, 16(9), available: http://tinyurl.com/c3vwwe3 (accessed 13 Apr 2015).

Mishra, P. and Koehler, M.J. (2006) 'Technological pedagogical content knowledge: A framework for teacher knowledge', *Teachers College Record*, 108(6): 1017–1054.

ONS (Office for National Statistics) Report (2011) 'Internet access – Households and individuals', available: http://www.ons.gov.uk/ons/rel/rdit2/internet-access – households-and-individuals/2011/stb-internet-access-2011.html (accessed 27 Jun 2015).

Pegrum, M. (2009) *From Blogs to Bombs: The Future of Digital Technologies in Education*, Perth: UWA Publishing.

Prensky, M. (2001) 'Digital natives, digital immigrants', *On the Horizon*, 9(5): 1–6.

Rushkoff, D. (2010) *Program or Be Programmed: Ten Commands for a Digital Age*, New York, NY: OR Books.

Sansone, M. (2008) *Hey Teachers! Your 'Digital Natives' Still Need You*, available: http://tinyurl.com/4m3dlq (accessed 13 Apr 2015).

Tapscott, D. (1999) 'Educating the net generation', *Educational Leadership*, 56(5): 6–11, available: http://tinyurl.com/yaxb4jl (accessed 13 Apr 2015).

# 9
# Evaluation in CALL
## Tools, interactions, outcomes

*Catherine Caws and Trude Heift*

As an ever-growing area of research, computer-assisted language learning (CALL) abounds with tools, systems or learning environments that are constantly changing to reflect the latest technology trends. Faced with the reality that quality control in CALL is not a simple task, researchers have been looking for new and more specific measures to assess the pedagogical and educational values brought about by these new technologies. In this chapter, we reflect on the changing nature of evaluation in CALL by focusing on three key issues that emerged from our research: the evaluation of tools, interactions and outcomes. In doing so, our reflections are based on data collections from two case studies: FrancoToile, an online oral corpus of French speakers, and E-Tutor, an online written, form-focused ICALL environment. We address the various stages of evaluation and focus on its iterative nature by emphasising the relationship between the tools, the interactions and the outcomes in relation to the task. As such, and while using these two specific yet distinct case studies, our analysis applies to any context where a digital platform becomes the focus of a language learning environment.

## Evaluation in the context of language learning and technology

Evaluation is a multifaceted concept. Traditionally, evaluation in education included a strong human dimension within a fairly stable learning system, anchored in a set institution. Assessment of learning generally followed a linear pattern of activities regulated by a behaviourist approach. However, with the advent of different types of technologies as well as the ubiquitous nature of computers, the core concepts of evaluation have been radically transformed. Learning takes place anywhere, anytime, in a nonlinear fashion, and in conditions that seemed impossible as recently as a few decades ago. Due to this ever-changing nature of learning, evaluation needs to address these changes, and the ways in which learning systems and contexts, learners and/or concepts are evaluated need to be diversified. Accordingly, evaluation in computer-assisted language learning (CALL) ideally includes several factors: (1) the learner, (2) the tool that is being utilised, (3) their interactions in relation to a task and (4) the learning outcomes.

This chapter mainly focuses on three of these aspects of CALL evaluation, namely the tool, the interactions and the outcomes, in addition to discussing some of the issues relating to the learner. Generally, our reflections will be in part based on qualitative and quantitative data that we collected over several years and that emerged from a series of case studies using two specific CALL tools: FrancoToile and E-Tutor. While these two systems constitute only two examples amongst the multitude of CALL tools, they illustrate and emphasise the fact that CALL evaluation needs to adapt to the diversification of CALL contexts by using a multitude of assessment measures.

*A need for evaluation*

In today's language learning context, CALL evaluation often depends on experiments that include different actors, tools and artefacts. Adopting a sociocultural perspective, we define the actors as anyone directly or indirectly involved in the learning process: learners, instructors, native speakers with whom learners may interact as well as developers involved in the initial design of an instrument, among others. The tools are as varied and as indefinable as the artefacts they can produce. For instance, with the advent of Web 2.0 and the central role of social-networking, tools for language learning range from a piece of software or digital repository, developed in-house to meet specific pedagogical goals and needs, to applications or systems created by a public or private enterprise in order to attract web traffic. As a consequence of this symbiosis of education and popular tools, the range of artefacts that language learners can produce nowadays has also grown exponentially: oral and written digital productions (sometimes published online), blog entries, vlogs, wikis, full sites and/or simple answers to language-related episodes, as well as more structured exercises. This variety of learner productions constitutes rich corpora and merits its own evaluation, and in fact has already nurtured multiple empirical studies. Moreover, the complexity of CALL has lead to an ever-growing need for evaluation. Levy and Stockwell (2006: 41) cite Johnson (1992), who differentiates *evaluation* from *research* by asserting 'the purpose of an *evaluation* study is to assess the quality, effectiveness and general value of a program or other entity. The purpose of *research* is to contribute to the body of scholarly knowledge about a topic or to contribute to theory'. Levy and Stockwell (see also Levy, Chapter 7 this volume), however, admit that the distinction between the two is not fully clear and, in fact, one might argue that CALL research does need to include proper evaluative methods. If evaluation is to be more limited than pure empirical research, then the need for evaluation resides in its potential for assessing learning tasks and outcomes by, at the same time, establishing the factors that need to be taken into account when designing CALL tools and/or tasks.

The need for evaluation is also summarised by Chapelle (2001: 53), who suggests 'an evaluation has to result in an argument indicating in what ways a particular CALL task is appropriate for particular learners at a given time'. Moreover, an additional argument in favour of including evaluation methods within research methods can be illustrated by a need to link evaluation to development of a CALL tool and its implementation in authentic learning settings. Hubbard (1996) framed this need for an integrated approach by, for instance, devising a CALL methodological framework that includes an evaluation module designed to assess the learner fit or the teacher fit of a system. In a similar manner, Levy and Stockwell (2006: 42) associate evaluation with design by claiming an obvious overlap between the two concepts, and recall important features of evaluation such as the fact that evaluation studies 'have a practical outcome' and 'draw value from the process as well as from the product of the evaluation'. Finally, the diversity of CALL contexts also motivates the ever-growing need for evaluation. As expressed by Stockwell, CALL is:

> a field that by nature is divergent and dynamic, and for this reason, we might argue that diversity in CALL is something that is not only inevitable, but also something that is necessary to provide the best options for the myriad of contexts in which it is used.
>
> *(Stockwell 2012: 5)*

## Types of evaluation

The diversity of CALL contexts, however, also nurtures diversity of CALL evaluation tools, methods and studies. The goals, objects and actors motivating the evaluation also affect the types of evaluation that will be required or designed. In addition, the current culture of CALL, and, more specifically, the growing role of digital media in the daily life of learners, cannot be ignored. With a goal to empower students to 'control technology', Selber (2004: 93) argues that for proper use of technology in education to happen, 'contexts of use deserve at least as much attention as contexts of design'. Indeed, by giving power to users to reflect and evaluate their own use of instruments, they are developing the type of meta-knowledge that they can use to properly manipulate, analyse and eventually resist some aspects of the digital world in which they live. As a result of this ever-changing nature of CALL and, while evaluation is typically understood as the assessment of instruments, we need to add a human factor to CALL evaluation to reflect the dynamic and diverse aspects of language learning.

Moreover, and as a result of the dynamic nature of CALL, evaluation requires as much, and probably more, scrutiny than ever (see e.g. Hubbard 1987; Dunkel 1990; Chapelle 2001; Felix 2005; Leaky 2011). Hubbard (1987), for instance, recommends that effectiveness of CALL software be checked in its relation to the language approach it reflects and thus promotes. For instance, a system promoting an acquisition approach of language learning will 'provide comprehensible input at a level just beyond that currently acquired by the learner' (Hubbard 1987: 236), while a system promoting a behaviourist approach will 'require the learner to input the correct answer before proceeding' (p. 231). Hubbard further argues that software evaluation must also address other aspects of the educational context in which the system is used: learner strategies and the institution-specific syllabus. Likewise, in her synthesis of effectiveness research in computer-assisted instruction (CAI) and CALL, Dunkel (1990: 20) calls for a need to produce effective ways to assess the impact of CALL using 'nontechnocentric', experimental and/or ethnographic research studies that highlight the 'importance of the central components of the education situation – the people and the classroom culture, and the contents of the educational software'. Accordingly, the current trend seems to shy away from comparative studies aiming to show that a group of learners or a certain tool performs better than another or none at all, mainly because their focus is limited to one aspect of the educational context, that is, the tool. Dunkel (1990: 19) notes that, for this reason, research is veering more towards descriptive and evaluative research that can address questions of validity and effectiveness of instruments for specific learners and language skills or define users' attitudes and perceptions towards CALL. This type of systematic evaluation of CALL in all its aspects is also what Chapelle (2001: 52) recommends. She considers that in order to improve CALL evaluation three conditions must be met:

> First, evaluation criteria should incorporate findings of a theory-based speculation about ideal conditions for SLA [...]. Second, criteria should be accompanied by guidance as to how they should be used; in other words, a theory of evaluation must be articulated. Third, both criteria and theory need to apply not only to software, but also to the task that the teacher plans and that the learner carries out.
>
> *(Chapelle 2001: 52)*

Along the same lines, Felix (2005: 16) also contests the value of numerous effectiveness research findings for their lack of focus because 'the ever pursued question of the impact of ICT on learning remains unanswerable in a clear cause and effect sense'. She argues for a more systematic approach to evaluative research based on limited variables and outcomes and with a potential for improving learning processes. Moreover, a recent exhaustive study by Leaky (2011) proposes a new framework for evaluating CALL research using a system that relies on the inherent synergy that occurs when, what he calls, the 'three Ps' (platforms, programs and pedagogies) intersect. His model is unique in the sense that, following previous recommendations for systematicity, it combines CALL enhancement criteria with qualitative and quantitative measures to enhance the evaluation of platforms, programs or pedagogies. For instance, the evaluation flowchart (Figure 9.1) includes twelve criteria: 'language learning potential, learner fit, meaning focus, authenticity, positive impact, practicality, language skills, learner control, error correction and feedback, collaborative CALL, teacher factor and tuition delivery modes' (Leaky 2011: 249).

Regarding instruments, evaluative studies use several approaches to test the effectiveness and validity of new materials or artefacts, be it a web application or software; a combination of qualitative and quantitative methods will potentially lead to the best results. Checklists, however, appear to be a very common instrument to evaluate educational software. Depending on the goal of the evaluation (be it to test the functionality of a tool, assess users' attitudes towards a tool or obtain specific feedback from students and instructors), the items included in the evaluation checklist will vary (see e.g. Hubbard 1987; Levy and Stockwell 2006; Leaky 2011). As per Chapelle's (2001: 53) recommendations, CALL software evaluation constitutes only the first level of CALL evaluation, followed by an evaluation of CALL activities planned by the teacher (level 2) and, most importantly, an evaluation of learners' performances during CALL activities (level 3). This paradigm is useful in helping us expand on the notion of evaluation; yet, it remains very focused on the idea that CALL implies 'opportunities for interactional modifications to negotiate meaning' (ibid.). In sum, such evaluation analysis falls within an interactional theory framework.

While evaluation of instruments remains the most common type of assessment in CALL, and too often the goal of the evaluative study, we argue here that a focus on other aspects of the

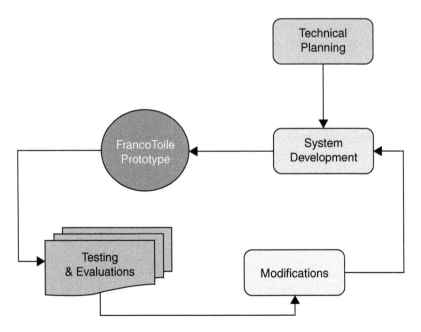

*Figure 9.1* Life cycle of the tool development and implementation

CALL context can lead to fruitful results in enhancing the overall experience with technology. Our argument falls within theoretical frameworks originally rooted in the sciences, in particular, activity theory, theory of affordances or complexity theory, because they share a common holistic, ecological view on learning (see Part I of this volume). Notions of interaction of various elements, continuous evolution of dynamic forces, adaptation and iteration of occurrences characterise the nature of CALL today. Such contexts of CALL learning and evaluation are intrinsically nonlinear. Moreover, pedagogy is one instance of the ecology of learning that is often neglected. Nokelainen (2006: 183), in an attempt to reflect the need to evaluate the pedagogical usability of digital learning material, uses criteria that combine learners' experience (control and activity) with such aspects as 'intuitive efficiency', 'motivation' or 'added value'. By pedagogical usability, Nokelainen (2006: 181) makes reference to the fact that learning is an unquantifiable concept and, when technical elements (i.e. computers or digital learning materials) are introduced to the learning context, they should constitute an added value that can be clearly identifiable. Combined with this concept of 'pedagogical usability', however, other approaches to evaluation need to be mentioned. Hémard (1997, 2003), for instance, proposes evaluation guidelines to address the design issues that many authors face when trying to conceive a CALL tool. Matching user and task, determining user-task feasibility and offering flexibility of use, among others, in addition to including instruments such as checklists and walk-throughs to assess usability and learnability of a system, will lead to a more accurate and thorough evaluation of both tools and learning processes (see also e.g. Smith and Mosier 1986; Brown 1988).

## The changing nature of evaluation

With an increasing number of CALL applications incorporating an increasing level of system complexity as well as opportunities for interactions, autonomous learning and creativity, evaluating the effectiveness of such systems is also changing drastically. In addition, the way in which the assessment of learners and learning occurs within and outside of such systems must be considered. Ultimately, the introduction of CALL in education has meant a significant impact on the learner, the context of learning and instruction; to this end, we see three aspects that qualify for further scrutiny: making a distinction between feedback and evaluation, taking advantage of peer and self-evaluations, and reexamining the role of the instructor in relation to these new learning models.

### Feedback versus evaluation

While feedback and evaluation are closely related in that both aim at some form of assessment, there are also important differences. Feedback generally refers to a more formative, interim assessment of learner performance that is aimed to coach the learner and, more generally, steer learning. In contrast, evaluation aims at a more summative assessment that usually reflects a goal, a standard and notions of validity and reliability. Furthermore, and as stated earlier, it not only takes into account the learner but, ideally, also the tool, their interactions as well as the outcomes. However, along with the changes brought about by new technologies, which have influenced CALL evaluation, similarly, the concept of feedback has undergone changes as well. Instead of feedback being restricted to automated system feedback, learners also provide feedback to each other when working collaboratively in various social media learning environments (see e.g. Ware and O'Dowd 2008).

Chapelle (1998) proposes an interdependence of design and evaluation of CALL learning activities. For instance, she suggests that when CALL materials are designed, they ideally 'include features that prompt learners to notice important aspects of the language' (p. 23). The noticing of particular features can be prompted and achieved, among others, when learners' performance is followed by computer-generated feedback during learner-system interactions. Such feedback can come from instructional materials containing explicit exercises aimed at providing learners with practice on particular grammatical forms and meanings (see e.g. Heift 2010a). Such materials, which can focus on specific areas of grammar or vocabulary, reading or listening, are aimed at providing learners with immediate feedback about the correctness of their responses to questions in a manner that engages learners in focused interactions that illuminate their gaps in their knowledge. For instance, this can be achieved with natural language processing (NLP), commonly implemented in Intelligent CALL (ICALL) applications (see Tschichold and Schulze, Chapter 37 this volume). Here, the automatic feedback is enhanced by a better match between the user and the task, leading to improved learnability, and more flexibility in terms of data display and/or data entry. Matching the previous language experience of the user is the ultimate goal to improve evaluation of the learner's ability. This type of information is commonly found in a learner model, which provides information not only on the learners' performance but also their learning preferences. Hémard (1997: 15) underlines the importance and significance of user models by highlighting that 'the more information on the potential users, the greater the designer can match the demands placed on the users with their cognitive characteristics', adding that a better 'understanding of tasks to be performed must inevitably lead to improved learnability and increased performance'.

*Peer evaluation/self-evaluation and learning*

As rightly expressed by Ellis and Goodyear (2011: 21), 'the increasing availability of ICT has widened the range of places in which students can learn, and they now expect greater flexibility in educational provision'. In addition, the affordances allowed by systems such as blogging, microblogging, vlogging, multiuser platforms or networked learning sites (such as Duolinguo, a site where language learners practice the target language by translating a text, which can be submitted by any user of the free language learning site) have greatly developed the concept of peer- and self-evaluation. Here, users are (often subconsciously) compelled to provide feedback and comments to their peers and assess their own contributions by adding to them or editing them. Ultimately learning (i.e. e-learning) and evaluating may become one process that engages users in self-awareness, develops meta-cognitive skills and self-regulation and elevates intrinsic motivation, by also leading to more learner autonomy. As Ellis and Goodyear (2011: 26) explain, 'learning can be understood as induction into a community of practice, in which appropriation of cultural tools and participation in cultural practices go hand in hand with increasing recognition and status in a community'.

In such a sustainable CALL environment, offering new possibilities for evaluation of users, tasks and instruments, the role of the various actors engaged in the CALL context may also be changing and/or may be reevaluated. Besides the CALL learner/user, however, another key actor is the instructor. To what extent and in what ways is that role evolving?

*The role of the instructor*

When evaluation becomes increasingly more diverse and allows for much flexibility and accountability on the part of the learner, what happens to the instructor? At a time when massive open online courses (MOOCs) are creating a buzz in and out of higher education milieus, the technophobes who years ago feared for the survival of the teacher now fear for the survival of the institution per se. We cannot deny the fact that, as learners become progressively digitally literate and dependent, the role of the instructor is also radically changing while, at the same time, becoming more critical. As we are reminded by many studies, instructors are still highly visible agents, actively communicating with students, mentoring, guiding and slowly transforming them into independent thinkers (Levy and Stockwell 2006; Warschauer 2012) – and yet, instructors need to disengage from the 'lecturing' mode to address changing learning environments. A recent study by Bates and Sangrà (2011) on managing technology in higher education, for instance, notes that while flexible access to learning has increased in recent years, the quality of instructing with technology has not increased in a similar manner due to a lack of investment in training. What does this mean for CALL evaluation?

Within a constructivist learning context where learners and instructors are interconnected via multiple digital channels, evaluation of computer-mediated tasks is complex. CALL evaluation by instructors is directly related to tracking interactions and new learning opportunities afforded by the instrument. In a full online context, access to all modes of interactions (i.e. student to student, student to instructor, student to system) help the instructor to guide the learner, set up appropriate tasks, and evaluate the quality of the interactions. In a blended learning environment, the face-to-face interactions often help to clarify difficulties that may have occurred during the online interactions by also ensuring proper communication among all actors involved in the CALL scenario. In addition to the mentoring role played by instructors, several systems have provided valuable interaction data to inform instructional design within CALL (Fischer 2012). One outcome of this interaction data analysis is the urgent need for further training of learners in CALL contexts (Hubbard 2004; Levy and Stockwell 2006; Hubbard and Romeo 2012). Training is needed to fill the gap between what users of technology do as independent or collaborative social agents and what they should do as independent or collaborative e-learners. Evaluating e-learning in such a way is meant to focus on the learner(s) and the learning activity. In their description of teaching-as-design, Ellis and Goodyear (2011: 119) state that 'regular evaluation, reflection and review are needed to close the loop between students' experiences of learning and the (re)design and on-going enhancement of all aspects of educational provision'.

In sum, within a Vygotskian approach and sociocultural view of learning (see Part I of this volume), instructors need to constantly assess the situation in which e-learning occurs to properly evaluate, amongst other agents, such feedback mechanisms as 'extrinsic feedback', which is provided by others through several channels and tools, and 'intrinsic feedback' as a result of self-monitoring (see Ellis and Goodyear 2011: 124).

Evaluation of CALL takes several forms and involves several agents and instruments. The following will examine some of these factors in more detail by focusing on two case studies involving two specific CALL tools.

## Core issues in evaluation: Analysis of two case studies

The two case studies that serve to illustrate our perspective on evaluation are linked to two tools, which were specifically designed within a L2 pedagogy context. These tools and the empirical data that they allowed to generate also illustrate that, in CALL, a balance of qualitative and quantitative data is needed in order to evaluate the values brought about by computer-mediated instruments and/or activities (see e.g. Felix 2005; Colpaert 2006). Leaky further explains:

> There is a general agreement on the need in a field such as CALL, anchored as it is between the humanities and the world of technology, to balance qualitative with quantitative data. It is not that the humanities can only be subject to qualitative study and the world

of technology only subject to quantitative analysis, but rather that human interaction, or 'inter-subjectivity', is so complex as not to be easily quantifiable and that technology so utterly dependent on empiricism and logic as to miss the affective, the 'human', the persona, and the synergistic.

*(Leaky 2011: 5–6)*

This statement emphasises the need for a well-informed approach to evaluation by assessing all aspects of the CALL context. In the following, we will focus on aspects of the tool (i.e. its effectiveness), the tasks and interactions that occur within a set activity (i.e. the process) and the outcomes of this activity (i.e. the product). Our basic precept is centred on the need for a cyclical approach to learning design in a view to recycle the outcomes of our evaluation into new learning processes (Caws and Hamel 2013).

## *Evaluating the tools: FrancoToile and E-Tutor*

When evaluating CALL tools or contexts of learning, the question of effectiveness arises. As pointed out by Colpaert (2006), measuring the effectiveness of a learning system is a difficult task because it involves many variables that are often overlooked or not taken into consideration when first designing a system. Effectiveness was a key factor in the development of both FrancoToile and E-Tutor.

FrancoToile (http://francotoile.uvic.ca) is a digital library of short videos featuring French-speaking individuals from around the world. Built as a web-based bilingual interface, the tool allows users to view videos, read transcripts and annotations, and search through the video database using various keywords combinations (see Kohn 2012). It was originally designed to fill a gap in the availability of authentic video documents featuring native speakers engaged in spontaneous discourse; the intent was also to mirror real-life interactions in 'normal' conditions (e.g. conversations with background street noise have not been edited) so that learners could prepare themselves to the authentic language that they will encounter when visiting or living overseas.

Following recommendations to adopt a conceptual and methodological approach to CALL design in order to create applications that are 'usable' as opposed to simply 'available' (see e.g. Hémard 2003, 2004; Colpaert 2006), we adopted the Analysis-Design-Development-Implementation-Evaluation (ADDIE) methodology (see e.g. Colpaert 2006; Strickland 2006). ADDIE is an instructional systems design (ISD) that is particularly well suited to guide developers in the creation and evaluation of language software or other language-related computer systems. One advantage of the ADDIE model is that 'each stage delivers output which serves as input for the next stage' (Colpaert 2006: 115). We applied this pedagogy and design-based research approach to create the system (see Figure 9.1) and also to design the annotation system.

CALL ergonomics also guided our study because it constitutes a methodological and theoretical framework that seeks to describe interactions between users and instruments in an attempt to ameliorate these interactions so that learning can be maximised. CALL ergonomics research – in particular, interaction-based research – adopts a user-centred approach which is grounded in mediated activity theories (see e.g. Raby 2005) or instrumented activity theory (Verillon and Rabardel 1995; see also Blin, Chapter 3 this volume). The basic precept of these theories is that human beings adapt, change and learn through their interactions with machines, tools or other human beings. In other words, these interactions are socially and culturally constructed (see e.g. Leont'ev 1981; Rabardel 1995).

Similarly, E-Tutor was also developed with an iterative research and development process in mind. E-Tutor is an ICALL system for beginner and intermediate learners of L2 German, which covers learning content distributed over a total of fifteen chapters. Each chapter begins with an introductory text (e.g. a story or dialogue) that highlights the focus of the chapter. Each chapter offers different learning activities that allow students to practise chapter-related vocabulary and grammar. In addition, there are learning activities for pronunciation, listening and reading comprehension, culture and writing. There are currently ten activity types implemented in the system (e.g. sentence building, reading comprehension, essay) in addition to an introductory unit on pronunciation.

The design underlying E-Tutor was strongly motivated by pedagogical considerations. We aimed at a CALL system that emulates a learner-teacher interaction by focusing on individualised interaction between the learner and the CALL system. For this, two main design criteria have to be met: first, the system needs a sophisticated answer-processing mechanism to be able to provide students with individualised, error-specific feedback; second, the system needs to collect and maintain information about its users and their behaviour while they are working with the CALL program. Accordingly, E-Tutor was designed as an ICALL system with a natural language processing (NLP) component that performs a linguistic analysis of learner input. It checks for correct syntax, morphology, and to a lesser extent, semantics, to provide error-specific feedback through an automatic evaluation of the learner's input. Moreover, the system offers a dynamic assessment of each learner by considering past and current learner performance and behaviour in relationship to a particular learning activity. As a result, the system's interaction with each student is individualised as to the kinds of errors in the student input as well as the ways they are communicated to the learner. To achieve this, however, an ongoing, iterative evaluation of learner progress is needed.

Colpaert (2006), in describing different approaches to software development, also advocates a pedagogically driven approach but, at the same time, alludes to a problem of system design, namely bridging the gap between language pedagogy and technology. A CALL program might include the latest technological fads but lack language pedagogy, or it might reflect sound language teaching pedagogy but not effectively exploit the technology. On the other hand, even the best team of CALL software designers cannot always anticipate the ways in which learners will use a CALL system. Accordingly, many CALL studies have shown a discrepancy between the intention behind certain software features and their actual use. For this reason, E-Tutor also followed an iterative, cyclical process of development, implementation and evaluation (see Colpaert 2006) to enhance the effectiveness and scope of the tool.

In both systems, FrancoToile and E-Tutor, evaluation of the tools is a condition for their dynamic development. In the case of FrancoToile, a series of case studies were implemented whereby the tool became the focus of specific learning activities in the form of guided and free explorations, within set pedagogical conditions and parameters, hence leading to interactions between learners and the system. Data were collected from multiple sources: pre- and postactivity online questionnaires, activity sheets (used by participants during interventions), computer screen video captures using Camstasia Studio and recorded focus group interviews (Caws 2013). While users were involved in *authentic learning tasks* that were measured and/or observed, the analysis of their interactions (as recorded with the screen video capture software and through online questionnaires and interviews) were used to define the degree to which the interface was conducive (or not) to performing a task. Results of this analysis were recycled into improvement of the tool itself. In the case of E-Tutor, evaluation of the tool resulted from an unceasing analysis of system performance and learner input with the goal to improve overall system functionality and system features as well as to create a learner corpus from recycled data on learner-system interactions that were collected over five years. Overall, cross-sectional as well as longitudinal data were collected from automated server logs, learner-system interactions and user questionnaires as well as retrospective user interviews. Initially, data analyses served to improve system performance with regards to error identification, system responses and interface design (Heift and Nicholson 2001), while later analyses focused on pedagogical issues such as improving learner feedback or enhancing learner-computer interactions by adding additional system features and learning tools (e.g. help options) (Heift 2010b).

## *Evaluating learner-system interactions: The process*

Knowing what exactly users do when they interact with our systems has been the focus of our iterations of evaluation. This kind of focus allowed us to concentrate on the *process* of learning rather than simply directing our analysis towards the outcomes of a particular task or focusing exclusively on the system itself. In her argument for more systematic CALL research focusing on processes, Felix (2005: 16) explains that investigating 'how technologies might be impacting learning processes and as a consequence might improve learning outcomes' is critical. Likewise, Leaky (2011) proposes a model of evaluating CALL that inherently requires 'stable' environments and takes into consideration processes of learning, processes of manipulating digital materials and processes of teaching with technology. Fischer (2012: 14) also adds that the study of tracking data 'gives a clear and discrete view of students' actions' and thus helps us to better understand how students use software, as opposed to how we think that they are using it (see also Fischer 2007: 40).

In the case of both FrancoToile and E-Tutor, the methods used to evaluate learning processes involved the analysis of a 'work situation', as per CALL ergonomics principles, namely the study of 'the association of subject and a task in set conditions' (Raby 2005: 181). Data collection instruments included both quantitative user logs that recorded learner-tool interactions as well as qualitative analyses of user responses from questionnaires, activity sheets and retrospective interviews. In addition, in the case of FrancoToile, video screen recordings provided further insight on learner-tool interactions. Data analyses focused on what learners did while they were immersed in the task. For instance, are they following directives given to them? Are they using the tools available to them most effectively? Are they using other digital tools to complete the tasks? How do they respond to system interventions? Do they seem to exhibit signs of cognitive overload? What are their own perceptions of the task? In sum, such a close analysis of user-task-tool interactions places the user at the centre of the analysis with a goal to improve the process (Rabardel 1995; Raby 2005; Bertin and Gravé 2010). As for both FrancoToile and E-Tutor, monitoring students' behaviours during our CALL tasks and/or activities provided essential data to improve the instruments we use, and thus improve the efficiency and effectiveness of a task process.

## *Evaluating learning outcomes: The product*

While it is essential to analyse the interactions to evaluate the processes of learning, we cannot discount the need to measure the degree of accuracy with which users complete their tasks, hence evaluating the overall learning outcomes of interactions with CALL tools. Assessments of outcomes occur either with or through technology, and while properly evaluating learning outcomes can be challenging (see e.g. Leaky 2011), ICALL systems such as E-Tutor do offer that possibility in that they aim at automated understanding and generation of natural human languages. This generation of CALL applications makes it possible to develop input-based instruction, whereas the NLP capabilities allow for the computer to provide an analysis of learners' language and relevant feedback. Moreover, the CALL activities can meet the individual needs of learners by modelling what the student knows based on the evidence found in his or her writing. Such models can then be used for making suggestions about useful areas of instruction (Heift and Schulze 2007).

Evaluating the outcome of a task or an activity is an essential part of the overall assessment for language learners who seek to position themselves in the learning context. This type of evaluation does not need to fall under the sole role of the instructor, as stated earlier. New instruments designed for language learning or other learning environments can help to transfer or share this role with other actors, especially learners themselves. While learning to self- and peer-evaluate, students will develop meta-cognitive skills along with other critical knowledge that they will be able to use in any environment where evaluation plays a crucial role.

## Future directions

This chapter aimed to illustrate that CALL evaluation involves activities, tasks and instruments that coexist within a holistic frame. When we create CALL activities, we need to take into account the users' present experiences and the fact that those are influenced by former experiences with similar systems. Moreover, these experiences have repercussions on their interactions with other instruments in future learning situations. As such, 'getting to know our learners in depth through pretask surveys and/or observations will help us better train participants to use systems, as well as adjust our systems to better match participants' functional skills' (Caws and Hamel 2013: 32).

Accordingly, one may ask whether a stronger and more informed focus on CALL evaluation has achieved a decline in the tenacious scepticism towards the use of technology in language learning of its early days along with the belief that its impact had yet to be asserted. We think yes, simply for two main reasons. First, the instrument in question has become a cultural artefact comparable to any other artefact used for learning (e.g. a notebook, a book or a film). Second, the questions that centre around issues of effectiveness have developed in such a way that they, by now, include a number of nontechnological components of the learning context such as learning strategies, learning tasks, the role of the instructor or the physical design of the learning space, among others.

Yet, evaluating processes with technology has never been as promising due to the diversity of the digital tools that have become available. These tools have not only changed the role of the instructor – who by now has become much more of a guide than the former dominant knowledge provider – but they also allow for self-evaluation, peer-evaluation and critical assessment of systems in shared practice and space. Thus they permit learners to freely reflect upon their own experiences as well as those of others. As Selber (2004: 141) explains, the development of critical literacy deserves much attention, and the development of a meta-knowledge about the role of technology in learning gives learners the power to be producer as much as user of technology. Accordingly, what does this imply for the development and use of CALL tools?

Given that digital tools, especially social networking tools, occupy most of our students learning and social spaces, whether consciously or not, we must ensure that they *interact* with CALL tools as opposed to *react* (see e.g. Hémard 2003). As rightly expressed by Lantolf and Pavlenko (2001: 148), engagement matters because 'it is the activity and significance that shape the individuals' orientation to learn or not'. As a result of the omnipresence of these tools, evaluation of and for CALL includes such instruments. This, amongst other benefits, will inevitably transform the relationship that language learners develop with technology.

While CALL evaluations through analysis of interactions (i.e. data on behaviours, or data on outcomes) may reveal important insights into different types of learner engagement with the instrument, distinct learning strategies (or lack of) for task completion or achievement of a learning outcome and/or technical issues of system benefits and deficiencies, an effective evaluation must focus more closely on *design*: namely the relationship between tool, interaction and learning outcome in relation to the task. Design is a multifaceted, complex concept and its role in enhancing learning is far from new (see e.g. Levy 2002); however, it is important to study the wider context that affects the success or failure of CALL activities instead of solely focusing on the tool. After all, a tool is not used in a vacuum but instead, learners as well as learning contexts are involved in learning processes, and thus none of them can be regarded and/or assessed in isolation.

## Further readings

Brown, C.M. (1988) *Human-Computer Interface Design Guidelines*, New York, NY: Ablex.
  This book offers a practical introduction to software design for the development of interfaces oriented towards the user. This guide is based on research on human performance and interactions, and on practical experience.
Hamel, M.-J. (2012) 'Testing the usability of an online learner dictionary prototype: Process and product oriented analysis', *Computer Assisted Language Learning*, 25(4): 339–365.
  The article describes a usability study on the quality of the learner-task-dictionary interaction in the context of the design and development of an online dictionary for L2 French. Study findings provide insight into the learners' dictionary search and look-up strategies and prompt suggestions for interface design and testing methodology.
Hubbard, P. (1988) 'An integrated framework for CALL courseware evaluation', *CALICO Journal*, 6(2): 51–72.
  The article provides a methodological framework for CALL software evaluation from which teachers can develop their own evaluation procedures. The interaction of the three main parts of the framework (i.e. operational description, teacher fit, learner fit) and their interactions are described and ideas for use are provided.
Rabardel, P. (1995) *Les hommes et les technologies: approche cognitive des instruments contemporains*, Paris: A. Colin.
  This book offers a good insight into interactions between human beings and machines within various disciplines. It explains the concept of instrumented tasks and principles of ergonomics within a cognitive approach.
Ware, P.D. and O'Dowd, R. (2008) Peer feedback on language form in telecollaboration. *Language Learning & Technology*, 12(1): 43–63.
  The article describes a longitudinal study on the impact of peer feedback on language development with L2 learners who engaged in weekly asynchronous discussions. Findings indicate that while all students preferred feedback on language form as part of their exchanges with peers, feedback only occurred when students were explicitly required to do so. Pedagogical suggestions are provided.

## References

Bates, A.W. and Sangrà, A. (2011) *Managing Technology in Higher Education: Strategies for Transforming Teaching and earning*, San Francisco, CA: Jossey-Bass.
Bertin, J.C. and Gravé, P. (2010), 'In favor of a model of didactic ergonomics', in J.C. Bertin, P. Gravé and J.P. Narcy-Combes (eds), *Second Language Distance Learning and Teaching: Theoretical Perspectives and Didactic Ergonomics*, Hershey PA: Information Science Reference, IGI Global USA: 1–36.
Brown, C.M. (1988) *Human-Computer Interface Design Guidelines*, New York, NY: Ablex.
Caws, C. (2013) 'Evaluating a web-based video corpus through an analysis of user interactions', *ReCALL*, 25(1): 85–104.
Caws, C. and Hamel, M.-J. (2013) 'From analysis to training: Recycling interaction data into learning processes', *Cahiers de l'ILOB*, 5: 25–36.
Chapelle, C. (1998) 'Multimedia CALL: Lessons to be learned from research on instructed SLA', *LLT Journal*, 2(1): 22–34.
Chapelle, C. (2001) *Computer Applications in Second Language Acquisition: Foundations for Teaching, Testing and Research*, Cambridge: Cambridge University press.

Colpaert, J. (2006) 'Toward an ontological approach in goal-oriented language courseware design and its implications for technology-independent content structuring', *Computer Assisted Language Learning*, 19(2): 109–127.

Dunkel, P. (1990) 'The effectiveness research on computer-assisted instruction and computer-assisted language learning', in P. Dunkel (ed), *Computer-Assisted Language Learning and Testing: Research Issues and Practices*, New York, NY: Newbury House: 5–36.

Ellis, R.A. and Goodyear, P. (2011) *Students' Experiences of E-Learning in Higher Education: The Ecology of Sustainable Innovation*, New York, NY: Routledge.

Felix, U. (2005) 'Analysing recent CALL effectiveness research – Towards a common agenda', *Computer Assisted Language Learning*, 18(1): 1–32.

Fischer, R.A. (2007) 'How do we know what students are actually doing? Monitoring students' behavior in CALL', *Computer Assisted Language Learning*, 20(5): 409–442.

Fischer, R.A. (2012) 'Diversity in learner usage patterns', in G. Stockwell (ed), *Computer-Assisted Language Learning Diversity in Research and Practice*, New York, NY: Cambridge University Press: 14–32.

Heift, T. (2010a) 'Developing an intelligent language tutor', *CALICO*, 27(3): 443–459.

Heift, T. (2010b) 'Prompting in CALL: A longitudinal study of learner uptake', *Modern Language Journal*, 94(2): 198–216.

Heift, T. and Nicholson, D. (2001) 'Web delivery of adaptive and interactive language tutoring', *International Journal of Artificial Intelligence in Education*, 12(4): 310–325.

Heift, T. and Schulze, M. (2007) *Errors and Intelligence in CALL: Parsers and Pedagogues*, New York, NY: Routledge.

Hémard, D. (1997) 'Design principles and guidelines for authoring hypermedia language learning applications', *System*, 25(1): 9–27.

Hémard, D. (2003) 'Language learning online: Designing towards user acceptability', in U. Felix (ed), *Language Learning Online: Towards Best Practice*, Lisse, the Netherlands: Swets and Zeitlinger: 21–43.

Hémard, D. (2004) 'Enhancing online CALL design: the case for evaluation', *ReCALL Journal*, 16(2): 502–519.

Hubbard, P. (1987) 'Language teaching approach, the evaluation of CALL software, and design implications', in W.F. Smith (ed), *Modern Media in Foreign Language Education*, Volume I, Lincolnwood, IL: National Textbook: 227–254.

Hubbard, P. (1996) 'Elements of CALL methodology: Development, evaluation, and implementation', in M. Pennington (ed), *The Power of CALL*, Houston, TX: Athelstan: 15–32.

Hubbard, P. (2004) 'Learner training for effective use of CALL', in S. Fotos and C. Browne (eds), *New Perspectives on CALL for Second Language Classrooms*, Mahwah, NJ: Lawrence Erlbaum Associates: 45–68.

Hubbard, P. and Romeo, K. (2012) 'Diversity in learner training', in G. Stockwell (ed), *Computer-Assisted Language Learning Diversity in Research and Practice*, New York, NY: Cambridge University Press: 33–48.

Johnson, D.M. (1992) *Approaches to Research in Second Language Learning*, New York: Longman.

Kohn, K. (2012) 'Pedagogic corpora for content and language integrated learning. Insights from the BACKBONE project', *The EUROCALL Review*, 20(2): 3–22.

Lantolf, J.P. and Pavlenko. A. (2001) '(S)econd (L)anguage (A)ctivity: Understanding learners as people', in M. Breen (ed), *Learner Contributions to Language Learning: New Directions in Research*, London, UK: Pearson: 141–158.

Leaky, J. (2011) *Evaluating Computer-Assisted Language Learning: An Integrated Approach to Effectiveness Research in CALL*, Bern, Switzerland: Peter Lang.

Leont'ev, A.N. (1981) 'The problem of activity in psychology', in J.V. Wertsch (ed), *The Concept of Activity in Soviet Psychology*, Armonk, NY: M.E. Sharpe: 37–71.

Levy, M. (2002) 'CALL by design: Discourse, products and processes', *ReCALL*, 14(1): 58–84.

Levy, M. and Stockwell, G. (2006) *CALL Dimensions: Options and Issues in Computer-Assisted Language Learning*, New York, NY: Lawrence Erlbaum A.

Nokelainen, P. (2006) 'An empirical assessment of pedagogical usability criteria for digital learning material with elementary school students', *Educational Technology and Society*, 9(2): 178–197.

Rabardel, P. (1995) *Les hommes et les technologies: approche cognitive des instruments contemporains*, Paris: A. Colin.

Raby, F. (2005) 'A user-centered ergonomic approach to CALL research', in J.L. Egbert and G.M. Petrie (eds), *CALL Research Perspectives*, New York, NY: Lawrence Erlbaum A: 179–190.

Selber, S. (2004) *Multiliteracies for a Digital Age*, Carbondale: Southern Illinois University Press.

Smith, S.L. and Mosier, J.N. (1986) 'Guidelines for designing user interface software', Report ESD-TR-86-278, Electronic Systems Division, MITRE Corporation, Bedford.

Stockwell, G. (2012) *Computer-Assisted Language Learning Diversity in Research and Practice*, New York, NY: Cambridge University Press.
Strickland, A.W. (2006) *ADDIE*. Idaho State University College of Education, Science, Math and Technology Education, available: http://ed.isu.edu/addie/ (accessed 10 Sept 2011).
Verillon, P. and Rabardel, P. (1995) 'Cognition and artifacts: A contribution to the study of thought in relation to instrumented activity', *European Journal of Psychology of Education*, 10(1): 77–101.
Ware, P.D. and O'Dowd, R. (2008) 'Peer feedback on language form in telecollaboration', *Language Learning & Technology*, 12(1): 43–63.
Warschauer, M. (2012) *Learning in the Cloud: How and Why to Transform Schools with Digital Media*, New York, NY: Teachers College Press.

# 10
# Language testing and technology

*James Dean Brown*

A number of overview articles have been published in the last two decades on the topic of language testing and technology. This chapter examines them and explores what we have learned about the drawbacks and benefits of using computers in language testing. The chapter will also examine where technology is likely to take language testing in the future. To those ends, the following questions will be discussed at length:

1. What have we learned about computers in language testing, and how have our perceptions evolved?
2. What are the drawbacks of using computers in language testing?
3. What are the benefits of using computers in language testing?
4. Have our views of the drawbacks and benefits of computer-delivered language tests changed?
5. Where is technology likely to lead language testing in the future?

Language testing combines both educational measurement and applied linguistics to deal with field-specific sets of issues and special problems at the conjunction of those two fields that other fields do not have to contend with. As indicated by the long list of references in this paper, one rapidly growing subarea within language testing focuses on use of technology to address the peculiar issues and special problems of assessing second language learning. Indeed a number of technology projects are well underway, as shown in Table 10.1, which also explains many of the acronyms used to describe these tests. I have supplied URLs in Table 10.1 for readers interested in finding more information about these tests or in seeing what such tests look like.

## What have we learned about computers in language testing and how have our perceptions evolved?

The overview publications on computers and technology in language testing in the last two decades have used a variety of different approaches. For instance, Brown (1997) simply provided an early overview of the literature on computer-delivered language tests (CDLTs),[1] while Gruba and Corbel (1997) concentrated on computer-adaptive language tests (CALTs).[2]

*Table 10.1* Acronyms used in this chapter for current computer-based tests and testing systems

| Acronym | Test Name | Where to Find More Information |
| --- | --- | --- |
| ACT ESL | ACT English as a Second Language Placement Test | http://www.act.org/compass/tests/esl.html |
| BEST Plus | Basic English Skills Test | http://www.cal.org/aea/ |
| BULATS | Business Language Testing Service | http://www.bulats.org/Bulats/The-Tests.html |
| CAPE | Computerized Adaptive Placement Exam | https://www.aetip.com/Products/CAPE/CAPE2.cfm |
| CB IELTS | Computer-Based International English Language Testing System | http://www.ielts.org/ |
| CELSA | Combined English Language Skills Assessment | http://www.assessment-testing.com/celsa.htm |
| DIALANG | A suite of diagnostics foreign language tests | http://www.lancaster.ac.uk/researchenterprise/dialang/about.htm |
| iBT TOEFL | Internet-Based Test of English as a Foreign Language | http://www.ets.org/toefl/ibt/about |
| NEPTON | New English Placement Test Online | http://www.unic.ac.cy/study-with-us/english-placement-test |
| PLEVALEX | Plataforma de Evaluación Valenciana de Lenguas Extranjeras | http://dialnet.unirioja.es/servlet/articulo?codigo=2201305 |

Alderson (2000) considered the present and future of technology in language testing, while Chalhoub-Deville (2001) reviewed the literature on CDLTs from 1985, arguing that CDLTs had fallen short of their potential and called for innovative thinking. Douglas (2000: 259–277) provided an overview of CDLTs in language for specific purposes contexts. Chapelle (2001) also provided an overview of research on CDLTs, focusing on validity issues and criteria for evaluating CDLT quality. Jamieson (2005) explained how CDLTs evolved in three stages: using traditional language items but in computer formats; adding item response theory (IRT) analyses to develop computer-adaptive tests (CATs); and using computers innovatively. Chapelle and Douglas (2006) discussed issues ranging from the place of CDLTs in language teaching and research to the influences of CDLT on language assessment and applied linguistics. Douglas and Hegelheimer (2007) purposely related their article to Jamieson (2005) by exploring the progress that had been made with regard to her three stages. Garcia Laborda (2007) reviewed the issues involved in designing CDLTs and using multiple-choice, writing and speaking items. Dooey (2008) focused on the effects of technology on language test reliability and validity. Ockey (2009) provided background from the general computer-based testing (CBT) literature and discussed the influences of CDLTs on how language abilities have been described and assessed. Finally, Brown (2013a) examined progression CDLTs in the past, present and future.

Table 10.2 lists those publications across the top and records the main topics covered down the left side. The x marks within the table indicate which of the topics each publication covered. Column totals are also given along the bottom and row totals are provided in the last column. Notice, in the column totals, that there is a general tendency for these overview publications to cover more topics as time goes by. For example, only five topics were covered in Brown (1997), but ten topics were covered in Brown (2013a). However, simple topic counts can be misleading. For example, Chapelle and Douglas (2006) clearly covered the most topics, but that is a natural consequence of the fact that it is the only book listed here.

Table 10.2 What we have learned about language testing and technology

| Topics | Brown 1997 | Gruba & Corbel 1997 | Alderson 2000 | Chalhoub-Deville 2001 | Douglas 2000 | Chapelle 2001 | Jamieson 2005 | Chapelle Douglas 2006 | Douglas & Hegelheimer 2007 | Douglas & Garcia Laborda 2007 | Dooey 2008 | Ockey 2009 | Brown 2013b | Row totals |
|---|---|---|---|---|---|---|---|---|---|---|---|---|---|---|
| Item banking | x | | | | | | | | | | x | | x | 3 |
| Using technologies | x | | | | | | | | | | | | x | 2 |
| CAT/CALT | x | | x | | | | x | | | | | | x | 4 |
| Benefits of CBLT | x | x | | | | | | | | | | | x | 3 |
| Future directions | x | x | x | | | | | x | | | | | x | 6 |
| Validity issues | x | | | | | x | | x | x | x | | | x | 5 |
| CBLT design issues | x | | x | | | | x | x | x | x | | | | 5 |
| CALT example projects | x | | | | | | x | | | | | x | x | 3 |
| Administration issues | x | | | | | | | | x | | | | x | 3 |
| Psychometric issues | x | | | | | | | | | | | | | 1 |
| Hardware issues | | x | | | | | | x | | | | | | 2 |
| Software development issues | | x | | | | | | x | x | | | | | 3 |
| CB TOEFL | | x | | | | | | | | | x | | | 2 |
| CB UCLES tests | | x | | | | | | | | | x | | | 2 |
| Other international CB tests | | x | | | | | | | | x | | | | 2 |
| Pedagogical benefits | | x | | | | | | x | | | | | | 2 |
| IBLT | | x | | | x | | | | | x | | | | 3 |
| Actual implementation falling short | | | x | | | | | | | | | x | | 2 |
| Disruptive technologies | | | x | | | | | | | | | | x | 1 |
| CBLT design: multidimensional | | | x | | | | | x | | | | | | 2 |
| CBLT for tracking learning | | | x | | | | | | | | | | | 1 |

(Continued)

Table 10.2 (Continued)

| | Brown Gruba & Corbel 1997 | Alderson 2000 | Chalhoub-Deville 2001 | Douglas 2000 | Chapelle 2001 | Jamieson 2005 | Chapelle & Douglas 2006 | Douglas & Hegelheimer 2007 | Garcia Laborda 2007 | Dooey 2008 | Ockey 2009 | Brown 2013b | Row totals |
|---|---|---|---|---|---|---|---|---|---|---|---|---|---|
| Technology in LSP | | | | x | | | | | | | | | 1 |
| IBLT example websites | | | | x | | | | | | | | | 1 |
| Uses of CBLTs and CALTs in LSP | | | | x | | | | | | | | | 1 |
| CBLT & test method effects | | | | | x | | | | | | | | 1 |
| Criteria for evaluating CBLTs | | | | | x | | x | | | | | | 2 |
| Standards for evaluating CBLTs | | | | | x | | x | | | | | | 2 |
| CBLT score reporting | | | | | | x | | x | | | | | 2 |
| Automatic scoring of writing | | | | | | x | x | x | | | x | | 4 |
| Automatic scoring of speaking | | | | | | x | x | x | | | x | | 4 |
| CBLT authentic task types | | | | | | x | | | | | x | | 2 |
| Scoring & feedback | | | | | | | x | x | x | x | x | | 5 |
| CBLT authoring | | | | | | | x | x | | x | | | 2 |
| CBLT design characteristics | | | | | | | x | | x | | | | 2 |
| CBLT in language teaching and research | | | | | | | x | | | | | | 1 |
| Influence on language testing and teaching | | | | | | | | | x | | x | | 2 |
| Security issues | | | | | | | | | x | | x | | 2 |

|  |  |  |  |  |  |  |  |  |  |
|---|---|---|---|---|---|---|---|---|---|
| Language learner communities |  |  |  |  |  |  |  | x |  | 1 |
| Test preparation issues |  |  |  |  |  |  |  | x |  | 1 |
| The learner's test-taking experience |  |  |  |  |  |  |  | x |  | 2 |
| Computer-human interface |  |  |  |  |  |  | x |  |  | 1 |
| CBLT flexibility in when to administer |  |  |  |  |  |  | x |  |  | 1 |
| CBLT flexibility in where to administer |  |  |  |  |  |  | x |  |  | 1 |
| CBLT & accumulating data for research |  |  |  |  |  |  | x |  |  | 1 |
| iBT TOEFL |  |  |  |  |  |  | x |  |  | 1 |
| CBLT content assessment |  |  |  |  |  |  |  | x |  | 1 |
| CBLT tools |  |  |  |  |  |  |  |  | x | 1 |
| CBLT resources |  |  |  |  |  |  |  |  | x | 1 |
| Column totals | 5 | 7 | 9 | 5 | 4 | 7 | 16 | 8 | 10 | 11 | 7 | 10 | 103 |

Turning now to the x marks furthest to the left in each row, notice, moving down Table 10.2, that there is a clear pattern of new topics being introduced progressively from left to right. That is true except in two cases (Douglas and Hegelheimer 2007; Ockey 2009), where the authors chose to revisit topics that had already appeared. Scanning down the topics column at the left, there also seems to be a general tendency for the nature of the topics to become more specific over time. For instance, at the top of the list, there are very general topics like item banking, using technologies, computer-adaptive testing/language testing (CAT/CALT) and so forth; at the bottom there are much more specific topics like the Internet-based TOEFL (iBT TOEFL), CBLT content assessment and so forth. The single most common topic covered was *Future directions*, which was in six of the thirteen articles. Other popular topics (appearing in four or more) were *CAT/CALT, Future directions, CBLT design issues, CALT example projects, Automatic scoring of writing and speaking*, and *Scoring and feedback*. I hope that readers will consider using this table both to examine for themselves how topics have changed over time and to find which publications they should read for more details on topics of particular interest to them.

## What are the drawbacks of using computers in language testing?

While focusing here on the drawbacks of CDLTs, I will rely primarily on the work cited earlier, but will draw on others as well, and on my own experiences. A summary of these drawbacks is outlined in Table 10.3. Notice that they are organised into physical drawbacks and performance drawbacks. Note also that four columns have been set up to indicate whether these drawbacks apply to computer delivery systems (i.e. computer-based CBLTs or computer-adaptive CALTs) or Internet delivery systems (e.g. Internet-based IBLTs or Internet-adaptive IALTs). On the right side, an additional column suggests potential solutions to each of the drawbacks. The minus signs indicate where each of the drawbacks is more likely to be a problem.

### Physical drawbacks

Obviously, *computer equipment availability* can be a drawback because computer equipment and Internet access are not universal around the world. Indeed, those of us who sit comfortably in industrialised countries often don't realise the extent to which even sources of electricity may not be universally available or reliable. Naturally, this drawback could dramatically affect examinees' test performances in negative ways. While such problems appear to be decreasing over time in many places, they still need to be taken into account in others. Clearly, the only solution to this potential drawback is to make sure that adequate power supplies, equipment and software are available, properly installed and working. It is also crucial that maintenance personnel be available because such technology tends to degrade if not actively maintained. In addition, given the rapidity of technological change, everything will need to be upgraded on a regular schedule by the maintenance personnel. This is the baseline without which all other issues discussed in this chapter become irrelevant.

Even when available, *equipment quality* can vary considerably. Screen, processing and graphics capacities may be uneven and otherwise present challenges for testing. For example, computer screens have limited amounts of space. Consider the effects of screen size on developing a reading test. Could a 1,500-word passage and accompanying items fit on the screen at the same time? Would the test be the same if it was administered on desktop computers with 30-inch screens versus laptops with 10-inch screens? The overriding worry here is that tests that rely on screen size, processing speed, graphs, screen resolution, animation and so forth may not be feasible on some machines, or may respond differently for examinees working on different machines.

*Table 10.3* Drawbacks of using computers in language testing

| Drawbacks | Computer | | Internet | | Potential Solutions |
|---|---|---|---|---|---|
| | CBLT | CALT | IBLT | IALT | |
| **A. Physical Drawbacks** | | | | | |
| 1. Computer equipment availability | – | – | – | – | Make sure adequate electricity, equipment and software; provide for maintenance personal and regular upgrades for all technology |
| 2. Equipment quality | – | – | – | – | See A1; ensure that all monitors and graphics adapters are adequate for all testing needs; for Internet-based tests, ensure that Internet connections, servers and browsers are working |
| 3. Limitations in item types | – | – | – | – | Recognise this problem; keep up with the literature on new ways for testing and scoring all skills on computers; use hybrid formats that involve human raters |
| 4. Need for large numbers of items | | – | | – | Adaptive tests need development, piloting and banking sufficient items for the purposes of the test; do it |
| 5. Expense of expertise & training | – | – | – | – | Budget sufficient personnel and funding for the purposes of the test including technical teacher training staff |
| **B. Performance Drawbacks** | | | | | |
| 1. Differences in CDLT and P&P results | – | – | – | – | Consider giving examinees a choice of taking P&P or CDLT; be sure to perform whatever research is necessary to make sure that the scores on the two are comparable |
| 2. Computer familiarity & anxiety | – | – | – | – | Check for computer familiarity before any CDLT & provide keyboard/computer familiarity training to those who need (or want) it |
| 3. Security & cheating | | | – | – | For high-stakes tests, careful monitoring can help to avoid security risks; for Internet delivery systems, develop encrypted scripts & use password controls; security is less problematic for adaptive testing with large item banks |
| 4. Reliability | – | – | – | – | Study, document and defend the reliability of each set of CDLT items and scores just like you should for any other test |
| 5. Validity | – | – | – | – | Study, document and defend the validity of each individual CDLT just like you should for any other test |

*Source*: Adapted considerably from Brown (2004).

In addition, as Roever (2001) pointed out, for Internet-based tests, servers may fail and browsers may prove to be incompatible. Some of the solutions to these potential problems have already been covered in A1 of Table 10.3, but it will also help to make sure that the monitors on each computer are large enough, the graphics adapters are fast enough, the screen resolution is sufficient, and for the Internet-based tests, the connections, servers and browsers are all stable enough for the needs of the test.

*Limitations in item types* is a common complaint associated with CDLTs largely because they have tended to rely on multiple-choice or cloze items due to the fact that other item types are 'harder to implement in a setting where responses must be machine-scorable' (Alderson 2000: 594). As a result, CDLTs have often been limited to testing knowledge skills (like grammar and vocabulary) and receptive skills (like reading and listening) rather than productive skills (like writing and speaking) or task-based performances. In terms of productive language skills like reading and writing, Chalhoub-Deville and Deville (1999: 276) put it this way: 'While test takers' performances on these types of items can be collected, human judgment is still required to score such performances'. More recently, a number of real-world test development projects have shown progress in the area of oral testing (see e.g. Yu and Lowe 2007; Blake, Wilson, Cetto and Pardo-Ballester 2008). In *writing assessment*, large-scale testing organisations have long been able to collect essay samples from examinees for centralised scoring by human markers. However, recent work also describes interesting advances in automated scoring (see e.g. Attali and Burstein 2006; Warschauer and Ware 2006; Chodorow, Gamon and Tetreault 2010).

The solution to this drawback (that is to say, limitations in item types) is to recognise the temptation to test only knowledge and receptive skills with multiple-choice items and not to succumb to that temptation, especially when teaching communicative language that involves speaking, writing or tasks. Once the problem is recognised, it will be necessary to keep up with the literature on new strategies for testing and scoring all skills on computers. In the interim, also consider using hybrid formats that involve gathering speaking and writing samples on computers, then turning to human markers for scoring.

One drawback peculiar to *adaptive* CALTs and IALTs is their *need for large numbers of items*. If the bank of prepiloted items is too small, a dedicated group of examinees can recreate the items after the test and compromise the test by revealing the items publicly. To thwart such activities, large numbers of items must be included in the item bank. This requirement may become an important consideration in deciding whether or not to pursue such adaptive techniques. However, once committed to an adaptive project, test developers must definitely develop, pilot and bank sufficient numbers of items for their purposes.

Another drawback of CDLTs is the *expense of expertise and training*. CDLTs require levels of expertise in computer technology that are not needed for traditional pen and paper (P&P) tests. Where *adaptive* techniques are applied, additional expertise in software programming is also needed as well as advanced knowledge of IRT. All of this expertise requires highly trained and experienced personnel who are presumably relatively expensive. Also, CDLTs generally require setting up and maintaining computer laboratories, equipment and software over long periods of time, as well as staffing these facilities with technicians who are trained and experienced in regularly maintaining and upgrading the equipment and software – all of which is proportionately expensive. Another aspect of expertise that tends to be overlooked is the need for training teachers in the expertise they will need to effectively use CDLTs (Garcia Laborda and Litzler 2011).

### *Performance drawbacks*

The first of the performance drawbacks results from the possibility of *differences in CDLT and P&P results*. The worry is that a CDLT version of a test could lead to results that are different from those on the same test in a P&P format. Differences could occur in the comparability of scores, in their relative reliability and validity, and even in relative fairness. For a brief overview of this issue, see Jones and Maycock, who also suggest a solution to this problem:

Providing candidates with the opportunity to be examined in the mode of their choice is clearly the best way to maximise fairness and may also improve test authenticity, which is an important aspect of validity. However, in order for stakeholders to be able to interpret results appropriately and to make comparisons between candidates who have taken the same examination in different test modes, comparability studies remain important.

(Jones and Maycock 2007: 3–4)

*Computer familiarity and anxiety* present another set of drawbacks, which are caused by the fact that examinees not familiar with computer technology and keyboard use may experience anxiety when they are confronted with a CDLT, which may in turn affect their scores. Research indicates that familiarity with technology is indeed somewhat related to examinee performance on CDLTs (Yu and Lowe 2007; Dooey 2008), but also that this relationship disappears when examinees are provided with a computerised testing tutorial (Kirsch et al.1997; Taylor et al. 1998). While anxiety does indeed appear to pose a problem, the best solution seems to be to check for computer familiarity before any CDLT and then provide adequate keyboard and computer-familiarity training for any examinees who need or want it.

*Security and cheating* issues are particularly important for high-stakes tests where a lack of security threatens the meaning of the scores for admissions or placement decisions. In contrast, for lower-stakes classroom diagnostic, progress or achievement assessments, the motivation to cheat is probably lower and the consequences of the decisions involve lower stakes. It should also be noted that cheating is more difficult on an *adaptive* CALT or IALT than on a *computer-based* CBLT or IBLT. As adaptive tests adjust the item difficulty levels until they have zeroed in on the examinee's precise performance level, different examinees are usually presented with different sets of items, thereby making it much more difficult to predict which items will be seen.

Notice that Table 10.3 shows, contrary to what I just wrote, that security is a problem for Internet IBLTs and IALTs but not for computer CBLTs and CALTs. I decided to present it this way because CBLTs and CALTs can be set up to be monitored in computer labs much like P&P tests, while IBLTs and IALTs pose considerable security challenges primarily because of the general difficulty of monitoring examinees who are taking a test individually or on their own computers. Of course, they could all be asked to bring their computers to a central location and be monitored while they take the test, but even then, examinees might have other materials on their computers in the form of crib-note files, prewritten compositions and so forth. In addition, Internet-savvy examinees could easily cheat by accessing all of the test items and answers in the web browser JavaScript (Roever 2001) or by hacking into the item bank and compromising items (Alderson 2000: 596). High-stakes tests should be administered in a way that can be carefully monitored to avoid all the problems listed earlier. This is true of any test, but there are additional potential problems on Internet-delivery systems. It is also true that adaptive tests with large item banks can help control security problems. In addition, encrypting scripts and using passwords can also help increase the security of Internet-delivery systems.

Another drawback has to do with *reliability*. In general, the reliability of a set of test scores has to do with the degree to which the scores are consistent, either over time, across forms or internally across the items. Reliability can be adversely affected by environmental factors, administration factors, scoring procedures, test format problems or examinees' personal problems (Brown 2005: 171–175). Test reliability is desirable because it helps ensure that all examinees will have the same treatment, opportunities and chances of success. Reliability becomes a drawback when the degree of reliability of a set of items is unknown, as is often the case with CDLTs. It is important to realise that reliability is not a characteristic of a test, but rather a characteristic of the scores on a test when it is administered to a particular group of people under specific conditions. As a result, reliability issues can only be adequately resolved when the reliability of the items and scores on each individual CDLT have been studied, documented and defended. This is true for CBLTs, CALTs, IBLTs and IALTs, just as it is for P&P tests.

*Validity* is often defined as the degree to which a test is measuring what it claims to measure. Nowadays, that definition is usually expanded to include the social values that underlie the items and the consequences of the decisions that are being made with the scores. There are many ways to argue for the validity of a test, but that is beyond the scope of this chapter. Here, I will focus on drawbacks in CDLT validity.

For example, some of the other drawbacks discussed earlier, especially the ones under physical drawbacks, can lead to compromises in the validity of CDLTs. In theory, language teaching has shifted from structural, situational and skills-based syllabuses to more communicative approaches involving functional and task-based syllabuses. The assessments associated with such communicative approaches have also had to shift to more performance-based tests. Unfortunately, to date CDLTs have not been able to keep up with these developments. As Dooey pointed out:

> the validity of computerized language tests may be compromised, as the second language (L2) field has long promoted performance based assessment, a form of assessment that does not lend itself as easily to computer administration as do more traditional test formats.
>
> *(Dooey 2008: 24, citing Chalhoub-Deville 2001)*

In one sense, this is not just a CDLT problem; similar issues have long been discussed for P&P task-based performance tests as well.

Like reliability, validity is not a characteristic of a test, but rather a set of characteristics for particular sets of scores when used for making particular types of decisions in specific settings. Hence, each set of items and scores in each setting must be studied, documented and defended regardless of the test delivery system. Dooey (2008: 24) suggests that 'the move to embrace technology needs to take place whilst at the same time conserving the underlying basic qualities of validity and reliability in language testing'.

## What are the benefits of using computers in language testing?

The drawbacks of using CDLTs are far from the whole story:

> Technology promises a range of capabilities, including speed, accuracy and efficiency – in the case of language testing, technology is being used partly because it is available, and partly because it is intended to offer improvements in the way the job has been done traditionally. [. . .] there is little doubt that computer-based testing has in many ways rendered the language testing process more practical.
>
> *(Dooey 2008: 24)*

But, that is not the whole picture, either.

Drawing on all of the work cited earlier and others, as well as on my own experiences, I have listed eighteen benefits in Table 10.4 in three categories: test designer benefits, test administrator benefits and examinee benefits. The columns have been set up to indicate whether these issues apply to computer delivery (CBLTs or CALTs) or Internet delivery (IBLTs or IALTs). The plus

*Table 10.4* Benefits of using computers in language testing

| Benefits | Computer | | Internet | |
| --- | --- | --- | --- | --- |
|  | CBLT | CALT | IBLT | IALT |
| **C. Test Designer Benefits** | | | | |
| 1. More accurate and reliable scoring | + | + | + | + |
| 2. Specific ability level targeting |  | + |  | + |
| 3. Minimising cheating |  | + |  | + |
| 4. Design flexibility | + | + | + | + |
| 5. Positive washback | + | + | + | + |
| 6. Enhanced validity | + | + | + | + |
| **D. Test Administrator Benefits** | | | | |
| 1. Data gathering | + | + | + | + |
| 2. Data transmission | + | + | ++ | ++ |
| 3. Data storage | + | + | + | + |
| 4. Remote scoring | + | + | ++ | ++ |
| 5. Shorter tests that take less time |  | + |  | + |
| 6. Administration flexibility | + | + | + | + |
| **E. Examinee Benefits** | | | | |
| 1. Many examinees enjoy computers | + | + | + | + |
| 2. Examinees can work at their own pace | + | + | + | + |
| 3. Less intimidating | + | ++ | + | ++ |
| 4. Less frustrating | + | ++ | + | ++ |
| 5. Walk-in convenience | + | + | ++ | ++ |
| 6. Immediate feedback | + | + | + | + |

*Source*: Adapted considerably from Brown (2004).

signs in the cells indicate where each of the benefits is most likely to be found. When I have used a ++, it indicates where the benefit is especially strong.

## *Test designer benefits*

CDLTs can provide *more accurate and reliable scoring* than humans can – at least for selected-response items (i.e. true-false, multiple-choice and matching). Naturally, this precision can only be as accurate as the human-produced answer keys. Beyond that problem, computers are strikingly accurate. In addition, strides have been made in scoring writing samples. For more information see Dikli (2006), who explores the advantages of automated essay scoring systems in terms of cost, time, reliability and generalisability of scores, and provides a synopsis of available systems. Another aspect of this scoring benefit is that CDLTs can provide quick and accurate score reporting. Once human test administrators ensure that examinee identification names or numbers are correctly aligned,[3] computers are virtually infallible with regard to the accuracy of reporting scores.

CALTs and IALTs are also capable of *specific ability level targeting*. Using IRT and computer-adaptive testing strategies, adaptive CALTs and IALTs can use the first several items to zero in on the specific ability levels of individual examinees.[4] Then, using items at or near the examinee's ability level, the test provides increasingly precise estimates of those abilities until a stopping rule says the estimate is sufficiently precise. In this way, computer-adaptive tests quickly target examinees' specific ability levels and do so more quickly and accurately than CBLTs, IBLTs or P&P tests.

*Minimising cheating* often requires test administrators to carefully monitor examinees while they are taking any CDLT. Another strategy for minimising cheating on adaptive tests (CALTs and IALTs) involves drawing on a large item bank; test designers can then arrange for the test to present examinees with different or substantially different sets of items that nonetheless can produce scores that are comparable on the same scale.

> This means that test security can be greatly enhanced, since tests can be created by randomly accessing items in the database and producing different combinations of items. Thus any one individual is exposed to only a tiny fraction of available items and any compromise of items that might occur will have negligible effect.
>
> *(Alderson 2000: 596)*

Indeed, if the item bank is large enough, this adaptive strategy can mitigate the effects of doing test preparation, of examinees recreating the item pool after the test, and of course, of examinees copying from other examinees.

In addition, CDLTs offer increased *design flexibility* for test designers. For instance, CDLTs can be designed to provide support for examinees, like online help screens, dictionaries, glossaries, clues and so forth (Alderson 2000). CDLTs can also gather additional information by querying examinees about how confident they are about the accuracy of their answers. Also, CDLTs can allow examinees to choose easier or more difficult items or item types that they want to be tested on. Design flexibility can also be enhanced by CDLT tools like test development templates and test authoring tools.

CDLTs also afford test developers the flexibility to create new and innovative item types that use pictures, maps, graphs and strategies like dragging objects, clicking buttons and connecting to websites, or to accommodate the special needs of certain examinees by providing large-print testing materials, volume controls and so forth (Chalhoub-Deville and Deville 1999). In addition, oral CDLT designers can create tests with a variety of different stimuli including 'text, audio, graphics, motion video, or a combination of these inputs' (Larson 1999: 56), and importantly, the quality of digital voice recordings on CDLTs is better than that of analogue recordings.

CDLTs also provide the flexibility needed to build classroom diagnostic assessments designed to quickly provide examinees with feedback on which items they answered incorrectly, and either provide hints (so they can try again) or correct their answers (possibly with explanations) – all of which would be very awkward in P&P formats. Such capabilities further allow the development of new types of continuous assessment,[5] and indeed, examinees could be allowed to choose the way they are tested in differential or individual differences assessment.[6]

I am of the opinion that many of the benefits that I am listing here, especially those in the previous subsection on *design flexibility* and in the section on *examinee benefits*, would or could be used to foster *positive washback* (i.e. any positive effects of tests on the curriculum that precedes or follows them). For example, it is easy to see how communicative classroom practices could be positively affected even for examinees steeped in grammar/translation methods if those examinees knew that they would be assessed on a CDLT that included pictures, maps, graphs and sound files in a test that required them to manipulate objects on the screen in response to what they are hearing in the target language and then describe a video that they are watching while the computer records them. Such a test might even increase their overall motivation to learn to communicate in English. That is just one example of how CDLTs could create positive washback if they were cleverly designed.

I have argued that CDLTs promise *enhanced validity*, but only if the reliability and validity of each CDLT is carefully studied, documented and defended. If a CDLT is designed to measure and/or give feedback on communicative abilities or performance-based or task-based assessment, those features will naturally become a part of how validity is defined and studied for that particular test. Test developers would also benefit from including the positive washback effects of each CDLT in their study of validity. This is certainly true for examining the degree to which the test scores are measuring what they were intended to measure. However, it is especially true for validity considerations like the social consequences of the testing and the values implications that underlie the assessment procedures and decisions based on the scores.

One last validity benefit that can be derived from CDLTs comes from the fact that computers can be infinitely patient. This means that computers can deliver tests with no time limits. Educators and examinees today are conditioned to think of tests as having time limits. As a result, those examinees who work quickly, efficiently and with great focus tend to score better because they are taking a *speeded test* (i.e. one that is timed, usually without enough time for all examinees). However, in the real world, time is not always limited. Hence, people can pace themselves and be more thoughtful. A test that could capture that process would be a *power test* (i.e. one that measures the ability to do something with as much time as is necessary to accomplish the task) that would capture each examinee's abilities when unconstrained by time. The patience of computers can be used to allow examinees as much time as they need to do whatever task is set before them. Imagine the potential effects of such assessment procedures on test validity.

## Test administrator benefits

One clear advantage of CDLTs over P&P tests is that *data gathering* is relatively easy and efficient. This applies to gathering crucial administrative data about test takers and their scores, but also useful research information about aspects of examinees' response times, changes they made in their answers, the number of times they consulted a help screen, glossary, or dictionary and so forth. *Data transmission* is also facilitated in CDLT systems, wherein all the data discussed earlier can easily be transmitted to other locations for storage, scoring or further transmission. However, it is particularly helpful, as I will explain in the next two subsections, that examinees' response data can be sent to a central location where all stakeholders in the decision-making can share the information.

A related advantage of CDLTs is their *data storage* capacity. With today's large capacity hard drives and cloud storage, there is no real limit to the amount of data that can be accumulated. This includes the additional possibility of creating, collecting and storing large databases of items in item banks. Indeed, the very possibility of having large item banks has led to the developments in adaptive CALTs and IALTs that in turn have made possible many of the other benefits discussed in this section. One of the primary benefits of item banking is enhanced test security, as noted under B3 in Table 10.3. The possibility of storing items in banks also allows for using IRT to study item bias, to select items, to assemble prepiloted and preequated tests (i.e. tests that produce scores that can be interpreted interchangeably) and to periodically assess and track examinees' language development.

The data gathering, transmission and storage capacities of CDLTs also make possible efficient *remote scoring*. While this is convenient when dealing with receptive item formats like multiple-choice, true-false, matching and so forth, it is crucial when dealing with *productive language* samples like compositions or recorded interviews that can be gathered, stored and sent to a central location or several locations for scoring by humans and/or for automated scoring.

Adaptive techniques also allow CALTs and IALTs to be *shorter tests that take less time*. Since adaptive tests have the capacity to quickly zero in on each examinee's language ability level,[7] they generally require fewer items to arrive at accurate scores. Because they require fewer items, CALTs and IALTs are generally much quicker for examinees to finish than traditional P&P tests, and therefore, they are much more efficient.

All of the benefits listed under D in Table 10.4 contribute to the *administration flexibility* of CDLTs generally, but particularly adaptive CALTs and IALTs. The fact that CDLTs can be administered individually or in groups makes organising test administrations easier and more flexible in terms of scheduling rooms, hiring and training proctors and so forth. Indeed, issues of time and geography tend to become more flexible when using CDLTs over their P&P cousins.

Fortunately, while CDLTs offer more administration flexibility, they also offer more standardised testing conditions (Chalhoub-Deville and Deville 1999) because each examinee can be presented with comparable language prompts, tasks and response requirements under exactly the same conditions. This is especially true for oral tests, which unlike face-to-face oral assessments can be designed to test all examinees under exactly the same or very similar conditions (Larson 1999).

## *Examinee benefits*

Stevenson and Gross (1991) observed early on that *many examinees enjoy computers* and even enjoy the testing process with CDLTs because such tests are simply more engaging than P&P tests. Early studies on CBLTs found that language learners generally had positive attitudes towards using computers in the classroom (see e.g. Phinney 1991). Indeed, it is no secret that examinees on a CDLT will probably be more comfortable with this technology than their teachers.

As pointed out in the discussion of C6 in Table 10.4, computers are infinitely patient. They also cost far less per hour to keep in place than paid proctors. As a consequence, tests can be designed so that *examinees can work at their own pace*, which will allow them to determine for themselves how much time they need to comfortably accomplish all the tasks on the test. I suspect that many students would appreciate being able to work at their own pace.

CDLTs also seem to be *less intimidating* for examinees than P&P tests. First, the items on a CDLT can be presented in smaller bites, one item at a time per screen, rather than in an intimidating P&P booklet full of hundreds of items. Second, if adaptive techniques are used, fewer items will be needed. And third, as mentioned earlier, CDLTs need not be speeded in nature (i.e. have a time limit).

Particularly on adaptive CALTs and IALTs, examinees should also find CDLTs *less frustrating* than they do P&P tests because they need only work on items that are pitched at their level of ability. In other words, since the items on adaptive tests quickly focus in on the specific ability level of each examinee, the examinees will be working on test items that are appropriate for their own ability levels, and not be presented with many items that are boringly easy or dishearteningly difficult.

In addition, CDLTs can be set up to provide examinees with *walk-in convenience*. Computer-delivered CBLTs and CALTs can be administered on stand-alone computers in monitored computer laboratories, which can be kept open 24/7 if resources are available. Internet-delivered IBLTs and IALTs can also offer the same convenience if they are administered in 24/7 laboratories. However, if security drawbacks can be overcome, Internet-based IBLTs and IALTs can offer even more convenience in the form of *anywhere-anytime convenience* because Internet tests by definition are available on any computer connected to the World Wide Web.

CDLTs can also be designed to provide examinees with *immediate feedback*, which most examinees and teachers would view as beneficial. At least for receptive item formats like multiple-choice, true-false and matching, examinees could get their scores immediately after finishing the test. For written or oral tests, examinees may have to wait a few minutes or hours for scoring, but even that scoring can be made much more immediate than it is in P&P tests. Importantly, feedback on such tests can take many other forms in addition to scores. For example, while score reports for examinees would usually include their numerical results, they might also provide verbal descriptions of performances and explanations for wrong answers. In addition, such feedback reports can include information about how the examinees performed on each subtest or for each course objective. Summary score reports can also be provided to teachers or administrators that can include this information for each examinee, or as class or institutional averages, as well as item analysis statistics, distractor efficiency analyses, reliability of information and so forth. Imagine how useful such feedback reports could be, and how they could facilitate continuous[8] or individual differences[9] assessment. Indeed, if the assessment tools and immediate feedback were integrated into regular classroom activities, examinees might even come to embrace the whole idea of assessment as part of the learning process.

## Have our views of the drawbacks and benefits of CDLTs changed?

A number of authors have examined different sets of advantages and disadvantages of CDLTs over P&P tests. Since I have been actively watching these articles evolve (in a number of articles from Brown 1992a, 1992b, 2013a), I feel I am therefore in a good position to distil what we have learned over that time and summarise how our perceptions of the issues have evolved.

It seems clear to me that our awareness and understanding of the drawbacks and benefits of CDLTs are increasing over time. In addition, we are increasingly finding solutions for the drawbacks. Indeed, in Table 10.3, I was able to suggest at least some solutions for each of the drawbacks. Fortunately now, the benefits of using CDLTs far outnumber the drawbacks, and in some cases, these benefits also help overcome the drawbacks. All in all, I would say that our views of the drawbacks and benefits of CDLTs have become much more sophisticated over the years: changing in number, shifting in the ways they are labelled and categorised, and increasing in the depth with which they are discussed. All of this is particularly true in terms of solving the problems and overcoming the drawbacks.

## Where is technology likely to lead language testing in the future?

While computer technology has already changed language testing profoundly, these changes are just the beginning. Table 10.2 shows the numerous CDLT-related topics that have been introduced and discussed over the last two decades. However, new topics will no doubt be identified and explored in the future. Unfortunately, the literature on technology and language testing may need to move even faster in order to keep up with the increasing speed of technological developments, which may mean that new technologies will need to be explored more quickly – just as soon as they are rolled out. To those ends, here are eleven questions that technology and language testing could address together in the future:

1  Much of the work on CDLTs has been on their use in standardised testing for admissions and placement decisions, but how can computers be applied in classrooms for giving students feedback, for continuous and differential assessment, and for record keeping, for example?

2   How can integrated learning management systems (e.g. the proprietary Blackboard or Edmodo, or the open-source Moodle or Sakai) and other classroom technologies be used for classroom assessment purposes?
3   If assessment is defined as any activity that provides feedback in the form of a score or verbal/written comments, corrections and explanations, how can computers improve the immediacy and effectiveness of the feedback?
4   How can language assessment best be integrated into online or hybrid courses?
5   How can voice recognition and automated scoring of audio files be improved, made more practical, more reliable, more valid and more widely accepted?
6   How can optical character recognition technology and automated scoring of text be improved, made more practical, more reliable, more valid and more widely accepted?
7   How could biometrics for identification be used to stop cheating and improve security on CDLTs of all kinds?
8   How can audio and video telephoning and teleconferencing systems be used in language testing?
9   Now that individual websites have become much easier to set up, how can they be used for language assessment (for instance, for setting up student portfolio websites and displaying course projects)?
10  How can new technologies resulting from the ubiquity of Internet access and cheap Wi-Fi equipment, audio and video streaming devices and cloud storage be developed for language assessment purposes?
11  What about language assessment using developing technologies (e.g. mobile phones, tablets, readers and MP3 players), resources (e.g. pdf files, social media, public domain sources and open source journals), and software (e.g. mobile apps and artificial intelligence)?

So much technology and so little time. That is why I suggested earlier that 'the literature on technology and language testing may need to move even faster in order to keep up with the increasing speed of technological developments'. Let's get moving.

## Further reading

Brown, J.D. (2013) 'Research on computers in language testing: Past, present, and future', in M. Thomas, H. Reinders and M. Warschauer (eds), *Contemporary Computer-Assisted Language Learning*, London, UK: Bloomsbury: 73–94.
  Brown examines progress in CDLT with regard to the past, present and future. For the past, this author identifies four trends, mostly practical in nature, that for the most part have been adequately addressed: the banking of items, the incorporation of new technologies, the development of CALTs and the effectiveness of CDLTs for testing languages. In recent years, this article notes that the CDLT literature had generally centred on five topics: overview articles, delivery issues, CDLT content, example CDLTs and tools/resources in CDLT.

Chapelle, C.A. and Douglas, D. (2006) *Assessing Language Through Computer Technology*, Cambridge: Cambridge University.
  This book by Chapelle and Douglas discusses: (1) the place of CDLTs in language teaching and research; (2) characteristics of CDLTs in temporal and physical conditions, instructions and rubrics, inputs and responses, input/response interactions, and assessment characteristics like construct definitions and scoring techniques; (3) drawbacks of CDLTs in with regard to various types of test performances, limitations on item selection, flaws in automatic scoring, issues of security and other negative effects; (4) issues in CDLT implementation related to authoring tools and a model for developing an assessment system; (5) guidelines for CDLT evaluation before, during and after the test is administered; and (6) influences of CDLT in advancing language assessment and applied linguistics.

Dooey, P. (2008) 'Language testing and technology: Problems of transition to a new era', *ReCall*, 20(1): 21–34.

Dooey focuses on the effects of technology on language test reliability and validity. She turns initially to research about the effects of computer-human interfaces on construct validity, especially the effects of computer familiarity and anxiety on test scores. She also surveys the benefits of CDLTs in terms of how flexible they can be in when and where examinees can take them; how effective item banking can be; how quick feedback can be; and how data can easily be accumulated for research. Her last section covered the relative effects of technology on the CB IELTS listening and reading tests, as well as on iBT TOEFL writing tests.

Ockey, G.J. (2009) 'Developments and challenges in the use of computer-based testing for assessing second language ability', *Modern Language Journal*, 93: 836–847.

Ockey provides background from the general CBT literature, then discusses the influences of CDLT on how language abilities have been described and assessed. He proposes that CDLTs can provide a number of benefits; they can be used to produce more authentic tasks and tests; and they can result in relatively easy, quick and reliable scoring of speech and writing samples. However, he also points to disadvantages: CDLTs still have security problems, and in particular, CALTs have failed to live up to earlier hopes that language testers had for them.

## Notes

1 Note that key acronyms are defined in Appendix 10A.
2 CALTs use item response theory statistics and programming algorithms to quickly zero in on each examinee's ability level with the following consequences: each examinee is presented with only items at or near their ability level; the test is ended when the algorithm locates the examinee's ability level with sufficient precision; and the test is typically short in both numbers of items and amount of time needed to take the test.
3 I mention this because I have repeatedly had problems with examinees on machine-scored tests not being familiar with (or particularly accurate at) recording their names or identification numbers. Functionally, this has meant that up to 5% of the score reports were effectively missing that information and needed special handling.
4 See note 2.
5 '*Continuous assessment* thoroughly integrates assessment into the curriculum, assessing and giving feedback to the students in constant, cyclical, and cumulative ways (including daily classwork, ongoing project work, portfolios, etc.), all of which is often contrasted with final examination systems'. Brown (2013b: 4)
6 '*Individual differences* assessment typically involves assessing differences among students in terms of motivation, anxiety, personality, multiple intelligences, willingness to communicate, learning preferences, learning strategies, literacy, and more. Knowing the students' strengths and weaknesses in terms of any of these factors allows teachers to then tailor their assessments to individual abilities and preferences'. Brown (2013b: 5)
7 See note 2.
8 See note 5.
9 See note 6.

## References

Alderson, J.C. (2000) 'Technology in testing: The present and the future', *System*, 28, 593–603.
Attali, Y. and Burstein, J. (2006). 'Automated essay scoring with e-rater®V.2', *Journal of Technology, Learning, and Assessment*, 4(3), 1–30.
Blake, R., Wilson, N.L., Cetto, M. and Pardo-Ballester, C. (2008) 'Measuring oral proficiency in distance, face-to-face and blended classrooms', *Language Learning & Technology*, 12(3): 114–127.
Brown, J.D. (1992a) 'Technology and language education in the twenty-first century: Media, message, and method', *Language Laboratory*, 29: 1–22.
Brown, J.D. (1992b) 'Using computers in language testing', *Cross Currents*, 19: 92–99.
Brown, J.D. (1997) 'Computers in language testing: Present research and some future directions', *Language Learning and Technology*, 1(1): 44–59.

Brown, J.D. (2004) 'Visionary view: For computerized tests, potential benefits outweigh problems', *Essential Teacher*, 1(4): 37–40.

Brown, J.D. (2005) *Testing in Language Programs: A Comprehensive Guide to English Language Assessment*, New edition, New York, NY: McGraw-Hill.

Brown, J.D. (2013a) 'Research on computers in language testing: Past, present, and future', in M. Thomas, H. Reinders and M. Warschauer (eds), *Contemporary Computer-Assisted Language Learning*, London, UK: Bloomsbury: 73–94.

Brown, J.D. (2013b) *New Ways of Classroom Assessment, Revised*, Alexandria, VA: TESOL.

Chalhoub-Deville, M. (2001) 'Language testing and technology', *Language Learning & Technology*, 5(2): 95–98.

Chalhoub-Deville, M. and Deville C. (1999) 'Computer adaptive testing in second language contexts', *Annual Review of Applied Linguistics*, 19: 273–299.

Chapelle, C.A. (2001) *Computer Applications in Second Language Acquisition*, Cambridge: Cambridge University Press.

Chapelle, C.A. and Douglas, D. (2006) *Assessing Language Through Computer Technology*, Cambridge: Cambridge University Press.

Chodorow, M., Gamon, M. and Tetreault, J. (2010) 'The utility of article and preposition error correction systems for English language learners: Feedback and assessment', *Language Testing*, 27(3): 419–436.

Dikli, S. (2006) 'An overview of automated scoring of essays', *Journal of Technology, Learning, and Assessment*, 5(1): 1–35.

Dooey, P. (2008) 'Language testing and technology: Problems of transition to a new era', *ReCall*, 20(1): 21–34.

Douglas, D. (2000) *Assessing Languages for Specific Purposes*, Cambridge: Cambridge University Press.

Douglas, D. and Hegelheimer, V. (2007) 'Assessing language using computer technology', *Annual Review of Applied Linguistics*, 27: 115–132.

Garcia Laborda, J. (2007) 'On the net: Introducing standardized EFL/ESL exams', *Language Learning & Technology*, 11(2): 3–9.

Garcia Laborda, J. and Litzler, M.F. (2011) 'Constraints in teacher training for computer assisted language testing implementation', *International Education Studies*, 4(2): 13–17.

Gruba, P. and Corbel, C. (1997) 'Computer-based testing', in C. Clapham and D. Corson (eds), *Language Testing and Assessment*, Dordrecht: Kluwer Academic: 141–149.

Jamieson, J. (2005) 'Trends in computer-based second language assessment', *Annual Review of Applied Linguistics*, 25: 228–242.

Jones, N. and Maycock, L. (2007) 'The comparability of computer-based and paper-based tests: Goals, approaches, and a review of research', *University of Cambridge ESOL Research Notes*, 27(4): 1–4.

Kirsch, I., Jamieson, J., Taylor, C. and Eignor, D. (1997) *Computer Familiarity Among TOEFL Examinees*. Unpublished manuscript, Princeton, NJ: Educational Testing Service.

Larson, J.W. (1999) 'Considerations for testing reading proficiency via computer-adaptive testing', in M. Chalhoub-Deville (ed), *Issues in Computer-Adaptive Testing of Reading Proficiency*, Cambridge: Cambridge University Press: 71–90.

Ockey, G.J. (2009) 'Developments and challenges in the use of computer-based testing for assessing second language ability', *Modern Language Journal*, 93: 836–847.

Phinney, M. (1991) 'Computer-assisted writing and writing apprehension in ESL students', in P. Dunkel (ed), *Computer-Assisted Language Learning and Testing: Research Issues and Practice*, New York, NY: Newbury House: 189–204.

Roever, C. (2001) 'Web-based language testing', *Language Learning & Technology*, 5(2): 84–94.

Stevenson, J. and Gross, S. (1991) 'Use of a computerized adaptive testing model for ESOL/bilingual entry/exit decision making', in P. Dunkel (ed), *Computer-Assisted Language Learning and Testing: Research Issues and Practice*, New York, NY: Newbury House: 223–235.

Taylor, C., Jamieson, J., Eignor, D. and Kirsch, I. (1998) *Measuring the Effects of Computer Familiarity on Computer-Based Language Tasks*, Princeton, NJ: Educational Testing Service.

Warschauer, M. and Ware, P. (2006) 'Automated writing evaluation: Defining the classroom research agenda', *Language Teaching Research*, 10(2): 1–24.

Yu, X. and Lowe, J. (2007) 'Computer assisted testing of spoken English: A study to evaluate the SFLEP college English oral test in China', in F. Khandia (ed), *11th CAA International Computer Assisted Assessment Conference: Proceedings of the Conference on 10th and 11th July 2007 at Loughborough University*, Loughborough Leicestershire, UK: Loughborough University: 489–502.

# Appendix 10A
# Acronyms used in this chapter

| Acronym | Stands for | Definition/additional notes |
|---|---|---|
| CALT | Computer-adaptive language test/testing | A language test or testing delivered on a computer that adapts to the level of ability of each examinee; specific to language testing |
| CAT | Computer-adaptive test/testing | A test or testing delivered on a computer that adapts to the level of ability of each examinee; general, in all fields |
| CB | Computer-based | Delivered on a computer (as in the computer-based or CB IELTS in Table 10.1); general, in all fields |
| CBLT | Computer-based language test/testing | A language test or testing delivered on a computer; synonym for computer-assisted language test/testing; specific to language testing |
| CBT | Computer-based test/testing | A test or testing delivered on a computer; general, in all fields |
| CDLT | Computer-delivered language test/testing | A language test or testing presented and taken on a computer; specific to language testing |
| IALT | Internet-adaptive language test/testing | A language test or testing delivered online that adapts to the level of ability of each examinee; specific to language testing |
| IBLT | Internet-based language test/testing | A language test or testing delivered online; specific to language testing |
| IRT | Item response theory | Statistical analyses that allow for designing and equating tests that can be independent of the person and item samples involved in piloting (this is a necessary component of most adaptive testing); general, in all fields |
| LSP | Language for specific purposes | Purpose-driven language teaching (e.g. English for business purposes); specific to language teaching |
| P&P | Paper and pencil | Taken on hard copy, usually by reading a test booklet and marking a paper answer sheet; general, in all fields |
| UCLES | University of Cambridge Local Examinations Syndicate | A well-known testing organisation in the UK; general, in all fields |

# 11
# From age and gender to identity in technology-mediated language learning

*Elisabeth (Hayes) Gee and Yoonhee N. Lee*

While there has been considerable interest in age and gender issues in language learning, there are far fewer studies that explore these issues in the context of technology-mediated learning environments. In this chapter, we describe key theoretical perspectives on age and gender that inform research and practice, noting implications for the use of technologies in language learning. Scholarship on language learning more broadly suggests that the significance of age and gender is mediated by a number of other individual, situational, social and cultural factors. We argue that understanding how learner identities, including but not limited to age and gender, are constructed and enacted in particular contexts can be useful in designing and implementing technology-mediated language learning in education. The chapter concludes with questions and implications for research and practice, with an emphasis on understanding the role of learner identities in technology-mediated language learning from a holistic perspective.

## A shift from age and gender to identity

The significance of age and gender in language learning has received considerable attention from language scholars over the last few decades. Overall, scholarly work on these topics has become more complex and nuanced, while at the same time a variety of contradictory perspectives and arguments coexist. Research and practical literature that addresses gender or age in relationship to technology-mediated language learning is more sparse and simplistic. In a review of empirical literature on the use of computer-assisted language learning (CALL) in English as a second language (ESL) instruction at the primary and secondary levels, Macaro, Handley and Walter (2012) found that most articles did not even specify the gender of participants. Of articles that did identify participant gender, the majority did not use it as a variable. Similarly, in a review of literature for this chapter, we found only a handful of empirical articles published in the last ten years that investigated the significance of learner age or gender in relation to any form of technologically mediated language learning. Even when participants' age or gender were described, they were not treated as central to understanding the learning process or outcomes.

This limited attention to age and gender, at least in connection to technology-mediated language learning and teaching, may be explained in part by the 'social turn' in language learning theory and research (Johnson 2006). This shift towards the application of sociocultural theories has led to a focus on learner *identity* rather than on certain dominant individual or group traits. Sociocultural perspectives tend to conceptualise identity as the intersection of multiple 'subject positions' – age, gender, race, ethnicity, social class, occupation and so on – in relation to students' language practices (ibid.). Accordingly, while we begin with a discussion of age and gender in this chapter, we move to a consideration of identity and its implications for understanding technology-mediated language learning.

In addition, the diversity of new digital technologies and the contexts in which they are used make it challenging to identify the particular role of gender or age in shaping any language learner's experience (Zhao 2003). For example, it has been popular to characterise young people as 'digital natives', assumed to be fluent with digital technologies and even to learn differently due to modern technology. However, the concept of the digital native has been shown to be simplistic and inaccurate, as the complex and diverse effects of young people's technology experiences have become evident (Bennett, Maton and Kervin 2008).

In the following section, we discuss key theoretical perspectives on age and gender in language learning. We organise these perspectives into two broad groups, what we call the 'individual trait' perspective and the 'sociocultural' perspective, and illustrate each perspective as it relates to understanding language learning and technology. We then move to a more detailed discussion of the concept of socially situated identities (Gee 2000), as a means of integrating a consideration of age and gender with other influential personal and social factors in technology-mediated language learning.

In this discussion, we focus primarily on age, gender and identity of students in second or foreign language learning. The gender, age or identities of teachers are also relevant to language learning, though these factors have received much less attention in the literature. We refer readers to Varghese, Morgan, Johnston and Johnson (2005), Johnson (2006) and Appleby (2013), as examples of literature on this topic.

## Theoretical perspectives

The theoretical perspectives that inform scholarship on age and gender in language learning are tied to broader theories of the language learning process. Scholarship on language learning has traditionally been dominated by theories informed by cognitive science and psycholinguistics (Zuengler and Miller 2006), and consistent with these perspectives, age and gender have been treated as individual variables that affect biological or cognitive development. Sociocultural perspectives on language learning, increasingly popular over the last few decades, treat age and gender as aspects of learner *identities*, shaped by the immediate and broader social and cultural contexts of language learning. Our brief summaries suggest key differences in the implications of these perspectives for understanding age and gender in relationship to technology-mediated language learning.

### *Individual trait perspectives*

Individual trait perspectives on age and gender in relation to language learning include theories based on neuropsychology, psycholinguistics and cognitive science that posit the existence of innate, developmental stages in which individuals have heightened language learning abilities. These perspectives attempt to explain apparent differences in, for example, how readily children acquire fluency in a second language as compared to adults, by stages of maturation and lateralisation in brain function or loss of neural plasticity. Similarly gender (or sex) differences in language acquisition are attributed to biological differences in male and female predispositions towards language learning. From this perspective, digital technologies might be used to customise language learning to meet the developmental or gender-specific needs of particular learners.

*Age*

Age has long been presumed to be an obvious factor influencing second language acquisition, for biological and in particular neurodevelopmental reasons. According to the Critical Period Hypothesis (CPH; also known as the sensitive period; Muñoz 2007), children have a biological predisposition to acquire their first language, and until puberty can achieve native-like fluency in a second language more readily than adults. The CPH has been used to argue for the incorporation of foreign language immersion programs into early elementary school and for intensive structured English language immersion for young bilingual students. However, the theory has been widely criticised for a lack of empirical evidence that age differences in second language learning are actually tied to developmental variations in brain physiology (Birdsong 2005; Singleton 2005; Muñoz 2007). Marinova-Todd, Marshall and Snow (2000) point out that *variations* among children and adults' language learning abilities tend to be overlooked; there is much more variation among adults than children in language learning outcomes, and some adults do achieve near native proficiency in a second language (which would be extremely difficult, if not impossible, according to the CPH).

Cognitive developmental perspectives offer a somewhat different approach to understanding the significance of age in language acquisition (Harley and Hart 2002; Robinson 2005). Rather than looking at age as a drawback for adolescents' and adults' language acquisition, scholars adopting this approach suggest that age influences individuals' preferred strategies for learning a language. Simply put, children tend to rely on memorisation and practice, acquiring fluency through long-term inductive and implicit learning. Adolescents and adults, who are capable of higher-order language awareness and learning strategies, rely more on analysis of linguistic rules and functions (DeKeyser 2003; Long 2005; Muñoz 2007). Because of their ability to formally articulate linguistic rules, older learners can outperform younger learners in the early stages of language acquisition (Muñoz 2007). This perspective suggests that language instruction should vary for older and younger learners; for example, multiplayer digital games might be a means of providing immersive language practices for children while explicit and direct instruction in language form and structure though computer-based tutoring systems might be preferable for adolescents and adults (for a larger discussion on issues related to games and language learning, see Part V of this volume).

Many chapters in a recent volume on new technologies and language learning (Motteram 2013) reflect the perspective that while age is important in affecting students' orientations to learning a language and their capabilities (e.g. adults may expect direct instruction in grammar based on their prior schooling), the context and goals of instruction may be just as important as learner age in determining how technologies be used to support language learning. In a chapter on the primary grades, Pim (2013) notes that there is no single best approach to teaching young language learners, and offers examples of how various technologies, from video conferencing to interactive games, have been integrated into engaging activities for primary grade students. Similarly, in the chapter on adult language learners, Slaouti, Onat-Stelma and Motteram (2013) discuss broad characteristics of adult learners, such as goal-directedness, but argue for specific applications of technology that are sensitive to particular contexts, learners and goals for language learning. They provide examples of technologies as varied as digitally recording and discussing peer interviews, a teacher-created class Moodle with information and language exercises, and a collaborative class wiki where students support each other's language learning.

Teachers' perceptions of the appropriateness of different technologies for particular age groups may be the strongest determinant of how they are incorporated into language teaching. For example, Pim's chapter on primary school learning has an extensive discussion of game-based language learning, with detailed examples of primary school teachers' use of games and related activities as well as links to tools that allow language teachers to create their own games. However, game-based learning can be appropriate and effective for learners of all ages; indeed, there has been little investigation of whether game-based learning is more or less effective for learners of different ages, in any language learning context.

## Gender

The term 'gender' originally referred to the socially constructed roles, behaviours and attributes that particular social and cultural groups consider appropriate for women and men, in contrast to 'sex', which referred to biological and physiological characteristics that define women and men. Within an individual trait perspective, gender is frequently used interchangeably with sex as a term to differentiate between women and men based on attributes that are presumed to be innate or learned. In scholarship on language acquisition and learning, both biological and social factors have been hypothesised to create differences in women's and men's use of language, their language learning abilities and preferences for particular learning strategies.

Cameron (2009) identifies two generalisations that reflect this individual trait perspective: (1) one sex (typically assumed to be women, but in some cases, men) has superior verbal abilities, and (2) women and men differ in their preferred communication styles, with men's speech characterised as more competitive and aggressive and women's speech characterised as more cooperative and empathetic. Men and women are thought to have different communicative goals: men tend to talk about things and facts, with the goal of 'getting things done', while women talk more about relationships and emotions, with the intent of building and sustaining relationships with others. The reasons offered for these differences vary in their emphasis on inherited biological traits or different patterns of socialisation into linguistic gender-norms in childhood. These generalisations often are used to support claims that female and male learners prefer different teaching and learning strategies, such as females prefer cooperative learning like paired tutoring, or that men might prefer texts of a factual nature while women might prefer narratives or stories (Ellis 1994).

There is a lack of evidence in support of these generalisations, and claims about sex differences in linguistic abilities can be contradictory. Hyde and her colleagues (Hyde and Linn 1988; Hyde 2005), in meta-analyses of hundreds of research articles, found little or no meaningful difference in women's and men's verbal abilities. Even when differences exist, the significance of these differences is small, and researchers often tend to minimise the considerable overlap in women's and men's patterns of language use and abilities.

An individual trait perspective is reflected in research that investigates gender differences in preferred learning styles with technology (Aliweh 2011), the impact of educational software features on girls' and boys' language learning (Luik 2011) and differences in males' and females' preferences for certain types of digital games (Intratat 2011), as a few examples. The results of such research tends to be inconclusive, with few to no significant gender differences and differing findings across studies.

Overall, individual trait perspectives do not offer conclusive evidence of generalisable age or gender differences in language acquisition. There are no consistent age or gender differences in learner preferences for different kinds of educational technology or in outcomes, and scholars acknowledge the need to consider age and gender as they interact with other variables to affect learning (Jones and Myhill 2007). Observed age or gender differences in language acquisition may reflect differences in the context of learning rather than in capacity to learn. How to conceptualise the context of learning is the focus of sociocultural perspectives.

## Sociocultural perspectives

While individual trait perspectives account for social factors in language learning, social phenomena tend to be treated as variables that are external to the learning process. In contrast, sociocultural perspectives view language learning as inextricably tied to particular social and cultural contexts. A variety of theories and frameworks are associated with sociocultural perspectives on language learning, including sociolinguistics, language socialisation, situated learning and critical theory (Zuengler and Miller 2006). While these theories vary in their core concepts and key concerns, they reflect common themes: to understand language learning, we must take into account how learners negotiate the complex social relationships that mediate their language use in and out of classrooms, how the acquisition of a new language is tied to learners' identities and social positioning and how learners actively choose to take up particular forms of language to accomplish various personal and social goals (Polat and Mahalingappa 2010). Developing fluency in a new language entails not simply mastering new vocabulary or grammar; learners also must learn to participate in social practices that require certain forms of language use (Belcher 2004). This emphasis on understanding language as a means of participating in social practice has led researchers to investigate language learning in a wide range of contexts within and beyond formal classrooms, more recently including technologically mediated environments such as virtual worlds, Internet chat rooms, and online interest communities (Thorne, Black and Sykes 2009).

The construct of identity is central to sociocultural perspectives. Identity has been conceptualised in various ways among sociocultural theorists, but they share the view that identity is dynamic, shaped by broader social norms and cultural models, as well as by the demands of local contexts; and multifaceted, that is, reflective of a person's sense of affiliation with multiple social groups at any given time (Duff 2012). Scholars working from sociocultural perspectives tend to consider the biological attributes of age and gender to be less significant than, or at least mediated by, the social and cultural construction of, for example, masculinity or adolescence. In language learning, gender has received far more attention than age from scholars adopting a sociocultural perspective, largely due to the influence of feminist theory (e.g. Norton 2000; Norton and Pavlenko 2004). In terms of technologies, a sociocultural perspective would emphasise involving students in use of technological tools, related activities, and talk in a manner consistent with the practices of the community to which they are being introduced (e.g. medicine, higher education, businesses) and engaging them in consideration of how identities, including gender and age, are enacted, reinforced, or suppressed through these practices.

## Age

The beliefs we have about the attributes and behaviours associated with age are shaped by cultural norms and social factors. The Western discourse of decline associated with aging can affect adults' (and teachers') views of their abilities to learn a new language (Andrews 2012). One reason that the CPH has been so appealing is its consistency with dominant cultural models of decline in learning ability. Saying that age is socially constructed suggests that a person's chronological age is associated with age-related social norms, which in turn mean that people of different ages are expected to behave in certain ways in any given social situation, including different expectations for their language use. For example, Ochs and Schieffelin (1984) described different expectations for children as interlocutors with caregivers in different cultures. In Anglo-American middle-class families, caregivers treat infants and children as conversational partners in dyadic social interactions. In contrast, in Kaluis and Samoan cultures, children need to learn how to position themselves in triadic and multiparty interactions from a very young age, rather than in dyadic interactions only between a caregiver and a child (ibid.).

Distinctive cultural and social contexts for language learning lead to the development of different abilities as well as different ways of evaluating children and adults' language skills and their identities as successful language learners. New technologies add another factor that can shape family and community expectations for children's and adults' linguistic practices. For example, bilingual children frequently serve as language brokers in immigrant families; with the introduction of digital technologies, these children now may be expected to broker their families' access to online information resources (Katz 2010).

## Gender

Scholars who adopt a sociocultural perspective typically use the term gender explicitly to exclude reference to biological or innate differences between women and men. Gender is viewed as 'performative', enacted rather than an individual trait. We 'do' gender in a myriad of ways, ranging from how we dress to how we interact with others to what occupations we choose. A key concept is 'gender ideology', a set of beliefs about appropriate roles, behaviours and responsibilities of women and men in society. Gender ideologies vary according to society and culture, and differing gender ideologies can exist within one society. Gender ideologies are typically associated with power and social status; the predominant scholarly focus has been on identifying how gender ideologies justify and enforce male dominance.

Language scholars have explored how particular social contexts offer different opportunities for women's and men's language learning, particularly in terms of how gender is tied to social status and power in these contexts. Inequitable classroom interactions have been the focus of much research. For example, Hruska (2004), in a study of second language learners in an English dominant kindergarten class, found that the children's gender ideologies, which reinforced gender segregation and same sex friendships, affected second language learners' access to high status friendships and opportunities for development of English language skills. Boys' tendency to engage in more competitive discourse in class discussions, in part to display their power and dominance over girls, tended to give them more opportunities to speak and control the conversations. These gendered interactions may persist in technology-mediated environments. In Lam's (2000) study of an L2 teenager learning to write online, the male English learner expressed preferences for female pen pals because of his perception that men and women differed in how they expressed encouragement and enhanced his self-confidence. Indeed, his female correspondents took on motherly, nurturing roles in the context of their online relationships with him.

Scholars have investigated how the process of learning a new language may challenge and transform learners' gender identities as well as contribute to broader challenges to gender ideologies. Typically, these transformations are tied to experiences in a new cultural setting in which language learning serves as a route to increased independence and new social roles, particularly for women (Gordon 2004).

Overall, sociocultural studies continue to find that age and gender play a role in language learning, though they do not seem to be implicated in predictable ways based on age or gender

Elisabeth Gee and Yoonhee N. Lee

in isolation. Research from these perspectives offers rich and detailed pictures of language learners' experiences, but is just as likely to describe how women or men act and speak in ways that contradict gender norms as conform to them. Digital technologies may contribute to this diversity, for example by offering learners access to online communities with different opportunities for and constraints on language learning and practice. In Lam's (2000) study, noted earlier, the male teenager adopted a 'feminine' nurturing discourse when interacting with his female pen pals, potentially because he was not limited by the norms of a face-to-face context.

It is widely acknowledged that understanding how learner identities – including but not limited to age and gender – are constructed and enacted in particular contexts can be useful in designing and implementing technology-mediated language learning in education. In the next section, we more fully explicate the nature of identity as it relates to language learning, using the concept of *socially situated identities*, before moving to a discussion of technology, identity and language learning.

## *Socially situated identities*

A considerable body of scholarship explores the relationship between identity, language learning and language teaching (Duff 2012). Identity can be treated as an individual trait; for example there is a considerable body of literature on 'gender identity' as a core psychological trait. However most scholars in language learning tend to adopt a more sociocultural perspective, viewing identities as socially situated; that is, tied to particular social contexts and social interactions in which particular kinds of identities are recognised, enacted and legitimated (Gee 2000, 2011; Menard-Warwick 2005; Duff 2012). People may conform to or resist particular identities that are expected in various situations, both consciously and unconsciously. Language is one way that people enact identities; for example, by using specialist language particular to certain groups or by expressing power, status or bonding in relation to others (Hayes and Lee 2012). The identities that people wish to assume or that are ascribed to them affect the kinds of language that they are exposed to, the ways of using language they are motivated to acquire and how others evaluate their language use.

Scholars working within this perspective try to account for multiple dimensions of identity and how they intersect, for example by discussing gender and ethnicity or socioeconomic class. Age is rarely discussed as an explicit aspect of identity in this literature. There are a variety of ways that identity can be conceptualised, ranging from identities associated with biological or genetic attributes such as sex or skin colour to identities associated with institutions (e.g. a college student), cultural models of individual attributes (e.g. a person who is 'shy' or 'aggressive') and affinities for particular groups and practices (i.e. a 'gamer' or a 'jock') (Gee 2000).

The significance of particular identities varies according to social context as well as by how they intersect with and are modified by other salient identities. Gender and age are significant in relationship to other aspects of a person's identity. Being a 'girl gamer' or an 'adult learner', for example, have specific connotations. This view of identities has several implications for technology-mediated language learning and teaching. The first is that learning a new language always involves identity; it involves taking on the identity of a language learner as well as other identities associated with the new language and the technology, whether that be a college student learning a new language through interacting with a tutor by video conferencing or a teen author practicing written English in an online fan fiction community, among many others. The second is that acquiring desired identities requires mastering *particular* forms of language and practice, such as the identity of a good student communicating with an instructor in an online course, a novice blogger responding to comments from peers, or an English language learner swapping gameplay strategies with native English speakers in a multiplayer game. The third implication is that learners' current and desired identities may work for or against language learning. This includes how teachers view students based on assumptions about who they are, their language abilities and their preferences for various technologies.

Digital technologies have become ways of expressing our identities; these technologies have also led to new identities: the computer geek, the gamer and the technophobe, for example. We next consider how digital technologies and identity are implicated in language learning.

## Identities, language learning and digital technologies

From a sociocultural perspective, people enact multiple aspects of their identities in part through their use of objects and tools like technologies (Wajcman 2010). The particular technical skills, expertise and orientations towards digital technology that learners bring to a learning experience are caught up not simply with their prior access to technology, but with how the use of digital media is tied to various identities and ideologies within and beyond the classroom. From this perspective, technology is not neutral; ideologies, or belief systems about technology, affect our views of the value of technology and what technologies are appropriate for particular people and purposes. For example, video games still tend to be viewed as a masculine pastime; parents still tend to buy game consoles for boys rather than girls, and girls may be less likely to admit that they like to play games, due to social norms about gaming (see also Sundqvist, Chapter 32 this volume).

A sociocultural perspective on technology stresses the importance of understanding how particular people and social contexts shape how technology is used, and in turn how technology shapes these people and contexts. Technological innovations change the nature and meaning of language practices in and out of the classroom, as well as introducing novel practices that can be caught up with identity. Eva Lam's (2004) research on the language and literacy practices of immigrant youth in online spaces such as chat rooms offers numerous illustrations of how young people use technology to construct new forms of language practice that are tied to new collective ethnic identities. As another example, Lee's (2012) study illustrated how a teenage girl in Spain became fluent in specialist language practices associated with graphic design through her participation in an online game modding (modification) community. The culture of this online affinity space, in which participants were encouraged to be both teachers and learners, gave her opportunities to interact informally with numerous people from diverse backgrounds, developing her vernacular English skills as well.

## Implications for technology-mediated language learning and teaching

This socially situated view of identity, language learning and technology as mutually shaping and fluid suggests the danger of stereotyping any particular group or assuming that any particular educational technology will be appropriate. The literature is replete with examples of how language teachers' unexamined assumptions about learners, based on categorical attributes like age, gender and ethnicity, negatively affect their language learning opportunities. Technologies are laden with symbolic meanings as well as material affordances, and learners will be variously positioned by teachers as well as peers in relation to these technologies according to their prior experiences and identities as well as how these technologies are incorporated into instruction.

As many chapters in this handbook illustrate, technology-based language teaching is not a method in itself, but is integrated into various pedagogical approaches with different goals and strategies (Kern 2006). Technologies can serve a variety of roles: as tutors, providing instruction and testing; as tools, providing reference material such as online dictionaries or databases; and as media, providing a means of communication and participation in new communities and groups (ibid.). Educators should take into account how a particular group of learners might relate to a particular use of technology within a desired pedagogical approach.

This more complex view of learner identity can be used to enhance the value of frameworks for designing technology-mediated learning, such as those proposed by Chapelle (2001), Doughty and Long (2003) and Hampel (2006). Chapelle's (2001) widely cited criteria for evaluating the appropriateness of CALL tasks and activities include: (1) language learning potential, (2) learner fit, (3) meaning focus, (4) authenticity, (5) positive impact and (6) practicality. 'Learner fit' is often defined in terms of how learner variables such as age, native language, proficiency level, gender or interests might make certain objectives or activities more or less appropriate (see e.g. Hubbard 2006). Teachers need to be aware of and critical about their assumptions about learners, including their orientations towards various forms of technology-mediated learning, which may not be consistent with learner self-perceptions or desired identities. For example, when choosing entertainment games, gamers can select from among a wide range of game genres, depending on their interests, skills and prior experience. Different types of games are associated with different gaming communities and even particular gamer identities. Many entertainment games let players choose how to play, whether to use supportive materials such as game guides, whether to play alone or with others and so forth. There is no one orientation to gaming, and educators should keep this in mind when choosing language learning games, or by extension, any other technology.

In addition, educators can make the symbolic meanings of technology and stereotypes about technology use based on age or gender an explicit focus of study. Feminist scholars such as Norton and Pavlenko (2004) describe ways in which teachers can address the gendered dimensions of language learning and use through the analysis of popular culture (e.g. soap operas) and students' personal storytelling. Extending this approach to technology-mediated language use and multiple forms of identity, educators might, for example, engage students in an analysis of language use and choices in popular social media or discussion forums. How do people's discursive choices contribute to the expression of particular identities and affiliations? Who is visible and invisible in such spaces? How do particular forms of language use and identity recruit different sorts of responses? Such analyses can support learners in developing a meta-awareness of language form and function and assist them in understanding how language use positions them in particular social contexts.

A related strategy is to engage learners in analysing technology-mediated language use specific to the educational setting, with the goal of identifying how learners engage with the technology and each other in various ways that may support or marginalise different individuals, as well as enhance or inhibit the learning of the group as a whole. Involving learners in this process can help them identify and challenge their own biases and assumptions about each other, language learning and technology.

These latter suggestions are consistent with Warschauer's (2004) argument that technology-mediated language learning might be construed more as about teaching language to help people use computers more effectively than about using computers as tools to teach a language effectively. In other words, a significant aspect of language fluency and literacy is the ability to participate in computer-mediated interactions, whether that be online courses, email, forums, blogs or some as yet unimagined digital mode, and such participation depends on learners' ability to negotiate and renegotiate new roles and identities.

## Future directions for research

As we have noted previously, the literature that focuses specifically on technology-mediated language learning in relation to age, gender or identity is sparse and further research is crucial. First is the need for multiple theoretical frameworks to account for the complex intersection of identities, technologies and language learning. While there is a growing body of work on identity and second language learning, the kinds of identities taken into account are frequently limited, and do not necessarily account for new forms of identity as well as language practices that language learners construct in technology-mediated environments. Scholars might draw from work on the social construction of technologies and feminist theories of technology (Wajcman 2010) to develop a more critical view of how technologies are developed, used and interpreted by different social groups in relation to language learning.

Second, researchers can develop more dynamic conceptions of learner identity, language learning and technology use by studying how learners move across different contexts, technology-mediated and not, to see how different contexts support, reinforce and/or contradict learning. There is a long tradition of studying language socialisation and identity across contexts such as school and home (Baquedano-López and Hernández 2011), but researchers have yet to give substantive attention to how technology affects learning across these settings or creates new contexts for language learning. The work of Eva Lam (2004, 2008) illustrates the potential of such research for illuminating the potential affordances and challenges of this movement. Leander, Phillips and Taylor (2010) offer a useful overview of work in related fields on young people's mobility and learning across technologically mediated and other settings that might serve as a starting point.

Finally, more insight is needed into how teachers' efforts to be responsive to learners' identities, gender, age or otherwise do and do not make a difference in technology-mediated language learning. Not all aspects of a learners' identity are relevant in any given situation, and one potential affordance of technology is the ability to construct, say, an online presence that is significant different from one's 'real-life' identity. In some cases, situational and pragmatic factors might make attention to learner identity, even in one-dimensional terms, unnecessary or impractical. Much of the work on identity and second language learning presumes a classroom or out of school setting in which learners are interacting with others, such as a teacher and other learners, and engaged in meaningful or authentic language practices. In other situations, such as automated tutoring or computer-based language drills, there may be no real opportunity to – or more importantly, no real gain from – efforts to address particular aspects of learner identities. The responsibility in this case will lie as much with the designers of the technology as with teachers or learners to determine how it might be most responsive and inclusive of different learner abilities and orientations to technology and language learning.

## Further reading

While these readings do not specifically address age, gender and technology in relation to language learning, they offer useful and relevant perspectives that can be applied by language learning teachers and researchers.

Center for Children and Technology (http://cct.edc.org)
 A site sponsored by the Education Development Center to report current research on how technology can be used to enhance teaching and learning for children.

Gee, J.P. (2000) 'Identity as an analytic lens for research in education', *Review of Research in Education*, 25: 99–125.
 A useful overview of different perspectives on identity and their implications for educational research.

Gee, J.P. and Hayes, E.R. (2010) *Women and Gaming: The Sims and 21st Century Learning*, New York, NY: Palgrave.

The book explores how gaming can be a vehicle for women and girls' learning, by examining how entertainment-focused games like *The Sims* serve as hubs for a wide range of individual and collective knowledge creation and sharing practices.

Motteram, G. (ed) (2013) *Innovations in Learning Technologies for English Language Teaching*, London, UK: The British Council.

This volume includes chapters on the use of technologies for language learners of varied ages and contexts, from primary school to postsecondary education.

Selwyn, N., Gorard, S. and Furlong J. (2006) *Adult Learning in the Digital Age: Information Technology and the Learning Society*, London, UK: Routledge.

This book offers insight into the ways in which adults in the 21st century interact with technology in different learning environments.

# References

Aliweh, A.M. (2011) 'Exploring Egyptian EFL students' learning styles and satisfaction with web-based materials', *CALICO Journal*, 29(1): 81–99.

Andrews, P. (2012) *The Social Construction of Age: Adult Foreign Language Learners*, Clevedon, UK: Multilingual Matters.

Appleby, R. (2013) 'Desire in translation: White masculinity and TESOL', *TESOL Quarterly*, 47(1): 122–147.

Baquedano-López, P. and Hernández, S.J. (2011) 'Language socialization across educational settings', in B. Levinson and M. Pollock (eds), *A Companion to the Anthropology of Education*, 1st edn, Malden: Blackwell Publishing Ltd: 197–121.

Belcher, D.D. (2004) 'Trends in teaching English for specific purposes', *Annual Review of Applied Linguistics*, 24(1): 165–186.

Bennett, S., Maton, K. and Kervin, L. (2008) 'The 'digital natives' debate: A critical review of the evidence', *British Journal of Educational Technology*, 39(5): 775–786.

Birdsong, D. (2005) 'Interpreting age effects in second language acquisition', in J.F. Kroll and A.M.B. DeGroot (eds), *Handbook of Bilingualism: Psycholinguistic Approaches*, New York, NY: Oxford University Press: 109–127.

Cameron, D. (2009) 'Sex/gender, language and the new Biologism', *Applied Linguistics*, 31(2): 173–192.

Chapelle, C.A. (2001) *Computer Applications in Second Language Acquisition*, New York, NY: Cambridge University Press.

DeKeyser, R. (2003) 'Implicit and explicit learning', in C.J. Doughty and M.H. Long (eds), *The Handbook of Second Language Acquisition*, Malden: Blackwell Publishing: 313–348.

Doughty, C. and Long, M.H. (2003) 'Optimal psycholinguistic environments for distance foreign language learning', *Language Learning and Technology*, 7: 50–80.

Duff, P. (2012) 'Identity, agency, and SLA', in A. Mackey and S. Gass (eds), *Handbook of Second Language Acquisition*, London, UK: Routledge: 410–426.

Ellis, R. (1994) *The Study of Second Language Acquisition*, Oxford, UK: Oxford University Press.

Gee, J.P. (2000) 'Identity as an analytic lens for research in education', *Review of Research in Education*, 25: 99–125.

Gee, J.P. (2011) *Social Linguistics and Literacies: Ideology in Discourses*, 4th edn, New York, NY: Routledge.

Gordon, D. (2004) '"I'm tired. You clean and cook." Shifting gender identities and second language socialization', *TESOL Quarterly*, 38(3): 437–457.

Hampel, R. (2006) 'Rethinking task design for the digital age: A framework for language teaching and learning in a synchronous online environment', *ReCALL*, 18: 105–121.

Harley, B. and Hart, D. (2002) 'Age, aptitude and second language learning on a bilingual exchange', in P. Robinson (ed), *Individual Differences and Instructed Language Learning*, Amsterdam/Philadelphia: John Benjamins Publishing Co., 301–330.

Hayes, E. and Lee, Y. (2012) 'Specialist language acquisition and trajectories of IT learning in a *Sims* fan site', in E. Hayes and S. Duncan (eds), *Learning in Video Game Affinity Spaces*, New York: Peter Lang, 186–211.

Hruska, B.L. (2004) 'Constructing gender in an English dominant kindergarten: Implications for second language learners', *TESOL Quarterly*, 38(3): 459–485.

Hubbard, P. (2006) 'Evaluating CALL software', in L. Ducate and N. Arnold (eds), *Calling on CALL: From Theory and Research to New Directions in Foreign Language Teaching*, San Marcos, TX: CALICO: 313–338.

Hyde, J.S. (2005) 'The gender similarities hypothesis', *American Psychologist*, 60(6): 581–592.

Hyde, J.S. and Linn, M. (1988) 'Gender differences in verbal ability: A meta-analysis', *Psychological Bulletin*, 104: 53–69.

Intratat, C. (2011) 'Alternatives for making language learning games more appealing for self-access learning', *Studies in Self-Access Learning Journal*, 2(3): 136–152.

Johnson, K.J. (2006) 'The sociocultural turn and its challenges for second language teacher education', *TESOL Quarterly*, 40(1): 235–257.

Jones, S. and Myhill, D. (2007) 'Discourses of difference? Examining gender difference in the linguistic characteristics of writing', *Canadian Journal of Education*, 30(2): 456–482.

Katz, V. (2010) 'How children of immigrants use media to connect their families to the community', *Journal of Children and Media*, 4(3): 298–315.

Kern, R. (2006) 'Perspectives on technology in learning and teaching languages', *TESOL Quarterly*, 40(1): 183–210.

Lam, W.S.E. (2000) 'Second language literacy and the design of the self: A case study of a teenager writing on the Internet', *TESOL Quarterly*, 34(3): 457–483.

Lam, W.S.E. (2004) 'Second language socialization in a bilingual chat room: Global and local considerations', *Language Learning and Technology*, 8(3): 44–65.

Lam, W.S.E. (2008) 'Language socialization in online communities', in P.A. Duff and N.H. Hornberger (eds), *Encyclopedia of Language and Education, vol. 8. Language Socialization*, New York, NY: Springer: 301–311.

Leander, K.M., Phillips, N.C. and Taylor, K.H. (2010) 'The changing social spaces of learning: Mapping new mobilities', *Review of Research in Education*, 34: 329–394.

Lee, Y.N. (2012) *Learning and Literacy in an Online Gaming Community: Examples of Participatory Practices in a Sims Affinity Space*, Unpublished dissertation, Arizona State University.

Long, M. (2005) 'Problems with supposed counter-evidence to the Critical Period Hypothesis', *International Review of Applied Linguistics in Language Teaching*, 43(4): 287–317.

Luik, P. (2011) 'Would boys and girls benefit from gender-specific educational software?', *British Journal of Educational Technology*, 42(1): 128–144.

Macaro, E., Handley, Z. and Walter, C. (2012) 'A systematic review of CALL in English as a second language: Focus on primary and secondary education', *Language Teaching*, 45:1–43.

Marinova-Todd, S.H., Marshall, D.B. and Snow, C.F. (2000) 'Three misconceptions about age and L2 learning', *TESOL Quarterly*, 34(1): 9–34.

Menard-Warwick, J. (2005) 'Both a fiction and an existential fact: Theorizing identity in second language acquisition and literacy studies', *Linguistics and Education*, 16: 253–274.

Motteram, G. (ed) (2013) *Innovations in Learning Technologies for English Language Teaching*, London: The British Council.

Muñoz, C. (2007) 'Age-related differences and second language learning practice', in R.M. DeKeyser (ed), *Practice in a Second Language: Perspectives from Applied Linguistics and Cognitive Psychology*, New York, NY: Cambridge University Press: 229–255.

Norton, B. (2000) *Identity and Language Learning: Gender, Ethnicity, and Educational Change*, Harlow, UK: Longman.

Norton, B. and Pavlenko, A. (2004) 'Addressing gender in the ESL/EFL classroom', *TESOL Quarterly*, 38(3): 504–514.

Ochs, E. and Schieffelin, B. (1984) 'Language acquisition and socialization: Three developmental stories and their implications', in R.A. Shweder and F. Levy (eds), *Culture Theory: Essays on Mind, Self, and Emotion*, Cambridge: Cambridge University Press: 277–320.

Pim, C. (2013) 'Emerging technologies, emerging minds: Digital innovations within the primary sector', in G. Motteram (ed), *Innovations in Learning Technologies for English Language Teaching*, London, UK: The British Council: 15–42.

Polat, N. and Mahalingappa, L.J. (2010) 'Gender differences in identity and acculturation patterns and L2 Accent Attainment', *Journal of Language, Identity, and Education*, 9: 17–35.

Robinson, P. (2005) 'Aptitude and second language acquisition', *Annual Review of Applied Linguistics*, 25(1): 46–73.

Singleton, D. (2005) 'The critical period hypothesis: A coat of many colours', *International Review of Applied Linguistics*, 43: 269–286.

Slaouti, D., Onat-Stelma, Z. and Motteram, G. (2013) 'Technology and adult language teaching', in G. Motteram (ed), *Innovations in Learning Technologies for English Language Teaching*, London: The British Council, 67–86.

Thorne, S.L., Black, R.W. and Sykes, J.M. (2009) 'Second language use, socialization, and learning in Internet interest communities and online gaming', *The Modern Language Journal*, 93(1): 802–821.

Varghese, M., Morgan, B., Johnston, B. and Johnson, K.A. (2005) 'Theorizing language teacher identity: Three perspectives and beyond', *Journal of Language, Identity and Education*, 4(10): 21–44.

Wajcman, J. (2010) 'Feminist theories of technology', *Cambridge Journal of Economics*, 34(1): 143–152.

Warschauer, M. (2004) 'Technological change and the future of CALL', in S. Fotos and C. Browne (eds), *New Perspectives on CALL for Second Language Classrooms*, Mahwah, NJ: Lawrence Erlbaum: 15–26.

Zhao, Y. (2003) 'A comprehensive review of research on technology uses in language education', *The CALICO Journal*, 21(1): 7–27.

Zuengler, J. and Miller, E.R. (2006) 'Cognitive and sociocultural perspectives: two parallel SLA worlds?', *TESOL Quarterly*, 40(1): 35–58.

# 12
# Culture, language learning and technology

*Robert Godwin-Jones*

Traditionally, language learning was seen as the gateway to high culture, meaning the ability to read and appreciate the masterworks of the target culture. This approach, however, has given way to the notion that language learning at all levels should incorporate elements of the target culture, that is, aspects of everyday life, behavioural norms, traditions and values. A result of that trend has been the desire to incorporate linguistically and culturally authentic texts in language instruction from the beginning levels. The proliferation of texts and media on the Web provides a rich resource for accomplishing that goal. A deeper and more personal insight into the target culture is possible through online exchanges. The many different modes of computer-mediated communication available today offer many opportunities for peer-to-peer networking, which serve to improve language competence but also to build cultural knowledge, allowing language students to discover first-hand how their peers in other cultures experience the world. In recent years there has been considerable interest among language educators in moving from bicultural experiences and learning to the development of intercultural competence, with language learning being part of a broader ecological system.

## Language and culture

Technological developments as well as increased international commerce and migration bring into contact more than ever before people representing different languages and cultures. In some cases, this results in conflict and strife; in others, it can lead to a desire to learn more about the culture encountered. That might well develop into an interest in learning the language of that culture. In today's Internet-connected world, both language learning and cultural understanding can be facilitated through technology. In fact, culture and language are, in most cases, tightly linked. That may be different for lingua francas, especially English, which represents a wide variety of cultures. In any case, one's native language tends to be an essential component of individual cultural identity.

The link between language and culture was famously described in the work of anthropologists Benjamin Whorf and Edward Sapir. The Sapir-Whorf hypothesis postulates that your native language has a profound influence on how you see the world, that you perceive reality in the context of the language you have available to describe it. From this perspective, all language use

173

– from the words we use to describe objects to the way sentences are structured – is tied closely to the culture in which it is spoken. Whorf wrote:

> The background linguistic system (in other words, the grammar) of each language is not merely a reproducing instrument for voicing ideas but rather is itself the shaper of ideas, the program and guide for people's mental activity, for their analysis of impressions, for their synthesis of their mental stock in trade. Formulation of ideas is not an independent process, strictly rational in the old sense, but is part of a particular grammar and differs, from slightly to greatly, among different grammars ... We dissect nature along lines laid down by our native languages.
>
> *(Whorf 1940: 231)*

Taken to its extreme, this kind of linguistic determinism would prevent native speakers of different languages from having the same thoughts or sharing a worldview. More widely accepted today is the concept of linguistic relativity, meaning that language shapes our views of the world but is not an absolute determiner of how or what we think. After all, translation is in fact possible, and bilinguals do exist, both of which phenomena should be problematic in a strict interpretation of the Sapir-Whorf hypothesis.

Second language learners quickly become aware of how aspects of the new language signal a different way of perceiving the world or emphasise aspects of life important to that culture. Native English speakers learn that pronouns for addressing others is not universal, that the 'you' which in English is used to address individuals, groups, friends, strangers and so forth may have multiple equivalents in other languages. That may go beyond the distinction between familiar and formal second person pronouns to a code of respect and politeness that dictates different vocabulary, intonation and speech patterns depending on one's relationship to the addressee. Students of Korean, for instance, learn the importance of those aspects of the language early on.

Language students from the beginning will also learn that the target language likely has different verbal (and nonverbal) conventions for participating in aspects of everyday life such as greetings, leave-taking, apologising or making requests. Such 'speech acts' were described and studied by John Searle and John Austin in the 1960s. These are uses of language to perform actions or to generate specific activities, and they can vary substantially from language to language. The field of sociolinguistics deals with speech acts, as well as with other aspects of how language is used in social contexts. An important aspect of this field of study is the examination of variations in languages, such as dialects and regional differences. This can involve clear cultural distinctions such as the existence of high prestige and low prestige versions of a language. Linguists also study language variation related to age, gender or occupation. Contact between cultures is another important area studied by sociolinguists. Such contact can bring about change, including new variations of a language, or even new languages. Creoles, for example, are languages that develop as hybrids from several different languages. Today, there is considerable interest in studying how language is used in and adapted to online environments, including in microblogging (Twitter), text messaging and social networks (see Lomicka and Lord, Chapter 18 this volume). Sociolinguists emphasise the changing nature of language as it comes into contact with social reality and with new ways of communicating.

## Incorporating culture into language learning

While the intersection of language and culture has been of considerable interest in linguistics and anthropology, that link has not always been an explicit part of second language instruction.

'Culture' has often been treated as distinct from language, as a discrete body of knowledge that can be taught separately from the ability to read, write, listen and speak. What constitutes culture, as taught in the language classroom, has varied considerably over the years. For most of the 20th century, it meant high culture with a capital C, the study of the great works of artistic and literary achievement, along with their historical development. This meant waiting to introduce culture until students had achieved enough facility with the target language to be able to read and discuss literary and historical texts. Sometimes, short literary passages, especially poems, were introduced at the intermediate level, with the message to students being that the ability to read, understand and interpret such works was the ultimate goal of language study.

With the proliferation of the communicative approach to language learning in the 1970s, it was small-c culture that was emphasised: the social elements of everyday life of the target country. Topics covered could range from political systems to holiday customs, with plenty of attention paid to culinary customs and school life. This approach to the presentation of culture in second language instruction is sometimes derisively described as the four Fs: festivals, food, folklore and facts. These kinds of 'culture capsules' were – and still are today – often incorporated into textbooks through short readings, dialogues or video clips. Typically, they are supplied as supplementary materials, to be used, if time allows, after the serious business of learning essential vocabulary and grammatical structures. In the treatment of both 'high' and 'low' culture in second language learning, the emphasis has been on gaining knowledge about a specific speech community, seen normally from the perspective of an assumed homogenous nation-state.

The popularity of the communicative approach to language instruction also brought a gradual shift in the nature of cultural materials used in language instruction. The emphasis was placed on the use of 'authentic' language texts, with the expectation that they would provide real-life exposure to linguistic features of the target language. Rather than describing aspects of the culture, realia should be used instead, such as train timetables, restaurant menus or native speaker letters/diaries. Such materials could then serve as the source for task-based communicative activities in the classroom, such as having small groups determine together how to travel from Hamburg to Frankfurt, or reading and discussing online movie reviews to decide which film to watch. The emphasis remained on developing practical communicative proficiency, the functional ability for learners to carry out tasks and conduct conversations in a variety of contexts.

With this approach, culture remains largely separated from language, its role being to supply content for communicative exchanges. The treatment of culture in the language classroom is still often today at a level that rarely goes beyond the easily understood surface manifestations of a foreign culture. Without explicit discussion of the social and historical contexts for cultural phenomena, students tend to view them in the context of their own native environment. Rather than understanding culture as a product, students should be guided to see it as a process, something that is dynamically created through a community's shared memories and experiences. In the traditional practice of culture as product, there might be a unit on French cities that highlights famous landmarks, without mention of the changing demographics of French cities or the very different real-world meaning of 'suburbs' in a French context. External manifestations of culture, such as the topics typically discussed in the second language classroom, can be used as a starting point for deeper explorations of the target culture. Pictures of food, for example, can be informative in terms of culinary traditions, but could also lead to discussion of topics such as vegetarianism, religious taboos and sustainability.

In recent years there has been a growing recognition that culture and language cannot be separated, and that culture permeates all aspects of language. If, for example, a language has different personal pronouns for direct address, such as the informal *tu* in French and the formal *vous*, both meaning 'you', that distinction is a reflection of one aspect of the culture. It indicates that there is a built-in awareness and significance to social differentiation and that a more formal level of language use is available. Typically, sociolinguistic knowledge is presented as standard and universal in a given culture, much as language is presented in the model of educated speakers using standardised, grammatically correct language forms. This can result in a somewhat unrealistic representation of the target culture. Foreign cultures are often viewed as monolithic and invariable, with distinctions based on age, occupation or locality either glossed over or presented as intriguing, exotic outliers ('what a strange dialect'). The reality of identity creation in today's world is quite different, with globalising economic trends and the spread of social media leading to multifaceted personal and cultural identities which may come to the fore at different times in different situations. The national culture in which a person is raised certainly is an important factor in determining one's values, beliefs and habits, but there are likely to be multiple additional influences, coming, for example, from membership of a minority group, gender identification, online gaming, the work environment or a chosen free-time activity.

In line with the view that language and culture are intertwined has come the recognition that this should be reflected in instructed language learning. This means that culture should not be a separate activity but should be integrated all along into the learning process. It also changes the nature of what culture represents. Cultural integration involves going beyond presenting specific facets of everyday life, to showing how values, beliefs and practices are embedded in the language. This entails, on the one hand, adding a 'reflexive component' to language study (Kramsch 2012), that is, guiding students to think about how the language elements introduced differ from their native language, and to consider what they might represent in the foreign culture. This necessitates students becoming cognisant of aspects of language in general as well as characteristics of their own language. On the other hand, this shift entails introducing linguistic features of the target language that reflect aspects of the culture. This might mean supplementing the standardised language presented in language textbooks by introducing varieties of language use that reflect different cultural contexts, including, as appropriate, migrant or other marginalised communities. Teaching German, for instance, without some discussion of the important role Turkish language and culture play in contemporary German life (food, literature and film) would give a distorted view of that society.

Textbooks present standard language and do not often introduce variations in language patterns that reflect different social, regional or situational contexts. This is done for practical, pedagogical reasons, with the goal of having students learn basic vocabulary and essential structural elements. Dialogues in textbooks typically present the speech of educated, well-behaved native speakers, who wait until their conversation partners are finished before speaking. These are idealised native speakers, intent on being agreeable, conversing in order to exchange information and to find consensus. Linguists know how far removed such exchanges are from real life. Real conversations are full of interruptions, false starts and repetitions. Conversations rarely focus on transmitting information. Interactions may be contentious, with open conflict and raw emotions on display. In any case, the language used will likely not resemble the nicely cooperative and grammatically correct sentences in a textbook (see Caines, McCarthy and O'Keeffe, Chapter 25 this volume). The use of discourse analysis in linguistics – transcribing and analysing recordings of real conversations – has shown how varied and spontaneous human speech really is.

In many contexts today, another characteristic of real language use often emerges – code-switching, or the mixing of languages together within a conversation. This can be simply substituting an occasional word of another language or, in other cases, it can involve a back and forth between languages for the entire conversation. As globalisation has increased international contact, more frequent travel has taken more people into unfamiliar cultures, and the explosion in the use of social networks has expanded exposure to multiple languages, code-switching is a phenomenon that increasing numbers of people are likely to experience. Claire Kramsch describes this phenomenon as 'language crossings' (Kramsch 1998). She provides examples of such acts of identity and sample conversations which show how choice of language within conversations can be clear markers of group membership or social distancing. Such language crossings are no longer limited to bilingual groups, but are particularly evident on the Internet, where discussion forums and social media frequently mix and match languages.

In the typical language learning environment, it is not possible to expose learners to all the varieties of language use they might encounter. However, it certainly is possible to increase learners' awareness of sociocultural issues. One of those is the existence of language registers, the fact that we adjust the language we use – in terms of formality, tone and even vocabulary – in response to the context in which we find ourselves. Learners need to be aware of how language use could be adjusted in formal face-to-face settings, as in a work environment, to highly informal, online settings, as in Facebook exchanges (see Lomicka and Lord, Chapter 18 this volume). This involves looking beyond grammatical correctness to language in use. Pragmatics, another field of interest in sociolinguistics, deals with the nature of language as it occurs in actual social use. The meaning of what is said in conversation may be quite different from the literal meaning of the words used. A statement made in an ironic, sarcastic or humorous tone may, in fact, have a meaning diametrically opposed to its surface meaning. Answering 'oh, sure' in American English to a statement or question can be a positive affirmation or be intended to ridicule what the interlocutor has said. Such nuances are important for being able to function in the target culture. This kind of sociocultural competence is not easy to acquire, as pragmatics does not involve learning a fixed set of rules. Rather, inference and intuition play a major role, as can emotions. Making students aware of the dynamics of language use in conversation can help make them better informed and literate speakers of any language they use. Pragmatic competence is particularly important in online exchanges, in which the nonverbal cues signalling intent and attitude are not available.

## Connecting to the target culture through the Internet

It used to be that one of the challenges in language learning was the difficulty in connecting learners to the foreign culture they were studying, both in reference to contact with native speakers and to the materials and media developed within that culture. Today the Internet provides a mechanism for both kinds of connections. It wasn't that long ago that language teachers would be sure to bring home a rich collection of cultural media and realia when travelling abroad. Now such materials can be found in abundance online. Learners of English have the widest choice of digital texts and other media available for language study. English remains the most widely used language on the Internet today, but it is closely followed now by Chinese, with most other major languages also having a substantial presence online. However, it may be more difficult for learners of some less commonly taught languages to find useful learning material in the target language, as in some cultures it has not become standard practice for newspapers or television broadcasts to be made publicly available in digital formats. For language learners, having such resources available can be a rich source of material for enhancing reading ability and listening comprehension (see Liou, Chapter 34 this volume). They are also an invaluable source for learning about the target culture. After all, such online resources have not been artificially created for the benefit of language learners, as is the case with textbooks, but represent resources used in the real, everyday lives of people living in those cultures.

Of course, just having access to online realia in the target language does not mean that such materials will be useful for an individual language learner. That will depend on the nature of the resource, its linguistic difficulty and its level of interest for the user. Search engines are typically of limited use in finding appropriate resources. In instructed language learning, teachers are likely to provide help in that process, an especially important service for students of less commonly taught languages. Professional organisations, individual instructors and language centres are increasingly finding it to be part of their instructional and service role to provide up-to-date and annotated links to appropriate online materials.

Another role instructors and language professionals play is to add a pedagogical framework to online texts and media. YouTube videos, for example, can have their instructional usefulness enhanced considerably through the use of transcripts or captions. In fact, YouTube includes the ability to generate automatically a transcript for English language videos, providing a useful rough draft that requires some degree of editing. The Flagship Media Library in the United States is building a system for storing, annotating, accessing and developing pedagogical materials around web-based audio and video. The authentic materials collected are being analysed, tagged and transcribed so they can be used in a variety of contexts, offering a combination of authenticity and flexibility.

Texts can be and have been glossed as well, providing learners with both linguistic and cultural annotations for working with authentic texts in the target language (see Liou, Chapter 34 this volume). Tools and services are available which will locate online texts that correspond to a specific set of characteristics, such as using a set number of items from a vocabulary list. REAder-specific Practice (REAP) is an example of such a service (Collins-Thompson and Callan 2004). It provides reader-specific practice for improved reading comprehension, incorporating an advanced search model that can find documents satisfying a set of diverse lexical requirements, including a passage's topic, reading level, use of syntax and vocabulary. Additionally, there are add-ons to web browsers which allow users to click on words or phrases for instant dictionary lookups.

A technique that can be quite useful for vocabulary development, checking for valid pragmatic use of phrases and learning about collocations (set word chunks) is to make use of language corpora (see Part IV of this volume on corpora and data-driven learning). A language corpus is a collection of texts that have been put into a database. A number of corpora exist for a variety of languages and typically include a rich selection of texts retrieved from online sources. Searches on words or phrases display that item in a KWIC (keyword in context) display, showing a truncated display of each sentence containing that item. Accessing a corpus can provide valuable insight into how a given item is actually used in context by native speakers. It is sometimes maintained that having learners access language corpora directly is too difficult. This may be less a factor for the more motivated and mature language learners, who, as Alex Boulton states, can be empowered by such a tool: 'it would seem disingenuous to coddle learners with simplified language, disempowering them and leaving them unprepared for the realities of the authentic language we are presumably preparing them for' (Boulton 2009: 89). He advocates creating homemade corpora that can match particular needs, a potentially valuable resource in self-directed language learning. In an experimental use of corpora with beginning learners, corpus use was shown to be of particular benefit in learning pragmatics (Belz and Vyatkina 2005). A learner corpus can provide sociocultural information about language use, such as frequency of occurrence of items in particular genres or contexts of use.

A more contextualised use of native language is available for learners through participation in one of the online services used by native speakers, such as a forum established for discussion of particular topics, like those set up for readers of a newspaper or fans of a television series. Such interactions can be valuable learning experiences, but they can also be linguistically and culturally challenging. Users of such forums often have a low tolerance for novices, particularly those who are unfamiliar with the rules and expectations of that particular forum. As with all writing, it is important to be able to adapt to the conventions and language register of that genre, just as it is with other types of online writing, such as Facebook updates or text messages. Participating in social networks which include the presence of multiple languages can be a less stressful experience, as the participants tend to have more in common and thus be less judgemental.

One such opportunity exists in the multiple fan sites associated with online gaming (see Part V of this volume on gaming and language learning). Multiplayer online games, such as *World of Warcraft*, include participants from many different cultures and so represent rich potential sources of intercultural contact. The game experience itself may also offer opportunities for culturally informed language learning. Games provide an immersive environment in which extensive use is made of the target language. To progress in a game, players must make active use of that language, interacting with game objects or other players. This means that they are using language in real and socially appropriate ways; in the game context pragmatic appropriateness trumps grammatical accuracy. Gamers are often exposed to cultural and linguistic insights that they are unlikely to have encountered in a textbook or in the classroom. An example of a digital game designed for both cultural and linguistic learning is *Croquelandia*, created with the goal of enhancing the ability to perform requests and apologies in Spanish. Students having played the game showed an increase in the awareness of meta-linguistic considerations and of the importance of pragmatic appropriateness (Sykes, Oskoz and Thorne 2008). The enhanced awareness of linguistic features tied to cultural norms and practices is an outcome likely to be achievable through gaming, more so than narrowly focused language goals. It is not likely that either gaming or participation in online chats/forums will result in users increasing knowledge of grammatical rules, but such activities are likely to result in a gain in sociolinguistic skills, which get scant attention in language classrooms.

## Online culture exchanges

In addition to the opportunities to connect with native speakers, discussed in the previous section, there are also mechanisms for connecting online with other language learners, either on a individual basis or as part of a group, as in an online class exchange (see Helm and Guth, Chapter 17 this volume). The conversation partners could be local – students in another class or members of a local ethnic community – but they could be located abroad. For maximum cultural benefit, the latter arrangement is preferable. One of the opportunities for individuals is to participate in a tandem learning experience. This involves finding language partners who are studying each other's languages. Partners split their time together between the two languages, with the exchanges being in written form (email, chat) or increasingly in audio or video formats. A number of services have been created to assist learners in finding appropriate partners, conforming not only to the language being learned, but also to age, gender and interest preferences. Such arrangements can provide direct, unfiltered exposure to the target language. On the other hand, the language partners may not be particularly helpful in terms of knowledge of grammar or other aspects of language use. This is not likely, however, to minimise the cultural value of the exchanges; they can provide valuable sociolinguistic and pragmatic knowledge.

Language classes have been engaging in exchanges going back to the days of pen pals. Today such telecollaboration can take place in a variety of ways, through email exchanges, discussion forums or common access to a standalone website or a course website within a virtual learning environment. Tools associated with Web 2.0 can also be used, including blogs, wikis and Twitter. Video conferencing is also possible through such services as Skype or Google Hangouts. Case studies of telecollaboration have shown that they work best if they are both monitored by instructors and prepared by participants. Having participants start communicating with one another without advance preparation can lead to a variety of misunderstandings and, in fact, to serious conflict and hurt feelings. Students typically need both linguistic and cultural preparation in order for the exchange to be successful. They need to know something about the conventions of language use in the target culture, including appropriate modes of address, turn-taking rules and communication style (e.g. degree of directness). They also need to be aware of which topics could be uncomfortable or contentious for the other side. One of the seminal projects in this area, Cultura, out of MIT, used a variety of ways to prepare students in advance of collaborating with partners abroad (Furstenberg, Levet, English and Maillet 2001). A jointly accessible website was established, which invited students to comment on a number of culturally loaded terms, such as *family* or *freedom*. Responses to these word associations were discussed in class and in online forums. This activity, along with joint readings and comments on texts and films, acquainted students with the values and beliefs of the other culture and also led them to analyse aspects of their own culture.

Other telecollaborative projects have used additional approaches, such as having students create cultural autobiographies or video self-portraits. Such activities also tend to lead to personal and cultural self-analysis, which can be valuable in establishing a basis for understanding both the other culture and reactions from the other side to aspects of one's own culture. Such exchanges can be vehicles for personal development in addition to learning opportunities. They can also be fraught with considerable emotional reactions, as students may be discovering and articulating for the first time feelings and opinions that may have been hidden beneath the surface. Given that dynamic, it is important for teachers to monitor exchanges and provide sufficient guidance and support throughout the process. A study by Kramsch and Thorne (2002) examined the use of synchronous and asynchronous communication between French and American students and found that there were misunderstandings and miscommunications based on different communication styles. The French chose 'factual, impersonal, dispassionate genres of writing' (Kramsch and Thorne 2006: 94) while the Americans used an oral style with many questions and exclamation marks, indicating a high level of effective involvement. In addition to different discursive styles, differences in cultures of use in reference to Internet communication tools may become apparent in online exchanges. Digital tools are not, as often assumed, culturally neutral. Many teachers today, for example, are likely to find that students associate email with a formal learning environment, whereas their personal communications are carried out through text messaging. Thus, course assignments requiring email may be less personally engaging for many students, resulting in lower levels of motivation and commitment.

Tensions and disappointments in online exchange are common; O'Dowd and Ritter (2006) provide an extensive list. However, conflict and miscommunication can provide powerful learning opportunities. Conflict is unavoidable, so instead of a fruitless effort to try to eliminate it from exchanges, it is advantageous to study its cause and the underlying cultural backdrop. It is an opportunity for learning about the target culture as well as about one's own cultural practices and preferences. In the language classroom we often assume communication is taking place between individuals with similar interests and common goals, but this hardly reflects real-world conversations. The communication difficulties that arise in online exchanges provide evidence of that. Often, however, we fail to take advantage of such conversational dynamics to reflect on their significance:

> The increased use of CMC [computer-mediated communication] to develop communicative competence in the L2 has led to a reorientation of language learning toward conversational fluency, online chatting ability, the negotiation of surface features of speech and a

focus on common experiences in the here-and-now. It has not, however, necessarily led to the in-depth exploration of cultural difference, the negotiation of incompatible worldviews and a focus on different interpretations of historical events.

*(Kramsch 2013: 71)*

The mostly decontextualised nature of online exchanges can lead to knee-jerk reactions and reinforcement of stereotypes. That is why, for maximum benefit, online exchanges should be well prepared and monitored, with students supplied with opportunities to reflect on the nature and origins of miscommunications. In that way conflict is not a problem, but rather a 'rich point' providing deep insight into cultural values and practices. Learning through real-world communicative experiences the conventions and appropriate language registers for different modes of online communication can be a valuable contribution to building students' practical communication skills in the target language, along with contributing significantly to the meta-linguistic knowledge students need to become effective autonomous language learners.

## Current trends: Towards intercultural competence

Engaging with speakers of other languages in online exchanges can be an exhilarating experience or, in other cases, deeply troubling. In any case it represents real communication with real people. In that sense it is quite different from the practice setting of the classroom or of traditional computer-assisted language learning, both of which function as rehearsals for the real thing. Online exchanges provide linguistic and cultural authenticity. Because of the personal developmental opportunities which online exchanges provide, having students maintain a journal during that process can be quite informative, both for the teacher and for the learner. This can provide evidence of both linguistic and sociocultural learning and serve as a reflective platform important in processing what takes place in the exchange. Increasingly today, the skills and knowledge language instructors are seeking to develop in students are not just related to the target language and culture but are culture-general insights into communicating with people from different cultural and linguistic backgrounds. In fact, this kind of intercultural communicative competence has become part of established standards for language learning, having been incorporated into the US American Council of Teachers of Foreign Languages (ACTFL) Guidelines and into the Common European Framework of Reference for Languages. Intercultural communication, in fact, is a field in which many disciplines have a vested interest, including anthropology, social psychology and applied linguistics. As societies across the world become more diverse, the importance of being interculturally competent has been recognised in a variety of professions, including business, health and tourism. Many of the telecollaborative projects in place today target the development of intercultural sensitivity, along with linguistic and sociocultural skills. Organisations have been established to promote such developments, such as the Soliya Connect Programme, for example, which brings together representatives from Western countries with Middle Easterners in an effort to ease tensions between the two sides and to foster intercultural understanding. Participants in the project engage in individual and group exchanges monitored by facilitators (Genet 2010).

As with all educational goals today, educators and administrators are seeking to be able to document and assess students' intercultural communicative competence. In the business context, this is often done through formal assessment instruments. In educational settings, it is more common to use portfolios. There are a number of tools and services for creating language portfolios, and increasingly these also incorporate cultural competence. This is the case, for example, with the Council of Europe's Autobiography of Intercultural Encounters. As recognition increases for extramural learning – the developmental experiences we all have outside the classroom – efforts are likely to increase to be able to include such activities in portfolios. Standards and tools for doing that are being developed by entities such as the Council of Europe. Eventually, it may be possible for electronic portfolios to document not only formal educational experiences and personal self-assessment, but also other potential learning experiences such as participation in study groups, open educational courses or even educational games.

Educational games, in fact, point towards another trend in the use of technology for cultural learning, namely using mobile devices for place-based games. Such digital games for mobile devices have been available for some time. The best-known are the high-end immersive language and culture simulations for the US military by Alelo. These are virtual environments in which users interact with virtual native speakers in environments that mimic the target culture. The virtual user-soldier, for example, may interact with elders in an Iraqi village, requiring use of the correct politeness etiquette and formulas. Such programs are expensive, however, and time-consuming to produce. An alternative is game authoring tools such as ARIS, short for Augmented Reality and Interactive Storytelling, an open source platform. ARIS has been used to develop a variety of language learning games. *Mentira* was created with ARIS and is a mobile game which combines virtual experiences with real-world visits to locations in Albuquerque, New Mexico (Holden and Sykes 2011). The object of the game is to solve a murder mystery and involves students gaining information from site visits and from conversations.

This kind of place-based augmented reality game is in line with the current interest in applied linguistics in localised language instruction. Rather than a standardised curriculum for all communities, language learning environments – whether face-to-face or virtual – should customise approaches and content based on student demographics, including cultural background, extent of technology available and motivation for learning the target language. Students in a foreign language learning context – users not living in the target culture – likely have a different set of needs and interests from those learners living in a foreign land struggling with practical language use in a day-to-day context. Learners of English represent a special case. Depending on their location and individual situations, learners of English may have widely varying reasons for their interest. That has a particular impact on the integration of culture in teaching English, as well as how and to what extent aspects of the cultures of English-speaking countries are presented. In fact, the cultural component of English as a second language is a complex issue, in that, as Kramsch (1993) points out, 'even as an international language, English instruction transmits such Anglo-Saxon values as efficiency, pragmatism, and individualism, that superimpose themselves on those of the learners' native culture' (Kramsch 1993: 12). This makes it all the more important in teaching English to take into account the learners' needs and aspirations, but also their native language and culture. It requires as well an awareness on the part of English as a second language (ESL) teachers of the implicit cultural values embedded in English.

The rise of interest in place-based language learning is in line with the recognition in applied linguistics of the importance of connecting academic learning to real-world experiences. An awareness of the essential cultural component of language naturally leads to the need for language teachers to take into account the lives of the learners beyond the classroom. It also requires the learner to acquire meta-linguistic knowledge and skills. Learning words and rules is not nearly enough to become functional in a second language. As Bourdieu writes:

> The competence adequate to produce sentences that are likely to be understood may be quite inadequate to produce sentences that are likely to be listened to, likely to be recognized as acceptable in all the situations in which there is occasion to speak . . . Social acceptability is not reducible to mere grammaticality.

*(Bourdieu 1991: 55)*

If we accept the importance of sociolinguistic and pragmatic competence, then that necessitates an integration of social realities into language instruction at all levels. Learners need to supplement their practical communicative competence with what Kramsch (2012) calls 'symbolic competence': 'What foreign language learners need to develop is an ability to recognise the discourses behind the words, what could have been said but was not, or could have been said differently' (Kramsch 2012: 23). Increasingly today, that kind of competence is both developed and demonstrated through participation in Internet-mediated activities.

## Further reading

Belz, J.A. and Thorne, S.L. (eds) (2006) *Internet-Mediated Intercultural Foreign Language Education*, Boston, MA: Heinle & Heinle.
   This is a collection of essays on the intersection between culture and technology, which features case studies showing advantages of online exchanges but also discusses potential problems. Included are studies dealing with the teaching of intercultural competence through online exchanges, the use of student ethnography, learner corpora and teacher education. There is also a chapter on the Cultura Project, a seminal study which pioneered a number of techniques widely used in online exchanges focusing on cultural learning.
Byram, M., Nichols, A. and Stevens, D. (2001) *Developing Intercultural Competence in Practice*, Bristol, UK: Multilingual Matters.
   This is an important study on intercultural competence, dealing not only with what that means, but also providing practical help for teachers who want to help their learners achieve intercultural competence. It contains descriptions of lessons and materials from a wide range of classrooms in several countries and for beginners to advanced learners.
Guth, S. and Helm, F. (eds) (2010) *Telecollaboration 2.0: Language, Literacies, and Intercultural Learning in the 21st Century*, Bern, Switzerland: Peter Lang.
   Included in this volume are essays by major scholars in the field, exploring the use of tools and services often associated with Web 2.0: blogs, wikis, social networking such as Facebook, virtual environments such as Second Life and video conferencing tools such as Skype. The main emphasis is on ways to integrate informal learning into instructed language learning. The essays also explore topics related to digital literacy, including the ability to adapt to different registers and conventions in online writing.
Kramsch, C. (2009) *The Multilingual Subject*, Oxford: Oxford University Press.
   This is a major study by one of the most important scholars in language learning and culture. The book deals with the complex issues of how learner identities are constructed with and through language. The author draws on three sources of data: testimonies of authors' experiences in a second language, written and spoken data from language learners and data from language learners in online collaborative activities. She analyses examples of online exchanges in which communication breaks down due to a variety of cultural issues, including the use of the medium itself.
Levine, G. and Phipps, A. (eds) (2010) *Critical and Intercultural Theory and Language Pedagogy*, Boston, MA: Heinle & Heinle.
   This is a set of essays exploring what it means to develop translingual and transcultural competence (as called for by an Modern Language Association Report), including issues of how critical theory can be integrated into language and culture teaching. Included are discussions of distance learning and telecollaboration in the context of postcolonial and postmodern theory. The volume also examines the teaching of literature in the context of language learning.

## References

Belz, J.A. and Vyatkina, N. (2005) 'Learner corpus research and the development of L2 pragmatic competence in networked intercultural language study: The case of German modal particles', *Canadian Modern Language Review/Revue canadienne des langues vivantes*, 62(1): 17–48.
Boulton, A. (2009) 'Testing the limits of data-driven learning: Language proficiency and training', *ReCALL*, 21(1): 37–51.
Bourdieu, P. (1991) *Language and Symbolic Power*, Cambridge, MA: Harvard University Press.

Collins-Thompson, K. and Callan, J. (2004) 'Information retrieval for language tutoring. An overview of the REAP project', in *Proceedings of the 27th Annual International ACM SIGIR Conference on Research and Development*, Sheffield, UK: AGM: 544–545.

Furstenberg, G., Levet S., English, K. and Maillet, K. (2001) 'Giving a virtual voice to the silent language of culture: The cultura project', *Language Learning & Technology*, 5(1): 55–102.

Genet, R. (2010) 'Case study: Soliya connect programme at ENSIMAG, France', in F. Helm and E. Guth (eds), *Telecollaboration 2.0 for Language and Intercultural Learning*, Bern, Switzerland: Peter Lang Publishing Group: 359–374.

Holden, C. and Sykes, J. (2011) 'Leveraging mobile games for place-based language learning', *International Journal of Game-Based Learning (IJGBL)*, 1(2): 1–22.

Kramsch, C. (1993) *Context and Culture in Language Learning*, Oxford: Oxford University Press.

Kramsch, C. (1998) *Language and Culture*, Oxford: Oxford University Press.

Kramsch, C. (2012) 'Theorizing translingual/transcultural competence', in G. Levine and A. Phipps (eds), *Critical and Intercultural Theory and Language Pedagogy*, Boston, MA: Heinle.

Kramsch, C. (2013) 'Culture in foreign language teaching', *Iranian Journal of Language Teaching Research*, 1(1): 57–78.

Kramsch, C. and Thorne, S. L. (2002) 'Foreign language learning as global communicative practice', in D. Block and D. Cameron (eds), *Globalization and Language Teaching*, London: Routledge: 83–100.

O'Dowd, R. and Ritter, M. (2006) 'Understanding and working with "failed communication" in telecollaborative exchanges', *CALICO Journal*, 23(3): 623–642.

Sykes, J., Oskoz, A. and Thorne, S. (2008) 'Web 2.0, synthetic immersive environments, and mobile resources for language education', *CALICO Journal*, 25(3): 528–546.

Whorf, B. (1940) 'Science and linguistics', *Technology Review*, 42: 229–248.

# 13
# Language learning and technology in varied technology contexts

*Hyun Gyung Lee and Joy Egbert*

As some authors (e.g. Warschauer 2003; Egbert and Yang 2004; Egbert 2010) have noted, there are many ways in which a language learning context may be technology-limited, and there are many causes for these limitations. However, as different types of technology and their uses become ubiquitous across a variety of language learning contexts, it becomes more accurate to say that these contexts are technology-varied. For example, in some countries such as India and Turkey, where personal computer use is not the norm in rural areas, mobile phones are widespread and used for all kinds of learning purposes (Egbert, ElTurki, Hussein and Muthrakrishnan 2012). In other places, such as Taiwan, language learning technologies are often lab-based; this is a very different context than, for example, a one-computer classroom or mobile-focused learning and comes with its own challenges.

The purpose of this chapter is to suggest effective strategies for technology use in varied technology contexts. The first section briefly discusses the different types of technological contexts where language learning takes place and some of the challenges found in these contexts. Next, goals for the use of technology in language learning are described. Finally, the chapter addresses specific educational settings to examine how teachers might use technology to meet the goals for language learning whatever the technological context.

## Understanding varied contexts for technology

Cummins, Brown and Sayers (2007) point out that, although governments' emphasis worldwide on the use of technology to enhance teaching and learning has equipped schools with more technology, teachers are not necessarily using the technology effectively. They argue that it is more important for teachers to use technology effectively than to buy more computers for schools. Egbert and Yang (2004) agree, claiming that the important difference among language learning contexts is not the ownership of hardware and software, which comprises what others have called the 'digital divide'. Rather, the issue is whether language teachers are provided with development opportunities to help students learn with available technologies. They noted:

> This divide is the result in part of the current emphasis on emerging technologies in the CALL literature and in CALL language teacher development that seems to indicate that

good CALL activities and lessons can only be carried out with the use of advanced and cutting-edge technologies . . . Given the reality that technology in many countries as well as in many ESL classrooms in the United States remains limited, this focus does not provide consideration for the majority of language teachers who work in contexts without cutting-edge technologies and de facto creates its own kind of covert digital divide in language classrooms.

*(Egbert and Yang 2004: 281)*

Further, they assert that it is critical to understand the challenges in varied technology contexts in order to make good use of technology for language teaching.

Egbert and Yang (2004) point out a variety of language classroom technology contexts that might be considered limited in some way, which they characterise as varied from the 'ideal' CALL classroom with new technologies, unlimited access and well-educated teachers. They focus on these challenges:

- Limited general access to technology
- Limited Internet connections
- No software
- Old software
- Mandated software
- Limited hardware
- Set curriculum
- Limited time
- Large classes
- Limited teacher training
- Limited funding for any aspect of technology
- Limited administrative support
- Lack of culturally relevant electronic resources
- Student lack of strategies for electronic media use.

These challenges have a variety of causes, from government reluctance to allow open resources to lack of funding in specific schools. Others have to do with how the process of education is conducted in some places. However, the point is that they vary, and each of these challenges can be addressed with thoughtful planning, creativity and an understanding of the goals of technology use.

## Goals for technology use

Regardless of the context, the purpose of technology use in language classrooms is to support learning. Learning happens when teachers offer their learners engaging opportunities (Spolsky 1989; Csikszentmihalyi 1990; Lin 2012), regardless of the technology that exists. Engagement, in general, suggests that learners are deeply involved in a task. According to the literature, this requires learners to perceive themselves capable of the task; to see value, purpose, and use in the task; to be free from anxiety during the task; and to have appropriate and relevant feedback (Meltzer and Hamann 2004; Egbert, Hanson-Smith and Chao 2007). Overall, an engaging task is authentic, meaningful and doable for students. Used well, technology can help support and provide engaging tasks for learners, regardless of whether it is cutting-edge or not-so-new.

Engaging tasks, Egbert claims, can help language teachers succeed in any technological context, but especially those where:

> the use of any digital technology (i.e., old, new, computer, cell phone, calculator) makes language learning more effective (leads to greater success by, for example, providing challenge, differentiating, supplying access to otherwise inaccessible interactions or data) and/or more efficient (speeds the rate of learning by, for example, allowing students and teachers to spend more time on effective language-focused tasks) in pursuit of whatever language and content goals, objectives, and standards are to be achieved.
>
> *(Egbert 2010: 2)*

In other words, when the use of technology makes the language task more engaging or more effective, greater learner achievement can be expected. On the other hand, when technology does not lead to engaging, effective and/or efficient language tasks, other materials should be considered.

## CALL in varied technology contexts

Based on Egbert and Yang's list of the challenges in varied technology language contexts and the goals for technology use outlined previously, this section describes classroom examples with multiple challenges and presents what effort was or can be made to solve the problem(s) and enhance language learning.

### *Primary and secondary education examples*

The following examples come from the limited literature available that addresses varied technology contexts directly.

#### Distance learning in rural Colombia

Nelson (2010) reports that he was invited to work as a voluntary technology consultant to set up a computer lab and English language teaching facilities located near Vélez, Colombia. The El Camino Foundation ran a small group or tutorial-based distance learning high school programme for about 5,000 students in remote rural areas as well as a residential school based on foreign donations and government support. Foreign donations were made to build a computer lab for computer and language skills teaching. Because the government mandated the curriculum to include English and information technology, the Foundation administrators thought a computer lab would be essential. The Foundation also wanted students in the residential school to have access to computers and to provide professional training to tutors on how to use computers for language teaching; however, they did not have money for computer hardware, software and skilled system administrators who could maintain the programme and also conduct teacher training. Due to the political situation in Colombia, the system administrator they hired was suddenly picked up on the street and conscripted into the army, a situation which made it hard for the Foundation to find good system administrators who could stay for long. Also, there was almost no Internet in the town where the Foundation was located. Another concern was related to the Colombian cultural context in which people do not often value technology very much. For example, one student took a computer mouse from the lab to use it as a clothesline, and people often wanted to use the lab for purposes they thought more important than learning about language or technology. Overall, the challenges in this context that provided barriers to effective and engaging technology use included limited general access to the lab, limited hardware and software, limited Internet connection, limited administrative support, limited funding, limited teacher/tutor training and cultural attitudes.

In order to solve these problems and meet the goals for technology use, project members:

- *asked for donations* of computers and called for volunteers. Although only five old computers in the residential school were available at the beginning, several computers were donated. Also, the Foundation had highly trained volunteers from other countries. Jeff Nelson was one of them and he set up the lab and gave teachers workshops on how to use computers for language teaching. In addition, he trained system administrators from the local town so they could gradually take over the system management and teacher training work.
- *started with what they had*. In order to set up a lab at virtually no cost, Jeff used the free open-source Linux operating system until more funding became available for Windows stations. Although the staff member they hired was not familiar with the system and thus had to be trained to use it well, it was cost-effective considering the lack of funding for system software. Also, Jeff connected multiple computers under one control server since most computers were old and not very reliable. In this way, old computers could run stably under one powerful central server.
- *used cheap and simple equipment*. Since available technology and funding were very limited, Jeff felt it was better to use simple technology which was cheap, stable, easy to learn and light to travel with, so students in remote rural towns could access the technology. For example, he purchased several used Alphasmart intelligent keyboards at $20 on eBay for writing classes. This hardware is similar to an ordinary computer keyboard but with a monochrome monitor to show the texts that the users type. Since it was very light, tutors in remote rural towns could check it out easily for their classes, which allowed the students with no access to the lab to access technology; students then had access to writing support and could learn basic technology skills. Since the Alphasmart was very popular with students and teachers in general, the Foundation purchased more to make them available for more classes.
- *provided teachers with training*. While Jeff was providing teachers with information technology (IT) workshops, he trained local staff who could travel to teach IT classes to teachers who could not come to the workshops. In this way, teachers could learn skills required to teach their classes without spending time travelling long distances to visit the lab, and the teacher trainer could provide more contextualised training based on the teaching context.
- *considered sociocultural/sociopolitical contexts before setting up a lab*. Considering cultural contexts in Colombia, the Foundation built computer tables with concrete and fixed the computers and other hardware to the tables; thus people could not take the technology or other physical resources away or reconfigure the lab to use it for other purposes. Also, after the male staff member was drafted by the army, they hired a female system administrator from the local town to avoid further disruptions to the project (there were strict male conscription policies in place at the time). As more funding and equipment became available, additional resources and skilled personnel were added.

Overall, this context provided the place for innovative and effective uses of technology for language learning. For example, by providing teachers with development opportunities, the project made it more likely that teachers would be able to engage students with the technology. In addition, effectiveness and efficiency were enhanced by using technology that was simple and aimed directly at writing in English. Although some educators would see this as a limited technology context, the available and varied technology, used well, made it possible to meet not only government mandates but administrative objectives as well.

## An urban elementary school context in Korea

In a very different context, Kim (2007) explains that Miss Lee was an English language teacher in Seoul, South Korea. According to Kim, in South Korea, the set curriculum by the Korean Ministry of Education mandates teaching English to third and fourth graders for at least one hour a week and to fifth and sixth graders for at least two hours a week. Furthermore, they strongly recommend that English teachers use information and communications technologies (ICT) for teaching; they provided a CD-ROM along with the English textbook. Miss Lee used the CD-ROM, like many other English teachers in Korea, because it was free and easy to use. It included videos of new vocabulary, dialogues and quizzes for each unit of the textbook. Although lab access was limited, each classroom had a computer connected to the Internet for teachers, so teachers could easily use it to do drills and practice in class. However, problems arose when Miss Lee found the vocabulary and sentences in the dialogues too easy for her students, in particular the sixth graders. This is because many students in urban Seoul area start to learn English early through private lessons. This caused an 'English divide' – a gap in English language achievement between students studying in Seoul and those from other provinces. Since the textbooks and the curriculum targeted the average student, the language goals for each chapter in the textbook were not very challenging for Miss Kim's students. Thus, she wanted to find other English language software for her sixth graders. However, there were some other concerns since she was going to use it in the school context. First, the software had to meet the goals and class time in the set curriculum from the Ministry of Education. Second, it had to be culturally responsive to the Korean context, unlike overseas software that was not very connected to Korean students' lives and cultures. Third, it had to be within the school's funding limits for teaching materials and ICT resources. In addition, she wanted to find software that provided more content and cognitive challenge than just language skill teaching, so her students would be more engaged.

The description of the context reveals challenges to engaging and effective technology use such as a set curriculum, mandated (or strongly recommended) software, large classes, limited funding, lack of culturally responsive resources, lack of cognitive challenge, limited access to technology and limited time for using technology. In order to overcome the challenges, Kim (2007) explains that Miss Lee:

- *asked for help.* Miss Lee discussed the issue with experts, school administrators, and parents. She found out about e-APPLE, an electronic news in education (e-NIEs) resource, through Professor Kim, who was conducting an e-APPLE project funded by her university and a news company. Miss Lee was very interested in the project and wanted to participate. After discussion with her school principal, she was given approval to use e-APPLE instead of the software the school mandated.
- *used software that can be easily integrated into the set curriculum.* There was some alternative English teaching software to serve the set curriculum, and e-APPLE was one of these. It provided lesson plans and activities for the whole class time to meet the curriculum goals for each grade and level. Thus, it could meet the goals of the curriculum and was relatively easy to adapt to her classes.
- *used software that included students' cultures and language.* Unlike other e-NIEs available in Korea, e-APPLE was developed by a Korean university with a news company, and thus it

included content related to Korean cultures and both Korean and English language. For example, one of the activities students liked was making a Mother's Day carnation after watching a video; this video included both Korean and American cultures. In Korea, there is no Mother's Day, but there is Parents' Day, and making carnations for Parents' Day is a common cultural activity for Korean children.
- *integrated engaging opportunities into language teaching.* Kim's research found that students were most engaged when Miss Lee taught a problem-solving activity, 'Seven Wonders of the World', which required students to decipher codes after watching a video about how to decipher old Egyptian numbers. This suggests that just like in the traditional language classroom, in CALL classes the use of technology can support integrating cognitive challenges and other aspects of engaging tasks.
- *was flexible and creative.* Although the lessons were designed to fit English classroom contexts in Korea, there were some difficulties in applying the lesson plans and the activities to her lessons without modifications. For example, some news articles and videos were too long and difficult, and took more time than she expected. Thus, she was selective with the activities in the lesson and modified some activities to serve her class better. For example, after watching the video about 'Seven Wonders of the World', she expanded the activity and told the students to create their own codes, which students also found engaging, according to Kim's research.
- *used paper-based materials.* Since the classroom has only one computer, which could be accessed only by the teacher, for newspaper reading activities after the video Miss Lee printed out the online newspaper and activities; thus all the students could have access to what was displayed on the monitor.

This context was quite different from that which Jeff Nelson faced in Colombia. However, the challenges required the same kind of initiative and creativity on the part of the teacher. Miss Lee was able to integrate authentic, meaningful and challenging tasks for her students and still stay within government and administrative guidelines. Not every teacher has a Dr Kim or a supportive administration to turn to, and another classroom with these same basic challenges may find different solutions. Important, regardless, is the focus on effective uses of technology so that students will be engaged and learn.

## *Varied technology in adult language education*

This section suggests strategies for technology use in varied technology contexts for teaching languages to adults. The examples are based on two CALL contexts: (1) an English as a second language (ESL) family literacy program in the United States and (2) a university in Turkey.

### Family literacy program in Santa Barbara, California

Herrity, Ho, Dixon and Brown (2006) describe a Santa Barbara elementary school where teaching is in English only, like most schools in California. Many students, particularly those from language-minority groups, struggled because they did not have basic English language skills. Also, because of the growth in technology, students were required to learn additional literacy skills such as digital literacy and media literacy, as well as the traditional literacy of reading and writing. Since many students' parents did not have the necessary literacy and English language skills to help their children, it was difficult for them to be involved in their children's academic literacy development. The Verizon Foundation provided $160,000 to the Gevirtz Research

Center and its collaborating schools in Santa Barbara County to provide quality literacy education for minority families to enhance (1) their multiple literacies, (2) English language proficiency, (3) home environment/culture, (4) parental involvement and (5) a sense of belonging to the community. The context of the focal elementary school reveals challenges such as the lack of culturally responsive resources/teaching and lack of students' and parents' strategies for electronic media use.

In order to deal with the challenges suggested, the program created the Parents, Children, and Computers Project which includes:

- *computer literacy classes for parents and their children*. It taught them how to use computers, the Internet and software for publication.
- *authentic tasks*. Parents and children worked together to write articles or fun stories based on their home cultures using the technology introduced in the class.
- *experience/interest/knowledge of family members*. Researchers found that by building upon family culture, interests and experience – in other words, engaging participants – in their first language, the project helped increase children's respect for their parents and parents' confidence; they suggested that this could lead to more active parent participation in the school and local community.

Funding from outside sources can sometimes fill needs that local governments or schools cannot. Of course, this project did not solve all of the school's issues, and additional solutions could have been sought. For example, the programme could have awarded parents a certificate for computer literacy and materials development, which could boost their confidence and sense of belonging to their community and allow inclusion in the parents' résumés. Expert groups of parents and children who had been through the programme could be viewed as a resource and tapped to work with the next group of participants and so on. However, the focus on families instead of just the children in this context was a creative and effective use of both funding and technology.

### University in eastern Turkey

In a language teacher education programme in a university in eastern Turkey, technology is not used either as a means of instruction or as the focus. Although there is much interest in the idea, Internet access at the university is limited to a few small labs, not many students have smartphones (or any kind of mobile phone) due to the huge expense, and electricity is unreliable. Still, the teacher education students are committed to engaging their future K-12 students in any way possible, and they are willing to try new things. The teacher educators, on the other hand, each have a computer in their office with intermittent Internet access, and most of them have smartphones. However, many of them look with scepticism on the use of technology in their instruction, and they do not ask the teacher education students to think about CALL for their future classrooms. This situation presents another kind of divide, between those who want to use CALL and those who do not perceive a need. This does not mean that the teacher education students do not have recourse to learn about CALL, only that they have challenges in getting access, finding and integrating resources, and helping their professors understand their points of view. Solutions for both teacher educators and teacher education students include:

- *taking advantage of technologies outside of the university context*. In the area of this university, there are a number of Internet cafés that offer inexpensive access to resources. Sometimes a printout of a web-based activity can be more effective than what is found in the regular textbook, and CALL educators can find these all over the Internet. For example, song lyrics sheets can be used along with an analogue tape recorder to learn songs in English, and printed idiom cards with pictures can help students learn informal language.

- *learning to work in a one-computer classroom.* Many educators have long championed the use of one computer for language teaching, and lessons abound that can be used successfully with one computer (see e.g. Teacher Tap at http://eduscapes.com/tap/topic84.htm and LT Technologies at http://www.lttechno.com/links/onecomputerclassroom.html). Many of these ideas work even without Internet access. Professors can take their computer to their classroom and use it in a variety of effective ways using these resources.
- *considering alternative technologies.* Although the use of computers and the Internet can help students acquire new literacies and engage in learning, their absence does not mean that engaging learning cannot take place. Teachers can teach effectively without using digital technologies, and they can also consider the use of time-tested technologies in new ways. For example, tape recorders, rather than being used only for listening exercises, can be used effectively for audio dialog journals (Akef and Nossratpour 2010), and overhead projectors can be used to provide visual support for any lesson. A quick Internet search uncovers multitudes of uses for these two tools.

Every CALL context is different, and teachers can explore ways to recognise the needs and challenges in their own classrooms. Lack of optimal technology-enhanced language learning environments can actually be an advantage when it supports teachers in looking carefully at the resources that are available and ways in which they can be used effectively and engagingly.

## Teacher development in varied technology contexts

Other chapters in this handbook (see Hanson-Smith, Chapter 15) describe teacher education and development that can occur in contexts with access to technology and opportunities for teacher educators to work with future and current teachers. However, even when such opportunities are not available, teachers have many resources to help them learn about and develop their knowledge of language teaching with technology. This section presents two very different examples; one concerns a high school teacher in the United States and the other a university teacher in Sudan.

### *A rural high school in the US Pacific Northwest*

Huff (2010) provides an example of Anne, a high school ESL teacher in a school context with few opportunities for professional development in technology use. Her school provided a computer lab for the class and money for software, but she rarely used the computers in her classes. Her school administrators and other teachers with more knowledge of technology encouraged her to integrate technology into her curriculum; however, they did not provide her with practical guidelines. Although she was excited about the benefits of using technology to teach language, she did not know how to use it effectively. Determined to implement CALL in her classes, she bought a software package that was highly recommended for fun and engaging English language teaching; however, her students were not engaged. She blamed her lack of experience and skills with technology, especially compared to her students, and her lack of CALL training. The biggest challenge Anne was facing in trying to engage her students with CALL was her own lack of professional development. Although her school provided her with a computer lab to enhance language teaching, they did not guide her in how to use technology and what software to use; this forced Anne, with her very limited knowledge, to make her own decisions.

# Varied technology contexts

In order for Anne to gain the skills and knowledge she needed, Huff (2010) makes two main suggestions:

- *Internet research.* According to Huff, there are many online opportunities for development, such as exploring free educational software, online tutorials, and CALL journals. For example, free Internet journals such as *CALL EJ* (http://tell.is.ritsumei.ac.jp/allejonline/index.php) and *Language Learning & Technology* (http://llt.msu.edu/) provide research on language classroom applications of technology and reviews on new language teaching software. Also, Atomic Learning (http://movies.atomiclearning.com/k-12/home) and other websites provide a range of tutorials both for beginners and more skilled users. Huff cautions CALL beginners like Anne not to get too intimidated by the large number of resources and opportunities to learn about CALL applications on the Web. According to Huff, it is important to try a few resources and tools suggested and gain some understanding of the technology available.
- *Collaboration.* Although the Internet covers a wide range of resources and tools, it may not be the best solution to Anne's problems because of the wide range of possibilities and her limited knowledge. She might not be able to find resources that fit her situation well and she might need others' help with her professional development. In these cases, collaboration might be a solution. Huff focuses on four ways of collaborating:
    - *Online teacher collaboration.* There are many online teacher communities providing support for teachers' use of technology in classes. Huff proposes Tapped In (http://www.tappedin.or), MERLOT (http://www.merlot.org), the Webheads in Action group (http://webheadsinaction.org) and the Becoming a Webhead course (http://baw09.pbworks.com) as examples. These online resources have spaces for content-specific discussions where teachers can help each other and exchange ideas on educational technology.
    - *Book groups.* Anne can join a book study with other interested teachers at her school or in the district to explore CALL. She can read books on CALL professional development to learn step-by-step and exchange thoughts and ideas with the teachers in the group who share similar teaching contexts and goals.
    - *Administrative support.* Anne can ask school administers for support. She can discuss her problems and ask what they can do to help her. For example, they might be able to arrange a teachers' meeting for CALL professional development.
    - *Local community support.* Anne can seek help from the local community because community organisations, universities or businesses are often interested in partnering with schools on a variety of projects. Community members might not know about teaching, but they could provide teachers with opportunities to develop technology skills and experiences.

Of course, Anne should also call on the expertise of her students to help her learn and collaborate about engaging CALL tasks. This could be the simplest and most effective way to work with students and provide authenticity and challenge.

## Universities in Khartoum, Sudan

Fawzi (2010) describes the context of teaching general English and English for specific purposes (ESP) classes to adults in Sudan. Most university students in Sudan are required to take

ESP courses because the Ministry of Education places great emphasis on English language education. Also, organisations like UNICEF and UNESCO Khartoum provided computers for schools and universities to help fulfil the policy requiring computers for classes. However, from her research with university English teachers, Fawzi found people's pedagogical awareness of CALL very low since it was still new to the country. Many teachers believed that CALL was something very different from language teaching. Also, although technology was available in fairly good labs, there was little administrative support for the technological problems that occurred during classes. Another problem in this context was teachers' limited time and lack of financial compensation; most university English teachers in Sudan teach many classes in multiple universities because one university does not pay them enough to support themselves. Integrating CALL into the curriculum was not compensated, and it appeared to the teachers to involve a lot of hard work and problems with no one to help. In addition, although the Internet was available, not all the resources were culturally appropriate for Sudanese students. In fact, YouTube was prohibited in Sudan because some of the videos went against local Islamic beliefs. As a result, many teachers were apprehensive about exposing their students to the Internet, and thus they found it challenging to select appropriate Internet materials with no morally questionable aspects.

According to Fawzi's description of the context, its main challenges were limited teacher training, limited administrative support and lack of culturally relevant electronic resources. In order to address the challenges discussed earlier, Fawzi suggested that the universities or the Ministry of Education should consider:

- *providing financial compensation or advantages for employment.* Teachers might feel motivated if they are paid for developing computer skills or if many universities give more credit to teachers with experience in integrating CALL when recruiting teachers.
- *providing online teacher training programmes and professional workshops.* There are some benefits of online teacher training programmes. First, a good online training programme can serve as a practical model of effective use of educational technology, considering both pedagogical and technological concerns. Second, class time and space are flexible for busy teachers. Also, professional workshops provide teachers and administrators with opportunities to learn technology skills and discuss how to apply them to their own teaching contexts.
- *having student volunteers or interns for technical support.* If there is no funding available for technical staff, program administrators can employ student volunteers and interns with technology skills who major in education or educational technology or who simply have the required skills.
- *using resources available in other media as well as on the Web.* If teachers and administrators are uncomfortable using unfiltered Internet resources, they can use resources from other media such as radio/TV shows or newspapers which include students' own cultures. For example, the BBC website (http://www.bbc.co.uk/religion/religions/islam/) includes rich resources including Muslim cultures with videos, TV shows, documentaries and music. Also, there are many English language newspapers for Muslims such as *Passion Islam* (http://www.passionislam.com/), which are available online.
- *using resources created by students.* Teachers can use resources created by students. For example, students can create videos or images using Windows MovieMaker or Paint. After reading a story or article in language class, students can develop digital reflections, which can be shared in class to motivate discussion. In this way, students can connect themselves to their reading and have opportunities to be creative.

It is clear that government and administrative support can help teachers use CALL effectively and in engaging ways. However, when such support is not forthcoming, these examples show that teachers have other useful sources, such as the Internet, colleagues and even students. The unifying thread among these varied contexts is the desire of the teachers to provide students with access to language learning materials and their willingness to discover how they may do so.

## Making good use of technology

The examples of varied CALL contexts presented in this chapter reveal that first, the solutions to the challenges in CALL classrooms need to be contextualised. In other words, a solution to one context does not necessarily work well in other contexts. For example, Nelson provided Alphasmart intelligent keyboards to solve the problem caused by limited or no access to the lab. He received positive responses from administrators, teachers/tutors and students since culturally, most people placed a low value on technology and had very little experience with computers. Thus, it was necessary to let them learn basic skills like typing and to give them the opportunity to first become familiar with computers. Miss Lee, in an urban Seoul classroom context, had a totally different approach to dealing with the challenges caused by limited access to the lab. She had only one classroom computer to present videos and activities. Instead of equipping the class with more computers, she focused more on providing students with opportunities to be creative. She did not insist on using technology all the time and used printouts for students without access to the computer. As students in urban Seoul areas generally have good ICT knowledge and skills and experience in CALL classes, it was not necessary for the teachers to provide students with opportunities to become familiar with computers in the CALL classroom.

Second, the examples suggest that different technology uses can enhance students' engagement. As shown in several of the cases, what is important is not to simply provide students with more access to computers but to engage them in the lessons and to let them use language creatively. For example, audio dialogue journals can allow students to speak with the teacher or another student on a one-to-one basis, practise their language as many times as they need to in order to be satisfied with their output and have the freedom to use language creatively.

Lastly, the examples reveal the importance of collaboration in CALL professional development. From students to parents to outside sources, collaboration can change how and why technology is used and can result in effective and engaging learning. Teachers and school administrators in all CALL contexts can consider how to build local and international partnerships for effective CALL professional development.

While many governments are encouraging language teachers to integrate technology into their curricula, many teachers are experiencing challenges in making *good use* of technology. As Huff notes, 'it's easy to talk about. It is much more difficult to do it effectively' (Huff 2010: 31). As discussed, there is no one-size-fits-all solution to varied CALL classroom contexts. This chapter suggests that it is important for governments and school administrators to work with teachers in sharing issues in similar CALL contexts, discovering opportunities to collaborate and exchanging ideas about how technology can be used to enhance students' engagement in language learning.

## Further reading

Burkhart, L. (1999) *Strategies and Applications for the One Computer Classroom*, available: http://www.lburkhart.com/elem/strat.htm.
   This web page lists many uses for one computer in the classroom, from using it as a multimedia 'flipchart' to letting students use it individually to prepare for a presentation. Although it is an older site, the tasks are still very relevant for varied technology environments.

Cennamo, K. (n.d.) 'Katherine Cennamo (Author)', *Amazon.com*, available: http://www.amazon.com/Katherine-Cennamo/e/B009HX52WM (accessed 25 Jan 2016).
  Visit Amazon's Katherine Cennamo Page. Find all the books, read about the author, and more.
Ross, J. and Ertmer, P. (2007; 2nd edn 2013) *Technology Integration for Meaningful Classroom Use: A Standards-Based Approach*, Independence, KY: Cengage Learning.
  This excellent text includes a variety of ideas for how to use technology for learning regardless of the context. It includes topics from tools to creativity and guidelines for creating technology-enriched learning environments.
Warschauer, M. (2002) 'Reconceptualizing the digital divide', *First Monday*, 7(7), available: http://firstmonday.org/ojs/index.php/fm/article/view/967/888 (accessed 30 May 2013).
  This article provides a preview of Warschauer's 2004 text by addressing issues of access to technology and providing an exploration of the digital divide as a social one.
Warschauer, M. (2004) *Technology and Social Inclusion: Rethinking the Digital Divide*, Cambridge, MA: MIT Press.
  This text redefines the digital divide in social terms and explores what can be done to overcome it.

## References

Akef, K. and Nossratpour, S. (Winter 2010) 'The impact of keeping oral dialogue journals on EFL learners' oral fluency', *Journal of English Language Studies*, 1(2): 127–142.
Cummins, J., Brown, K. and Sayers, D. (2007) *Literacy, Technology, and Diversity: Teaching For Success In Changing Times*, Boston, MA: Pearson.
Csikszentmihalyi, M. (1990) *Flow: The Psychology of Optimal Experience*, New York, NY: Harper Collins.
Egbert, J. (ed) (2010) *CALL in Limited Technology Contexts*, San Marcos, TX: CALICO.
Egbert, J., ElTurki, E., Hussein, I. and Muthrakrishnan, R. (2012) 'Applying principles for new literacies in differing call contexts: Conceptualizing issues for teaching, research, and policy', *CALL-EJ*, 13(1): 1–11.
Egbert, J., Hanson-Smith, E. and Chao, C. (2007) 'Foundations of CALL', in J. Egbert and E. Hanson-Smith (eds), *CALL Environments: Research, Practice, and Critical Issues* (Chapter 1), Alexandria, VA: TESOL, Inc.
Egbert, J. and Yang, D. (2004) 'Mediating the digital divide in CALL classrooms: Promoting effective language tasks in limited technology contexts', *ReCALL Journal*, 16(2): 145–157.
Fawzi, H. (2010) 'Bleeding edge challenges in Sudan: Limits on using CALL in EFL classrooms at the tertiary level', in J. Egbert (ed), *CALL in Limited Technology Contexts*, San Marcos, TX: CALICO: 189–200.
Herrity, V.A., Ho, H-Z., Dixon, C.M. and Brown, J.H. (2006) *The Verizon OPTIONS Initiative: Supporting Families' Multiple Literacies*, Paper prepared for the American Educational Research Association Annual Meeting, San Francisco, April 7–11.
Huff, L. (2010) '"There's too much stuff": Professional development', in J. Egbert (ed), *CALL in Limited Technology Contexts*, San Marcos, TX: CALICO: 31–41.
Kim, H. (2007) 'ICT-integrated English language curriculum for elementary school students: A case study of Apple Project', *Multimedia-Assisted Language Learning*, 10(1): 177–200.
Lin, T. (2012) *Student Engagement and Motivation in the Foreign Language Classroom*, Unpublished thesis, Washington State University.
Meltzer, J. and Hamann, E. (2004) *Meeting the Needs of Adolescent English Language Learners for Literacy Development and Content Area Learning; Part One: Focus on Motivation and Engagement*, Providence, RI: Education Alliance at Brown University, Northeast and Islands Regional Educational Laboratory.
Nelson, J. (2010) 'Implementing technology in rural Colombia', in J. Egbert (ed), *CALL in Limited Technology Contexts*, San Marcos, TX: CALICO: 7–17.
Spolsky, B. (1989) *Conditions for Second Language Learning*, Oxford: Oxford University Press.
Warschauer, M. (2003) 'Dissecting the "digital divide": A case study in Egypt', *The Information Society*, 19(4): 297–304.

# 14
# Limitations and boundaries in language learning and technology

*Richard Kern and Dave Malinowski*

Technology shapes our sense of what is possible by modifying, reframing or eliminating existing limits and boundaries. For example, writing made it possible for humans to communicate beyond the limits of the here and now. The telephone allowed spoken conversation to reach far beyond the natural range of the human voice. Eyeglasses corrected poor vision, and X-rays made it possible to inspect the inside of the human body. As Marshall McLuhan (1964) put it, technologies and media are extensions of man; they extend our capabilities by overcoming the natural limitations of our bodies, our perception and our consciousness.

Great hopes have been hung on the promise of technology to improve language teaching and learning. Over the past thirty years, computer-assisted tutorials, exercises, drills, simulations, instructional games, tests and concordancers have been developed to foster students' autonomous learning. The Internet has introduced a wealth of searchable, authentic multimedia materials that have not been designed specifically for language learning but can be potentially exploited for that purpose. Email, chatrooms, online forums and social media have created spaces where language learners can meet and communicate with native speakers or other learners, inside or outside of a formal learning setting, getting practice with a wide range of genres and registers used in global communication environments.

The hopes attached to technology have been bolstered by the rhetoric of globalisation, which emphasises the erasure of national boundaries and far-reaching flows of people, goods, information and capital. Technology amplifies that rhetoric and applies it to the individual. Online, it is said, one can go anywhere, do anything, be anyone. Technology, it would seem, removes limits and dissolves boundaries. Our argument in this chapter is that the reality of technology use is more complex than that. Where technology eliminates certain limitations and boundaries, it creates others. Moreover, limits and boundaries are not always negative things; as we will see, they often give rise to inventive responses as people think of creative ways to circumvent them.

We begin by defining and exemplifying limitations and boundaries, followed by a discussion of how limitations and boundaries relate to a range of different media, and how those relations may vary across languages and cultures. We end with a prospective view of the boundaries and limitations of new technologies yet to come.

Richard Kern and Dave Malinowski

## Technology, limitations, boundaries: Examples and definitions

Let's consider two examples of teachers learning to incorporate new technologies into their teaching and some of the challenges they face. Each vignette is followed by a brief discussion, in which we offer definitions and commentaries on the two central concepts in our chapter: technology (Vignette 1) and limitations and boundaries (Vignette 2).

### Vignette 1: Nadia's experience with technology

Nadia is an experienced teacher of German at the university level. For several years, she has used the learning management system (LMS) supported on her campus to distribute her syllabi and other course materials, manage her roster, make announcements, host discussions, assign grades for assignments and exams, and perform other teaching and administrative functions. Although she and her colleagues appreciate its ease of use, she has heard that her school will soon adopt a newer LMS that offers features such as real-time monitoring of students' viewing of class materials, the ability for participants to make video and audio recordings where they had previously only been able to enter written text, and new tools for engaging in collaborative work with a variety of media and materials. Although Nadia is excited by all these new features, she is worried that the number and scope of the changes will be too much for her to follow. What, she wonders, do all these new features actually do? How is she to monitor and assess the increasing amount of student work on the new LMS? Can she continue to teach, keep attendance, and record grades as she has always done, or will she need to do more online now? Will she be able to continue using the same course design and materials, or will this change to a new technology require Nadia to rethink her German classes from the ground up?

### 'Technology': Definitions and considerations

Nadia's questions about her university's new LMS – and the struggles, accommodations and transformations that will take place in her own teaching as she learns to use it – bespeak a need to consider the meaning and significance of the term 'technology' in language teaching and learning contexts. The word *technology* comes from the Greek words *technê* (art, craft, know-how) and *logos* (word, discourse) and originally referred to a systematic treatment of grammar. It was not until the mid-19th century that technology came to refer to a science of mechanical and industrial arts, which was about the transformation of raw materials into finished products.

In recent decades, with the advent of electronic devices and digital communications tools of all sorts, theorists of technology have reminded us that it is important not just to think about hardware and software but also the linguistic, cognitive, social and behavioural practices that evolve through, around and with the use of technologies. Feenberg (2002), for instance, makes a distinction among instrumental, substantive and critical theories of technology (see Hubbard and Levy, Chapter 2, and Blin, Chapter 3 this volume for further discussion of theoretical approaches). The instrumental view sees technologies as culturally neutral tools, serving just as well in one social context as in another. The substantive view (represented in writings of Jacques Ellul and Martin Heidegger) treats technology as an autonomous cultural force that restructures the social world, creating a technology-based way of life. Feenberg proposes a third stance, which he calls a critical theory of technology. This view adopts certain aspects of the instrumental and substantive views, but sees technology as 'ambivalent' rather than 'neutral', and as a site of struggle between technology designers and users rather than as an autonomous force in and of itself.

Reflecting on Nadia's situation, an instrumental view would suggest that the new LMS will be equally beneficial for all teachers, regardless of their discipline or personal approach. This might be the view adopted by her administration or IT department, but it might be met with more scepticism by Nadia and her faculty colleagues, who might fear that some features of the new LMS could impose a particular way of teaching and interacting with students that they would not necessarily welcome (a substantive view). For example, would she feel pressured to monitor her students as they access resources, read and participate online because she *can*? Will she be forced to grade only in ways the *computer understands*? Will her workload actually increase with the new demands that the LMS places on her? A critical view would empower Nadia and her colleagues to evaluate the changes in the new LMS and to decide individually which features would in fact be useful and supportive of their teaching goals, which features would be worth trying out and which would not.

## Vignette 2: 'Limitations and boundaries' and Ayo's experience

Ayo, a seasoned university instructor of Yoruba in face-to-face classroom settings, has recently partnered with an African language programme at a neighbouring institution to offer his class to a number of students there as well. The language class is to be one of a growing number of shared courses offered for credit at both institutions, and taught synchronously with room-to-room videoconferencing. Students on both sides are able to see and hear the teacher and their peers in their respective classrooms; cameras in both classrooms can be panned and zoomed to focus on different scenes, and the teacher can broadcast an interactive whiteboard or other content from an in-room computer to the other site. Ayo has recently undergone training in the use of the videoconferencing and whiteboard tools and feels confident in his ability to perform basic operations such as dialling the partner classroom, muting and enabling both rooms' microphones and selecting the appropriate output source. But as his class begins and he strives to teach in his usually interactive, student-centred and fast-paced style, he wonders how this is to work in practice. Because he has no physical access to the students on the other side, Ayo has to devise new ways to distribute handouts, assignments and quizzes ahead of class time, and to collect them at a distance after class has finished. In his traditional classes, Ayo can move among his students and have them move about as well, but in his shared classroom clearly they cannot. To compensate, he often tries to address the distally located students directly by speaking at the camera, but this requires that he turn his body and his gaze away from the students nearby. Although there is usually little perceptible delay between image and sound across classrooms, he has noticed that it is difficult to know where students are looking, and even more challenging to facilitate dialogue and pair work across the video connection. At the same time that Ayo teaches his lesson, he has to constantly select what (and how much, at what angle) the screens in both classrooms are to show, while never being entirely sure that students on both sides can see and hear the same thing. Although Ayo hears that monitoring his and his students' images on the screen will eventually become second nature, he meanwhile struggles to keep his mind on the lesson and his focus in the moment.

## 'Limitations and boundaries': Definitions and considerations

Ayo's use of videoconferencing to teach Yoruba simultaneously on two campuses shows how using technology to overcome certain boundaries and limitations gives rise to others. The networked cameras, screens, microphones and speakers in the two classrooms eliminate the distance between students and teacher with respect to their synchronous, spoken communication. But, as illustrated earlier, this distance becomes a barrier again every time Ayo and his students carry out the everyday tasks of the language classroom. At a more general level, Ayo and his students must all learn how to learn in a mediated environment that is marked by persistent uncertainty about who can see and hear what at any moment in time.

Boundaries and limitations can be identified in a variety of domains: spatial, temporal, cultural, material, virtual, cultural and human. 'Limitation', and 'boundary' especially, are terms that derive their original meanings from constraints on physical movement and geographic markers of the sort that have for centuries set one territory apart from another. In the spaces and screens of the language classroom, boundaries and limitations are physical realities, as we have seen in the case of Ayo's shared Yoruba class: TVs, projector screens and computer monitors are examples of the *interface*, which Friedberg (2006: 220) defines as 'a geometric term for the surface that forms the common boundary between two three-dimensional figures'. While opening up new vistas and opportunities for language students, interfaces also powerfully constrain perspective, as Friedberg illustrates by extending Wittgenstein's epigram, 'The limits of my language are the limits of my world', to its visual corollary: 'the limits and multiplicities of our frames of vision determine the boundaries of our world' (Friedberg 2006: 7).

Just as they can be seen as pervasive physical elements of the mechanically, electrically and digitally tool-rich world, boundaries and limitations may also be understood as powerful metaphors, organising disparate facets of language learners' and teachers' experience. Warschauer illustrates this point with respect to the notion of 'access' as he argues that securing learners' ability to utilise information and communication technology is not a one-dimensional affair:

> Meaningful access to ICT comprises far more than merely providing computers and Internet connections. Rather, access to ICT is embedded in a complex array of factors encompassing physical, digital, human, and social resources and relationships. Content and language, literacy and education, and community and institutional structures must all be taken into account if meaningful access to new technologies is to be provided.
> 
> *(Warschauer 2003: 6)*

As video, audio, and virtual mediation becomes more and more salient in today's language classrooms, identifying invisible boundaries may be just as crucial for language learners as overcoming the visible ones. In the next section, we present a conceptual model to facilitate this task.

## *The kaleidoscope of boundaries: A metaphor for thinking about technological ecologies*

In their critique of what they term the 'technocratic', instrumental perspective on educational technologies, Burbules and Callister (2000: 15) write, 'The dangers and possibilities of information and communication technologies are not opposed to one another – they are aspects of one and the same capacities. We cannot simplistically choose one over the other'. This is, as Burbules and Callister term it, a *relational* view of technology, one that sees people as culturally, psychologically and physically changed by the technologies they use, and one that posits that 'choices in technology use (to the extent that these are consciously and collectively decided) always stand in relation to a whole host of other changing practices and social processes' (Burbules and Callister 2000: 6–7).

In the previous section, we suggested that as spatial, temporal, cultural and material boundaries are overcome by the use of technology, others arise in the process. In this section, we develop a model for visualising this relationship, and present examples for consideration in Table 14.1.

*Table 14.1* Examples of technology both creating and transcending limits and boundaries

| Boundaries/limits blurred/overcome by technology | Boundaries/limits created by technology |
| --- | --- |
| Spatial boundaries, e.g. geographical, national borders, local (rooms/labs) | Interface constraints (window and screen size, view frame, hardware/software features and functionality); limitations to in-class mobility, mutuality of perception |
| Temporal boundaries, e.g. international time zones, what is 'in-class' and 'out-of-class' time | Constraints on modes and forms of expression (e.g. capacity of the medium to represent speech, writing, gesture, graphics) |
| Linguistic boundaries made permeable by online automated translation, cross-linguistic dictionaries | Variable access to Internet, hardware, software; learners' decreased access to and awareness of context, connotation, contingency in language use |
| Material boundaries between image, sound, video, etc. blurred by common digital data structure | Constraints related to users' digital literacies and technological know-how |
| Intra- and extra-institutional roles and relationships transformed: teacher-student; classroom-community, etc., leading to greater individual access and power | Variable access and accessibility to facilities, tools, networks; privatisation of knowledge and resources; redistribution of institutional authority |
| Text boundaries: in the case of hypertext, where does 'the text' end? Textual practices reimagined, with focus on procedural knowledge | Search, filtering, censorship of content assume new roles and authority; divisions between 'writers' and 'designers', 'authors' and 'coders' |
| Boundaries between author and reader – production and consumption are blurred by social media, computer-mediated communication (CMC), hypertext | Keyboard configuration (e.g. alphabetic keyboard for nonalphabetic writing systems), character encoding, online language support etc. highly unequal among languages |

The examples in Table 14.1 are just a few of the changes that can attend the use of technology in language teaching. Yet if we imagine ways in which items from each of these two columns relate to one another in practice, visualising hypothetical paths of movement between elements on the left and the right, we can appreciate that there might be patterns that appear and disappear with some regularity, much as what one sees as one turns a kaleidoscope. These shifting patterns are illustrated in Figure 14.1, with solid lines representing various kinds of boundaries that are blurred through the use of a given technology at a certain time and place, and dashed lines representing boundaries of a different nature emerging in their place.

As anyone who has looked through a kaleidoscope can attest, the coloured patterns that are visible in any one fixed position change in size, shape and complexity as the shaft is twisted. Some colours and shapes disappear quickly, others bloom with a flourish, while still others that were previously invisible suddenly emerge. Importantly, there is always opposition between different colours and different shapes. Moreover, it is not the static view of a particular patterned configuration of shapes and colours that is so pleasing to the eye; rather, it is the dynamic morphing and emergence of new patterns that delights the viewer.

It is precisely this kind of dynamic disappearance and emergence among patterns of cultural, temporal, spatial, linguistic and subjective relations that is brought about through the introduction and use of various technologies for language teaching and learning. Moreover, just as each

*Figure 14.1* Kaleidoscope analogy

person who picks up and views the kaleidoscope will see something different from what others see, each language learner, teacher and administrator will experience the use – and limitations – of any given technological medium in a unique way. Teachers' experiences of technology are particularly complex because they often play several roles simultaneously: they manage students' behaviour, facilitate their learning by directing activities, serve as resources and mentors and evaluate their students' performance. A given use of technology may look different from the perspective of each of these roles. For example, in Nadia's case, we saw that the LMS offered new tools for administering her class. If these tools are easy to learn, we might assume they would support Nadia's administrative role. However, there may be little in the LMS that she finds useful in her role as instructor and mentor. Moreover, if the LMS's administrative features are too overwhelming, time-consuming or hard to adapt to, they might not support that role at all – and the distraction might be detrimental to her instructional role as well.

## The relational nature of limitations

Among the many technological platforms that have been used for language learning over the past several decades, each one presents potential benefits as well as limitations. So, for example, writing email or text messages, participating in online forums and communicating in online chatrooms all encourage dialogic written exchange, but they tend to affect how language is used differently. Factors such as the synchronicity of writing (e.g. email tends to be asynchronous, whereas chat is typically synchronous), length of messages, size of audience, anonymity of participants, purpose, genre and tone of expression each enable certain kinds of interaction and learning while constraining others (see Herring 2007).

Limitations are often subtle. In the case of videoconferencing, for example, participants think of their interaction occurring in real time, like face-to-face interaction, yet the audio and visual signals they perceive are always slightly delayed due to transmission distance and bandwidth limitations. Most of the time, this delay is inconsequential, but sometimes it leads to disfluencies and confusion: one may wonder if the interlocutor's smile, gesture or facial expression is in response to what one is saying right now (as one is speaking) or whether it is in response to what one said previously. Often it is unclear whether one is making the appropriate discursive linkages, and videoconferencing thus asks for a greater degree of interpretive flexibility than face-to-face conversation.

It is important, however, not to conceive of potential benefits and limitations in static, absolute terms (i.e. 'these are the benefits of this medium, and these are its limitations'). Rather, benefits and limitations need to be understood in a dynamic, context-specific way (i.e. in this particular context, with this particular task and with these particular students, medium X supports these particular learning goals). For example, Constantin de Chanay (2011) shows how two students asked to write a summary of their videoconferencing session used a chat window that was integrated into the videoconferencing interface. What they wrote as 'chat' was radically different from what one normally recognises as 'chat', in that it involved a formal register and appeared as a monologic text that was perfectly typical in terms of the institutionally based expectations of the 'summary' genre. Indeed, in Japan, best-selling novels have been written (and read) on mobile phones (Onishi 2008). Because it is not only the medium but also the genre demands that shape discourse, it is important to recognise that mediums can be called into action to do things that are not typically done in that medium.

Furthermore, features that people typically assume to be advantageous may sometimes turn out to impede communication and learning. Videoconferencing, for example, ostensibly affords ideal conditions for communication at a distance because participants can see and hear one another in real time. However, some studies of videoconferencing interactions reveal that sometimes what appears on the screen (and what is heard online) is misinterpreted because of ambiguities introduced by the medium itself (Malinowski 2011; Kern 2014). A tutor who sees her student looking at the screen as she talks to him on Skype assumes he is looking at her, but when she gets no response to her questions, she wonders if there is a problem with the sound. Unbeknownst to her, the student is watching a music video that the tutor had mentioned moments earlier. The window for the video covers the Skype window on the student's screen, so he actually cannot see her, and the sound of the video obscures the tutor's voice. Here, the features of the technological system literally block communication while giving the appearance of facilitating it.

Conversely, technological limitations can sometimes produce positive outcomes if they spur creative innovation and learning. Let's consider another videoconferencing example: during an exchange between language learners and tutors, the sound went out due to a server problem. The students and their tutors were confronted with having to rely on alternative channels to communicate. They immediately responded creatively with gestures, handwritten signs held up in front of the webcam, and especially written chat, which became the mainstream channel for the remainder of the session. What was interesting was the effect this shift to writing had on the pedagogical dynamics of the interactions our research team observed. In one case, a student's query about a vocabulary item led the tutor to teach her how to swear in French. In another case, the student persisted in asking about personal side topics the tutor had introduced earlier in the interaction, even after the tutor had moved to the formal lesson content of the day. In a follow-up interview, this student remarked on how much he had enjoyed this 'written' session because (1) it was easier for him to write in French than to speak and (2) because 'it was much more cultural than the other sessions'. To speculate a bit, it might be the case that if the tutor had established the topic in speech it would have had a more authoritative effect and that the student would have gone along with the lesson (since that was what had been observed in earlier sessions). Similarly, the first tutor might be less likely to teach his student how to swear if they were using spoken language. In other words, the distance provided by writing may have made it 'safe' to swear and made it 'safe' to deviate from the tutor's lesson. In this context, writing allowed a certain degree of transgressiveness that learners found to be very productive.

Taken together, these examples illustrate that limitations are not necessarily intrinsic to the technological medium itself. Rather, they are found in the interaction between the material medium, an individual user and a particular context of use.

## Limited by language: Separate worlds of technology

Pointing to the global imbalance of languages on the Internet, and particularly to the early dominance of English online, Danet and Herring (2007: 4) wrote that 'hundreds of millions of people are already participating online today in languages other than English, in some form of non-native English, or in a mixture of languages, and this trend is projected to continue in the years to come'. By 2008, China had replaced the United States as the country with most users (17.0% of the worldwide total compared to 13.4% in the United States), while India and Japan held the third and fourth largest positions (Computer Industry Almanac). Another current index of the presence of multiple languages online, *List of Wikipedias*, shows a growing diversity as well: wikipedias exist in 287 different languages, including 11 languages with 1,000,000 or more articles, and an additional 41 languages with 100,000 articles or more.

Such statistics point to what Leppänen and Peuronen (2012: 2) describe as the first of two perspectives on 'multilingualism on the Internet': that of the 'visibility, accessibility and status' of the various languages used for communications on the Internet. The second phenomenon, that of the actual multilingual practices of Internet users, can be considerably more difficult to assess on a large scale. Yet it is this second perspective on multilingualism on the Internet – in particular, language learners' and teachers' personal experiences and online practices – that informs our discussion in this section of technological limitations that can vary by language. In the ensuing discussion, we focus on three sample issues that give a sense of the extent to which limitations and possibilities may be linked to specific languages.

## Language and the computer keyboard

The notion that some machines are better suited to represent certain peoples and cultures appears to fly in the face of the universalist, technocratic perspective behind many of the tools and conveniences we use today, but a quick exploration of keyboard design should give us pause for thought. The QWERTY keyboard used in English-speaking parts of the world was originally intended to slow typists' fingers by arranging the letters in an unfamiliar pattern, to avoid jamming the typewriter's typebars. Although typewriters have disappeared, and despite rival key layouts shown to be more efficient (e.g. the Dvorak keyboard), QWERTY persists on today's digital keyboards. However, different languages use different layouts (e.g. French uses AZERTY, Italian uses QZERTY), and this can present mild challenges to learners who must type on foreign keyboards. Much more significant, however, are the limitations of the computer keyboard for nonalphabetic languages. Unlike the technologies of handwriting and print, which do not favour certain scripts over others, typewriter and digital keyboards have a clear structural bias towards alphabetic writing. Typing also imposed horizontal writing, which clashed with languages such as Japanese that were most commonly formatted vertically – a clash that has been resolved with computer technology. Japanese computer keyboards retain the QWERTY keyboard, but they also print *kana* characters on the keys, facilitating the inputting of multiple scripts. Writing Chinese involves a more complex process. The most common way to write Chinese characters on computers is to use the standard Roman alphabet keys on a QWERTY keyboard to write in pinyin (Roman phonetic transliteration), which activates a menu of Chinese characters that correspond to that phonetic representation. The user then chooses the appropriate Chinese character from the menu, and this is inserted into the text. An alternative procedure (called Wubi) maps components of Chinese characters (radicals and strokes) onto the QWERTY keyboard. One enters these character components in the same sequence as one would handwrite them on paper. As these examples show, particular technologies may impose more obstacles for certain languages than for others. Nevertheless, people inevitably work around technological limitations in culturally specific ways.

## *Availability of pedagogical materials*

In a 2005 UNESCO report, John Paolillo asked: 'Has linguistic difference become a barrier to information access, that provides unfair advantages to some, and disadvantages to others?' (Paolillo 2005: 44). While the status and implications of the 'digital divide' have been debated widely (and have changed substantially over the years), this question is of continued significance to language learners and teachers who want to find, create, edit and share learning materials.

The lack of resources to support the learning of less commonly taught languages (LCTLs) has been frequently noted (e.g. MLA Ad Hoc Committee on Foreign Languages 2007; Jackson and Malone 2009). Garrett (2009: 726) points out the particular importance of digital and online materials for LCTLs because 'few language textbook publishers can afford to publish print materials for languages with small enrolments'. Many language resource centres have established initiatives designed to support such languages. The teacher training courses created by the Language Institute at the University of Wisconsin–Madison and the National Council of Less Commonly Taught Languages is an example; the compilation of professional development and learning materials by the University of Minnesota's Center for Advanced Research on Language Acquisition (CARLA) is another. Such institutions also frequently support the development of resources for particular languages: examples are the Open Access Textbook for Yoruba, *Yoruba Yemi*, and the Open Access Website for Arabic, *Aswaat Arabiyya*, supported by the Center for Open Educational Resources and Language Learning at the University of Texas.

However, these examples stand out as successes in a broader context of limited funding and human resources required for the ongoing and robust support for the learning of any one language. Hundreds of LCTLs are taught in North America alone, while the overwhelming majority of US students study – and the overwhelming majority of resources support – the more commonly taught languages such as French, German, Italian and Spanish.

## *Cultures, genres and styles of use*

A growing body of research in intercultural communication and online language learning recognises how all technologies are embedded in cultural and linguistic practices, meaning that a given technological artefact can be used in radically different ways, and for different purposes by different groups of people. Researchers in telecollaboration (see Helm and Guth, Chapter 17 this volume) have long recognised that the kinds of experiences learners have with electronic communication shapes their expectations as well as their language use with foreign partner classes. In light of linguistic, cultural, institutional and other differences in such partnerships, learners' varying familiarity with the tools and practices of online communication can contribute to miscommunication and even breakdown in cross-cultural learning partnerships. However, even when learners have more or less the same technical facility with a given tool, they might use it with substantially different expectations and understandings. Kramsch and Thorne (2002) argued that culturally specific genres may be less identifiable when they are mediated by technology. Thorne (2003) focused more specifically on cultural historical processes of mediation that inhere in the material tools of intercultural communication and posited the term 'cultures-of-use', which refers to the 'historically sedimented characteristics that accrue to a CMC [computer-mediated communication] tool from its everyday use' (Thorne 2003: 40). Just as the rudimentary objects of everyday life (utensils, pens and pencils, chairs) are used in different ways to suit different purposes and traditions, so may online communication tools like email, Facebook, Skype or Twitter come to be used for diverse, culturally specific genres, styles and purposes.

## Looking forward

As mentioned at the outset, technology is often thought of as something that eliminates or minimises limitations and boundaries. In language classrooms like Nadia's and Ayo's, it is technology that gives students access to authentic materials, texts and speakers of target languages beyond geographic divisions, time differences and income gaps. Technology is what enables students to instantly view online translations for unknown words (overcoming barriers of language), to carry out learning activities outside the classroom and in 'real-world' contexts (overcoming limitations of mobility) and to question narrow cultural worldviews through telecollaborative exchange (transcending boundaries of culture).

On the other hand, we have also seen that the use of any given technology introduces new boundaries and limitations that may be inherent in the technological medium itself, but also may emerge from the interaction of that medium with particular purposes, tasks, settings and participants in a cultural context. We also saw that some limitations and boundaries can be viewed positively to the extent that they lead people to invent fresh ways of using and thinking about language, whether it is at the level of compensatory strategies during interactions or at the level of designing new social configurations. With our metaphor of the kaleidoscope we have suggested that boundaries and limitations of some sort will *always* accompany the teaching and learning languages with technology, and that what is of paramount importance is learning to see what new patterns emerge when a new technology is used.

As we look towards the future, a number of areas will be interesting to observe with respect to boundaries and limitations. One is machine translation, which attempts to reduce or eliminate language barriers. Behind the scenes, machine translation blurs boundaries between speech and writing when it takes an audio speech signal in language A, converts it to writing, translates the written rendition into language B, and then converts it into audible speech. Computer scientists fully realise the limitations of such an approach and recent programs combine speech-to-writing algorithms with direct speech translation so that subtle details of articulation (such as speaking while smiling) can be taken into account.

A second area has to do with the limits of texts. Texts have traditionally been bounded; but in the electronic age, as texts are amended, reshaped, repurposed, multi-authored (as in wikis) and hypertextually linked to one another, it becomes increasingly difficult to delimit text boundaries in space and time. Texts may be fluid in the sense that they are changeable and frequently updated, and also in the sense that they may appear differently depending on the device on which they are displayed. This is important in the classroom, because students and teachers may think they have read the 'same' text, and had the same reading experience, when in fact they have not.

The permeable nature of the boundaries between people and technology, and between selves and others mediated through technology, is a third broad area of concern for the future. Near the beginning of the chapter, we pointed to Burbules and Callister's (2000) relational view of technology to make the point that users of technology may themselves be culturally, psychologically and even physically changed by the technologies they use. What is at stake for language learners and teachers may be the ability to know whom they are speaking to, to know what consequences (intended or unexpected) might come of their interaction and, indeed, to know just who they are. According to Kramsch:

> the computer has given the self-procedural authority and spatial agency, it has dramatically increased the potential for distributed authorship and inter-subjectivity, it offers borderless spaces for play and creativity – but at a price. The virtual self, together with others, must reinvent the contextual boundaries without which there can be no agency, authorship, or creativity – indeed, there can be no subject.
>
> (Kramsch 2009: 185)

Social media, collaborative writing, multimedia appropriation and mashups, identity play and anonymity are among the many phenomena of contemporary online life and learning that have led to doubts about the stability of boundaries that had previously seemed solid – notions of 'the author' and related notions of 'authenticity' and 'plagiarism', for instance. From a teacher's perspective, the blurred boundaries that accompany the use of new technologies confront us with new questions concerning how we define and assess learning, where we situate accountability, and how we instil in our students a sense of moral responsibility in the use of those technologies.

In this chapter, we have taken a glimpse into the German classroom of Nadia, whose school has just adopted a new learning management system. We can easily imagine that she might now feel more able to track her students' discussion forum posts and comments with the new system's enhanced analytics functions, while also being less sure about how to evaluate those posts, as they represent a new, more personal genre of expression. Similarly, we have considered the situation for students and teacher in a small Yoruba class, where lessons are now shared via videoconferencing with students in a partner classroom. We have seen how participants on both sides benefit from the sense of proximity and shared space opened up by the audio/video connection between them, while at the same time they must reconcile themselves to new ambiguities (e.g. reading eye gaze and body language) and new immobilities (e.g. the need to stay on-camera and on-screen) in their learning environments.

Everywhere we celebrate previously unsurpassable limitations being overcome with the use of technology for language learning and teaching, we must also be aware of new boundaries and limitations emerging. This is not, however, a zero-sum game, since the qualities of the two sets of boundaries and limitations may be quite different. What is crucial for language teachers and learners alike is to adopt a critical stance with respect to the technologies they use and, specifically, to be attentive to:

- how technologies mediate language use and behaviour in particular ways;
- what communicative consequences (in terms of understanding and learning) might accompany that mediation;

- what social consequences might follow the choice of using one form of technology versus another (in terms of who is included or excluded, how participant interactions might be reconfigured and how cultural processes and products might be affected).

## Further reading

Dooly, M. (2011) 'Crossing the intercultural borders into 3rd space culture(s): Implications for teacher education in the twenty-first century', *Language and Intercultural Communication Research*, 11: 319–337.
This article reports on how student teachers in Spain and the United States transcended the limits of their individual course programmes by engaging in a year-long online exchange using Skype, Moodle, Voicethread and Second Life. Participants' interaction with their foreign partners varied according to the available communication modes. Dooly argues that the affordances of the various modes may make traditional categorisations of culture less salient to participants when they are engaged in 'emergent' cultures in virtual communities, suggesting that researchers need to revise models of intercultural competence especially in the context of such exchanges.

Hanna, B.E. and de Nooy, J. (2009) *Learning Language and Culture via Public Internet Discussion Forums*, Basingstoke, UK: Palgrave Macmillan.
This book discusses the use of public discussion forums to engage with native speakers on a wide range of topics and to be exposed to other cultures' takes on the topic at hand. The study shows that online intercultural *contact* does not necessarily produce successful intercultural *communication*, and that learners' language competence per se is not as important as their understanding of the social genres and practices associated with different online environments. The authors argue that the Internet is 'far from the utopia of the borderless world', and can often reinforce borders, stereotypes and racist hostility, rather than increasing understanding.

Tenner, E. (1996) *Why Things Bite Back: Technology and the Revenge of Unlimited Consequences*, New York, NY: Alfred A. Knopf.
This is a classic work on technology, limits and mediation in many realms of life. As people's work is mediated by tools, they become further removed from direct contact with their work (e.g. writing has become far less physical over the centuries; airline pilots no longer manipulate mechanical controls but rather manage tools that manage other tools). Labour-saving technologies often require surprising amounts of vigilance, however, and Tenner reviews sometimes untoward social consequences. One particularly relevant section raises questions about whether computer networks are democratic or authoritarian.

## Websites

*Aswaat Arabiyya* (http://laits.utexas.edu/aswaat/)
Computer Industry Almanac Internet user forecast by country (http://www.c-i-a.com/internetuser.htm)
List of Wikipedias (http://en.wikipedia.org/wiki/List_of_Wikipedias)
National Council of Less Commonly Taught Languages Online Teaching Course (http://www.ncolctl.org/resources-links/online-teaching-course)
University of Minnesota's Center for Advanced Research on Language Acquisition (http://www.carla.umn.edu/lctl/)
*Yoruba Yemi* (http://coerll.utexas.edu/yemi/)

## References

Burbules, N.C. and Callister, T.A. (2000) *Watch IT: The Risks and Promises of Information Technologies for Education*, Boulder, CO: Westview Press.
Constantin de Chanay, H. (2011) 'La construction de l'éthos dans les conversations en ligne', in C. Develotte, R. Kern and M.-N. Lamy (eds), *Décrire la conversation en ligne: le face à face distanciel*, Lyon: ENS Éditions: 145–172.
Danet, B. and Herring, S.C. (eds) (2007) *The Multilingual Internet: Language, Culture, and Communication Online*, Oxford: Oxford University Press.
Feenberg, A. (2002) *Transforming Technology: A Critical Theory Revisited*, Oxford: Oxford University Press.

Friedberg, A. (2006) *The Virtual Window: From Alberti to Microsoft*, Cambridge, MA, MIT Press.

Garrett, N. (2009) Computer-assisted language learning trends and issues revisited: Integrating innovation. *The Modern Language Journal*, 93: 719–740.

Herring, S.C. (2007) 'A faceted classification scheme for computer-mediated discourse', *Language@Internet*, available: http://www.languageatInternet.org/articles/2007/761 (accessed 13 Nov 2014).

Jackson, F.H. and Malone, M.E. (2009) *Building the Foreign Language Capacity We Need: Toward a Comprehensive Strategy for a National Language Framework*, Washington, DC: Center for Applied Linguistics.

Kern, R. (2014) 'Technology as pharmakon: The promise and perils of the Internet for foreign language education', *Modern Language Journal*, 98: 330–347.

Kramsch, C. (2009) *The Multilingual Subject: What Foreign Language Learners Say About Their Experience and Why It Matters*, Oxford: Oxford University Press.

Kramsch, C. and Thorne, S.L. (2002) 'Foreign language learning as global communicative practice', in D. Block and D. Cameron (eds), *Globalization and Language Teaching,* London, UK: Routledge.

Leppänen, S. and Peuronen, S. (2012) 'Multilingualism and the Internet', in C.A. Chapelle (ed), *The Encyclopedia of Applied Linguistics*, New York, NY: Blackwell Publishing Ltd.

Malinowski, D. (2011) *Where Is the Foreign?: An Inquiry into Person, Place, and the Possibility of Dialogue in an Online French Language Class. Graduate School of Education*, Berkeley, MA: University of California.

McLuhan, M. (1964) *Understanding Media: The Extensions of Man*, New York, NY: McGraw-Hill.

MLA Ad Hoc Committee on Foreign Languages (2007) 'Foreign languages and higher education: New structures for a changed world', *Profession*, 12: 234–245.

Onishi, N. (2008) 'Thumbs race as Japan's best sellers go cellular', *New York Times*. 20 January.

Paolillo, J. (2005) 'Language diversity on the Internet: Examining linguistic bias', In U. I. F. Statistics (ed), *Measuring Linguistic Diversity on the Internet*, Paris: UNESCO.

Thorne, S.L. (2003) 'Artifacts and cultures-of-use in intercultural communication', *Language Learning & Technology*: 7: 38–67.

Warschauer, M. (2003) *Technology and Social Inclusion: Rethinking the Digital Divide*, Cambridge, MA: MIT Press.

# 15
# Teacher education and technology

*Elizabeth Hanson-Smith*

Past and current practices in language teacher education have often relegated training in technology to elective coursework, or even worse, left student teachers to their own devices. However, computers and mobile technologies have the potential to help teacher education catch up; they enable rich and varied global access to education for language teachers. This chapter provides a brief overview of the problems in current teacher education and highlights programs, approaches, tools and online resources that can expand and enrich teacher professional development. The final section discusses the role of technology standards in incorporating technology into teacher education.

## Problems in teacher education technology

Recently a fellow teacher educator in South America remarked that for her teachers, technology still 'meant a Xerox' (Albers, personal communication, 2014, referring to Negroponte, of the MIT Media Lab). While global business proceeds at the speed of the latest computer chip and Internet connection, education in the pedagogical uses of technology has marched along at a crawl. We are still not far from the days when a colleague of mine in the English department declared he would not let students use word processors for their essays because he feared the computer would write the paper for them. The gap between the current realities of global computer use – especially for business, economics and (sadly) warfare and politics – and the capabilities of teachers to educate their students in and through technology has never seemed greater. Kessler's (2007) survey of students in MATESOL programmes indicated widespread dissatisfaction with their preparation in using technology tools. Hubbard (2008) reported that the majority of MATESOL programmes in the US and Canada did not offer technology training courses, and many that did offered them only as electives. Since then, little has changed.

Currently, the general practice in schools of education is to relegate training in technology uses to one course (two to three hours weekly), which might include the use of projectors, scanners and interactive whiteboards (if the school has one), word processor templates and presentation makers such as Microsoft PowerPoint, and possibly some Internet-based flashcard creators and so-called educational games, whether on a desktop computer, a mobile device or the Internet. The focus is more often than not the physical or technological apparatus: how to open and save files or how to input content, rather than a close examination of how and why such tools might be used for pedagogical purposes in the classroom or at home. Healey et al. (2011: 143–144) note an additional problem, that teacher educators themselves may be slightly technophobic and may in fact resist technology, or they may feel that the rising generation of digitally adept new teachers may not need technology education. Additionally, teachers who are technologically able may be hired as the sole expert in technology and may spend most of their time answering pleas for help with mundane problems; they may have little time left to work on their own skills and interests in teaching with technology.

For many teachers, then, even relatively modest goals for education in technology are not attained through their schooling. Teachers and parents often remark that the students themselves can find a way to understand and use mobile apps and software. And indeed, youngsters use technology on a per-hour basis far more than do their elders (Pew Research Center 2010: 3). However, on close examination, these uses of new technologies are generally not for the purposes of furthering education. A recent study at the University of Maryland (2014) indicated that many entering students felt 'expert' at social sites like Facebook (67%; $n$ = 1,698–1,702), but very few felt the same level of confidence in using wikis or blogs (5% and 8% respectively) or multimedia software (11%; University of Maryland 2014: 3). Most teachers find that students have to be weaned from violent games, social chatting and other forms of mobile and Internet use, and redirected to more productive educational goals. They may discover a surprising lack of understanding about such fundamental tools as word processors, online dictionaries, and collaborative technologies to create papers and projects. In a recent MOOC (massive open online course) offered by the University of Oregon and the US Department of State, community teaching assistants remarked that they hadn't realised how much difficulty the participants (mainly teachers and teachers-in-training) would have with such simple tasks as opening PDF files or saving their own work in a nonstandard format, such as a plain text file, rather than the default word processor format (personal communication during MOOC course, May/June 2014). Teachers and administrators need to ask serious questions about how further professional development can take place as the pace of computer and Internet software and mobile application development continues to increase. At present, without further training or education, any teachers five years out of college will find themselves hopelessly behind the times.

Fortunately, some signs of good technology practices in education are surfacing and possibly snowballing into a genuine self-help movement that may yet strongly influence the way teachers approach new technologies for their students.

## Self-help for educators interested in technology: Personal learning environments

Some answers to the problem of rapidly expanding technology use can be found in tools and websites specifically designed to further teacher education. By exploring, collecting and curating knowledge, individual teachers can create personal learning environments (PLEs) that support their learning mission. This section looks at several sites where teachers may find encouragement in exploring tools for and approaches to pedagogically appropriate technology.

Several dedicated teachers keep very accurate and useful blogs or provide regular email news of technological tools of interest to teachers, and they explain how to use them in the classroom or lab, or online in a flipped classroom (i.e. one where lectures and instructional material are viewed or read outside of class online, and the classroom itself is used primarily for discussion and further explorations). One example of such a teacher is Richard Byrne (2014), whose weekly blog, *Free Technology for Teachers*, discusses a set of tools with a particular use – for instance a variety of Web tools to create digital stories, or new presentation programs. The advantage of Byrne's site is that he gives tips in brief on how to use the tools with students. Byrne offers paid 'camps' for teachers both on land and online as webinars for professional development. However, his newsletter articles are free to anyone and can be subscribed to using a free email service, FeedBlitz, through an RSS feed, or by notification through social media such as Facebook or Twitter. This 'push' connection means that teachers do not have to go out hunting for new information; it arrives weekly to their email inbox, a reminder to stay current.

Another teacher, Russell Stannard, records screencasts showing how to use technology of interest to educators (Stannard 2014). As Stannard describes the tools, he also discusses how he uses them in his own classroom. These easy to view, short screencasts do not require special software for viewing and are completely accessible on his own website – thus solving the problem in some countries of YouTube blockage. Stannard walks the viewer through even the simple steps of signing up or registering to use a program. Again, while Stannard works for the Norwich Institute for Language Education and offers paid workshops for teachers, his TTV (Teacher Training Videos) site is accessible for free, and a user can subscribe to be sent an email when new recordings become available. Like Byrne, Stannard makes a point of describing how he uses each tool with his own students.

Other places to find good educational web, software and mobile applications include Kathy Schrock's webinars and accompanying resource lists (Schrock 2014) and Larry Ferlazzo's 'Best of . . .' websites linked from his explanatory blog (Ferlazzo 2014). Schrock's webinars show how specific tools and applications might be used through screencasts of the technology. They are recorded, so the viewer need not be present at a certain date or time. Ferlazzo's blog links to an enormous variety of resources on pedagogy, current news, sports, culture and so forth. While there is no doubt something for every teacher, these sites will require a certain dedication to searching and/or a taste for the serendipitous.

Other sites, though not specifically focused on computers and educational technology for language learning, also offer the teacher professional development through videos and webinars created by teachers themselves. The Teaching Channel focuses on pedagogy, mainly in American schools, viewed in videos that show classrooms using specific pedagogical approaches and teaching skills and interviews with their teachers. Many recent videos have focused on the US Common Core standards. BBC Active offers videos set mainly in British classrooms. These cover discipline as well as 'new techniques employed by teachers to reinforce learning'. Titles include such topics as virtual learning and differentiated classrooms. The BBC's Teaching English site also provides an enormous number of teacher resources, lesson plans, and training videos. Registration gives access to free educational online workshops and teaching tips videos as well. EdWeb, another prolific site for educators, produces and archives webinars on a wide variety of topics for teachers, and awards continuing education certificates for participation.

At the university level, MERLOT (Multimedia Educational Resource for Learning and Teaching Online) is a website sponsored by the California State University System. Areas of the site are categorised by academic discipline, but the focus throughout is teaching with technology at the university level, whether in the classroom, online or in a blended course. Teachers are expected to search for content and methods appropriate to their classes and their level of comfort. While primarily US-focused, MERLOT welcomes participation from libraries, publishers, other state systems and individuals in using and contributing to its resources. There are strong resource libraries in the content areas of science and technology as well as teaching of various languages.

The dedicated teacher could create an entire system of regular self-improvement, a PLE, by using just the sites mentioned in this section. By finding blogs, recommended tools, instructional websites and webinars, then collecting them through such archiving resources as Twitter, Diigo, Scoop.it or Pinterest, the educator can continually update knowledge. However, learning is always easier when done in the company of others, and most teachers probably require something more organised to improve their technological expertise systematically. Fortunately, there are a number of free online courses or MOOCs, that can provide at least some of the needed discipline.

## The rise of the MOOC

The rise of MOOCs has barely touched the needs of language educators in the field of technology. However, free online courses have the potential to meet a real need among teachers around the world. There are many advantages to taking a MOOC, particularly in the field of educational technology:

- Courses need not go through an extensive review system; anyone can offer a course, but university sponsorship can give it more credibility. MOOC courses can adapt rapidly to changes in technology and incorporate new teaching ideas.
- Courses can be relatively short; many are five to six weeks in length, and can thus fit into the schedule of working professionals, though many are also the traditional ten to fourteen weeks.
- Courses are online twenty-four hours a day and thus can be accessed in any time zone.
- Courses are often free, though many also offer an optional extension study certificate or statement of accomplishment as a way of recognising the time and effort put into such a course. Verified certificates usually are accompanied by a fee, but this is generally quite modest compared to enrolling in a university.
- Course materials can be viewed in any of a number of popular world languages; courses are offered by universities around the world in the local language.
- Course materials are usually made downloadable, so even in low-access situations (such as dial-up Internet) students can save materials to their own computers for future use.
- Most interfaces also run on mobile devices, such as tablets and cellular phones, used by over 2 billion people on the planet.
- Most universities make a point of including handicapped-accessible features, such as closed-captioning for videos and descriptive text for images.
- Student teachers usually have access to materials after the course has closed so that they can continue to review and study; some courses are open indefinitely.
- Teachers are an ideal audience, as they are generally self-motivated and eager to have further professional development; MOOC students have to be self-starters.

Thus far, I have found two or three MOOCs in Coursera (2014) relating to technology and pedagogy every six months or so – for example, the recent University of London course, *ICT for Primary Education* (May 2014), or *Learning to Teach Online* by the University of New South Wales (July 2014), although these are not specific to language teaching. A free set of two courses offered by the US Department of State and the University of Oregon/Applied English Institute, *Shaping the Way We Teach English*, targeting international teachers of EFL, was offered in 2014 and 2015 and probably will be offered again in succeeding years. While focusing more on classroom pedagogy than technology, the *Shaping* series includes examples of online collaborative learning for K-12 and adults, and discussion forums include questions about technology uses for those teachers with access. Other institutions, such as the OpenupEd.eu (2014) consortium, have also had a handful of courses, for example, *E-learning*, a fourteen-week course offered last in 2013. Admittedly, this is a small sample compared to the thousands of courses offered by a wide variety of institutions that seem to focus on the traditional content areas of maths, sciences, computer science, social sciences, business and the humanities. However, many of these courses also have a technology component and would be appropriate for teachers of content-based language teaching and learning.

MOOCs offer a unique opportunity to bring language teacher education in technology up to date on a regular basis, an opportunity that will no doubt expand in future. A search of the *MOOCs Directory* (2014) is a good way to begin looking for free online learning in the area of technology and education. While it is not a simple matter to create materials for a MOOC, schools of education might find in them a way to keep their graduates informed and up to date in a systematic way. Courses taught on a campus as a 'flipped' course could be offered simultaneously as a MOOC, or as a paid course with reduced registration fees for graduates. Discussion forums would take the place of in-class sessions, and 'human assessment' (i.e. peer evaluations) would be given for papers and lesson plan assignments.

One of the more interesting features of MOOCs and online distance courses in general is the desire of participants to communicate with each other and to form subgroups within the course itself. One might expect that a course with 20,000–30,000 students would be a largely impersonal experience. On the contrary, I found that in the *Shaping* courses, students who participated in the text chat forums were extraordinarily solicitous of others' needs, and many shared lesson plans with each other, cheered each other on, offered to exchange email addresses, gave assistance freely, and so on. Possibly the fact that there was not a competitive grading system – where a large percentage of the students were taking the course to learn, rather than to get a certificate – meant that the natural human tendency to create community could rise to the surface, and students began to form personal learning networks (PLNs) spontaneously. That is, some participants sought to extend the information they were receiving to interconnections with teachers in similar classroom or cultural situations.

In the *Shaping* courses, the instructional materials encouraged participants to collaborate with others in developing their lesson plans. In addition, the US Department of State, in some instances, offered offices and cultural centres as places for local teachers to meet regularly to watch the instructional videos together and discuss them and the assignments. This was especially valuable where Internet access was limited. In a few areas, a local teacher brought others together for the same purposes, and in one instance, the teacher downloaded all the videos to his personal laptop so others could watch. The land-based connections no doubt contributed to greater interest in the materials and a better completion rate, but similar PLNs can be made online through email lists and discussion forums. This type of community building within MOOCs would be interesting to explore in further research.

Both PLEs and PLNs have an element of chance (for an extended discussion of the difference between PLEs and PLNs, see Morrison 2013). In the busy life of a teacher, it is difficult to maintain a regimen of consistent learning over time, particularly on one's own. The disappointing completion rate of free MOOCs (usually below 10%) is one demonstration of this problem. Nonetheless, it should be remembered that that figure represents some 2,000 teachers who have completed the course requirements. Further, the communal tendencies possible within MOOCs point to the need for more formalised ways to bring teachers together to collaborate in learning. Communities of practice, where shared learning is deliberately cultivated within a PLN, offer a solution.

## Personal learning networks and communities of practice for technology-using teachers

Professional associations offer the first line of continuing professional development, sometimes in unusual ways. In addition to regular professional conventions, which provide networking opportunities as well as papers and presentations on technology, some professional associations have created the means to establish learning networks with a focus on technology for pedagogy.

IATEFL (the Europe-based International Association of Teachers of English as a Foreign Language) provides a busy and intensive weeklong convention annually that includes an entire day of technology presentations sponsored by its Learning Technology Special Interest Group (LTSIG). Presentations are recorded and archived for future use. Outside the convention, the LTSIG also offers an annual Virtual Round Table (Virtual-round-table.com 2014), a three-day web conference on topics of interest in technology. The web conferences are also recorded for later use by those who cannot attend the live presentation. For example, one 2014 webinar was on the topic Gaming and Gamification, a joint effort with the US TESOL association's CALL-IS (Teachers of English to Speakers of Other Languages; Computer-Assisted Language Learning Interest Section). Participants receive links to the sites under discussion and are encouraged to participate with presenters – and each other – in the live text chat. Those who sign up at the Virtual Round Table website receive regular notices of upcoming events. The site also hosts a lively discussion list. Since many participants return repeatedly for these round tables, it is possible to connect personally with others in the field and include them in a PLN.

To offer an example of how a PLN can develop through conferencing and webinars, one might take the example of the IATEFL plenary at the recent 2014 convention, given by Sugata Mitra (2014). The presentation on 'SOLEs' (self-organised learning environments) for children was accompanied by a SOLE 'toolkit' to bring the idea to the teacher's own community. Numerous bloggers followed up Mitra's talk with wide-ranging comments. To follow just one of these threads, Part two of Graham Stanley's three-part blog post about the plenary (2014), in turn, included a video (contributed by another person, Carol Goodey) of Emma Crawley, a teacher at St Aidan's Primary School in Gateshead, who was using the SOLE approach (Crawley 2013). The post then led to comments by a variety of people on Facebook, with links to their respective blogs, which had additional resources. Stanley's blog was eventually noted in the community of practice, Webheads in Action (described in more detail later), with further comments and queries. Michael Coghlan, of this community, then created a podcast with his own considered thoughts (Coghlan 2014) and sent the link to Webheads. If one traced the embedded video in Stanley's blog back to YouTube, there were many additional videos by Mitra linked in the sidebar, as well as comments by other teachers on the video, and notes on a question-and-answer follow-up with Mitra (Pinard 2014). Any one of the points of contact – plenary comments, blog comments, podcasts, video comments – could allow the teacher to join in the discussion and gain further access to those educators already online. This kind of webbing, meshing, interlacing and cross-referencing is the way self-learning or professional development is provided by PLNs. One need only join the conversation.

In many ways comparable to IATEFL, but headquartered on the American side of the Atlantic (and with a much larger membership), TESOL (Teachers of English to Speakers of Other Languages, an international professional organisation) offers paid courses that include topics in technology, and a Principles and Practices of Online Teaching Certificate Program; however, TESOL's Computer-Assisted Language Learning Interest Section (CALL-IS) is very active in several unique, free, all-volunteer projects for technology-using teachers. In the early 1990s, CALL-IS instituted an Electronic Village (EV) at the TESOL convention, which consisted of a room full of computers and volunteers from the IS who helped newcomers understand computers and technology-driven pedagogy for language learning. The EV has evolved into three days of short round-robin talks, brief webcast presentations that can be joined for free by non-convention-goers and free time to consult with expert volunteers.

In the early 2000s, CALL-IS instituted the Electronic Village Online (EVO) project, at first an extension of the convention EV and convention themes, but eventually a MOOC-like stand-alone source of online education. In January and February each year, EVO volunteers offer 12–15 five-week online courses that are free to participants from around the world. The 2014 offerings had over 4,000 participants. For examples of typical offerings of EVO, see the Call for Participation for 2014 (Electronic Village Online 2014). Many participants have been following topics and themes, such as Drama in Education, Becoming a Webhead, Digital Storytelling, Moodle for Teachers and so forth for a number of years in succession, thus broadening and expanding their personal connections into PLNs. The sessions usually include text forums for communication, an archive wiki to store resources, and also live webcasts to discuss session topics with guest speakers. Many sessions focus on one set of applications and their uses, such as Podcasting for Teachers or Video Online. Other sessions revolve around themes or issues, such as teachers as mentors or nonnative-speakers as teachers of EFL. A full list of sessions offered over the past fifteen years may be seen at *EVO Previous Sessions* (2014). Many participants return year after year to take courses; bonds among moderators, coordination team members and participants have become very strong over the years.

An additional benefit of professional organisations are connections to resources such as the TESOL Blog (2014) and the CALL-IS Virtual Software Library (VSL) at Diigo (TESOL CALL-IS's Public Library 2014). The TESOL Blog has frequent contributions by guest writers on a wide variety of topics, such as using effective peer feedback, creating flashcards with Quizlet, games to reinforce vocabulary and so forth. Anyone may read the blog, but first one must know it exists. The VSL is also free and open to anyone, as is the related Diigo group, where members may contribute URLs. The archive may be searched by tags (such as 'content-based' or 'very-young-learners') or by lists, which may be viewed as a slideshow of front pages. The archive is a ready-made PLE, with the potential to allow personal contacts within the Diigo group, or PLN.

While professional organisations may be relatively expensive for teachers in developing countries to join, they are well worth the effort in the variety and quality of resources and materials they offer for teachers attempting to stay abreast of the world of technology. Interest section newsletters and association newsletters are free sources of information, as are connections with fellow members worldwide. Conventions and smaller local academies offer additional opportunities for professional growth and put teachers in touch with others locally who are attempting to improve their own knowledge about technology and online resources. Every school of education should insist that their teacher candidates join and participate in one of the several professional associations that exist to help language teachers.

Communities of practice (CoPs) are perhaps the most convenient and efficient way to solve the problem of continuing teacher education, both during and after schooling. And in fact, the distinction between pre- and in-service training is of far less importance in a CoP than elsewhere, as individuals can contribute at their own level. Lave and Wenger (1991) are usually attributed with coining the term 'communities of practice', which they discuss as forming naturally in social settings where problems need to be solved. Wenger subsequently has written on CoPs in several contexts (see Wenger 1998), and Stevens has discussed the concept of 'distributed' CoPs, where communities form at a distance, that is, through the Internet rather than in person (e.g. Stevens 2009, and elsewhere). In essence, members of a CoP will share knowledge, assist or mentor apprentices and collaborate in practising the skills needed in the environment or domain where the CoP has formed. In distributed CoPs, members of the community use Internet tools to create their support system and social interactions. (See Coverdale 2008 for an extensive bibliography on the subject of distributed CoPs.)

Wenger and Traynor (2014, n.p.) have carefully distinguished between networks and communities, the former being a set of information 'nodes and links', as well as personal interactions, the latter expressing the intention 'to steward a domain of knowledge and to sustain learning about it'. The essentials of a CoP in the context of teacher education have been discussed by several authors (Johnson 2003; Stevens 2005; Hanson-Smith 2006). They include the following aspects (see Hanson-Smith 2006 for fuller elaboration):

- *A domain or purpose.* In the domain of teaching languages through or with technology, in a university setting, teacher educators could encourage their student teachers to seek out international communities that would help foster and encourage their participation. One such community is the Webheads in Action (*WebheadsinAction.org* 2014), described later. Or a class or department of education might start its own collaborative group with the intention of extending it beyond one limited class, as discussed by Dahlman and Tahtinen, who created a 'reflective electronic support network' for their pre-service teachers (2006: 225), to serve them after the end of a semester of instruction.
- *A collaborative 'praxis'*, or an approach to continuing education that includes hands-on work with technology in a collaborative educational environment. Instead of just sitting in on or observing a class, peers in a CoP might take part as a guest speaker or interviewee of students to assist them in hearing and interacting with an authentic native speaker. In the Webheads, an email message might put out a call for help with a class or a new technology, and peers would respond based on their available time and expertise. Peer support in a CoP should always be at hand. Immediate support and collaboration is possible through readily available tools on the Internet.
- *Tools* for collaboration at a distance would be required, since teachers will disperse after graduation, though the need for support will increase as technology develops. Online communities generally use email lists (e.g. via a Yahoo Group or Google+ community), live chat and video conferencing (e.g. Adobe, Blackboard or Skype), and a means to archive websites, training videos and screencasts and software discoveries (e.g. Diigo or a wiki). Thus, the tools that teachers need to be trained in are themselves the interfaces that bind the community together. Often in online meetings, the Webheads create a 'backchannel' through a familiar tool, such as a text chat, while experimenting with a new technology, such as a video conference site or a Second Life venue.
- *Social support and peer mentoring.* Creating bonds between and among teacher candidates will take more than a single class or one mutual experiment. If a CoP is to be of enduring value to teacher educators it should have the potential to be a lifelong commitment to online friendships and peer collaboration. In a CoP such as the Webheads, such bonds have lasted over ten years. A school of education could encourage successive classes to join a CoP, so that newcomers are welcomed and 'inducted' into an ongoing social collaboration where 'old hands' can help them.

Stevens (2009), in referring to the Webheads in Action (WiA) as a distributed CoP, offers us a diagram of CoPs and PLNs (Figure 15.1). Networks or PLNs may have a wider range of associations, but the bonds are closer in CoPs. Without the social bonding, CoPs tend to decline fairly rapidly, although the resulting PLEs and PLNs still serve very useful functions.

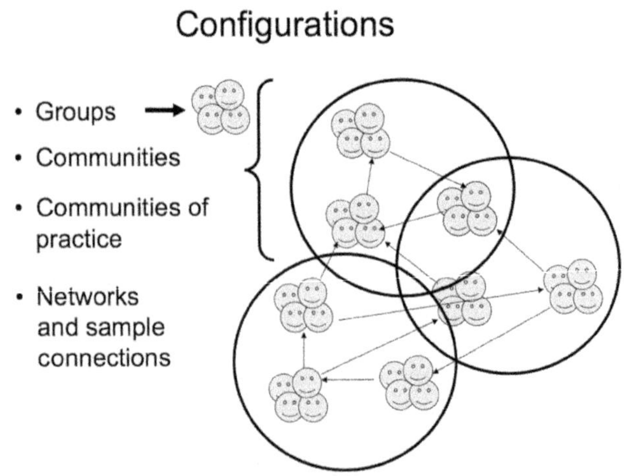

Elizabeth Hanson-Smith

## Configurations

- Groups
- Communities
- Communities of practice
- Networks and sample connections

*Figure 15.1* Communities of practice in relationship to networks, communities and groups
Source: Stevens (2009), slide 9 (with permission of the author).

Short of developing one's own CoP, there are several online communities that teachers can find with the potential to be CoPs; however, very few fulfil all the criteria for a satisfying community. For example, MERLOT, mentioned earlier, also has 'communities', which are really more like collections of materials contributed by teachers and eventually commented upon by other teachers. There is really little actual communication among members who make comments, so it is more like a PLE than a network or community.

Another centralised place to find like-minded teachers is Google Educator Groups (GEG), which are divided roughly by geographical location/primary language (though the 'Central Valley' California group currently has members from Canada and Baja California, Mexico). Some GEGs are just getting under way, and often the conversation focuses on specific Google tools; however, there is a sense of welcome and camaraderie within the groups I have visited. It is necessary to see how these groups might coalesce and further develop before claiming them as true CoPs. Nonetheless, any teacher educator could start a Google Educator Group and work to build a community within it. The interface provides a way to communicate easily, with email notifications to members and threads posted with the contributor's picture on discussion boards. Teachers would have to create their own archives in blogs or Diigo collections, however. As Google Classroom is put into place, this community may develop further.

The best example of a fully functioning CoP is the Webheads in Action, mentioned earlier. Founded by Vance Stevens as part of an Electronic Village Online session, the Webheads have continued from 2002 to the present. An annual session of EVO is used to induct new members by introducing them to the tools used by Webheads as well as to the camaraderie and social aspects that make this international group unique. Their domain is teaching languages, primarily English, with and through technology, whether computer, mobile or Internet. Stevens has also instituted a weekly webcast on topics of interest to the community, 'Learning2gether', offered by community members themselves (see Stevens 2014). Peer mentoring and hands-on praxis are at the heart of the Webheads collaborations, and the regular weekly live meetings encourage solidarity and community, bolstered by the email list. In addition, individuals in the community host their own archival web pages, blogs, podcasts and so forth. Often, a typical exchange will begin with a call for help on the community's email list, whether in using a new tool or in conducting a class online. Volunteers always step forward to assist and will take an active role in completing a survey, participating in a class or setting up an exchange between classes. The active intervention within a class and the interclass collaborations would be of great use to novice teachers who might make use of a CoP to continuously develop their technology skills.

## The role of standards in teacher education in technology: Prospects for the future

One of the most significant developments in technology and language education in recent years has been the creation of an extensive set of standards specifically designed for language educators who seek to use contemporary technologies: the TESOL Technology Standards (Healey et al. 2011; see also Kessler, Chapter 4 this volume). A set of standards demonstrates to teachers, teacher educators, administrators, curriculum writers, publishers and students what is meant by competency in the pedagogical uses of current technologies. Without such a road map, it would be difficult to determine what students (or teachers) know and what they should study next. The TESOL Standards lay out this road map in great detail.

The TESOL Standards include reference to current research in language teaching and technology, and to other standards created by such institutions as the ISTE (International Society for Technology in Education; ISTE.org 2014; these standards are not specifically for language teachers). The definition of student levels of proficiency are also articulated with reference to commonly used criteria, for example, the Common European Framework of Reference for Languages. The TESOL Standards include both a set of teacher standards and a separate set of student standards. The standards and goals within each standard increase in difficulty, although successive goals do not always depend on mastery or near-mastery of previous goals. Thus student Standard 1 Goal 1 includes such simple tasks as turning devices on and off and recognising when someone is online. Standard 3 goals include understanding aspects of Internet safety, while Standard 4 includes the ability to troubleshoot common problems (such as volume control of media), file search and when to ask for technical help. The TESOL Standards also include a simple checklist for self-assessing one's current abilities.

The TESOL Technology Standards are performance based. They include an explicit checklist of can-do statements that the teacher or student could directly apply to their own capabilities. In addition, each of the goals is illustrated by a set of vignettes or short examples of lesson plans that show how students or teachers could demonstrate their competencies. Each set of vignettes is explained in terms of low-level, mid-level, and high-level access to technology. Low-level access might be a situation where students share a single computer in the classroom, or even use the teacher's mobile phone. High-level technology access might mean a language lab full of computers with high-speed Internet or every student with a personal mobile device. Thus, the standards are not linked to specific brand-name technologies or software, but to types of devices and uses, including those that are freely available.

The TESOL Standards also include a range of classroom settings as well as labs and flipped classes, very young learners as well as adult learners, administrators as well as teachers and teacher-educators, and a set of goals specifically for advanced or expert-level technology users. To ensure its widespread availability, TESOL has made the vignettes downloadable for free online at TESOL.org (2014). They will no doubt be updated as needed when new technologies are invented. The standards' accessibility online ensures their immediacy and usefulness for teachers and teacher-educators. Added benefits are that school districts will have a set of criteria by which to judge the accomplishments of their students, teachers and administrators; publishers and curriculum writers will be able to use the standards as criteria for lessons incorporated into texts and other materials.

It is difficult to underestimate the utility of a complete set of standards for technology-using teachers and students. Administrators can use the standards to measure their programmes' improvement. As teacher educators become aware of the standards, they can incorporate them into their curricular goals and into any extended communities they create with and for their student teachers. The standards can be considered a culminating step in the quest for professional development in educational technology that will go beyond the brief semesters of teacher diplomas or graduate education.

## Further reading

Egbert, J. and Hanson-Smith, E. (eds) (2007) *CALL Environments: Research, Practice, and Critical Issues*, 2nd edn, Alexandria, VA: TESOL, Inc.
   The definitive text for graduate teacher education courses in CALL, this collection of essays illustrates the theory of second language acquisition in practical applications of digital technologies. Topics include interaction, authentic audience and task, exposure and production, time and feedback, intentional cognition, atmosphere, autonomy and prospects for the future.

Healey, D., Hanson-Smith, E., Hubbard, P., Ioannou-Georgiou, S., Kessler, G. and Ware, P. (2011) *TESOL Technology Standards*, Alexandria, VA: Teachers of English to Speakers of Other Languages, Inc.
   The TESOL Standards include a summary of various aspects of research in CALL, the standards framework for both teachers and students, an analysis of other sets of standards, a description of learner proficiency levels, self-assessment checklists and so forth. Vignettes (brief lesson plans) based on various levels of technology make up a large proportion of the work and provide excellent models for classroom use.

Hubbard, P. and Levy, M. (eds) (2006) *Teacher Education in CALL*, Amsterdam, Netherlands: John Benjamins.
   A comprehensive set of articles by noted authors in the field of CALL and teacher education. Topics include suggestions for CALL teacher education curricula, pre-service and in-service courses and projects for technology-using teachers, and a discussion of alternatives to formal CALL training.

Wenger, E. (1998, June) 'Communities of practice: Learning as a social system', *Systems Thinker*. n.p., available: http://iatefl.britishcouncil.org/2012/sites/iatefl/files/session/documents/learning_as_a_social_system_cofp_wenger.pdf (accessed 1 Jul 2014).
   A foundational article defining communities of practice more extensively than possible here. Wenger has long been associated with CoPs, and has expanded his definition to include online communities as well.

## Websites

*BBC Active* (2010) Available from: <http://www.bbcactive.com/BBCActiveIdeasandResources/VideosforTeacherTraining.aspx> [30 June 2014].

Byrne, R. (2014) *Free Technology for Teachers*. Available from: <http://www.freetech4teachers.com/> [20 June 2014].

Coursera.org (2014) *Coursera*. Available from: <http://www.coursera.org> [1 July 2014].

*edWeb: A professional online community for educators* (2012) Available from: <http://home.edweb.net/> [26 June 2014].

Electronic Village Online (2014) *Electronic village Online/FrontPage* | TESOL CALL-IS. Available from: <http://evosessions.pbworks.com/ Call_for_Participation2014> [30 June 2014].

*EVO Previous Sessions* (2014) Available from: <http://evosessions.pbworks.com/EVO%20Previous%20Sessions> [30 June 2014].

Ferlazzo, L. (2014) *Larry Ferlazzo's Websites of the Day . . .*, Available from: <http://larryferlazzo.edublogs.org/> [20 June 2014].

Google.com (2014) *Google Educator Groups*. Available from: <https://www.google.com/landing/geg/> [1 July 2014)].

ISTE.org (2014) *ISTE Standards*. Available from: <http://www.iste.org/STANDARDS> [4 July 2014].

Merlot.org (2014) *MERLOT II*. Available from: <http://www.merlot.org> [26 June 2014].
*MOOCs Directory* (2014) *Higher Education MOOCs: Massive Open Online Courses*. Available from: <http://www.moocs.co/Higher_Education_MOOCs.html> [1 July 2014].
OpenupEd.eu (2014) *OpenupEd*. Available from: <http://www.openuped.eu/> [1 July 2014].
Schrock, K. (2014) *Kathy Schrock's Guide to Everything*. Available from: <http://www.schrockguide.net/> [20 June 2014].
Stannard, R. (2014) *TTV: Teacher Training Videos*. Available from: <http://teachertrainingvideos.com/> [20 June 2014].
Stevens, V. (2014) *Volunteersneeded: Learning 2gether*. Available from: <http://learning2gether.pbworks.com/volunteersneeded> [28 June 2014].
Teachingenglish.org.uk (2014) *TeachingEnglish | British Council | BBC*. Available from: <http://www.teachingenglish.org.uk/> [30 June 2014].
*TESOL Blog* (2014) Available from: <http://blog.tesol.org/category/blog/> [30 June 2014].
*TESOL CALL-IS's Public Library* (2014) Available from: <http://www.diigo.com/user/call_is_vsl> [1 July 2014].
TESOL.org (2014) *TESOL Technology Standards*. Available from: <http://www.tesol.org/docs/books/bk_technologystandards_framework_721.pdf?sfvrsn=2> [4 July 2014].
*The Teaching Channel: Videos, Common Core Resources and Lesson Plans for Teachers* (2014) Available from: <https://www.teachingchannel.org> [28 June 2014].
Virtual-round-table.com (2014) *Virtual Round Table Web Conference*. Available from: <http://www.virtual-round-table.com/> [28 June 2014].
WebheadsinAction.org (2014) *WebheadsinAction.org: Communities of Practice Online*. Available from: <http://webheadsinaction.org/> [1 July 2014].

# References

Albers, M.I. (2014) *Survey of Teacher Education in Technology, Message in Yahoo Group, evonoline2002*, available: https://groups.yahoo.com/neo/groups/evonline2002_webheads/conversations/messages/31112
Byrne, R. (2014) *Free Technology for Teachers*, available: http://www.freetech4teachers.com/ (accessed 20 Jun 2014).
Coghlan, M. (2014) *Thoughts on Sugata Mitra's SOLE (Self-Organised Learning Environment)*, available: http://michaelc.podomatic.com/entry/2014-06-11T06_23_58-07_00 (accessed 30 Jun 2014).
Coverdale, A. (2008) *Distributed Communities of Practice – PhD Wiki*, PhD prospectus, submitted to University of Nottingham, available: https://sites.google.com/site/andycoverdale/texts/distributed-communities-of-practice (accessed 3 Jul 2014).
Crawley, E. (2013) 'Lessons from the SOLE by Emma Crawley, St Aidan's Primary School, Sept 2013' [video], available: http://youtu.be/oNau8XVcwgU (accessed 30 Jun 2014).
Dahlman, A. and Tahtinen, S. (2006) 'Virtual basegroup: E-mentoring in a reflective electronic support network', in E. Hanson-Smith and S. Rilling (eds), *Learning Languages Through Technology*, Alexandria, VA: TESOL, Inc.: 221–232.
Electronic Village Online (2014) *Electronic village Online/FrontPage | TESOL CALL-IS*, available: http://evosessions.pbworks.com/ Call_for_Participation2014 (accessed 30 Jun 2014).
Ferlazzo, L. (2014) *Larry Ferlazzo's Websites of the Day . . .*, available: http://larryferlazzo.edublogs.org/ (accessed 20 Jun 2014).
Hanson-Smith, E. (2006) 'Communities of practice for pre-and in-service teacher education', in P. Hubbard and M. Levy (eds), *Teacher Education in CALL*, Amsterdam, Netherlands: John Benjamins: 301–315.
Healey, D., Hanson-Smith, E., Hubbard, P., Ioannou-Georgiou, S., Kessler, G. and Ware, P. (2011) *TESOL Technology Standards*, Alexandria, VA: Teachers of English to Speakers of Other Languages, Inc.
Hubbard, P. (2008) 'CALL and the future of language teacher education', *CALICO Journal*, 25(2): 175–188.
Johnson, C.M. (2003) 'Establishing an online Community of Practice for instructors of English as a Foreign Language', Unpublished PhD dissertation, Nova Southeastern University.
Kessler, G. (2007) 'Formal and informal CALL preparation and teacher attitude toward technology', *Computer Assisted Language Learning*, 21(3): 173–188.
Lave, J. and Wenger, E. (1991) *Situated Learning: Legitimate Peripheral Participation*, Cambridge: Cambridge University Press.
Morrison, D. (2013, Jan 22) 'How to Create a Robust and Meaningful Personal Learning Network [PLN]', in *Online Learning Insights: A Blog About Open and Online Education*, available: http://onlinelearninginsights.

wordpress.com/2013/01/22/how-to-create-a-robust-and-meaningful-personal-learning-network-pln/ (accessed 28 Jun 2014).

Pew Research Center (2010) *Global Attitudes Project*, available: http://pewglobal.org/files/2010/12/Pew-Global-Attitudes-Technology-Report-FINAL-December-15–2010.pdf (accessed 20 Jun 2014).

Pinard, L. (2014) IATEFL 2014: *Q and A with Sugata Mitra – Saturday 17.00 BST: A Summary | Reflections of an English Language Teacher*, available: http://reflectiveteachingreflectivelearning.com/2014/04/19/iatefl-2014-q-and-a-with-sugata-mitra-saturday-17–00-bst-a-summary/ (accessed 30 Jun 2014).

Schrock, K. (2014) *Kathy Schrock's Guide to Everything*, available: http://www.schrockguide.net/ (accessed 20 Jun 2014).

Stanley, G. (2014, April 18) *The Rise of SOLES (part 2): At the Heart of a SOLE | blog-efl: reflections on teach and learning by @grahamstanley*, available: http://blog-efl.blogspot.com.au/2014/04/the-rise-of-soles-part-2-at-heart-of.html (accessed 30 Jun 2014).

Stevens, V. (2005) 'Multiliteracies for collaborative learning environments', *TESL-EJ*, 9.2: n.p., available: http://tesl-ej.org/ej34/int.html (accessed 2 Dec 2015).

Stevens, V. (2009, March 27) *The Webheads and Distributed Communities of Practice* [slide presentation], available: http://www.slideshare.net/vances/the-webheads-and-distributed-communities-of-practice (accessed 1 Jul 2014).

Stevens, V. (2014) *Volunteersneeded: Learning 2gether*, available: http://learning2gether.pbworks.com/volunteersneeded (accessed 28 Jun 2014).

University of Maryland (2014, July) 'First year perceptions of blended learning', *CAWG Snapshot of Student Experiences*, 4: 1–6, available: https://www.irpa.umd.edu/CAWG/Reports/2014/snapshot_jul14.pdf (accessed 5 Jul 2014).

Wenger, E. (1998, June) 'Communities of practice: Learning as a social system', *Systems Thinker*, 1998: n.p.; reprinted (2014), as *CoP: Best Practices*, available: http://www.co-i-l.com/coil/knowledge-garden/cop/lss.shtml (accessed 1 Jul 2014).

Wenger, E. and Traynor, B. (2014) *Communities Versus Networks?* available: http://wenger-trayner.com/resources/communities-versus-networks/ (accessed 1 July 2014).

# 16
# Sustainable CALL development

*Françoise Blin, Juha Jalkanen and Peppi Taalas*

The rapid pace of technological development, along with the uncertainty and unpredictability that characterise the knowledge society, have brought to the fore the issue of sustainability and sustainable development on various international, national and local educational research and policy agendas. Sustainability is a complex concept that gives rise to many definitions and interpretations. In this chapter, we draw on environmental/ecological definitions of sustainability and sustainable development, as well as system theories, to propose a multidimensional framework for sustainable CALL development. Following a definition of sustainability that employs systems theories and ecological economics, we briefly review the literature on sustainable e-learning in general and CALL in particular. We then propose a systemic view of sustainable CALL and discuss two models, the 'institutional model' and the 'CALL ecosystem model', that can be used to help integrate sustainability in our CALL designs and development.

## What is sustainability? Preliminary definitions

Sustainability has become a hot topic in the 21st century, in relation to society, economics, politics, education and most of all, the environment. Environmental scientists warn us against the impact of climate change that threatens our lifestyle, businesses strive to remain sustainable in a rapidly changing economic context and universities struggle to sustain their teaching and research activities in the face of increased competition and reduced funding. But what is sustainability?

Sustainability is a complex concept that gives rise to many definitions and interpretations. Everyday definitions, as found in most dictionaries, refer to 'the capacity to endure, to maintain or prolong' (Wikipedia), 'the ability to be sustained, supported, upheld, or confirmed' (dictionary.com), or the 'ability to maintain or support an activity or process over the long term' (BusinessDictionary.com). Systems, actions, or processes are said to be sustainable when they are supported by sufficient material, human or financial resources (dictionary.com). With regards to the environment, the United Nations published, in June 1987, the *Report of the World Commission on Environment and Development: 'Our Common Future'*, also known as the Brundtland Commission report (Brundtland 1987). This report introduced the concept of *sustainable development*, defined as 'development that meets the needs of the present without compromising the ability of future generations to meet their own needs' (Brundtland 1987: chap. 2, item 1). The report further identifies two key concepts: 'the concept of needs' and 'the idea of limitations imposed by the state of technology and social organization on the environment's ability to meet present and future needs' (ibid.).

Since the publication of the Brundtland Commission's report, sustainable development has been seen as 'a combination of three dimensions or "pillars": namely, the environmental (ecological), economic, and social dimensions' (Lehtonen 2004: 200). The nature of the relationship or interaction between these three pillars has given rise to controverted interpretations (Lehtonen 2004), represented by different visualisations as illustrated by Figure 16.1. According to Lehtonen (2004: 201), in the 'institutional version' represented by a Venn diagram, the three dimensions are hierarchically equal and mutually interacting. No priority is given to any of them, and 'the model gives the impression of pillars as independent elements that can be treated, at least analytically, separately from each other' (ibid.). By contrast, in the bioeconomy model represented by concentric circles, the environment circumscribes the social dimension, and the economic dimension constitutes the innermost circle (Figure 16.1). According to Lehtonen:

> this reflects the idea that economic activities should be in the service of all human beings while at the same time safeguarding the biophysical systems necessary for human existence. The social would thus be in the command of the economic, but at the same time submitted to the ultimate environmental constraints.
>
> *(Lehtonen 2004: 201)*

Different political philosophies underpin each model, and an in-depth discussion of these would go far beyond the scope of this chapter. However, both provide a useful starting point to explore the concept of sustainable development and its possible applications to CALL development, as we will see later on in the chapter.

The environmental/ecological concept of sustainable development outlined earlier, and more particularly the 'institutional model', underpins most current debates on sustainability at all levels of society. According to the US Environmental Protection Agency (EPA n.d.)

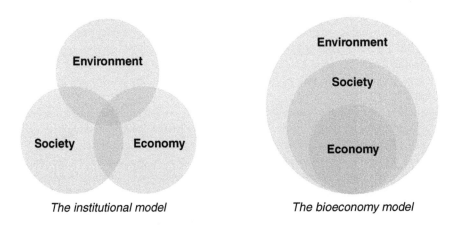

*Figure 16.1* Two models for sustainable development

Source: Adapted from Lehtonen (2004).

website, 'sustainability creates and maintains the conditions under which humans and nature can exist in productive harmony, that permit fulfilling the social, economic and other requirements of present and future generations'. In the business world, sustainability can be defined as the 'continued development or growth, without significant deterioration of the environment and depletion of natural resources on which human well-being depends' (BusinessDictionary. com), or as 'managing the triple bottom line – a process by which companies manage their financial, social and environmental risks, obligations and opportunities' (*Financial Times* Lexicon). In a blog post, Bent (2011) argues for the adoption by organisations of a 'sustainable business model', which must be commercially successful, future-ready and part of a sustainable society.

Universities around the world are also embracing this tripartite definition of sustainability, which increasingly drives higher education developments. For example, the Vanderbilt University (US) website defines sustainability from an institutional perspective as 'the development of a process or management system that helps to create a vibrant campus economy and high quality of life while respecting the need to sustain natural resources and protect the environment'. They further define sustainable programmes as 'those that result from an institution's commitment to environmental, social and economic health' (Vanderbilt University n.d.). In the UK, Kingston University is 'committed to fostering a culture of sustainable practice throughout the University, ensuring [the university community] contribute[s] positively to the economy, environment and society from the local to the global scale'. This is done by 'facilitating and promoting best practice in the development of [their] campus operations, curriculum, research and partnerships' (Kingston University n.d.).

A sustainable curriculum or programme of studies does not necessarily mean that any or all three sustainability pillars are core components of a given study programme. While a university may offer 'flagship' programmes or courses on different aspects of sustainability (including development education or 'green finance'), a sustainable programme can be defined in terms of its capacity to respond to present and future societal or economic needs within the limitations imposed not only by the institution business model and funding opportunities, but also by its 'human capital', physical and technological infrastructure, and by the local or national culture and values. In most cases, however, the sustainability of programmes, courses or simply of new pedagogical initiatives is likely to be conceived in its more basic form, that is, as *the capacity to be maintained or prolonged* through adequate funding and resources. This seemingly narrower view of sustainability is also espoused by the European Commission in relation to international cooperation projects under the auspices of the now defunct Lifelong Learning Programme (2007–13). For example, in the context of Tempus projects, a project is deemed sustainable 'when it continues to deliver benefits to the project beneficiaries and/or other constituencies for an extended period after the Commission's financial assistance has been terminated' (EC Directorate General Education and Culture 2006: cover page). This extended period usually covers two years after the end of the allocated funding. Similarly, in the context of Leonardo projects:

> sustainability means that *crucial* activities and results of the project are maintained and continue to deliver benefits to the target group, structure, sector or system *after* the end of the EU funding. Ideally, the sustainability of a project should also generate impact, meaning direct or indirect long-term effects on actors, structures, sectors or systems *beyond* the original project environment.
>
> (*EC Directorate-General Education and Culture,*
> *Lifelong Learning Programme 2007–13, emphasis in the original*)

## Towards a definition of sustainable CALL

Interestingly, the environmental/ecological dimension of sustainability also tends to be absent from the institutional or academic discourse surrounding the development and diffusion of e-learning, including CALL. However, concepts and principles of sustainable development, as well as the need for the implementation of a development education framework, are often implicit in the e-learning literature, at least in its social and economic dimensions, through the renewed emphasis on lifelong learning that accompanies many curriculum and e-learning developments within and across disciplines. Lifelong learning, according to UNESCO, is 'the philosophy, conceptual framework, and organizing principle for education in the 21st century' (2013: 3), and is regarded as essential to empowering the citizens of the world to respond to the global environmental, social, cultural, economic and technological changes that characterise the 21st century. A lifelong learning framework must 'provide comprehensive and flexible pathways combining formal, non-formal and informal opportunities, in order to cater to the diversity of learning needs' (UNESCO 2013: 3). E-learning has been hailed by governments, higher education authorities and third-level education providers, either public or private, as crucial to the operationalisation of the global educational vision and goals formulated by international organisations such as UNESCO or the Organisation for Economic Co-Operation and Development (OECD). However, this requires the *sustainable embedding* of successful e-learning initiatives in institutional contexts (Sharpe, Benfield and Francis 2006; Nichols 2008; Robertson 2008) as well as in nonformal or informal settings.

The sustainable embedding of an e-learning initiative or innovation is normally defined in terms of its diffusion within an institutional (or cross-institutional) context, and of its adoption by a wider community, beyond the immediate context of its development (see e.g. Nichols 2008: 599), leading to its sustainable embedding, that is, to a 'sustainable and effective uptake of technologies that improve[s] the student experience' (Sharpe et al. 2006: 136) and learning outcomes. Robertson (2008: 819) defines sustainable e-learning as 'e-learning that has become normative practice and which has the capacity to meet the needs of the present and the future'. The notion of a 'normative practice' points to the concept of CALL *normalisation*, which has been the focus of much of Bax's (2000, 2003; Chambers and Bax 2006) work. According to Bax (2003: 23), 'this concept is relevant to any kind of technological innovation and refers to the stage when the technology becomes invisible, embedded in everyday practice and hence "normalised"'. If CALL normalisation and sustainability are not identical concepts, they nevertheless share some features, more particularly those that focus on the diffusion and adoption of CALL initiatives or innovations by the wider community and on change and development (see e.g. Chambers and Bax 2006: 466). Keeping with Robertson's (2008) definition of sustainable e-learning, we thus define *sustainable CALL* as CALL initiatives or innovations that have been or are in the process of being normalised – and thus will be maintained and prolonged – and which have the capacity to meet the needs of present and future language teachers and learners.

The capacity to meet language teachers' and learners' present and future needs is often assessed through the investigation of factors that may impede or promote normalisation and/or sustainability, such as logistics, stakeholders' conceptions, knowledge and abilities, syllabus and software integration, and training, development and support (Chambers and Bax 2006: 476). Looking at CALL development, within one institution and against rapid technological change, Kennedy and Levy (2009: 446) argue that the success of a new initiative requires that it is tailored to the particular context, integrated into the curriculum, and that it goes through an iterative development process. They identify a range of factors that have shaped, over a fifteen-year period, the 'genesis, development and longevity' of a number of CALL projects for

Italian within their own institution: key factors include institutional support (i.e. funding, reliable infrastructure, adequate technical support), the practitioners' skills, attitudes and collective strategic decisions, and student evaluation and feedback, with the latter being fully integrated into an iterative enhancement process (Kennedy and Levy 2009: 455). In doing so, they stress that rapid technological change is not incompatible with a long-term approach to CALL projects, nor does it require that 'we have to continually upgrade or convert to new platforms' (Kennedy and Levy 2009: 460).

While Kennedy and Levy (2009) discuss CALL sustainability at a macro level, and more specifically at the institutional level, other researchers have focused on CALL sustainability at the level of learners (micro level), and are more particularly concerned with online language learning practices that can be sustained over time thanks to the development and integration of language learning technologies. For example, Hiroya Tanaka et al. (2013) developed Lexinote, an e-portfolio system designed to help Japanese learners of English to sustain their vocabulary learning over time. Sustaining vocabulary learning outside the classroom is also the motive behind Stockwell's (2013) study, in which he investigates the effect of a 'push' mechanism (via the sending of notifications to students' mobile phones) on learners' engagement with 'pull' web-based vocabulary learning activities. His conclusions suggest however that push notifications via their mobile phone do not result in students immediately carrying out the suggested activities. They seem to prefer to engage with these activities on a PC at home or at the university, and thus appear to 'make calculated decisions about which platform to use depending on their particular learning needs' (Stockwell 2013: 322; see also Stockwell, Chapter 21 this volume). In this case, pushing notifications and reminders via learners' mobile phones may have very little impact on helping them sustain their vocabulary learning activities outside the classroom. In an earlier study, Stockwell and Levy (2001) investigate the relationship between the sustainability of email exchanges between native and nonnative speakers of English on the one hand and learner online profiles on the other. Starting from the commonly held view that email exchanges that are sustained over time are likely to have an impact on the development of language proficiency, these authors seek to determine whether or not a relationship exists between the number and length of email interactions and L2 proficiency gains, and if so, what factors have an effect on the sustainability of these interactions. The results of their study suggest that students who produce higher numbers of messages are indeed more likely to demonstrate L2 gains. However, they also show that higher proficiency learners are more likely 'to be more prolific e-mail writers than those with a lower proficiency' (Stockwell and Levy 2001: 437). They derive some suggestions for learner training, in particular in the area of strategic training:

> In the same way that students need strategies to initiate and maintain face-to-face interactions, which have their own particular dynamic, students will also need strategies for the on-line interactional environment.
>
> *(Stockwell and Levy 2001: 437)*

Finally, Chow (2013) reports on a longitudinal study (over a two-year period) that sought to establish the degree of sustainability of informal language learning via Livemocha, which combines social networking and more traditional online language learning activities. Not only does she show that the use of the Livemocha platform gradually increased over the two-year period, thus suggesting the emergence of a sustainable language learning practice, she also highlights the significant role of environmental factors (e.g. the Livemocha platform itself, students' professional and social environments) and learner characteristics (e.g. learning styles, attitudes and everyday engagement with social networks).

While looking at different aspects of sustainability and CALL in various educational settings and technological environments, the aforementioned studies all point to factors that can facilitate or impede sustainable language teaching and learning mediated by technology. Such factors may include institutional support, tools development and maintenance, teacher and learner training and development, and last but not least, the building of a community of teachers and/or learners collectively contributing to the establishment of new language teaching and learning practices. In line with Chambers and Bax (2006), we believe that these various factors interact with each other. What is true for CALL normalisation also applies to sustainable CALL: 'in working towards normalisation it is therefore important to address more than one factor at a time, taking account of the "ecological complexity" of the whole context in each case' (Chambers and Bax 2006: 477).

Sustainable CALL, even in its most basic representation, that is the 'capacity to maintain and to prolong' language teaching and learning practices mediated by technology, can only be realised to its full potential if we look at CALL from an ecological perspective (see Blin, Chapter 3 this volume), and more specifically, by adopting a system view of the world, which 'helps us to understand the true nature of education as a complex, open, and dynamic human activity system that operates in ever-changing multiple environments and interacts with a variety of societal systems' (Banathy 1992: 17).

## A systematic view of sustainable CALL

The systems view or systems theories have emerged in recent decades both in education and in the corporate world to help understand and manage sustainable change. These theories describe and highlight the dynamic nature of complex systems, such as language or bio systems. In CALL, these ecological approaches have also become an area of interest and inquiry (see Blin, Chapter 3 this volume). These approaches offer many useful concepts and metaphors for understanding how the different levels and elements of a CALL complex system are always affected by changes in any other part of the system. Thus, a systemic approach to sustainability organises and conceptualises these different components, as well as documents and analyses the interaction between them. In other words, sustainability is built on understanding and acknowledging the relationships between the different components of the system across different timescales.

### An example of systemic thinking for sustainable CALL

To illuminate the sustainability approach further, an EU-funded project under the auspices of the Lifelong Learning Programme, SpeakApps (http://www.speakapps.org), is provided as an example to show how systemic thinking can be applied in CALL research and development projects. The main objective of the project was to create online tools for oral practice and to design pedagogical templates and examples of tasks for their use. Four main areas, seen as key components of a complex system that was to become SpeakApps, were to form the basis not only for the various work packages that constituted the project, but also for the development of a sustainability framework that would underpin the research and development work throughout the life cycle of the project. These areas were (1) development of a platform and tools enabling the learning and practice of spoken skills online, (2) pedagogical and professional development, (3) building of a community of practitioners and (4) development of an exploitation plan and of a business model that would ensure the sustainability and the financial viability of the system beyond the funding period.

While the fourth and last area directly relates to the overall sustainability of the SpeakApps system (and was required by the funders), the other three were integrated into a sustainability framework from the very beginning of the project (Blin, Jalkanen, Taalas, Nic Giolla Mhichil and Ó Ciardubháin 2012). From a sustainability perspective, the tools and platform component is primarily *technological* and refers to the longer term maintenance and development of the SpeakApps technologies in response not only to future technological changes but also to the changing needs of language learners with regards to the learning and practice of spoken skills online. The pedagogical and professional development component is *developmental* and relates to initial and continuing professional development through the creation of pedagogical designs and artefacts, by and for language teachers, that can respond to the present and future needs of teachers and learners. Finally, the third component is *social* and concerns not only the building and maintenance of a community of SpeakApps practitioners, but also the community's capacity to transform itself and to create new knowledge and practices.

The aforementioned components can be seen as interacting subsystems, whose elements were identified and linked to factors that could either support or constrain the objectives and sustainability of other subsystems. Relationships within and between the four main components were drawn in order to better understand their interconnectedness (see Figure 16.2).

Using Figure 16.2 as a roadmap throughout the project made it possible to see which component could be affected by changes in another. For instance, the modification of a particular tool would require changes in a planned training workshop or in the design of pedagogical tasks. Similarly, the creation of new tasks, in response to a new emerging need, may require the available tools to be modified. Guiding questions were formulated with respect to each component and their main elements (see Blin et al. 2012). They could then serve as a checklist to assist project partners in their efforts to define sustainable objectives and strategies during the development phase. In order to measure progress and achievements with regards to the sustainability of the project (i.e. platform and tools, pedagogical and professional development, community building), provisional indicators were developed for each component (see Table 16.1 for examples). Indicators such as these can help identify the potential for further development as well as emerging sustainability issues.

The SpeakApps sustainability framework is not restricted to a commercialisation plan. While it does include an exploitation plan that should ensure the medium-term financial viability of the project (e.g. through a license fee structure), it does not seek to maintain products and services that are no longer relevant nor does it seek to preserve existing organisational structures and processes. Rather, it views SpeakApps as an open and flexible system, whose technological tools and pedagogical artefacts will be used in ways or for purposes that were not part of the developers' initial plan. It seeks to enable the self-organised continuation of the project and the self-sustainability of its operations, activities and communities as they evolve over time and across multiple spaces (Blin et al. 2012). In other words, the SpeakApps sustainability framework is primarily concerned with the *sustainable development* of the SpeakApps system, which needs to take into account the present and future needs of its users, both teachers and learners, as well as their current language teaching and learning practices. The framework is useful for evolving the three dimensions or elements of sustainability discussed earlier in this chapter into a model for sustainable CALL development.

## The four pillars of sustainable CALL development

The four main areas of activity identified in the SpeakApps project need to be renamed to make them more general, adaptable and scalable. The tools and platforms become environments and tools for learning, the pedagogical and professional development remain as is, community building is expanded to community and knowledge building, and the business model is incorporated

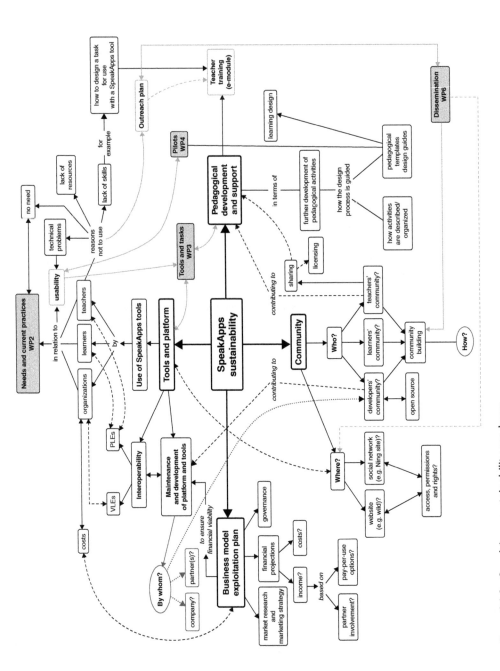

*Figure 16.2* SpeakApps sustainability roadmap

*Source:* http://speakapps.org.

*Table 16.1* Examples of SpeakApps sustainability indicators

| Component | Sustainability indicators | Description |
| --- | --- | --- |
| Pedagogical and professional development | Number and types of artefacts (e.g. resources and materials for the language classroom or professional development) being used by users of the system | Defines the basic needs for the resources and materials available to users |
| | Number, types, and origin of new artefacts contributed by users of the system | Defines the basic needs for the resources and materials available to users and the system capacity to meet them |
| Community building | Number and type of users | Defines the ongoing basic needs for the project services and resources |
| | Focus and quality of users' contributions with regards to the teaching and learning of the skills and competences that are the focus of the project | Indicates possible changes in the community primary focus |
| Platform and tools | Number of successful integrations into institutional VLEs | Defines the institutional needs for the products and services, and measures the system capacity to meet these needs |
| | Evidence of additional tools used to perform project related tasks | Indicates whether the project tools meet the needs of the target users |
| Business model and exploitation plan | Number of paying users over time | Defines the needs for products and services and users' willingness to pay for these products and services; indicates the actual market size for the project products and services |
| | Exploitation Consortium Annual Report | Indicates viability of commercial entity and effectiveness of governance structure |

Source: From Blin et al. (2012).

into an organisational structures component. These are proposed as the 'four pillars of sustainable CALL' and they will be explained further in the coming sections.

## Environments and tools for learning

From a sustainability aspect, it is important to analyse the various technological tools and environments from the points of view of potential and their added value and always in relation to the current practices and how these practices are affected by the infusion of technology. It is important to realise that different environments and tools provide different affordances, that is, action possibilities that are offered by the environment (see Blin, Chapter 3 this volume for a more detailed discussion) for different types of learners and in different types of activities and task designs. Affordances are realised depending on the learner's perception, motivation and capacity (Gibson 1986; van Lier 2000), meaning that the technologies don't necessarily have self-sustained value, but their potential or affordance will become reality through activities that are contextualised and purposefully planned for the specific group of learners and with realistic expectations for the outcome and added value. As Jones, Dirckinck-Holmfeld and Lindström (2006: 51) point out, 'technologies do not have affordance within them, affordances occur in relationships with active agents or actants'. In other words, 'it is the activity that determines what is picked up, not the complex environment' (van Lier 2004: 93). To summarise, for the creation and use of the tools and environments to be sustainable, they need to be planned and chosen for the intended users, learning goals and existing practices in mind.

## Pedagogical and professional development

There is a great deal of discussion and even debate around the role of pedagogical innovation in relation to pedagogical development. Teachers develop their teaching and themselves as professionals through their everyday practice. When trying out different types of activities they eventually develop a tacit understanding of what works and what does not. In the middle of the constantly hurried life in schools and universities, they develop new teaching materials and, when interacting with students in the classroom situation, aim at fixing things that do not work (in more academic terms, this could be called a local configuration). Whereas they have adopted a certain theoretical approach to language and learning during their studies and the 'pedagogical atmosphere' of institutions might encourage a certain type of pedagogy, in the classroom they are very much on their own.

Fullan (2007: 30) reminds us of the multidimensionality of pedagogical innovation. According to him, there are at least three dimensions or levels of 'new' in terms of introducing a change in education whether at the policy or practice level:

1. The possible use of new or revised *materials* (instructional resources such as curriculum materials or technologies);
2. The possible use of new *teaching approaches* (i.e. new teaching strategies or activities);
3. The possible alteration of *beliefs* (e.g. pedagogical assumptions and theories underlying particular new policies or programs).

All of these dimensions are needed to bring about a systemic change, but very often the change takes place at the first level only (e.g. in the case of introducing new technologies). To ensure a systemic, and thus more sustainable integration of technology, continuous professional development is a must. It will also make it possible for the teachers to gain ownership and agency over the technological changes and to redesign the pedagogical approaches to align with the changes in the learning environment. The underlying ideology in all professional development is to help the teachers to eventually become familiar with, for instance, an e-learning platform, not as a technological tool but as a vehicle to expand the teachers' pedagogical thinking as well as learning opportunities and optimal conditions for the different learner groups in different contexts.

## Community and knowledge building

Community as a more or less stable entity has for quite some time been the unit of focus for many researchers. The basic premise behind *communities of practice* (Lave and Wenger 1991) has been that there is a community of people who share a way of communicating in certain ways, and gradually, by interacting with the members of the community, a new member becomes part of this community. This process has also been seen as a shift from a novice to an expert. In their attempt to define a new culture of learning, Thomas and Brown contrast communities with collectives:

> As the name implies, [a collective] is a collection of people, skills, and talent that produces a result greater than the sum of its parts. For our purposes, collective is not solely defined by shared intention, action, or purpose (though those elements may exist and often do). Rather they are defined by an active engagement with the process of learning. [...] In communities, people learn in order to belong. In a collective, people belong in order to learn.
>
> *(Thomas and Brown 2011: 52)*

The idea of community put forward by Thomas and Brown (2011) is that of a more dynamic collection of people. A similar notion is characteristic of Engeström's work (see e.g. Engeström 2008), who has extensively studied learning that takes place within and across the contexts of workplace. In his many studies he has demonstrated how a great deal of learning in the workplace occurs in dynamic formations in which 'the center does not hold' and which are created around a task, a purpose or a goal. The same can be seen in today's youths' informal learning communities that can involve quite sophisticated and ambitious goals for learning, for instance in 3D design or for creating new guitar riffs. From a sustainability perspective, teacher communities or collectives need to exist not only to maintain, but also to recreate and reinvent the understanding and purpose of the implementation and use of certain tools and environments.

## *Organisational structures*

Designing for sustainable development necessitates a systems view of the learning setting that represents the whole organisation as one ecology. In such a system most development is planned and carried out together with all levels of the organisation and with the larger organisational goals and factors in mind, while also recognising the possibility that something completely unplanned and unexpected might emerge as a result.

As noted by Boreham and Morgan:

> most contemporary researchers define learning as organizational to the extent that it is undertaken by members of an organization to achieve organizational purposes, takes place in teams or other small groups, is distributed widely throughout the organization and embeds its outcomes in the organization's system, structures and culture.
>
> *(Boreham and Morgan 2004: 308)*

In her framework for sustainable information and communications technologies (ICT) integration that builds on the systems view, Taalas (2005) identifies teacher and learner support, mental and financial resources, and theoretical links to learning, language learning and assessment as integral components. Based on the data from the SITES-M2 study, Owston (2007) proposes a model with almost identical elements. The main difference is that Owston's model lacks the theoretical aspect and instead highlights the importance of the role of educational policies. However, as Taalas et al. (2008: 243) point out, the aspects of theory or research 'are often separated from both the practice and policy levels and thus form an isolated existence adjacent to both these levels, but without a real linkage to either'. In addition, Owston (2007) maintains that some of these factors are essential whereas others can be seen as merely contributing to sustainability.

Jalkanen and Taalas (2013) discuss the idea of designing *for* sustainability and link sustainable pedagogical development to organisational learning. They maintain that whereas organisational structures are important, there must also be room for emergence, discovery and new pedagogical initiatives. The sustainability of environments for learning also needs to be considered, as these environments need to be both negotiated and rooted in the transforming organisational and pedagogical practice. In this way funding periods and project time frames will no longer be the sole determining factors for the lifespan of the environments and new practices.

## Two models for sustainable CALL development

The four pillars of CALL sustainable development briefly described earlier bear some analogy to the three pillars of environmental/ecological sustainability introduced at the beginning of this chapter. The economic and environmental pillars have been replaced by the organisational structures and learning environment pillars, respectively. The social pillar has been divided into two components reflecting its collective and individual elements, as well as the interaction between them. In line with Lehtonen's (2004) discussion of the three pillars of environmental sustainability, we can conceptualise the relationships and interactions between the four pillars with the help of two distinct models (see Figure 16.3).

The first model, or *institutional model*, takes as a starting point that the four pillars are equal and mutually interacting. However, they are likely to be treated as separate and independent entities during the design, development and deployment of the CALL project. In line with Lehtonen (2004: 201), we can voice a number of criticisms against such a model, such as the risk of maintaining a status quo (e.g. the nontransformation of existing pedagogical practices), a potential overemphasis on 'productivity' (e.g. the efficient delivery of courses to increasing numbers of students) as opposed to the quality of the language learning experience and outcomes, and the emergence of potential conflicts between the different pillars that may prove difficult to resolve. For example, the development of new pedagogical practices within an institution may conflict with the existing organisational structures, or with the learning environment available to language teachers and students at a point in time. The institutional model does however provide a useful sustainability roadmap for large collaborative projects, such as the SpeakApps project briefly discussed earlier, where different partners, usually from different countries and institutions, bring different contexts and practices that have to be taken into account in the collective design for sustainability.

The second model, which we identify as the *CALL ecosystem model*, assumes a form of hierarchy between the four pillars, which constitute nested systems. By analogy to the bioeconomy system discussed by Lehtonen (2004), the *environments for learning* circle circumscribes the social components and the *organisational structures* component constitutes the innermost circle. According to this model, and drawing on Lehtonen (2004), organisational structures should be in the service of all actors in the learning environment, while ensuring that the technologies, tools and language learning artefacts are adequately maintained and developed in response to the changing needs of teachers and learners. At the same time, the social components should drive the organisational structures while being 'submitted to the ultimate environmental constraints' (Lehtonen 2004: 201) and ensuring that the affordances of the learning environment are realised. The environmental constraints and affordances for language learning are however frequently changing as a result not only of rapid technological changes, but also of institutional and national (or even international) priorities and policies in relation to e-learning. Borrowing from Lehtonen (2004: 202), and in line with Kennedy and Levy (2009), this does not mean however that the learning environment, and more particularly the technologies, 'would necessarily always be the most important and relevant dimension'. Depending on the context, the development of individual teachers' pedagogical and professional development and the community or collective to which they belong, or the organisational structures supporting (or impeding) the existing pedagogical practice may be 'the most relevant and meaningful point of departure' to ensure the

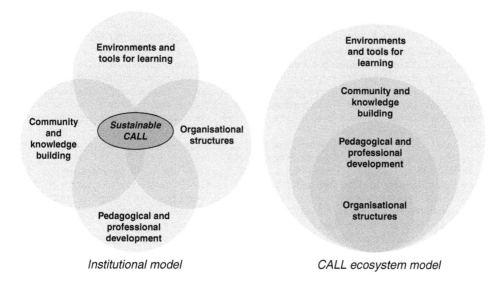

*Figure 16.3* The four pillars of sustainable CALL

sustainability of a CALL initiative. We believe that the CALL ecosystem model is particularly suited, at the local level, to CALL innovations that aspire to be self-organised and self-sustainable in the medium or longer term.

## A glance into the future

Throughout this chapter, we have highlighted the multidimensional facets of sustainable CALL from a systemic perspective while drawing on the literature on environmental/ecological sustainability. What we have called the *four pillars of sustainable CALL*, by analogy to the *three pillars of sustainable development* discussed at the beginning of the chapter, constitute the foundations on which to build sustainable CALL initiatives and innovations, whatever their initial scope and context of deployment. Indeed, as mentioned earlier, designing for sustainability, as well as for teaching and learning (see Blin and Jalkanen 2014), and more specifically for sustainable CALL development, should be an integral part of all CALL designs from the outset.

The two models for sustainable CALL development we presented earlier are still very much in their infancy and require further work. They provide nevertheless a useful point of departure for developing CALL sustainability frameworks that take into account the dynamic interactions between the four dimensions within a particular context. In line with Lehtonen (2004: 211), we indeed believe that 'different geographical and temporal scales as well as situational contexts require their own framework, which do not necessarily provide a coherent picture, but a mosaic of partly contradicting views of reality'. Context-specific sustainability measurements and indicators are also needed to evaluate the sustainability of a CALL innovation as well as trace the transformation of its different components and elements across multiple timescales.

When applied to CALL development, and when combined with systemic and ecological views of language, language teaching and language learning, the concepts and principles of environmental/ecological sustainability are powerful tools that can only enrich the CALL research agenda and ensure that our designs and development activities will be maintained and prolonged while addressing the present and future needs of language learners and teachers.

## Further reading

Banathy, B.H. (1992) *A Systems View of Education: Concepts and Principles for Effective Practice*, Englewood Cliffs, NJ: Educational Technology Publications.

In this book, Banathy defines his pioneering concept of systems thinking. His thinking has been used to help design strategies and methods in various contexts, for instance in the Educational Design System (EDS). In Banathy's work, design process is viewed as a creative, iterative, holistic, decision-oriented process resulting in a model of a new system. He also emphasises that the designers must transcend current approaches and solutions to design a completely new model of a system appropriate for the specific, unique context.

Lehtonen, M. (2004) 'The environmental–social interface of sustainable development: capabilities, social capital, institutions', *Ecological Economics*, 49(2): 199–214.

In this article, Lehtonen explores the social dimension of sustainable development and the environmental-social interface. Although this work is located in ecological economics and not in CALL (nor in any cognate domain), the concepts presented and discussed provide an interesting starting point to explore the multidimensional features of sustainable CALL, and more particularly the role of the social dimension and of its dynamic interactions with other components.

Ludvigsen, S., Lund, A., Rasmussen, I. and Säljö, R. (eds) (2011) *Learning Across Sites. New Tools, Infrastructures and Practices*. EARLI publications series, London, UK: Routledge.

This collection of articles brings together a diverse range of contributions from leading international researchers to examine the impacts and roles which evolving digital technologies have on our navigation of education and professional work environments. Viewing learning as a socially organised activity, the contributors explore the evolution of learning technologies and knowledge acquisition in networked societies through empirical research in a range of industries and workplaces.

Owston, R. (2007) 'Contextual factors that sustain innovative pedagogical practice using technology: an international study', *Journal of Educational Change*, 8(1): 61–77.

In this article, Owston offers an explanatory model of sustainability that is based on the analysis of a great number of cases in the SITES-M2 project. He has identified two sets of contextual factors that are either essential for or contributing to sustainable innovative teaching practices using technology. This model functions as a valuable point of departure for rethinking development projects and processes in CALL.

Sterling, S. (2004) 'Higher education, sustainability and the role of systemic learning', in P.B. Corcoran and A.E.J. Wals (eds), *Higher Education and the Challenge of Sustainability: Problematics, Promise, and Practice*, Dordrecht: Kluwer Academic, 49–70.

In this paper, Sterling argues for a fundamental change in educational cultures and practices. Instead of approaching sustainability as an add-on to existing structures and curricula, he advocates a systemic learning approach, which places the transformation of practices and structures at the core of pedagogical and organisational development. The ideas presented in the paper are useful in repositioning and expanding the discussion of sustainable CALL development.

## References

Banathy, B.H. (1992) *A Systems View of Education: Concepts and Principles for Effective Practice*, Englewood Cliffs, NJ: Educational Technology Publications.

Bax, S. (2000) 'Putting technology in its place', in C. Field (ed), *Issues in Modern Foreign Languages Teaching*, London, UK: Routledge: 208–219.

Bax, S. (2003) 'CALL – Past, present and future', *System*, 31(1): 13–28.

Bent, D. (2011) 'Characteristics of a sustainable business model' [online], *Forum for the Future*, available: http://www.forumforthefuture.org/blog/characteristics-sustainable-business-model

Blin, F. and Jalkanen, J. (2014) 'Designing for Language Learning: Agency and languaging in hybrid environments', *Apples – Journal of Applied Language Studies*, 8(1): 147–170.

Blin, F., Jalkanen, J., Taalas, P., Nic Giolla Mhichil, M. and Ó Ciardubháin, C. (2012) 'A framework for sustainability' [online], Project Nr 2010–4210 / 511552-LLP-1-2010-1-ES-KA2-KA2MP-SPKApps, available: http://langblog.test.speakapps.org/webspeakapps/files/2013/02/5-1_sustainabilityframework.pdf

Boreham, N. and Morgan, C. (2004) 'A sociocultural analysis of organizational learning', *Oxford Review of Education*, 30(3): 307–325.

Brundtland, G.H. (1987) *Report of the World Commission on Environment and Development: 'Our Common Future'* [online], United Nations, available: http://www.un-documents.net/ocf-02.htm

Chambers, A. and Bax, S. (2006) 'Making CALL work: Towards normalisation', *System*, 34(4): 465–479.

Chow, G.S.-M. (2013) 'Pedagogy 2.0 for teaching English as an international language: Sustainability of Livemocha as an informal learning resource', paper presented at the WorldCALL 2013 Conference – Global Perspectives on Computer-Assisted Language Learning, Glasgow, UK, 10–13 July 2013.

Engeström, Y. (2008) *From Teams to Knots: Activity-Theoretical Studies of Collaboration and Learning at Work*, Cambridge: Cambridge University Press.

European Commission Directorate-General Education and Culture (2006) *Sustainability of International Cooperation Projects in the Field of Higher Education and Vocational Training: Handbook on Sustainability* [online], Luxembourg: Office for Official Publications of the European Communities, available: http://ec.europa.eu/dgs/education_culture

European Commission Directorate-General Education and Culture, Lifelong Learning Programme (2007–13) *Leonardo da Vinci, Transfer of innovation: Sustainability of European Cooperation Projects in VET – Check list for Project Coordinators* [online], available: http://www.oapee.es/dctm/weboapee/pap/leonardo-da-vinci/proyectos-multilaterales-de-toi/2013/sustainability-check-list-for-project-coordinators.pdf?documentId=0901e72b8175a659

Fullan, M. (2007) *The New Meaning of Educational Change*, London, UK: Routledge.

Gibson, J.J. (1986) *The Ecological Approach to Visual Perception*, Hillsdale, NJ: Lawrence Erlbaum Associates.

Jalkanen, J. and Taalas, P. (2013) 'Designing for sustainable pedagogical development in higher education language teaching', in E. Christiansen, L. Kuure, A. Mørch and B. Lindström (eds), *Problem-Based Learning for the 21st Century: New Practices and Learning Environments*, Aalborg: Aalborg University Press: 73–99, available: http://vbn.aau.dk/files/187818413/PROBLEM_BASED_LEARNING_FOR_THE_21st_CENTURY_WEB.pdf

Jones, C., Dirckinck-Holmfeld, L. and Lindström, B. (2006) 'A relational, indirect, meso-level approach to CSCL design in the next decade', *Computer Supported Collaborative Learning*, 1(1): 35–56.

Kennedy, C. and Levy, M. (2009) 'Sustainability and computer-assisted language learning: Factors for success in a context of change', *Computer Assisted Language Learning*, 22(5): 445–463.

Kingston University (n.d.) 'Sustainability' [online], available: http://www.kingston.ac.uk/aboutkingstonuniversity/sustainability/

Lave, J. and Wenger, E. (1991) *Situated Learning: Legitimate Peripheral Participation*, Cambridge: Cambridge University Press.

Lehtonen, M. (2004) 'The environmental–social interface of sustainable development: capabilities, social capital, institutions', *Ecological Economics*, 49(2): 199–214.

Livemocha (na) [online], available: http://livemocha.com/

Nichols, M. (2008) 'Institutional perspectives: The challenges of e-learning diffusion', *British Journal of Educational Technology*, 39(4): 598–609.

Owston, R. (2007) 'Contextual factors that sustain innovative pedagogical practice using technology: An international study', *Journal of Educational Change*, 8(1): 61–77.

Robertson, I. (2008) 'Sustainable e-learning, activity theory and professional development', *Ascilite*: 819–826, available: http://ascilite.org.au/conferences/melbourne08/procs/robertson.pdf?origin=publication_detail (accessed 6 Apr 2014).

Sharpe, R., Benfield, G. and Francis, R. (2006) 'Implementing a university e-learning strategy: Levers for change within academic schools', *ALT-J, Research in Learning Technology*, 14(2): 135–151.

Stockwell, G. (2013) 'Sustaining out-of-class mobile learning through a mobile phone based "push" mechanism', *WorldCALL 2013 Proceedings – Global Perspectives on Computer-Assisted Language Learning* [online], 341–344, available: http://www.arts.ulster.ac.uk/worldcall2013/userfiles/file/shortpapers.pdf

Stockwell, G. and Levy, M. (2001) 'Sustainability of e-mail interactions between native speakers and non-native speakers', *Computer Assisted Language Learning*, 14(5): 419–442.

Taalas, P. (2005) *Change in the Making: Strategic and Pedagogical Challenges of Technology Integration in Language Teaching*, Jyväskylä: Centre for Applied Language Studies, University of Jyväskylä, available: https://www.jyu.fi/hum/laitokset/solki/tutkimus/julkaisut/pdf-julkaisut/changeinthemaking.pdf

Taalas, P., Kauppinen, M., Tarnanen, M. and Pöyhönen, S. (2008) 'Media landscapes in school and in free time – two parallel realities?', *Digital Kompetanse – Nordic Journal of Digital Literacy*, 3(4): 240–256.

Tanaka, H., Suzanne M., Yonesaka, S.M., Ueno, Y. and Ohnishi, A. (2013) 'Developing an e-portfolio to enhance sustainable vocabulary learning in English', *WorldCALL 2013 Proceedings – Global Perspectives on Computer-Assisted Language Learning* [online], 341–344, available: http://www.arts.ulster.ac.uk/worldcall2013/userfiles/file/shortpapers.pdf

Thomas, D. and Brown, J.S. (2011) *A New Culture of Learning: Cultivating the Imagination for a World of Constant Change*, Lexington, KY: CreateSpace.

UNESCO (2007) 'The UN Decade of Education for Sustainable Development (DESD 2005–2014) – The First Two Years' [online], available: http://www.unesco.org/education/desd

UNESCO (2013) *Principles on Education for Development Beyond 2015* [online], available: http://en.unesco.org/post2015/sites/post2015/files/UNESCOPrinciplesonEducationforDevelopmentBeyond2015.pdf

US Environmental Protection Agency (EPA) [online], available: http://www.epa.gov/sustainability/basicinfo.htm

Vanderbilt University (n.d.) 'What Is Sustainability?' [online], available: http://www.vanderbilt.edu/sustainvu/who-we-are/what-is-sustainability/

van Lier, L. (2000) 'From input to affordance: Social-interactive learning from an ecological perspective', in J.P. Lantolf (ed), *Sociocultural Theory and Second Language Learning*, Oxford: Oxford University Press: 245–259.

van Lier, L. (2004) *The Ecology and Semiotics of Language Learning : A Sociocultural Perspective*, Boston, MA: Kluwer Academic.

# Part III
# Interactive and collaborative technologies for language learning

# 17
# Telecollaboration and language learning

*Francesca Helm and Sarah Guth*

The ever-increasing access to the Internet across the globe has made it possible for language educators to implement telecollaboration, which can be defined as online intercultural exchange between classes of foreign language students in geographically distant locations. Reflecting what has been defined as the 'intercultural turn' in foreign language education and the 'crucible of new media' (Thorne 2010), the aims of most telecollaboration projects go beyond the development of language competence to include the fostering of intercultural communicative competence (Byram 1997) as well as new online literacies (Guth and Helm 2010). This chapter begins with an outline of the divergent theoretical frameworks which justify the practice of telecollaboration, that is, interactionist and sociocultural theories of SLA (see Hubbard and Levy, Chapter 2 this volume). The authors then describe several models of telecollaboration which have been developed and expanded upon over the past twenty years. The next section focuses on considerations that need to be made when planning and implementing telecollaboration projects as regards collaborating with partner teachers, task design, communication modes and assessment. Subsequently the authors address the many challenges of implementing telecollaboration and making it a sustainable practice in higher education. The chapter concludes by looking at the future and the possibility of mainstreaming telecollaboration as a form of virtual mobility which could become a mainstay of foreign language courses in our increasingly interconnected and interdependent world.

## Theoretical frameworks for telecollaboration

Telecollaboration is the practice of engaging distant classes of language learners in interaction with one another using Internet-based communication tools to support intercultural exchange and foreign language learning. It developed as a form of network-based language teaching (NBLT) in the 1990s, which entailed the use of computers connected to one another in networks. Initially most NBLT was intraclass, and had learners within the same class communicating with one another. As the Internet became more widely available and accessible, foreign language teachers began to look for opportunities to engage learners in authentic interaction with expert speakers across the globe.

Telecollaboration was the first term to be used to describe this practice in foreign language education and appeared in the title of Warschauer's (1996) edited volume *Telecollaboration in Foreign Language Learning*. However, various other terms have been coined to define this activity, such as online intercultural exchange (OIE) (O'Dowd 2007) and Internet-mediated intercultural foreign language education (ICFLE) (Belz and Thorne 2006). This practice is also increasing in popularity outside of language learning contexts, and this has led to the coining of other terms such as globally networked learning (Starke-Meyerring and Wilson 2008), collaborative online international learning (COIL) (Rubin and Guth 2015) and virtual exchange. Although there are slight differences in the objectives of the practice each term refers to, they all share the goal of increasing students' understanding of their own and others' cultures by connecting them with peers in geographically distant locations using Internet technologies.

Theoretical justification for the practice of telecollaboration has been found both in interactionist perspectives on second language acquisition (SLA) and in sociocultural theories of foreign language development. Whilst initially telecollaboration activity focused on interaction for language development, this century has been characterised by an 'intercultural turn' in foreign language education and the 'crucible of new media' (Thorne 2010), which have brought the aims of most telecollaboration projects beyond the development of language competence to include the fostering of intercultural communicative competence (Byram 1997) as well as new online literacies (Guth and Helm 2010).

Interactionist SLA theory (see Hubbard and Levy, Chapter 2 this volume), which is based on the notions of comprehensible input and the output hypothesis, holds that the process of interaction encourages learners to attend to linguistic form as they monitor their interlocutor's comprehension and adjust their output to foster understanding (Chapelle 2008). It is particularly at moments when there is a lack of understanding that interlocutors are forced to pay attention to and adjust their linguistic output as they 'negotiate meaning'. The process of 'noticing' (Schmidt 1990), that is, directing attention to key linguistic features to facilitate understanding, is seen to foster language acquisition. Though it was developed in the context of face-to-face language learning, the interaction hypothesis clearly has relevance for telecollaboration, which is based on interaction between peers mediated by technology. Computer-mediated communication (CMC) has been found to have several characteristics that favour the negotiation of meaning and noticing, in particular the permanence of the written form over the spoken, which allows learners to go back to their interactions with the support of their teachers and to focus on form. Different modes of CMC have been analysed for the advantages they offer: synchronous text chat tends to be motivating and immediate for learners, while asynchronous communication gives learners time to reflect on their communication, to prepare and plan their interventions. The focus of educators and researchers working within this framework has been on designing tasks for interaction that offer opportunities for the negotiation of meaning and that lead interlocutors to draw one another's attention to form and correct each other's and their own errors.

Interactionist approaches have been problematised, however, for the focus on grammatical over pragmatic knowledge and meaning, and for fostering nonnaturalistic use of language as learners engage in tasks which are not authentic, but specifically designed to foster the negotiation of meaning. There is also an implicit assumption in the theories that if negotiation of meaning does not take place, no learning is taking place. However, the main issue for many telecollaboration researchers is that these approaches do not take into account the social and intercultural aspects of foreign language learning, but assume a purely cognitive view, which sees learners as individually internalising stable systems of language knowledge.

More social approaches to language development, in particular sociocultural theory based on the work of the Russian scholar Vygotsky (Lantolf and Thorne 2007), have been gaining ground and represent a shift from the purely cognitive view that characterises the interactionist paradigm. From a sociocultural perspective, cognitive development is interdependent with social activity. Learning is viewed as a social process in which culturally and historically situated participants engage in social activity, using culturally and socially produced artefacts. Language is one such artefact, as is technology, and these dynamic tools mediate and transform social activity and learning.

Sociocultural theory has been interpreted and developed in many ways, with different scholars emphasising different aspects such as the concept of mediation, activity theory, situated learning or communities of practice (for a fuller discussion of theoretical frameworks, see Hubbard and Levy, Chapter 2, and Blin, Chapter 3 this volume). Sociocultural theory has also been applied to the area of new literacy studies (see Dudeney and Hockly, Chapter 8 this volume) and how language learning through CMC relates to issues of culture, literacy and identity. Telecollaboration practices based on the sociocultural paradigm do not focus exclusively on language development, but very much on the development of intercultural communicative competence (ICC) and more recently also online literacies or multiliteracies and learner identities.

The model of ICC that has been most widely embraced in the telecollaboration literature stems from the work of Byram (1997), who views a person with a degree of intercultural competence as someone who can see relationships between different cultures and can interpret each in terms of the other. It is someone who recognises that their own perspective is culturally determined. Byram's construct of intercultural competence comprises five different *savoirs*: *savoir être*, attitudes of openness and curiosity; *savoir apprendre/faire*, skills of discovery and interaction; *savoirs*, knowledge of how social groups and identities function; *savoir comprendre*, that is skills of interpreting and relating; and finally the most complex, *savoir s'engager*, critical cultural awareness, the ability to evaluate critically perspectives, practices and products in one's own and other cultures.

Given the increasing importance placed on multiliteracies in addition to intercultural and language learning, Helm and Guth (2010) expanded Byram's model of ICC by integrating it with notions from the literature on new online literacies (Lankshear and Knobel 2006) and foreign language learning. The aim was to develop a broader framework for the definition of learning objectives for telecollaboration (see Table 17.1). It is beyond the scope of this chapter to enter into a detailed description of the model, so only a brief description will be provided here. The table is divided into the three areas mentioned earlier while the rows are divided into three dimensions: the operational, the cultural and the critical.

The operational dimension refers to the 'means' or 'tools' of literacy, language, tools and procedures, that is, the practical skills required for online intercultural communication. Lankshear and Knobel (2006) divided this dimension into the 'the technical stuff' and 'the ethos stuff'. This works well within the context of telecollaboration since effective intercultural communication inherently requires not only language skills, but attitudes and interest as well. In Byram's model of ICC, the cultural dimension is broadly defined as 'knowledge of social groups and their products and practices in one's own and in one's interlocutor's country, and of the general processes of societal and individual interaction' (Byram 1997: 58). In addition to this factual knowledge, learners must also be aware of the 'culture' of the web-based tool they are using to interact as well. The third dimension is what Lankshear and Knobel call 'the critical dimension' and Byram 'critical cultural awareness'. The aim of this third dimension is to arrive at an honest, in-depth dialogue based on trust. Given the complexities involved in terms of teachers being prepared to facilitate such discussions (see further discussion later) and the time required to establish a safe environment for dialogue, not all telecollaboration projects get to this level.

*Table 17.1* Framework for the goals of telecollaboration proposed by Helm and Guth (2010)

| New online literacies | ICC | Foreign language learning |
|---|---|---|
| **Operational: The 'technical stuff'** | | |
| Computer literacy | *Savoir apprendre/faire*: skills of discovery and interaction | Spoken production |
| Information literacy | | Spoken interaction |
| New media literacies | *Savoir comprendre*: ability to interpret a document or event from another culture, to explain it and relate it to one's own | Written production |
| | | Reading |
| | | Listening |
| | | Code switching |
| **Operational: Attitude: The 'ethos stuff'** | | |
| Willingness to explore, learn from, participate in, create, and collaborate and share in online communities | *Savoir-être*: attitude of openness and curiosity | Autonomy |
| | | Motivation |
| | | Willingness to communicate |
| **Cultural** | | |
| Knowledge of literacy practices and appropriate ways of communicating online | *Savoirs*: knowledge of social groups and their products and practices in own and other cultures; knowledge of the processes of interaction | Linguistic knowledge |
| | | Sociolinguistic knowledge |
| Propositional knowledge of topic | | Pragmatic knowledge |
| **Critical** | | |
| Critical literacy awareness | *Critical cultural awareness* | Critical language awareness |

## Models of telecollaboration

The first models of telecollaboration to be developed in foreign language education were bilingual, bicultural models, which are still widely practised today. They are based on the partnering of foreign language students with 'native speakers' of the target language, usually by organising exchanges between two classes of foreign language students studying one another's native language. The most well-established models are the eTandem and the Cultura models.

### *eTandem*

eTandem is a development of face-to-face tandem learning, which began to gain popularity in the 1980s in foreign language learning. Tandem is based on mutual language exchange between partners where traditionally each learner is a native speaker of the language their partner is learning. This model is based on the principles of reciprocity, with equal amounts of time spent on each of the languages of the exchange, and learner autonomy, whereby learners independently meet, establish objectives and select learning materials.

eTandem has been widely adopted by individual learners who seek partners on the many available educational websites which offer to find partners and suggest activities for tandem partners to engage in. However, when teachers adopt the eTandem model to institutionalised telecollaboration projects, they establish specific objectives, tasks and/or topics for discussion. The actual communication with partners can take place within or outside of the classroom context, but debriefing of what took place during the conversations takes place within the local classes facilitated by the teacher. The main focus of eTandem-style exchanges tends to be on the development of linguistic competence, with learners encouraged to provide feedback on their partners' foreign language performance, correct errors and offer new formulations.

## Cultura

The other main model is based on the Cultura project (Furstenberg, Levet, English and Maillet 2001), which was developed by teachers of French as a foreign language at MIT with the aim of making culture the focus of their telecollaborative activities. This model takes its inspiration from the words of the Russian philosopher Mikhail Bakhtin: 'It is only in the eyes of another culture that foreign culture reveals itself fully and profoundly [. . .] A meaning only reveals its depths once it has encountered and come into contact with another foreign meaning' (Bakhtin in Furstenberg et al. 2001: 58). Some of the activities students undertake are completing questionnaires such as word associations, sentence completion and situation reactions. Students in both classes post answers to the questionnaires in their native/institutional language and can then see everyone's answers side by side for analysis. The comparison and analysis of responses takes place through a detailed process of individual reflection as homework, discussion in class of linguistic and intercultural issues, and then follow-up between partners using online discussion forums. Other types of data which students compare and analyse include news stories, national surveys, films (different versions of the same films, for example American remakes of French films, or films which address the same theme), or sharing personal artefacts such as images (e.g. 'my home').

What characterises the original Cultura model is that while it is bilingual, like eTandem, the language learners communicate in their L1, that is, native/institutional language, and the communication is asynchronous. The rationale behind this is twofold: first, learners can more accurately describe cultural subtleties in their native language and, second, in this way learners provide rich linguistic input for each other. Though originally designed for French/English exchanges, the model has been used for different language configurations but also adapted to different approaches, with students interacting in the foreign language at various points of the project and using other modes of communication such as videoconferencing.

## Emerging models

The bilingual models described earlier assume that the native speaker is the ideal interlocutor for the language learner and can act both as a cultural informant and language expert, providing error correction and feedback. However, the assumptions behind these models have been questioned primarily for two reasons: (1) the recognition that cultures are not static, but rather liquid and constantly evolving and (2) the fact that in an increasingly globalised world characterised by transnational flows and migrations, it is ever more unlikely to find homogenous classes of learners who all share the same native language and culture. Also, particularly in the case of English language teaching (ELT), there has been a gradual recognition that most communication in the English language does not occur with native speakers, but rather in a multiplicity of contexts, predominantly with nonnative speakers.

In response to this, many new approaches to telecollaboration have emerged, with different configurations of languages, users, technologies and pedagogical design. A recent survey of over

100 telecollaboration practitioners in Europe (Guth, Helm and O'Dowd 2012) found that while bilingual, bicultural models are still predominant, the implementation of these online intercultural exchanges in a diversity of contexts has extended the scope of telecollaboration so that it now also includes exchanges between groups of participants who are not necessarily all language learners, but also student teachers 'practising' their online tutoring skills with foreign language learners, heritage speakers, classes of a variety of subjects from media studies to engineering collaborating with students of their foreign language. Exchanges may be multilateral, involving more than two groups in any one exchange; and they may be multilingual, bilingual or monolingual, involving just one of the partners' languages or a lingua franca, that is, foreign language shared by both groups. These findings reflect the flexibility of telecollaboration, with different ways in which language can be used and also different ways classes can be partnered for projects.

More recently, attention has focused on what has been described as 'intercultural communication in the wild' (Thorne 2010), or rather tapping into the language learning that takes place in noninstitutional, informal contexts such as fan fiction communities, online gaming and social networks (see Parts III and V of this volume). The rationale behind this model is that learners are motivated when driven by their specific interests and engage not as foreign language learners but rather as authentic members of particular communities. In these contexts, participants activate multiple modes of meaning-making and plurilingual resources to make and maintain relationships and position themselves within the communities in order to successfully integrate. This informal language learning outside of the classroom can be integrated in the foreign language classroom through a pedagogical framework which Thorne and Reinhardt (2008) have described as 'bridging activities', building on principles of language awareness. Within this framework students observe and collect digital vernacular texts and contexts, analyse and explore them with guidance in the classroom, comparing and contrasting with more conventional literacy and genre forms (Thorne 2010). Once again, these new approaches demonstrate the flexibility that underscores the practice of telecollaboration.

## Planning and implementing telecollaboration

Telecollaboration is a complex activity: two (or more) teachers working in different institutional contexts and cultures, with cohorts of students who speak two or more different languages come together to develop a project, with shared content and tasks, and must engage students in collaborative online work. Teachers need to allow sufficient time to plan the project and should have a solid, structured outline with objectives, tasks and a calendar before implementation. The success of a project and its sustainability over time require both teachers to contribute equally throughout the entire process. In order to create a trusting relationship, they have to be clear and effective communicators with one another. Through this process teachers also start to engage in the kind of communication and collaboration that will then be required of their students, as will be shown later.

Sharing contact information and establishing guidelines for communication is an important starting point. It is likely that email will serve as a main source for communication, but there are other options as well, from instant messaging and/or text chat tools such as Google Chat and WhatsApp, which allow for synchronous text communication, to Skype, which allows for real-time communication using audio and/or video. Some form of audio/video communication, particularly when teachers have never met in person, can help develop a stronger relationship. The same holds true for student-to-student interaction.

Teachers and students alike should establish guidelines for their online communication. When planning a course, teachers often agree on a regular day and time when they will commit to some form of synchronous communication; the same holds true when students are asked to engage in synchronous communication outside of the classroom. Similar guidelines should also be set for asynchronous communication, be it through email between teachers or on a discussion forum between students, regarding expectations for receiving a reply. The issue here is predominantly one of expectations: rather than assuming a partner will behave as we would, it is important to discuss, for example, how much time both parties should expect to pass from when they send an email/text message/post on a discussion forum to when they receive a reply.

Since telecollaboration is a form of institutionalised exchange, when planning a project it is also important to consider institutional cultures and contexts. The degree of academic freedom that teachers have to determine when, where and how to teach their courses varies significantly across cultures and institutions. Although telecollaborative projects may involve both partners co-developing a new course from scratch, more often they only involve adapting existing parts of the two courses that overlap. If, for example, one teacher cannot make any changes to their course before implementation and the telecollaboration activity becomes merely an additional activity to their course, while the partner teacher reduces their students' workload during the weeks of the exchange, there may very well be an imbalance in participation and commitment to the project. Similarly, if one group of students is going to be assessed on aspects of the telecollaborative project whereas the other is not, this may also lead to imbalanced participation on the part of students.

Teaching practice may also differ significantly, so partner teachers must share what is the norm at their respective institutions and through negotiation arrive at pedagogical and assessment practices that are acceptable in both institutional contexts. Some discussion points might regard the number of hours per week students are expected to be in the classroom and to dedicate to study and work outside of the classroom, how much of a students' grade is typically determined by a final exam, if regular class attendance and participation are expected and contribute to the final grade and so forth.

In many institutional contexts, course objectives and contents are determined not by teachers but at a higher institutional level. However, in order to be successful, the teachers planning a telecollaboration project must find a way to conciliate these differences and arrive at a solution that works for both groups. In order to be as equitable as possible, a good starting point is for both partners to write down three or more objectives they have for the telecollaboration project, since they may not always be the same. This is particularly relevant when, as was mentioned earlier, the configuration of classes is not two language classes but rather mixed groups. For example, in the case of student teachers partnered with foreign language students, the former will be focused on their students' ability to effectively teach the target language online whereas the latter will need to improve their linguistic production and/or reception. The goal is to find shared objectives, which might involve improving intercultural awareness and digital literacies.

Once both partners have agreed upon shared objectives, they can then move on to creating the activities that will make up the telecollaborative exchange. The methodological approach adopted in telecollaboration is generally task-based language learning (Guth and Helm 2012). O'Dowd and Ware (2009) developed a categorisation of telecollaborative tasks that is divided into twelve general types, grouped into three macro areas that reflect the type of communicative activity involved: information exchange, comparison and analysis, and collaboration and product creation.

The first stage of an exchange generally involves tasks characterised by relatively straightforward information exchange or 'icebreakers'. These are activities where learners answer a series of questions or share pictures or videos in order to get to know one another as people and/or the contexts they live in. This type of activity is followed by comparison and analysis tasks that may involve further investigation of the artefacts shared during the first stage or, for example, an analysis of how the same news story is reported in the media of the respective countries. The final stage then engages learners in intense negotiation on tasks that involve the production of an artefact. The key here is interdependence, that is, the task must require learners to depend on one another rather than information they might easily find on the Internet. In this stage it is important to guarantee that tasks do not lead to a 'you do this, I'll do that' approach, but rather an 'I cannot do my part without your contribution' approach. For example, learners may be asked to create a presentation on a given topic based on interviews partners carry out locally. Only with one another's description/transcription of the interviews can the partners then produce the presentation.

Regarding task design, it is important to point out that each task works within a cycle: preparatory pretask, interactive task, reflective posttask. The pretask activity is aimed at preparing learners for the task, be it linguistically, technologically and/or cognitively, and this may be done independently as homework or as part of classroom activities. After this, learners engage in the actual task in pairs or in groups with their international peers. Finally, there is a reflective, posttask phase in which issues that have emerged, for instance language issues, cultural misunderstandings, communication breakdowns and so forth can be discussed. Reflection can take place in various forms, through guided class discussions or, for instance, in structured journal writing (Helm 2009). If students keep a written record of their reflections through, for example, a learner diary, then this can be used for portfolio-like assessment at the end of the course.

The final missing element at this point is the technology. The choice of what tool to use should be determined by the objectives and tasks agreed upon by partner teachers, not the other way around. In today's world, there is a plethora of diverse free and proprietary tools for every mode of communication from asynchronous audio to synchronous image sharing. In telecollaboration, the choice of tool should consider not only which is the 'best' tool available, but other factors as well. For example, if one institution's learning management system (LMS), for example, Moodle, is used and is familiar to that group, but the other cohort has no LMS, this will lead to an imbalance, particularly at the beginning, that needs to be taken into consideration. Similarly, if access to the Internet is only available via smartphones in one partner's country, then an LMS is not a valid choice, and possibly more smartphone–friendly apps such as Facebook should be considered as alternatives. The speed at which tools come and go, change and develop, improve and disappear is such that teachers (presumably supported by technical or instructional design staff) need to focus on objectives, tasks and technological constraints before choosing a tool.

## Challenges of telecollaboration

As has been explained so far in the chapter, telecollaboration has the potential to foster the development of language skills, intercultural communicative competence and new online literacies (see Kern, Ware and Warschauer 2004 for an overview of research studies in these three areas) as well as subject-specific content through an intercultural lens. Yet research findings have also pointed to the many challenges of telecollaboration. They can primarily be divided into two areas: implementation and support.

Difficulties, tension and failure in the implementation of telecollaboration have been attributed to a wide range of factors. In a review of the telecollaboration literature, O'Dowd and Ritter (2006) identified four levels at which factors can contribute to 'failed communication':

- *Individual level*: learners' level of intercultural communicative competence, knowledge, motivations and expectations and the stereotypes that participants may bring with them to an exchange.
- *Class level*: teacher-to-teacher relationship, task design, the matching of learners and local group dynamics.
- *Socio-institutional level*: the mediating technologies and their design; the general organisation of the students' courses of study including differences in timetables, contact hours, workload and assessment or recognition of student participation in telecollaboration activity; the value placed on the particular languages studied by participants and what they are graded on.
- *Interactional level*: cultural differences in communication styles and behaviours, such as different attitudes to directness, nonverbal communication, use of humour and irony.

Most of these issues could potentially be avoided if partners dedicated time for planning, as outlined in the previous section. The more the teachers communicate prior to an exchange and try to understand each other's contexts and specific course needs, the better prepared they will be to create tasks that will engage students in productive communication. Nonetheless, this begs the question of what skills are required of teachers engaged in telecollaboration. While they may be prepared to support students in discussions about generic cultural differences, they may not be prepared to scaffold student engagement at deeper levels of interaction.

It has been found that in order to avert miscommunication, that is, misunderstandings or tensions in communication with their peers, students may avoid deep engagement through probing questions on sensitive issues. Ware reports that these avoidance strategies 'can lead to "missed" communication, or missed opportunities for approximating the kind of rich, meaningful intercultural learning that instructors often intend with telecollaborative projects' (Ware 2005: 66). These findings point to the need for both instructors to be prepared to not only identify missed communication, but to have the skills to facilitate communication when there is misunderstanding. Language teachers might argue that conflict resolution is not part of their skill set and they would be more comfortable with noncontroversial topics. This does point to the need for professional development for in-service teachers and including such topics in teacher education (O'Dowd 2013).

Without the support on the part of institutions to invest in professional development for in-service teachers interested in telecollaboration, the lack of sustainability that currently characterises the practice in Europe (Guth et al. 2012) cannot change. Despite the increasing implementation of telecollaborative projects over the last decade, these projects are primarily the initiatives of individual educators who are not provided with institutional support in terms of technical support, time release from teaching commitments, consideration in career progression and so forth. Consequently, telecollaboration in universities across Europe and beyond tends to be connected to specific teachers, and when these people leave the institution or choose to pursue other activities, the telecollaboration component disappears (O'Dowd 2013).

## The normalisation of telecollaboration

Internationalisation is a key word for policy makers in Europe as well as many other developed and developing countries. This term, however, is generally associated with physical mobility, that is, study abroad, internships abroad and so forth. Given that the large majority of students do not participate in physical mobility (only about 1% of US students have a study abroad experience, compared to less than 10% in Europe), attention has now shifted to what is called 'curricular internationalisation' or 'internationalisation at home'. Outside of English-speaking countries, such efforts have aimed at providing more English-medium instruction to attract foreign students, and across Europe attempts have been made to add global content to existing courses. Although telecollaboration might seem to be a valid response to the need for curricular internationalisation, it remains the exception in higher education rather than the norm. For telecollaboration to become normalised and an integral part of education, it needs to be introduced into educational policy both within institutions and at the European level.

At the institutional level, efforts could be made to make a telecollaborative experience a criterion for degree completion. Currently telecollaboration is commonly an add-on to an existing foreign language course, and there is rarely recognition of this either in the form of credits for telecollaboration or recognition in the European Diploma Supplement. Despite the practice having predominantly come out of foreign language programmes, as has been stated, telecollaboration can extend far beyond this discipline and recognition of the practice is the only way it will become normalised. Finally, just as an Erasmus experience is recognised as an intercultural study period (without any assessment of the intercultural learning that has taken place), so should telecollaboration be recognised as an intercultural study experience. If the indications for planning and implementation earlier are followed, a telecollaborative project can be an intense intercultural experiential learning opportunity.

The introduction of telecollaboration exchanges in teacher education programmes is another way to contribute to more widespread adoption of this practice. Telecollaboration in this context can help student teachers connect the dots between theory and practice by gradually immersing them in more and more complex online learning interactions by promoting both 'doing' and 'reflecting on doing' (Dooly and Sadler 2013). It offers the opportunity for 'exploratory' teaching practice and 'experiential modelling' (Guichon and Hauck 2011), not to mention the development of multimodal communicative competence, multiliteracy, autonomy and the teacher competences required for teaching with multimodal technologies (Fuchs, Hauck and Müller-Hartmann 2012). These references all refer to foreign language teaching contexts, but if telecollaboration exchanges were extended to all teacher education programmes, teachers would enter the teaching context prepared to set up telecollaborative projects. Consequently, students entering the university system would have the expectation that telecollaboration will be a part of their academic experience.

In Europe, at a school level, the eTwinning project was developed by the European Commission and has been hugely successful in many respects, with projects connecting classes across Europe – mostly foreign language classes but also other subjects and in interdisciplinary projects. However, it is worth noting that eTwinning projects tend to promote teacher-to-teacher communication, with students collaborating at the local level but not so much at the international level (Education for Change 2013). In response to the absence of such a project in higher education, the EU-funded INTENT project developed a platform called UNICollaboration to support telecollaboration in this context (see Figure 17.1).

The platform, which is freely accessible, offers a partner-finding function, tasks and task sequences for telecollaboration projects, training materials and sample projects for educators to learn more about telecollaboration, and an e-portfolio for assessing the learning that takes place in telecollaboration in the three domains – foreign language, intercultural competence and online literacies – and forums for the community of practising telecollaborators to exchange news, papers and experiences. It is important to note, however, that this project takes place at

*Figure 17.1* The UNICollaboration platform homepage

a grassroots level. Despite the benefits of such initiatives, such as motivation and interest on the part of the partner teachers, they will only become sustainable once there is institutional buy-in. This perhaps remains the greatest challenge to the normalisation of telecollaboration.

## Further reading

Several books have been published on telecollaboration and are extremely useful for learning about this practice in greater depth.

Belz, J.A. and Thorne, S.L. (eds) (2006) *Internet-Mediated Intercultural Foreign Language Education*, Boston, MA: Heinle & Heinle.
 Though it was first published nearly ten years ago, this volume offers important contributions from lead researchers in this field which are still highly relevant today. The book is divided into three sections: part one looks at the pedagogy of Internet-mediated intercultural foreign language education (ICFLE); part two looks at research in this field; and part three looks at new developments. The book includes chapters on the Cultura project, telecollaboration for teacher education, the use of videoconferencing, psycholinguistic and sociocultural studies of telecollaboration, communication breakdown, learner corpus analysis and closes with a critical look at technologies and ideologies in ICFLE.

Dooly, M. and O'Dowd, R. (eds) (2012) *Researching Online Foreign Language Interaction and Exchange: Theories, Methods and Challenges*, Bern, Switzerland: Peter Lang.
 This book looks at the research of telecollaboration rather than the practice itself, and is an invaluable resource for those who want to embark on research into this area. It begins with a section on theoretical

approaches to researching online exchange, with a chapter offering an overview of the divergent psycholinguistic and sociocognitive frameworks, an introduction to cultural historical activity theory and then a look at mixed methods approaches. The next section looks at key areas of research, beginning with multimodal communicative competence, followed by classroom-based action research, virtual worlds and finally intercultural competence. The volume closes with a section on research methods and has a chapter on the application of learner corpus analysis and then another on eye-tracking to investigate gaze behaviour.

Guth, S. and Helm, F. (eds) (2010) *Telecollaboration 2.0: Language, Literacy and Intercultural Learning in the 21st Century*, Bern, Switzerland: Peter Lang.

This focuses on the state of the art of telecollaboration at the end of the first decade of the 21st century. The first section focuses on new trends and environments in telecollaboration, many of which were discussed in this chapter. This is followed by sections on the new skills and competences required of language learners and teachers engaging in telecollaboration. The book ends with a series of eight case studies that provide examples of practical implementations of telecollaboration.

*Language Learning & Technology Journal*, Special Issue on Telecollaboration

This 2003 edition of the *Language Learning & Technology Journal* is specifically dedicated to telecollaboration and offers a valuable collection of articles on the theme by top researchers in the field, such as Julie Belz, Robert O'Dowd and Steve Thorne. The articles can be freely accessed at http://llt.msu.edu/vol7num2/default.html.

O'Dowd, R. (2007) *Online Intercultural Exchange: An Introduction for Foreign Language Teachers*, Clevedon, UK: Multilingual Matters.

Specifically designed for language teachers wishing to embark on telecollaboration, this book offers an accessible overview of telecollaboration. The first section offers three chapters which describe the three main models of telecollaboration (eTandem, Cultura and eTwinning). This is followed by a section with chapters on important issues in the practice and research of telecollaboration, such as focus on form, the development of intercultural communicative competence, the role of the teacher, telecollaboration with young learners and the choice of communication tools. The final section includes practical accounts and experiences of online exchange.

## Websites

Cultura (http://cultura.mit.edu/)

The Cultura site offers a comprehensive guide to the Cultura approach to telecollaboration, plenty of advice for teachers on methodology, activities for French/English students and an archive of past exchanges which in itself could be used as a resource in class, even if teachers are not involving students in telecollaboration.

eTandem (http://www.slf.rub.de/)

The eTandem site offers resources for teachers to learn more about the eTandem approach, tips for teachers and a partner-finding service both for individuals and teachers. It is available in many different languages.

eTwinning (http://www.etwinning.net)

eTwinning is the European Commission's website for schoolteachers interested in learning more about telecollaboration in school contexts. A strong community of schoolteachers has developed within this multilingual site which offers information about eTwinning, training materials and information on workshops in member countries, eTwinning projects to browse, support in finding partners to set up projects with and collaboration tools.

UNICollaboration (http://www.unicollaboration.eu)

UNICollaboration is a hub for telecollaboration practitioners in higher education. It offers partner-class finding functions, sample projects and training resources to learn more about the practice of telecollaboration, a database of tasks and task sequences that can be used, adapted and uploaded for telecollaboration projects, a customisable e-portfolio tool and a discussion forum with regular updates of conferences and published papers.

## References

Belz, J.A. and Thorne, S.L. (2006) *Internet-Mediated Intercultural Foreign Language Education*, Boston, MA: Thomson Heinle.

Byram, M. (1997) *Teaching and Assessing Intercultural Communicative Competence*, Clevedon, UK: Multilingual Matters.

Chapelle, C., A. (2008) 'Interactionist SLA theory in CALL research', in J.L. Egbert and G.M. Petrie (eds), *CALL Research Perspectives*, New York, NY: Routledge: 53–64.

Dooly, M. and Sadler, R. (2013) 'Filling in the gaps: Linking theory and practice through telecollaboration in teacher education', *ReCALL*, 25(01): 4–29.

Education for Change (2013) *Study of the Impact of eTwinning on Participating Pupils, Teachers and Schools*, Luxembourg: European Union.

Fuchs, C., Hauck, M. and Müller-Hartmann, A. (2012) 'Promoting learner autonomy through multiliteracy skills development in cross-institutional exchanges', *Language Learning & Technology*, 16(3): 82–102.

Furstenberg, G., Levet, S., English, K. and Maillet, K. (2001) 'Giving a voice to the silent culture of language: The CULTURA project', *Language Learning & Technology*, 5(1): 55–102.

Guichon, N. and Hauck, M. (2011) 'Editorial: Teacher education research in CALL and CMC: More in demand than ever', *ReCALL*, 23(3): 187–199.

Guth, S. and Helm, F. (eds) (2010) *Telecollaboration 2.0: Languages, Literacies and Intercultural Learning in the 21st Century*, Bern, Switzerland: Peter Lang.

Guth, S. and Helm, F. (2012) 'Developing multiliteracies in ELT through telecollaboration', *ELT Journal*, 66(1): 42–51.

Guth, S., Helm, F. and O'Dowd, R. (2012) *University Language Classes Collaborating Online: A Report on the Integration of Telecollaborative Networks in European Universities*, available: http://intent-project.eu/sites/default/files/Telecollaboration_report_Final_Oct2012.pdf (accessed 20 Jan 2014).

Helm, F. (2009) 'Language and culture in the online context: What do the learners gain?' *Language and Intercultural Communication*, 9(2): 91–104.

Helm, F. and Guth, S. (2010) 'The multifarious goals of telecollaboration 2.0: Theoretical and practical implications', in F. Helm and S. Guth (eds), *Telecollaboration 2.0: Languages, Literacies and Intercultural Learning in the 21st Century*, Bern, Switzerland: Peter Lang: 69–106.

Kern, R., Ware, P. and Warschauer, M. (2004) 'Crossing frontiers: New directions in online pedagogy and research', *Annual Review of Applied Linguistics*, 24: 243–260.

Lankshear, M. and Knobel, M. (2006) *New Literacies: Everyday Practices and Classroom Learning*, Maidenhead: Open University Press.

Lantolf, J. and Thorne, S.L. (2007) 'Sociocultural theory and second language learning', in B. van Patten and J. Williams (eds), *Theories in Second Language Acquisition*, Mahwah, NJ: Lawrence Erlbaum: 201–224.

O'Dowd, R. (2007) *Online Intercultural Exchange*, Clevedon, UK: Multilingual Matters.

O'Dowd, R. (2011) 'Online foreign language interaction: Moving from the periphery to the core of foreign language education?', *Language Teaching*, 44(03): 368–380.

O'Dowd, R. (2013) 'Telecollaborative networks in university higher education: Overcoming barriers to integration', *Internet and Higher Education*, 18: 47–53.

O'Dowd, R. and Ritter, M. (2006) 'Understanding and working with 'failed communication' in telecollaborative exchanges', *CALICO Journal*, 61(2): 623–642.

O'Dowd, R. and Ware, P. (2009) 'Critical issues in telecollaborative task design', *Computer Assisted Language Learning*, 22(2): 173–188.

Rubin, J. and Guth, S. (2015) 'Collaborative online international learning: An emerging format for internationalizing curricula', in A. Schultheis Moore and S. Simon (eds), *Globally Networked Teaching in the Humanities: Theories and Practice*, New York and London: Routledge: 15–27.

Schmidt, R.W. (1990) 'The Role of Consciousness in Second Language Learning', *Applied Linguistics*, 11(2): 129–158.

Starke-Meyerring, D. and Wilson, M. (eds) (2008) *Designing Globally Networked Learning Environments: Visionary Partnerships, Policies, and Pedagogies*, Rotterdam, Netherlands: Sense Publishers.

Thorne, S., L. (2010) 'The 'Intercultural Turn' and language leaning in the crucible of new media', in S. Guth and F. Helm (eds), *Telecollaboration 2.0: Languages, Literacies and Intercultural Learning in the 21st Century*, Bern, Switzerland: Peter Lang: 139–164.

Thorne, S., L. and Reinhardt, J. (2008) '"Bridging Activities", New media literacies and advanced foreign language proficiency', *CALICO Journal*, 25(3): 558–572.

Ware, P.D. (2005) '"Missed" communication in online communication: Tensions in a German-American telecollaboration', *Language Learning & Technology*, 9(2): 64–89.
Warschauer, M. (1996) *Telecollaboration in Foreign Language Learning*, Honolulu: Second Language Teaching and Curriculum Center.

# 18
# Social networking and language learning

*Lara Lomicka and Gillian Lord*

---

Our increasing dependence on and use of various technological tools has impacted every facet of our lives, and language teaching and learning are no exception. Educators regularly incorporate a variety of tools (Thorne and Payne 2005) to engage their students and to allow them to interact in new and different ways, both in class and beyond the walls of the classroom. In particular, popular social networking sites (SNSs) such as Facebook, Edmodo, and LinkedIn offer educators even more ways to help students increase motivation and reinvigorate the classroom climate.

(*Mazer, Murphy and Simonds 2007*)

Social networking tools such as these and others also provide opportunities for language learners to enhance digital and multiliteracy skills, interact in and through the target language, work collaboratively and enhance their linguistic and pragmatic proficiency (Blattner and Fiori 2011; Mills 2011; Blattner and Lomicka 2012b; Lomicka and Lord 2012). This chapter examines the theoretical underpinnings of using social networking in language learning, as well as how social networking tools can be effective in the classroom. Specifically, we look at current pedagogical practices that are linked to social networking communities. Moreover, we examine prominent studies thus far in the field that help to shed light on key issues and considerations in the use of social networks in the language classroom.

This chapter explores second language (L2) learning and teaching with technology, specifically in the area of social networking (SN). SN represents one aspect of social media, which has the broader focus of creating and transmitting information to others. SN is more about the tools used to make that content available to others and to allow users to connect, engage and build communities. According to Grahl (2013), social media can be categorised into six different but overlapping categories, which include: (1) social networks (e.g. Facebook, LinkedIn); (2) bookmarking sites (e.g. Delicious, StumbleUpon); (3) social news (e.g. Digg, Reddit); (4) media sharing (e.g. Instagram, YouTube, Flickr); (5) microblogging (e.g. Twitter); and (6) blogging, particularly comments and forums. The popularity of SN tools has increased dramatically in the last several years. The upsurge of online social interaction may be attributed in part to a desire to connect with new people, to share opinions, to stay in touch with old friends and colleagues and to share different types of information with a widespread community of followers. Simply put, there is a desire to develop and maintain online relationships that lead to community building, self-expression and interaction with others (Thorne 2010). In situations that involve L2, these types of relationships can be built or maintained in a language other than one's own within a shared community, which makes them appealing to language educators.

Yet, despite this potential, and despite SN's popularity for personal interaction, it has not been as widely embraced in education. Lepi (2013: n.p.) reports on a recent study by the Babson Survey Research Group and Pearson Education of 8,000 faculty members, and notes that while 'faculty have adopted some social media use in their personal life, fewer have done so professionally'. Although there are an increasing number of academic studies related to various social media tools, many of them are not empirically based, nor do they offer strong theoretical advances. In the area of L2 learning, recent studies have only begun to investigate the potential that social networking sites (SNS) have for the classroom (Blattner and Fiori 2009, 2011; McBride 2009; Stevenson and Liu 2010; Mills 2011; Reinhardt and Zander 2011, 2013; Sykes and Holden 2011; Blattner and Lomicka 2012a, 2012b; Mitchell 2012), as will be discussed later.

The next section of this chapter addresses various theoretical approaches that have been associated with SN in the L2 classroom. We then examine the principal contributions that research-based studies have provided, and address the practical aspects of incorporating SN tools into the classroom. We conclude by looking at the future of SN in language learning.

## Theoretical approaches to L2 learning and SN

For educators interested in incorporating aspects of SN with their learners, it is crucial to keep in mind the theory and current pedagogical stances that underlie language learning with technology (see Part I of this volume for a fuller discussion). According to Blyth (2008), there are four distinct categories to language learning research: technological, psycholinguistic, sociocultural and ecological. Technological approaches include studies that report on new technologies as they move from being used in society to their pedagogical application in the classroom, as well as how teachers and students react to their use. Studies driven by psycholinguistic theories integrate the interaction hypothesis and noticing, while sociocultural research, based on Vygotsky's theories of social learning within communities, looks at how learning is mediated within those contexts (see Hubbard and Levy, Chapter 2 this volume). Finally, ecological approaches attempt to consider the whole context of a project and examine how all of the parts of a learning environment, such as the students, teachers, environment and technological tools, work together to form the whole. Each of these four approaches to language learning is examined in turn to explore how SN fits within the various perspectives.

### Technological approaches

Technological theories are those that Blyth (2008) describes as a development stage, consisting of explorative and descriptive studies. These types of studies aim at assessing the potential benefits of the particular tool. Although, as Blyth points out, these studies are often criticised for their perceived lack of theoretical framework, they do contribute to the field by introducing new technologies to educators in L2 contexts. They also discuss how these tools may change the perception of traditional learning in the classroom. In terms of SN, preliminary studies such as Stevenson and Liu's (2010) analysis of three SNS (Livemocha, Palabea and Babbel) investigate how they are used for language learning and social purposes. Their 2010 study showed that learners initially showed a greater interest in Web 1.0 technology. Consistent with Blyth's claims, studies such as this one are helpful for teachers seeking to use a particular social networking tool and pave the way for further research in the area of social networking.

## Psycholinguistic approaches

Psycholinguistic approaches to language acquisition are focused on the importance of social interaction and noticing. For example, Long's (1985, 1996) interaction hypothesis holds that language development is brought about by person-to-person communication and the linguistic interactions that take place. Proponents of such interactionist approaches (e.g. Chapelle 1997, 1998) highlight the crucial role that input, interaction and output have on language learning. Input in the target language is essential (e.g. Krashen 1994), and input that is comprehensible but slightly beyond the level of the learner ($i + 1$) provides direct information about the language and serves to illustrate what patterns are and are not evidenced in language. Additionally, input that is comprehensible is most likely to be noticed (e.g. Schmidt 1990, 1995) and processed by learners. When negotiation of meaning is required, either due to a gap in the learner's knowledge or through a breakdown in communication and the need for comprehension checks and communication strategies, it leads in turn to the output that a learner produces. Swain and Lapkin (1995), for example, have proposed the comprehensible output hypothesis to explain how learning is facilitated precisely by the need to produce language.

Such interactionist approaches seem to be ideally suited as a basis for exploring the role of SN tools in language learning, given their emphasis on connecting learners to provide increased input, engage in negotiation of meaning and require output. In fact, seminal research in CALL has long advocated the exploration of acquisition issues within an interactionist, psycholinguistic framework (e.g. Chapelle 1997, 1998; Salaberry 1999). For example, students can attend to the linguistic characteristics of the input from the speakers with whom they interact, they can reflect on their own language system and take note of their own errors, and use their computer-enhanced communication opportunities to improve their own production, be it oral or written.

## Sociocultural approaches

Researchers such as Lantolf (2000) have advocated that the sociocultural approach (based on work by Vygotsky 1978) is ideally suited to examining the process of language acquisition, thanks to its emphasis on interaction from within a community of learners. Language and social interaction play a role in human development, and serve as cultural practices that can lead to the construction of knowledge shared by members of the community. In terms of how this might contribute to social networking, virtual connections with other learners and experts around the world can potentially offer a rich environment for sociocultural language exchange (Harrison and Thomas 2009; Harrison 2013). Social networking spaces can also provide virtual spaces and offer promising opportunities to learn through observation, where students can observe others, interpret their behaviours and adjust their own styles of interacting in SNSs (Ryberg and Christiansen 2008). Through interaction in these spaces, learners can gain confidence by working with others and by establishing recognition as members of a particular community. Over time, virtual encounters within a community can even help learners to become experts. As proposed by Reinhardt and Zander (2011), SNSs allow users to interact in a myriad of communication exchanges due to the fact the SNSs combine many technological features into one platform. This interaction can lead to developments in both identity and in relationships and can expose students to current, real and meaningful language use for specific tasks. He notes that because social networks offer spaces shared by communities of individuals, they can be considered social practices (Scribner and

Cole, cited in Lankshear and Knobel 2008). Mills (2011) advocates that social networking tasks can allow users to 'write [themselves] into being' (Rosen 2007: 87). This formation of identity or writing into being takes place, as Mills notes, through shared postings, feedback from the community, and reflection and self-appraisal. Identity can be constructed virtually in these social spaces by posting, sharing ideas, media preferences and news items (Pempek, Yermolayeva and Calvert 2009). Thus, from a sociocultural perspective, interaction, work within specific communities and perceived identity construction are all plausible areas that can further be explored.

## Ecological approaches

In the fourth and final theoretical stance discussed here, van Lier (2004) advocates for an ecological approach in which context is not only central but also crucial to understanding the dynamic interrelations among various personal and environmental factors. Within this approach, the learner 'acts and interacts within and with his environment' (van Lier 2004: 246), rather than the learning taking place individually in an isolated context. At times, this interaction can be mediated by affordances (Gibson 1979) available in the environment, and by which the learner may reach various goals. Affordances can be objects, places, events or things; however, the learner must be made aware of these affordances and their potential in order to make use of them (van Lier 2004). The existence of the affordance alone does not necessarily encourage action, rather it is the responsibility of the teacher and other interlocutors to help to make the affordances available and accessible to the learners so that they can use them to their benefit (van Lier 2004). Ducate and Lomicka's (2013) study is grounded in this approach, as they examine how students use a mobile device 'on the go' both within and outside of the language classroom, at a time and place that accommodates them, and suggests the types of affordances that are possible within mobile language learning (see also Stockwell, Chapter 21 this volume). Their findings suggest that intermediate language students who are offered the use of mobile devices will take advantage of their affordances for personal and academic uses, thereby allowing themselves more exposure to the target language and culture. Although this study did not specifically explore social networks, the findings can be applicable to all virtual spaces. Many of the studies mentioned in this section will be revisited in the next section in more detail, where primary contributions from research-based studies are considered.

## Primary contributions from research-based studies

With these theoretical perspectives in mind, we now turn to recent studies in the area of SN to explore what they have contributed to the field of L2 learning. Kárpáti (2009) has argued that social web tools can, in general, facilitate educators in setting up collaborative learning, as they place students at the core of the learning experience while at the same time allowing the teacher to function as the mentor and guide of knowledge construction and sharing. He also highlighted the fact that such tools provide authentic language education settings, an important consideration for achieving high communicative competence in a foreign language. Likewise, Komatsu (2011) conducted a survey of SNSs and Web 2.0 and concluded that these networks are potential forums of learning because they can be learner-centred, active and collaborative. While survey-based research of this type is not designed to push the research agenda forward in terms of gains to learning and teaching, it does provide general information about social networking.

Educators, though, have claimed that relatively little empirical research exists on how (and if) social networking can facilitate language learning (Stevenson and Liu 2010; Zourou 2012; Lamy and Zourou 2013). Many studies report increased motivation for learning (Clark and Gruba 2010;

Stevenson and Liu 2010; Liu et al. 2013), and indicate that SNS can generate meaningful output and stimulate students' interest in language learning (Chartrand 2012). Other studies have investigated sociopragmatic competence (Blattner and Fiori 2009; Reinhardt and Zander 2011; Blattner and Lomicka 2012a, 2012b) and the potential to develop and explore online relationships and identities (e.g. Thorne 2010; Mills 2011; Chen 2013; Klimanova and Dembovskaya 2013; Reinhardt and Chen 2013), where expression, interaction and community building are all important factors in the language learning experience. The following sections address this research in greater detail.

## Motivation and user profiles

One benefit that has emerged with regard to the use of SNS is motivation and student enjoyment. McBride (2009) suggested that daily engagement with Facebook could be a motivating factor for pedagogically useful foreign language experiences. Stevenson and Liu (2010) explored the pedagogical and technical use of three language-related SNS (Livemocha, Palabea and Babbel) in the context of foreign language learning. Five participants tested the three SNS as they engaged in different tasks (exploratory, closed-ended and open-ended). The results of their exploratory survey study showed that the participants were interested and excited about the possibilities of collaboration on SNS in terms of learning directly from other users including native speakers. However, the data also revealed that the perceived user-friendliness of the sites also impacted students' reactions.

Similarly, Liu et al. (2013) looked at twenty-one university-level ESL learners' use of SNS (buusu, Livemocha and English Café) for language learning, and their perceptions of these experiences. Twenty-one ESL students completed a survey (Likert-type and open-ended questions) to look at their usage and perception of SNS for language learning. Factors identified that are important to learner satisfaction of social spaces include comfort level, language proficiency level, preferred communication modes and the design of the sites. Additionally, Mitchell (2012) suggests that creating and developing friendships in SNS can increase motivation. Using a qualitative case study, her study explored Facebook with nine learners of English and a second language. Data were coded from interviews and analysed to identify salient themes, and the findings suggest that students were able not just to communicate with friends but also to improve their linguistic and cultural competency. In a related study, Clark and Gruba (2010) found that motivation is key to working in SNS like Livemocha. While using an auto-ethnographic approach including self-aware participation, learner diaries and peer debriefing, their results indicate that a number of pedagogical impediments such as flaws in site design exist but may not affect growth in the number of site users.

In addition to motivation, other work has focused on student profiles. Harrison and Thomas (2009), for example, investigated Livemocha with a small group of learners, who used the SNS one hour per week. Overall, students responded positively to the materials and experience. Results also suggest that profiles are central to the dynamic of interaction in online communities and thus play a role in learning. Finally, they propose that SNS such as Livemocha can 'transform language learning, by providing environments that allow new modes of active learning' (Harrison and Thomas 2009: 121).

## Development of sociopragmatic competence

Blattner and Fiori (2009) considered the potential of Facebook to encourage positive student relationships, provide constructive educational outcomes and immediate, individualised opportunities to interact and collaborate with peers, instructors and native speakers of a variety of foreign languages. They found that meaningful integration in Facebook in the language classroom can lead to a sense of community and impact the development of sociopragmatic competence in language learners. Likewise, Blattner and Lomicka (2012a, 2012b) examined pedagogical practices using a social forum and a Facebook forum in the context of an intermediate French course. They administered structured linguistic tasks and questionnaires. Students were asked to identify information in posts made by forum members: types of salutations, use of pronouns, question formation and colloquial vocabulary (i.e. abbreviations, syllabograms). The results suggest that language analysis on Facebook forums can enhance the awareness of important sociopragmatic elements by transcending national and cultural boundaries. Finally, informed by a bridging activities model, Reinhardt and Zander (2011) conducted a sociopragmatic study with nine participants. Their study implemented activities using Facebook for elementary Korean with the goal of developing sociopragmatic awareness of Korean honorifics. Trends emerging from his work suggest that there is evidence of sociopragmatic awareness, understanding of contextual constraints on use and creative use of Facebook affordances.

## Identity issues

Several studies have explored identity issues in SN communities. For example, Mills (2011) conducted a study that highlighted the nature of student participation, knowledge acquisition and relationship development within SN communities. Facebook was used as an interactive tool where students could share collective reflection and access resources that enhanced the various topics discussed in class. Mills noticed that students made connections to course content, developed identities through the enhancement of interpersonal, presentational, and interpretative modes of communication, engaged in meaningful learning experiences and contextualised interactions within these social communities in the L2. Similarly, Iskold (2012) examined the concepts of self-authorship and performing identity among L2 learners on Facebook. She concluded that Facebook may enhance face-to-face learning, especially in the areas of critical thinking, and by providing additional opportunities to interact, increased motivation and the ability to experiment with character identity. Reinhardt and Chen (2013) also investigated how SN is used to invest in new identities that lead to socialisation in imagined communities. From an ecological perspective, their study shows how a learner made use of affordances to establish identity; results suggest that Facebook was used as a way to socialise and invest identity in the context of graduate studies, and to interact with broader communities and networks.

Chen (2013: 143) looked at two multilingual writers and how they design and construct identities in literary practices in Facebook. Findings indicated that writers adopted various strategies, subject positions and even reappropriated 'symbolic resources afforded by the SNS as they aligned themselves with particular collective and personal identities at local and global levels'. Klimanova and Dembovskaya (2013) provided an analysis of a comparable SN community, VKontakte, in Russian classes. Online activities, phenomenological interviews and interactions with native speaker students all focused on identity construction through interaction.

Taken together, these studies show that even in its beginning stages, research on SNS indicates a beneficial impact of using such sites in the context of L2 learning. The next section examines the more practical issues related to developing and incorporating SNS-based tasks and activities in L2 learning.

## Incorporating social networking tools in the classroom

As should be clear from the foregoing, the case for incorporating social media into our language classes is compelling. Not only can these sites be used to share classroom resources, news and work, but they have also been shown to foster greater student engagement and, as emerging evidence indicates, linguistic gains as well. With that in mind, this section addresses key considerations in incorporating SN tools in the language classroom.

## Types of SNS

Although SNS are pervasive, they are also constantly changing, and for that reason we frame our discussion here around a few general types of social networks: tools that offer learners opportunities to engage in written discourse (e.g. Facebook, LinkedIn or Twitter); those that focus primarily on oral discourse (e.g. PodOmatic, VoiceThread or video messaging sites); and those that highlight the sharing of images (e.g. Instagram, Pinterest, or Snapchat). Table 18.1 displays

*Table 18.1* Representative SNS

| Name | Description | URL |
|---|---|---|
| Edmodo | Education-oriented site, shares layout of popular SNS. Provides a safe and easy way for your class to connect and collaborate, share content and access homework, grades and school notices. | http://www.edmodo.com |
| Facebook | Online social networking service, originally designed for college students but now extended to general population. | http://www.facebook.com |
| Google Hangout | Hangouts bring conversations to life with photos, emoji and even free group video calls. Connect with friends across computers or Android or Apple devices. | http://www.google.com/hangouts |
| GroupMe | A mobile group-messaging app owned by Microsoft. | http://www.groupme.com |
| Instagram | An online photo-sharing, video-sharing and social networking service that enables its users to take pictures and videos, apply digital filters to them, and share them on a variety of social networking services, such as Facebook, Twitter, Tumblr and Flickr. | http://www.instagram.com |
| LinkedIn | A business-oriented social networking service with similar functionality to Facebook. | http://www.linkedin.com |
| Pinterest | A visual discovery tool that people use to collect ideas for their different projects and interests. People create and share collections (called 'boards') of visual bookmarks (called 'Pins') that they use to do things like plan trips and projects, organise events or save articles and recipes. | http://www.pinterest.com |
| PodOmatic | A website that specialises in the creation of tools and services that enable users to easily find, create, distribute, promote and listen to both audio and video podcasts. | http://www.podomatic.com |
| Snapchat | A mobile app that lets users take photos and short videos. Users decide how long data will be visible once opened – up to 10 seconds – and then it supposedly disappears forever. | http://www.snapchat.com |
| Twitter | An online social networking and microblogging service that enables users to send and read short 140-character text messages, called 'tweets'. Registered users can read and post tweets. | http://www.twitter.com |
| VoiceThread | An interactive collaboration and sharing tool that enables users to add images, documents, and videos, and to which other users can add voice, text, audio files or video comments. | http://www.voicethread.com |

a selection of current popular and freely available SNS that, based on the aforementioned theoretical perspectives, have promising potential for use in language classes.

The tools listed in Table 18.1, and many others like them, offer language educators unique opportunities to engage their students and develop their cultural and linguistic awareness at the same time. The spectrum of skills and task types that educators can incorporate through various social platforms is limitless (see also Liou, Chapter 34 this volume on reading and writing using social media), and SN tools can be exploited for a variety of languages and proficiency levels by focusing on different linguistic elements as the situation requires.

## Sample task types using SNS

The sites listed in the previous section can be adapted and incorporated in a variety of productive ways, depending on the pedagogical goals. For example, tools that tend to focus on written discourse can be used at beginning or intermediate levels to create self-descriptions and to engage in self-expression tasks, as was mentioned earlier. Other aspects of these tools may lend themselves nicely to longer, blog-type posts, which can be used for the development and interpretation of extended discourse. As learner proficiency increases, these same sites and tools can be maximised to promote meta-linguistic awareness of language structures and sociocultural aspects of language use. Similarly, observing group interaction on these sites provides rich material for further sociolinguistic and sociocultural discussions that more advanced learners will appreciate.

Likewise, as we have seen in Table 18.1, SN is no longer limited to printed text, and the proliferation of podcasts and similar sites opens the door for the development of listening and speaking. In addition to similar discourse development – but oral, rather than written – these sites can offer learners the opportunity to observe native spoken language. They can use these sites to develop their comprehension skills, as well as to improve their own spoken speech. Depending on the level, learners can be encouraged to focus on their pronunciation and suprasegmental features like pitch and rhythm, or to assess their own fluency through such indicators as temporal aspects and discourse markers. Alternately, learners can analyse these features in the speech of native speakers from a variety of backgrounds, open up the door for comparisons between native and nonnative speech, dialectal variation and sociopragmatic variation.

Finally, networking sites that revolve primarily around sharing photos and images are rapidly increasing in popularity. In addition to lending themselves to the development of descriptive language, these visual elements can often lead nicely into cultural issues and development of cultural awareness and competence. It should be noted here as well that even though some sites work exclusively with images (such as Instagram), most other SNS have adapted to the ubiquity of photos and images, so virtually any of the tools listed earlier can be used in this way.

It is important for instructors to keep in mind that social interaction is the main goal of any of these sites, and thus their successful incorporation into language curricula also depends on social interaction. Any activity using an SNS should depend upon the interaction and the connectedness it was designed to promote. If an activity or project does not allow for and encourage participation from multiple students, it is probably not truly maximising the potential of the tool. Similarly, a passive SNS will be far less successful than one that is monitored frequently. Therefore, some students, depending upon their learning styles and preferences, may react better and engage more willingly if they know there is an audience of followers and if they are actively encouraged to produce their own content.

## Key considerations when using SNS

Having considered various SN tools, we now look to several considerations when using SN. Rodriguez (2011) suggests that educators keep in mind the following: ownership, privacy and security, accessibility and compliance, stability of technology, intellectual property rights and copyright law. Here we will address a few of these considerations.

### Codes of conduct

As a teacher, especially if teaching in online or hybrid environments, it is important to establish codes of conduct so that students know how to behave in SNS while they are in a course. A good place to begin would be to check with the institution to see what guidelines for SN conduct are already in place. As an educator, you can work from those guidelines and supplement with specific guidelines for the course. Obviously, it can be suggested that students be respectful of others and use common sense when making posts. It might also be helpful to include what the instructor has a right to remove and what happens if a violation occurs. It is important to go over rules for conduct at the beginning of a term or semester, and if necessary, ask students to sign a document specifying that they have read and agree to the specific terms.

### Privacy

Students need to be made aware of and reminded of privacy issues, especially since what constitutes a 'classroom' today is often archived and available for public viewing. Classroom spaces, whether within the traditional four walls or in cyberspace, are now public spaces and students should be aware that comments and posts are potentially archived and can impact hiring and future references. It is also crucial to know what hosting sites do with data collected from users, especially in cases where students are required to use a certain SN tool for a course. Finally, students and instructors should consider maintaining separate personal and educational/professional sites, in order to avoid complications or violations of privacy in a classroom setting.

### Accessibility

Faculty members must be prepared to accommodate diverse student needs, especially with regard to students with disabilities and accessing materials online. Educators should be familiar with accessibility issues that these particular groups of users face so that everyone will have opportunities to an inclusive learning environment. For example, when a spell checker is not available within a particular tool, educators can inform students to compose text in a word processor with a spell-checking tool and then copy it into the other tool.

As educators today are using more new and innovative technologies, they must also be aware of associated considerations and issues. Code of conduct, privacy, and accessibility have been identified in the literature as legitimate concerns and ones that should be addressed in the classroom before embarking on projects using social media. In addition to these issues, copyright, anonymity and fraud are all issues that users should be aware of. While addressing these issues in depth would be well beyond the scope of this chapter, educators do need to consider these topics. According to Barretta (2014), educators can follow nine simple policies to guide them in their use of social networking (her article references Twitter specifically, but the principles apply to any social networking site). She breaks her recommendations down into the four Cs and the 5 Rs: credibility, consistency, correctness and creativity; and relevancy, reactivity, responsibility, responsibility and respect. Robinson (2010) also offers some valuable considerations, ranging from public records laws to freedom of speech, and provides guidelines for those interested in incorporating any kind of social media into classes.

## Looking to the future of social networking

Three emerging trends that will likely characterise the future of SN both in personal and (eventually) in educational settings include (1) a move towards mobility, (2) a focus on ephemerality and digital tribalism and (3) a reduction of text and subsequent increase in images (Friedman 2013; Beck 2014).

SN is projected to become increasingly mobile. As tablets and smartphones grow faster and more powerful, more and more users are accessing popular SN apps on mobile devices. Recent data published by comScore and analysed by Statista.com indicate that mobile devices have become the main channel for SN. Statista.com shows Instagram, Pinterest, Facebook and Twitter as the apps receiving the most time spent on mobile devices, whereas Tumblr and LinkedIn were accessed more from desktop locations (Richter 2014). There is already a push towards mobility in language learning, demonstrated by the increased attention MALL is receiving in the literature (e.g. Stockwell and Sotillo 2011; Ballance 2012; Stockwell, Chapter 21 this volume).

Second, young people are migrating away from Facebook in favour of more ephemeral applications such as Instagram and Snapchat. The emerging trend for these ephemeral networks, where content literally vanishes seconds after being received (as is the perceived case with Snapchat), is claimed by some to imply a more genuine and unfiltered exchange. These so-called self-destructing apps assure their users that their communication is more privately exchanged and may alleviate a fear of an archived and publicly available record of communications.

In addition, others have also noted that while the basic need to connect, communicate and share has not changed, the way in which that is accomplished is changing. Beck (2014) explains that earlier generations of SN have relied heavily on status updates, likes, followers, connections and notifications, creating a challenge to keep up with everything. The second generation of SN, though, is shifting its focus away from 'networking' and towards 'ephemerality and digital tribalism' (Beck 2014: n.p.), the push towards smaller subpopulation groups with shared interests. He says that this generation of users:

> will follow a small circle of close friends on Instagram, pin with a small handful of followers on Pinterest, message with a girlfriend or schoolmate on WhatsApp or Snapchat, or follow a co-worker's check-ins on Foursquare. Or, they will build the next platforms and apps that don't exist yet.
>
> *(Beck 2014: n.p.)*

While this trend offers the potential for slightly different ways to communicate, it also muddles the ease with which research can be carried out and data can be collected, for example, with Snapchat user-controlled settings allowing for text and pictures to disappear, it is difficult to imagine how L2 projects could be built around this particular tool. Likewise, with Instagram, it is a challenge to collect data from a mobile device, so it is difficult to integrate the app effectively into L2 teaching and learning when certain aspects of the tool are not accessible from a laptop or desktop (posting, sharing, etc.).

The third predicted trend will be a reduction of text and corresponding increase in images, as well as an increased use of hashtags. By the close of 2014, 140 characters may be too much text. Photos were the predominant social share in 2013. This focus today is on developing a sense of Internet presence by sharing material/posts/pictures and increasing knowledge by assessing, analysing, retaining and sharing information. Photos on Facebook, according to a recent study by Kissmetrics, receive 53% more likes, 104% more comments and 84% more click-throughs on links than text-based posts. The focus on the visual aspect of SN is also related to mobility, and that fact that more people access social media and engage with it on the go, as photos can communicate information clearly and quickly. Ward confirms:

> When we moved to status updates on Facebook [from blogs], our posts became shorter. Then micro-blogs like Twitter came along and shortened our updates to 140 characters. Now we are even skipping words altogether and moving towards more visual communication with social-sharing sites like Pinterest.
>
> *(Ward cited in Walter 2012: n.p.)*

Engaging students with shorter amounts of text, increased hashtags and pictures is something that can be appealing to the L2 learner. Shorter amounts of text can encourage students to be succinct, and may motivate them to contribute more in the long run. Hashtags, if carried out in the target language, may pose complications, so students could benefit from first studying common L2 hashtags. Finally, photos can be accompanied by short descriptions in the L2 to engage readers in the post.

This chapter has illustrated how language teaching and learning can benefit tremendously from the incorporation of various aspects of SNS. Regardless of the theoretical approach to the acquisition of second and foreign languages that one adopts, the features of the social tools such as those discussed here open the door for students to engage in and with the target language in ways that were not possible before. Instructors who are well informed about these social sites and are able to develop pedagogically sound activities for their students are in the best position to foster linguistic and cultural development in their classes.

In spite of the benefits discussed here, there continues to be some reluctance when it comes to using SNS in L2 learning. Educators may be intimidated by the need to learn new tools, and both educators and students may be reluctant to risk crossing inappropriate social boundaries or merging professional and personal social worlds (Schwartz 2009). These concerns are well founded, but can be remedied by careful planning and sound task design that takes maximum advantage of the SNS while also providing solid technological guidance and advice to learners. SNS have created a unique way to bring individuals, communities and groups together to share information and engage in meaningful discussion, reflection and learning. These new and exciting venues will impact both teachers and learners, and so we all must continue to explore and learn about new ways to expand collective knowledge and relationships to new horizons.

## Further reading

Blattner, G. and Fiori, M. (2011) 'Virtual social network communities: An investigation of language learners' development of socio-pragmatic awareness and multiliteracy skills', *CALICO Journal*, 29(1): 24–43.
    Blattner and Fiori found that meaningful integration of Facebook in the language classroom can lead to the development of community and sociopragmatic competence.

Blattner, G. and Lomicka, L. (2012) '*Facebook*-ing and the Social Generation: A New Era of Language Learning', *Apprentissage des langues et systèmes d'information et de communication)*, available: http://alsic.revues.org/2413 (accessed 28 Apr 2014).
    This study examines pedagogical and sociopragmatic practices using a social forum and a Facebook forum in the context of an intermediate French course.

Iskold, L. (2012) 'Imagined identities: An examination of self-authorship on Facebook', in P. Chamness Miller, M. Mantero and J. Watzke (eds), *Readings in Language Studies: Language and Identity*, Grandville: MI: International Society for Language Studies, Inc.: 119–210.

This study examines the concepts of self-authorship and performing identity in Facebook with twelve intermediate-level students studying Russian.

Lomicka, L. and Lord, G. (2012) 'A tale of tweets: Analyzing microblogging among language learners', *System*, 40: 48–63.

This study explores the use of Twitter among French learners who connected with each other and with native speakers of French. Evidence of cultural and linguistic gains is provided, along with student attitudes and reactions.

McBride, K. (2009) 'Social-networking sites in foreign language classes: Opportunities for re-creation', in L. Lomicka and G. Lord (eds), *The Next Generation: Social Networking and Online Collaboration in Foreign Language Learning*, San Marcos, TX: CALICO Monograph Series: 35–58.

This chapter discusses the potential for creating mash-ups from various SNS, and how these can be used in language learning endeavours.

Mills, N. (2011) 'Situated learning through social networking communities: The development of joint enterprise, mutual engagement, and a shared repertoire', *CALICO*, 28(2): 345–368.

In this study, Facebook was used as an interactive tool where students could share collective reflection and access resources that enhanced the various topics discussed in class.

# References

Ballance, O.J. (2012) 'Mobile language learning: More than just "the platform" (A commentary on Glenn Stockwell's "Using mobile phones for vocabulary activities: Examining the effect of the platform")', *Language Learning and Technology*, 16(3): 21–23, available: http://llt.msu.edu/issues/october2012/index.html (accessed 12 May 2014).

Barretta, A.G. (2014) '9 rules of etiquette for academic Twitter use', *eCampus News: Technology News for Today's Higher-Ed Leader*, available: http://www.ecampusnews.com/top-news/twitter-etiquette-academic-241/

Beck, M.B. (2014) 'The future of social media is mobile tribes', available: http://readwrite.com/2014/04/18/social-media-future-mobile-tribes#awesm=~oE4yit9h86UDXW (accessed 12 May 2014).

Blattner, G. and Fiori, M. (2009) 'Facebook in the language classroom: Promises and possibilities', *International Journal of Instructional Technology and Distance Learning*, 6(1): 17–28, available: http://itdl.org/journal/jan_09/article02.htm (accessed 8 Apr 2014).

Blattner, G. and Fiori, M. (2011) 'Virtual social network communities: An investigation of language learners' development of socio-pragmatic awareness and multiliteracy skills', *CALICO Journal*, 29(1): 24–43.

Blattner, G. and Lomicka, L. (2012a) '*Facebook*-ing and the social generation: A new era of language learning', *Alsic (Apprentissage des langues et systèmes d'information et de communication)*, available: http://alsic.revues.org/2413 (accessed 28 Apr 2014).

Blattner, G. and Lomicka, L. (2012b) 'A sociolinguistic study of practices in different social forums in an intermediate French class', *International Journal of Instructional Technology and Distance Learning*, 9(9): 3–24.

Blyth, C. (2008) 'Research perspective on online discourse and foreign language learning', in S. Magnan (ed), *Mediating Discourse Online*, Philadelphia, PA: John Benjamins Publishing Company: 47–72.

Chapelle, C.A. (1997) 'CALL in the year 2000: Still in search of research paradigms?', *Language Learning and Technology*, 2(1): 22–34, available: http://polyglot.cal.msu.edu/llt/vol1num1/chapelle/default.html (accessed 12 May 2014).

Chapelle, C.A. (1998) 'Multimedia CALL: Lessons to be learned from research on instructed SLA', *Language Learning and Technology*, 2(1): 22–34, available: http://polyglot.cal.msu.edu/llt/vol2num1/article1/index.html (accessed 12 May 2014).

Chartrand, R. (2012) 'Social networking for language learners: Creating meaningful output with Web 2.0 tools', *Knowledge Management and E-learning: An International Journal*, 4(1): 97–101.

Chen, H.I. (2013) 'Identity practices of multilingual writers in social networking spaces', *Language Learning and Technology*, 17(2): 143–170.

Clark, C. and Gruba, P. (2010) 'The use of social networking sites for foreign language learning: An autoethnographic study of Live Mocha', in *Proceedings ascilite*, Sydney: 164–173, available: http://ascilite.org.au/conferences/sydney10/procs/Cclark-full.pdf (accessed 12 May 2014).

Ducate, L. and Lomicka, L. (2013) 'Going mobile: Language learning with an iPod touch in intermediate French and German Classes', *Foreign Language Annals*, 46(3): 445–468.

Friedman, P. (2013) '6 social media trends of 2013 and what they mean for the future', available: http://www.huffingtonpost.com/peter-friedman/social-media-trends-of-2013_b_4463802.html (accessed 12 May 2014).

Gibson, J.J. (1979) *The Ecological Approach to Visual Perception*, Boston, MA: Houghton Mifflin.

Grahl, B. (2013) 'The media of social media', available: http://tristantreadwell.wordpress.com/tag/grahl/ (accessed 12 May 2014).

Harrison, R. (2013) 'Profiles in online communities: Social network sites for language learning – *Live Mocha* revisited', in M.-N. Lamy and K. Zourou (eds), *Social Networking for Language Education*, Basingstoke, UK: Palgrave Macmillan: 100–116.

Harrison, R. and Thomas, M. (2009) 'Identity in online communities: Social networking sites and language learning', *International Journal of Emerging Technologies and Society*, 7(2): 109–124.

Iskold, L. (2012) 'Imagined identities: An examination of self-authorship on Facebook', in P. Chamness Miller, M. Mantero and J. Watzke (eds), *Readings in Language Studies: Language and Identity*, Grandville: MI: International Society for Language Studies, Inc.: 119–210.

Kárpáti, A. (2009) 'Web 2 technologies for net native language learners: A "social CALL"', *ReCALL*, 21 (2): 139–156.

Kissmetrics. (2013) Available: http://blog.kissmetrics.com/wp-content/uploads/2013/06/how-to-get-more-likes-on-fb.pdf (accessed 14 May 2014).

Klimanova, L. and Dembovskaya, S. (2013) 'L2 identity, discourse, and social networking in Russian', *Language Learning and Technology*, 17(1): 69–88.

Komatsu, S. (2011) 'Sosharu media to gaikokugo gakushu, education – furansugo no atarashii manabi no tameni (Social media and learning foreign languages: A new approach for learning French)', *Archives of Rencontres Pédagogiques du Kansai*: 76–80, available: http://www.rpkansai.com/bulletins/pdf/025/076_080_Komatsu.pdf (accessed 23 Jan 2014).

Krashen, S. (1994) 'The input hypothesis and its rivals', in N.C. Ellis (ed), *Implicit and Explicit Learning of Languages*, San Diego, CA: Academic Press: 45–78.

Lamy, M.-N. and Zourou, K. (eds) (2013) *Social Networking for Language Education*, Basingstoke, UK: Palgrave Macmillan.

Lankshear, C. and Knobel, M. (eds) (2008) *Digital Literacies: Concepts, Policies and Practices*, New York, NY: Peter Lang.

Lantolf, J.P. (2000) *Sociocultural Theory and Second Language Learning*, Oxford, UK: Oxford University Press.

Lepi, K. (2013) 'How social media is being used in higher education', available: http://www.edudemic.com/social-media-in-education/ (accessed 12 May 2014).

Liu, M., Evans, M., Horwitz, E., Lee, S. McCrory, M., Park, J.B. et al. (2013) 'A study of the use of language learning websites with social network features by university ESL students', in M.-N. Lamy and K. Zourou (eds), *Social Networking for Language Education*, Basingstoke, UK: Palgrave Macmillan: 137–157.

Lomicka, L. and Lord, G. (2012) 'A tale of tweets: Analyzing microblogging among language learners', *System*, 40: 48–63.

Long, M. (1985) 'Input and second language acquisition theory', in S. Gass and C. Madden (eds), *Input in Second Language Acquisition*, Rowley, MA: Newbury House: 377–393.

Long, M. (1996) 'The role of the linguistic environment in second language acquisition', in W. Ritchie and T. Bhatia (eds), *Handbook of Second Language Acquisition*, San Diego, CA: Academic Press: 413–468

Mazer, J. P., Murphy, R. E. and Simonds, C. J. (2007) 'I'll see you on "Facebook": The effects of computer-mediated teacher self-disclosure on student motivation, affective learning, and classroom climate', *Communication Education*, 56(1): 1–17, available: http://dx.doi.org/10.1080/03634520601009710 (accessed 18 Nov 2015).

McBride, K. (2009) 'Social networking sites in foreign language classes: Opportunities for re-creation', in L. Lomicka and G. Lord (eds), *The Next Generation: Social Networking and Online Collaboration in Foreign Language Learning*, San Marcos, TX: CALICO: 35–58.

Mills, N. (2011) 'Situated learning through social networking communities: The development of joint enterprise, mutual engagement, and a shared repertoire', *CALICO Journal*, 28(2): 345–368.

Mitchell, K. (2012) 'A social tool: Why and how ESOL students use Facebook', *CALICO Journal*, 29(3): 471–493.

Pempek, T.A., Yermolayeva, Y.A. and Calvert, S.L. (2009) 'College students' social networking experiences on Facebook', *Journal of Applied Developmental Psychology*, 30(3): 227–238, available: http://dx.doi.org/10.1016/j.appdev.2008.12.010 (accessed 20 May 2014).

Reinhardt, J. and Chen, H. (2013) 'An ecological analysis of social networking site-mediated identity development', in M.-N. Lamy and K. Zourou (eds), *Social Networking for Language Education*, Basingstoke, UK: Palgrave Macmillan: 11–30.

Reinhardt, J. and Zander, V. (2011) 'Social networking in an intensive English program classroom: A language socialization perspective', *CALICO Journal*, 28(2): 326–344.
Richter, F. (2014) 'How mobile are social networks?', available: http://www.statista.com/chart/2091/mobile-usage-of-social-networks/ (accessed 12 May 2014).
Robinson, J. (2010) 'Educational use of social media: Some logistics and legal concerns', *The 21st Century Principal: Technology, Teach, and Public Education Advocate*, available: http://the21stcenturyprincipal.blogspot.com/2010/12/educational-use-of-social-media-some.html (accessed 29 Sept 2014).
Rodriguez, J. (2011) 'Social media use in higher education: Key areas to consider for educators', *The Journal of Online Learning and Teaching*, 7(4), available: http://jolt.merlot.org/vol7no4/rodriguez_1211.htm (accessed 12 May 2014).
Rosen, L.D. (2007) *Me, Myspace, and I: Parenting the Net Generation*, New York, NY: Palgrave Macmillan.
Ryberg, T. and Christiansen, E. (2008) 'Community and social network sites as technology enhanced learning environments', *Technology, Pedagogy & Education*, 17: 207–219.
Salaberry, R. (1999) 'CALL in the year 2000: Still developing the research agenda', *Language Learning and Technology*, 3(1): 104–107.
Schmidt, R. (1990) 'The role of consciousness in second language learning', *Applied Linguistics*, 11: 129–158.
Schmidt, R. (1995) 'Consciousness and foreign language learning: A tutorial on the role of attention and awareness in learning', in R. Schmidt (ed), *Attention and Awareness in Foreign Language Learning*, Honolulu, HI: University of Hawaii, Second Language Teaching and Curriculum Center: 1–63.
Schwartz, H.L. (2009) 'Facebook: The new classroom commons?', *The Chronicle Review*, available: http://blog.csustudents.org/?p=423 (accessed 12 May 2014).
Stevenson, M.P. and Liu, M. (2010) 'Learning a language with Web 2.0: Exploring the use of social networking features of foreign language learning websites', *CALICO Journal*, 27(1): 233–259.
Stockwell, G. and Sotillo, S. (2011) 'Call for papers for special issue of LLT. Theme: mobile language learning', *Language Learning and Technology*, 15(3): 130, available: http://llt.msu.edu/issues/october2011/call.pdf (accessed 12 May 2014).
Swain, M. and Lapkin, S. (1995) 'Problems in output and the cognitive processes they generate: A step towards second language learning', *Applied Linguistics*, 16: 371–391.
Sykes, J. and Holden, C. (2011) 'Communities: Exploring digital games and social networking', in N. Arnold and L. Ducate (eds), *Present and Future Promises of CALL: From Theory and Research to New Directions in Language Teaching*, San Marcos, TX: CALICO: 311–336.
Thorne, S.L. (2010) 'The 'Intercultural turn' and language learning in the crucible of new media', in F. Helm and S. Guth (eds), *Telecollaboration 2.0 for Language and Intercultural Learning*, Bern, Switzerland: Peter Lang: 139–164.
Thorne, S. L. and Payne, J. S. (2005). 'Evolutionary trajectories, Internet-mediated expression, and language education', *CALICO Journal*, 22(3): 371–397.
van Lier, L. (2004) *The Ecology and Semiotics of Language Learning*, Boston, MA: Kluwer Academic Publishers.
Vygotsky, L. (1978) *Mind in Society: The Development of Higher Psychological Processes* (M. Cole, V. John-Steiner, S. Scribner and E. Souberman, eds), Cambridge, MA: Harvard University Press.
Walter, E. (2012) 'The rise of visual social media', *Fast Company* blog, available: http://www.fastcompany.com/3000794/rise-visual-social-media (accessed 12 May 2014).
Zourou, K. (2012) 'On the attractiveness of social media for language learning: a look at the state of the art', in F. Demaizière and K. Zourou (eds), Special issue "language learning and social media: (r)evolution?" *ALSIC*, 15(1), available: http://alsic.revues.org/2436 (accessed 14 Mar 2014).

# 19
# Computer supported collaborative writing and language learning

*Muriel Grosbois*

This chapter sets out to probe the potential of computer supported collaborative writing (CSCW) for foreign and/or second language (L2) development. In order to do so, CSCW will first be defined. It will then be examined in view of what research highlights as core issues: the interplay between collective and individual actions, as well as the dynamics involved in the complex process of co-writing. Implications in terms of teacher education will then be addressed. Finally, further perspectives will be encompassed considering the evolving nature of writing in an environment which is critically mediated by technologies.

## Defining CSCW

Today, Web 2.0 tools allow shared content creation among participants, turning writing into a collective activity referred to as CSCW. Whilst the impact of word processing on students' individual writing is still being investigated (e.g. Grégoire and Karsenti 2013), the spread of Web 2.0 applications with open editing and review structures (such as wikis or public pads) now also calls for the study of how co-writers jointly create and transform a common text, often within a distant, shared space. A brief overview will first help to grasp the parallel between the evolution of writing mediated by digital tools and that of the theoretical reference frameworks.

During the 'computer as tool' era (Levy 1997: 83, 178–184), technology had already started to provide 'a dynamic medium for exploring plans and ideas', as Sharples and Pemberton (1990: 38) put it. Interestingly, the model presented by Hayes and Flower (1980) considered writing no longer as a linear process but rather as a recursive one (with planning, formulating, reviewing and executing phases). This dynamic has gone one step further with CSCW, because the 'writable web' as Kárpáti (2009: 140) names it provides users with the opportunity to express themselves and interact in many ways. Blogs, for instance, tend to be personal sites where visitors can post messages. Wikis are made up of pages that can be modified by others, and some cloud-based supports are specifically designed for collaborative writing (e.g. Google Drive Document or TitanPad). It is worth noting that the reference writing model has evolved accordingly: in 1996 Hayes added the social environment, that is, the co-authors, the audience (be it real or fictive) and the physical environment (likely to entail modifications of the planning and executive phases). Grabe and Kaplan (1996) also added situational variables such as the participants, the setting, the task, the topic and the knowledge necessary for writing (i.e. linguistic and discursive knowledge on how to write a text in a second/foreign language).

Such landmarks help to situate CSCW in today's context so as to analyse it with a language learning perspective. To do so, the term 'collaborative' first needs to be considered, since CSCW can encompass a large array of activities ranging from an individual writer producing a text through interaction with others to a group of writers jointly writing a shared text. For Forman and Cazden (1985: 329), 'collaboration requires a mutual task in which the partners work together to produce something that neither could have produced alone'. They distinguish between co-authorship – characterised by a group-owned product – and the product of an individual achieved thanks to the contributions of others. In the same vein, Haring-Smith defines collaborative writing by distinguishing between serial writing, compiled writing, and co-authored writing. Although she defines co-authoring as producing a text in which it 'is difficult (indeed, often impossible) to distinguish the work of one writer from another' (Haring-Smith 1994: 363), it must be noted that individual participation can now be traced, thanks to a colour code, for example, which identifies each writer in some Web 2.0 tools.

In fact, when going back to the distinction established between collaboration and cooperation by Henri and Lundgren-Cayrol (2001), the former corresponding to shared teamwork and the latter based on division of labour, the term 'collaborative writing' sometimes proves inappropriate, as pointed out by some researchers (e.g. Pellet 2012). The following examples will illustrate the difference.

Figure 19.1 shows an excerpt of a text produced as a result of distant collaboration by participants simultaneously engaged in a CSCW task included in a pedagogical scenario (during a workshop at the University of Caen, France, in 2013). Their shared teamwork appears through the intertwined turns, materialised by typographic marks here, but originally distinguished by colours with TitanPad. (Only the initials of the participants' surnames have been kept to preserve anonymity.)

---

7 **Syrie et Lybie: des conflits vécus par des natifs** *depuis la France*

9 A l'heure où la diplomatie suisse tente de mettre sur pied une conférence pour la paix en Syrie, nous vous proposons un entretien exclusif avec H, syrien d'origine, qui vit en France depuis 4 ans et qui nous donne sa vision du conflit qui sévit en Syrie depuis plus de 2 ans. **F, lui, est Lybien d'origine et vit en France depuis 9 ans.**

11 Une façon pour nos lecteurs Suisses et d'ailleurs d'appréhender de manière neuve cette problématique complexe. Bonne lecture

13 **La Rédaction – De nos envoyés à Caen: M et JP**

16 Quel a été l'élément déclencheur de la crise en Syrie?

18 *Suite à la révolution égyptienne et libyenne, le souffle de la révolution est* aussi *arrivé en Syrie.* C'est un *événement marquant,* qui a eu lieu au Sud du pays, qui a déclenché *le* soulèvement du *peuple syrien pour la dignité* et *la liberté.* Toute l'histoire a commencé suite à une *conversation téléphonique entre une enseignante et son amie,* qui parlaient de leur espoir de voir aussi un vent de liberté atteindre la Syrie, et qui a *malheureusement* été entendu par *les services secrets* qui contrôle le pays d'une *main de fer.*

21 **H, tu nous as dit tout à l'heure que tu étais arrivé en France avant le début du conflit syrien. Comment as-tu vécu le début des événements sur un plan personnel?**

---

*Figure 19.1* Abstract of text produced as a result of collaborative practice

The corresponding chat exchange (Figure 19.2) leading to this resulting document also reveals that the participants worked together in a collaborative manner.

But when examining the notion of shared teamwork in Wikipedia for instance, one may wonder whether this online encyclopaedia is not more cooperative than collaborative, although it is defined as 'written collaboratively by volunteers around the world'. This may be due to the fact that content creation in Wikipedia cannot be planned by a 'group' since anyone can participate at any time (unless Wikipedia is diverted for pedagogical purposes).

Placing the cursor on collaboration or cooperation may then depend on the context, which is also likely to vary over time. The hypernym 'collective' will therefore be favoured and used in this chapter. Since CSCW actually involves individuals working together to various degrees towards a common goal, it is now the interplay between the individual and the collective that will be considered from L2 learning perspectives.

## L2 learning and CSCW: Individual and collective interplay

It is first worth noting that individual and collective interplay is precisely at the core of both the socioconstructivist paradigm and second language acquisition (SLA) theories, and that it is favourable to L2 learning in both frameworks (for a full discussion of CALL-related theories, see Hubbard and Levy, Chapter 2 this volume.)

Within the socioconstructivist paradigm, learning itself is viewed as an individual and collective process: each person fosters his/her own cognitive and linguistic development through interaction with others (Vygotsky 1978; Leontiev 1981; Bruner 1983). In this theoretical framework, mediation is essential: learning relies on help between an expert and a novice. In other words, what learners manage to achieve thanks to more advanced peers or a tutor or teacher is greater than they would have achieved by themselves. Given the importance attributed to interactions in the learning process, and that CSCW precisely allows learners to participate jointly in the process of writing, the socioconstructivist approach can be considered relevant to studying how CSCW can foster L2 development, as suggested by Brown and Adler (2008).

CSCW can also be examined in light of SLA theories. Based on Swain's notions of 'pushed output' and 'comprehensible output' (1985: 249), CSCW is likely to play a significant role in L2 development because this problem-solving type of activity requires the participants to confront solutions and explanations, suggest changes and revisions, and interact and negotiate meaning in order to write a common text. By so doing, each learner can notice a gap between his/her L2 linguistic knowledge and the target language, test new hypotheses about language (in terms of structure and meaning) and receive feedback on those hypotheses, which benefits L2 acquisition according to Gass and Selinker (2001).

In fact, the individual and collective endeavours operate at the levels of both content and form in CSCW. Indeed, exchanges between participants engaged in CSCW are essential for common coherent content to emerge. In the case of distant CSCW, they can be sustained by tools such as chat, as illustrated in Figure 19.2. Clearly, the nature of writing in the chat exchange (Figure 19.2) is different from that of the joint text in the shared writing support (Figure 19.1). But both are complementary since organisation and brainstorming discussed through chatting prepare for the resulting common text. Figure 19.2 also shows that the participants discussed content and organisation at the very beginning of the task, thus laying the foundation for the synchronous CSCW activity. It suggests that coordination is prior to co-producing text, in this type of context at least, which is in keeping with Elola and Oskoz who noticed that 'in the individually-produced wiki drafts learners defined their thesis and worked on the essay structure throughout the entire writing process. When working collaboratively, learners established the

Muriel Grosbois

14:38 **JP: Bonjour**

14:38 *M: on pose une question déclencheuse?*

14:38 *H: salut*

14:38 **JP: d accord**

14:38 *H: ok on commence par des question réponses*

14:38 *M: j eme lance*

14:39 *H: une petite introduction puis l'interview*

14:39 unnamed: *je me suis trompé de la place*

14:39 unnamed: *c'est bon maintenant*

14:39 **JP: on effqce tout le texte et on recommence**

14:40 *M: yes*

14:40 *M: j'ai anticipé*

14:40 **JP: on pourrqitavoir un cqdre plus personnel qqvqnt cette pre,iere auestion, non**

14:41 *F: c'est un peu compliqué ce que vous écrivez JP*

14:41 *F: peut-etre vous écrivez avec un clavier anglai*

14:42 *M: oui bonne idée*

14:42 **JP: faut trouver un titre qussi**

14:42 *M: Genre le conflit syrien*

14:42 *M: ca vou irait?*

14:43 *F: quand le partie Baat est arrivé au pouvoir H*

14:44 *M: JP il faudrait placer ta question avant la mienne*

14:44 *M: non?*

14:44 **JP: oui mais le coinflit syrien vu pqr Syrien alors qu'il est en Frqnce**

14:46 *M: mais il est quand même syrien*

14:46 *M: tu veux dire qu'il faudrait être plus précis dans notre titre?*

14:46 **JP: oui!**

14:47 *M: Genre: le conflit syrien vu d'Europe par un Syrien*

14:47 **JP: donc ce nest pqs lq vision occidentale mqis ce n est pas non plus tout a fait la vision de quelqu un qui est reste sur plqce$**

*Figure 19.2* Chat exchange preparing for common text (displayed in Figure 19.1)

\* The typographical errors in this chat exchange are due to the fact that one of the participants (JP) was used to typing on a Querty keyboard (not an Azerty one).

structure early in the initial wiki drafts' (2010: 62–63). Does this imply that structure and content are a greater concern than form for learners engaged in CSCW? In the literature, there is evidence that form is also attended to but in a way that differs from individual writing. Lee (2010) pointed out that peer scaffolding in a wiki task improves language accuracy in the revision process, and Elola and Oskoz (2010) concluded that learners tended to polish the essays while developing the multiple drafts (not towards the end of the writing process as when working individually). Yet, for Kessler (2009), learners were not particularly concerned with the accuracy of their writing as long as grammatical errors did not interfere with meaning. It is interesting to consider these results in light of findings on discussion-board writing in bicultural interactions: Ware and O'Dowd (2008) found that learners were more likely to provide feedback on form when they were encouraged to do so than when it was just suggested. Attention to form may then depend on the task and the assignment. But it could also depend on the socioaffective context (a dimension which matters in online distance tutoring), and hence on the link between public and private spaces.

In that respect it is worth stressing, in line with Elola and Oskoz (2010), that learners prefer revising their own subtexts (rather than the global product). Several interpretations might account for that. Learners may be relatively unconcerned with the accuracy of their partners' writing. But they may also not be willing to correct a partner's text publicly, unless encouraged or asked to do so, as in Figure 19.3.

Because writing publicly can be inhibiting, private spaces provided by some tools that allow one-to-one exchanges can prove useful. They permit lateral sequences which can operate like a 'whisper' channel to solve a linguistic problem without interrupting the general activity taking

---

14:50 *H: vous pouvez corriger s'il y a des fautes*
14:50 **JP: laissons les fautes pour l'instant**
14:51 *M: oui c'est une bonne idée de poser la question du titre dans le texte*
14:51 *M: car je pense aussi que la crise syrienne ce n'est pas assez précis*
14:51 **JP: il faut qu'on construise un chappeau pour situer l'entretien**
14:54 *M: c'est le genre d'exercice plus facile à réaliser quand le texte est construit*
14:54 *H: je rappelle que vous devez lire mon texte et le corriger*
14:54 *H: pour eux ils aiment voir l'arc en ciel dans nos textes*
14:55 *M: excellent le début du chapeau*
14:55 *M: ca fait grand reporter!*
14:56 **JP: F, pourrais tu me dire depuis combien de temps tu es en France? pour commencer à écrire le chapeau**
14:57 **JP: oui; il aut egqlement intégrer F**
14:57 *M: ok je relis!*
14:57 *H: Merci M ^_^*
14 :58 *F: ça fait presque 9 ans*
15:05 **JP: M je te laisse relire et corriger le chapeau**
15:06 *M: ok*

---

*Figure 19.3* Chat excerpt about attention to form

\* The typographical errors in this chat exchange are due to the fact that one of the participants (JP) was used to typing on a Querty keyboard (not an Azerty one).

place on the public co-construction space. Private spaces thus give co-authors the possibility to carry out the revision of their contributions (on a one-to-one basis) before communicating or including them in the shared document. Learners can thereby develop their L2 interlanguage through interaction and negotiation of meaning generated by their writing and the reaction of all, or just some, of the other co-present participants.

On the other hand, it should be added that the public nature of CSCW can also be stimulating: some studies indicate that the social implication of writing in an electronic public sphere impacts the output of language learners in a positive and constructive way (Abraham and Williams 2009). Examining CSCW with an L2 development perspective therefore implies considering not only the individual/collective interplay, but also the local/global, public/private spheres and their interrelations, which leads to a further discussion of CSCW and L2 learning in terms of complexity.

## Complexity of CSCW and L2 learning

Interestingly, the fundamental characteristics of a complex system find an echo in CSCW. In line with Larsen-Freeman and Cameron (2008), who developed a complex systems approach to applied linguistics (with vivid examples in their chapter 2, taken from the natural world as well as from applied linguistics), Mercer (2011) explains that a complex system is defined by the following features: the various components constantly interact with one another and constantly evolve; the context is an integral part of the system; changes cannot be predicted; and nonlinearity prevails. Yet, despite the seemingly general instability and chaotic behaviour generated by the numerous factors always in process, a kind of dynamic stability emerges thanks to internal and external adaptation. Those key features precisely apply to CSCW. Consequently, the analysis of CSCW for L2 learning can also benefit from being studied in light of complexity theory (provided this framework is coherent with the research objective). In fact, exploring the potential of CSCW for L2 learning within complexity theory is likely to help understand the complex dynamic nonlinear iterative process which sustains CSCW and results in a common text. For researchers, putting into parallel the exchanges between the participants (as in Figure 19.2) and the joint text (displayed in Figure 19.1) enables one to go beyond the product and to access the complex process of co-writing because, as Leblay (2011: 3) stresses: 'the product is not the true picture of the production: seeking to understand the writing process from the product would be an illusion'. Hence research interests have shifted from the product towards the process (e.g. Blin and Appel 2011).

In order to investigate the process, it should first be noted that each contributor's involvement in the phases implied in co-writing can now be traced thanks to widgets (web application tools used to present dynamic content) such as a time slider, which not only keeps track of the changes made by the participants but allows the display of such data in a time-aware manner. Visualising temporal data (e.g. showing cumulative data to a point in time, or data that falls within a time range) thanks to this type of tool, helps to grasp precisely the dynamics behind the process of CSCW by giving access to the layers of information which correspond to the changes made by the various participants. More exactly, only part of the dynamic process of co-(re)writing is displayed that way, because the writing process itself is never entirely accessible and visible (for instance, the thinking or the retrieval and manipulation of content from memory). Such widgets nevertheless reveal how organisation, content and form are tackled by the participants during the activity and how they lead to a common text. Researchers can then examine the process across the data at a macro level as well as at a micro level, in order to grasp the intricate interplay between the various components at various levels and at various moments. By so doing, they can also analyse how the end-product emerges from the numerous interrelated components that constantly interact (agents, artefact, context, L2), and hence better comprehend the unpredictable nature of the final product.

Given the complexity of CSCW, it is difficult to draw pedagogical guidelines to help learners become efficient L2 writers and/or learn L2 through CSCW. However, given that the position favoured here is that of teacher education sustained by research, elements to take into consideration in order to design pedagogically meaningful CSCW activities will be examined, based on key research findings.

## CSCW and L2 teacher education

Because no 'recipe' can possibly be applied, the implementation of CSCW in teaching practice will be analysed through relevant questions triggered by research, centred mainly on task design and mediation, the expert/novice distinction, the balance between public/group interactions and an individual approach to L2 learning.

Considering task design necessarily implies considering the objective. Is the objective L2 learning through CSCW, or learning how to become an efficient L2 writer? Are learners expected to further their linguistic and/or cultural development, or build content knowledge, or develop their creativity (in terms of language and/or content), or understand particular writing conventions depending on genres as noted by Harklau (2002) and Ortega (2009)?

Task design also implies taking the context into account. As previously mentioned, there is, for instance, a major difference between a formal pedagogical task designed for a set group of learners during a set period of time (as in Figures 19.1 and 19.2) *versus* a free participatory informal activity undertaken by anyone on the social web over an infinite time span, even if both practices can coexist. In the first case, several issues need to be addressed, including the need for consideration of mediation.

In the task corresponding to Figures 19.1 and 19.2, teacher mediation consisted first of introducing TitanPad to the participants and giving them instructions: 'Generate a striking news headline of your choice'. Second, it centred on guiding reflection regarding the potential of CSCW for L2 learning purposes, the objective of the workshop being to introduce CSCW to in-service L2 teachers of French and to reflect upon major pedagogical issues with them. But a CSCW activity can also benefit from being peer-mediated, once the collaboration is underway. Kessler, for instance, highlights the impact of the teacher's presence in a wiki-based task in those terms:

> While many tasks in a content-based class may involve elements of, or even a focus on, form, it may be equally important to provide students with tasks that do not introduce the power dynamics of the teachers' presence. In fact, there may be an unseen benefit for the advanced-level students in the form of greater output (Oxford 1997), more opportunity for practice (Ortega 2009), or a greater sense of autonomy (Benson 1997). Each of these characteristics may contribute to linguistic development, particularly for more advanced language learners. The task and environment may influence these fluency building practices as well as their attention to accuracy.
>
> *(Kessler 2009: 91)*

Interestingly, the author points to a difference related to the L2 level of the students. Another distinction worth examining when setting up a CSCW activity is the one between expert and novice writers.

When investigating the process of writing, Leblay (2009) showed that the expert writer works on his draft differently from the novice writer, the former tending to proceed in a circular way with a lot of revising work while the novice tends to proceed in a linear way with hardly any insertion, modification or revision work. It is therefore interesting to reflect upon the potential benefit of expert/novice teamwork when engaging students in CSCW.

Moreover, as mentioned by Lundin (2008) with regard to wikis in particular, the students' social practice may have already shaped their use of CSCW tools. On the other hand, contrary to what is expected of 'digital natives', it could happen that students may not be used to CSCW. A CSCW task should then be regarded as an activity which requires particular guided instruction. Hyland (2003), for instance, suggests that it is necessary first to develop a well-structured writing course based on genre-specific pedagogy: the instructor models texts and helps learners to analyse features of language and structure. Then, the integration of web-based tools can make learners become active participants who gradually develop familiarity with one another as writers and, by so doing, acquire the necessary linguistic and writing conventions of the target language. Lin and Kelsey (2009) also stress the importance for students to learn collaborative writing practices through three phases of wiki use: exploration, adaptation and collaboration.

Further to the necessity to consider students' histories with writing, another crucial issue for CSCW and L2 teacher education relates to the difficulties teachers may encounter in balancing the potential of public/group interactions and the individual approach required to meet the needs of each learner.

Whether a teacher can spare the time to use the widgets to visualise the co-writing process the students are engaged in, and single out those who most need guidance, is questionable. However, when the focus is on form, for instance, such tools could prove useful to point out some recurrent individual errors and give personalised feedback to the students. Instructors should then keep in mind that error correction in public spaces is a serious concern and that precautions need to be taken in order to avoid students losing face. In that respect, the differences associated with cultures of individuals and groups across different types of learning contexts and cultures are worth taking into account.

It should finally be reminded that students may prefer writing individually when performing a pedagogical task since co-writing implies that they have less control over both the process and the end product. They therefore depend more on the others for the achievement of the task and for the evaluation, if any. Hence the necessity for teachers to make assessment criteria clear: Is only the end-product evaluated or each learner's contribution, or both? Is priority given to form or content or collective creativity? Reflecting upon those issues can contribute to a successful experience and can therefore be considered relevant for pre-service and in-service L2 teacher education. But beyond that, it is also judicious to reconsider the nature of writing and the concept of literacy.

## Further perspectives: Literacies, CSCW and L2 learning

Today's technology-mediated environment urges us to reconsider the very nature of writing and the concept of literacy. As Cazden et al. underline, there is:

> [an] increasing multiplicity and integration of significant modes of meaning-making, where the textual is also related to the visual, the audio, the spatial, the behavioral, and so on. This is particularly important in the mass media, multimedia, and in an electronic hypermedia.
> *(Cazden et al. 1996: 64)*

One may therefore wonder whether writing still means writing a text, or something else. Such an evolution implies revisiting conventional literacy practices through multiliteracies defined by

Cazden et al. (1996: 63) as 'the multiplicity of communications channels and media, and the increasing saliency of cultural and linguistic diversity'. A broader view of literacy is also suggested by Thomas et al. (2007: n.p.) who define transliteracy as 'the ability to read, write and interact across a range of platforms, tools and media from signing and orality through handwriting, print, TV, radio and film, to digital social networks'.

Furthermore, Musser, O'Reilly and the O'Reilly Radar Team (2007: 30) explain that 'the key to Web 2.0 is not just user participation, it is participation leading to reuse'. In fact, users 'modify', 'multiply' and '(re)mix' content, as Zourou (2012) stresses. As a consequence, Web 2.0 developments and the evolution of the concept of literacy sustain a (re)mix of content in which different types of expression end up being merged, which blurs the frontiers between the usual oral/written competencies and provides a new challenge for L2 learning. All the more so as the communicative genres which interact with each other in the informal social media practices are likely to have some consequences on the final document produced by learners engaged in CSCW, in terms of both content and form. The complexity inherent to CSCW for L2 learning is thereby increased. How then can one best help participants to learn a second/foreign language or to become efficient L2 writers through CSCW practice?

To foster L2 learning, the complex L2 content which emerges out of CSCW may require 'bridging activities', as suggested by Thorne and Reinhardt (2008: 563) for gaming (see also Reinhardt and Thorne, Chapter 30 this volume). As regards linguistic diversity, the learners' remix could be analysed along an inductive approach with the objective of developing meta-linguistic awareness among the participants. Inviting them to reflect upon language by analysing the varied input emanating from their co-'writing', input that is therefore situated, should help them deal with the unpredictability of the end product. As regards the multimodal nature of (re)'writing', the issue of learning how to 'write' in a second/foreign language could be addressed by adopting a holistic approach based on connectedness as suggested by Frau-Meigs:

> 'medi@education.century21st' refers to the fact that old and new media are digitizing and allowing for yet unsuspected forms of education in the 21st century, owing to coming generations of Web 2.0, 3.0, . . .
>
> So, establishing connectedness implies a number of positive actions and the abolition of antiquated binary oppositions to accommodate for today's complexity. This can be done within complexity theory.
>
> *(Frau-Meigs 2008: 56)*

Revisiting the concept of literacy thus leads to the consideration of an extra layer in terms of complexity when probing the potential of CSCW for L2 learning.

It is too soon to examine fully the contribution of the multifaceted-nature of CSCW on L2 learning, and to do so with hindsight. However, taking part in L2 CSCW can be regarded as an activity that is likely to contribute to the development of communication skills that are necessary in today and tomorrow's society.

The author would like to warmly thank all the participants of the L2CSCW workshop given during the research seminar 'Didactique et Langues' in July 2013 at the University of Caen, France.

## Further reading

Blin, F. and Appel, C. (2011) 'Computer supported collaborative writing in practice: An activity theoretical study', *CALICO Journal*, 28(2): 473–497.
    This article enables the reader to understand further the complexity and the dynamics inherent to CSCW in a second language. Through the example of an EFL course, this paper provides an analysis

of CSCW as an activity system. More precisely, it aims at grasping the mediational and collaborative structures of the activities and subactivities implied in the process. Studying the interactions among the participants also gave the authors the possibility to bring to light deviations from planned procedures (when the instructions were ignored for instance) thus revealing that the activity is likely to unfold in unexpected ways.

Fuchs, C. and Snyder, B. (2013) 'It's not just the tool: Pedagogy for promoting collaboration and community in CMC', in M.-N. Lamy, and K. Zourou (eds), *Social Networking for Language Education*, New York, NY: Palgrave Macmillan: 117–134.

In this chapter, the authors consider the link between pedagogical design and learning outcomes. They focus on how interactions can foster L2 development when carrying out a task using Google Wave. They also highlight the complexity of writing (due to the various functions of the collaborative tool) and reflect upon the usefulness of genre analysis so as to help students to be autonomous in their writing practice. This is worth considering in light of what Lamy and Mangenot discuss in the paragraph about genres in the same book, in their chapter titled 'Social Media-Based Language Learning: Insights from Research and Practice'.

Kessler, G. and Bikowski, D. (2010) 'Developing collaborative autonomous learning abilities in computer mediated language learning: attention to meaning among students in wiki space', *Computer Assisted Language Learning*, 23(1): 41–58.

This study addresses how students constructed meaning when performing a long-term wiki-based collaborative activity. The authors give a clear review of the literature in the domains of autonomy, collaboration, collaborative writing and computer mediation in language learning. They show how the students manipulated language independently and as collaborative team members.

Strobl, C. (2014) 'Affordances of Web 2.0 technologies for collaborative advanced writing in a foreign language', *CALICO Journal*, 31(1): 1–18.

Based on a comparison between text produced individually and collectively by advanced proficiency L2 writers, the results of this study emphasise the positive impact of collaboration on organisation during the planning phase. The author also establishes a link between online collaboration and recursive writing, which is worth considering in light of Leblay's findings regarding the distinction between expert and novice writers, as mentioned earlier in this chapter.

Thorne, S. and Fischer, I. (2012) 'Online gaming as sociable media', *Alsic, Apprentissage des langues et systèmes d'information et de communication*, 15(1).

This paper comes as an interesting complement to the last section of the present chapter insofar as it explores the nature of the linguistic environment in specialised literacies that go beyond conventional forms of literacy. The authors consider the emergence of informal communicative practices and analyse them in light of L2 learning. By so doing, they probe into the linguistic complexity inherent to communication in a technology-enhanced context and defend a critical language awareness approach to sustain L2 learning.

## References

Abraham, L.B. and Williams, L. (2009) *Electronic Discourse in Language Learning and Language Teaching*, Amsterdam, Netherlands: John Benjamins.

Benson, P. (1997) 'The philosophy and politics of learner autonomy', in P. Benson and P. Voller (eds), *Autonomy and Independence in Language Learning*, London, UK: Longman: 18–34.

Blin, F. and Appel, C. (2011) 'Computer supported collaborative writing in practice: An activity theoretical study', *CALICO Journal*, 28(2): 473–497.

Brown, J.S. and Adler, R.P. (2008) 'Minds on fire: Open education, the long tail, and learning 2.0.', *EDUCAUSE Review*, 43(1): 16–32.

Bruner, J.S. (1983) *Child's Talk: Learning to Use Language*, New York, NY: Norton.

Cazden, C. et al. (1996) 'A pedagogy of multiliteracies: Designing social futures', *Harvard Educational Review*, 66(1): 60–92.

Elola, I. and Oskoz, A. (2010) 'Collaborative writing: Fostering foreign language and writing conventions development', *Language Learning & Technology*, 14(3): 51–71, available: http://llt.msu.edu/issues/october2010/elolaoskoz.pdf

Forman, E.A. and Cazden, C.B. (1985) 'Exploring Vygotskian perspectives in education: The cognitive value of peer interaction', in J.V. Wertsch (ed), *Culture, Communication and Cognition: Vygotskian Perspectives*, Cambridge: Cambridge University Press: 323–347.

Frau-Meigs, D. (2008) 'Media literacy and human rights: Education for sustainable societies', *DC/74/EL/CP Editions, Council of Europe*, 14(1): 51–82.
Gass, S. and Selinker, L. (2001) *Second Language Acquisition – An Introductory Course*, Mahwah, NJ: Lawrence Erlbaum Associates.
Grabe, W. and Kaplan, R.B. (1996) *Theory & Practice of Writing*, Harlow, Essex: Addison Wesley Longman Limited.
Grégoire, P. and Karsenti, T. (2013) 'Le processus de révision et l'écriture informatisée – Description des utilisations du traitement de texte par des élèves du secondaire au Québec' *Alsic, Apprentissage des Langues et Systèmes d'information et de communication*, 16, available: http://alsic.revues.org/2598; DOI: 10.4000/alsic.2598
Haring-Smith, T. (1994) *Writing Together: Collaborative Learning in the Writing Classroom*, New York, NY: HarperCollins College Publishers.
Harklau, L. (2002) 'The role of writing in classroom second language acquisition', *Journal of Second Language Writing*, 11: 329–350.
Hayes, J.R. (1996) 'A new framework for understanding cognition and affect in writing', in C.M. Levy and S. Ransdell (eds), *The Science of Writing*, Hillsdale, NJ: Lawrence Erlbaum Associates.
Hayes, J.R. and Flower, L.S. (1980) 'Identifying the organization of writing processes', in L.W. Gregg and E.R. Steinberg (eds), *Cognitive Processes in Writing*, Hillsdale, NJ: Lawrence Erlbaum Associates: 3–30.
Henri, F. and Lundgren-Cayrol, K. (2001) *Apprentissage collaboratif à distance*, Sainte-Foy: Presses de l'Université du Québec.
Hyland, K. (2003) 'Genre-based pedagogies: A social response to process', *Journal of Second Language Writing*, 12: 17–29.
Kárpáti, A. (2009) 'Web 2 technologies for net native language learners: A "social call"', *ReCALL*, 21(2): 139–156.
Kessler, G. (2009) 'Student-initiated attention to form in wiki-based collaborative writing', *Language, Learning & Technology*, 13(1): 79–95, available: http://llt.msu.edu/vol13num1/kessler.pdf
Larsen-Freeman, D. and Cameron, L. (2008) *Complex Systems and Applied Linguistics*, Oxford: Oxford University Press.
Leblay, C. (2009) 'En deçà du bien et du mal écrire. Pour une saisie en temps réel des invariants opérationnels de l'écriture', *Écrits de savoir, Pratiques*, 143/144: 153–167.
Leblay, C. (2011) *Le temps de l'écriture. Genèse, durée, représentations*, unpublished thesis, University of Jyväskyla.
Lee, L. (2010) 'Exploring wiki-mediated collaborative writing: A case study in an elementary Spanish course', *CALICO Journal*, 27(2): 260–276.
Leontiev, A.A. (1981) *Psychology and the Language Learning Process*, Oxford: Pergamon Institute of English.
Levy, M. (1997) *Computer-Assisted Language Learning – Context and Conceptualization*, New York, NY: Oxford University Press.
Lin, H. and Kelsey, K.D. (2009) 'Building a networked environment in wikis: The evolving phases of collaborative learning in a wikibook project' *Journal of Educational Computing Research*, 40(2): 145–169.
Lundin, R.W. (2008) 'Teaching with wikis: Toward a networked pedagogy', *Computers and Composition*, 25: 432–448.
Mercer, S. (2011) 'Understanding learner agency as a complex dynamic system', *System*, 39: 427–436.
Musser, J., O'Reilly, T. and the O'Reilly Radar Team. (2007) *Web 2.0 Principles and Best Practices*, Sebastopol, CA: O'Reilly.
Ortega, L. (2009) Understanding second language acquisition, London, UK: Hodder Education.
Oxford, R. (1997) 'Cooperative learning, collaborative learning, and interaction: Three communicative strands in the language classroom', *The Modern Language Journal*, 81(6): 443–457.
Pellet, S.H. (2012) 'Wikis for building content knowledge in the foreign language classroom', *CALICO Journal*, 29(2): 224–248.
Sharples, M. and Pemberton, L. (1990) 'Starting from the writer: Guidelines for the design of user-centred document processors', *Computer Assisted Language Learning*, 2: 37–57.
Swain, M. (1985) 'Communicative competence: Some roles of comprehensible input and comprehensible output in its development', in S. Gass and C. Madden (eds), *Input in Second Language Acquisition*, Rowley, MA: Newbury House: 235–255.
Thomas, S., Joseph, C., Laccetti, J., Mason, B., Mills, S., Perril, S. et al. (2007) 'Transliteracy: Crossing divides', *First Monday*, 12(12), available: http://firstmonday.org/article/view/2060/1908

Thorne, S.L. and Reinhardt, J. (2008) '"Bridging activities", new media literacies, and advanced foreign language proficiency', *CALICO Journal*, 25(3): 558–572.

Vygotsky, L.S. (1978) *Mind in Society: The Development of Higher Psychological Processes*, Cambridge, MA: Harvard University Press.

Ware, P.D. and O'Dowd, R. (2008) 'Peer feedback on language form in telecollaboration', *Language Learning & Technology*, 12(1): 43–63, available: http://llt.msu.edu/vol12num1/pdf/wareodowd.pdf

Zourou, K. (2012) 'On the attractiveness of social media for language learning: A look at the state of the art', *Alsic, Apprentissage des langues et systèmes d'information et de communication*, 15(1), available: http://alsic.revues.org/2436

# 20
# Interactive whiteboards and language learning

*Euline Cutrim Schmid*

Since the late 1990s, interactive whiteboards (IWBs) have progressively established their role in the field of computer-assisted language learning (CALL). The academic literature produced so far has highlighted the potential of this technology for enhancing language teaching and learning (Cutrim Schmid 2009; Mathews-Aydinli and Elaziz 2010), but has also drawn attention to potential drawbacks, such as increasing teacher-centredness (Gray 2010) or causing cognitive overload (Cutrim Schmid 2008b). This chapter starts by providing a short introduction to this technology and its development as an educational tool. The next section draws on theories of second language acquisition to discuss the potential of IWBs for enhancing language teaching and learning. The chapter then goes on to discuss academic research findings that shed light on the opportunities and challenges involved in the integration of IWBs into the language classroom. The following section incorporates the insights gained from practice-based and practice-oriented research. It presents examples of professional development tools that aim at supporting and guiding language teachers in the process of integrating the IWB into their teaching in ways that are consistent with current theories of language teaching methodology. The chapter concludes with a look into the future of this technology. It points towards classroom scenarios in which IWBs are used in combination with other interactive systems, such as learner response systems, tablet PCs or multiuser/multitouch environments, to provide a technology that is more interactive and individualised.

## How did the IWB find its way into language classrooms around the world?

The first IWB was manufactured by SMART Technologies in 1991. Some of the early adopters of this technology were educators who used it in distance education programmes in universities and colleges. Since the early nineties, classroom adoption of IWBs has grown steadily in many parts of the world and this technology is becoming increasingly commonplace in educational institutions, from primary schools through to universities. The UK was the first school-level market to invest heavily in IWBs. As early as 2004, 63% of secondary schools and 92% of all primary schools were equipped with IWBs (DfES 2004). The British Council was one of the first language organisations to introduce IWBs in their language teaching centres all over the world (Wightman 2006).

The UK continues to be the largest interactive whiteboard market in the world. As the figures provided by Futuresource show (see Figure 20.1), 100% of British classrooms are already equipped with IWBs. The figures also show a general trend towards IWB in schools in many parts of the world. In fact, according to the latest quarterly research from Futuresource, sales of interactive whiteboards in the education and corporate sectors increased 42% in the first half of 2015, despite the increasing presence of tablet devices in the educational sector.

In the early stages of IWB integration in the UK context, the popularity of this technology was largely a product of the education reforms introduced by the New Labour government, which emphasised the need to increase the amount of whole-class interaction, particularly in relation to young children, with the aim of improving standards of attainment in literacy and numeracy. However, the integration of IWBs can also be situated in a much wider context, as simply reflecting a growing presence of ICTs in education over the last two decades.

First insights into the use of IWB in the foreign language (FL) context were provided by informal Internet reports produced by language teachers, where they wrote about the general benefits of using IWB technology, without providing any details on how the technology was in fact being used (e.g. Walker 2003). In the early 2000s, authors who discussed the development of CALL (e.g. Davies 2003) included the use of IWB technology as an important tendency in this field, and a few reports were produced by British Council teachers and teacher trainers (e.g. Banks 2004; Orr 2008), who conducted small-scale studies to examine the reactions of students and teachers to the introduction of IWBs in their teaching contexts.

From approximately 2005 onwards a new phase can be identified, in which findings from university-based research (Gray et al. 2005, 2007; Cutrim Schmid 2006) and reports funded by government agencies (e.g. Moss et al. 2007) were published, and the focus shifted to the analysis of classroom use and more importantly the implications for pedagogical practice and professional development. Since then, a great number of publications on IWBs in language education have explored a wide variety of topics, such as IWB affordances for FL teaching, the impact of IWB use on classroom practice and learning outcomes, recommendations for teacher professional development and the future of IWBs. In what follows, the main findings of these studies will be presented and discussed. The next section draws upon principles and theories relative to second language acquisition and language teaching methodology to discuss the potential of IWBs for facilitating classroom language learning. For further discussion of related theories please see Hubbard and Levy, Chapter 2, and Blin, Chapter 3 this volume.

## How can the use of IWBs in the language classroom be theoretically justified?

The basic principles of current methods of second language teaching, such as for instance task-based learning (Nunan 2006) and project-based learning (Legutke and Thomas 1991; Becket and Miller 2006) include an emphasis on learning to communicate through interaction in the target language, the inclusion of the learner's own personal experiences and needs, and the linking of classroom language learning with language use outside the classroom. The current movement on 'focus on form', meaning to provide some type of explicit focus on grammar during communicative language teaching, is also becoming an increasingly important factor in FL syllabus design. Considering such theoretical principles, how can the interactive whiteboard

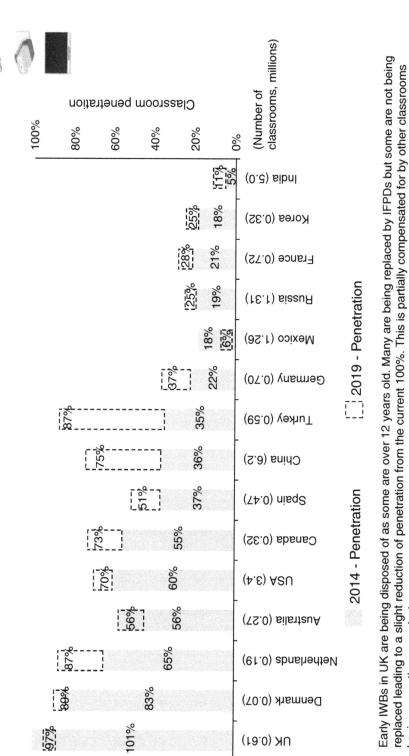

Figure 20.1 Classroom interactive display penetration

Source: © Futuresource Consulting Ltd (reproduced with permission from Futuresource).

support language learning? In the following section, some of the main IWB affordances for FL teaching that have been documented in the literature are discussed.

## *Enhancing interaction and collaborative learning*

The literature has discussed the potential of IWBs for improving the levels of interaction in the language classroom and for promoting whole-class collaborative language learning (e.g. Cutrim Schmid 2008c; Bettsworth 2010). Several authors (e.g. Cutrim Schmid 2007, 2009; Bannister, Hutchinson and Sargeant 2010; Cardoso 2011) provide examples of classroom activities in which peripherals, such as slates and learner response systems, are used to enhance the scope of interactivity in the language classroom. Other authors present concrete examples of IWB-based FL pedagogical materials that create opportunities for enhanced interaction, collaboration and negotiation of meaning (e.g. Cutrim Schmid and van Hazebrouck 2010; Kegenhof 2014; Sailer, Cutrim Schmid and Koenraad 2014; Whyte and Cutrim Schmid 2014).

## *Bringing authenticity into the classroom*

The IWB has also been found to facilitate the process of opening up the classroom to the outside world through seamless access to web-based multimedia materials which can help to create an authentic and stimulating learning environment and to integrate cultural aspects into language lessons (Cutrim Schmid and van Hazebrouck 2010; Gray 2010). Some authors have also discussed the advantages of combining IWB use with various software applications to create a more authentic language learning environment. For instance, the use of IWB-supported videoconferencing allows for real-time communication, screen-sharing and collaboration with experts, native speakers or students from other classrooms or institutions (e.g. Whyte 2011; Whyte and Cutrim Schmid 2014) and digital games can be used in conjunction with IWBs to present content in new and engaging ways (Stanley 2014).

## *Facilitating comprehension of input and supporting output production*

The literature also discusses special IWB affordances that can facilitate the presentation and structuring of content and language material and assist learners in expressing understanding (e.g. Cutrim Schmid 2008b; Sailer et al. 2014). The IWB software includes many of the forms and tables necessary for graphic organisers, which can help teachers create multimodal materials and provide effective scaffolding for the comprehension of complex input. The multimedia environment, which is facilitated by the use of an IWB, can provide the resources for input modification, for instance by creating links to various kinds of resources, which can be activated or ignored depending on the needs and actual responses of the learners. The IWB can also be used to implement output-oriented scaffolding techniques since the pupils can demonstrate their understanding by using symbolic representations found in charts or pictures.

## *Meeting the needs of students with diverse learning styles and facilitating long-term retention of vocabulary and input*

Several authors have pointed towards the IWB affordances that allow language teachers to deliver instruction in a way that covers the three modalities of learning (visual, auditory and tactile), thus meeting the needs of students with diverse learning styles (Cutrim Schmid 2008b; Cutrim

Schmid and van Hazebrouck 2010). The ease of integrating images, sound and the written word in multisensory presentations allows language learners to have access to the same information in various formats (e.g. video, audio, diagrams), which provide the scaffolding support to their language learning processes and facilitates long-term retention of vocabulary and concepts. Although the same goals could be achieved with a computer-projector setup, some authors emphasise the role of the IWB in providing teachers with seamless, easy and effective access to these multimedia resources and increased possibilities for interactive use of these resources.

### *Drawing attention to particular features of language (noticing and conscious awareness)*

Some authors have emphasised the IWB affordances that support learning skills like 'noticing' (Schmidt 1990) and conscious awareness. Some examples of classroom activities in which the IWB was used to facilitate the understanding of grammar concepts and rules have been presented. For instance, in activities that focus on reordering words in a sentence, categorising words or phrases or demonstrating specific features of word order in the target language (e.g. Bettsworth 2010) and the potential to use colour, font size and other annotation tools to facilitate noticing and memorisation of grammar content (Bettsworth 2010; Cutrim Schmid and van Hazebrouck 2010, 2012).

### *IWBs for specific purposes*

Researchers have also investigated the potential applicability of this technology for supporting specific types of learners and methods. For instance, IWBs were seen as facilitating the presentation and structuring of content and language material and to assist learners in expressing understanding in the content and language integrated learning (CLIL) context (Sailer et al. 2014), supporting inclusion of pupils with special educational needs (SEN) in mainstream second language learning by exploiting multimodality and the versatility of IWB tools, and enhanced possibilities to model activities (Hillier and Beauchamp 2014) and facilitating the implementation of digital storytelling (Kegenhof 2014).

Following this review of the main affordances of IWBs for language education, the next section discusses research findings regarding the impact of IWB use on pedagogical practice and learning outcomes.

## What does the research say about the impact (positive or negative) of IWB use on pedagogical practice and learning outcomes?

Research findings on the use of IWB technology in the language classroom reveal considerable variety, both in the ways in which the IWB is exploited pedagogically by the teachers and in the degree to which they change their classroom teaching practices. Most of the data described in the FL learning literature seem to point towards a pattern of IWB use that is mostly based on a behaviouristic approach to CALL (see Hubbard and Levy, Chapter 2 this volume) (e.g. Gray et al. 2005, 2007; Cutrim Schmid 2010, 2011; Coyle, Yañez and Verdúa 2010; Cutrim Schmid and Whyte 2012). However, some studies provide more optimistic language teaching scenarios (e.g. Cutrim Schmid 2009; Miller and Glover 2009; Cardoso 2011; Cutrim Schmid and Whyte 2014a) in which IWBs are used in conjunction with other tools (e.g. Web 2.0 tools, learner response systems, videoconferencing software and mobile technology) to enhance learners' active participation and to support constructivist practice in the language classroom.

## The challenges

Critics of the IWB have pointed out that one of the main drawbacks of integrating this technology into the language classroom is the fact that it can be easily assimilated into teachers' traditional pedagogical practice, thus leading to patterns of technology use that simply replicate previous (traditional) practice. As Moss et al. (2007: 96) point out, 'the clear advantage IWBs seem to have in terms of uptake – that their use fits quite easily with existing patterns of whole-class pedagogy – may also be their weakness'.

A central issue in the concerns expressed by a number of researchers is the question of whether IWBs may be used to enhance teachers' control of the learning environment, thus reinforcing a transmission model of education. Early IWB research conducted in schools run by the British Council in Lebanon, Tunisia and Hong Kong (e.g. Pearson 2006; Orr 2008) showed that most of the teachers saw the introduction of IWBs as a positive step because it facilitated the integration of multimedia into their lessons, but the great majority also found that the use of this technology tended to encourage teacher-centredness, which was seen as a negative side effect. More recent findings obtained from research conducted in state schools in the UK, France, Germany and Spain (e.g. Gray et al. 2007; Cutrim Schmid 2008b; Cutrim Schmid 2011; Yañez and Coyle 2011; Cutrim Schmid and Whyte 2012) also point towards patterns of technology use which focused mainly on demonstration by the teacher with little manipulation by the pupils. Research on learners' and teachers' perceptions also reveals dissatisfaction with levels of interaction during lessons (e.g. Yáñez and Coyle 2011; Sailer et al. 2014).

Another issue discussed in the literature is related to the use of multimedia materials in connection with IWBs. Since the technology allows seamless access to multimedia resources, there is 'a potential danger of using the technology mainly to give lessons a crisp pace, instead of focusing on making the best pedagogical use of these resources' (Cutrim Schmid 2008b: 1566). This issue was also discussed by Jewitt, Moss and Cardini (2007: 311), who questioned the relationship between fast pace and effective learning and point out that 'the use of such prepared presentational texts may result in a rigid scaffolding and superficial interactivity'.

Aspects of interaction and interactivity are also often discussed in the IWB literature, since a real understanding of these concepts is crucial to the effective use of this technology. As pointed out by Smith, Hardman and Higgins (2006: 445), 'there is a lack of empirical evidence to support many of the assertions made about the benefits of IWBs in promoting and enhancing teacher pupil interaction', and there are debates about the nature and quality of such interaction (Gray et al. 2007; Jewitt et al. 2007; Beauchamp and Kennewell 2010; Cutrim Schmid 2010, 2011). In most research, the interactivity found in the classroom was limited to 'physical interactivity', where the focus is on students going up to the front and manipulating elements on the board (e.g. Gray et al. 2005, 2007; Cutrim Schmid 2010, 2011).

Another challenge has to do with the availability of teaching materials. The lack of communicative-based materials for the IWB from publishing houses leads to an increasing responsibility for teachers as materials designers (Russell 2010). More specifically in the EFL context, several authors (Cutrim Schmid 2010, 2011; Cutrim Schmid and Whyte 2012; Whyte and Alexander 2014; Whyte 2015) have shown research findings suggesting that language teachers are still prone to design a superficial interactivity into IWB-based activities, 'leading to patterns of technology use in which students interact with the IWB mainly to reveal answers embedded in the electronic files or to move pictures or textboxes across the screen without modification or creation of new content' (Cutrim Schmid and van Hazebrouck 2010: 127).

Research tracing language teachers' developmental paths in the process of IWB integration has revealed that teachers often go through different stages: the first phase is replication and the subsequent ones are concerned with transformation (e.g. Walker 2003; Glover et al. 2007; Cutrim Schmid 2010, 2011; Whyte and Alexander 2014). According to these findings, teachers often go from using the IWB as a 'large board' for operating software that they already used before (in phase one) to discovering and exploiting the specific features of the technology (in phase two) to using it as a platform for collaboration and by having students coming to the board and presenting material or participating on a regular basis (in phase three).

The findings discussed earlier indicate that currently most users of IWB technology are probably in phases one or two. However, several authors argue that IWB technology has the potential to go beyond a simple presentational device and reveal examples of the IWB being used for supporting more learner-centred approaches. In what follows, some of these findings are discussed.

*The opportunities*

Some authors have discussed the significant steps already taken by teachers in exploiting the potential affordances of IWB technology to support constructivist practice. Cutrim Schmid and Whyte (2012), for instance, discussed the specific competencies developed by one of the researched teachers taking part in an IWB professional development programme. Their findings show how the teacher was able to provide students with stimulating and relevant input via the IWB, motivate them to engage with the various learning tasks and create IWB-based opportunities for co-construction of knowledge.

Some results of action research projects presented in the literature also show language teachers' concerns towards the implementation of more learner-centred approaches to IWB use. Soares (2010) analyses the use of IWBs to support the implementation of podcasting projects in a language school in Brazil. The author concludes that IWBs can be useful in learner-centred contexts, provided that teachers revisit their practices and give their students more autonomy in class. Bettsworth (2010) examined how effective the IWB can be in promoting understanding and retention of specific grammar points in her French secondary classroom. Her results revealed that, although the IWB-based lessons involved more whole-class teaching than usual, this was not seen negatively, as it generated an unexpected depth of discussion and debate among the pupils, thus facilitating their understanding of grammar. Cutrim Schmid and van Hazebrouck (2010) described an IWB-supported task-based lesson and discussed various strategies used by a German teacher to enhance learner involvement and participation, for instance by encouraging the students to explain their reasoning and their actions as they manipulated objects on the screen, thus ensuring that the IWB would provide genuine opportunities for pedagogical interactivity.

Other research findings show IWBs being used in combination with other interactive technologies to enhance the scope of interactivity in the language classroom. Cutrim Schmid (2007, 2008a), Bannister, Hutchinson and Sargeant (2010) and Cardoso (2011) discuss the educational potentials of learner response systems and present several examples of classroom use of these devices. Whyte and Cutrim Schmid (2014) investigated the use of IWBs for supporting live communication between distant classes of young EFL learners. They show how the combination of IWB tools and other interactive technologies, such as collaborative videoconferencing software, can provide multiple opportunities for authentic target language use.

These findings indicate that IWB affordances can be used to enhance language learning and teaching. However, in order to become proficient 'constructivist' IWB users, teachers need to go through a process of technology development that goes beyond the familiarisation with IWB presentation tools (Cutrim Schmid 2010, 2012; Cutrim Schmid and Whyte 2012; Whyte 2015).

The literature has thus discussed various competencies that IWB users need to develop in order to be able to fully exploit this technology. The following section will summarise some of these competencies and provide examples of professional development tools that aim at supporting and guiding language teachers in the process of integrating the IWB into their teaching.

## How can teachers be supported in developing the necessary competencies for exploiting the IWB in ways consistent with current theories of language teaching pedagogy?

### Key competencies

The IWB literature has discussed various competencies that language teachers need to develop in order to be able to use this technology in accordance with current models of language teaching pedagogy. These competencies can be subdivided into four main categories: (1) balancing technology use, (2) designing and evaluating IWB-based resources, (3) managing IWB-based interaction and (4) combining IWB use with other interactive technologies.

Research (e.g. Gray et al. 2007; Cutrim Schmid and Whyte 2012) has shown that teachers, especially in early stages of technology integration, tend to 'overgeneralise' the use of IWB technology to all stages of the lesson and thus forget other traditional repertoires they possess, for example, the use of real objects or physical activity such as miming, role plays and pair- and group-work activities. Therefore, an important competency to be developed by teachers is the ability to make the right judgement regarding when to use the technology and when not to use it. As discussed earlier in this chapter, the ability to find the right balance of technology use can also enable teachers to cater to different learning styles and provide learners with increased opportunities for language practice (Cutrim Schmid and van Hazebrouck 2010).

The literature also highlights important competencies in the area of materials design. For instance, (1) the ability to design materials that create space for pupils' contributions and ideas in order to allow adequate room for learner experimentation and discovery (Cutrim Schmid and van Hazebrouck 2012; Oberhofer, Simons and Smits 2014); (2) the ability to exploit IWB software tools to add elements of physical and conceptual interactivity to teaching materials (e.g. drag and drop, hide and reveal tools, point and click programming) and visual, audio and tactile input (e.g. embedding of audio, image and video files) while considering issues of pace, cognitive load and learners' active processing of these materials (Cutrim Schmid 2008b; Jewitt et al. 2007; Cutrim Schmid and Schimmack 2010); and (3) the ability to use effective search strategies for finding relevant and useful IWB-based material in online teaching communities or other databases, and apply effective criteria for the evaluation of these resources (Celik 2014; Cutrim Schmid and Whyte 2014b).

Research has also shown (Cutrim Schmid 2010; Gray 2010; Cutrim Schmid and van Hazebrouck 2012) that teachers need to learn the appropriate management of interaction around IWBs in a way that ALL learners (not only the one at the board) are provided with opportunities to become actively involved in the learning process (e.g. through the use of printed copies of IWB-displayed materials for annotation or manipulation). Teachers also need to develop classroom interactional competencies for supporting reflection-in-action and peer evaluation during IWB-based activities and for engaging students emotionally and intellectually in the creation of new IWB-based content (Coyle et al. 2010).

Current statistics on technology penetration in schools (Futuresource 2013) show that language classrooms are becoming increasingly more equipped with different types of mobile technology (e.g. learner response systems, tablets, smartphones) and collaborative software (e.g. videoconferencing software), which can enhance the functionality of IWBs. This increasing availability of various types of interactive technologies in the language classroom creates new challenges for teachers, who need to develop new competencies in order to be able to harness these technological developments to enhance meaningful interaction in the target language.

*Resources for professional development*

Since the IWB is a relatively new technology in language education, there is still a shortage of resources for professional development in this area. Current textbooks focusing on the technology-enhanced language classroom (e.g. Dudeney and Hockly 2007; Sharma and Barrett 2007; Stanley 2013) still dedicate little space to this topic. Meanwhile, other textbooks focusing specifically on the use of IWBs in language education (e.g. Martin 2009; Sharma, Barrett and Jones 2013) make relatively little reference to the theoretical principles guiding the design and implementation of IWB-based activities. Another problem is the fact that most textbooks are aimed at language teachers working with adult learners in private institutions and in technology-rich environments. However, the increasing availability of IWBs in primary, secondary and tertiary education has led researchers and publishing houses to dedicate more efforts towards providing resources for practitioners working in a wider context. Two recent publications (Thomas and Cutrim Schmid 2010; Cutrim Schmid and Whyte 2014a), for instance, present illustrative examples of IWB-enhanced language teaching which is embedded in school curricula and practice.

The availability of open educational resources in this area has also grown rapidly in the last five years. Major IWB providers (e.g. SMART, Promethean, Hitachi) are actively involved in offering teachers online platforms where they can share and get access to a huge number of interactive materials by teachers for teachers. Examples of online sharing communities available for this purpose are Promethean Planet, SMART's Exchange, Hitachi StarBoard Community and eI Community. However, a recent analysis of these websites (Oberhofer et al. 2014) has shown that the availability of IWB materials for languages is limited compared to other subjects, and among the language teaching materials the large majority is for English (including EFL/ESL).

In Europe, there have been some research initiatives aiming to provide teachers with open educational resources (OERs) for professional development in this area. The iTILT (Interactive Technologies in Language Teaching) project (Whyte et al. 2014) is one of these initiatives. It was conceived as an OER for teacher education in the use of IWBs as a tool for improving opportunities for communication in the second language classroom. The main outcome of the project is a searchable online repository of professional development materials including a training manual and classroom illustrations in the form of video clips, descriptions of lessons and participant commentaries. Other European projects, such as SmartVET (Interactive Whiteboards in Vocational Education and Training) and iTEC (Innovative Technologies for Engaging Classrooms) have also produced professional development and teaching resources that can be useful for the language teacher.

## What can be predicted about the future of IWBs?

The future of the IWB is currently the focus of much debate in the field of educational technology (Bax 2010), and particularly English language teaching circles (Dudeney 2006; Hockly 2013), and the main IWB brands are already rethinking their technology to accommodate the challenge of mobile devices. Most agree, however, that the pedagogical need for a shared screen to focus whole-class attention will remain, though perhaps in a less central position in the classroom and in teaching (Bax 2010; Hockly 2013). These authors believe that the technology will evolve in order to better accommodate learner-centred approaches. As Bax pointed out:

> Perhaps one day decades hence we will indeed walk through a dim museum corridor and glimpse a lonely IWB gathering dust alongside the record player and video machine. However, I suggest that it is unlikely that the whole of IWB technology will now simply disappear; it is far more likely that it will evolve, perhaps converging with other technologies by taking on functions previously reserved for separate different devices.
>
> *(Bax 2010: 275)*

Since the introduction of the first IWBs in 1990s, this technology has evolved continuously in order to respond to the needs of a constructivist-based curriculum. The IWB-dedicated software has been constantly updated to include a wider range of interactive tools, and more recently the development of multitouch functionality extended collaborative learning opportunities. IWB manufacturers have also developed a wide range of peripherals (interactive systems) to provide a technology which is more interactive and individualised. In the late 1990s, graphic slates and learner response systems started to be used in conjunction with IWBs. However, the functionality of these devices was and is still rather restricted. More recently multitouch horizontal displays (e.g. tabletops) allow for collaboration in small groups and creates better synergy between IWB-based whole class and group work, but their production is still limited to specific age groups (e.g. SMART tables are designed specifically for the primary educational sector).

Currently, however, IWB manufacturers are focusing on the development of learner response software rather than physical devices. This has the potential to allow learner response tools and other types of collaborative software to be installed on other handheld devices such as iPads, mobile phones or laptops. Very recently, two major IWB manufacturers (SMART and Promethean) have developed cloud-based classroom presentation and management tools that enable teachers to create lessons, deliver interactive content across multiple devices and assess student learning, thus facilitating the integration of mobile technology into IWB-based lessons and creating new possibilities for collaboration in and outside the classroom. As pointed out by Hockly (2013), publishers themselves are moving away from creating IWB-compatible versions of course books to course book–related content online, which is accessible not just by the teacher via the IWB but by students themselves with their own devices in a connected classroom.

As mentioned earlier in this chapter, some manufacturers have also developed their own video communication and conferencing software which support online collaboration by allowing learners in different locations to share their whiteboard screens and interact with each other's documents by annotating directly on the whiteboard (e.g. SMART Bridgit conferencing software). It is expected that this type of technology, which is still not easily accessible to schools, and mostly used by companies, will become more widely used in educational sectors, thus enhancing the functionality of IWBs for the implementation of more learner-centred forms of teaching and learning. As Bax suggests, these are desirable technological developments:

> And so long as such a device succeeds in putting the learner and learning first, and therefore putting itself in the background, I suggest that it might well succeed in eventually becoming the norm in our classrooms, as normal and as normalized in the education of the future as the pen and pencil are today.
>
> *(Bax 2010: 275)*

Apart from the evolution of the technology itself, there are other crucial factors determining the future of this technology. The central role played by teachers in shaping technology integration has often been discussed in the literature. In spite of widespread technological investment, research has shown that teachers are able to resist educational and pedagogical hegemonies within their individual classrooms (e.g. Gray 2010; Cutrim Schmid and Whyte 2012). Therefore, the quality and quantity of pedagogical training available to teachers will be critical in shaping the uptake of this technology in the next years.

Another crucial factor is the direction of government policy. As mentioned earlier in this chapter, the National Literacy and Numeracy strategies in the UK, and the emphasis on whole-class teaching operated with political forces and indeed with economic strategies in the process of widespread IWB adoption in that country in the last two decades. Therefore, it is important to consider the role of larger political, economic and social forces, far beyond the school walls, in shaping the future of IWBs.

Considering the fact that ICTs are usually promoted as symbols of progress, modernity and economic prowess, it is reasonable to expect a continuous investment in ICT in education. As discussed earlier, statistics show an increasing tendency to invest in the use of mobile technologies in schools and research findings point towards the need for more learner-centred technological environments. This section has discussed aspects of the evolution of IWBs showing that the technology is not incompatible with mobile technology use. Therefore, one can speculate that IWBs will continue to find their way into language classrooms for the years to come, serving as a digital hub for seamless transition across different media and devices.

This chapter provided a state-of-the-art overview of the challenges and opportunities involved in the integration of IWBs into the language classroom. IWB affordances for FL teaching have been well documented in the literature, but so far the evidence on whether the use of this technology improves student attainment is inconclusive. Findings from classroom-based research also indicate that language teachers tend to use the IWB in ways that do not reflect clear pedagogical transformation towards constructivist practices. A discussion about the future of this technology also indicates an increased tendency towards combining IWB use with mobile technologies to create a more learner-centred approach in the language classroom. Based on these facts, what are the main challenges of IWB research in the language teaching context for the years to come?

As discussed in this chapter, most of the research on the use of IWB in language education does not allow any definite conclusions to be drawn about the effects of technology use on learning outcomes. Therefore, there should be more research focusing on the investigation of specific approaches to IWB use in order to evaluate their impact on language learning. There is also a need for more longitudinal studies of teachers' use of the IWB, as most research conducted so far are short-term studies, which are unlikely to reveal much about genuine sustained impact.

The review presented in this chapter also reveals that most research on IWBs has been conducted in primary, secondary and vocational education, probably due a lack of technological investment in the higher education context. Therefore, further work needs to be done to establish how IWBs can be implemented in pedagogically sound ways in tertiary education in order to explore various strategies to deal with the specific challenges of that context, such as possible IWB-related teaching techniques for large classes, design of IWB-based teaching materials and resources specially tailored for university students, and ways of exploiting IWB for facilitating understanding and discussion of complex concepts.

There is also a need for more qualitative and ethnographic research into the particular contexts of use of the IWB around the world. So far, little focus has been given to the analysis of classroom processes in order to gain insights into the everyday pedagogical practices which using the technology involves. One way to obtain a more accurate account of classroom context is by including teachers' voices, observations and concerns. Therefore, there should be more focus on collaborative action research (Burns 1999), where teachers are supported in a process of structured reflection involving data collection and analysis to improve teaching and learning. The findings of such research could also provide useful insights for the design and implementation of effective IWB professional development programmes.

## Further reading

Cutrim Schmid, E. (2009) *Interactive Whiteboard Technology in the Language Classroom: Exploring New Pedagogical Opportunities*, Saarbruecken, Germany: VDM Verlag Dr. Mueller.

This book is the result of a PhD study concerning the use of IWBs in the teaching of English for academic purposes in the higher education context. It discusses several pedagogical benefits of using IWBs in language education. Special focus is given to the use of IWBs in conjunction with learner response systems for implementing novel ways of assessing, engaging and motivating students in the context in question.

Cutrim Schmid, E. and Whyte, S. (eds) (2014) *Teaching Languages with Technology: Communicative Approaches to Interactive Whiteboard Use: A Resource Book for Teacher Development*, London, UK: Bloomsbury.

This book presents seven case studies which focus on the use of interactive whiteboards for the teaching of languages in primary, secondary, vocational and higher education contexts. The main topics covered are special educational needs, teacher training, materials design, teaching young learners, gamification and CLIL. The final chapter proposes a set of recommendations for interactive whiteboard use drawn from the studies presented in the book.

Thomas, Michael and Cutrim Schmid, Euline (eds) (2010) *Interactive Whiteboards: Theory, Research and Practice*, Hershey, PA: IGI Global.

This edited collection provides an overview of research on IWBs in education. Several chapters examine influential research-based studies on classroom learning environments in the compulsory sector from leading IWB researchers. The book also includes chapters discussing analytical frameworks for the evaluation of teachers' use of IWB technology and models of training and professional development. The final section of the book presents international case studies and research projects from teacher practitioners.

Whyte, S. (2015) *Implementing and Researching Technological Innovation in Language Teaching: The Case of Interactive Whiteboards for EFL in French Schools*, London, UK: Palgrave Macmillan.

This book reports on a case study investigating the integration of IWBs into the teaching of EFL in French schools. It presents an analytical framework for the evaluation of teachers' use of IWB technology and for documenting the development of their IWB-mediated teaching practice. The qualitative findings presented in the book enhance our understanding of the challenges and opportunities inherent in the process of technological innovation involving IWB use.

## References

Banks, T. (2004) *Interactive Whiteboards – Way Forward or Costly Gimmick?* Paper presented at IATEFL, Liverpool, April 2004.

Bannister, D., Hutchinson, A. and Sargeant, H. (2010) 'Effective implementation of learner response systems: Moving beyond the right response', in M. Thomas and E. Cutrim Schmid (eds), *Interactive Whiteboards for Education: Theory, Research and Practice*, Hershey, PA: IGI Global: 144–161.

Bax, S. (2010) 'Magic wand or museum piece? The future of the interactive whiteboard in education', in M. Thomas and E. Cutrim Schmid (eds), *Interactive Whiteboards for Education: Theory, Research and Practice*, Hershey, PA: IGI Global: 264–277.

Beauchamp, G. and Kennewell, S. (2010) 'Interactivity in the classroom and its impact on learning', *Computers and Education*, 54(3): 759–766.

Beckett, G. and Miller, P. (2006) *Project-Based Second and Foreign Language Education: Past, Present and Future*, Greenwich, CT: Information Age Publishing, Inc.

Bettsworth, B. (2010) 'Using interactive whiteboards to teach grammar in the MFL classroom: A learner's perspective', in M. Thomas and E. Cutrim Schmid (eds), *Interactive Whiteboards for Education: Theory, Research and Practice*, Hershey: Information Science Reference: 216–224.

Burns, A. (1999) *Collaborative Action Research for English Teachers*, Cambridge: Cambridge University Press.

Cardoso, W. (2011) 'Learning a foreign language with a learner response system: The students' perspective', *Computer Assisted Language Learning*, 24(5): 393–417.

Celik, S. (2014) 'Exploring IWB use for language instruction in Turkish higher education settings', in E. Cutrim Schmid and S. Whyte (eds), *Teaching Languages with Technology: Communicative Approaches to Interactive Whiteboard Use: A Resource Book for Teacher Development*, London, UK: Bloomsbury: 182–205.

Coyle, Y., Yañez, L. and Verdúa, M. (2010) 'The impact of the interactive whiteboard on the teacher and children's language use in an ESL immersion classroom', *System*, 38(4): 614–625.

Cutrim Schmid, E. (2006) 'Investigating the use of interactive whiteboard technology in the language classroom through the lens of a critical theory of technology', *Computer Assisted Language Learning*, 19(1): 47–62.

Cutrim Schmid, E. (2007) 'Enhancing performance knowledge and self-esteem in classroom language learning: The potential of the ACTIVote system component of interactive whiteboard technology', *System*, 35(2): 119–133.

Cutrim Schmid, E. (2008a) 'Using a voting system in conjunction with interactive whiteboard technology to enhance learning in the English language classroom', *Computers and Education*, 50(1): 338–356.

Cutrim Schmid, E. (2008b) 'Potential pedagogical benefits and drawbacks of multimedia use in the English language classroom equipped with interactive whiteboard technology', *Computers and Education*, 51(4): 1553–1568.

Cutrim Schmid, E. (2008c) 'Facilitating whole-class collaborative learning in the English language classroom: The potential of interactive whiteboard technology', in A. Müller-Hartmann and M. Schocker-v. Ditfurth (eds), *Aufgabenorientiertes Lernen und Lehren mit Medien: Ansätze, Erfahrungen, Perspektiven in der Fremdsprachendidaktik*, Frankfurt am Main, Germany: Peter Lang: 325–335.

Cutrim Schmid, E. (2009) 'The pedagogical potential of interactive whiteboards 2.0', in M. Thomas (ed), *Handbook of Research on Web 2.0 and Second Language Learning*, Hershey, PA: IGI Global: 491–505.

Cutrim Schmid, E. (2010) 'Developing competencies for using the interactive whiteboard to implement communicative language teaching in the English as a foreign language classroom', *Technology, Pedagogy and Education*, 19(2): 159–172.

Cutrim Schmid, E. (2011) 'Video-stimulated reflection as a professional development tool in interactive whiteboard research', *ReCALL*, 23(3): 252–270.

Cutrim Schmid, E. and Schimmack, E. (2010) 'First steps towards a model of interactive whiteboard training for language teachers', in M. Thomas and E. Cutrim Schmid (eds), *Interactive Whiteboards: Theory, Research and Practice*, Hershey, PA: IGI Global: 197–214.

Cutrim Schmid, E. and van Hazebrouck, S. (2010), 'Using the interactive whiteboard as a digital hub', *Praxis Fremdsprachenunterricht*, 4: 12–15.

Cutrim Schmid, E. and van Hazebrouck, S. (2012) 'Materials development and task design for the interactive whiteboard in the foreign language classroom', in K. Biebighäuser, M. Zibelius and T. Schmidt (eds), *Aufgaben 2.0 – Konzepte, Materialien und Methoden für das Fremdsprachenlehren und-lernen mit Digitalen Medien*, Tübingen: Narr: 119–140.

Cutrim Schmid, E. and Whyte, S. (2012) 'Interactive whiteboards in state school settings: Teacher responses to socio-constructivist hegemonies', *Language Learning and Technology*, 16(2): 65–86.

Cutrim Schmid, E. and Whyte, S. (eds) (2014a) *Teaching Languages with Technology: Communicative Approaches to Interactive Whiteboard Use: A Resource Book for Teacher Development*, London, UK: Bloomsbury.

Cutrim Schmid, E. and Whyte, S. (2014b) 'Ongoing professional development in IWB mediated language teaching: Evening up the odds', in E. Cutrim Schmid and S. Whyte (eds), *Teaching Languages with Technology: Communicative Approaches to Interactive Whiteboard Use: A Resource Book for Teacher Development*, London, UK: Bloomsbury: 244–259.

Davies, G. (2003) 'Computer-assisted language learning: Where are we now and where are we going?', available: http://www.nestafuturelab.org/viewpoint/learn23.htm (accessed 8 Jun 2005).

DfES (2004) 'Information and communications technology in schools in England 2004 – First Release: DfES Research & Statistics', available: http://www.dfes.gov.uk/ (accessed 23 Aug 2005).

Dudeney, G. (2006) 'Interactive, quite bored IATEFL', *CALL Review*, Summer: 8–10.

Dudeney, G. and Hockly, N. (2007) *How to Teach English with Technology*, London, UK: Longman.
Futuresource Consulting Ltd (2015) Classroom interactive display penetration (report), available: http://futuresource-consulting.com/2015-02-Edu-InteractiveDisplays-2378.html (accessed 11 Nov 2015).
Glover, D., Miller, D., Averis, D. and Door, V. (2007) 'The evolution of an effective pedagogy for teachers using the interactive whiteboard in mathematics and modern languages: An empirical analysis from the secondary sector', *Learning, Media and Technology*, 32(1): 5–20.
Gray, C. (2010) 'Meeting teachers' real needs: New tools in the secondary modern foreign languages classroom', in M. Thomas and E. Cutrim Schmid (eds), *Interactive Whiteboards for Education: Theory, Research and Practice*, Hershey, NY: Information Science Reference: 69–85.
Gray, G., Hagger-Vaughan, L., Pilkington, R. and Tomkins, S. (2005) 'The pros and cons of interactive whiteboards in relation to the key stage 3 strategies and framework', *Language Learning Journal*, 32(1): 38–44.
Gray, G., Hagger-Vaughan, L., Pilkington, R. and Tomkins, S. (2007) 'Integrating ICT into classroom practice in modern foreign language teaching in England: Making room for teachers' voices', *European Journal of Teacher Education*, 30(4): 407–429.
Hillier, E. and Beauchamp, G. (2014) 'IWB in language education for learners with special educational needs: Learning Welsh at primary school', in E. Cutrim Schmid and S. Whyte (eds), *Teaching Languages with Technology: Communicative Approaches to Interactive Whiteboard Use: A Resource Book for Teacher Development*, London, UK: Bloomsbury: 25–49.
Hockly, N. (2013) 'Interactive whiteboards', *ELT Journal*, 67(3): 354–358.
Jewitt, C, Moss, G. and Cardini, A. (2007) 'Pace, interactivity and multimodality in teachers' design of texts for interactive whiteboards in the secondary school classroom', *Learning, Media and Technology*, 32(3): 303–317.
Kegenhof, A. (2014) 'Digital storytelling in the primary EFL classroom', in E. Cutrim Schmid and S. Whyte (eds), *Teaching Languages with Technology: Communicative Approaches to Interactive Whiteboard Use: A Resource Book for Teacher Development*, London, UK: Bloomsbury: 80–116.
Legutke, M.K. and Thomas, H. (1991) *Process and Experience in the Language Classroom*, London, UK: Longman.
Martin, D. (2009) *Activities for Interactive Whiteboards: Educational Teacher's Handbook*, London, UK: Helbling Languages.
Mathews-Aydinli, J. and Elaziz, F. (2010) 'Turkish students' and teachers' attitudes toward the use of interactive whiteboards in EFL classrooms', *Computer Assisted Language Learning*, 23(3): 235–252.
Miller, D. and Glover, D. (2009) 'Interactive whiteboards in the Web 2.0 classroom', in M. Thomas (ed), *Handbook of Research on Web 2.0 and Second Language Learning*, Hershey, PA: IGI Global.
Moss, G., Carrey, J., Levaaic, R., Armstrong, V., Cardini, A. and Castle, F. (2007) *The Interactive Whiteboards Pedagogy and Pupil Performance Evaluation: An Evaluation of the Schools Whiteboard Expansion (SWE) Project: London Challenge*, London, UK: Institute of Education, University of London.
Nunan, D. (2006) *Task-Based Language Teaching*, Cambridge: Cambridge University Press.
Oberhofer, M., Simons, M. and Smits, T. (2014) 'Academic teacher training and the IWB: Coaching pre-service teachers in Belgium', in E. Cutrim Schmid and S. Whyte (eds), *Teaching Languages with Technology: Communicative Approaches to Interactive Whiteboard Use: A Resource Book for Teacher Development*, London, UK: Bloomsbury: 206–234.
Orr, M. (2008) 'Learner perceptions of interactive whiteboards in EFL classrooms', *CALL-EJ Online*, 9(2), available: http://www.tell.is.ritsumei.ac.jp/callejonline/journal/9-2/orr.html (accessed 6 Jun 2009).
Pearson, R. 'Teachers and new technology: interactive whiteboards at British Council Hong Kong', Paper presented at the CALL conference, Beijing, 4 June 2006.
Russell, B. (2010) 'Designing resources for IWBs: The emerging roles of educational publishers and materials writers', in M. Thomas and E. Cutrim Schmid (eds), *Interactive Whiteboards: Theory, Research and Practice*, Hershey, PA: Information Science Reference: 53–68.
Sailer, H, Cutrim Schmid, E. and Koenraad, T. (2014) 'The IWB in the CLIL classroom: Using visuals to foster active learning with young beginners', in E. Cutrim Schmid and S. Whyte (eds), *Teaching Languages with Technology: Communicative Approaches to Interactive Whiteboard Use: A Resource Book for Teacher Development*, London, UK: Bloomsbury: 129–158.
Schmidt, R. (1990) 'The role of consciousness in second language learning', *Applied Linguistics*, 11: 129–158.
Sharma, P. and Barrett, B. (2007) *Blended Learning*, London, UK: Macmillan.
Sharma, P., Barrett, B. and Jones, F. (2013) *400 Ideas for Interactive Whiteboards: Instant Activities Using Technology*. Oxford: Macmillan Education.

Smith, F., Hardman, F., and Higgins, S. (2006) 'The impact of interactive whiteboards on teacher-pupil interaction in the national literacy and numeracy strategies', *British Educational Research Journal*, 32(3): 443–457.

Soares, D.A. (2010) 'IWBs as support for technology-related projects in EFL education in Brazil', in M. Thomas and E. Cutrim Schmid (eds), *Interactive Whiteboards for Education: Theory, Research and Practice*, Hershey, PA: Information Science Reference: 238–249.

Stanley, G. (2013) *Language Learning with Technology: Ideas for Integrating Technology in the Classroom*, Cambridge: Cambridge University Press.

Stanley, G. (2014) 'Using the IWB to support gamification in order to enhance writing fluency in the secondary language classroom', in E. Cutrim Schmid and S. Whyte (eds), *Teaching Languages with Technology: Communicative Approaches to Interactive Whiteboard Use: A Resource Book for Teacher Development*, London, UK: Bloomsbury: 146–181.

Thomas, M. and Cutrim Schmid, E. (eds) (2010) *Interactive Whiteboards: Theory, Research and Practice*, Hershey, PA: IGI Global.

Walker, R. (2003) 'Interactive whiteboards in the MFL classroom', *TELL & CALL*, 3: 14–16.

Whyte, S. (2011) 'Learning to teach with videoconferencing in primary foreign language classrooms', *ReCALL*, 23(3): 271–293.

Whyte, S. (2015) *Implementing and Researching Technological Innovation in Language Teaching: The Case of Interactive Whiteboards for EFL in French Schools*, London, UK: Palgrave Macmillan.

Whyte, S. and Alexander, J. (2014) 'Implementing tasks with interactive technologies in classroom CALL: Towards a developmental framework', *Canadian Journal of Learning and Technology*, 40(1): 1–26.

Whyte, S. and Cutrim Schmid, E. (2014) 'A task-based approach to video communication with the IWB: A French-German primary EFL class exchange', in E. Cutrim Schmid and S. Whyte (eds), *Teaching Languages with Technology: Communicative Approaches to Interactive Whiteboard Use: A Resource Book for Teacher Development*, London, UK: Bloomsbury: 50–79.

Whyte, S., Cutrim Schmid, E., van Hazebrouck Thompson, S. and Oberhofer, M. (2014), 'Open educational resources for CALL teacher education: The iTILT interactive whiteboard project', *Computer Assisted Language Learning*, 27(2): 122–148.

Wightman, B. (2006) 'The future of interactive whiteboards in ELT', *IATEFL CALL Review* (Winter): 8–12.

Yáñez, L. and Coyle, Y. (2011) 'Children's perceptions of learning with an interactive whiteboard', *ELT Journal*, 65(4): 446–457.

# 21
# Mobile language learning

*Glenn Stockwell*

Mobile language learning is a field that brought with it a large amount of expectation and, to some degree, disappointment at the same time. Very few would doubt the potential of learning through mobile devices, given the fact that they provide access to text, images and video, as well as allowing learners to interact with other people through various communication and social networking tools. At the same time, problems continue to exist regarding the types of activities that are suitable for mobile devices given the physical characteristics of the screen and input and overcoming the general attitudes towards engaging in learning activities through mobile devices.

Indeed, the very view of what mobile devices are has not been a fixed construct either. The portable laptop computer was most definitely a mobile device, yet the literature into mobile learning did not seem to place a great deal of importance on the use of this tool in any way that differed from more conventional computer-assisted language learning. It was not until the advent of smaller handheld devices such as MP3 players and PDAs (personal digital assistants) that mobile learning really began to attract the interest of language teachers. Since that time, these small portable technologies have achieved an amazing penetration rate, with the vast majorities of both teachers and learners at almost all levels of education possessing them.

While the initial boom regarding specific mobile technologies – in particular smartphones and tablet computers – often focused on the potential of the technologies as a tool for learning languages, recent research has started to take advantage of the affordances associated with mobile devices rather than trying to simply replicate computer-based activities. This chapter will look specifically at the theories that are applicable to mobile learning, provide some suggestions as to how mobile learning may be implemented, outline the key considerations regarding learning languages through mobile devices and put forward some thoughts regarding the future.

## Theory in mobile language learning

Theory in computer-assisted language learning (CALL) in general has always been an area of contention, and there has been an increasing amount of attention paid to this issue in the past few years (see Hubbard and Levy, Chapter 2 this volume for a discussion of theory in CALL research and practice). One of the biggest criticisms directed towards the field of CALL is that theory often has a peripheral position in research articles using CALL technologies, with CALL practitioners tending to be consumers of theories developed by others depending on their specific purposes (Levy and Stockwell 2006). An observation of literature suggests that the theories that are applied to CALL tend to be more based on second language acquisition (SLA) or learning theory (see Chapelle 2005, 2007; Hubbard 2008), and the consideration of the role of technology in the learning process seems to take far less prominence (see Stockwell 2014 for further discussion). Given that the field of CALL is primarily concerned with learning languages, it is neither surprising nor inappropriate that theories associated with SLA or learning theory have prominence in the literature, but at the same time there is a need to bear in mind that the technology does make a difference to the environment, and this needs to be factored into the equation. Bax (2003) has argued that technology will become normalised, that is, that it will no longer be noticed as a part of the learning environment, in much the same way as pen and paper. Be that as it may, it does not follow that the technology does not continue to have an impact on the environment even when it is not noticed, and as such there is clearly a need to be aware of the fact that technology does alter the learning environment in some ways.

The spread of mobile technologies means we are less aware of but perhaps more dependent on these devices as a part of our daily lives. At one point, we might have carried multiple mobile devices with us, including a mobile phone, an MP3 player, and perhaps a PDA. Research using all three of these types of tools has emerged such as using mobile phones for email, SMS (Kiernan and Aizawa 2004; Kennedy and Levy 2008) or web-based activities (Stockwell 2008); MP3 players for podcasting (Rosell-Aguilar 2007); and PDAs for interactive web-based applications (Chang and Hsu 2011). The relatively limited functionalities of many early mobile devices meant that 'learning content tended to be . . . stripped down versions of their more complex desktop predecessors' (Squire 2009: 71), and this is likely to have had an impact on not only tools that were available but the way in which they were viewed. The increased capabilities of smartphones and tablets, however, has meant that there has been a merger of many of the aforementioned functionalities into a single device, and learners are less likely to carry multiple devices around when they can use the Internet, access social networking, listen to music, and play games on the one device. To this end, mobile technologies such as the mobile phone have largely become transparent, but the impact that they have on our daily lives cannot be ignored. While earlier research focused on the individual functionalities of these devices, we are starting to see more and more research that can capitalise on the full range of multimedia tools (Hwang and Chen 2013), communication and social networking tools (Al-Shehri 2011) and Internet capabilities (de Jong, Specht and Koper 2010) that these devices possess.

A range of theories has also begun to appear in the literature related to mobile language learning. Early research focused more on the affordances of the technology, but as the field developed, theory started to find its way into the literature into mobile learning research. Theory mainly takes one of three forms: research that relies on SLA theory in much the same ways as more traditional CALL did; research founded in psychological theories as a rationale for their studies; and, although less common, studies that apply theories that attempt to describe the role of the technology in the language learning process. Each of these will be described in turn.

## SLA theories

As described earlier, in many cases the rationale for using mobile devices for learning a language is derived from various SLA theories, depending on what it is the teacher/researcher is setting out to achieve. As with CALL, this is not surprising, and SLA theories can do a great deal to inform researchers about what can be achieved when learning through mobile devices. For example, Lan, Sung and Chang (2009) refer to *constructivist approaches* to learning as the foundation for their study of elementary school-aged children in Taiwan using tablet PCs in order to learn English. In this particular case, the collaboration that took place between the learners was face-to-face, where learners used the mobile device as a means of completing reading and vocabulary activities and then shared the results with others, and taught what they had learned to other members in their group.

In contrast, de la Fuente (2014) applied the *noticing hypothesis* to listening tasks for learning Spanish by English native speakers, making targeted items more salient in order to allow the learner to attend to them more easily. Learners using iPods in class were compared with learners using computers in a computer lab, and the study suggested that learners using the iPods achieved higher scores than learners using the computers, which may have been due in part to the fact that learners had more control over the input in the iPods compared with the computers, where the input was controlled by the teacher. There are also examples where multiple theories are used. Nah, White and Sussex (2008) use the *interaction hypothesis* in conjunction with *sociocultural theory* as a rationale for engaging in collaborative learning of English in a Korean university using a specially designed learning management system (LMS) that enabled learners to communicate with one another through their mobile phones. Unlike the two studies described earlier, in this case the learners were able to use their own mobile phones outside of class, and therefore had to take responsibility for the times and places where they chose to undertake the activities and found that collaboration helped them to view assigned activities more positively, and the bulletin board system (BBS) was intended as a means through which learners could maintain their motivation to engage in the activities.

These examples serve to illustrate how a particular theory (or theories) of second language acquisition may be used as a rationale for the design of activities through mobile devices. The types of activities described here do not vary greatly from activities that take place through more traditional types of CALL, and in many ways, the activities also reflected a simpler interface than might be found when using desktop computers, as Squire (2009) pointed out. There is certainly a place for this type of activity, but at the same time, in some cases the interactivity and multimedia features that modern mobile devices bring with them may have been capitalised upon more fully, which must then be reflected in the theories that are used.

*Cognitive psychology theories*

The examples provided here are not meant to be exhaustive but rather serve to show the types of theories related to educational psychology that are being employed with regard to mobile learning. Two commonly appearing theories are *dual coding theory* and *cognitive load theory*. While these theories are certainly applicable without technology, technology does lend itself rather well to the application of these theories, both of which share the common feature of awareness of individual or personalised elements of learning. It is likely that the personal nature of learning through mobile devices is one of the reasons that it has attracted the attention of researchers.

Dual coding theory was originally conceived by Paivio in the early 1970s, but it has been updated a number of times due to findings from related psychological research (Paivio 2007). In essence, dual coding theory claims that learning occurs through a combination of verbal (or text) and nonverbal (visual) codes, and that this allows for different means through which information is processed, resulting in two separate mental representations of concepts. One of the most common applications of dual coding theory is as a rationale for using multiple annotation types for aspects such as listening, vocabulary or even grammar. Huang, Kuo, Lin and Cheng (2008), for example, describe a system where Taiwanese learners of English could access video content and could interact with one another using text-based methods regarding this content, such as responding to questions posed to them by the teacher via SMS. Through this method, they suggest that learners can form representations of knowledge through both the visual and text channels, supporting learning that is suited to their own individual learning styles.

Cognitive load theory considers the quantity and quality of information that is required to be processed, and how the interrelationship between intrinsic cognitive load (the load related to the difficulty of the task), extraneous cognitive load (how unnecessary or excessive the load is) and effective cognitive load (the load imposed by instructional design) impacts on working memory and long-term memory (Paas, Renkl and Sweller 2003). This theory is of particular interest to educators in that it deals directly with the difficulty of the task, the information presented to learners, and the way in which it can be presented in order to make it more manageable to them. Hsu, Hwang and Chang (2013) provide an example of how they designed their system for Taiwanese learners of English that provides various annotations and personalised recommendations to learners as a means of easing the cognitive load on learners during reading.

The two theories described in the studies here were used as a means of attempting to take the impact of the technology into account to a certain degree, but in both cases, the mobility and ubiquity of the technology still take a rather minor role. An extension of these theories specifically related to technology is *multimedia learning*, was proposed by Mayer (2001, 2009), who suggested that humans have the ability to learn more effectively if there are multiple channels of input, such as a combination of auditory and visual input, and that this can serve to reduce the cognitive load. This theory was applied by Chang, Tseng and Tseng (2011), who provided their learners with PDAs that could interact with the environment around them in the Taipei Zoo. They suggested that the interactive nature of the materials contributed to a lower cognitive load, and the balance of the dual channels of visual and textual queues allowed for increased opportunities to acquire the content.

### *Theories considering the role of mobile devices*

Despite their size and input limitations, modern mobile devices have the potential to go beyond the role of more traditional computers (be they desktop or laptop) in two main ways. First, they can be carried around at any time of the day, including to nonlearning locations, meaning that they can be used at any time. This was initially seen as a way of having learners access learning materials from anywhere, but without detracting from the potential of this, there is also the advantage of learners being able to access reference materials whenever they need them. Second, mobile devices make it possible to interact with the surroundings. This can be done through global positioning systems (GPS) that can enable the mobile device to 'know' where it is, but it also makes it possible for the device to receive input that is relevant to a particular event or action as necessary. To truly make sense of the impact of mobile technologies on the learning process, it is necessary to consider theory that can account for how the mobility of these devices can alter the learning environment.

Despite its potential, one theory that has yet to be applied to learning contexts is called *distributed cognitions*. Originally coined in the 1990s, it was popularised by Hutchins (1995a, 1995b) who claimed that any theory of human memory needed to take into account the fact that a significant proportion of our memory function takes place outside of the body. For example, a calendar helps us to know what day of the year it is, and a watch tells us the time without the need to constantly remember it. Developments in technology have meant that we are becoming increasingly dependent upon the mobile devices we carry with us to almost everywhere, and we are remembering fewer and fewer facts. Although many of us might remember the telephone numbers of our childhood, we may have difficulty in remembering numbers of close friends or even our own telephone number because they are all stored in the mobile device(s) we carry. This has quite a large potential impact on how mobile devices are used, and indeed even on how education may be carried out, as will be discussed later in this chapter. Information can be retrieved 'just in time' to deal with a need, and this may also apply to linguistic needs as well. Thus, when learning reaches the point where some things no longer need to be learned, the way in which devices are used may change the face of the teaching and learning process in a major way.

The mobility and portability of modern mobile devices can also lend themselves to another type of learning, where the learners can interact with their surroundings in order to facilitate meaningful learning. Although not a theory per se, *situated learning* (Lave and Wenger 1991) is a model of learning that views the context in which the learning takes place as an essential part of the learning process. Simply put, it advocates that learning occurs in the context in which it is applied, rather than the simple decontextualised transmission of information. The fact that mobile devices can be carried to any location means that they can be a means of instruction in authentic contexts where learners require information in order to complete a task. For example, if a learner wishes to learn about ordering in a restaurant, rather than just learning phrases in the classroom, they may be able to access the information they require from their mobile device to order food or ask about the menu, and apply this immediately to an authentic context. Although cited periodically in language learning research, it is yet to feature much in literature into learning a language through mobile devices, although there have been a small number of notable exceptions (e.g. Song and Fox 2008; Wu, Huang, Chao and Park 2014). In the study by Song and Fox, learners were able to use PDAs as a part of their learning process for a year, and could use the devices to assist them in learning new vocabulary that they encountered as a part of their lives while studying abroad in Hong Kong. In this case, the mobile aspect of the device was factored into the learning process and it is used in a way that capitalises upon this capability.

Theory can inform us of the potential of learning approaches and the tools we use to achieve particular teaching and learning goals, and it follows that this is also relevant to the use of mobile technologies. It is important, however, to bear in mind not only the aspects associated with language learning, but also to step back and consider the potential impact of using mobile devices in order to achieve these goals, and understand that learning outcomes and even learning objectives may alter when such tools are used.

## Primary outcomes from research into mobile language learning

Research into mobile learning has come an incredibly long way in the comparatively short period that it has been in existence. According to Burston (2013), there were as many 570 works related to mobile language learning over a period of nearly two decades from 1994 to 2012, looking at how mobile devices are viewed by teachers, students and institutions, as well as at the ways in which they are used. This large body of research has enabled us to gain quite solid insights into the possibilities regarding mobile language learning, but at the same time, it must also be pointed out that this research hasn't been without its limitations. The choice of device has definitely had an impact on the ways in which mobile learning has been viewed, with a significant proportion of studies being carried out under controlled conditions, likely as a result of data collection methods (see Stockwell 2012 for a discussion). Because of the nature of mobile devices, it is very difficult to know how they are being used in naturalistic learning environments, and as a result, a lot of research has been conducted in class or where the researcher can directly observe their usage. In many cases, devices are provided to learners, and there have been several studies where learners have used PDAs or tablets that were lent to them for the duration of the study. While this enables consistency in the device and eliminates gaps that might occur for socioeconomic or other reasons, the use of these types of devices does differ from having learners use their own devices in the real world. The nature of these two types of research is quite different, with the former primarily considering design principles, and the latter looking more at usage patterns and attitudes towards learning through mobile devices. Thus, research described here will be divided into two sections, the first looking at research under controlled conditions, and the second at research in unsupervised conditions outside of the classroom.

## Research under controlled conditions

Research into the use of mobile devices has shed some very interesting light on the ways in which mobile technologies can be used, and there has been a large body of work that examines different system designs that can be used individually, in groups with other students or with the teacher. As described earlier, the technologies used have predominantly been PDAs and tablets, and these are usually provided in class sets that learners borrow at the beginning of a class, and usually return on completion of each session. There have been a smaller number of studies that have used these devices outside classroom settings, but these have also typically required learners to return the devices they have used at the end of each session under investigation.

Studies that take place under these controlled conditions generally describe systems that have been specifically designed to develop a particular skill, with the majority of studies centring around vocabulary (Song and Fox 2008) and listening (Chen and Chang 2011) and, to a somewhat lesser degree, reading (Lan et al. 2009). Given the concerns with screen size and inputting on mobile devices (e.g. Stockwell 2008), it is perhaps not that surprising that vocabulary and listening have been the main focus of studies using mobile devices. These studies have contributed to our understanding of the design of systems to assist learners in vocabulary and listening using mobile devices, and collectively have advocated the need for personalised learning and adaptivity to learners' abilities and preferences, as well as to enable learners to gain exposure to new content through multiple modes. Though very small in number, there have also been studies under controlled conditions that have investigated learners using their own mobile phones, such as Huang and Lin (2011) who looked at learners' preferences for text-length reading passages through sending messages via Bluetooth to their mobile phones in class.

The studies that have been carried out under controlled conditions such as those listed earlier are far too broad to do all of them justice in the brief description provided here, but in essence, they tend to be concerned with the affordances of the technology, and how teaching materials may be adapted to mobile devices. Apart from studies such as Chang et al. (2011), where the learners carried the devices outside and interacted with the real world, the mobility of the device has not really been an area under investigation in these types of studies. Learners have typically given very positive evaluations of the systems being investigated, but questions remain as to how learners would react to mobile learning in their own time without direct supervision.

## Research of mobile devices outside of the classroom

Research that examines how mobile devices are used for pedagogical purposes outside the classroom differs quite significantly from that which looks at classroom contexts in that it tends to focus more on attitudes towards usage and patterns of engagement. There have been numerous studies looking at how learners engage in activities using various mobile technologies including MP3 players, PDAs and mobile phones, but despite the enthusiasm shown for using mobile devices under controlled conditions, research has shown there is often resistance to using their mobile devices, particularly when other options such as a computer are available (Stockwell 2008; Kim et al. 2013). This has been an outcome that has been perplexing to educators, as learners have often expressed positive attitudes towards using mobile devices for educational purposes, but this has not been translated directly into high levels of engagement to the tools that are provided to them.

Stockwell (2010), for example, provided vocabulary activities to Japanese learners of English that could be carried out on mobile phones or desktop computers, but ultimately as many as 40% of learners never even attempted to use their mobile phones to undertake the activities despite responding in a presurvey that they felt that learning through mobile devices would be convenient. Similar results were found by Petersen, Divitini and Chabert (2008), who showed that learners of French in Norway indicated that they believed a mobile blog was a good idea but ultimately very few learners actually used it. This trend has been evident even in the nonlanguage learning literature, where more than 30% of their learners in the United States (Abdous, Camarena and Facer 2009) never tried to listen to podcasts provided for them because they didn't think they would be useful. The noteworthy point to bear in mind here is that many learners did not come to this conclusion based on their experience of engaging in mobile-based activities, but rather they made this decision without actually ever having tried them.

While this trend has persisted to a degree, not all feedback about mobile learning has been negative, and Gutierrez-Colon Plana et al. (2013) and Ma and Wang (2013) indicated that student perceptions to using mobile devices for learning were very positive in Spain and Hong Kong, respectively. An overview of perceptions towards mobile learning by learners from a various cultural backgrounds by Hsu (2012) provides some insights into this phenomenon, suggesting that learners who are used to more traditional teaching environments show a greater resistance to the use of mobile devices for language learning.

Attempts have been made to use the 'push' aspect of mobile learning in order to promote more active participation in students' learning outside of class, such as Kennedy and Levy (2008), who sent SMS learning reminders to learners of Italian in Australia; Nah et al. (2008), who encouraged learners to interact with one another using SMS to maintain their motivation; and Stockwell (2013), who sent learners lists of vocabulary they had difficulty with in online activities. Results have been somewhat inconclusive, suggesting that while the technology itself can play a role in promoting learner engagement in mobile-based activities, there is a need to look deeper into the reasons why learners have not always embraced unsupervised mobile learning as enthusiastically as expected.

## Applying mobile devices to language learning environments

The use of mobile devices for language learning is surprisingly complex, and goes beyond just the design of the system or the way in which the mobile component is integrated into the larger teaching and learning context. Stockwell and Hubbard (2013: 8–10) outline ten principles for the implementation of mobile language learning that are based on practice as represented in the relevant literature. A simplified version of the principles follows:

1. Consider the affordances and limitations of both the mobile device and the environment in which the device will be used in light of the learning goals.
2. Limit multitasking and environmental distractions.
3. Use the push mechanism but respect boundaries.

4  Strive to maintain equity, including catering for a range of mobile devices and provide for nonmobile alternatives.
5  Acknowledge and plan for accommodating language learner differences.
6  Be aware of language learners' existing uses and cultures of use for their devices.
7  Keep mobile language learning activities and tasks short and succinct when possible, dividing longer tasks into smaller chunks.
8  Let the language learning task fit the technology and environment, and let the technology and environment fit the task.
9  Provide guidance and training to use mobile devices for language learning most effectively.
10 Recognise and accommodate multiple stakeholders, including teachers, learners and administrators.

The first three principles relate more directly to the design of materials to be used with mobile devices, and stress the need to ensure that the learning activities or tools are suitable to both the device and the language learning goals, and that there is not an overly heavy burden placed on the learner. Related to this are Principles 7 and 8, as these also indicate the need to ensure that tasks and activities are kept at a reasonable length and that these suit the anticipated language learning environment. Principles 4 through 6 are founded on having a clear understanding of the learners, the technologies they possess, and their preferences for using (or not using) mobile devices, whereas Principle 10 goes beyond the learners to the others that are involved in the educational context, including the teachers and the administrators, who may be responsible for implementing and maintaining the technologies that are used.

Principle 9 on learner training is an issue that is of particular importance. There is often an assumption that learners are capable users of technology, and that they are able to use them competently for a range of uses, including educational uses. As some of the examples listed earlier point out, this is not necessarily the case, and in many instances the learners are unwilling to use them when the teacher is not there to constantly support them. Learner training has not featured very much at all in the literature in mobile language learning, and in many cases this is limited to a simple explanation of what the technology is and how to operate it. This type of training would fit into the category of 'technical training', according to Romeo and Hubbard (2010), which is only one element of training they deem as essential to maximise learning through technology. In addition to these two elements, they also point out the need for strategic training (training in how to use the technology for language learning purposes) and pedagogical training (making it clear to learners why it is important to undertake particular tasks or activities). According to a study by Stockwell and Hubbard (2014), moving past simple technical training and including strategic and pedagogical training has been shown to have a significant impact not only on the amount of time that learners spend on the tasks, but also on their attitudes towards mobile learning and on their performance in the target language.

## Key considerations for mobile language learning

There are two main areas that need to be considered when implementing mobile language learning. The first of these is the context in which the language learning tools will be used, and the second is the actual design of the tools themselves. These two elements cannot be separated from one another, and the design of any learning tools will be dependent upon the context in which they are to be used.

A useful overview of how to consider mobile context and the impact that this can have on the learning process is provided by Sampson and Zervas (2013). They define the mobile context as including the following:

- learner temporal information (current state of mind and how this impacts the learner's willingness to participate in the learning process);
- people (how other people influence the learning process);
- place (including the current location, private and public spaces, cultural background and learning setting);
- technological artefacts (the mobile device itself) and nontechnological artefacts (books and other tools that can be used to help learning);
- time (duration of a task, scheduled time of a task, time availability of the learner, a peer or an expert);
- physical conditions (illumination level, noise level and weather conditions).

A look at this list shows that the context itself is indeed very complex, and while it may not be possible to control for all of these variables, at the very least it is important to be aware of the fact that there are several factors at play when designing for learning through mobile devices.

With regard to designing mobile applications, Lecheler and Hosack (2014) provide a list of seven areas to be considered, as follows:

1. Mode of interaction
2. Context of use
3. Scope
4. Data management
5. Mode of access
6. Design scale
7. Incentives.

The mode of interaction refers to whether the input is by keypad, touch screen and so forth, and the type of output, be it video, audio, text or any combination of these. The context refers to knowing when, where and how the application will be used, as it will alter the way in which it is designed. With regard to the scope, it is necessary to decide what the application will include and what it will not, and how it can fit in with other applications or tools. Data management is important if the application will record data pertaining to the learner, be this for the development of a learner profile or for teacher reference, but the way in which these data are stored and transmitted needs to be taken into consideration. The mode of access refers to the way in which the learner will access the learner materials, be it through their mobile phone, a tablet or even a desktop computer, as each of these have different screen sizes and even different operating systems that will alter the way in which the material is presented. The design scale is the degree to which an application can be minimised in order to make it run more smoothly on mobile devices in terms of memory or screen design. Finally, incentives refers to the benefits to the learner for completing activities on the mobile devices. It is a combination of each of these factors that leads to successful design and use of applications for language learning, and it is essential that these factors are considered within the entire language learning context.

## Looking to the future of mobile language learning

Mobile language learning is still a maturing area, but at the same time, the development of mobile devices has marked a potentially enormous change in the face of education itself. Learners are carrying highly sophisticated equipment in their pockets that enables access to an almost unlimited wealth of resources, and this means that the way in which we think about learning may take on different forms from in the past. As an example of this, Dikkers (2014) questions the degree to which learners in the future will actually need to memorise everything when this information is readily available at their fingertips. The implications for language learning are also immediately obvious in that learners can pull out dictionaries that can help them with necessary vocabulary, supported with various kinds of multimedia that can help to contextualise the information that they retrieve.

One feature of mobile language learning that is likely to become increasingly important in the future is how devices interact with the world around the learner. Sampson and Zervas (2013) argue that context-aware adaptive and personalised mobile learning systems can provide educational resources and activities that suit the mobile context, and thereby maximise the learning experience, which is an idea that fits with the concept of situated learning. Being able to access information that is personalised not only to learners' abilities and preferences but also to the context in which they find themselves is an area where there is an enormous range of possibilities. This is also one of the key defining features separating mobile learning from other forms of learning through technology, and will allow for learning opportunities that can complement learning with or without technology. Being aware of the full capabilities of mobile devices and how this form of learning can fit in with teaching and learning goals is the first big step towards developing not only hardware and software, but also pedagogies that capitalise upon the changing affordances of mobile devices.

## Further reading

Burston, J. (2013) 'Mobile-assisted language learning: An annotated bibliography of implementation studies 1994–2012', *Language Learning & Technology*, 17(3): 157–255.
This is an excellent resource covering nearly two decades of mobile learning, looking at studies implementing mobile language learning. For nearly all of the studies listed, there is a detailed annotation showing where the study was carried out and some of the major outcomes of the study.

Romeo, K. and Hubbard, P. (2010) 'Pervasive CALL learner training for improving listening proficiency', in M. Levy, F. Blin, C. Siskin and O. Takeuchi (eds), *WorldCALL: International Perspectives on Computer Assisted Language Learning*, New York, NY: Routledge: 215–229.
In this chapter, Romeo and Hubbard outline three types of learner training which have the potential to lead to more effective use of CALL-based materials. Although it is not specifically targeted towards mobile language learning, the ideas expressed here are very relevant to helping learners to use mobile-based resources more effectively and consistently.

Stockwell, G. and Hubbard, P. (2013) 'Some emerging principles for mobile-assisted language learning', *TIRF Report*, 2013: 1–14.
This discussion paper provides an overview of principles for mobile language learning based on the literature of mobile assisted language learning, CALL and mobile learning. These principles provide practical advice regarding how to use mobile devices more effectively for language learning that are applicable to a range of teaching and learning contexts.

## References

Abdous, M., Camarena, M.M. and Facer, B.R. (2009) 'MALL technology: Use of academic podcasts in the foreign language classroom', *ReCALL*, 21(1): 76–95.

Al-Shehri, S. (2011) 'Mobile social networking in language learning: A transformational tool', *International Journal of Mobile Learning and Organisation*, 5(3–4): 234–259.

Bax, S. (2003) 'CALL – Past, present and future', *System*, 31: 13–28.

Burston, J. (2013) 'Mobile-assisted language learning: An annotated bibliography of implementation studies 1994–2012', *Language Learning & Technology*, 17(3): 157–255.

Chang, C.-C., Tseng, K.-H. and Tseng, J.-S. (2011) 'Is single or dual channel with different English proficiencies better for English listening comprehension, cognitive load and attitude in ubiquitous learning environment?', *Computers & Education*, 57: 2313–2321.

Chang, C.-K. and Hsu, C.-K. (2011) 'A mobile-assisted synchronously collaborative translation annotation system for English as a foreign language (EFL) reading comprehension', *Computer Assisted Language Learning*, 24(2): 155–180.

Chapelle, C. (2005) 'Interactionist SLA theory in CALL research', in J. Egbert and G.M. Petrie (eds), *CALL Research Perspectives*, Mahwah, NJ: Lawrence Erlbaum Associates: 53–64.

Chapelle, C. (2007) 'Technology and second language acquisition', *Annual Review of Applied Linguistics*, 27: 98–114.

Chen, I.-J. and Chang, C.-C. (2011) 'Computer presentation modes in mobile language listening tasks: English proficiency as a moderator', *Computer Assisted Language Learning*, 24(5): 451–470.

de Jong, T., Specht, M. and Koper, R. (2010) 'A study of contextualised mobile information delivery for language learning', *Educational Technology & Society*, 13(3): 110–125.

de la Fuente, M.J. (2014) 'Learners' attention to input during focus on form listening tasks: The role of mobile technology in the second language classroom', *Computer Assisted Language Learning*, 27(3): 261–276.

Dikkers, S.M. (2014) 'The future of mobile media for learning', in C. Miller and A. Doering (eds), *The New Landscape of Mobile Learning: Redesigning Education in an App-Based World*, New York, NY: Routledge: 103–119.

Gutierrez-Colon Plana, M., Gimeno, A., Appel, C., Hopkins, J., Gibert, I. et al. (2013) 'Improving learners' reading skills through instant short messages: A sample study using WhatsApp', Paper presented at the WorldCALL Conference, Glasgow, July 2013.

Hsu, C.-K., Hwang, G.J. and Chang, C.-K. (2013) 'A personalized recommendation-based mobile learning approach to improving the reading performance of EFL students', *Computers & Education*, 63: 327–36.

Hsu, L. (2012) 'English as a foreign language learners' perception of mobile assisted language learning: A cross national study', *Computer Assisted Language Learning*, 26(3): 197–213.

Huang, L.-L. and Lin, C.-C. (2011) 'EFL learners' reading on mobile phones', *The JALT CALL Journal*, 7(1): 61–78.

Huang, Y.-M., Kuo, Y.-H., Lin, Y.-T. and Cheng, S.-C. (2008) 'Toward interactive mobile synchronous learning environment with context-awareness service', *Computers & Education*, 51: 1205–1226.

Hubbard, P. (2008) 'Twenty-five years of theory in the CALICO Journal', *CALICO Journal*, 25(3): 387–399.

Hutchins, E. (1995a) *Cognition in the Wild*, Cambridge, MA: MIT Press.

Hutchins, E. (1995b) 'How a cockpit remembers its speeds', *Cognitive Science*, 19: 265–288.

Hwang, W.-Y. and Chen, H. (2013) 'Users' familiar situational contexts facilitate the practice of EFL in elementary schools with mobile devices', *Computer Assisted Language Learning*, 26(2): 101–125.

Kennedy, C. and Levy, M. (2008) 'L'italiano al telefonino: Using SMS to support beginners' language learning', *ReCALL*, 20(3): 315–330.

Kiernan, P.J. and Aizawa, K. (2004) 'Cell phones in task based learning: Are cell phones useful language learning tools?', *ReCALL*, 16(1): 71–84.

Kim, D., Rueckert, D., Kim, D.-J. and Seo. D. (2013) 'Students' perceptions and experiences of mobile learning', *Language Learning & Technology*, 17(3): 52–73.

Lan, Y.-J., Sung, Y.-T. and Chang, K.-E. (2009) 'Let us read together: Development and evaluation of a computer-assisted reciprocal early English reading system', *Computers & Education*, 53: 1188–1198.

Lave, J. and Wenger, E. (1991) *Situated Learning: Legitimate Peripheral Participation*, Cambridge: Cambridge University Press.

Lecheler, L. and Hosack, B. (2014) 'Seven design considerations for mobile learning applications', in C. Miller and A. Doering (eds), *The New Landscape of Mobile Learning: Redesigning Education in an App-Based World*, New York, NY: Routledge: 85–102.

Levy, M. and Stockwell, G. (2006) *CALL Dimensions: Options and Issues in Computer Assisted Language Learning*, Mahwah, NJ: Lawrence Erlbaum Associates.

Ma, Q. and Wang, L. (2013) 'An evidence-based study of Hong Kong University students' mobile assisted language learning (MALL) experience', Paper presented at the WorldCALL 2013 Conference, Glasgow, July 2013.

Mayer, R.E. (2001) *Multimedia Learning,* New York, NY: Cambridge University Press.
Mayer, R.E. (2009) *Multimedia Learning*, 2nd edn, New York, NY: Cambridge University Press.
Nah, K.C., White, P. and Sussex, R. (2008) 'The potential of using a mobile phone to access the Internet for learning EF listening skills within a Korean context', *ReCALL*, 20(3): 331–347.
Paas, F., Renkl, A. and Sweller, J. (2003) 'Cognitive load theory and instructional design: Recent developments', *Educational Psychologist*, 38(1): 1–4.
Paivio, A. (2007) *Mind and Its Evolution: A Dual Coding Theoretical Approach*, Mahwah, NJ: Lawrence Erlbaum Associates.
Petersen, S.A., Divitini, M. and Chabert, G. (2008) 'Identity, sense of community and connectedness in a community of mobile learners', *ReCALL*, 20(3): 361–379.
Romeo, K. and Hubbard, P. (2010) 'Pervasive CALL learner training for improving listening proficiency', in M. Levy, F. Blin, C. Siskin and O. Takeuchi (eds), *WorldCALL: International Perspectives on Computer Assisted Language Learning*, New York, NY: Routledge: 215–229.
Rosell-Aguilar, F. (2007) 'Top of the Pods – In search of a podcasting "podagogy" for language learning', *Computer Assisted Language Learning*, 20(5): 471–492.
Sampson, D.G. and Zervas, P. (2013) 'Context-aware adaptive and personalized mobile learning systems', in D.G. Sampson, P. Isaias, D., Ifenthaler and J.M. Spector (eds), *Ubiquitous and Mobile Learning in the Digital Age*, New York, NY: Springer: 3–18.
Song, Y. and Fox, R. (2008) 'Using PDA for undergraduate student incidental vocabulary testing', *ReCALL*, 20(3): 290–314.
Squire, K. (2009) 'Mobile media learning: Multiplicities of place', *On the Horizon*, 17(1): 70–80.
Stockwell, G. (2008) 'Investigating learner preparedness for and usage patterns of mobile learning', *ReCALL*, 20(3): 253–270.
Stockwell, G. (2010) 'Using mobile phones for vocabulary activities: Examining the effect of the platform', *Language Learning & Technology*, 14(2): 95–110.
Stockwell, G. (2012) 'Mobile-assisted language learning', in M. Thomas, H. Reinders and M. Warschauer (eds), *Contemporary Computer-Assisted Language Learning*, London; New York, NY: Continuum Books: 201–216.
Stockwell, G. (2013) 'Tracking learner usage of mobile phones for language learning outside of the classroom', in P. Hubbard, M. Schultz and B. Smith (eds), *Human-Computer Interaction in Language Learning: Studies in Honor of Robert Fischer, CALICO Monograph Series*, San Marcos, TX: CALICO: 118–136.
Stockwell, G. (2014) 'Exploring theory in computer-assisted language learning', in X. Deng and R. Seow (eds), *Alternative Pedagogies in the English Language & Communication Classroom: Selected Papers from the Fourth CELC Symposium for English Language Teachers*, Singapore: Centre for English Language Communication, National University of Singapore: 25–30.
Stockwell, G. and Hubbard, P. (2013) 'Some emerging principles for mobile-assisted language learning', *TIRF Report*, 1–14.
Stockwell, G. and Hubbard, P. 'Learner training in mobile language learning', Paper presented at the XVIth International CALL Research Conference, Antwerp, July 2014.
Wu, T.-T., Huang, Y.-H., Chao, H.-C. and Park, J.H. (2014) 'Personalized English reading sequencing based on learning portfolio analysis', *Information Sciences*, 257: 248–263.

# 22
# Virtual worlds and language learning
## An analysis of research

*Mark Peterson*

Virtual worlds have long been of interest to language researchers and educators, as it is claimed that these computer-based simulations hold great promise as arenas for foreign and second language learning. This chapter provides a description of significant features of the major virtual worlds that have been investigated in computer-assisted language learning (CALL) research. Following this overview, the findings of fourteen learner-based studies focusing on the use of these environments is subject to critical analysis. The discussion highlights a number of encouraging findings. The analysis further reveals that to date, although research in this area is expanding, it remains incomplete and is subject to significant limitations. Moreover, the discussion draws attention to a number of potential issues that have been identified in the literature. This chapter concludes by emphasising the need for additional research, and identifies a number of promising areas for future investigation.

### Virtual worlds: Design features

Of the numerous environments for network-based communication produced by advances in computer technologies, virtual worlds are identified in the CALL literature as tools with significant potential (Stevens 2006; Cooke-Plagwitz 2008; Peterson 2011). The first virtual worlds explored in CALL research drew on elements of early 2D role-playing and adventure games. These desktop worlds present users with persistent simulations of environments described in text and on-screen graphics. However, in contrast to computer games that require players to undertake predesigned activities (e.g. engaging in trading), virtual worlds are designed primarily to support communication (Peterson 2013; see also Part V of this volume). A well-known example of a 2D virtual world explored in CALL research is known by the acronym MOO (multiuser object orientated domain). In a MOO world, users are immersed in a theme-based simulation that provides the option of maintaining anonymity through the adoption of a unique online identity known as a character. Characters can engage in role play and communicate in real time by using an onscreen text chat system. They can also navigate through the virtual user-created rooms that constitute a MOO world by use of typed commands. Commands further facilitate the creation of virtual content such as new rooms and objects. A number of MOOs have been established in order to provide language learners with immersion in target language (TL) cultures. Language learning MOOs currently in use include Schmooze University, an EFL MOO hosted at Hunter College; MOOssiggang, a German language MOO created at Vassar College; and MundoHispano, a MOO world designed for students of Spanish based at the University of Missouri–St. Louis.

As technology has advanced, virtual worlds have emerged that retain elements of their predecessors while incorporating new developments. In contemporary virtual worlds such as Second Life and Active Worlds, users are immersed in engaging browser-based simulations known as worlds. In common with MOOs, these are theme-based and persistent. Worlds can be programmed to reflect user requirements and are frequently designed to facilitate social interaction. Unlike the majority of MOOs, virtual worlds are large scale and provide access to diverse and growing online user communities. Worlds are user-created and incorporate high-quality 3D graphics. Highly realistic avatars that can be customised to reflect individual preferences have replaced the text-based characters used in MOOs. Moreover, individual avatars can traverse virtual space by walking or flying and can move between worlds, an activity known as teleporting. Avatars can further display a limited range of physical actions and emotional states in real time. In contrast to MOOs, contemporary virtual worlds provide users with multiple real-time communication tools and sources of feedback. These include voice chat, scripted note cards and instant messaging.

## Hypothesised benefits of the use of virtual worlds in CALL

Researchers identify a number of features of virtual worlds that may facilitate language learning (Stevens 2006; Sykes, Oskoz and Thorne 2008). The theme-based nature of many virtual worlds provides for authentic real-time TL interaction with a wide variety of interlocutors including native speakers. Immersion in this type of potentially beneficial communication context is frequently challenging to replicate in language classrooms (Milton, Jonsen, Hirst and Lindenburn 2012). Virtual worlds are seen as providing exposure to rich TL input and valuable opportunities to produce TL output, thus supporting the development of fluency (Peterson 2011). These environments further provide opportunities to engage in the social interaction and meaning negotiation that are identified as playing a central role in language acquisition (Sykes et al. 2008). Moreover, interaction with native speakers and more proficient peers in the TL may enhance intercultural awareness (Schneider and Von der Emde 2000; Thorne 2008). The anonymity provided and the reduction of social context cues such as age and status are viewed as beneficial, as these aspects of the interaction in virtual worlds can enhance motivation, reduce anxiety and encourage the risk-taking that supports learning (Schwienhorst 2002b). The ability to create content is perceived as encouraging participation and the development of learner autonomy (Shield 2003). The open access nature of virtual worlds facilitates the implementation of task-based learning (Jauregi et al. 2011). The availability of data recording provides educators with a potentially valuable resource that may be used to assist the process of conscious reflection on language use, thus raising meta-linguistic awareness (Peterson 2001). Additional beneficial factors identified in research include opportunities for role-play, sense of immersion, and the emotional engagement engendered by the creation and use of personal avatars (Svensson 2003; Cooke-Plagwitz 2008). These features of virtual worlds and their learner-centred nature are perceived as combining to reduce inhibition, creating conditions in which language acquisition may occur (Peterson 2011).

Speculation regarding the possible benefits of the use of virtual worlds has led researchers to conduct a variety of studies (Peterson 2011). As work in this area is increasing, an analysis of findings is now appropriate in order to support future research. In order to be included in this analysis, each study met the following criteria: investigated some type of virtual world, was learner-based and peer-reviewed. A keyword search of major databases and four major CALL journals (*Language Learning and Technology*, *ReCALL*, *Computer Assisted Language Learning*, and the *CALICO Journal*) identified fourteen learner-based studies published between 1999 and 2012. Data collection was completed by January 2013. The following discussion focuses on an analysis of findings from this body of work. Studies will be analysed in depth in order to draw attention to the strengths and weaknesses of current research. Discussion first focuses on research involving MOOs and then moves on to examine use of the 3D virtual worlds Active Worlds and Second Life. The analysis further highlights significant findings that have implications for future research.

## Research on the use of virtual worlds: Significant findings

In an early study, Donaldson and Kötter (1999) conducted qualitative research that examined the MOO-based interaction of two learner groups located in Germany and the United States. One group were intermediate level English as a second language (ESL) learners. The other participants were native speakers of English who studied German as a foreign language. The learners undertook a number of tasks including participation in online discussions on comparative topics related to the TL culture and the joint creation of virtual content within a MOO world. Transcript analysis demonstrated that both learner groups displayed a high degree of engagement and used a number of strategies found in face-to-face communication in order to overcome communication problems. This included the translation of single unknown words, code switching, correction and the production of simplified TL output. Although exploratory in nature, the findings of this research suggest that MOOs are viable venues for CALL.

Von der Emde, Schneider and Kötter (2001) reported the findings of a year-long longitudinal study that analysed learner interaction in a MOO world designed to facilitate the study of German as a foreign language. This web-based MOO provides a text and graphics-based simulation of a town in Germany. Two groups of undergraduates located in Germany and the United States participated in this research. Students studying German as a foreign language at an American college were paired with advanced students of English based at a university in Germany. In the first term, the learners undertook grammar-based learning activities and assignments. In the following term, they undertook joint research projects focusing on cultural differences between Germany and America in the MOO. The learners also maintained learning portfolios. The researchers found that the learners engaged in role play and experimentation. This supported collaborative interaction in the TL that involved frequent instances of negotiation of meaning and peer teaching. The researchers claim that the learner-centred nature of the interaction reduced anxiety and facilitated exploratory learning regarding aspects of the TL culture (Von der Emde et al. 2001: 219). The data further indicate that regular interaction elicited extensive TL output, risk-taking, and appeared to enhance cross-cultural knowledge. The researchers also examined the role of the teachers. They claimed that as the project progressed, the teachers adopted facilitator roles and this phenomenon encouraged learner autonomy (Von der Emde et al. 2001: 215–218). Although this study reports positive findings, the number of participants was not specified.

In longitudinal research conducted over a nine-week period, Schwienhorst (2002a) investigated the MOO-based interaction of two distinct learner groups. One group consisted of twenty-nine native speakers of English based in Ireland who possessed beginner level proficiency in German. Their partners were twenty-two native speakers of German located in Germany. The majority of the German group possessed advanced level English proficiency. The main focus of this study was the repair strategies used by the participants during communication problems. The analysis focused on text chat transcripts and feedback to a poststudy questionnaire. Data shows that the MOO provided a beneficial context for TL practice. Furthermore, during TL interaction, both groups used a number of strategies to successfully resolve communication problems. These involved use of clarification requests, translation, repetition and paraphrase. Instances of learners avoiding discussion of unknown vocabulary were infrequent. The data indicated that both groups engaged in risk-taking and displayed autonomy by actively managing their interaction and adapting to the needs of their partners.

In a mixed methods study, Kötter (2003) explored the semester long interaction of twenty-nine undergraduates in a MOO designed to facilitate the study of German as a foreign language. The participants formed two groups. One group was composed of native speakers of German based in Germany. The other group consisted of intermediate and advanced level learners of German as a foreign language based in the United States. Data was collected from text chat transcripts and learner self-reports. Analysis of this data revealed that the learners took responsibility for managing their discourse, initiating and sustaining TL interaction focusing on language tasks. This interaction was found to elicit communication problems that resulted in instances of meaning negotiation. Data show that the most frequent strategies used by the learners were explicit in nature and focused on clarification requests and confirmation checks. The researcher speculated that the computer-based nature of the interaction and the associated reduction in paralinguistic cues, coupled with differences in proficiency levels and the need to complete the tasks in real time, led to the frequent use of direct repair strategies, and the absence of the indirect repair strategies found in oral communication (Kötter 2003: 157).

Warner (2004) investigated the TL use of undergraduate students in a MOO. The text chat of two distinct learner groups was analysed. The first group comprised nineteen beginner level students of German who undertook text chat in a MOO as part of a regular language course. The sessions were held on four occasions during a semester. The sixteen students in the second group were advanced level learners of German as a foreign language who met in a MOO three times over the course of a semester. The majority of the learners were novice users. Data shows that the learners in both groups undertook social interaction in the TL and that this was characterised by risk-taking and the extensive use of language play. The analysis further reveals that the participants actively managed their interaction and engaged in peer correction.

Experimental research by Toyoda and Harrison (2002) investigated the interaction of learners of Japanese as a foreign language with native speakers in a purpose-built world within Active Worlds. The participants undertook weekly hour-long sessions held over a semester. Qualitative analysis of text chat transcript data indicated that the learners engaged in the negotiation of meaning, and that this type of interaction was triggered in the majority of cases by the use of unknown TL vocabulary. Other causes of negotiation included vocabulary misuse, pronunciation errors, inappropriate segmentation, sudden topic change, slow response and intercultural communication gaps. Instances of negotiation caused by the use of abbreviations and grammatical errors occurred but were infrequent. The data further showed that not all communication problems were successfully resolved. This research also emphasised potential problematic aspects of using 3D worlds. The aforementioned researchers draw attention to the complex nature of the communication environment and note that it appeared cogitatively demanding for the participants (Toyoda and Harrison 2002: 97). Observation revealed that the learners made little use of their avatars, preferring instead to concentrate on the text chat. Moreover, they encountered difficulties managing the interface and in following multiple topic threads as they scrolled in real time. These aspects of the interaction resulted in instances of technostress.

An experimental qualitative study undertaken by Peterson (2006) represents one of the few attempts to examine use of specific language tasks in a 3D virtual world. In this research, twenty-four intermediate EFL learners undertook an orientation and then worked in dyads to complete three one-hour sessions in Active Worlds. Three task types were administered: decision-making, jigsaw and opinion-exchange. Text chat transcripts were collected and this data source was supplemented with researcher observation and learner feedback to a poststudy questionnaire. Analysis revealed that the learners used both interactional and transactional strategies to manage their TL interaction. These strategies presented an effective means to deal with the computer-based nature of the interaction. Transactional strategies were found to be more frequent. Adaptive transactional strategies identified in the data included use of abbreviations, split turns and emoticons. These were used extensively to signal feedback and save time. Data further shows that participants made frequent and appropriate use of the interactional strategy of politeness in order to reduce the risks of misunderstandings arising in the absence of many social context cues such as age and status (Peterson 2006: 93–96).

In a noteworthy finding, it was found that negotiation was infrequent and that the highest incidence occurred in the decision-making task. The researcher speculated that low incidences of negotiation may reflect the project configuration and nature of the communication environment presented by Active Worlds, where learners need to keep up with messages and complete tasks in real time (Peterson 2006: 99). Moreover, the aforementioned factors coupled with sociocultural concerns may have led to occasions when participants avoided signalling that a communication problem had arisen. Learner feedback suggests that the presence of individual user-controlled avatars enhances the sense of presence experienced and facilitates communication. The earlier researcher acknowledged limitations of this study. Due to institutional constraints, the duration and number of participants were limited.

Deutschmann and Panichi (2009) examined use of Second Life in an English course. The course involved seven participants supported by two instructors. The participants were doctoral students who possessed intermediate and advanced levels of English proficiency. These learners undertook six ninety-minute online voice-chat sessions in which they undertook informal interactions regarding private interests, professional matters and formal presentations on their research interests. Data collected from the first and final sessions was subject to discourse analysis. The researchers examined participation including floor space, turn-taking and supportive moves such as backchanneling and the use of elicitors. The data shows that there was little difference in the floor space distribution between the two sessions. However, it was found that turn-taking patterns differed significantly between the sessions. As the research progressed, the learners displayed increasing autonomy and took the initiative in managing their interaction. Moreover, there were significantly more student support moves in the final session in comparison to the first session where teacher-initiated support moves predominated. The researchers claimed that although the communication environment provided by Second Life is challenging, if the teacher adopts a supportive facilitating role then learner engagement may be enhanced (Deutschmann and Panichi 2009: 325). Although the findings of this study are encouraging, the small number of sessions analysed represents a limitation. This factor draws attention to the provisional nature of the findings.

Peterson (2010) conducted an exploratory case study that analysed learner participation patterns, discourse management strategies and attitudes. Seven intermediate level EFL students undertook three seventy-minute task sessions in Second Life with an instructor present in-world. The sessions were held over a six-week period in the world known as USQ Island. This virtual world provides users with a high-quality simulation of a university campus located in Australia. Tasks involved treasure hunts, opinion exchange and completion of a short presentation. Data was collected from text chat transcripts, researcher observation and learner feedback to pre- and poststudy questionnaires. Analysis revealed that the interaction was highly learner-centred with the majority of interactions occurring between participants. Data showed that the learners were able to manage their TL interaction effectively through use of the interactional and transactional discourse management strategies identified in prior research (Peterson 2006). In a significant finding, it was found that the interaction was task focused. Researcher observation confirmed the high degree of engagement and interest displayed by the participants. Learner feedback was broadly positive, with the majority claiming that the interaction was enjoyable and motivating.

Research conducted by Jauregi et al. (2011) utilised a case study in order to examine the efficacy of tasks designed to utilise specific venues in Second Life. The tasks were designed to maximise opportunities for authentic social interaction and raise intercultural awareness. This study focused on learner oral interaction involving voice chat. Two learners of Spanish and two pre-service teachers undertook training. Participants then completed four tasks that involved visiting specific locations in the virtual world. In the first task, participants met in a specific venue to complete and then discuss their responses to an online questionnaire designed to elicit discussion of cultural similarities and differences. In the second and third tasks, learners worked in dyads undertaking in-world tours of Spanish-themed locations where they interacted with native and nonnative speakers. The final evaluation task involved opinion-exchange regarding experiences of interacting in Second Life. Data was collected from four one-hour long voice chat sessions, questionnaires, and informal debriefing interviews. Analysis established that the tasks elicited extensive and authentic TL interaction. The task design facilitated learner-centred discussion of intercultural issues and the interaction was conducted in an informal atmosphere that was characterised by familiarity and spontaneous displays of rapport. Instances of meaning negotiation appeared in the data. In their feedback, participants expressed positive views. They claimed that the interaction was useful and enjoyable. The learners noted that talking in the TL raised confidence. Learners drew attention to problematic aspects of using Second Life. These included issues with the real-time audio and the reduction of paralinguistic cues during interaction. Participants claimed that this later factor made turn management challenging.

Wehner, Gump and Downey (2011) undertook longitudinal research that examined how interaction in Second Life influenced learner motivation. This study represents one of the few attempts to compare use of Second Life with participation in a conventional classroom language course. Learners on a beginning level Spanish course were divided into two groups. One group of twenty-one students undertook training, and then completed ten one-hour sessions in Second Life. The tasks included interaction with native speakers, visits to Spanish-themed locations, and mini-presentations. The other group consisted of twenty-one learners who undertook a regular language course. At the end of the semester, both groups were given a twenty-minute survey based on Gardner's (1985) Attitude/Motivation Test Battery, in order to establish the potential of Second Life as a tool to enhance learner motivation. Statistical analysis indicated that there was a small increase in motivation of the learners who used Second Life compared to the control group. The researchers claimed that this finding suggests that virtual worlds may be a useful means to lower learner anxiety (Wehner et al. 2011: 286). However, they noted that the small number of participants and use of a nonrandom sample limits the generalisability of their findings. They further acknowledged the potential of other variables to influence learner motivation.

A study by Milton et al. (2012) investigated learner-based interaction in Second Life. In this research, the in-world task-based interaction of three dyads composed of native speakers of English and Hungarian was recorded during four one-hour sessions. Participants undertook English role-plays, and tasks designed to elicit the production of Hungarian words and phrases. These activities took place in various venues in Second Life including a virtual bank, travel agency, estate agent, supermarket and clothes shop. Analysis of speech and text data drawn from the first three sessions indicates that as the research progressed, the participants increased their TL output significantly. Data shows that the balance of speech between learners and native speakers was even. These findings led the researchers to speculate that Second Life may be a suitable venue for language learners to improve their fluency (Milton et al. 2012: 110). During the task-based interaction, it was found that vocabulary uptake was good and comparable with traditional classroom vocabulary-learning activities. However, the researchers claim that interaction outside of the tasks was lexically poor (Milton et al. 2012: 110). As the research unfolded, a number of limitations of the environment became apparent. For the participants in this study, following the interaction and turn-taking was challenging particularly during group discussions. Further issues highlighted by the researchers include financial costs and the considerable time required to set up a secure and controlled learning environment.

Research conducted by Liou (2012) investigated the use of language tasks in Second Life with twenty-five novice learners. The tasks included pair work involving joint essay writing, use of note cards, participation in tours, text chats and in-class presentations. The tasks formed part of a course focusing on the use of new technologies in English language education. Tasks were implemented over eighteen weeks and were completed in a computer lab, at home and in a classroom. An instructor and three graduate students participated in the text chats. Data was collected from responses to a background questionnaire, poststudy questionnaire and follow-up interviews. The researcher asserted that the majority of learner feedback was positive. Most participants claimed that the environment was engaging and provided immersion in realistic simulations that enhanced knowledge of the TL culture. Other positive features of undertaking the tasks identified by the participants included improved vocabulary, motivation, reduced anxiety and opportunities for self-expression. The learners also noted problems. On occasion, bandwidth issues and system failures restricted participation and this induced frustration. Some learners further claimed that mastering the commands required was time-consuming. Based on their analysis of the text chat, the researcher asserted that Second Life provides an authentic context for TL interaction and collaboration, and that transcripts provided a valuable resource for peer review (Liou 2012: 377). This research is significant as it represents a rare attempt to explore the integration of Second Life into a wider course. However, it is also subject to significant limitations. Only twelve of the twenty-five participants were interviewed. Moreover, in evaluating the learner feedback, the researcher did not acknowledge the possibility that as the learners were novice users their claims may have been influenced by the novelty of the environment.

Peterson (2012) analysed the task-based interaction of eight Japanese EFL learners in the Second Life world USQ Island. Three task types were administered: decision-making, opinion-exchange and presentation. The tasks required teleporting to specific venues in USQ Island. The decision-making task took place in a student recreation facility. The opinion-exchange tasks occurred in the campus garden and utilised an in-world graphing tool where participants moved their avatars in order to express agreement or disagreement with various statements. The presentation task took place in an outdoor lecture theatre. The interaction occurred over four seventy-minute sessions held once a week. During the tasks, the participants used the text chat system.

Analysis shows that the learners engaged in types of interaction hypothesised as beneficial in sociocultural accounts of SLA. Data indicated that the more proficient learners provided ongoing support to their peers focusing on lexis and correction. The interaction was characterised by a high degree of social cohesion, with the participants making appropriate use of various forms of politeness in order to establish and maintain collaborative interpersonal relationships that supported participation. This facilitated a shared perspective and the consistent production of coherent TL output focused on the tasks. Learner attitudes were investigated through a post-study questionnaire and interviews. In their feedback, the majority of the participants claimed that although the interaction could be challenging, it was enjoyable. The use of personal avatars appeared to enhance the sense of immersion and the anonymity provided reduced inhibition. Learners claimed that this feature of Second Life supported participation. They further claimed that the availability of scrolling was helpful. Additional beneficial aspects noted by the learners included exposure to new vocabulary and opportunities for TL practice. The researcher draws attention to the limitations of this research (Peterson 2012: 37). For example, the number of participants and duration of the sessions was limited by institutional constraints. Moreover, this factor prevented participation in content creation, leaving the potential of this activity unexplored.

## Common themes and issues in research

The discussion in this chapter shows that current research provides limited evidence to support the claims made in the literature regarding the value of 2D and 3D virtual worlds as environments for language learning. Studies have produced encouraging findings that mirror research on the use of other computer-based real-time communication tools (Darhower 2002; Smith 2003; Lee 2008). As Table 22.1 shows, positive findings that are consistently reported in research on the use of MOOs and 3D virtual worlds include high degrees of participation and opportunities to develop autonomy (Donaldson and Kötter 1999; Von der Emde et al. 2001; Schwienhorst 2002a; Kötter 2003; Deutschmann and Panichi 2009; Peterson 2010). A common theme in the research is that interaction in virtual worlds facilitates the production of TL output (Donaldson and Kötter 1999; Peterson 2012). Longitudinal studies are consistent in demonstrating that interaction in virtual worlds when combined with specific language tasks, elicits purposeful and authentic TL interaction that provides valuable fluency practice (Warner 2004; Peterson 2006; Milton et al. 2012). This frequently involves forms of TL interaction that are claimed to facilitate language development including opportunities for meaning negotiation and peer teaching (Von der Emde et al. 2001; Schwienhorst 2002a; Kötter 2003; Jauregi et al. 2011; Peterson 2012). A noteworthy feature of the research is that social interaction in virtual worlds appears to be based on reciprocity and collaboration (Peterson 2012). In addition, the data is consistent in showing that learner interaction is frequently characterised by spontaneity and social cohesion (Jauregi et al. 2011). These findings suggest that carefully designed projects provide access to conditions in which language development may occur.

Research further suggests that the computer-based nature of the interaction in virtual worlds appears to offer a number of advantages. The literature contains limited evidence that interaction in virtual worlds supports learner motivation (Wehner et al. 2011). However, the majority of studies have not investigated this factor in detail. Although findings are provisional, studies suggest that the use of personal avatars in 3D worlds combined with access to realistic simulations supports a high degree of engagement and immersion (Peterson 2006, 2012; Milton et al. 2012). Moreover, findings indicate that the anonymity provided may reduce inhibition and anxiety (Wehner et al. 2011; Peterson 2012). The reduction of social context cues may also support risk-taking. In addition, the availability of data recording offers learners a potentially valuable resource for raising meta-linguistic awareness (Liou 2012). As this discussion shows, there is evidence in the literature that regular interaction in virtual worlds with native speaker interlocutors enhances knowledge of the TL culture (Von der Emde et al. 2001; Liou 2012). Although interaction in virtual worlds may be challenging, learner feedback in the majority of studies emphasises that it is frequently enjoyable and perceived as valuable (Jauregi et al. 2011; Peterson 2012). The

Mark Peterson

*Table 22.1* Significant findings on the use of virtual worlds in CALL

| Positive findings | Negative findings |
|---|---|
| Learner-centred interaction | Need for network access and modern hardware |
| Engagement and participation enhanced | Time-consuming training may be required due to the learning curve |
| TL output elicited | Discourse management may be challenging |
| Meaning negotiation | Risk of technostress |
| Social interaction involving peer collaboration in the TL | Environments are complex and may be inappropriate for lower-level learners |
| Exploratory learning | Costs |
| Risk-taking | Sociocultural concerns may influence learner behavior leading to avoidance |
| Inhibition and anxiety reduced | |
| Development of learner autonomy | |
| Motivation enhanced | |
| Knowledge of the TL culture increased | |
| Avatars may support immersion | |

literature further indicates that virtual worlds foster learner-centred interaction (Peterson 2010). However, research highlights the central role of the teacher in the design and implementation of pedagogically appropriate tasks (Deutschmann and Panichi 2009). This factor remains critical to ensuring successful learning outcomes.

Although current research indicates that virtual worlds are viable and potentially beneficial venues for language development, this discussion draws attention to a number of potential issues associated with their use. Studies suggest that for learner groups with limited computer skills there is a need for time-consuming training. A significant finding identified in several studies is that virtual worlds present a complex and challenging communication environment that may not be suitable for lower-level learners (Toyoda and Harrison 2002; Jauregi et al. 2011). These studies have also identified instances of technostress and this finding is a cause for concern. A related issue identified in the literature is that contemporary virtual worlds require modern computer hardware and network access in order to function effectively (Liou 2012). As is noted in the CALL literature, these conditions are not found in all educational institutions (Maftoon and Shahini 2012).

Another potential drawback of virtual worlds lies in the costs of access. Milton et al. (2012) draw attention to the high costs associated with virtual worlds. In another interesting finding, studies suggest that contrary to the widely held view that online communication is beneficial, the complex interfaces provided in virtual worlds coupled with the reduction of paralinguistic cues may make aspects of interaction such as turn management problematic for language learners (Toyoda and Harrison 2002; Milton et al. 2012). Furthermore, research indicates that in contrast to findings reported elsewhere, although interaction in virtual worlds may reduce social context cues, these influences on communication are not removed during online interaction. Studies report findings mirrored in research conducted on other types of real-time communication tools that learner behaviour in virtual worlds appears influenced by sociocultural concerns such as, for example, maintaining status with peers (Peterson 2006, 2010). Moreover, as this analysis of findings indicates, this phenomenon may lead learners to avoid signalling that a communication problem has occurred, leading to potentially valuable opportunities for learning being lost.

This analysis further draws attention to limitations of the current research base. Although the majority of studies on MOO worlds involved significant numbers of participants, contemporary research has in most cases involved only small numbers of learners. In addition, with the exception of the work undertaken by Peterson (2006, 2010, 2012), there is an absence of follow-up studies leading to a situation where many of the valuable insights gained from early work appear to have been lost. A further issue associated with research is the small number of comparison and replication studies. As has been noted in the literature (Chun 2012; Porte 2013), this represents a significant limitation and makes the generalisability of findings challenging. The aforementioned features of current work coupled with the fragmented nature of the research base require acknowledgement. This later phenomenon may in part reflect the lack, at present, of methodologies that are specifically designed to evaluate the potential of virtual worlds as arenas for language learning (Chapelle 2010). Another limitation of current research is the emphasis on qualitative studies that are heavily reliant on learner self-reporting. In reporting their results, few researchers have explicitly recognised the drawbacks associated with learner self-reporting and the potential influence of novelty effects. Although qualitative research continues to produce valuable insights, in order to obtain a more balanced and comprehensive understanding of the potential of virtual worlds there remains a need for additional studies that utilise quantitative methods.

## Future directions

As this analysis demonstrates, although current research has expanded in recent years it is far from definitive. However, the promising findings that have been obtained to date suggest that further investigation is merited. The following discussion draws attention to a number of areas that appear promising and remain in need of further investigation.

A noteworthy feature of the current literature is the limited number of studies that explore how beneficial forms of TL interaction can be elicited though the use of tasks. Although Peterson (2006, 2012) and Jauregi et al. (2011) have conducted preliminary work in this area, there is a need for further research that explores how tasks can be designed to maximise opportunities for the types of TL interaction that are held to facilitate SLA (Chapelle 1997). As longitudinal studies on the use of virtual worlds remain limited, future research that explores the use of specific tasks over a sustained period offers the prospect of revealing valuable new insights into the role of interaction in facilitating language development. As the majority of studies have focused on text chat, additional work on the use of audio chat may shed new light on possible benefits of this type of interaction. Research that explores educator roles in optimal task design and the conduct of successful learner-based projects appear promising areas in need of further investigation. Moreover, research is required into teacher beliefs towards the use of virtual worlds in order to establish the influence of this factor in securing beneficial learning outcomes.

An area requiring investigation is the influence of participation in virtual worlds on motivation. As this factor is identified as playing a central role in language learning, additional large-scale studies are necessary in order to establish if the positive effects on motivation reported in some studies are sustainable or the product of novelty. Another area that appears promising in future research is the exploration of how the specific affordances provided by virtual worlds can be utilised to support learning. Recent work by Peterson (2012) draws attention to the benefits of engaging learners with activities that utilise specific in-world venues and tools. This line of inquiry could be expanded to examine how content creation can be utilised in order to facilitate social interaction and the collaboration that is central to TL development. The analysis conducted here draws attention to findings emphasising the potential of integrating virtual worlds into regular courses (Deutschmann and Panichi 2009; Liou 2012). However, as work in this area remains limited, more research is needed in order to establish the feasibility and benefits of this approach.

The current literature also highlights the influence of sociocultural factors such as status concerns on learner behaviour (Peterson 2006). Further exploration of this area may open up new lines of inquiry that enhance understanding of how these factors influence language development in virtual worlds. As this discussion shows, international projects open up interesting possibilities for research that investigates how virtual worlds can be harnessed to develop communicative competence and knowledge of the TL culture. A related area that would benefit from additional research is learner use of virtual worlds in informal noninstitutional contexts. As has been noted in the literature, the rapid expansion of the Internet and network technologies has opened up new opportunities for language learning that occur outside the confines of traditional language classrooms (Thorne, Black and Sykes 2009). As this phenomenon remains poorly understood (Thorne 2008), research that investigates learner use of virtual worlds in informal contexts may offer valuable insights. Finally, as has been noted previously, the literature indicates that additional comparative studies are needed in order to establish the potential of virtual worlds versus alternative modes of instruction.

## Further reading

Molka-Danielsen, J. and Deutschmann, M. (eds) (2009) *Learning and Teaching in the Virtual World of Second Life*, Trondheim, Norway: Tapir Academic Press.
   This book describes experiences and lessons learned from educational projects and courses based in Second Life.
Nelson, B.C. and Erlandson, B.E. (2012) *Design for Learning in Virtual Worlds*, New York, NY: Routledge.
   This book explores the history and evolution of virtual worlds and theories proposed to justify their use in education. Further areas examined include design guidelines for curricula and learning activities.
Sadler, R. (2012) *Virtual Worlds for Language Learning: From Theory to Practice*, New York, NY: Peter Lang.
   This text investigates the use of virtual worlds in language education.
Savin-Baden, M. (2010) *A Practical Guide to Using Second Life in Higher Education*, Glasgow: Open University Press.
   This handbook is designed to assist educators seeking to utilise virtual worlds in their courses.

## References

Active Worlds Inc. (1995) *Active Worlds*, available: http://www.activeworlds.com/ (accessed 24 Oct 2014).
Chapelle, C. (1997) 'CALL in the year 2000: Still in research of research paradigms?', *Language Learning & Technology*, 1(1): 19–43.
Chapelle, C. (2010) 'The spread of computer-assisted language learning', *Language Teaching*, 43(1): 66–74.
Chun, D. (2012) 'Replication studies in CALL research', *CALICO Journal*, 29(4): 591–600.
Cooke-Plagwitz, J. (2008) 'New directions in CALL: An objective introduction to second life', *CALICO Journal*, 25(3): 547–557.
Darhower, M. (2002) 'Interactional features of synchronous computer-mediated communication in the intermediate L2 class: A sociocultural case study', *CALICO Journal*, 19(2): 249–277.
Deutschmann, M. and Panichi, L. (2009) 'Talking into empty space? Signalling involvement in a virtual language classroom in Second Life', *Language Awareness*, 18(3–4): 310–328.
Donaldson R.P. and Kötter, M. (1999) 'Language learning in cyberspace: Teleporting the classroom into the target culture', *CALICO Journal*, 16(1): 531–557.
Gardner, R.C. (1985) *Social Psychology and Second Language Learning: The Role of Attitudes and Motivation*, London, UK: Edward Arnold.
Hunter College (1994) *Schmooze University*, available: http://schmooze.hunter.cuny.edu/ (accessed 24 Oct 2014).
Jauregi, K., Canto, S., de Graff, R., Koenraad, T. and Moonen, M. (2011) 'Verbal interaction in Second Life: Towards a pedagogic framework for task design', *Computer Assisted Language Learning*, 24(1): 77–101.

Kötter, M. (2003) 'Negotiation of meaning and codeswitching in online tandems', *Language Learning & Technology*, 7(2): 145–172.

Lee, L. (2008) 'Focus-on-form through collaborative scaffolding in expert-to-novice online interaction', *Language Learning & Technology*, 12(3): 53–72.

Linden Research Inc. (2003) *Second Life*, available: http://secondlife.com/ (accessed 24 Oct 2014).

Liou, H.C. (2012) 'The roles of Second Life in a college computer assisted language learning (CALL) course in Taiwan, ROC', *Computer Assisted Language Learning*, 25(4): 365–382.

Maftoon, P. and Shahini, A. (2012) 'CALL normalization: A survey on inhibitive factors', *JALTCALL Journal*, 8(1): 17–32.

Milton, J., Jonsen, S., Hirst, S. and Lindenburn, S. (2012) 'Foreign language vocabulary development through activities in an online 3D environment', *The Language Learning Journal*, 40(1): 99–112.

Peterson, M. (2001) 'MOOs and second language acquisition: Towards a rationale for MOO-based learning', *Computer Assisted Language Learning*, 14(5): 443–459.

Peterson, M. (2006) 'Learner interaction management in an avatar and chat-based virtual world', *Computer Assisted Language Learning*, 19(1): 79–103.

Peterson, M. (2010) 'Learner participation patterns and strategy use in second life: An exploratory case study', *ReCALL*, 22(3): 273–292.

Peterson, M. (2011) 'Toward a research agenda for the use of three-dimensional virtual worlds in language learning', *CALICO Journal*, 29(1): 67–80.

Peterson, M. (2012) 'EFL learner collaborative interaction in Second Life', *ReCALL*, 24(1): 20–39.

Peterson, M. (2013) *Computer Games and Language Learning*, New York, NY: Palgrave Macmillan.

Porte, G. (2013) 'Who needs replication?', *CALICO Journal*, 30(1): 10–15.

Schneider, J. and Von der Emde, S. (2000) 'Brave new (virtual world): Transforming language learning into cultural studies through online learning environments (MOOs)', *ADFL Bulletin*, 32(1): 18–26.

Schwienhorst, K. (2002a) 'Evaluating tandem language learning in the MOO: Discourse repair strategies in a bilingual Internet project', *Computer Assisted Language Learning*, 15(2): 135–145.

Schwienhorst, K. (2002b) 'The state of VR: A meta-analysis of virtual reality tools in second language acquisition', *Computer Assisted Language Learning*, 15(3): 221–239.

Shield, L. (2003) 'MOO as a language learning tool', in U. Felix (ed), *Online Language Learning: Towards Best Practice*, Amsterdam, Netherlands: Swets & Zeitlinger: 97–122.

Smith, B. (2003) 'Computer-mediated negotiated interaction: An expanded model', *The Modern Language Journal*, 87(1): 38–57.

Stevens, V. (2006) 'Second Life in education and language learning', *TESL-EJ*, 10(3), available: http://www.tesl-ej.org/ej39/int.html

Svensson, P. (2003) 'Virtual worlds as arenas for language learning', in U. Felix (ed), *Online Language Learning: Towards Best Practice*, Amsterdam, Netherlands: Swets & Zeitlinger: 123–142.

Sykes, J., Oskoz, A. and Thorne, S.L. (2008) 'Web 2.0, Synthetic Immersive Environments, and Mobile Resources for Language Education', *CALICO Journal*, 25(3): 528–546.

Thorne, S.L. (2008) 'Transcultural communication in open Internet environments and massively multiplayer online games', in S. Magan (ed), *Mediating Discourse Online*, Amsterdam, Netherlands: John Benjamins: 305–327.

Thorne, S.L., Black, W. and Sykes, J.M. (2009) 'Second language use, socialization, and learning in Internet interest communities and online gaming', *The Modern Language Journal*, 93(1): 802–821.

Toyoda, E. and Harrison, R. (2002) 'Categorization of text chat communication between learners and native speakers of Japanese', *Language Learning & Technology*, 6(1): 82–99.

University of Missouri–St. Louis (1997) *MundoHispano*, available: http://www.umsl.edu/~moosproj/mundo.html (accessed 24 Oct 2014).

Vassar College. (1998) *MOOssiggang*, available: http://german.vassar.edu/projects/moossiggang.html (accessed 24 Oct 2014).

Von der Emde, S., Schneider, J. and Kötter, M. (2001) 'Technically speaking: Transforming language learning through virtual learning environments (MOOs)', *The Modern Language Journal*, 85(2): 211–225.

Warner, C.N. (2004) 'It's just a game right? Types of play in foreign language CMC', *Language Learning & Technology*, 8(2): 69–87.

Wehner, A.K., Gump, A.W. and Downey, S. (2011) 'The effects of Second Life on the motivation of undergraduate students learning a foreign language', *Computer Assisted Language Learning*, 24(3): 277–289.

# 23
# Online and blended language learning

*Pete Sharma and Kevin Westbrook*

The Internet has changed the teaching and learning of languages forever. Increasing numbers of language learners are opting to take online language courses, either wholly web-based or blended, that is, distance combined with a face-to-face (F2F) classroom component. The extent to which effective language learning can take place in an online environment, and whether blended learning offers more successful outcomes than either F2F courses or wholly online courses, has been much debated. First, we examine how language learning in online learning (OL) and blended learning (BL) contexts is informed by theory, and review the literature of blended learning. Next we draw on the literature in order to describe the practicalities of teaching OL and BL. We then illustrate OL and BL through a number of case studies. Finally, we argue that these terms, while open to interpretation, remain relevant and useful for language teachers.

## Theory

Defining OL and BL can be problematic. BL in particular has a wide range of definitions, some of which can apply to purely classroom learning, or purely distance learning.

'The integrated combination of traditional learning with web based on-line approaches' (Oliver and Trigwell 2005: 17) can be viewed as the classical definition of BL. Variations include a 'mixture of face-to-face . . . and distance learning' (Frendo 2005: 40) and 'combining e-learning with f2f' (Smith and Baber 2005: 13). The definition we will use here is:

> A course designed as a mix of face-to-face and distance learning, with both elements being an important part of the whole.

Other common definitions describe BL as 'the combination of media and tools employed in an e-learning environment' (Oliver and Trigwell 2005: 17) and 'the combination of a number of pedagogic approaches, irrespective of the learning technology used' (Oliver and Trigwell 2005: 17) – definitions which can be applied to both purely classroom and wholly distance courses. There is an argument that the term is, in fact, redundant, as very few courses designed in recent years would not fit a definition of BL, thus making it a term that defines the norm, not the exception. However, we believe that it remains a useful concept, given that there is still widespread uncertainty surrounding it.

Whereas BL has a range of specific definitions, OL is a vaguer concept. Felix (2003: 8) identifies 'two major forms of online learning' as follows: 'Stand-alone online courses that strive to operate as virtual classrooms' and 'add-on activities to classroom teaching or distance education courses in which technology is used primarily as a tool and a communication device'. Moore, Dickson-Deane and Galyen (2011: 130) come to the conclusion that many authors see a relationship between the terms 'distance learning' and 'online learning'. NIACE (2005: 1) defines online learning as 'formal or informal learning that involves purposeful use of the Internet for educational content delivery or support'.

We identify an overlap here between BL and OL. The definitions we have found cover situations where students are being taught synchronously using tools such as Skype, Adobe Connect, Wiziq and Blackboard Collaborate – in effect, face-to-face learning at a distance – as well as situations that include anything that does not take place in the classroom. We will, therefore, focus our discussion on what we consider to be the most important areas where BL and OL differ from the solely F2F situation.

The clearest areas of difference are those that are affected by distance and time, in particular, motivation and autonomy. Figure 23.1 illustrates these two concepts.

Having established working definitions for OL and BL, we will now cover some of the language learning theories that underpin language learning and technology as it relates to OL and BL.

Whether a course is partially or completely conducted with the learner outside of the classroom, greater responsibility is placed on the learner and their ability to learn autonomously. Both Nunan (1997: 201) and Godwin-Jones (2011: 4) stress that learners are often ill-equipped to learn in an autonomous manner, and emphasise that time needs to be allowed to provide guidance. Consideration should also be given to starting with a low level of autonomy demands and gradually increasing them with appropriate support, following a scheme such as that proposed by Nunan (1997: 195). It also means that suitable, on-demand support must be available. This includes access to assistance from the teacher and also to technology support when things fail to work as expected: the most motivated student will have to give up if they cannot get the technology to work.

Given the integral nature of the distance element of a BL course, motivation is vital. It underpins any autonomous behaviour and is especially important in a distance learning environment. One problem with trying to address motivation directly in a BL environment is the multiplicity of motivations within a group, allied with the different theories of motivation, making it difficult

| Same time, same place (e.g. traditional classroom, F2F) | Different time, different place Asynchronous (e.g. email, forums) |
|---|---|
| Same time, different place Synchronous (e.g. chat, virtual classrooms) | Different time, same place (e.g. messages left in a self-access centre) |

*Figure 23.1* Blended learning: Synchronous and asynchronous communication

to directly address individuals' motivation. Intrinsic motivation can be successfully addressed (Bate, Robertson and Smart 2003: 30) by making material relevant to the learner (see later). Extrinsic motivation can be provided by making face-to-face activities reliant on the completion of distance activities. For example: 'In the next lesson we will discuss the best place to go on holiday. Research a holiday destination and prepare arguments for this being the best place'. This kind of motivation can be strengthened by linking the distance activities to some form of assessment. However, Lim, Morris and Kupritz (2006: 809) point out that online learning (defined in this case as learning that takes place using a computer network) has a limited ability to engage learners who are not already self-motivated.

Second language acquisition (SLA) refers to the processes by which learners acquire a new language. A clear link has been established between the conditions for learning implied by SLA research and the types of activities which learners encounter when using typical interactive exercises delivered across learning platforms. Willis (1996: 11) outlines three essential conditions as: exposure, opportunities for real use of language, and motivation; and also a further desirable condition: instruction, in order to focus on form. Brett (1995: 77) argued that multimedia 'may prove to be a useful tool for second language learning' since programs provide motivation; authentic tasks provide exposure; and subtitled video can facilitate intake through form-focused tasks. Multimedia offers learners choice as to how they work through a programme or how many times to revisit an exercise. In that BL offers variety, studies about learner styles and modalities are also relevant, as is work on learner strategies.

However, scepticism is often expressed over the types of 'noncommunicative' exercise found in some online materials; such programmes can at best offer only guided practice. Much web-based material has been criticised for providing mechanical drills. Critics claim they draw on largely discredited behaviourist theories of learning. Hubbard and Levy (Chapter 2 this volume) suggest that second language acquisition theories have a central role within the theoretical sources used in computer-assisted language learning (CALL). The three that they describe as being most prominent are all based on interaction. There is wide scope for different forms of interactivity (spoken, written, synchronous, asynchronous, audio, video, graphical) in a BL context, with learners engaged in online exercises which provide feedback. Interactivity outside the classroom can allow time for thinking, rewriting, reflection and so forth that can be very beneficial to learners who find F2F activities with no thinking time quite difficult.

Walker and White (2013) describe with the arrival of the Internet, how the role the computer plays in learning now includes computer-mediated communication (CMC). 'Sociocultural theories of learning argue that learning occurs more effectively when people are working together' (Walker and White 2013: 6), an opportunity provided by the Internet, with learners dispersed across the world, coming together in a collaborative environment such as a virtual classroom. Walker and White (2013) describe the concept of community, which is important in online language learning.

Interactivity can be explicit in activities that involve discussion forums, wiki and blog writing and so forth, or it can be more subtle where comments are invited from classmates on online activities such as pinboard sites, individual blogs or podcasts. Interactivity is arguably less well supported by a purely synchronous OL programme. The time factor is similar to F2F lessons, and the range of forms of interactivity is limited by the time available and the resources offered by the platform being used.

Relevance is considered a key factor (Bate et al. 2003: 30; Arnold 2008: 3) in improving learning, especially among adult learners, and blended learning provides greater opportunities to make this possible. Providing activities that are relevant to the learner's context and personal preferences is both a function of course/materials design and of opportunity. Where activities are done at a distance, learners have the possibility of incorporating sources and information that are relevant to them, which would be very difficult to do in a classroom environment and which, even if possible, would consume large amounts of contact time that could be better used in other ways. Providing participants with the flexibility to choose when and where they do an activity can be very beneficial, especially to those who are not in full-time education. Inputs can be consumed while commuting, during a break or even while jogging, for example. This is clearly a specific difference between F2F-only courses and BL, and not only makes it more likely that the individual will listen to/watch/read the material, it also releases valuable F2F time for activities where the presence of the teacher can be most useful. One caveat here is that if tasks are viewed as optional, uptake may be lower.

We have mentioned some of the learning theories which underpin OL and BL. We now turn to the literature of BL and OL. Blended learning has a long history in the corporate sector (Driscoll 2002; Bonk and Graham 2006), and extensive research also exists in the tertiary area (Oliver and Trigwell 2005; Sharpe, Benfield and Francis 2006). In language learning, Barrett and Sharma (2007) and Dudeney and Hockly (2007) explore the term within ELT (English language teaching) contexts. For example, Barrett and Sharma (2007: 10–11) discuss the interactive feedback given to language learners using the Macmillan English campus learning platform; Dudeney and Hockly (2007: 138–143) explore course design for online language learning.

Gruba and Hinkelman (2012) describe four considerations for blended approaches: purpose, appropriateness, multimodality and sustainability. Regarding purpose, they 'advocate BL approaches be introduced in an incremental manner, keeping in mind a raft of related concepts' (2012: 8). Regarding appropriateness, they suggest 'pedagogies, processes and content levels (should be) suitable to the academic context' (2012: 9). Concerning multimodality, they suggest BL maintains a balance between F2F and electronic and print-mediated modalities, and that it is varied, so the technologies encompass a range of options: digital material is authorable, and it should be comprehensible to learners. Finally, concerning sustainability, they suggest 'resources are managed in ways that seek to ensure long-term results' (2012: 11).

The key question, whether blended approaches lead to better learning outcomes, should in our view be the central concern of educators. While much anecdotal evidence exists that BL produces better outcomes, there is still more to be done. Neumeier wrote (2005: 163) 'that a systematic investigation into the factors that shape the Blended Learning (BL) experience in the context of language learning and teaching is missing and urgently needed'. This is a daunting task. Scientific research techniques, where blended classes and/or online classes are compared with nonblended classes in terms of achievement, leave much to be desired, as 'classrooms are far too complex to control all the variables required in experimental types of research' (Allright and Bailey cited in Gruba and Hinkelman 2012: 74). Reports on the efficacy of BL and OL approaches from the US Department of Education such as that produced by Means, Toyama, Murphy, Bakia and Jones (2010) are not primarily situated within language learning contexts, and claims about the superiority of BL and online learning need to be taken cautiously.

Stracke's study (2007: 3) of a blended language learning (BLL) environment lists 'the most important qualities of the successful BLL environment, as valued by the learners' as including 'a teacher's presence and guidance'. We believe that teachers should be concerned with the interconnectedness of what happens in the classroom and what happens in the distance mode. For example, in the teaching of grammar, teachers concern themselves with fuzzy areas of language, while crisp areas are dealt with using programmable, self-access software. Within online contexts, the teacher orchestrates the course. Many purely self-study programmes have high dropout rates, and the absence of the teacher may be a key factor in this.

Many of the arguments revolving around BL and OL are common to those relating to the use of technology in language teaching in general. The argument is no longer about whether a given approach is better, but about the way in which the learning experience can be enhanced in some way by such approaches. We will now focus on the practicalities of teaching a blended course, and teaching online.

## From theory to practice

We have previously identified useful definitions for blended and online teaching. We described some of the theories which have impacted on these ways of teaching. We will now examine the factors to be taken into account when setting up successful blended or online courses.

There are many contexts for BL. We agree with Lamping (2004: 7) that 'there is, of course, no single perfect blend – the concept is grounded on the notion of flexibility'. Whittaker and Tomlinson (2013) present forty case studies involving BL, including tertiary, English for academic purposes (EAP), English for specific purposes (ESP) and business English. These involve using a learning platform housing publisher-produced content, or an educational social media platform, like Edmodo. Similarly, there are many contexts for online learning, from freelance teachers using Skype and online schools such as Global English to MOOCs, or massive open online courses (see Hanson-Smith, Chapter 15 this volume for more on MOOCs).

Rather than constantly pursue a mythical 'perfect blend', we suggest practitioners recognise the multiplicity of course types and work through the practical checklist for those wishing to create blended courses provided by Whittaker and Tomlinson (2013: 243). This has four stages: examination of context, course design, considerations about learners and teachers and evaluation. We will summarise key points from each stage.

Stage one – context. The first thing to decide on are the reasons for blending. Whittaker and Tomlinson (2013) note a high degree of agreement between the reasons given in the literature for blending and the reasons given by language providers in the case studies they describe, in particular with regard to increased access, flexibility and 'improved pedagogy' (2013: 14). The latter is often cited, but it is difficult to pin down what is meant and it is generally left unsupported. They explore additional reasons such as motivation, autonomy, collaboration and market reach and experiential learning.

Stage two – course design. This involves deciding what you are going to blend. The two modes which are generally under consideration are 'face-to-face' and 'technology'. The technology may be computer-assisted language learning or online. Whittaker (2013) adds a third mode, that of self-study. The choices to be made include deciding on the lead mode. Typically, this is the face-to-face mode, which is frequently used to present language, with the online mode used to consolidate. Practical considerations include timetabling: the optimal length of sessions and how the modes complement each other. Variety is important, 'so as to appeal to as many learning styles as possible' (Whittaker 2013: 233). 'Getting the balance right in terms of time spent on each of the modes, and the way they are integrated, is significant' (Whittaker 2013: 19).

Stage three – learners and teachers. 'The learners and teachers play [. . .] a key role in any blend' (Whittaker 2013: 235). Both may need support in the move towards a blended approach (Whittaker 2013: 235).

Stage four – evaluating the blend. Designers will 'need to determine which aspects of the blend to evaluate' (Whittaker 2013: 239). Many areas can be evaluated, such as the choice of software, the balance of time spent on each mode, teacher and student attitudes, and exploring the effects on student achievement.

Sharma (2014) argues that successful blended learning involves three essential ingredients 'appropriacy, integration and attitude'. Concerning appropriacy, Stacey and Gerbic (cited in Murphy and Southgate 2011: 21) agree that 'any combination should be based on an understanding of the strengths and weaknesses of the tools as well as their appropriateness to the learners involved'. For example, classroom discussions are ideal to promote fluency, whereas deeper, critical thinking is best developed in a forum, giving students time to draft and edit a reply before posting.

Integration of the face-to-face and distance elements accords with the notion of complementarity, as described by Marsh (2012: 6), who states 'it is important for different "ingredients" of the blend to complement each other'. Attitude, linked to teacher beliefs (Freeman 1989), is critical, as it is often the teacher's job to communicate to students the validity of a blended approach positively.

We have described the practicalities of setting up blended courses. We now examine online teaching. Purely OL courses exhibit certain differences to F2F classroom teaching that Hannum (2001: 13–19) summarised in three categories: logistical, instructional and economic, with advantages and disadvantages in each category. Advantages include the fact that physical premises and travelling are not required and there are reduced delivery costs. Disadvantages include connection speeds, which remains an issue in large parts of the world. Other disadvantages are limitations on interaction compared to F2F and the learning curve for using the tools (see Kern and Malinowski, Chapter 14 this volume).

Fein and Logan (2003: 51) explore the challenges for OL instructors. They mention the additional skills necessary, such as knowledge of the different tools in use for OL (including virtual whiteboards, chat streams and application sharing). The instructor needs to recognise different indications of the students' involvement, due to the lack of body language. Monitoring student engagement and checking for questions, either in a chat stream or via a 'hands up' system, can be quite demanding. The instructor will also need to be able to help with technical difficulties.

When faced with the daunting move from teaching in a classroom to teaching online, it is important to establish first to what extent the course you are delivering is part of a blended solution or whether it is 100% online. Hockly and Clandfield (2010) describe a range of scenarios: mainly face-to-face, half-and-half, mainly online and fully online. They mention that 'liveware', the online tutor, plays a critical role in the success of a course. Salmon (2002) offers a useful five-stage framework for teaching and learning online, outlining progression from getting familiar with the tools to the eventual construction of knowledge building.

According to Warnecke and Lominé (2012: 127), 'the adoption of synchronous online tools has revolutionised course design and delivery'. They provide a helpful checklist of the most common tools in synchronous online conferencing. According to Green et al. (2011: 169), asynchronous online tools 'exploit potential learner enthusiasm for communication'. These tools allow 'learners to work both individually and together', developing learning independence. They provide a useful framework for potential online tutors, consisting of questions, such as 'what functions do I want the tool (forum/wiki/blog) to perform?' and deciding on how much time should be spent by tutors and students in writing, reading and responding to online contributions.

In this section, we have provided an essentially practical checklist for setting up blended and online courses. In the next two sections, we will look at such courses in practice.

## Online learning: Case studies

We will describe the experiences of two institutions running online language courses. The five following cases reflect the diversity of language teaching within online and blended contexts, and are situated in a range of contexts and locations. They are not academic studies, but they are intended to show OL and BL in action.

## Case study: Net Languages

Net Languages is an online language school, based in Barcelona, which produces and sells online language courses. It was established in 1998. Net Languages uses its own learner management system (LMS), custom developed to provide users with an easy-to-use interface to access course materials, communication tools and reporting systems. Tutors on the courses work from home as well as from company premises. The courses are structured, ready-to-go online courses created by the institution. The exercises are created using specific templates common in online learning, and include twenty-five different types of exercises including mix and match, type-in and multiple choice. The materials include text, video and audio files. Students enrol from across the world and are given an access code for their specific course of study.

One of the successful course series which Net Languages offers is English for Work, which is designed for people who need to use English in the workplace. Communication with customers using these modules showed a need for a module which would help people to deal more effectively with the public in English. Market research was carried out to establish the course content, which had to be suitable for people working in different cultural contexts.

The course module consists of six sections and includes twenty-two to twenty-five hours of study time. There are two modules, one for students at B1 level and another for students at B2 level (Common European Framework of Reference). Students complete the material at their own pace, although courses do have a fixed start and end date. At the end of three of the sections, they contact their tutor to arrange an online speaking tutorial, thirty minutes long. This is an open-ended, personalised role play which provides learners with the chance to put the language they have been working on in the online interactive exercises into practice.

In order to be able to analyse its success, a feedback form was included at the end of the module. This, and feedback from training managers and tutors, showed the popularity of the module and indicated a high level of satisfaction among both students and tutors. It identified two areas requiring attention:

1   The positioning of the final speaking tutorial at the end of the last section of the course put unnecessary pressure on the tutors to schedule in the tutorials, as many students only complete the course at the last minute.
2   One section called 'introductions and greetings' was set in a context which many students felt was irrelevant to them. The context was highlighted in the description of the course objectives, focusing students' attention unnecessarily on this rather than the language being practised.

This example of a wholly online course shows the importance of continuous evaluation, as feedback led to both issues being rectified. It also provides insights into learner motivation.

## Case study: The Ceibal English Project

Uruguay lacks trained teachers of English in its primary school system with only 150 trained teachers for 120,000 pupils in years four to six of primary school.

The British Council successfully bid for the Ceibal English Project, which consists of two elements. First, online language improvement for classroom teachers, using the LearnEnglish

Pathways (LEP) course. Second, remote teaching using telepresence technology, using teachers in Argentina, the UK, Uruguay and the Philippines who deliver a forty-five-minute lesson each week to children in primary schools in real time via a fifty-inch screen. The classroom teachers are themselves learning English alongside the children, and teach two forty-five-minute practice lessons each week, following up on what the remote teacher taught. The course for primary pupils is blended in that part is taught via videoconferencing and part is taught face-to-face by class teachers with very limited knowledge of the language content. For this to work, lesson content has to be quite tightly scripted. To achieve this, the LEP course was tailored to the needs of the Uruguayan class teachers including translating the instructions for the lower levels into Spanish. For the children, a team of four Argentinian materials writers produced detailed lesson plans for the remote lessons, taught by remote teachers, and for the practice lessons – making use of Learn English Kids materials and specially produced audio and video clips downloaded onto the pupils' OLPC (one laptop per child) laptops.

It was essential for the remote and classroom teachers to work as a team. The Filipino teachers needed a 120-hour Spanish course to enable them to communicate effectively with the Uruguayan classroom teachers. It was necessary to motivate the classroom teachers to first log onto the LEP course, and then not to drop out. This involved a team of e-moderators, who provided online clinics and asynchronous support via Facebook groups and email. Class teachers were further motivated by receipt of a certificate on completion of each level of the LEP course.

To date, evaluation of the LEP course has involved tracking how many teachers have completed each level of the course. The dropout rate has been lower than anticipated, although 30% of teachers never logged on. Student progress was measured by achievement tests. Results to date show that all groups have made significant progress.

The pupils are clearly learning English through the combination of a trained and qualified remote teacher and a classroom teacher with very limited content knowledge but who acts as a guide and facilitator, pointing them to materials on their laptops and practising content introduced by the remote teacher. There has been a lower dropout rate for the LEP course for classroom teachers than might normally be expected for a largely online course.

This case clearly shows the realisation of the part motivation plays in successful delivery of online courses, and the need for teacher training. It involves a groundbreaking approach to the use of technologies across continents and clearly demonstrates the need to consider not only materials development when designing a new course but also teacher training.

## Blended learning case studies

We will describe the experiences of three institutions running blended learning courses.

### Case study: Laureate

Laureate International Universities is a private international network of degree-granting post-secondary institutions. This network includes over seventy-five institutions in thirty countries, operating both campus-based and online programs. Enrolment exceeds 800,000 students.

Laureate saw BL as an opportunity to promote learner autonomy, as students tend to be dependent on the teacher for explanations, as a way of providing better and more time-efficient learning outcomes, and of encouraging learners to see the classroom as a place of activity rather than of academic study.

Cambridge University Press's Touchstone product was selected for reasons of design. This is an example of study using publisher-produced online materials. Touchstone is a four-level series covering beginner to intermediate levels (Common European Framework of Reference [CEFR]: A1–B2). Interactive content is based on research into the Cambridge English Corpus (see Caines, McCarthy and O'Keeffe, Chapter 25 this volume). There are three modes of study: print, blended (print + online workbook) and premium blended (print + online workbook + online course).

Blended learning was based on the premise of student online preparation followed by language production and personalisation in F2F sessions. Implementation involved three phases:

Phase 1: students were provided with online content and urged to use it to prepare for class. Less than 5% of students actually accessed the platform; there was no real change.

Phase 2: students were given weekly deadlines to complete that week's unit. The completion of this work was a prerequisite for doing the corresponding unit quiz. This added compulsion resulted in 95% of students completing the work prior to the deadline. However, very few students did the work prior to the class, but rather, they procrastinated, doing the work in a marathon five-hour session prior to the deadline, which was not deemed an effective way to assimilate content.

Phase 3: involved three deadlines during the week, requiring students to study the content prior to the F2F class. Teachers verified completion of the work prior to the class, awarding points according to an established rubric.

In a student satisfaction survey, students were pleased with the change to phase 3, and welcomed the imposition of deadlines. Students felt a positive impact on the face-to-face learning, with classes becoming 'more dynamic and enjoyable'. Teachers designed classes with the assumption that students had received the language input and proceeded directly to practice and production tasks. They no longer felt the need to 'cover' course book content and were able to run activities activating what was studied online. Students reported improvements in language performance and confidence, although some concerns remain about the workload of the online preparation.

This case shows a change in the F2F experience. It is interesting because the lead mode here is online, with the material providing input. The fact that phases 1 and 2 were deemed unsuccessful bears out the fact that online is less successful when it is viewed as an optional add-on. It also highlights the need for continuous review.

## Case study: Go English

Go English has been providing BL learning services to corporate clients in Spain since 2007. Blended learning is seen as offering benefits to large companies with offices and employees spread over large geographical locations in terms of training management, quality assurance, course and content delivery, learning objectives and verifiable/comparable learning outcomes. Other benefits identified by the provider were the possibility of self-paced learning; flexibility in terms of time and space; relinquishing of some control to the learner as to what they study and when; and providing learners with engaging multimodal content which would be impossible in the classroom context.

A decision was made to use the English360 Platform by T-Systems. This is an example of an open platform, which allows the designing and creating of content using various templates and dovetailing this tailored content with Cambridge-authorised materials. It provides authoring tools and communication tools, such as private and group messaging, and a forum. All progress can be monitored effectively and remedial action taken where necessary.

Courses ran from October 2012 to July 2013 with a total of fifty hours of F2F tuition (ninety minutes per week over thirty-four weeks) and around sixty hours of online content, divided into eight units of study. Learners were evaluated on the retention of different language and vocabulary covered in the course, and on their language skills in reference to what is expected of learners at their level on the CEFR. Learners' completion rates of the online content and attendance in the F2F class were taken into account in the final evaluation of learners. A prerequisite of 70% completion of online content and a minimum attendance rate of 60% in the F2F class was required for learners to pass the course. Of 300 participants, 90 respondents answered the end-of-course survey. In general, the response from learners was positive in terms of the usefulness of the course. Of the learners who responded:

- Sixty-seven percent agreed or strongly agreed that the course class content and online content were fully integrated.
- Sixty-seven percent agreed or strongly agreed that the online content was useful for their work.
- Sixty-two percent agreed or strongly agreed that they enjoyed the course.

Most learners had participated in traditional F2F language training prior to joining the blended programme. Feedback indicated some resistance to the change partly due to the negative perceptions of these learners of computer-based learning, a feeling of having their training reduced by their company, as face-to-face time was effectively halved, and/or resentment of the fact that they were expected to complete the language learning online in their own time.

This case shows the suitability of customising the digital content of courses for business English learners. Again, the importance of training teachers to work with the platform was recognised, and in this instance resulted in the creation of a teacher training course run using English360, allowing teachers to experience the platform from a learner's perspective.

## Case study: AVO-Bell

AVO-Bell Language and Examination Centre, Sofia, was established in 1990. The centre has been designing and providing blended courses since 2007. Blended learning was introduced to respond to changing students' attitudes. Feedback from focus groups and end-of-course questionnaires showed a desire for language courses providing more flexibility in terms of virtual classes and F2F sessions. Another reason was to improve the effectiveness of courses by incorporating online and interactive components to provide individual, extra language practice on specific areas of weakness. The course, based on published materials (Market Leader, Longman), combines three modes:

1. virtual classes, once a week in the evening;
2. F2F sessions at the weekend;
3. online, interactive course materials – available 24/7.

The course required 70% session attendance covering at least 70% of the online material. The course book VLE (virtual learning environment) allows for the assignment of whole-class, small-group and individual tasks. Students are given access to all the materials (units) at different stages, depending on lesson aims. There are two main approaches:

## Approach one

- input during the virtual classroom, followed by the assignment of online homework for controlled and semi-controlled practice;
- F2F sessions – freer/free practice, with a focus on oral production;
- online work – consolidation, production.

## Approach two

- pretasks – usually reading/listening activities on the platform;
- virtual classroom – elicitation of the target language based on the pretasks, input, controlled practice;
- online work – controlled practice, semi-controlled practice;
- F2F sessions – freer practice, production.

The approach and the procedure varied depending on the lesson aims and needs analysis. Moodle was chosen as the learning platform, an open-source platform for delivering content, assessment and tracking. The Big Blue Button feature was added, which provides synchronous communication during the virtual classes. The same final test was given to the BL groups and entirely face-to-face groups at the same level. Both groups used the same course book: a print version in F2F classes and the online course book in blended courses. Results suggested that more progress was made by the blended learning groups (see Table 23.1).

Students reported that they enjoyed the atmosphere in both virtual and face-to-face classes, expressing surprise at the positive learning atmosphere which also existed online. Among other benefits perceived was the fact that students received more individual and frequent feedback from their tutors through a variety of channels. The virtual classroom allowed for deepening a particular topic, vivid discussions, and active reflection. This course demonstrates the complex interplay between online and F2F elements, and a high degree of flexibility in the way a given course can be delivered. The virtual classes and F2F classes are interconnected. The test results show that positive outcomes are possible within blended contexts.

*Table 23.1* Test results, general English courses, Level B2, January 2014

|  | Traditional course | Blended course |
| --- | --- | --- |
| Reading | 75% | 82% |
| Listening | 78% | 90% |
| Language systems | 66% | 76% |
| Writing | 72% | 76% |
| Speaking | 74% | 78% |

## Current and future trends

We have illustrated through five very different cases many of the theoretical issues surrounding blended and online courses, concerning the pursuit of better learning outcomes, flexibility, learner motivation, customisation, feedback and the impact on teacher training. In this section, we examine current and future trends.

Current discussions in BL include consideration of the 'flipped classroom'. Flipping involves moving the input given in class to preclass work. Students receive input through videos, PowerPoint presentations or podcasts beforehand. In class, they engage with content by asking questions, discussions and individual work with the teacher. Current discussions in OL revolve around MOOCs. These are massive open online courses, which can be taken by anyone anywhere over the Internet. The British Council are trialling the use of MOOCs for language learning (see http://blog.britishcouncil.org/2014/08/14/how-thousands-of-people-can-join-an-english-language-online-course-for-free/).

M-learning (mobile learning; see Stockwell, Chapter 21 this volume) is relevant here, since nowadays many students bring smartphones and tablets to class and therefore have access to their learning materials and platforms on such devices. The future of blended learning is therefore inextricably bound with m-learning. Dudeney, Hockly and Pegrum (2013: 38) describe one result of the rise of mobile as 'learning spreading into wirelessly networked physical spaces anywhere in the world. This is part of the promise of m-learning, or more accurately perhaps, u-learning'.

We have mentioned that many platforms track useful detail regarding learners' use. As VLEs develop, we believe that more such data will be available, and may be linked to further attempts to prove the elusive statement 'blended is best' through quantitative studies aiming to show better outcomes. We believe such statements should continue to be viewed with caution. The qualitative feedback from learners and teachers will continue to be relevant.

Whittaker (2013: 19) states: 'Clearly more studies to investigate the pedagogical effectiveness of blended learning in ELT are required that provide us with empirical rather than impressionistic evidence in its favour'. Johnson and Marsh, writing about Laureate (2013: 53), say the university 'has acknowledged that research is central to informed decision making in order to provide for effective blended learning'. While we agree to some extent with these statements, we also believe that the rich variety of contexts for BL mean that no single study can be applied universally.

The search for a single definition of the term blended learning is, in our view, illusory. Gruba and Hinkelman (2012: 159) suggest 'blended learning is a transitory phenomenon that may [...] disappear soon, simply to be replaced by "learning"'. This echoes Bax's (2003) use of the term 'normalisation'. However, we have delineated clear differences between classroom activities and distance learning. These differences will continue to be relevant to language teachers, and the term 'blended' for mixing F2F and online will remain a useful term.

## Acknowledgements

The authors would like to thank a number of people and institutions for their invaluable help in providing data: Paul Woods and Graham Stanley, British Council Uruguay; James Hoyle, Timothy Crook and Catherine Maughan, Go English, Spain; Cleve Miller, English360, Fiona Thomas, Net Languages, Spain; Nataliya Yordanova, AVO-Bell, Bulgaria; Daniel Lowe, Unitec, Honduras.

## Further reading

Gruba, P. and Hinkelman, D. (2012) *Blended Learning Technologies in Second Language Classrooms*, Basingstoke: Palgrave Macmillan.
   Highly academic, in-depth analysis of blended learning.
Hockly, N., with Clandfield, L. (2010) *Teaching Online*, Surrey: Delta.
   Highly practical teaching guide for teaching languages online.
Nicolson, M., Murphy, L. and Southgate, M. (eds) (2011) *Language Teaching in Blended Contexts*, Edinburgh: Dunedin.
   Academic book which draws on the experience of the writing team at the OU (Open University, UK).
Whittaker, C. and Tomlinson, B. (eds) (2013) *Blended Learning in English Language Teaching: Course Design and Implementation*, London, UK: British Council.
   Compendium of practical case studies in a variety of language teaching contexts.

## References

Arnold, L. (2008) 'Experiential work-integrated online learning: Insights from an established UK Higher Education Program', *Innovate – Journal of Online Education*, 4(3): 5, available: http://www.innovateonline.info/index.php?view=article&id=494&action=article (accessed 13 Feb 2008).

Barrett, B. and Sharma, P. (2007) *Blended Learning: Using Technology in and Beyond the Language Classroom*, Oxford: Macmillan.

Bate, F., Robertson, I. and Smart, L. (2003) *Exploring Educational Design: A Snapshot of Eight Case Studies Using E-Learning in Australian VET*, Brisbane: Australian National Training Authority, available: http://flexiblelearning.net.au/projects/resources/educational-design.pdf (accessed 3 Jun 2014).

Bax, S. (2003) 'CALL – Past, present and future' *System*, 31(1): 13–28.

Bonk, C.J. and Graham, C.R. (eds) (2006) *Handbook of Blended Learning: Global Perspectives, Local Designs*, San Francisco, CA: Jossey-Bass.

Brett, P. (1995) 'Multimedia for listening comprehension: The design of a multimedia-based resource for developing listening skills', *System*, 2(1): 77–85.

Driscoll, M. (2002) 'Blended learning: Let's get beyond the hype', http://www-07.ibm.com, available: http://www-07.ibm.com/services/pdf/blended_learning.pdf (accessed 5 Jul 2009).

Dudeney, G. and Hockly, N. (2007) *How to . . . Teach English with Technology*, Harlow, UK: Pearson Education Limited.

Dudeney, G., Hockly, N. and Pegrum, M. (2013) *Digital Literacies*, Harlow, UK: Pearson.

Fein, A.D. and Logan, M.C. (2003) 'Preparing instructors for online instruction', *New Directions for Adult and Continuing Education*, 100: 45–55, available: http://onlinelibrary.wiley.com/doi/10.1002/ace.118/abstract (accessed 21 May 2014).

Felix, U. (ed) (2003) *Language Learning Online: Towards Best Practice*, Lisse, Netherlands: Swets & Zeitlinger B.V.

Freeman, D. (1989) 'Teacher training, development and decision making: A model of teaching and related strategies for language teacher education', *TESOL Quarterly*, 23(1): 27–45.

Frendo, E. (2005) *How to Teach Business English*, Harlow, UK: Longman.

Godwin-Jones, R. (2011) 'Emerging technologies: autonomous language learning' *Language Learning & Technology*, 15(3): 4–11, available: http://llt.msu.edu/issues/october2011/ (accessed 15 Jan 2014).

Green, H. St. John, E., Warnecke, S. and Atkinson, V. (2011) 'Asynchronous online teaching', in M. Nicolson, L. Murphy and M. Southgate (eds), *Language Teaching in Blended Contexts*, Edinburgh: Dunedin.

Gruba, P. and Hinkelman, D. (2012) *Blended Learning Technologies in Second Language Classrooms*, Basingstoke, UK: Palgrave Macmillan.

Hannum, W. (2001) 'Web-based training: Advantages and limitations' in B.H. Khan (ed), *Web-Based Training*, Englewood Cliffs, NJ: Educational Technology Publications.

Hockly, N. and Clandfield, L. (2010) *Teaching Online Tools and Techniques, Options and Opportunities*, Surrey, UK: Delta Publishing.

Johnson, C. and Marsh, D. (2013) 'The Laureate English Program taking a research informed approach to blended learning', *Higher Learning Research Communications*, March 3(1).

Lamping, A. (2004) 'Blended language learning', http://www.bbc.co.uk, 45–55, available: http://www.bbc.co.uk/languages/tutors/blended_learning/ (accessed 3 Jun 2014).

Lim, D.H., Morris, M.L. and Kupritz, V.W. (2006) 'Online vs. blended learning: Differences in instructional outcomes and learner satisfaction', http://eric.ed.gov, available: http://eric.ed.gov/ERICWebPortal/contentdelivery/servlet/ERICServlet?accno=ED492755 (accessed 9 Nov 2007).

Marsh, D. (2012) *Blended Learning: Creating Opportunities for Language Learners*, New York, NY: Cambridge University Press.

Means B., Toyama, Y., Murphy, R., Bakia, M. and Jones, K. (2010) 'Evaluation of evidence-based practices in online learning: A meta-analysis and review of online learning studies', *U.S. Department of Education*, available: http://eprints.cpkn.ca/7/1/finalreport.pdf (accessed 3 Jun 2014).

Moore, J.L., Dickson-Deane, C. and Galyen, K. (2011) 'e-Learning, online learning, and distance learning environments: Are they the same?' *The Internet and Higher Education*, 14(2): 129–135, available: http://www.sciencedirect.com/science/article/pii/S1096751610000886 (accessed 21 May 2014).

Murphy, L. and Southgate, M. (2011) 'The nature of the "blend": Interaction of teaching modes, tools, and resources', in M. Nicolson, L. Murphy and M. Southgate (eds), *Language Teaching in Blended Contexts*, Edinburgh: Dunedin: 13–28.

Neumeier, P. (2005) 'A closer look at blended learning – Parameters for designing a blended learning environment for language teaching and learning', *ReCALL*, 17(02): 163–178.

NIACE (2005) 'What is online learning?', available: http://www.niace.org.uk, available: http://www.niace.org.uk/sites/default/files/56-What-is-online-learning.pdf (accessed 21 May 2014).

Nicolson, M., Murphy, L. and Southgate, M. (eds) (2011) *Language Teaching in Blended Contexts*, Edinburgh, New Zealand: Dunedin.

Nunan, D. (1997) 'Designing and adapting materials to encourage learner autonomy', in P. Benson and P. Voller (eds), *Autonomy and Independence in Language Learning. Applied Linguistics and Language Study*, Harlow, UK: Pearson Education Ltd.

Oliver, M. and Trigwell, K. (2005) 'Can "blended learning" be redeemed?' *E-Learning*, 2(1): 17–26, available: http://dx.doi.org/10.2304/elea.2005.2.1.2 (accessed 21 May 2010).

Salmon, G. (2002) *E-tivities: The Key to Active Online Learning*, Abingdon, UK: RoutledgeFalmer.

Sharma, P. (2014) 'Success with blended learning', http://www.teachitelt.com, available: http://www.teachitelt.com/custom_content/newsletters/TWN_Jan14_long.html

Sharpe, R., Benfield, G., Roberts, G. and Francis, R. (2006) 'The undergraduate experience of blended e-learning: A review of UK literature and practice', http://www.heacademy.ac.uk, available: http://www.heacademy.ac.uk/assets/York/documents/ourwork/research/literature_reviews/blended_elearning_exec_summary_1.pdf (accessed 5 Jul 2009).

Smith, D.G. and Baber, E. (2005) *Teaching English with Information Technology*, London, UK: Modern English Publishing.

Stracke, E (2007) 'Spotlight on blended learning: A frontier beyond learner autonomy and computer assisted language learning', in *Proceedings of the Independent Learning Association*, available: http://www.independentlearning.org/uploads/100836/ILA2007_036.pdf (accessed 8 Dec 2014).

Walker A. and White, G. (2013) *Technology Enhanced Language Learning: Connecting Theory and Practice*, Oxford: Oxford University Press.

Warnecke, S. and Lominé, L. (2011) 'Planning and preparing for synchronous online teaching', in M. Nicolson, L. Murphy and M. Southgate (eds), *Language Teaching in Blended Contexts*, Edinburgh: Dunedin: 126–139.

Whittaker, C. and Tomlinson, B. (eds) (2013) *Blended Learning in English Language Teaching: Course Design and Implementation*, London, UK: British Council.

Willis, J. (1996) *A Framework for Task-Based Learning*, Harlow, UK: Longman.

# Part IV
# Corpora and data-driven learning

# 24
# Introduction to data-driven learning

*Martin Warren*

This chapter introduces a highly innovative language learning methodology formally known as data-driven learning (Johns 1991), but usually simply referred to as DDL. This approach to language learning owes much to the development of computer readable corpora and the notion that learners of a language can also be researchers of the language they are learning. This notion of the learner as language researcher (Johns 1991: 2) is central to DDL and requires the teacher to be a facilitator of language study rather than a traditional language teacher. This form of DDL would not be possible without learners having access to corpora and an understanding of how to use corpus linguistics software. Once these basics are mastered, students need some training to enable them to analyse the raw data generated by their corpus searches. Of course, all of this places additional demands on the language teacher and students, and so the undoubtedly strong case for DDL needs to be made in order to justify its use inside and outside the language classroom. This chapter details what this entails with examples from DDL studies. It also examines the pros and cons of DDL and the logistics of implementing it. Finally, the chapter concludes with a discussion of possible future developments in DDL.

## What is DDL?

Data-driven learning (DDL) is an approach to language learning which is rooted in corpus linguistics. Corpus linguistics has become increasingly mainstream within the wider fields of linguistics and applied linguistics over the last thirty years. There are now numerous corpora freely available on the Internet, such as the 100-million-word British National Corpus (BNC) and the Corpus of Contemporary American English, COCA (over 410 million words), which are both general reference corpora; and the many specialised corpora representing different registers and genres, such as the Hong Kong Engineering Corpus (9.2 million words) and the 1.7-million-word Michigan Corpus of Academic Spoken English (see Murphy and Riordan, Chapter 28 this volume). As corpus linguistics has grown, it has become increasingly influential in English language learning and teaching, although the pace of such developments has been much slower. As language learning reference materials and activities have begun to incorporate corpus linguistics and its findings in, for example, dictionaries, grammars and textbooks, DDL has been at the centre of some of the independent language learning and language classroom developments. These new language learning and teaching methodologies have resulted in a number of related studies (see e.g. Burnard and McEnery 2000; Ghadessy, Henry and Roseberry 2001; Hunston 2002; Römer 2009; Gilquin and Granger 2010; Sripicharn 2010; Cheng 2012). A number of these specifically examine some of the ways in which DDL can be applied and the benefits of DDL to be gained by students (see e.g. Johns 1997; Tribble 1997; Sinclair 2003; Hafner and Candlin 2007; Boulton 2010; Gao 2011; Smith 2011; Lee 2011). The first proponent of DDL was Tim Johns (see e.g. 1989, 1991, 1997), then based at Birmingham University in the UK, who believed that language learners are also language researchers. This means that in order to be able to effectively learn the target language, learners need access to as much authentic linguistic data as possible (Johns 1991). Hence the term DDL given by Johns to this innovative approach to language learning, which emphasises that the authentic linguistic data are behind the conclusions reached. Both the research process and the conclusions drawn provide students with a unique and valuable deep-learning experience.

## How does DDL differ from other forms of self-directed learning?

Using corpora as the source of spoken and written texts, DDL brings to the language learner abundant examples of authentic language in use that can be studied and exploited in many ways. This is significantly different to traditional language learning and teaching because, as Chambers (2010: 345) notes, DDL 'not only uses corpus data in the preparation of language learning materials, but it gives learners access to more substantial amounts of corpus data than can be found in a dictionary, grammar or course book'. Language corpora provide instances of naturally occurring language, and corpus-linguistic methods enable exploratory and discovery learning (Bernandini 2004). This in turn facilitates autonomous learning, which is another important benefit of DDL. Even if the size of the corpora used in DDL are unable to represent all linguistic features, they are a useful resource to test intuitive claims made about a language and can serve to motivate the learning of linguistic features (Gavioli and Aston 2001).

DDL is based on the notion that language learners can be both active learners and language researchers if they are granted direct access to corpus data in order to critically analyse the data. Johns provides a useful summation of the distinguishing features of DDL:

> What distinguishes the DDL approach is the attempt to cut out the middleman as much as possible and give direct access to the data so that the learner can take part in building his or her own profiles of meanings and uses. The assumption that underlines this approach is that effective language learning is itself a form of linguistic research, and that the concordance printout offers a unique resource for the stimulation of inductive learning strategies – in particular, the strategies of perceiving similarities and differences and of hypothesis formation and testing.
>
> *(Johns 1991: 30)*

In Johns's view, therefore, 'research is too serious to be left to the researchers' (Johns 1991: 2). DDL is a 'research-then-theory' (Johns 1991: 30) approach to language learning; this is also the defining characteristic of the corpus-driven approach to language research advocated by Tognini-Bonelli (2002), among others, and is seen to be the most effective way to exploit corpora if the aim is to uncover new knowledge and develop new theories. DDL, then, is a radical departure from former approaches to language learning and requires both learners and teachers to take on new roles if it is to succeed. This is because DDL requires the dismantling of the traditional roles of learners and teachers. The teacher must take on the role of facilitator of language study and drop the role of being the sole language expert in the language learning process. Learners must take on the new role of language researcher as well as that of language learner. Johns (1991: 2) argues that assuming these new roles is at the heart of the DDL approach because 'research is too serious to be left to the researchers'.

Other distinguishing features of DDL are described by Gilquin and Granger (2010: 359), who list some of the advantages of DDL. For example, DDL brings authenticity into the language classroom and can contribute to 'vocabulary expansion and heightened awareness of language patterns' (Gilquin and Granger 2010: 359). They also note that it has a corrective function when learners compare their own language use with that of expert users in the corpus, and DDL has an important discovery element which can help to motivate students' learning and make it more enjoyable (Gilquin and Granger 2010: 359). Moreover, DDL empowers learners and this in turn can boost learners' self-esteem and confidence (Gilquin and Granger 2010: 359). O'Sullivan (2007) also makes the important and often overlooked point that DDL improves a number of generic skills such as observing, critical thinking, analysing, interpreting, comparing, drawing inferences, theorising and hypothesising, which are useful not only for language learning, but for academic study generally and in many other contexts other than formal education.

## How can DDL be applied in language classrooms?

The basic requirements for DDL are access to a corpus or corpora and software with which to conduct searches. In practice, DDL activities can range from teacher-mediated (see e.g. Boulton 2010) to those that position the language learner as language researcher (see e.g. Cheng, Warren and Xu 2003).

A comprehensive hands-on introduction to acquiring some of the skills needed if language learners are to become language researchers is provided by Sinclair (2003). He illustrates the analysis of concordances of words and phrases in terms of grammar, lexis, patterns of co-selection and semantic prosody, which together serve as an effective means of learning many of the skills required for successful DDL. Sripicharn (2010: 372–374) identifies a number of tasks for which DDL is particularly suited: hypothesis testing, error correction, contrastive studies and translation, genre analysis and self-study, especially in specialised areas. In order to have a positive learning experience with DDL, Sripicharn notes that solid preparation of the learners before embarking on DDL activities is key. The preparation of learners to participate in DDL can take a number of forms. For example, it can be useful for learners to compile a mini-corpus of their own so that they understand some of the fundamental design principles in corpus building (Cheng et al. 2003). This suggestion is endorsed by Smith (2011), who advocates that for more successful DDL, learners should go beyond consulting existing corpora and build their own corpora best suited to their own specific needs and fields of study. Smith found that the learners who compiled their own corpora had a 'sense of ownership and therefore a motivational impetus' (2011: 291). Training is needed before learners interrogate a corpus in terms of what it can be searched for. Basic search functions need to be taught: word frequencies, key words, clusters, collocates and concordance generation. Training is also required to enable learners to identify patterns of co-selection for words and phrases in context. The random sampling of large outputs and help from the teacher in editing outputs can help learners new to DDL to handle large quantities of data. Sripicharn also states that there is a need for caution in terms of statements such as 'overuse' or 'underuse' when comparing corpora, especially learner versus expert corpora (Sripicharn 2010: 382). It is better to use expressions such as 'higher' or 'lower' frequencies rather than immediately assuming that there is a problem if learners' usages are not in line with those of the expert users of the language under investigation.

A number of studies detail specific applications and uses of DDL in a variety of contexts. Hafner and Candlin (2007) make use of a corpus of approximately 800,000 words from 114 legal cases together with a concordancer to provide online writing support for students in a university law department who were learning how to draft the legal texts which form part of their coursework requirements. While they found that the students made good use of the resources for checking their own usage, there were some who found the corpus tools technically difficult to use and the outputs hard to make sense of (Hafner and Candlin 2007: 316); more training was recommended for such learners. Another study (Gao 2011) showed that L2 learners are able to improve their translation skills when independently using a parallel concordancer. This approach was particularly useful in enhancing the learners' use both of word choices and of phraseology, which in Gao's study inclusively encompassed various forms of word combinations. The successful use of a small corpus of film transcripts to enable learners improve their conversational skills by using the corpus to identify characteristic features of conversation is described by Basanta and Martín (2007: 141). These features include speech acts such as requests, hedges, adjacency pairs, hesitation devices and backchannels (Basanta and Martín 2007: 152–153). Greaves and Warren (2007) describe DDL language learning activities covering aspects of phraseology. These activities also help to develop computing and critical analytical skills for arriving at the phraseological profile of a text and then determining which of the phraseologies are specific to that particular text compared with a corpus of texts of the same genre (Greaves and Warren 2007).

Sometimes advocates of DDL do not use a corpus in the sense of a collection of texts and use DDL in the study of one specific text. One example is a study which uses corpus linguistics software to facilitate the learning of the use of English prepositions in one book written by J.K. Rowling (Lee 2011). She found that the learners in her study were able to search for prepositions, identify patterns of use and then apply their findings in their own writing.

In a study of university level English language majors in Hong Kong, Cheng et al. (2003) describe an application of DDL which required students to design and conduct corpus-driven language projects. First, the students were introduced to a number of corpora such as the BNC, COCA, and the International Corpus of English (ICE), which is comprised of equal quantities of spoken and written texts taken from different varieties of English. The students were trained to use several software programs and, once they were familiar with the corpora and the software, they had to come up with a research topic of their own. To help them in this task, Cheng et al. introduced them to the kibbitzers (a 'kibbitzer' is another Johns's coinage and roughly translates as 'interested observer'), available online thanks to the original work of Tim Johns (http://lexically.net/TimJohns/, hosted on Mike Scott's website) and others, such as those developed by the MICASE team (http://micase.elicorpora.info/micase-kibbitzers). These kibbitzers are a rich resource and source of ideas for mini-research projects. In the case of Tim Johns, the kibbitzers are intended for language learning based on real-world language problems he encountered in his work teaching English for academic purposes to overseas postgraduate students at Birmingham University. For example, he explores the differences between *incessant* versus *steadfast*, *as* clauses versus *that* clauses, *by* versus *using*, logical connectives, *population who* versus *population which*, *closely related* versus *deeply related*, *so far* versus *hitherto*, *reason to* versus *reason for*, and *read widely* versus *widely read*. Similarly, the MICASE team provide a number of kibbitzer tasks on their website which require the user to search the MICASE corpus and then analyse the search results to answer the questions posed. Here are four examples taken from the MICASE website:

1 'Among' or 'Between'?

   The traditional rule recommends 'between' for two things and 'among' for more than two. Do MICASE speakers follow this rule?

2 'Less' and 'Fewer'?

   Do MICASE speakers use 'less' with uncountables (for example, less money) and 'fewer' with countables (for example, fewer dollars)? Or are there other factors at play?

3 The Distribution of Anaphoric 'So' in MICASE

   The use of 'so' in such phrases as 'I guess so' is not that common in MICASE. With which verbs does it occur? In which speech-events? Do other languages use a similar structure?

4 'End up' in MICASE

   This phrasal verb is one of the five most common in MICASE. Why is this? What are its functions?

*(http://micase.elicorpora.info/micase-kibbitzers)*

In their application of DDL, Cheng et al. (2003) introduced to their students the main (overlapping) areas of study conducted by corpus linguists: lexical, syntactic, discoursal, collocation and colligation. The students then worked on their individually chosen research topic independently. This approach to DDL has been termed the 'hard version' by Gabrielatos (2005: 11) in that it places the maximum demands on students by requiring them to be competent in the use of corpora and corpus linguistics programs, set their own language learning agenda, and be able to critically analyse the search results and discuss their findings. However, the hard version is not the only version of DDL, and there are many who adopt a full or partial teacher-mediated form of DDL (see e.g. Römer 2008; Boulton 2010). A teacher-mediated approach to DDL means that it is the teacher who has identified, for example, a language feature or perceived language problem, and it is the teacher who has searched the corpus to find instances to share with learners as hard copy. This reduces the demands on the learners and the need for classroom-based computer facilities, and makes DDL more accessible to learners who, for whatever reason, are unable to handle the pure learner-as-language-researcher approach.

## What are the advantages and disadvantages of DDL?

In a number of studies, DDL has been found to be a useful language learning methodology, and there is evidence that learners can indeed benefit from being both language learners and language researchers (see e.g. Cheng et al. 2003; Chambers and O'Sullivan 2004; Lee and Swales 2006; Gao 2011). One of the main benefits of combining DDL with a corpus-driven approach in language studies is learning the corpus linguistics techniques and procedures that enable the learner to uncover and understand the connection between language theories and corpus findings (Tognini-Bonelli 2002). In addition, according to Cheng (2012), conducting DDL research projects can help the learner to develop valuable generic attributes such as analytical reasoning, critical thinking and problem solving which can be put to good use in a variety of other contexts.

Surveys of how learners who have used DDL respond to this approach show differing results. The survey conducted by Cheng et al. (2003) after their students had completed their DDL mini-research projects found that 87% of students found it a very useful or useful learning experience and only 13% considered it not very useful. The students had positive views about both the process and the outcome of corpus-driven language research. For example, they stated that they had a better understanding of the characteristics of corpora, namely that corpora can help supplement one another and help provide researchers with information regarding the distribution, positions, functions and collocates of words. They gained insights into gender and cross-cultural similarities and differences in language use, and some noted that corpora could help them to better understand and check the meanings of words provided by dictionaries. However, 76% of the students said that they had encountered difficulties in doing the mini-research project.

There are a number of problems which have become associated with DDL. These problems are often cited as possible reasons why DDL is still not mainstream in language learning and teaching contexts. One is the logistics of using the DDL approach in terms of requiring computers and corpus linguistics software in order to provide learners with a DDL experience. Obviously, these facilities are not available to all learners and teachers or may not be available often enough to be able to make meaningful use of the DDL approach. In addition, teachers may lack the expertise and/or confidence or interest to engage with DDL. To rectify this, there also needs to be a considerable investment of time to train learners before they can benefit from DDL. Another problem is that the contents of the available corpora might not fit the learners' needs, and even if the contents are suitable, the search results might be too meagre to discern patterns of use or so plentiful that learners feel overwhelmed and unable to process them in a coherent fashion.

In their survey of students at the end of their mini-research project, Cheng et al. (2003) also uncovered some problems encountered by the students. For example, students observed that existing corpora may not represent all language in use, as new uses are coined every day, and some words could not be found in the International Corpus of English – Great Britain (ICE-GB), for example, because the word or phrase studied is mainly used in American English. Other difficulties described by the students encountered during the DDL process of research were of three main types: those that occurred at the different stages of the project, those related to corpus-driven language research and those due to the nature of the corpus data (Cheng et al. 2003). Some found it difficult to decide on the topic and devise research questions or hypotheses. Another difficulty was lacking the ability to fully critically analyse the data and discuss their findings. Others felt they lacked the knowledge and skills when it came to choosing the most appropriate corpus/corpora and which function and searches to select in the corpus linguistics programs to best achieve their research goals. The third type of difficulty concerned handling the corpus data generated in their study. These included the laborious nature of obtaining and analysing data from the corpora, and the tedious business of, for example, counting frequencies of occurrence, classifying data into word classes and calculating out percentage distributions. Some students were uncertain as to how best to classify instances from the corpus into useful and meaningful categories. However, it needs to be added that even though there were multiple difficulties to overcome, the students all successfully completed their mini-research projects (Cheng et al. 2003).

At least some of the kinds of problems described by Cheng et al. (2003) still seem to persist in DDL. A study by Pérez-Paredes, Sánchez-Tornel and Calero Alcaraz (2012) looked at EFL learners' use of BNC searches to improve their writing proficiency versus another group of learners who also had access to other Internet resources. They found that only using the BNC was not so effective due to the 'unsophisticated queries' employed by the learners (2012: 482). They conclude that there needs to be a significant investment in training learners how to fully exploit corpora as a language learning resource and they present a 'taxonomy of learner searches' (2012: 482) which might provide the basis for such training.

The problem regarding insufficient corpus data is the subject of a study by Sha (2010), who argues that the limited size of existing corpora means learners often cannot find what they are looking for, or find too few instances, which makes the identification of patterns difficult. Sha found that using the contents of the Web as one big super-corpus is better in terms of 'usability, search speed, number of solutions and above all, preference investigations' (2010: 377). The one not inconsiderable problem with this conclusion is the very basic issue as to the status of what is available on the Web: can it be treated as if it is one enormous corpus? Those who believe that a corpus must be designed and compiled based on rigorous principles (see e.g. Sinclair 2005) would say 'no, the contents of the web are not a corpus'. There are others, such as Baroni and Kilgariff (2006) and those behind Webcorp (i.e. the Research and Development Unit for English Studies at Birmingham City University, UK) who argue that the contents of the Web (when edited using fully automated techniques) can constitute a corpus (or multiple corpora). The Webcorp website (http://www.webcorp.org.uk/live/) houses a number of corpora which the team has collated from the Web using web crawlers.

Another problem raised by some studies is whether or not DDL best suits the range of learning styles to be found among language learners. For example, Cresswell (2007) looks at the effectiveness of DDL with learner corpora to improve learners' writing skills with regard to their use of connectors. He concludes that DDL is 'moderately effective', but advocates more research into learners' preferred learning styles as the effectiveness of DDL is uneven across the learners in his study. Cresswell's conclusion is supported by another study of learners (Yoon and Hirvela 2004) who used a corpus to help to improve their writing. They found the DDL approach was thought by learners to be helpful in the development of their writing skills and also increased their confidence, but Yoon and Hirvela suggest that a staged introduction to DDL via teacher mediation is preferable in order to cater for learners' differing proficiency levels, and that there is a need to provide clear guiding principles for DDL implementation. They also observe that not all advanced language learners readily take to the DDL approaches, regardless of whether or not they are more or less teacher mediated. They therefore advise that learner's learning preferences should be established at the beginning to offset potential difficulties and resistance from learners (Yoon and Hirvela 2004).

As for the difficulties experienced by some learners when it comes to analysing concordance lines, McGee proposes an interesting alternative. McGee (2012) uses monolingual collocation dictionaries for DDL and compares their effectiveness with the use of concordance lines when learners have to answer questions posed by the teacher. McGee concludes that collocation dictionaries can be used for more teacher-led inductive language learning rather than learners trying to identify patterns in concordance lines, which can be a daunting task for some.

The difficulties encountered by some of those wishing to adopt or adopting DDL mentioned earlier do not necessarily negate the DDL approach to language learning but rather underline the need for larger and more comprehensive corpora in order to better support corpus linguistics and data-driven learning, more user-friendly corpus linguistics programs, and better training of both teachers and learners. These actions might go some way in overcoming an unfortunate tendency that exists, at least in Germany, where Römer (2006: 122) found a 'strong resistance towards corpora from students, teachers and materials writers'. This is unfortunate because studies such as those in Hong Kong by Cheng and Warren (2005, 2007) found consistent mismatches between naturally occurring English spoken in business contexts in

Hong Kong and the English that is portrayed in the business English textbooks used in schools. They recommend that writers of language learning materials should draw on the findings from corpora of naturally occurring language in use when they design and write their activities and materials. This is not a problem confined to Hong Kong: in general there is still a gulf between corpus evidence and the language presented in many of the textbooks used by language educators. Some notable exceptions to this general observation are covered in Caines, McCarthy and O'Keeffe, Chapter 25 this volume.

## DDL in the future

A more flexible and inclusive definition as to what constitutes DDL is the likely compromise in the future. Currently, teacher-mediated DDL is seen by some as lacking some of the key ingredients proposed by Johns (see e.g. 1989, 1991, 1997). However, mounting research evidence, such as the study by Boulton (2010), suggests that there is good reason to accept that DDL can exist on a cline between fully teacher-mediated DDL and learner as researcher DDL. Boulton demonstrates that DDL is more effective than traditional learning and teaching methods and the learners in his study prefer DDL. Importantly, however, in his study the teacher provides paper-based corpus activities rather than having the learners access the corpora themselves via a computer. Boulton makes the case that this then avoids the need for extensive training on how to exploit a corpus, and this applies to the teacher as well. Also, he claims it is a more efficient use of time, as many teachers have experienced the frustration of taking a class into a computer lab and finding that little is accomplished due to the logistical difficulties involved, as learners quickly head off in different search directions and so on.

Boulton's claims are supported by Chang and Sun's (2009) study in which two separate groups of students were taught how to do a proofreading task. One group was taught without exposure to DDL and the other group was taught how to perform the task using a DDL approach which specifically focused on verb + preposition collocations. They conclude that the latter group which had been introduced to scaffolded DDL (i.e. the use of teacher-led prompts) improved their ability to accurately proofread compared with the control group. Students were able to 'induce a rule from many examples and helped them to work as linguistics researchers to figure out common collocation use' (Chang and Sun 2009: 294).

It is interesting to note that the number of textbooks or online language learning materials dedicated to DDL remains small compared with the attention DDL has received from its advocates. For example, the guide to reading concordances by Sinclair (2003) and Thurstun and Candlin's (1998) workbook, which introduces some of the language features of academic essay writing by means of concordance printouts, are not recent publications and yet are among the few in existence which can be described as essentially DDL language learning materials, albeit teacher-mediated DDL rather than wholly learner as researcher DDL. For this reason, the future of DDL will depend in part on greater efforts being made to provide DDL support and DDL materials to both language learners and language teachers. McCarten (2010: 425) provides a comprehensive overview of the kinds of corpus-informed language learning materials we might expect to see in the future. She predicts the demise of hard copy books in language classrooms and thanks technological advances in 'virtual learning environments which users can access individually in addition to, or independently of, the classroom'. McCarten sees DDL as being one of the beneficiaries of these developments (2010: 425). She does, however, mention a few caveats which need to be taken care of if DDL is to be foregrounded in Internet-based or blended learning contexts. For example, she argues that concordancing software needs to be more user-friendly and its applications and advantages made clearer to a nonspecialist audience. She also suggests, citing

Allan (2009), that the corpora used in DDL could be designed to benefit students' needs and graded in terms of language difficulty to guide learners and teachers as to which to use.

Another future development for DDL, and all of those engaged in corpus linguistics, is the compilation of more and more multimodal corpora. While challenging to create (see e.g. Knight, Evans, Carter and Adolphs 2009), and equally challenging to access via user-friendly software interfaces (see e.g. Gu 2006), these corpora will be needed if we are to be able to fully describe communication and how lexical, prosodic and gestural features combine to create meaning (Knight et al. 2009). The complexities involved in analysing multimodal corpora will also make the necessary user-friendly interfaces that much harder to realise.

There are many possibilities for DDL to become mainstream both inside and outside the language learning classrooms of the future. Römer (2009: 91–95) notes that English language teachers in Germany, amongst other things, want more authentic learning and teaching materials, textbooks which reflect actual language use, and reliable and accessible resources. She argues that DDL can provide all of these from the more teacher-mediated approach with activities such as simple gap filling and making use of carefully prechosen concordance lines to the discovery-based learner-as-researcher DDL approach. A major step towards achieving this objective, according to Römer, would be the provision of a compulsory new course for language teachers titled 'Corpus linguistics and language teaching' (2009: 92). This is echoed by Flowerdew (2012: 197) who, along with other researchers, points out that a key factor as to why DDL is still not mainstream in language learning contexts – more than twenty years after Tim Johns (1989, 1991) first published his seminal papers – is that there is a pressing need to offer adequate DDL training to future language teachers in university language education programmes.

## Further reading

Boulton, A. (2009) 'Testing the limits of data-driven learning: Language proficiency and training', *ReCALL*, 21(1): 37–51.
    This article is one of the few that has successfully evaluated the effectiveness of different forms of DDL in the language classroom. It makes the case for a flexible approach as to whether fully teacher-mediated DDL, learner as researcher DDL or something in between these two extremes should be adopted.
Cheng, W. (2012) *Exploring Corpus Linguistics: Language in Action*, London, UK: Routledge.
    Aimed primarily at postgraduate students, this book provides the knowledge and theories needed to analyse and interpret corpus data. It is probably one of the best sources for what has become known as the Sinclairian approach in corpus linguistics circles, with an emphasis on the contribution of John McHardy Sinclair's ideas to the field. In addition, the book provides numerous examples of concordance-based analyses, tasks for the reader to carry out along with a detailed key, plus an excellent glossary of the terminology of corpus linguistics. It is therefore useful both at the conceptual level and as a practical guide to corpus linguistics.
Flowerdew, L. (2012) *Corpora and Language Education*, Basingstoke: Palgrave Macmillan.
    This book gives an overview of corpus linguistics which covers both the history of the field, the main concepts and some of the main approaches adopted by corpus linguists. The potential contributions that corpus linguistics can offer to language study are exemplified by drawing on studies from a variety of fields such as forensic linguistics, testing, translations studies, stylistics, second language acquisition, lexicography and business and healthcare contexts. The pedagogical implications of corpus linguistics are also covered in considerable detail.
O'Keeffe, A., McCarthy, M. and Carter, R. (2007) *From Corpus to Classroom*, Cambridge: Cambridge University Press.
    With its emphasis on spoken data in the CANCODE corpus and the Cambridge International Corpus, this volume summarises recent studies in corpus linguistics. It explains how to design a corpus and how to use it for corpus-informed pedagogy. It shows how corpora can be used by course designers, materials writers and language teachers and learners. Throughout, the writers explain key concepts and corpus applications with examples drawn from their corpora.

# References

Allan, R. (2009) 'Can a graded reader corpus provide "authentic" input?', *ELT Journal*, 63(1): 23–32.
Baroni, M. and Kilgariff, A. (2006) 'Large linguistically-processed web corpora for multiple languages', in *EACL '06 Proceedings of the Eleventh Conference of the European Chapter of the Association for Computational Linguistics*: 87–90.
Basanta, C. and Martín, M.E.R. (2007) 'The application of data-driven learning to a small-scale corpus: using film transcripts for teaching conversational skills', in E. Hidalgo, L. Quereda and J. Santana (eds), *Corpora in the Foreign Language Classroom*, Amsterdam, Netherlands: Rodopi: 141–158.
Bernandini, S. (2004) 'Corpora in the classroom: An overview and some reflections on future developments', in J. McH. Sinclair (ed), *How to Use Corpora in Language Teaching*, Amsterdam, Netherlands: John Benjamins: 15–36.
Boulton, A. (2010) 'Data-driven learning: Taking the computer out of the equation', *Language Learning*, 60(3): 534–572.
Burnard, L. and McEnery, T. (eds) (2000) *Rethinking Language Pedagogy from a Corpus Perspective*, Frankfurt: Peter Lang.
Chambers, A. (2010) 'What is data-driven learning?', in A. O'Keeffe and M. McCarthy (eds), *The Routledge Handbook of Corpus Linguistics*, London, UK: Routledge: 345–358.
Chambers, A. and O'Sullivan, I. (2004) 'Corpus consultation and advanced learners' writing skills in French', *ReCALL*, 16: 158–172.
Chang, W.L. and Sun, C.S. (2009) 'Scaffolding and web concordancers as support for language learning', *Computer Assisted Language Learning*, 22(4): 283–302.
Cheng, W. (2012) *Exploring Corpus Linguistics: Language in Action*, London, UK: Routledge.
Cheng, W. and Warren, M. (2005) '// → well have a DIFferent // ^ THINking you know //: Disagreement in Hong Kong business discourse: A corpus-driven approach', in M. Gotti and F. Bargiela (eds), *Asian Business Discourse(s)*, Frankfurt main: Peter Lang: 241–270.
Cheng, W. and Warren, M. (2007) 'Checking understandings in an intercultural corpus of spoken English', in A. O'Keeffe and S. Walsh (eds), *Corpus-Based Studies of Language Awareness. Special issue of Language Awareness*, 16(3): 190–207.
Cheng, W., Warren, M. and Xu, X. (2003) 'The language learner as language researcher: Corpus linguistics on the timetable', *System*, 31(2): 173–186.
Cresswell, A. (2007) 'Getting to 'know' connectors? Evaluating data-driven learning in a writing skills course', in E. Hidalgo, L. Quereda and J. Santana (eds), *Corpora in the Foreign Language Classroom*, Amsterdam, Netherlands: Rodopi: 267–287.
Flowerdew, L. (2012) *Corpora and Language Education*, Basingstoke: Palgrave Macmillan.
Gabrielatos, C. (2005) 'Corpora and language teaching: Just fling, or wedding bells?', *TESL-EJ*, 8(1): 1–35.
Gao, Z.M. (2011) 'Exploring the effects and use of a Chinese-English parallel concordancer', *Computer Assisted Language Learning*, 24(3): 255–275.
Gavioli, L. and Aston, G. (2001) 'Enriching reality: Language corpora in language pedagogy', *ELT Journal*, 55(3): 238–246.
Ghadessy, M., Henry, A. and Roseberry, R.L. (eds) (2001) *Small Corpus Studies and ELT: Theory and Practice*, Amsterdam, Netherlands: John Benjamins.
Gilquin, G. and Granger, S. (2010) 'How can data-driven learning be used in language teaching?', in A. O'Keeffe and M. McCarthy (eds), *The Routledge Handbook of Corpus Linguistics*, London, UK: Routledge: 359–370.
Greaves, C. and Warren, M. (2007) 'Concgramming: A computer-driven approach to learning the phraseology of English', *ReCALL Journal*, 17(3): 287–306.
Gu, Y.G. (2006) 'Multimodal text analysis: A corpus linguistic approach to situated discourse', *Text & Talk*, 26(2): 127–167.
Hafner, C.A. and Candlin, C.N. (2007) 'Corpus tools as an affordance to learning in professional legal education', *Journal of English for Academic Purposes*, 6: 303–318.
Hunston, S., (2002) *Corpora in Applied Linguistics*, Cambridge: Cambridge University.
Johns, T. (1989) 'Whence and whither classroom concordancing?', in T. Bongaerts, P. de Haan, S. Lobbe and H. Wekker (eds), *Computer Applications in Language Learning*, Dordrecht, Netherlands: Foris: 9–33.
Johns, T. (1991) 'Should you be persuaded: Two samples of data-driven learning materials', in T. Johns and P. King (eds), *Classroom Concordancing* (English Language Research Journal 4), Birmingham: ELR: 1–16.

Johns, T. (1997) 'Contexts: The background, development and trailing of a concordance-based CALL program', in A. Wichmann, S. Fligelstone, T. McEnery and D. Knowles (eds), *Teaching and Language Corpora*, London; New York, NY: Longman: 100–115.

Knight, D., Evans, D., Carter, R. and Adolphs, S. (2009) 'HeadTalk, HandTalk and the Corpus: Towards a framework for multi-modal, multi-media corpus development', *Corpora*, 4(1): 1–32.

Lee, D. and Swales, J. (2006) 'A corpus-based EAP course for NNS doctoral students: Moving from available specialized corpora to self-compiled corpora', *English for Specific Purposes*, 25(1): 56–75.

Lee, H.C. (2011) 'In defense of concordancing: An application of data-driven learning in Taiwan', *Procedia Social and Behavioral Sciences*, 12: 399–408.

McCarten, J. (2010) 'Corpus-informed course book design', in. A. O'Keeffe and M. McCarthy (eds), *The Routledge Handbook of Corpus Linguistics*, London, UK: Routledge: 413–427.

McGee, I. (2012) 'Collocation dictionaries as inductive resources in data-driven learning: An analysis and evaluation', *International Journal of Lexicography*, 25(3): 319–361.

O'Sullivan, I. (2007) 'Enhancing a process-oriented approach to literacy and language learning: The role of corpus consultation literacy', *ReCall*, 19(3): 269–286.

Pérez-Paredes, P., Sánchez-Tornel, M. and Calero Alcaraz, J.M. (2012) 'Learners' search patterns during corpus-based focus-on-form activities: A study on hands-on concordancing', *International Journal of Corpus Linguistics*, 17(4): 482–515.

Römer, U. (2006) 'Pedagogical applications of corpora: Some reflections on the current scope and a wish list for future developments', *Zeitschrift für Anglistik und Amerikanistik*, 54(2): 121–134.

Römer, U. (2008) 'Corpora and language teaching', in A. Lüdeling and M. Kytö (eds), *Corpus Linguistics: An International Handbook* (Vol. 1), Berlin: Mouton de Gruyter: 112–130.

Römer, U. (2009) 'Corpus research and practice: What help do teachers need and what can we offer?', in K. Aijmer (ed), *Corpora and Language Teaching*, Amsterdam, Netherlands: John Benjamins: 83–98.

Sha, G.Q. (2010) 'Using Google as a super corpus to drive written language learning: A comparison with the British National Corpus', *Computer Assisted Language Learning*, 23(5): 377–393.

Sinclair J. McH. (2003) *Reading Concordances,* London, UK: Pearson Longman.

Sinclair J. McH. (2005) 'Corpus and text: basic principles', in M. Wynne (ed), *Developing Linguistic Corpora: A Guide to Good Practice*. AHDS Guides to Good Practice (AHDS Literature, Languages and Linguistics), Oxford, UK: University of Oxford.

Smith, S. (2011) 'Learner construction of corpora for general English in Taiwan', *Computer Assisted Language Learning*, 24(4): 291–316.

Sripicharn, P. (2010) 'How can we prepare learners for using language corpora?', in A. O'Keeffe and M. McCarthy (eds), *The Routledge Handbook of Corpus Linguistics*, London, UK: Routledge: 359–370.

Thurstun, J. and Candlin, C., (1998) 'Concordancing and the teaching of the vocabulary of academic English', *English for Specific Purposes*, 17: 267–280.

Tognini-Bonelli, E. (2002) 'Functionally complete units of meaning across English and Italian: Towards a corpus-driven approach', in B. Altenberg and S. Granger (eds), *Lexis in Contrast: Corpus-Based Approaches*, Amsterdam, Netherlands: John Benjamins: 73–96.

Tribble, C. (1997) 'Improvising corpora for ELT. Quick and dirty ways of developing corpora for language teaching', in B. Lewandowska-Tomaszczyk and P. Melia (eds), *Palc '97: Practical Applications in Language Corpora*, Lodz: Lodz University Press: 106–118.

Yoon, H. and Hirvela, A. (2004) 'ESL student attitudes towards corpus use in L2 writing', *Journal of Second Language Writing*, 13: 257–283.

# 25
# Spoken language corpora and pedagogical applications

*Andrew Caines, Michael McCarthy and Anne O'Keeffe*

In comparison with written corpora, spoken corpora have not developed at the same rate. The reasons for this are largely to do with the huge costs and time involved in compilation and transcription, as well as access to recordable data. What has developed over the last twenty years, however, is an acknowledgement of the importance of spoken corpora in creating a fuller understanding of everyday spoken language, especially casual conversation. Whereas spoken corpora were initially small appendages to much larger written corpora, they are now increasingly valued and created in their own right. Two broad types of spoken corpora are of relevance to language pedagogy: large, demographically sampled corpora which attempt to grab a snapshot of a language as a whole (e.g. for contemporary British English, the British National Corpus, hereafter BNC) and carefully targeted corpora aimed at collecting data for more specialised purposes such as spoken business language, spoken academic language, teenage language, spoken language in the broadcast media and so forth. These latter corpora are often smaller, yet nonetheless yield invaluable insights into particular kinds of speaking. Sizeable research output has accrued over the years into the two types of spoken corpora, and this has enhanced our understanding of the differences between spoken and written language in general, as well as offering insights into variation on a number of parameters. However, the pedagogical potential of these research findings has not always been fully exploited. This chapter reviews key findings from research into spoken corpora and current pedagogical applications and discusses how spoken-corpus-informed pedagogy might be expanded and brought further into the domains of conventional classrooms and blended and online learning.

## Spoken corpora: What are they?

### Defining spoken corpora

Spoken corpora are collections of recordings of speaking which have been transcribed to form a database or corpus. A distinction is generally made between spoken corpora and 'speech corpora', which are usually collections of speech (such as recordings of people reading out loud) that are compiled for purposes such as the analysis of the phonetic substance of speaking or the creation of voice-to-text applications and telephone technology (Harrington 2010).

The growth in the number of spoken corpora can be seen as having gone in tandem with the emergence and development of recording technology (see Murphy and Riordan, Chapter 28 this volume).

## The evolution of large spoken corpora

McCarthy and O'Keeffe (2008) note that many early spoken corpora were developed as add-ons to much larger written corpora. This is a function of the time and expense involved in collecting spoken data relative to written texts. For example, the BNC (Crowdy 1993) contains over 100 million words of data, with the spoken component accounting for only 10% of this. The 10 million words of spoken data comprise informal conversations recorded by volunteers selected from different ages, regions and social classes in a demographically balanced way. Also important in the evolution of spoken corpora is the ICE (International Corpus of English) project, designed to bring together parallel corpora of 1 million words from 18 different countries where English is either the main language or an official language. The samples in the ICE corpus include 300 spoken texts, although these include many scripted samples, and broadcast interviews and discussions, with only 90 samples being face-to-face informal conversations (see Nelson 1996).

Other notable large-scale spoken corpora that were developed internationally include the 5-million-word Longman Spoken American Corpus (see Chafe, Du Bois and Thompson 1991). By the turn of the millennium, the American National Corpus (ANC) was set up as a comparative corpus to the BNC (Ide and Macleod 2001). It is available as an online resource including a total of over 14.5 million words, 3.2 million of which are spoken data (see http://www.anc.org/data/oanc/contents/).

The largest available online corpus of one variety of English now available is the 450-million-word Corpus of Contemporary American English (COCA), which includes 85 million words of spoken data, including unscripted conversation from nearly 150 different TV and radio programs (Davies 2010). Despite the availability of substantial amounts of spoken American English data, there is a dearth of spontaneous face-to-face conversation. An exception to this is the Santa Barbara Corpus of Spoken American English (SBCSAE), a collection of approximately 249,000 words of recordings of natural speech, representing a wide variety of speakers (Du Bois, Chafe, Meyer, Thompson and Martey 2003).

English spoken corpora still tend to dominate but spoken corpora for many other languages now exist, including Bulgarian, French (both European and Canadian), Mandarin Chinese, Vietnamese, Egyptian Arabic, Farsi, German and Greek, amongst others. Many of these are available from the Linguistic Data Consortium at the University of Pennsylvania (see http://www.ldc.upenn.edu). ELDA, the Evaluations and Language Resources Distribution Agency in Europe also makes available a number of spoken corpus resources in different languages (see http://www.elda.org).

## The evolution of smaller spoken corpora

Apart from the large-scale corpora of particular languages, there has also been parallel growth in the development of smaller, specialised or domain-specific corpora. These are often designed to meet a particular research need where a research question focuses on one particular context of use. Specialised corpora are usually quite small (around 1 million words). Some of the major developments in specialised spoken corpora have taken place in the domain of academic discourse and include, for example, the Michigan Corpus of Academic Spoken English (MICASE) and its British counterpart, the British Academic Spoken English Corpus (BASE). A subcategory of these are learner corpora. While most learner corpora consist of written texts, some spoken learner corpora exist, for instance the Louvain International Database of Spoken English Interlanguage (LINDSEI) (Gilquin, De Cock and Granger 2010; see also Meunier, Chapter 27 this volume). Other interesting developments have been corpora of expert users of English such as the Vienna-Oxford International Corpus of English (VOICE) (Breiteneder, Pitzl, Majewski and Klimpfinger 2006) and the English as a Lingua Franca in Academic Settings (ELFA) Corpus (Mauranen 2003).

Research into small, specialised spoken corpora has been particularly fruitful in the area of pragmatics (see O'Keeffe, Clancy and Adolphs 2011). Small domain-specific corpora allow for concentrated patterns of use to emerge, particularly those features which have become pragmatically specialised. Some examples of domain-specific studies that have yielded insights into pragmatic specialisations include Koester (2006), who looks at office talk, while Adolphs, Atkins and Harvey (2007) explore health communication. Cotterill (2003) looks at the language of courtrooms, O'Keeffe (2006) examines radio phone-ins, and academic seminars are explored by Evison, McCarthy and O'Keeffe (2007).

## Key findings from research into spoken corpora

### Studies of lexical frequency

Leech, Rayson and Wilson (2001) present comprehensive English word lists for the spoken and written components of the BNC, showing which items are significantly more frequent in speaking or in writing. In addition to backchannel items such as *er*, *erm* and *mm*, words such as *yeah*, *oh* and *no*, and the verbs *know*, *think* and *mean* rank very high among the items distinctively characteristic of the spoken language, owing to their frequency of occurrence in the discourse-marking items *you know*, *I think* and *I mean*. Other discourse markers such as *well*, *right*, *okay*, *really* and *actually* also achieve high ranks in the spoken list. These items reveal a lot about the nature of everyday spoken English interaction: *you know*, *I think* and *I mean* all form part of the web of interpersonal relations and the monitoring of shared and nonshared knowledge. Other items in Leech et al.'s (2001) list include hedges such as *just*, *sort of* and *a bit*. The prominence of all of these items in the lexis of spoken English is indicative of the real-time, constant monitoring of the interpersonal stratum that speakers engage in as the discourse unfolds (see also Stenström 1990). Notably, the computer gives to vocalisations such as *er* and *mm* the same status as conventional words, thus underpinning the work of conversation analysts on backchannel behaviour and reinforcing the ubiquity of such 'nonwords' in conversation.

Carter and McCarthy (2006: 830–831) provide lists of lexical chunks for written and spoken English of up to five words long. Their written lists are dominated by prepositional phrases and noun-phrase elements with embedded prepositional phrases, in contrast with the spoken lists, which remain characterised by the presence of verbs such as *know* and *mean* and vague expressions such as *and that sort of thing* and *it's a bit of a*. Other studies have also attempted to assess the use of recurring clusters or chunks and the general conclusion is that chunks are an important characteristic of speaking (Altenberg 1991; Biber et al. 1999; Erman and Warren 2000; McCarthy and Carter 2002; Sinclair and Mauranen 2006).

Buttery and McCarthy (2012) compared the top 2,000 words in the spoken list of the BNC with the top 2,000 words in its written list. They found that approximately 65% of the words were common to both lists, leaving some 35% of words that were unique to either the spoken or written list. On examination of those unique to the spoken list, Buttery and McCarthy noted that, as reported in McCarthy and Carter (1997a), the spoken list was characterised by words that support face-to-face interaction (including pragmatic markers such as *well, like* and *right*), as well as informal words (e.g. *y*-suffix adjectives such as *yucky, stroppy* and *comfy*).

## Research on items characteristic of speaking

Alongside bird's-eye-view studies of spoken corpora as a whole are studies of individual items that are frequent in spoken data, especially everyday conversation. These items tend to be words and multiword strings of high frequency in spoken data and/or items notably higher in frequency than in comparable written data. Tottie (1991) investigated backchannel behaviour in British and American English spoken data, and looked at vocalisations such as *mm, mhm* and *uh-(h)uh* alongside 'bona fide words and phrases' (Tottie 1991: 255). Tottie's work underpinned the body of backchannel research in corpus linguistics and conversation analysis (Yngve 1970; Gardner 1997, 1998) and shed light on the problem of establishing boundaries between vocalisations, short responsive turns and full, floor-grabbing turns (Duncan and Niederehe 1974; Zimmerman 1993; Tottie 2011).

Aijmer (2002) examined 'discourse particles' (e.g. *now, oh, just, sort of, and that sort of thing, actually*), and focused on contextual cues such as text type, position in the talk, prosody and collocation. Aijmer's numerous studies of pragmatic markers, including common words and phrases such as *actually, well, of course, it's okay, I think, sort of* and *kind of* (Aijmer 1984, 1996, 2001, 2003) reveal items of high frequency in talk which are not easily amenable to reflection and objective analysis without the evidence of corpus data. All these studies stand as a powerful counteraction against public prejudice about the use of many of the pragmatic markers, which may be perceived as of low status and negatively evaluated (Watts 1989).

## Spoken grammar

Biber et al. (1999) investigated differences of distribution and function of grammatical items as between written registers (fiction writing, news writing and academic writing) and conversation. Carter and McCarthy (1995) had also listed common grammatical features found in their conversational corpus that were rare or which functioned differently in writing; they also drew attention to cases where grammatical items and features are particularly associated with either speaking or writing (Carter and McCarthy 2006). Rühlemann (2007: 11) notes that much of the work done on grammar in spoken corpora should perhaps be better termed 'conversational grammar', since it is there that the most outstanding differences between speaking and writing have been brought to light. Leech (2000) also notes how it is often conversational data which stands out as different from the rest. Leech discusses the fact that conversational speaking reflects its online, linear nature in the brevity of utterances (where words and phrases predominate rather than long clauses or heavily embedded structures).

Situational ellipsis is a good example of how spoken grammar reflects the conditions under which spontaneous speech occurs. In informal English conversation, pronouns, copular and auxiliary verbs and articles may be regularly absent from places where they would be considered obligatory in most forms of writing (Quirk, Greenbaum, Leech and Svartvik 1985: 895–900; Carter and McCarthy 2006: 181ff). Rühlemann (2007: 55–58) sees situational ellipsis as reflecting the shared context of face-to-face conversation and real-time processing factors. Caines and Buttery (2010) report that, in their British English corpus, in 27% of questions with second-person subjects involving progressive aspect (e.g. *What you doing? You been working?*), the auxiliary was not used, as compared to only 5.4% of occurrences in comparable written data. They demonstrate that ellipsis of this kind is not random, and surrounding grammatical contextual features (e.g. subject pronoun type, tense-aspect configuration) can be used in the creation of a predictive model for training computers in natural language processing, resulting in a high level of success in automated searching which may relieve the drudgery of manual analysis.

Other spoken grammatical features reflecting the conditions under which conversational speaking occurs include preposed and postposed items, sometimes referred to as left- and right-dislocated items (Geluykens 1992) or, by Carter and McCarthy (2006: 782–783) as headers and tails. These are features not totally excluded or proscribed from the grammar of writing, but rather ones which are overwhelmingly preferred in speaking. Extract 1 is a typical example of the way a noun phrase or phrases focusing in on the topic may occur before the main subject of the verb (in this case the pronoun *he*), forming the header, a sort of lead-in for the listener (marked in bold). In formal written grammar, the pronoun *he* would be considered unnecessary or even ill-formed:

### Extract 1

[The speaker is reminiscing on his years working in the maritime lighthouse service.]

And er when the anchor man always had his hand on the rope you know and you'd hear him saying, 'Anchor coming home sir anchor coming home sir'. And **the engine man he** was on his knees beside the engine.

*(BNC)¹*

Extract 2 exemplifies the postposed tail phenomenon, where a pronoun is later reiterated in the form of its fully lexical noun-phrase referent (marked in bold):

### Extract 2

[The speaker is talking about a wristwatch which she changed for a smaller one because the face was too big.]

<$1> Oh that's beautiful isn't it?
<$2> Yeah, got a small little face and+
<$1> It's gorgeous that
<$2> +it had to change that for me, cos **it** was so big **the other one**
<$1> Mm

*(BNC)*

McCarthy and Carter (1997b) found that tails of this kind correlated strongly with evaluative contexts (see also Aijmer 1989). Headers and tails are indicative of the real-time, online construction that is characteristic of spoken grammar, where items may be only loosely related in terms of conventional written structures and where the grammatical output is essentially linear and listener-sensitive.

Phenomena such as headers and tails and particular types of ellipsis, for example, ellipsis of determiners, existential *there*, conditional *if* (see Carter and McCarthy 2006: 185–187 for examples), because of their low likelihood of occurrence in written corpora, can easily be overlooked or relegated to nonstandard or low-status usage. Their presence in spoken corpora from the mouths of speakers of all regional and social backgrounds, ages, and educational achievements show them to be anything but rare or nonstandard. In this respect, one of the achievements of spoken corpus analysis has been to raise questions about the nature of 'standard' grammar, and the sources from which the grammatical canon is conventionally derived (see in particular the papers by Carter and Cheshire in Bex and Watts 1999).

## Discourse and pragmatics

A notable pragmatic feature that spoken corpus research has brought to light is the ubiquity of vague language in conversation, with vague category markers such as *and things like that, or something, or whatever, and that sort/kind of thing* (see Carter and McCarthy 2006: 835–836 for examples) revealing how speakers project assumptions of shared context, shared knowledge, shared meanings and worldviews among interlocutors (O'Keeffe 2003; Cutting 2007; Evison et al. 2007).

Another area of spoken corpus analysis that has been fruitful is the study of turn-construction. Although the onset and construction of any individual turn in informal conversation may be quite unpredictable (apart from highly ritualised turns such as greetings, congratulations, thanks, etc.), corpus analysis shows that a surprisingly small repertoire of words can account for a large number of turn-openings. Tao (2003) searched in his corpus for the words immediately following a new speaker tag and found a notable consistency in how speakers opened their turns. Turn-openings, in Tao's data, utilise a small repertoire of items (e.g. *yeah, uh-huh, oh, and, well, so, right, okay, no* and personal pronouns). Tao's overall conclusion, that turn-openers are syntactically free forms that function as links or bridges between turns, is a powerful indicator of the way speakers work to create continuity or 'flow' in conversation, a phenomenon which McCarthy (2010) refers to as 'confluence'. McCarthy (2002, 2003) had already noted how, in conversational corpora, responsive turns routinely consisted of single-word adjectives or adverbs such as *fine, great, absolutely, definitely*, along with responses consisting of clusters of such items (e.g. *Okay, great, fine!*) or reduplications of particular items (*Good, good.*) (see also O'Keeffe and Adolphs 2008).

Research into spoken corpora, both general and specialised, has brought to light features of everyday interaction that are difficult to access through intuition or reflection alone. Spoken corpus investigations have often served to add large-scale, quantitative underpinning to the explanations and insights of conversation analysts, discourse analysts and pragmaticians, as well as offering ways of investigating phenomena such as speaking turns or problematic grammatical phenomena such as ellipsis. Discourse analysts, pragmaticians and conversation analysts have much to gain from large-scale corpus analysis through the ratification of or challenge to findings based on small amounts or individual pieces of data. In the realm of grammar, spoken corpora might be said to have disturbed the soil more fundamentally, raising debates that will no doubt continue for some time, while in the lexical domain, confirmation and hard evidence of the ubiquity of chunking has provided a new perspective and a renewed interest in the vocabulary of conversation.

## Key pedagogical implications from the research into spoken corpora

### Lack of application

Römer (2008) provides a survey of direct and indirect influences of corpora on language teaching. There is no gainsaying that the influence of corpora has been extensive and is increasing. However, many of the research findings outlined in the previous section are, at the time of writing, poorly represented in language teaching materials. Generally, in the teaching of oral skills most attention is given to the more monodirectional notion of 'speaking skills' as opposed to bi- or multidirectional conversation skills. Equally, when textbooks focus on 'listening skills' they usually separate them from the concept of speaking and focus almost solely on developing listening comprehension skills, where students listen and then complete content-related questions about what they have just listened to. As the research from spoken corpora illustrates, real conversational listening involves responding and co-constructing, with a speaker, across turns. One possible reason for the lack of widespread application of the findings of research into spoken corpora could be their general absence from language teacher education programmes as discussed by O'Keeffe and Farr (2003) and McCarthy (2008).

*Examples of materials which have applied research findings*

A small number have taken on the challenge of translating spoken corpus findings into classroom materials, for example the Touchstone and Viewpoint series (McCarthy, McCarten and Sandiford 2005–2011, 2012–2013). The syllabus of this English for adults series, which covers the main language teaching levels from false beginner to advanced, has a strong focus on conversation and includes input and practice in conversation strategies in every unit at every level, based on insights from spoken corpus data. Learners are presented with conversational extracts based on spoken corpus evidence to illustrate target items. Frequency patterns are explicitly presented (e.g. adjectives most frequently used after *That's* in response tokens, which grammatical pattern is most common in speaking, for instance, the choice between *isn't* and *'s not* as the negative of *be*). One of the main tenets underpinning the course is the notion of promoting 'noticing' (Schmidt 1990, 1993), based on the belief that learners generally need to be assisted in developing observation and awareness of spoken features, which are unlikely to simply come to them as second nature without pedagogical intervention and input enhancement (Sharwood Smith 1993). The Touchstone/Viewpoint series also attempts to bring together the skills of speaking and listening by highlighting appropriate responses to incoming talk and giving learners opportunities not only to listen to and comprehend audio input but also to react and respond in a contextually suitable manner.

The concept of spoken grammar has also become established in grammar reference books written (partly or wholly) with second language learners in mind. Biber et al. (1999) and Carter and McCarthy (2006) clearly affirm the distinction between spoken and written grammar and bring spoken corpus research insights into the purview of language teaching. Other grammars aimed at learners and/or supplemented with exercises, which also feature corpus-based material on spoken language, include Carter et al. (2011a, 2011b) and Bunting, Diniz and Reppen (2013).

## A case study of a key finding from spoken corpora and how it might be applied pedagogically

*Case study: Ellipsis in the context of 'zero auxiliary' progressive*

We now turn to findings from a corpus study and consider how these might be applied to a teaching context. Our case study features an example of ellipsis in British English – omission of the auxiliary verb in progressive (continuous) aspect constructions – the so-called 'zero auxiliary' progressive. Such constructions do not feature a tensed auxiliary verb, as in 1a where forms of

*BE* and *HAVE* which would be obligatory in formal writing and formal speaking are not used (cf. 1b):

1a   What you doing? Who you looking for? You been working?
1b   What are you doing? Who are you looking for? Have you been working?

According to standard grammatical conventions, especially those derived from writing, the auxiliary verb is an obligatory feature of such constructions. But the 'rule' is not always adhered to in the production of informal spoken language, as shown by 2–4 from the BNC:[2]

2   How you feeling now? KBK 3474
3   You not having any cake? KBW 13888
4   What you been buying? KPV 5313

However, nonuse of the auxiliary gains no mention in one of the major reference works of recent times on the grammar of English (Huddleston and Pullum 2002) and is only given passing mention in the footnotes of another (Quirk et al. 1985). With the evidence of spoken corpora, we consider the progressive construction in a new light and point out the pedagogical implications of the corpus statistics presented here.

## Corpus study

We extracted every progressive construction from the 10-million-word spoken section of the BNC (sBNC). Auxiliary realisation (full, contracted or zero) was noted along with various linguistic and extralinguistic properties at situational, clausal and lexical levels. These included subject type (pronoun, other noun, or 'zero') and subject person (first through third, singular or plural, or 'zero'), clause type (declarative or interrogative), clause tense, clause polarity and finally 'spontaneity' level (i.e. the formality of the recording context, from sermons to meetings to casual conversations).

As a result, we had a subcorpus of 93,253 annotated sentences, in which the majority of progressive constructions have pronominal subjects (most frequently third person singular), the clause is an un-negated present tense declarative and the auxiliary is contracted. The majority of the progressives occur at the informal spontaneity level even though overall this makes up only 4 million of the 10 million words contained in sBNC.

When we overlay these variables and investigate the interaction of factors, we find that the zero auxiliary occurs in almost every context available, with the exception of interrogatives at the formal, scripted level, for which frequencies are very low anyway. That is, the zero auxiliary is near-ubiquitous in terms of the contexts in which it can occur, although it only occurs at low frequencies, proportionally speaking, for all but the zero subject and interrogatives at the informal spontaneity level. Here in the interrogatives we find that the zero auxiliary is most frequent in the second person (at 34.1%), followed by the first person plural (23.6%) and then third person plural pronouns (20.2%). These three construction types are exemplified next:

5   You still using that monitor? (KD5 9846)
6   You been waiting long? (KDK 510)
7   Who we talking about? (KBW 15230)
8   We opening them now? (KD0 5133)

9   They rising to the top a lot Zoe? (KB6 478)
10  What they charging him with? (KDP 556)

We also found that zero subject + zero auxiliary constructions are a highly frequent type, and this is the main way in which declarative zero auxiliaries occur. For all spontaneity levels the proportion of zero subject progressives without an auxiliary is at least 50%. This type of zero auxiliary is pervasive across registers; from the most formal to the least formal, the zero subject + zero auxiliary is found:

11  Yeah hold on just looking at something (KD1 920)
12  Trying to decide whether to take them down off my windows and put some poles up (KCX 1178)
13  It's pretty decent. Thinking of buying myself one (KNY 565)

On the other hand, for zero auxiliaries with a subject noun or pronoun, we can infer a stylistic dimension to their use. In the more formal registers the zero auxiliary is a rare occurrence, whereas at the informal spontaneity level its use, especially for interrogatives, rises markedly. This stylistic dimension is one that we will return to when considering the pedagogical implications of our findings later.

A final point from our corpus study is that certain constructions correlate strongly with zero auxiliary use. We used the 'collostructional' statistical method (Stefanowitsch and Gries 2003) to identify the verbs most 'attracted' to and 'repulsed' by the zero auxiliary. On the plus side, *doing*, *going/gonna* and *laughing* were attracted to a statistically significant degree, whilst *saying*, *taking*, *working* and *happening* were strongly repulsed. Further investigation reveals that a small number of constructional patterns account for more than half of the second person zero auxiliary interrogatives, as shown in Table 25.1.

In this section, we have shown that a feature of English that is thought to be obligatory – the progressive aspect auxiliary verbs *BE* and *HAVE* – is in fact at times omitted by native speakers of English. Furthermore, our BNC survey demonstrates that such omission occurs more frequently in certain lexico-syntactic contexts. In the next section, we take the observations from this corpus study into account in our discussion of pedagogical implications.

*Table 25.1* Highly frequent second person interrogative zero auxiliary patterns in the spoken section of the BNC

| Constructional patterns | Frequency | % accounted for |
| --- | --- | --- |
| wh- you going/gonna + V | 189 | 14 |
| what you doing | 185 | 14 |
| you going/gonna + V | 132 | 10 |
| where you going | 101 | 7.5 |
| how you doing | 49 | 3.5 |
| what you looking for/at | 24 | 2 |
| what you talking about | 23 | 2 |
| what you having | 11 | 1 |
| what you laughing for/at | 7 | 0.5 |
| Subtotal | 721 | 54.5 |
| 2nd person interrogative zero auxiliary | 1330 | 100 |

## Pedagogical implications

These results bring to light an issue which is both methodologically challenging for corpus linguists and English language teachers in that they relate to researching and teaching a feature which involves variable *absence*. The case study shows how corpus research into spoken data can unearth the key patterns of ellipsis in spoken language, in this case in relation to auxiliary verbs, and can dispel erroneous intuitions about what we feel is 'obligatory'. In the sBNC data, for the participants at least, nothing is 'missing' and the utterances are perfectly grammatical.

Our case study shows that a grammatical item thought to be obligatory in progressive constructions – the auxiliary verb *BE*, or *HAVE* in perfect constructions – is in fact not always used by native speakers, especially in interrogative clauses, in zero subject constructions, and even more so in less formal registers. Since these auxiliaries are thought to be obligatory, they will generally always have been taught as such, both in first and second language teaching.

The challenge for the teacher then is how to 'teach' something which is absent. The first step is 'noticing' (Schmidt 1993). A simple drill such as the following would bring to students' attention what typically happens in spoken language:

> Below are real examples of what people say, taken from recordings of conversations. How would these differ if they were written rather than spoken? What is the effect of the changes in the written versions?
>
> 1   How you doing?
> 2   [Talking about food] What you having?
> 3   Think you don't need one.
> 4   Where you going Mum?
> 5   Trying to think.
>
> *(BNC data)*

Second, once the students' attention has been brought to some of the typical differences between (casual) spoken English and (formal) written English, the teacher may encourage appropriate practice in nonuse of the auxiliary: that is in less formal situations, when asking questions, and with second person subjects above all. Patterns such as *what/how you doing*, *where you going*, and *wh- you going/gonna* + V are especially appropriate skills to teach, as these are the types of zero auxiliary most frequently used by native speakers and most likely to be heard by students in encounters with native usage in films, Internet chat and other forms of media, as well as in face-to-face encounters.

The teacher could then move on to similar examples of informal ellipsis in appropriate situations: for instance with the omission of copular *be*, omission of subject pronouns, or the omission of determiners in spoken English. As with the earlier zero auxiliaries, corpus resources could be used to demonstrate and enhance such teaching.

## Looking to the future

In this chapter, we have attempted to demonstrate the potential use and benefit of spoken corpus research in language teaching. In order that this potential may be fully realised, there is a need for greater awareness of corpus resources and new findings from corpus research among language teachers. Academic networks such as the English Profile Project (http://www.englishprofile.org/)

can help in this regard, as can journals aimed at language teachers, such as *Language Teaching*, *ELT Journal* and *Language Teaching Research*.

To underpin any such development, major corpora themselves need to be enhanced with a greater amount of spoken data, as well as greater coverage of different contexts and registers. Equally, corpus linguists need to work with increased zeal towards making their findings accessible and transferable to pedagogy. As advocated in O'Keeffe and Farr (2003), corpus linguists need to present their research at teacher conferences and in language teaching journals in greater numbers than at the time of writing. This would add weight to the importance of including corpus linguistics as part of language teacher education programmes.

There also needs to be a wider availability of corpus-based teaching tools which allow for live concordance searches, visualisation of corpus frequencies and audio examples, at the very least. While there is a substantial amount of spoken data available online, for example via the COCA corpus, it is often scripted or media data. This is not quite representative of the most frequent human activity, that of everyday face-to-face conversation. In this regard, multimodal corpora, where audio and video data are combined and analysed in tandem, offer the prospect of further enhancing the language learning experience with video examples allowing for an additional focus on gesture and body language. Focusing on an innovative tool developed to make corpus use easier to access for language teaching, Farr (2010) details the potential of the SACODEYL (System Aided Compilation and Open Distribution of European Youth Language, a European Commission–funded project) corpus. This is a corpus of interviews with teenagers in seven different languages, available as a multimodal corpus (audio files, video files and transcriptions). This, and similar teacher-led innovations, will be key to bringing the benefits of spoken corpora directly to the language classroom.

Recently, too, debates have arisen over the status and positioning of speaking in blended learning and online environments. Decisions on which aspects of the classroom to 'flip' to a computer-mediated environment and which to retain in the face-to-face classroom could be positively underpinned by an awareness of the findings of spoken corpus investigations (e.g. the need to offer opportunities for active, responsive listening, as discussed earlier, or the need to develop noticing skills). At the time of writing, computer-mediated learning activities offer limited resources for recreating face-to-face spoken interaction in terms of controlled exercises, though sophisticated adaptive learning technologies may, in the future, replicate more convincingly the experience of listener feedback and bi-directional conversational flow (the 'confluence' referred to earlier). However, the addition to the blended learning environment of online social networking in the form of blogs, wikis, email exchanges or synchronous computer-mediated chat (SCMC) does offer contexts in which the patterns of informal dialogue immanent in spoken corpus data are seen as both natural and appropriate to the process of engaging with one's peers and teachers when learning a language (see Stevenson and Liu 2010 for a discussion of social networking in online language learning).

## Further reading

Aijmer, K. and Stenström, A.-B. (2005) 'Approaches to spoken interaction', *Journal of Pragmatics*, 37: 1743–1751.
   This paper forms the introduction to a series of articles on spoken interaction as evidenced in spoken corpora. It explores how spoken corpus linguistics relates to other linguistic subdisciplines such as conversation analysis and discourse analysis and provides a useful overview of the rest of the equally important papers in the journal's special issue.

McCarthy, M.J. (1998) *Spoken Language and Applied Linguistics*, Cambridge: Cambridge University Press.
McCarthy describes the genesis of the 5-million-word CANCODE spoken corpus, offers corpus-informed answers to the question of what can and should be taught about the spoken language and reports on findings relevant to the teaching of grammar, vocabulary and other features of speaking.

O'Keeffe, A., McCarthy, M.J. and Carter, R.A. (2007) *From Corpus to Classroom: Language Use and Language Teaching*, Cambridge: Cambridge University Press.
This book gives and introduction to corpora for language teachers. It brings together the findings from corpus research and their applications in the language classroom, with an extensive focus on spoken data and suggestions for practical applications in relation to some of the features in the present chapter.

Reppen, R. (2010) *Using Corpora in the Language Classroom*, Cambridge: Cambridge University Press.
This book is designed to help teachers and teacher trainers better to understand corpus linguistics and the ways in which corpus resources can be brought into the classroom. It features a directory of available corpus resources and comes with an informative companion website.

## Notes

1 All rights in the texts cited from the BNC are reserved (Oxford University Computing Services on behalf of the BNC Consortium).
2 Each extract is followed by a unique text identifier and sentence number.

## References

Adolphs, S., Atkins, S. and Harvey, K. (2007) 'Caught between professional requirements and interpersonal needs: vague language in healthcare contexts', in J. Cutting (ed), *Vague Language Explored*, Basingstoke: Palgrave Macmillan: 62–78.

Aijmer, K. (1984) '*Sort of* and *kind of* in English conversation', *Studia Linguistica*, 38: 118–128.

Aijmer, K. (1989) 'Themes and tails: The discourse function of dislocated elements', *Nordic Journal of Linguistics*, 12(2): 137–154.

Aijmer, K. (1996) 'I think – An English modal particle', in T. Swan and O.J. Westvik (eds), *Modality in Germanic languages. Historical and Comparative Perspectives*, Berlin: Mouton de Gruyter: 1–47.

Aijmer, K. (2001) 'It's okay', in M. Ljung (ed), *Language Structure and Variation*, Stockholm: University of Stockholm, *Stockholm Studies in English*, 92: 1–17.

Aijmer, K. (2002) *English Discourse Particles: Evidence from a Corpus*, Amsterdam; Philadelphia: John Benjamins.

Aijmer, K. (2003) 'Discourse particles in contrast: The case of *in fact* and *actually*', in A. Wilson, P. Rayson and T. McEnery (eds), *Corpus Linguistics by the Lune. A Festschrift for Geoffrey Leech*, Bern, Switzerland: Peter Lang: 23–35.

Altenberg, B. (1991) 'Amplifier collocations in spoken English', in S. Johansson and A.-B. Stenström (eds), *English Computer Corpora: Selected Papers and Research Guide*, The Hague: Mouton de Gruyter: 127–147.

Bex, T. and Watts, R.J. (eds) (1999) *Standard English: The Widening Debate*, London, UK: Routledge.

Biber, D., Johansson, S., Leech, G., Conrad, S. and Finegan, E. (1999) *The Longman Grammar of Spoken and Written English*, London, UK: Longman.

Breiteneder, A. Pitzl, M.-L., Majewski, S. and Klimpfinger, T. (2006) 'VOICE recording – Methodological challenges in the compilation of a corpus of spoken ELF', *Nordic Journal of English Studies*, 5(2): 161–188, available: http://hdl.handle.net/2077/3153

Bunting, J. and Diniz, L. with Reppen, R. (2013) *Grammar and Beyond*, Level 4, Cambridge: Cambridge University Press.

Buttery, P. and McCarthy, M.J. (2012) 'Lexis in spoken discourse', in J. Gee and M. Handford (eds), *The Routledge Handbook of Discourse Analysis*, Abingdon, Oxon; New York, NY: Routledge: 285–300.

Caines, A.P. and Buttery, P.J. (2010) 'You Talking to Me? A predictive model for zero-auxiliary constructions', in *Proceedings of the 2010 Workshop on NLP and Linguistics: Finding the Common Ground, ACL-2010*, Uppsala: Association for Computational Linguistics: 43–51.

Carter, R.A. and McCarthy, M.J. (1995) 'Grammar and the spoken language', *Applied Linguistics*, 16(2): 141–158.

Carter, R.A. and McCarthy, M.J. (2006) *Cambridge Grammar of English*, Cambridge: Cambridge University Press.

Carter, R.A., McCarthy, M.J., Mark, G. and O'Keeffe, A. (2011a) *English Grammar Today*, Cambridge: Cambridge University Press.

Carter, R.A., McCarthy, M.J., Mark, G. and O'Keeffe, A. (2011b) *English Grammar Today Workbook*, Cambridge: Cambridge University Press.

Chafe W., Du Bois J. and Thompson S. (1991) 'Towards a new corpus of spoken American English', in K. Aijmer and B. Altenberg (eds), *English Corpus Linguistics*, London, UK: Longman: 64–82.

Cotterill, J. (2003) *Language and Power in Court: A Linguistic Analysis of the O. J. Simpson Trial*, Basingstoke: Palgrave Macmillan.

Crowdy, S. (1993) 'Spoken corpus design', *Literary and Linguistic Computing*, 8: 259–265.

Cutting, J. (ed) (2007) *Vague Language Explored*, Basingstoke: Palgrave Macmillan.

Davies, M. (2010) 'The Corpus of Contemporary American English as the first reliable monitor corpus of English', *Literary and Linguistic Computing*, 25(4): 447–465.

Du Bois, J.W., Chafe, W.L., Meyer, C., Thompson, S.A. and Martey, N. (2003) *Santa Barbara Corpus of Spoken American English Part II*, Philadelphia, PA: Linguistic Data Consortium.

Duncan, S. and Niederehe, G. (1974) 'On signalling that it's your turn to speak', *Journal of Experimental Social Psychology*, 10(3): 234–247.

Erman, B. and Warren, B. (2000) 'The idiom principle and the open choice principle', *Text*, 20(1): 29–62.

Evison, J.M., McCarthy, M.J. and O'Keeffe, A. (2007) 'Looking out for love and all the rest of it: Vague category markers as shared social space', in J. Cutting (ed), *Vague Language Explored*, Basingstoke: Palgrave Macmillan: 138–157.

Farr, F. (2010) 'How can corpora be used in teacher education?', in A. O'Keeffe and M. McCarthy (eds), *The Routledge Handbook of Corpus Linguistics*, London, UK: Routledge: 620–632.

Gardner, R. (1997) 'The listener and minimal responses in conversational interaction', *Prospect*, 12(2): 12–32.

Gardner, R. (1998) 'Between speaking and listening: The vocalisation of understandings', *Applied Linguistics*, 19(2): 204–224.

Geluykens, R. (1992) *From Discourse Process to Grammatical Construction: On Left-dislocation in English*, Amsterdam, Netherlands: John Benjamins.

Gilquin, G., De Cock, S. and Granger, S. (2010) *Louvain International Database of Spoken English Interlanguage*, Louvain-la-Neuve: Presses Universitaires de Louvain, available: http://www.uclouvain.be/en-352660.html

Harrington, J. (2010) *Phonetic Analysis of Speech Corpora*, Oxford: Wiley-Blackwell.

Huddleston, R. and Pullum, G.K. (2002) *The Cambridge Grammar of the English Language*, Cambridge: Cambridge University Press.

Ide, N. and Macleod, C. (2001) 'The American National Corpus: A standardized resource of American English', in P. Rayson, A. Wilson, T. McEnery, A. Hardie and S. Khoja (eds), *Proceedings of Corpus Linguistics 2001*, Vol. 13, Lancaster: University of Lancaster: 274–280.

Koester, A. (2006) *Investigating Workplace Discourse*, Abingdon, Oxon: Routledge.

Leech, G. (2000) 'Grammars of spoken English: New outcomes of corpus-oriented research', *Language Learning*, 50(4): 675–724.

Leech, G., Rayson, P. and Wilson, A. (2001) *Word Frequencies in Written and Spoken English: Based on the British National Corpus*, London, UK: Longman.

Mauranen, A. (2003) 'The Corpus of English as Lingua Franca in academic settings', *TESOL Quarterly*, 37(3): 513–527.

McCarthy, M.J. (1998) *Spoken Language and Applied Linguistics*, Cambridge: Cambridge University Press.

McCarthy, M.J. (2002) 'Good listenership made plain: British and American non-minimal response tokens in everyday conversation', in R. Reppen, S. Fitzmaurice and D. Biber (eds), *Using Corpora to Explore Linguistic Variation*, Amsterdam, Netherlands: John Benjamins: 49–71.

McCarthy, M.J. (2003) 'Talking back: "Small" interactional response tokens in everyday conversation', *Research on Language in Social Interaction*, 36(1): 33–63.

McCarthy, M.J. (2008) 'Accessing and interpreting corpus information in the teacher education context', *Language Teaching*, 41(4): 563–574.

McCarthy, M.J. (2010) 'Spoken fluency revisited', *English Profile Journal*, 1(1): e4.

McCarthy, M.J. and Carter, R.A. (1997a) 'Written and spoken vocabulary', in N. Schmitt and M.J. McCarthy (eds), *Vocabulary: Description, Acquisition, Pedagogy*, Cambridge: Cambridge University Press: 20–39.

McCarthy, M.J. and Carter, R.A. (1997b) 'Grammar, tails and affect: constructing expressive choices in discourse', *Text*, 17(3): 405–429.

McCarthy, M.J. and Carter, R.A. (2002) 'This that and the other: multi-word clusters in spoken English as visible patterns of interaction', *Teanga* (Yearbook of the Irish Association for Applied Linguistics), 21: 30–52.

McCarthy, M.J. McCarten, J. and Sandiford, H. (2005–2011) *Touchstone, Student Books 1–4, and Blended/Online Program*, Cambridge: Cambridge University Press.

McCarthy, M.J. McCarten, J. and Sandiford, H. (2012–2013) *Viewpoint, Student Books 1 and 2*, Cambridge: Cambridge University Press.

McCarthy, M.J. and O'Keeffe, A. (2008) 'Corpora and the study of spoken language', in A, Ludeling, K. Merja and T. McEnery (eds), *Handbook of Corpus Linguistics*, Berlin: Mouton de Gruyter: 1–16.

Nelson, G. (1996) 'The design of the Corpus', in S. Greenbaum (ed), *Comparing English Worldwide: The International Corpus of English*, Oxford: Oxford University Press: 27–35.

O'Keeffe, A. (2003) '*Like the wise virgins and all that jazz* – Using a corpus to examine vague language and shared knowledge', in U. Connor and T.A. Upton (eds), *Applied Corpus Linguistics: A Multidimensional Perspective*, Amsterdam, Netherlands: Rodopi: 1–20.

O'Keeffe, A. (2006) *Investigating Media Discourse*, Abingdon, Oxon: Routledge.

O'Keeffe, A. and Adolphs, S. (2008) 'Using a corpus to look at variational pragmatics: response tokens in British and Irish discourse', in K.P. Schneider and A. Barron (eds), *Variational Pragmatics*, Amsterdam, Netherlands: John Benjamins: 69–98.

O'Keeffe, A., Clancy, B. and Adolphs, S. (2011) *Introducing Pragmatics in Use*, London, UK: Routledge.

O'Keeffe, A. and Farr, F. (2003) 'Using language corpora in language teacher education: pedagogic, linguistic and cultural insights', *TESOL Quarterly*, 37(3): 389–418.

Quirk, R., Greenbaum, S., Leech, G. and Svartvik, J. (1985) *A Comprehensive Grammar of the English Language*, London, UK: Longman.

Römer, U. (2008) 'Corpora and language teaching', in A. Lüdeling and K. Merja (eds), *Corpus Linguistics. An International Handbook* (Vol. 1). Berlin: Mouton de Gruyter, 112–130.

Rühlemann, C. (2007) *Conversation in Context: A Corpus-Driven Approach*, London, UK: Continuum.

Schmidt, R. (1993) 'Awareness and second language acquisition', *Annual Review of Applied Linguistics*, 13: 206–226.

Sharwood Smith, M. (1993) 'Input enhancement in instructed SLA: theoretical bases', *Studies in Second Language Acquisition*, 15: 165–179.

Sinclair, J.M. and Mauranen, A. (2006) *Linear Unit Grammar: Integrating Speech and Writing*, Amsterdam, Netherlands: John Benjamins.

Stefanowitsch, A. and Gries, S.T. (2003) 'Collostructions: investigating the interaction between words and constructions', *International Journal of Corpus Linguistics*, 8(2): 209–243.

Stenström, A.-B. (1990) 'Lexical items peculiar to spoken discourse', in J. Svartvik (ed), *The London-Lund Corpus of Spoken English*, Lund: Lund University Press: 137–175.

Stevenson, M.P. and Liu, M. (2010) 'Learning a language with Web 2.0: Exploring the use of social networking features of foreign language learning websites', *CALICO Journal*, 27(2): 233–259.

Tao, H. (2003) 'Turn initiators in spoken English: A corpus-based approach to interaction and grammar', in P. Leistyna and C.F. Meyer (eds), *Corpus Analysis: Language Structure and Language Use*, Amsterdam, Netherlands: Rodopi: 187–207.

Timmis, I. (2010) '"Tails" of linguistic survival', *Applied Linguistics*, 31(3): 325–345.

Tottie, G. (1991) 'Conversational style in British and American English, the case of backchannels', in K. Aijmer and B. Altenberg (eds), *English Corpus Linguistics*, London, UK: Longman: 254–271.

Tottie, G. (2011) '*Uh* and *um* as sociolinguistic markers in British English', *International Journal of Corpus Linguistics*, 16(2): 173–197.

Watts, R.J. (1989) 'Taking the pitcher to the "well": Native speakers' perception of their use of discourse markers in conversation', *Journal of Pragmatics*, 13: 203–237.

Yngve, V. (1970) 'On getting a word in edgewise', *Papers from the 6th Regional Meeting, Chicago Linguistic Society*, Chicago, IL: Chicago Linguistic Society.

Zimmerman, D. (1993) 'Acknowledgement tokens and speakership incipiency revisited', *Research on Language and Social Interaction*, 26(2): 179–194.

# 26
# Written language corpora and pedagogical applications

*Angela Chambers*

This chapter begins by showing how the study of academic writing as a research area has come to underpin publications which investigate how learners can benefit from corpus data to improve their writing skills. This raises the issue of what types of corpora are best suited to the teaching environment, and the concept of the pedagogical corpus is thus investigated. Then some uses of pedagogical corpora are examined, focusing mainly on academic writing but also referring to the use of corpora of other written genres in the learning and teaching context. On the one hand, the use of easily accessible corpora for learning vocabulary and lexico-grammatical patterns is discussed, while on the other the issue of the potential of corpora at the level of discourse is raised. While the majority of the references cited involve English, it is important to remember that there are also applications of corpora in relation to other languages, and this is the focus of the next section. Examples involving French will be included here, as the author has experience of teaching that language at the undergraduate and postgraduate levels. Finally, as studies of corpus consultation by learners have shown negative as well as positive reactions, the chapter deals with some of the challenges which have to be faced by the teacher who wishes to integrate written corpus data in the curriculum.

## Written corpora: From research to teaching

As acquiring competence in writing is a major part of the language learning and teaching environment, and as corpora provide access to increasingly vast collections of written texts, it is not surprising that the potential of using corpus data in this context is being investigated by researchers and teachers alike. Academic writing, in particular, has been the focus of attention of many researchers, most notably Swales (1990, 2004) and Hyland (2002, 2008). It is clear that the relevance of this type of research is to a large extent rooted in the need for students and academics to write and publish in a language which is not their native language, which in the vast majority of cases is English. This type of research and practice is thus based on the concept of genre. This is no doubt one of the reasons why researchers are increasingly focusing on the role of corpus data in their disciplines, and why the potential of using corpus data in teaching writing skills (Lee and Swales 2006) is being investigated.

Research on academic writing, mainly in English, has understandably taken advantage of developments in corpus linguistics. While it is generally corpus-based and takes quantitative data as the starting point, the approaches used are mainly qualitative in nature. Hyland's 2008 study of the ways in which authorial stance is conveyed in eight academic disciplines, for example, uses a corpus of 240 research articles of 1.4 million words in English, as well as interviews with academics, as the source of data on how stance and engagement are expressed in the eight disciplines. Stance is defined as 'the writer's textual "voice" or community recognised personality. This is an attitudinal, writer-oriented function, and concerns the ways we present ourselves and convey our judgments, opinions and commitments' (ibid.: 5). It is expressed through hedges (including adverbials such as 'possibly' and phrases such as 'these results may suggest that'), boosters (including adverbs such as 'certainly' and phrases such as 'these results clearly show that'), attitude markers and self-mention. All of these are illustrated from the corpus. Engagement, on the other hand, is defined as 'the ways writers rhetorically recognise the presence of their readers to actively pull them along with the argument, include them as discourse participants, and guide them to interpretations' (ibid.). Engagement is illustrated by examples from the corpus of reader mention, directives, such as 'see Smith 1999' (Hyland 2008: 10), questions, knowledge reference and asides. As we shall see later in the chapter, research such as this can inform practical applications of using corpus data in the classroom.

O'Sullivan (2010) similarly provides a qualitative study of an aspect of academic writing, in this case citation practices. The starting point is the use of concordancing software to search for occurrences of *19??* and *20??* to provide a list of all the citations in the 1-million-word corpus of academic writing in French (Chambers and Le Baron 2007) which she is investigating. The 758 citations which this produces are then analysed to reveal aspects of language use when citing, which in turn can be of use to novice writers, for example, the types of reporting verbs and the ways in which these convey the authorial stance of the writers. The pedagogical applications of these data are then discussed, including the indirect consultation of the data by students using examples prepared in advance by the teacher, and the potential for direct consultation of the corpus by learners using the concordance to investigate language use by expert writers both in the drafting and revision stages of writing. These are just two examples of how the vast area of research in academic writing can provide the teacher with valuable information which can be used to raise awareness of novice writers in these disciplines.

## The pedagogical corpus

Research on the use of corpora in the teaching of writing has centred mainly on higher education – understandably so, as the researchers are often engaging in action research, with their publications reporting on experimentation and innovation in their own practice. The substantial body of publications which has developed in this area often does not rely on the existing large reference corpora, but on smaller specialised corpora which the teacher/researchers have created to meet their learners' needs. (For further information on small specialised corpora, see Murphy and Riordan, Chapter 28 this volume). This section will briefly consider how these researchers define the pedagogical corpus, and the following section will then discuss how they have integrated corpus data into their classes. Two approaches are commonly used, namely the indirect approach, in which the learners work on concordances prepared in advance by the teacher, and the more challenging but arguably more rewarding direct approach, where learners have direct access to the corpora and the concordancing software and can carry out their own corpus searches. Studies in which learners compare their own writing with that of expert writers will be discussed. Finally, as small corpora of academic writing are relatively easy to create, the use of such corpora as resources for postgraduate study, for example at the doctoral and master's levels, will be explored.

The pedagogical corpus, as its name suggests, is primarily intended to serve as a resource for teaching rather than research, although many can serve both functions. In an early reference to the practice of making specialised collections of texts available to learners, Tribble (1990: 11) describes what would later be termed a pedagogical corpus, although he does not use the term: 'A collection of business letters can give an invaluable insight into the types of wording and grammar appropriate to a variety of commercial transactions'. Terms referring to the pedagogical purpose of the corpus would later be used by Willis (1998: 46), Braun (2005) and others. Corpora such as these often focus on one genre, usually relating to the specific interests of the learners. As Nesi points out, they are usually small corpora, although this is not necessarily a disadvantage:

> Corpora for specific research or pedagogical purposes, however, are usually created by time-poor academics and teachers, as Krishnamurthy and Kosem (2007) point out. They therefore tend to be smaller, although they can still be representative of a specific language variety because the narrower the corpus domain, the fewer texts will be needed to represent it.
>
> *(Nesi 2013: 408)*

In the case of academic writing, the pedagogical corpus will often consist of research articles as examples of expert writing for postgraduate students and early career-stage researchers, in some cases for comparison with their own writing. Information on a number of these studies will be provided later. It is important to note that pedagogical corpora, while they often consist of or include academic writing, are certainly not limited to this genre, and can include both written and/or spoken texts. The SACODEYL[1] and BACKBONE[2] corpora, for example, focus on spoken texts, consisting of interviews with teenagers and adults of various ages respectively in several European languages. (For information on corpora, including academic writing, which are publicly, although not necessarily freely available, see Nesi 2013. See also Murphy and Riordan, Chapter 28 this volume.)

## Pedagogical corpora for writing skills

The simplest way for a teacher to introduce corpus data into the classroom is to prepare exercises based on concordances which they have produced themselves, as in the example from business letters given earlier. Thus Tribble (1990: 12) provides learners with a concordance from which he has omitted two commonly confused prepositions, *in* and *at*, and asks them to work in groups to complete the exercises. An exercise such as this can obviously be prepared to cater for different levels of learners. In this case, the learners discover that in the expression 'at Vienna and Helsinki' (ibid.: 13) the preposition is 'accounted for by the following term being a metonymy standing for "at the Vienna conference": an institution rather than a physical location containing the event'. A particularly easy way for a teacher to prepare concordances in support of teaching is by using Lextutor,[3] a website which includes access to a number of written and spoken resources in English, French, German and Spanish, and which has a simple built-in concordancer which can be used with very minimal training. The written texts available in English, for example, include 1 million words from the BNC and 174,000 words of academic abstracts, namely abstracts of master's and doctoral theses from a number of disciplinary areas. A search for the word *thesis* in the abstracts provides 332 occurrences, and includes quantitative

> is=32 examines=23 presents=17 will=16 argues=12 proposes=10 explores=9 develops=5 makes=5 describes=4 discusses=4 provides=4 suggests=4 addresses=3 aims=3 considers=3 demonstrates=3 focuses=3 investigates=3 seeks=3 uses=3 applies=2 attempts=2 begins=2 centres=2 concludes=2 contains=2 documents=2 draws=2 integrates=2 studies=2 was=2

*Figure 26.1* Verbs following *thesis* in Lextutor

> 1  This THESIS ADDRESSES both of these issues.
> 2  The THESIS ADDRESSES this lack using an in-depth, situated case study of the
> 3  This THESIS ADDRESSES two main issues; first, the incorporation of the multiface
>
> ---
>
> 1  The THESIS AIMS to document and interpret this reappearance of the traditional techniques of historical archaeology as applied to cultural landscapes
> 2  The THESIS AIMS to examine the engagement between squatters and the landscape.
> 3  This THESIS AIMS to offer a theoretical foundation for the concept of mobility,

*Figure 26.2* Phrases including *thesis* in Lextutor

data at the bottom of the concordance on the collocates. This is particularly interesting in relation to the verbs which follow the noun *thesis*, as shown in Figure 26.1.

The teacher can thus easily prepare a concordance of a variety of these verbs to complement an occurrence in a single text which is being studied. As an example, the occurrences of 'thesis addresses' and 'thesis aims' are given in Figure 26.2. By clicking on an individual occurrence, access is provided not to the whole corpus, but to several lines of co-text, which can be of help in making the context clear.

Showing the whole concordance online to a class, the teacher could illustrate a number of aspects of these abstracts, for example, that the present tense is more common than the future, which represents only sixteen occurrences. With Internet access available in the classroom, other aspects of the abstracts could also be investigated in support of the classroom activities, such as the use of the first person, or citation practices. Other online resources can also be used in similar ways. Wordandphrase.info, for example, provides access to the Corpus of Contemporary American English (COCA), and allows searches of words and phrases limited to specific genres, including academic writing.

The direct approach involves giving the learners direct access to the corpus and providing them with training in the use of concordancing software and guidance in corpus consultation and analysis techniques. There has been an increasing number of studies since Tim Johns (1986) and others published studies reporting on their use of concordance data with learners. At this early stage of research in corpora and language learning, Johns (1986: 161) even mentioned that he was experimenting with the practice of placing a 'C' in the margin when assessing to suggest to his students that they could improve their language use in the relevant area by consulting a corpus. The Lextutor corpora, for example, could easily be consulted in this way by learners. Later studies (see e.g. Yoon and Hirvela 2004; Chambers 2005; O'Sullivan and Chambers

2006) provide detailed reports on learner reactions to direct corpus consultation, revealing both positive and negative reactions. The positive reactions include appreciation of the availability of multiple examples of real language use (Cheng, Warren and Xun-feng 2003: 181; Yoon and Hirvela 2004: 275; Chambers 2005: 120), while the negative reactions tend to focus on the time-consuming and laborious nature of analysing large amounts of data (Cheng, Warren and Xun-feng 2003: 183; Yoon and Hirvela 2004: 274; Chambers 2005: 120). Kennedy and Miceli (2001: 81) provide recommendations on the steps a teacher can follow when guiding learners in corpus analysis. They recommend a four-step process: '(a) formulating the question; (b) devising a search strategy; (c) observing the examples found and selecting relevant ones; and (d) drawing conclusions'. Finally, Yoon and Jo (2014: 107) examine the learning strategies used by students in direct and indirect corpus consultation. Their study reveals that the learners use a variety of strategies: meta-cognitive strategies such as self-evaluation and monitoring; cognitive strategies such as association, grouping and translation; affective strategies such as self-encouragement; and social strategies such as consulting the teacher. While the learners in the study 'preferred the interactive aspect of direct corpora use, which also raised their learning awareness' (ibid.: 112), the authors emphasise that 'indirect corpus use can be a great learning method for lower-level students in its own right' (ibid.: 113).

With the exception of Lee and Swales (2006), the studies of corpora and academic writing cited so far have been corpora of native speaker writing. However, according to Granger (2002), learner corpora also have an important role to play. Aston (2000: 10) points out that using corpora of native speaker texts as models provides no information on difficulty, learnability, or the productivity of features from the learner's perspective. Learner corpus research can thus make an important contribution to the area of corpora and language learning by revealing what corpus-based resources are necessary (Granger 2009). While Granger (2002: 26) accepts that giving learners significant exposure to erroneous data would be problematic, she argues for the relevance of learner data in two contexts, namely form-focused instruction and drawing attention to the gap between learner writing and expert writing. The latter of these has been the focus of a number of studies. Wen-Ming and Hsien-Chin (2008), for example, created two small corpora, fifty abstracts of research articles published in journals, and fifty abstracts of papers given at conferences, written by novice, nonnative speaker (NNS) writers. They included the NNS data in one lesson, and observed that the students showed interest in comparing their writing with that of expert writers. Other studies also exist in which teachers create corpora of current or former students' writing and also corpora of expert writing for use in the development of teaching materials (Mukherjee and Rohrbach 2006; Bloch 2009, 2010; Rankin and Schiftner 2011). Outside the context of academic writing, Belz and Vyatkina (2008) created an integrated bilingual corpus involving telecollaboration between learners of German and native speakers. An important feature which emerges from reading these studies is that a significant amount of time and effort is required on the part of the teacher to collect and analyse the data and to create the relevant exercises. While this makes for very interesting applied research projects, replicability may be limited for the majority of teachers who are not researchers.

The work of Lee and Swales (2006) is perhaps more easily replicable by teachers, as the learners themselves play an important role in the creation of the corpora. In their study PhD students create specialist micro-corpora as part of a course in corpus-informed EAP. They compile a corpus of their own writing and another of 'expert' writing, and subsequently compare their texts with those of established writers in the field. While the evaluation by the students was very positive, the authors point out that this success may have been largely attributable to the fact that the participants consisted of a small, highly motivated and very computer-literate group (ibid.: 72). As the learning and teaching of academic writing, particularly at the

> In this paper we have adopted a novel approach to investigate the molecular requirements for Cd36 to bind modified LdL.
>
> In order to explore this issue and to develop an improved understanding of the repertoire of p16 modulators, we have undertaken a genome-wide siRNA screen in normal finite life-span human mammary epithelial cells in which p16-mediated senescence is well established.
>
> To identify such genes we used a combination of suppressive subtractive hybridisation (SSH) and cDNA arrays.

*Figure 26.3* The use of *we* in statements of purpose
*Source*: Martin (2013: 44).

postgraduate level, may often be undertaken in a specialised rather than a general context, this is perhaps the area where the potential of small genre-specific corpora has the greatest potential for development.

There is also scope for the underlying principle in Lee and Swales's study, namely the creation by postgraduate students of small corpora of academic writing, to be undertaken by students of applied linguistics at the master's and doctoral levels, not necessarily for the improvement of their own written skills, but as a resource for the analysis of academic writing for the master's dissertation. Research projects such as these can, in turn, provide relevant information and guidance for teachers of academic writing wishing to use corpus data in their teaching. Martin (2013), for example, created a corpus of sixty biomedical research articles. This was then used as the basis for a study of the lexico-grammatical patterns found in statements of purpose in the introductions. A comparison with how this aspect of the research article introductions is dealt with in three relevant course books reveals that this small corpus provides a much richer learning environment for NNS writers, and also in the context of materials development for teachers. For example, Martin found that almost half (45.6%) of the occurrences of the personal pronoun *we* in the research article introductions are found in the statements of purpose. More than 98% of the articles in the corpus use *we* in the statements of purpose. Examples are listed in Figure 26.3.

In contrast, the examples provided in the course books examined in this research place much less emphasis on the degree to which authors use the personal pronoun in statements of purpose (Martin 2013: 34–35). She emphasises that this is not in any way to criticise the course books analysed, but rather to suggest that corpus data can greatly enhance the necessarily limited number of examples provided by course books, grammars or dictionaries. As we shall see in the following section, postgraduate research projects such as this can also be carried out in a multilingual context.

## Written corpora in a multilingual context

While the first reference corpora, namely the Brown Corpus and the LOB Corpus, were in English, corpora are now commonly available in many other languages. Although most of the research on corpora of academic writing relates to English, there are nonetheless a number of publications in relation to other languages. (For an overview of research in academic writing in languages other than English, see Fløttum, Dahl and Kinn 2006: 26–28.) Fløttum and her colleagues (2006) created Cultural Identity in Academic Prose (in Norwegian: Kulturell Identitet j Akademisk Prosa, or KIAP), a corpus of 450 research articles, 150 in each of three disciplines:

linguistics, economics and medicine. Equivalent publications were selected in three languages: English, French and Norwegian. This was then used to compare language use in the research cultures represented by the three languages, and the researchers discovered, for example, that differences between disciplines were more significant than differences between languages, although some instances of the latter were found (2006: 267). The researchers analysed various aspects of the texts, focusing in particular on aspects of authorial stance and on the roles of the author as writer, researcher and arguer (p. 26).

In the context of corpora and language learning, research relating to English once again dominates, although other languages are nonetheless represented. Kennedy and Miceli (2001) have investigated direct corpus consultation by intermediate learners of Italian, and O'Sullivan and Chambers (2006) have reported on research on corpus consultation by learners of French as a means of improving a text which they have written in the target language. Smaller pedagogical corpora of written texts have also been created in languages other than English. As we have seen, Lextutor includes texts in English, French, German and Spanish, including a variety of written and spoken genres which teachers of these languages can use as a source of examples. The search shown here was carried out in a few minutes using one of the Lextutor French corpora, consisting of approximately 1 million words from the newspaper *Le Monde* in 1998. *Permet*, the third person singular form of the present tense of the verb *permettre* (to permit or allow), was chosen as it is commonly used in formal written genres such as journalism and academic writing, and in my experience is underused by learners, even at advanced level. Examples from the 198 occurrences are listed in Figure 26.4.

Lack of space prevents a longer list here, but the three examples earlier have been chosen to exemplify a variety of grammatical structures which can easily be illustrated in a concordance. A longer list of thirty or forty lines, approximately an A4 page, where the different structures are not classified and grouped by the teacher, could be used to provide additional examples of one occurrence of *permettre* encountered in a text which was being studied in class. The learners could then be asked to identify patterns in the concordance to work out how the verb is used – a simple example of data-driven learning. The third example could have easily been extended to a sentence using the facility on Lextutor to access several lines of co-text by clicking on the search word. In this case a long sentence with scientific terminology relating to doping in sport was produced, which a teacher might decide not to include, as the phrase in the concordance makes the context meaningful.

Another aspect of using concordancing in this way is also illustrated in these few lines. The reference to former German Chancellor Helmut Kohl in the second example somewhat dates the source of the examples (1998). A more contemporary source can be seen as an advantage by

---

Ses bandes dessinées ne sont qu'un prétexte qui lui permet de délivrer un message politique. [His manga are simply pretexts which allow him to convey a political message.]

Le nombre d'indécis reste toujours élevé, ce qui permet à M. Kohl d'assurer qu'il sera réélu. [The number of undecided voters remains high, thus allowing Kohl to be certain of reelection.]

Le volume total de sang (sachant qu'une mesure au-delà de 50% permet de supposer que le sportif a absorbé des produits dopants). [The total volume of blood (given that a count above 50% suggests that the sportsperson has taken illegal substances).]

---

*Figure 26.4* Permettre in *Le Monde* in 1998

the learners. In one study (Chambers 2005: 120), where the learners were investigating a small corpus of journalistic texts created a few months previously, the fact that the examples were up-to-date and familiar was greatly appreciated by the learners, making for what one student termed 'easy memorizing'. On the practical side, however, for most teachers the instant access to examples which are generally on familiar topics provided by Lextutor will greatly outweigh the fact that references to individual names date very quickly.

The use of *permettre* is a useful and a relatively straightforward example. Others can be more complicated. In a study of the use of corpora in the teaching of the subjunctive in French (Chambers 2013), for example, a teacher could easily find examples of the use of the subjunctive with the modal verb *falloir* (to have to), where no variation was found in the occurrences, although one example included taboo language. However, when two other uses of the subjunctive were examined, namely with *il semble que* (it seems that) and with rare tenses such as the imperfect subjunctive and the pluperfect subjunctive, variation was very evident in the first case, and performance errors by native speakers were present in the second. The use of corpora can thus pose a challenge for teachers in that it forces them to choose what examples to present to the learners. On the one hand it may not be appropriate to give learners at a lower level too many examples of variation or performance errors in native speaker use, while on the other advanced learners may benefit greatly from such exposure, as it allows them to appreciate the richness and complexity of actual language use. The point at which it is appropriate to put this distinction into operation, however, is not always easy to determine.

In the context of teaching academic writing to advanced learners, corpora of the genre which the learners wish to master can be an invaluable resource. An example which I have used in French is to ask postgraduate students to study the use of *nous* (*we*, *us*) in a subcorpus of single-authored research articles in French (created from Chambers and Le Baron 2007) and to decide to whom the pronoun refers: to the author or the author and the reader, or whether it is a more inclusive use of the pronoun. On a simple level this can remind the students that it is normal practice in academic writing in French to use the plural form rather than the singular for self-mention. It can also provide the basis for a study of the variety of verbs used with *nous* to describe the author's activities as a writer, researcher and arguer. On a more sophisticated level it can enable them to discover examples of the reader engagement studied by Hyland (2008), referred to earlier. Examples are given in Figure 26.5.

In several examples it is clear that the plural pronoun simply refers to the single author (1, 3, 6, 7, 10, 11 and 13). In other examples it seems more likely that the author and the reader are included in the use of *nous* (2, 4, 5, 8, 9, 12 and 14). Classification is not entirely straightforward here; example 14, for example, could refer either to the author or to the author and the reader. Example 5 could also have a wider field of reference, a generic use of *nous* referring to the research community in general. Author roles can also be investigated. In examples 1, 3 and 13, it is clearly the role of writer which is emphasised, while the role of researcher predominates in examples 6, 7 and 14. The role of arguer is evident in examples 2, 8, 9 and 11. In examples 2, 4 and 5, the author is clearly attempting to engage with the readers. Thus, even at the level of indirect corpus consultation, these examples illustrate how a concordance can be used to encourage discovery learning in group work, and to focus on what Charles (2007: 290) describes as the need for research on corpora and language learning to 'help students to tackle their higher level discourse concerns'.

As in the case of monolingual corpora, studies of academic writing can be carried out by postgraduate researchers using small genre-specific corpora. Curry (2014), for example, carried out a contrastive analysis of the use of direct questions in French and English in a subcorpus of the KIAP corpus (Fløttum et al. 2006), which is described at the start of this section. The

Angela Chambers

> 1 Nous présentons les variables retenues dans cette régression et nous proposons une analyse descriptive rapide de l'évolution de ces variables
>
> 2 Comment pouvons-nous expliquer une telle logique? Étant donné que les télécommunications dominent
>
> 3 Comme nous l'avons indiqué plus haut, les premières critiques furent formulées
>
> 4 celui de la géographie régionale, de Marc Bloch, de Roger Dion ou, plus près de nous, de Jean-Robert Pitte
>
> 5 Nous sommes loin d'un modèle d'échange et de discussion, qui serait le fondement
>
> 6 Pour mieux saisir cette interaction, nous avons choisi de nous pencher sur la communauté de Saint-Roch-de-l'Achigan
>
> 7 En tenant compte des remariages, la démarche nous a conduit à effectuer la généalogie courte de 304 individus.
>
> 8 Un indice peut cependant nous être fourni à une date postérieure dans les registres
>
> 9 en mettant en avant l'interaction entre les deux protagonistes qui nous intéressent directement : le promoteur Infonie et la presse.
>
> 10 Arrivée à un certain seuil, une telle recherche défierait, nous le pensons, les limites du « raisonnable », du « normal »
>
> 11 Si les SACI sont, comme nous le prétendons, des dispositifs communicationnels à part entière
>
> 12 C'est en examinant leur mise en oeuvre que nous pouvons juger les normes et valider les systèmes de représentation
>
> 13 Dans cet article, nous nous concentrerons sur la question de l'autonomie de l'apprenant.
>
> 14 Sans prétendre du tout à l'exhaustivité sur ce point difficile du spinozisme, nous pouvons distinguer deux types d'approche de la nature du corps humain

*Figure 26.5* The use of *nous* (*we*, *us*) in single-authored research articles in French (an English translation is available in Appendix 26A)

subcorpus includes the articles in French and English in the area of linguistics. The analysis, which examines the forms and functions of the questions, reveals that direct questions are more common in French than in English. Contrastive studies of academic writing in English and French (Salager-Meyer, Alcaraz Ariza and Zambrano 2003: 232, cited in Curry 2014: 38) suggest that academic writing in English tends to prefer techniques such as hedging, while equivalent writing in French is more direct and passionate. Curry's analysis also reveals that the functions which the questions fulfil are similar in the two languages, corresponding to categories defined by Hyland (2002). A notable difference is observed in the form of the questions, in that alternative and declarative questions, as defined by Carter and McCarthy (2006: 722–724) are more common in French. Alternative questions offer the reader an option, for example: 'Perspectives de recherche foisonnantes ou suggestions oiseuses?' ['An abundance of possibilities for research or idle suggestions?'] (Curry 2014: 32). Declarative questions do not involve inversion, but simply take the form of a statement, for example: 'Une voix imperceptible qui s'entend?' ['An imperceptible voice which is heard?'] (ibid.). These and the other results from this analysis provide useful information for teachers of academic writing in either French or English, in that the differences in patterns in the two languages could be used to inform the teaching of this aspect of writing. The examples in this section thus show that there is scope for teachers of languages other than English to use corpus data with their learners, either by using easily and freely available resources or by benefitting from even small-scale research projects involving specific language pairs.

## The challenges of integrating corpora in the teaching of writing

On a practical level, the question arises as to whether research such as that described earlier actually influences the teaching of writing. We have seen that corpus data are now increasingly used for research on their potential for teaching, and on ways in which teachers can make corpus data available to learners to help them to improve their writing skills. It is difficult to discover, however, to what extent this type of experimentation influences practice by teachers who are not researchers. In the context of corpora and teaching applications, Nesi (2013: 418, citing Römer 2010) comments that 'researchers still need to communicate more with teachers and materials developers'. While dictionaries and course books, such as the *Oxford Hachette French-English Dictionary* and the Touchstone series of course books (McCarthy, McCarten and Sandiford 2004–2006) are now increasingly corpus-based, the number of publications addressed directly to teachers and providing guidance on the uses of corpora in the classroom remains limited. Tribble and Jones (1990) and Reppen (2010) are among the few examples, although they do not focus solely on academic writing.

The fact that corpus consultation is not believed to be widely adopted outside the research community may be explained by a number of factors. We have already seen that in many studies a considerable amount of work is required by the teacher/researcher to create corpora and prepare teaching materials. Flowerdew (2012: 204–205) puts forward a number of other reasons for 'the lack of uptake of corpus-driven pedagogy by the teaching community', based on an overview of reasons given in publications in the field. First she suggests that the medium rather than the methodology may be the problem, as 'some tools try to meet the needs of both researchers and teachers' (ibid.). She also points out that the naturally occurring data in corpora will often be too advanced for the majority of learners who are not at advanced level. Finally she stresses the importance of strategy training for teaching and learners.

It has been suggested by a number of researchers that a possible solution to this problem lies in the inclusion of corpora in language teacher education programmes (see, for example, Farr 2008). Such developments would have to take account of the needs of learners at secondary level, in contrast to the majority of publications on the subject to date, which involve undergraduate and postgraduate students at university level. Braun (2007) is an exception, in that her study involves secondary school learners. Johns (1997) carried out a study of teachers' use of a concordancing program. Finally, another limitation of corpus research in the educational context to date is that it is dominated by English, and more particularly, by English in a global context, in other words with little reference to the specific needs of learners who are speakers of a particular language. Mur Dueñas (2009) is an example of a study which is situated in the context of a specific language pair, Spanish learners of English. All of these factors indicate a need for further research in the various areas mentioned, as well as for collaboration with teachers both within and outside higher education who are not also researchers in corpora and language learning.

## Further reading

Ädel, A. (2010) 'Using corpora to teach academic writing: Challenges for the direct approach', in M. Carmen Campoy, B. Bellés-Fortuno and M.-L. Gea-Valor (eds), *Corpus-Based Approaches to English Language Teaching*, London, UK: Continuum: 39–55.

This book chapter is intended to complement the studies of the use of corpus data in language learning such as those cited earlier in the present chapter and examined in Boulton's (2012) review article, described earlier. The author asks 'why there are so few examples of teaching academic writing using corpora, especially above the level of vocabulary and collocation' (Ädel 2010: 41). Pointing out that these are only a small proportion of the issues covered in academic writing courses, she identifies and examines the following obstacles to wider use of corpora in this context, namely lack of corpus availability, the difficulty of knowing what to look for, the risk of 'drowning in data' (ibid.: 46) and interpreting and evaluating patterns.

Boulton, A. (2012) 'Corpus consultation for ESP: A review of empirical research', in A. Boulton, S. Carter-Thomas and E. Rowley-Jolivet (eds), *Corpus-Informed Research and Teaching in ESP: Issues and Applications*, Amsterdam, Netherlands: John Benjamins: 261–291.

This study reviews twenty empirical evaluations of the use of corpora by learners of English for specific purposes. Boulton notes the variety of course objectives, experiment design and research questions. His qualitative analysis concentrates on corpus consultation for the acquisition of vocabulary and for assistance with writing, and in both cases the results are generally positive.

Flowerdew, L. (2012) *Corpora and Language Education*, Houndmills: Palgrave Macmillan.

This book gives a comprehensive overview of corpus linguistics, both in research and teaching. Much of the book is devoted to pedagogical applications, focusing on both written and spoken corpora. A number of case studies based on published research are included, two of which involve academic writing. Research articles in the area of business in Spanish and English are the subject of one study (pp. 241–245), based on Mur Dueñas (2009), while the other focuses on intermediate learners of EAP (pp. 260–263), based on Boulton (2010).

## Notes

1 http://www.um.es/sacodeyl (accessed 27 June 2014).
2 http://www.um.es/backbone (accessed 27 June 2014).
3 http://www.lextutor.ca (accessed 27 June 2014).

## References

Ädel, A. (2010) 'Using corpora to teach academic writing: Challenges for the direct approach', in M. Carmen Campoy, B. Bellés-Fortuno and M.-L. Gea-Valor (eds), *Corpus-Based Approaches to English Language Teaching*, London, UK: Continuum: 39–55.

Aston, G. (2000) 'Corpora and language teaching', in L. Burnard and T. McEnery (eds), *Rethinking Language Pedagogy from a Corpus Perspective*, Frankfurt: Peter Lang: 7–17.

Belz, J. and Vyatkina, N. (2008) 'The pedagogical mediation of a developmental learner corpus for classroom-based language instruction', *Language Learning & Technology*, 12(3): 33–52.

Bloch, J. (2009) 'The design of an online concordancing program for teaching about reporting verbs', *Language Learning & Technology*, 13(1): 59–78.

Bloch, J. (2010) 'A concordance-based study of the use of reporting verbs as rhetorical devices in academic papers', *Journal of Writing Research*, 2(2): 219–244.

Boulton, A. (2010) 'Data-driven learning: Taking the computer out of the equation', *Language Learning*, 60(3): 534–572.

Boulton, A. (2012) 'Corpus consultation for ESP: A review of empirical research', in A. Boulton, S. Carter-Thomas and E. Rowley-Jolivet (eds), *Corpus-Informed Research and Teaching in ESP: Issues and Applications*, Amsterdam, Netherlands: John Benjamins: 261–291.

Braun, S. (2005) 'From pedagogically relevant corpora to authentic language learning contents', *ReCALL*, 17(1): 47–64.

Braun, S. (2007) 'Integrating corpus work into secondary education: From data-driven learning to needs-driven corpora', *ReCALL*, 19(3): 307–328.

Carter, R. and McCarthy, M. (2006) *Cambridge Grammar of English*, Cambridge: Cambridge University Press.
Chambers, A. (2005) 'Integrating corpus consultation in language learning', *Language Learning & Technology*, 9(2): 111–125.
Chambers, A. (2013) 'Learning and teaching the subjunctive in French: The contribution of corpus data', *Bulletin Suisse de Linguistique Appliquée*, 97: 41–58.
Chambers, A. and Le Baron, F. (eds) (2007) *The Chambers–Le Baron Corpus of Research Articles in French/Le Corpus Chambers–Le Baron d'articles de recherche en français*, Oxford: Oxford Text Archive, available: http://ota.ahds.ac.uk/headers/2527.xml (accessed 10 Nov 2013).
Charles, M. (2007) 'Reconciling top-down and bottom-up approaches to graduate writing: Using a corpus to teach rhetorical functions', *Journal of English for Academic Purposes*, 6(4): 289–302.
Cheng, W., Warren, M. and Xun-feng, X. (2003) 'The language learner as language researcher: Putting Corpus Linguistics on the timetable', *System* 31(2): 173–186.
Curry, N. (2014) 'Direct questions in applied linguistics research articles in English and French: A corpus-based contrastive analysis', unpublished master's thesis, University of Limerick.
Farr, F. (2008) 'Evaluating the use of corpus-based instruction in a language teacher education context: Perspectives from the users', *Language Awareness*, 17(1): 25–43.
Fløttum, K., T. Dahl and T. Kinn (2006) *Academic Voices: Across Languages and Disciplines*, Amsterdam, Netherlands: John Benjamins.
Flowerdew, L. (2012) *Corpora and Language Education*, Houndmills: Palgrave Macmillan.
Granger, S. (2002) 'A bird's-eye view of learner corpus research', in S. Granger, J. Hung and S. Petch-Tyson (eds), *Computer Learner Corpora, Second Language Acquisition and Foreign Language Teaching*, Amsterdam, Netherlands: John Benjamins: 3–33.
Granger, S. (2009) 'The contribution of learner corpora to second language acquisition and foreign language teaching: A critical evaluation', in K. Aijmer (ed), *Corpora and Language Teaching*, Amsterdam; Philadelphia: John Benjamins: 13–32.
Hyland, K. (2002) 'What do they mean? Questions in academic writing', *Text*, 22(4): 529–557.
Hyland, K. (2008) 'Persuasion, interaction and the construction of knowledge: Representing self and others in research writing', *International Journal of English Studies*, 8(2): 1–23.
Johns, T. (1986) 'Micro-concord: A language learner's research tool', *System*, 14(2): 151–62.
Johns, T. (1997) 'Contexts: The background, development, and trialling of a concordance-based CALL program', in A. Wichmann, S. Fligelstone, T. McEnery and G. Knowles (eds), *Teaching and Language Corpora*, London; New York: Longman: 100–115.
Kennedy, C. and Miceli, T. (2001) 'An evaluation of intermediate students' approaches to corpus investigation', *Language Learning & Technology*, 5(3): 77–90.
Lee, D. and Swales, J. (2006) 'A corpus-based EAP course for NNS doctoral students: Moving from available specialized corpora to self-compiled corpora', *English for Specific Purposes*, 25(1): 56–75.
Krishnamurthy, R. and Kosem, I. (2007) 'Issues in creating a corpus for EAP pedagogy and research', *Journal of English for Academic Purposes*, 6: 356–373.
Martin, C. (2013) 'Metadiscourse and lexicogrammar of statements of research aims in biomedical research articles: A corpus linguistics and discourse analysis study', unpublished master's thesis, University of Limerick.
McCarthy, M., McCarten, J. and Sandiford, H. (2004–2006) *Touchstone* (four levels), Cambridge: Cambridge University Press.
Mukherjee, J. and Rohrbach, J-M. (2006) 'Rethinking applied corpus linguistics from a language-pedagogical perspective: New departures in learner corpus research', in B. Kettemann and G. Marko (eds), *Planning, Gluing and Painting Corpora: Inside the Applied Corpus Linguist's Workshop*, Frankfurt am Main: Peter Lang: 205–232.
Mur Dueñas, P. (2009) 'Logical markers in L1 (Spanish and English) and L2 (English) business research articles', *English Text Construction*, 2(2): 246–264.
Nesi, H. (2013) 'ESP and corpus studies', in B. Paltridge and S. Starfield (eds), *The Handbook of English for Specific Purposes*, Oxford: Wiley-Blackwell: 407–426.
O'Sullivan, Í. (2010) 'Using corpora to enhance learners' academic writing skills in French', *Revue Française de Linguistique Appliquée*, XV(2): 21–35.
O'Sullivan, Í. and Chambers, A. (2006) 'Learners' writing skills in French: Corpus consultation and learner evaluation', *Journal of Second Language Writing*, 15: 49–68.
*Oxford-Hachette French Dictionary* (2001), 3rd edn, Paris: Hachette.

Rankin, T. and Schiftner, B. (2011) 'Marginal prepositions in learner English: Applying local corpus data', *International Journal of Corpus Linguistics*, 16(3): 412–434.

Reppen, R. (2010) *Using Corpora in the Language Classroom*, Cambridge: Cambridge University Press.

Römer, U. (2010) 'Using general and specialised corpora in English language teaching: Past, present and future', in M. Carmen Campoy, B. Bellés-Fortuno and M.-L. Gea-Valor (eds), *Corpus-Based Approaches to English Language Teaching*, London, UK: Continuum: 18–38.

Salager-Meyer, F., Alcaraz Ariza, M. and Zambrano, N. (2003) 'The scimitar, the dagger and the glove: Intercultural differences in the rhetoric of criticism in Spanish, French and English medical discourse (1930–1995)', *English for Specific Purposes*, 22(3): 223–247.

Swales, J.M. (1990) *Genre Analysis*, Cambridge: Cambridge University Press.

Swales, J.M. (2004) *Research Genres: Explorations and Application*, Cambridge: Cambridge University Press.

Tribble, C. (1990) 'Concordancing and an EAP writing programme', *CAELL Journal*, 1(2): 10–15.

Tribble, C. and Jones, G. (1990) *Concordances in the Classroom: A Resource Book for Teachers*, Harlow, UK: Longman.

Wen-Ming, H. and Hsien-Chin, L. (2008) 'A case study of corpus-informed online academic writing for EFL graduate students', *CALICO*, 26(1): 28–47.

Willis, J. (1998) 'Concordances in the classroom without a computer: Assembling and exploiting concordances of common words', in B. Tomlinson (ed), *Materials Development in Language Teaching*, Cambridge: Cambridge University Press: 44–66.

Yoon, H. and Hirvela, A. (2004) 'ESL student attitudes towards corpus use in L2 writing', *Journal of Second Language Writing*, 13: 257–283.

Yoon, H. and Jo, J. (2014) 'Direct and indirect access to corpora: An exploratory case study comparing students' error correction and learning strategy use in l2 writing', *Language Learning & Technology*, 18(1): 96–117.

# Appendix 26A
# Translation of concordance lines in Figure 26.5

1 We present the variables present in this regression and we propose a brief descriptive analysis of the development of the variables

2 How can we explain such a logic? Given that telecommunications dominate

3 As we have shown earlier, the first critiques were expressed

4 that of regional geography, of Marc Bloch, Roger Dion or, closer to us, Jean-Robert Pitte

5 We are a long way from a model of exchange and discussion which would be the foundation

6 For a fuller understanding of this interaction, we will examine the community of Saint-Roch-de-l'Achigan

7 Taking remarriages into account, the procedure led us to draw up a brief genealogy of 304 individuals

8 We can however find an indication at a later date in the registers

9 focusing on the interaction between the two actors of particular interest here, the promoter Infonie and the press

10 At a certain level such research would in our view go beyond the limits of what is 'reasonable' and 'normal'

11 If the SACI are, as we claim, purely intended for the purpose of communication

12 By examining their implementation we can evaluate the norms and justify the systems of representation

13 In this article we concentrate on the issue of learner autonomy

14 Without in any way claiming to deal exhaustively with this difficult aspect of Spinozism, we can distinguish two types of approach to the nature of the human body

Figure 26.5 The use of *nous* (*we, us*) in single-authored research articles in French

# 27
# Learner corpora and pedagogical applications

*Fanny Meunier*

This chapter shows how learner corpora can be used to help design pedagogical applications. The first section contains a brief description of learner corpora and addresses some of the key issues in learner corpus collection and analysis. In the ensuing sections four types of learner corpus–informed pedagogical applications are presented, namely grammar books, learners' dictionaries and writing aids, automatic assessment, annotation and rating, and finally pre- and in-service teacher training for nonnative teachers. The final section of the chapter offers suggestions for further reading.

## What are learner corpora and why do we need them?

Granger (2004: 538) defines a learner corpus as 'an electronic collection of authentic texts produced by foreign or second language learners'. To be labelled as a learner corpus, the corpus must fulfil a number of conditions. As is the case for any type of language corpus, metadata (i.e. data about data) must be collected. Burnard (2004) explains that metadata collection is needed to describe any digital resource in sufficient detail and with sufficient accuracy for potential future users to determine whether or not the resource (in our case, the corpus) is relevant to a particular enquiry. The Text Encoding Initiative (TEI) is one of the existing consortia proposing sets of standardised metadata for language data in general. The TEI insists, among others, on the need to collect contextual information related to text, participant and setting description. Text description metadata may include topic, register, channel mode (informal face-to-face conversation, formal writing, etc.), factuality type (mostly factual, fictional, etc.), preparedness (spontaneous vs. prepared) and purpose type (to inform, to entertain, etc.). Participant descriptors typically include participant identification (often via anonymised coding) but also turn-taking identifications (in the case of interactions between various participants), age, sex and geographical origins or socioeconomic status of the participant(s). As for setting descriptors, they can include date and time of collection, 'locale' (namely a brief informal description of the kind of place concerned, for example, a room, a restaurant or a lecture hall) or activity (a brief informal description of what a participant in a language interaction is doing other than speaking, if anything). Keeping separate files and coding schemes for each type of linguistic annotation added is also of paramount importance. Additional and more specific types of metadata are also needed for learner corpus collection. They include, among others: information on the home country, the native language, the various language(s) spoken at home, the knowledge of foreign language(s) and their respective proficiency levels (as self-assessed or as officially assessed by educational organisations or internationally recognised proficiency tests), the language(s) of instruction in the learner's educational background, the amount of target language instruction (e.g. number of years spent studying the target language), the type and amount of input received in class or during extracurricular activities, the time spent in a country where the target language is the official language, and the potential use of reference tools (dictionaries or other) to prepare the text. In the case of longitudinal learner corpus collections, each individual participant and his/her language productions over time must also clearly be identified to ensure easy traceability. All those variables and metadata must be coded and integrated in the corpus environment so that they can later be used to select some learner productions on the basis of searchable features (e.g. only essays produced by learners who have spent at least six months in the target language country), and learners' agreements to use the data for research purposes must be obtained.

The main purpose in collecting such corpora is to gather objective data to describe learner language either cross-sectionally (i.e. at one particular point in time) or longitudinally (i.e. over time). As is the case for any corpus type, in addition to the metadata made available when collecting the corpus, various levels of interpretative and linguistic annotations (Leech 1997: 2) can also be added once the corpus has been collected (see also Reppen, Chapter 29 this volume for more detailed information on annotation). Such linguistic annotations may include part-of-speech tagging, syntactic parsing, error tagging or prosody annotation. For more details on corpus annotation, see Leech (1997), Meunier (1998) and Meurers (2009), among others.

In an earlier publication (Meunier 2012: 211), I described the main aims of learner corpus research as follows: to better describe learner language use and development through cross-sectional and longitudinal approaches, to foster the understanding of second language acquisition processes (see Myles 2008; Granger and Meunier 2010) and to enhance pedagogical materials (see Gabrielatos 2005; Meunier and Gouverneur 2009; Römer 2011) and the creation of data-driven learning activities (see Boulton 2008, 2009a, 2009b; Gilquin and Granger 2010).

The aim of the present chapter is to illustrate the pedagogical applications of learner corpora. Given space constraints, the list of pedagogical applications presented here does not claim to be exhaustive; the selection has simply been made to be representative of various trends in pedagogy. Before presenting the various illustrations, however, a key issue to consider when using learner corpora for pedagogical purposes is that it inevitably means presenting learners with error-prone input. The issue of whether or not learners should only be presented with correct input has often been debated in second/foreign language teaching circles, with some believing that only comprehensible (i.e. correct and understandable) input is valuable and useful in learning a second/foreign language (e.g. Krashen 1982), and others stressing the potential of also working with what can be called incomprehensible input. White (1987), for instance, stated that confronting language learners with incomprehensible input often leads to negative feedback being provided by the teacher (and sometimes also by peers), and that this negative feedback enhances the process of SLA as it draws the learner's attention to specific features that need to be corrected or edited in order to facilitate communication and comprehension. Keogh, Dabell and Naylor (2008: 33) concur with the aforementioned view and state that 'presenting errors to learners is an effective way to develop understanding' (readers are also referred to Bahrani 2013 for an in-depth survey and discussion on the benefits of using various types of input in SLA). The awareness-raising power of learner corpora is often linked to the notions of 'pedagogical relevance' and 'authentication' in second/foreign language learning and teaching. Belz and Vyatkina (2008) explain that corpora will be used by language learners if they can interpret, analyse and understand them in a personally meaningful way. This corresponds to what Granger (2009: 25) calls 'corpora for immediate pedagogical use (IPU)', that is, data 'collected by teachers as part of their normal classroom activities [. . .] [and where] the learners are at the same time producers and users of the corpus data'. This IPU is, for instance, found in telecollaborative projects where L2 learners interact (orally or in writing) with native speakers or other nonnative speakers of the target language. Belz and Vyatkina (2008: 35) describe their study as part of a 'language learning configuration in which distally located learners use Internet communication tools for social interaction, dialogue, and debate with NS age peers [. . .] in genuine interactions', which naturally creates this feeling of authentication. Such genuine interactions do include erroneous input and/or output from the part of the participants, but this in no way undermines their use in the language classroom. Their pedagogical relevance is ensured by what Braun (2006) calls the 'homogeneity' and 'topical relevance' of such types of corpora, which she adds are more important than the issues of corpus size or representativity that are often deemed central in corpus research. Ruiz-Madrid (2007: 57) advocates the use of web resources 'not to teach the same thing in a different way but rather to help our students to enter a new realm of collaborative inquiry and construction of knowledge', and that is exactly what those corpora offer, as they can be characterised as what Seidlhofer (2002) calls 'learner-centred', 'context-dependent' and 'culture-bound'.

After this brief presentation explaining what learner corpora are, how they are collected, and the various main purposes they serve, the following sections will present concrete examples of their integration in pedagogical applications.

## Learner corpora as input for grammar books

Conrad (2000: 549) listed the various changes that corpus-based studies of grammar would have on the teaching of grammar in the 21st century, namely (1) monolithic descriptions of English grammar would be replaced by register-specific descriptions; (2) the teaching of grammar would become more integrated with the teaching of vocabulary; and (3) the emphasis would shift from structural accuracy to the appropriate conditions of use for alternative grammatical constructions. Whilst such changes have partly taken place (see Meunier and Reppen 2015 for a detailed discussion) they were clearly led by native corpus analysis. Learner corpus research (henceforth LCR), whilst not mentioned at the time by Conrad in her article, has also brought some changes to the teaching of grammar.

A first and concrete illustration of the use of learner corpora in grammar books is Carter et al.'s *English Grammar Today* (2011). The book is described as a guide to contemporary English grammar and usage. It is accompanied by a practical workbook and comes with a CD-ROM which provides access to the book content, 200 additional grammar explanations in a fully searchable format, and audio recordings for all examples and dialogues. Many of the examples included in the book come from the Cambridge International Corpus (CIC) which contains written and spoken text from different national varieties of English (e.g. British, Irish, American) and genres (newspapers, popular journalism, advertising, letters, literary texts, debates and discussions, service encounters, university tutorials, formal speeches, friends talking in restaurants and families talking at home). (See also Murphy and Riordan, Chapter 28 this volume for more details on the CIC.) Whilst the CIC constitutes the core material used for the book, some of the entries contain (usually at the end of the entry) information about the typical errors made by learners. Those errors come from the Cambridge Learner Corpus (CLC), which is considered to be the world's largest learner corpus, with over 200,000 exam scripts from students speaking 148 different mother tongues and living in 217 different countries and territories.

Another example of how learner corpora can be integrated in pedagogical material is Blass, Iannuzzi, Savage and Reppen's (2012) *Grammar and Beyond* (level 3) course book. This recent contextualised grammar series (four levels are available) is also based on research and analysis of the CIC and the CLC. The emphasis of the series is on modern North American English; it identifies and teaches differences between the grammar of spoken and written English and focuses more attention on the structures that are commonly used. The book is also informed by experienced classroom teachers, and reading and writing topics that will naturally elicit examples of the target grammar structure have been included in the book. The learner corpus is used to inform the 'Avoid common mistakes' and 'Editing task' sections included in all the units. The 'Avoid common mistakes' sections contain warnings and examples of mistakes that learners have a tendency to make (e.g. using the present perfect instead of the simple past – unit 2, overuse of the past perfect – unit 4, use of infinitive instead of gerundive complementation – unit 13). The 'Editing task' is typically a text containing mistakes that have to be spotted and corrected.

The two illustrations presented earlier show that corpora of authentic native and learner data can be used concurrently to enhance learners' understanding and acquisition of grammar as they constitute complementary types of input for pedagogical materials.

## Learner corpora as input for learners' dictionaries and other writing aids

Learner corpora can also prove useful in lexicography, particularly for learners' dictionaries. Lexicographers today often use native corpora and corpus linguistics tools and methods to easily access neologisms, word frequencies, typical word usages, contextualised definitions and authentic examples to feed the dictionary entries (see Biber, Conrad and Reppen 1994; Hurskainen 2003; Krishnamurthy 2008; Hanks 2012; and Wild, Kilgarriff and Tugwell 2013 for discussions on how native corpora can inform lexicography). Learner corpora are, however, also sometimes used to flesh out specific dictionary sections. Concrete examples are the 'Usage Notes' in the *Longman Active Study Dictionary*, the 'Avoid common mistakes' sections in the *Longman Learner's Dictionary*, and the 'Get it right' and 'Writing' sections included in the *Macmillan English Dictionary for Advanced Learners* (MEDAL). Rundell and Granger (2007: 16–17) stress the added value of integrating the results of learner corpus studies in the MEDAL and argue that it helps focus on behaviour that is both recurrent and characteristic[1] of learners and it also helps learners to negotiate known areas of difficulty in their writing. The authors distinguish two key domains: lexical and grammatical accuracy on the one hand, and writing fluency on the other. More specifically, lexical and grammatical accuracy refers to problems in areas such as lexical choice, register, countability, the use of articles and quantifiers, and syntactic patterning or complementation. The 'Get it right' boxes included in the MEDAL provide learners with authentic examples of typical learners' errors, together with a clear explanation of the source of the problem and recommended alternatives. As for problems relating to writing fluency (namely the fact that learners tend to rely on a limited range of devices which they might overuse and also misuse), specific writing sections have been included on the accompanying CD-ROM. The authors have focused on a number of key functions in academic and professional writing (introducing topics, drawing conclusions, paraphrasing, contrasting and quoting from sources, concluding, etc.) and have provided a rich description of the words and phrases typically used when performing such functions, thereby providing learners with detailed documentation and a number of alternatives to express their views.

In addition to dictionaries, which can be characterised as relatively traditional reference tools, new generation corpus-derived lexical resources have been designed to meet second/

foreign language learners' (digital) needs. Some recent intelligent computer-aided language learning (ICALL) applications offer real-time automated error analysis and the provision of immediate feedback to learners. Such applications rely on natural language processing (NLP) tools and aim to offer 'an individualized learning experience by providing a unique set of system responses and interactions between a learner and the computer' (Heift 2012: 2; see also Tschichold and Schulze, Chapter 37 this volume, for details on ICALL and NLP). A first illustration of ICALL using learner corpora is the IWiLL environment (Wible, Kuo, Tsao, Liu and Lin 2003). This Intelligent Web-based Interactive Language Learning (hence IWiLL) was initially used as a learning platform to collect learners' essays. A large learner corpus was collected and part of it was manually error-annotated by several teachers. After some much needed harmonisation of the error tags, Wible et al. developed a number of CALL tools, among them an automatic system for the recognition of English verb-noun miscollocations. Once miscollocations are spotted, correction suggestions (based on the analysis of large English native corpora) are subsequently presented to the learners.

Another example of ICALL is Heift's (2010) E-Tutor. The E-Tutor is aimed at L2 learners of German and can be used to check syntax and morphology. It contains an artificial intelligence component which 'provides a dynamic assessment of each learner by considering past and current learner performance and behaviour in relationship to a particular learning activity' (Heift 2010: 446). In addition to the automatic detection of syntax and morphology errors, this system thus makes it possible to individualise feedback as it compares the learner's productions with his/her previous productions.

The few examples presented earlier show that learner corpora are useful resources for both more traditional large scale reference tools such as dictionaries and more modern digital writing aids. New technologies also make it possible to individualise the feedback that learners receive.

## Learner corpora as input for automatic annotation, assessment and rating

Meurers (forthcoming) distinguishes three types of NLP uses for the analysis of learner corpora: to annotate learner corpora, to provide specific analyses of learner language and to train NLP tools. In this section, only the first two dimensions will be illustrated.

As regards the annotation of learner corpora, the most common NLP tools are part-of-speech taggers and syntactic parsers (see first section for general references on corpus annotation). Annotating learner corpora poses specific challenges as the texts that serve as input for the NLP tools sometimes deviate from the native norms (word order problems, missing words, spelling mistakes, erroneous morphology, lexical mistakes, etc.). For instance, Van Rooy and Schäfer (2002, 2003) have studied the impact of error-prone texts on the accuracy of part-of-speech taggers. Despite some inevitable problems and inaccuracies which might require some human postediting to eliminate some of the errors, part-of-speech taggers initially designed for native language analysis prove to be reliable tools for learner corpus annotation. This is particularly true when the corpora are of intermediate to advanced levels and it is mainly due to the probabilistic and context sensitive approach (preceding and following words, for instance) used by many taggers which can often guarantee accurate part-of-speech tagging even for nonexisting or misspelled words.

In contrast, automatic error annotation (which is one of the key types of annotations in LCR) is much less accurate than automatic part-of-speech tagging. Researchers have shown that automatic error detection works much better for more overt-type errors (e.g. certain spelling and morphological errors) than for more covert-type errors (e.g. wrong lexical word choice) (see e.g. Izumi, Uchimoto, Saiga, Supnithi and Isahara 2003; Izumi and Isahara 2004; Dodigovic 2005; Chen 2007; Chodorow, Tetreault and Han 2007: Tetreault and Chodorow 2008; Thewissen 2012). In that domain, human error detection/correction and manual error coding are still needed.

Once the corpus has been annotated, it can subsequently be submitted to specific analyses. Meurers (forthcoming) lists the following types of analyses:

1. L1 identification: tools are trained to automatically determine the native language of the learners (see for instance Tetreault, Blanchard and Cahill 2013).
2. proficiency level assessment (see Pendar and Chapelle 2008; Yannakoudakis, Briscoe and Medlock 2011).
3. analysis of developmental sequences and criterial features of different stages of proficiency (see Granfeldt et al. 2005; Alexopoulou et al. 2010, 2013).
4. automatic essay grading (see Shermis and Burstein 2013).

One concrete example of proficiency level assessment is Thewissen's (2013) study. The author aims to capture general L2 accuracy developmental patterns in an error-tagged EFL learner corpus. To do so, she uses learners' productions from three L1 backgrounds (French, German and Spanish) which have been collected synchronically (with over seventy learners per mother tongue background, for a grand total of 223 learners) but have each been annotated for proficiency levels ranging from the B1 to C2 levels of the Common European Framework of Reference (CEFR, Council of Europe 2001). The author uses potential occasion analysis to analyse the paths of development of over forty error types along the B1-C2 proficiency continuum. Thewissen shows that EFL error developmental patterns are dominated by progress and stabilisation trends, with regression rarely featuring. Progress, at group levels, is generally found to be located between B1 and B2, rather than between the more general B and C levels. She also stresses the fact that both stabilisation and regression should not de facto be negatively interpreted as they may be the result of growing L2 capacities, with increasing levels of complexity being attempted by learners. Beyond offering clearer descriptors of accuracy for various CEFR levels, her study also has considerable implications for language testing, namely the question of whether it is worth distinguishing between B2, C1 and C2 in terms of accuracy, or if two macro levels, namely B (current B1) and C (current B2/C1/C2) would not tally more closely with the developmental reality of foreign language learners.

An example of the analysis of developmental sequences and criterial features of different stages of proficiency is Briscoe, Medlock and Andersen (2010). The authors use machine learning techniques to automate the assessment of the Cambridge First Certificate in English (FCE) exam (exploitation of textual linguistic features including part-of-speech (POS) tagged words and n-grams). Alexopoulou, Yannakoudakis and Salamoura's (2013) work, based on earlier work by Briscoe et al., shows for instance that a discriminative feature set includes combinations of lexical and POS n-grams. Each feature carries a weight, either negative or positive, showing its association with either passing or failing the exam. For instance, *the_people* word bigram followed by a verb is labelled negative, as the definite article should not be used in generic contexts. In contrast, the 'VM_RR' POS bigram (verb + adverb, as in *could clearly*) has a positive weight. One single feature cannot discriminate between passing and failing scripts, but a combination of the full set of features is used to make a prediction.

Some of the NLP methods applied to (learner) corpus data can be rather complex and require the use of sophisticated programming and logarithms. As the aim of this chapter is not to go into the details of such methods and models, we will stick to the few illustrations presented here and refer the reader to the source articles for more information on the procedures. The examples included in this section (even if cursorily presented) show, however, that the pedagogical applications of combining NLP and learner corpora are numerous and varied.

## Widening the understanding of the learner corpus concept: A corpus of nonnative teacher talk

The learner corpus concept is often associated with the collection of data from 'students' (younger or older) who are in the process of acquiring an L2. In this section I would like to present a less traditional type of learner corpus, that is, a corpus of nonnative teacher talk. The debate of whether nonnative teachers should still be called learners of the language or whether they should be labelled as expert users will not be discussed here. Regardless of the label used (and of the pros and cons of using each label), many foreign language teachers in the world are nonnative speakers of the target language they teach, and in addition, many of those teachers aim to go on learning and improve their mastery of the language. Several corpora of nonnative teacher talk have been collected and analysed (often in comparison with corpora of native teacher talk). The main aim of such projects is to empower nonnative teachers by suggesting concrete ways of improving their mastery of the target language and of efficiently using pedagogical language in the classroom. Walsh's latest book on classroom discourse and teacher development (2013) stresses the centrality of classroom discourse given the complex interplay between teacher language, classroom interaction and learning as such. Teachers, native and nonnative alike, need to make optimal use of their verbal behaviour to foster ideal learning interactions. The mastery of and reflective practices related to teacher talk are particularly challenging for nonnative teachers as they cannot rely on native language intuitions and have to attend, in addition to both to teaching content and pedagogy, to their own use of the target language. In that respect, teacher talk corpora are an essential resource to access authentic transcriptions of classroom interactions. Tang (2011), for instance, analyses the lexical input of nonnative teachers in the foreign language classroom. She argues that in countries where target input outside the classroom is poor, teachers become a (if not the) major source of language input for learners. Her analysis of the lexical variation (LV) ratio of nonnative teacher talk reveals that teachers' oral input fails to provide a lexically rich environment as it is limited in both variation and frequency range. She then suggests ways to enhance the lexical environment. Kwon (2012) compares the formulaic language of nonnative and native English teachers. To do so, she collected two corpora of EFL teacher talk from general EFL courses offered by six different universities in South Korea: a nonnative EFL teacher corpus and a native EFL teacher corpus. She recorded and transcribed over twenty hours of instruction in each condition and her goal was to provide nonnative teachers with meaningful lists of chunks useful in teaching. Another example is Nicaise's work (forthcoming) on the CoNNECT corpus (*Corpus of Native and Non-native EFL Classroom Teacher Talk*). The corpus contains the transcripts of native and nonnative English lesson audio-recordings carried out in secondary education (classes ranging from A1 to B2 levels). Data collection spread over a twenty-six-month period, starting in January 2009 and running until March 2011. Recordings were made in French-speaking Belgium and in Britain. The native English recordings include twenty-four lessons, and the nonnative English recordings include fourteen lessons taught by seven francophone EFL teachers, all of which took place in French-speaking Belgium. The corpus is used to analyse the salient linguistic features of native speaker teachers' classroom language (including prosody) that could be useful to nonnative foreign language teachers within the framework of their most common teaching functions. The native English-lesson recordings serve as a baseline for comparison with the nonnative subcorpus. In addition to the (to be expected) partial use of the learners' L1 by some teachers, for better or worse depending on the cases, preliminary findings on the CoN-NECT corpus include, among others, the fact that native teachers use prosody as a strategic pedagogical tool (e.g. rising intonation to draw the learners' attention, longer pauses to prompt learners' feedback and reactions). Another finding is related to the rephrasing strategies. Native teachers not only rephrase guidelines, feedback, or task descriptions more often than nonnative teachers do, but they also use several types of rephrasing for the same turn (with sometimes up to three variants being offered). Nonnative teachers also tend to use the full forms of terms in spoken interactions (e.g. *are not, could not, is not, is going to*) whilst the contracted forms are more natural in spoken interactions. Research on native and nonnative teacher talk corpora is still rare and very promising results are expected in the future. Such results will undoubtedly prove very useful in creating awareness raising activities meant for teachers, and for reflective practices in language learning and teaching in general.

The various sections and concrete examples provided in this chapter have shown that learner corpora are multipurpose in nature and lend themselves to numerous and relevant pedagogical applications: traditional references tools, new generation digital tools, classroom activities, teacher training, testing and assessment and so forth. Learner corpora are also sustainable resources (see Meunier 2012) which can be built on progressively over time, stored and reused. It has also been shown that learner corpora do not necessarily have to be big in order to be useful. The range of automaticity has also been illustrated in this chapter, with some methods of analysis being fully automatic and some almost fully manual. Whilst working with learner corpora enables individualisation of both teaching and learning (teachers can go back to an individual learner's productions and learners can also go back to or use their own productions), it also makes it possible to tailor make teaching applications to larger groups, be they specific L1 groups or proficiency level groups.

## Further reading

Aijmer, K. (2009) *Corpora and Language Teaching*, Amsterdam, Netherlands: John Benjamins.
Although not exclusively devoted to learner corpora, the articles in this edited volume represent a broad coverage of areas. They discuss the role and effectiveness of corpora and corpus-linguistic techniques for language teaching but also deal with broader issues such as the relationship between corpora and second language teaching and how the different perspectives of foreign language teachers and applied linguists can be reconciled. A number of concrete examples are given of how authentic corpus material can be used for different learning activities in the classroom. It is also shown how specific learner problems, for example in the area of phraseology, can be studied on the basis of learner corpora and textbook corpora. On the basis of learner corpora of speech and writing, it is further shown that even advanced learners of English are uncertain about stylistic and text type differences.

Granger, S., Gilquin, G. and Meunier, F. (eds) (2013) *Twenty Years of Learner Corpus Research – Looking Back, Moving Ahead*, Louvain: Presses Universitaires de Louvain.
This proceeding volume of the Learner Corpus Research conference held in Louvain-la-Neuve in 2011 offers a collection of papers by researchers who collect, annotate, and analyse computer learner corpora and/or use them to inform SLA theory or develop learner-corpus-informed tools (courseware, proficiency tests, automatic spell- and grammar-checkers, etc.). At first limited to English as a foreign language, LCR has spread to a wide range of languages, and as a result the community group of learner corpus researchers is rapidly growing and diversifying. Great advances have been made in learner corpus design, collection and annotation, and the range of learner data has expanded with the addition of spoken and multimedia learner corpora. The field has also greatly benefited from growing links with related disciplines – in particular, second language acquisition, teaching methodology, contrastive linguistics, cognitive linguistics, lexicography, language testing and natural language processing. The papers included in the volume illustrate twenty years of learner corpus research, take stock of the advances that have been made in methodology, theory, analysis and applications, and think up creative ways of moving the field forward.

Granger, S., Hung, J. and Petch-Tyson, S. (eds) (2002) *Computer Learner Corpora, Second Language Acquisition and Foreign Language Teaching*, Amsterdam, Netherlands: John Benjamins.
This classic read in learner corpus research should be of particular interest to teachers and researchers looking to assess the relevance of learner corpus research to SLA theory and ELT practice. Throughout the volume, emphasis is placed on practical, methodological aspects of computer learner corpus research, in particular the contribution of technology to the research process. The advantages and disadvantages of automated and semi-automated approaches are analysed, the capabilities of linguistic software tools investigated and the corpora (and compilation processes) described in detail. The volume is divided into three main sections: a general overview of learner corpus research; illustrations of a range of corpus-based approaches to interlanguage analysis; and illustrations of the pedagogical relevance of learner corpus work.

Meunier, F., De Cock, S., Gilquin, G. and Paquot, M. (eds) (2012) *A Taste for Corpora*, Amsterdam, Netherlands: John Benjamins.
The eleven contributions to this volume, written by expert corpus linguists, tackle corpora from a wide range of perspectives and aim to shed light on the numerous linguistic and pedagogical uses to which corpora can be put. They present cutting-edge research in the authors' respective domains of expertise and suggest directions for future research. The main focus of the book is on learner corpora, but it also includes reflections on the role of other types of corpora, such as native corpora, expert users corpora, parallel corpora or corpora of new Englishes. For readers who are already familiar with corpora, this volume offers an informed account of the key role that corpus data play in applied linguistics today. For readers who are new to corpus linguistics, the overview of approaches, methods and domains of applications presented will undoubtedly help them develop their own taste for corpora. This volume has been edited in honour of Sylviane Granger, who has been one of the pioneers of learner corpus research.

## Note

1 Learners' behavior that is recurrent in several mother-tongue backgrounds has been considered as 'characteristic' and has been selected for inclusion in the MEDAL.

## References

Alexopoulou, T., Yannakoudakis, H. and Briscoe, T. (2010) 'From discriminative features to learner grammars: A data driven approach to learner corpora', presentation at the Second Language Research Forum, Maryland, October 2010, available: http://purl.org/net/Alexopoulou.ea-10.pdf (accessed 12 Jul 2014).

Alexopoulou, T., Yannakoudakis, H. and Salamoura A. (2013) 'Classifying intermediate learner English: A data-driven approach to learner corpora', in S. Granger, G. Gilquin and F. Meunier (eds), *Twenty Years of Learner Corpus Research: Looking Back, Moving Ahead*. Corpora and Language in Use – Proceedings 1, Louvain-la-Neuve: Presses universitaires de Louvain: 11–23.

Bahrani, T. (2013) 'Comprehensible or incomprehensible language input', *International Journal of Language Learning and Applied Linguistics World*, 4(1): 34–42.

Belz, J. and Vyatkina, N. (2008) 'The pedagogical mediation of a developmental learner corpus for classroom-based language instruction', *Language Learning & Technology*, 12(3): 33–52.

Biber, D., Conrad, S. and Reppen, R. (1994) 'Corpus-based approaches to issues in applied linguistics', *Applied Linguistics*, 15(2): 169–189.

Blass, L., Iannuzzi, S. Savage, A. and Reppen, R. (2012) *Grammar and Beyond – 3*, Cambridge: Cambridge University Press.

Boulton, A. (2008) 'DDL: reaching the parts other teaching can't reach?', in A. Frankenburg-Garcia (ed), *Proceedings of the 8th Teaching and Language Corpora Conference*, Lisbon, Associação de Estudos e de Investigação Cientifica do ISLA-Lisboa: 38–44.

Boulton, A. (2009a) 'Testing the limits of data-driven learning: Language proficiency and training', *ReCALL*, 21(1): 37–54.

Boulton, A. (2009b) 'Data-driven learning: Reasonable fears and rational reassurance', *Indian Journal of Applied Linguistics*, 35(1): 81–106.

Braun, S. (2006) 'ELISA – A pedagogically enriched corpus for language learning purposes', in S. Braun, K. Kohn and J. Mukherjee (eds), *Corpus Technology and Language Pedagogy: New Resources, New Tools, New Methods*, Frankfurt: Peter Lang: 25–47.

Briscoe, E.J., Medlock, B. and Andersen, O. (2010) *Automated Assessment of ESOL Free Text Examinations*. Technical Report, Cambridge University Computer Laboratory, TR-790.

Burnard, L. (2004) *Metadata for corpus work*. Electronic document available from http://users.ox.ac.uk/~lou/wip/metadata.html (accessed 1 Apr 2004).

Carter, R., McCarthy, M., Mark, G. and O'Keeffe, A. (2011) *English Grammar Today*, Cambridge: Cambridge University Press.

Chen, H. (2007) 'Developing statistic-based and rule-based grammar checkers for Chinese ESL learners', paper presented at the CANDLE meeting, Antwerp (Belgium), 22 November 2007.

Chodorow, M., Tetreault, J. and Han, N-R. (2007) 'Detection of grammatical errors involving prepositions', in *Proceedings from the Fourth ACL-SIGSEM Workshop on Prepositions*, Prague (Czech Republic), available: http://www.ling.upenn.edu/~nrh/acl07-prep-final.pdf

Conrad, S. (2000) 'Will corpus linguistics revolutionize grammar teaching in the 21st century'? *TESOL Quarterly*, 34: 548–560.

Dodigovic, M. (2005) *Artificial Intelligence in Second Language Learning. Raising Error Awareness*. Clevedon/Buffalo/Toronto: Multilingual Matters Ltd.

Gabrielatos, C. (2005) 'Corpora and language teaching: Just a fling or wedding bells?', *TESL-EJ Journal*, 8(4): 1–35.

Gilquin G. and Granger, S. (2010) 'How can data-driven learning be used in language teaching?', in A. O'Keeffe and M. McCarthy (eds), *The Routledge Handbook of Corpus Linguistics*, London, UK: Routledge: 359–370.

Granfeldt, J., Nugues, P., Persson, E., Persson, L., Kostadinov, F., Ågren, M. et al. (2005) 'Direkt profil: A system for evaluating texts of second language learners of French based on developmental sequences', in J. Burstein and C. Leacock (eds), *Proceedings of the Second Workshop on Building Educational Applications Using NLP*, Ann Arbor: Association for Computational Linguistics: 53–60.

Granger, S. (2004) 'Practical applications of learner corpora', in B. Lewandowska-Tomaszczyk (ed), *Practical Applications in Language and Computers (PALC 2003)*, Frankfurt: Peter Lang.

Granger, S. (2009) 'The contribution of learner corpora to second language acquisition and foreign language teaching: A critical evaluation', in K. Aijmer (ed), *Corpora and Language Teaching*. Studies in Corpus Linguistics 33, Amsterdam: Benjamins: 13–33.

Granger, S. and Meunier, F. (2010) 'SLA research and learner corpus research: Friend or foe?', Paper presented at the 20th Annual Conference of the European Second Language Association. Reggio Emilia, Italy, 1–4 September 2010.

Hanks, P. (2012) 'The corpus revolution in lexicography', *International Journal of Lexicography*, 25(4): 398–436.

Heift, T. (2010) 'Developing an intelligent language tutor', *CALICO Journal*, 27(3): 443–459.

Heift, T. (2012) 'Intelligent computer-assisted language learning', in C.A. Chapelle (ed), *Encyclopedia of Applied Linguistics*, New York, NY: Wiley-Blackwell: online ISBN: 9781405198431.

Hurskainen, A. (2003) 'New advances in corpus-based lexicography', *Lexikos*, 13: 111–132.

Izumi, E. and Isahara, H. (2004) 'Investigation into language learners' acquisition order based on an error analysis of a learner corpus', in *Proceedings of IWLeL: An interactive workshop on language e-learning*, available: http://dspace.wul.waseda.ac.jp/dspace/bitstream/2065/1396/1/07.pdf

Izumi, E., Uchimoto, K., Saiga, T., Supnithi, T. and Isahara, H. (2003) 'Automatic error detection in the Japanese learners' English spoken data', in *Proceedings of the Association for Computational Linguistics*, Sapporo (Japan), available: http://acl.ldc.upenn.edu/P/P03/P03-2026.pdf

Keogh, B., Dabell, J. and Naylor, S. (2008) *Active Assessment in English: Thinking, Learning and Assessment in English*, London; New York: Routledge.

Krashen, S. (1982) *Principles and Practice in Second Language Acquisition*, Oxford: Pergamon Press.

Krishnamurthy, R. (2008) 'Corpus-driven lexicography', *International Journal of Lexicography*, 21(3): 231–242.

Kwon, E. (2012) 'Formulaic sequence uses of non-native and native English teacher talks', *The Journal of Studies in Language*, 28(1): 1–27.

Leech, G. (1997) 'Introducing corpus annotation', in R. Garside, G. Leech and A. McEnery (eds), *Corpus Annotation: Linguistic Information from Computer Text Corpora*, London, Longman: 1–18.

Meunier, F. (1998) 'Computer tools for the analysis of learner corpora', in S. Granger (ed), *Learner English on Computer*, London, UK: Longman: 19–37.

Meunier, F. (2012) 'Learner corpora in the classroom: A useful and sustainable didactic resource', in L. Pedrazzini Luciana and A. Nava (eds), *Learning and Teaching English: Insights from Research*, Milano: Polimetrica: 211–228.

Meunier F. and Gouverneur, C. (2009) 'New types of corpora for new educational challenges: Collecting, annotating and exploiting a corpus of textbook material', in K. Aijmer (ed), *Corpora and Language Teaching*, Amsterdam, Netherlands: Benjamins: 179–201.

Meunier, F. and Reppen, R. (forthcoming 2015) 'Corpus- versus non-corpus informed pedagogical materials: Focus on grammar', in D. Biber and R. Reppen (eds), *The Cambridge Handbook of Corpus Linguistics*, Cambridge: Cambridge University Press.

Meurers, D. (2009) 'On the automatic analysis of learner language: Introduction to the special issue', *CALICO Journal*, 26(3): 469–473.

Meurers, D. (forthcoming 2014) 'Learner corpora and natural language processing', in S. Granger, G. Gilquin and F. Meunier (eds), *The Cambridge Handbook of Learner Corpus Research*, Cambridge: Cambridge University Press, 537–566.

Myles, F. (2008) 'Investigating learner language development with electronic longitudinal corpora: Theoretical and methodological issues', in L. Ortega and H. Byrnes (eds), *The Longitudinal Study of Advanced L2 Capacities*, New York, NY: Routledge: 58–72.

Nicaise, E. (forthcoming) 'Aiming for native competence: an analysis of the classroom language of English-speaking language teachers as a database reference for non-native EFL teachers', PhD thesis, Louvain-la-Neuve: Université catholique de Louvain.

Pendar, N. and Chapelle, C. (2008) 'Investigating the promise of learner corpora: Methodological issues', *CALICO Journal*, 25(2): 189–206.

Römer, U. (2011, forthcoming) 'Corpus research applications in second language teaching', *Annual Review of Applied Linguistics*, 31: 205–225.

Ruiz-Madrid, M.N. (2007) 'Pedagogical boundaries for web resources. An Integrative proposal for the FL classroom', *CORELL: Computer Resources for Language Learning*, 1: 56–67.

Rundell, M. and Granger, S. (2007) 'From corpora to confidence', *English Teaching Professional*, 50: 15–18.

Seidlhofer, B. (2002) 'Pedagogy and local learner corpora: Working with learning-driven data', in S. Granger, J. Hung and S. Tyson (eds), *Computer Learner Corpora, Second Language Acquisition and Foreign Language Teaching*, Amsterdam, Netherlands: John Benjamins: 213–234.

Shermis, M.D. and Burstein, J. (eds) (2013) *Handbook on Automated Essay Evaluation: Current Applications and New Directions*, London; New York, NY: Routledge.

Tang, E. (2011) 'Non-native teacher talk as lexical input in the foreign language classroom', *Journal of Language Teaching and Research*, 2(1): 45–54.

Tetreault, J., Blanchard, D. and Cahill, A. (2013) 'A report on the First Native Language Identification Shared Task', in *Proceedings of the Eighth Workshop on Building Educational Applications Using NLP*, Atlanta, GA: Association for Computational Linguistics.

Tetreault, J.R., and Chodorow, M. (2008) 'Native judgments of non-native usage: Experiments in preposition error detection', in *Proceedings of the Workshop on Human Judgements in Computational Linguistics*, Manchester: 24–32.

Thewissen, J. (2012) 'Accuracy across proficiency levels and L1 backgrounds: Insights from an error-tagged EFL learner corpus', unpublished PhD dissertation, Louvain: Université catholique de Louvain.

Thewissen, J. (2013) 'Capturing L2 accuracy developmental patterns: Insights from an error-tagged EFL learner corpus', *Modern Language Journal*, 97: S1, 77–101.

Van Rooy, B. and Schäfer, L. (2002) 'The effect of learner errors on POS tag errors during automatic POS tagging', *Southern African Linguistics and Applied Language Studies*, 20: 325–335.

Van Rooy, B. and Schäfer, L. (2003) 'An evaluation of three POS taggers for the tagging of the Tswana learner English corpus', in D. Archer, P. Rayson, A. Wilson and T. McEnery (eds), *Proceedings of the Corpus Linguistics 2003 Conference Lancaster University (UK)*, Lancaster: University Centre For Computer Corpus Research on Language Technical Papers: 835–844.

Walsh, S. (2013) *Classroom Discourse and Teacher Development*, Edinburgh: Edinburgh University Press.

White, L. (1987) 'Against comprehensible input: The input hypothesis and the development of L2 competence', *Applied Linguistics*, 8: 95–110.

Wible, D., Kuo, C.-H., Tsao, N.-L., Liu, A. and Lin, H-L. (2003) 'Bootstrapping in a language learning environment', *Journal of Computer Assisted Learning*, 19: 90–102.

Wild, K., Kilgarriff, A. and Tugwell, D. (2013) 'The Oxford Children's Corpus: Using a children's corpus in lexicography', *International Journal of Lexicography*, 26(2): 190–218.

Yannakoudakis, H., Briscoe, T. and Medlock, B. (2011) 'A new dataset and method for automatically grading ESOL texts', in *Proceedings of the 49th Annual Meeting of the Association for Computational Linguistics: Human Language Technologies* – Volume 1, Stroudsburg: Association for Computational Linguistics: 180–189.

# 28
# Corpus types and uses

*Bróna Murphy and Elaine Riordan*

This chapter provides a broad overview of corpus types and uses. It surveys five types of corpora: general, specialised, parallel, historical and multimodal. In each section, we provide a description of the corpus type, the key issues associated with the type as well as its applications in pedagogical contexts. The overview is not meant to be exhaustive, as there are many more corpora than we have space to mention. However, our aim is to introduce the main types and uses so that readers may then seek to explore the types more fully themselves, depending on their interests (see Appendix 28A for further information).

## General corpora

General corpora, or reference corpora, can be spoken, written or both, and aim 'to provide information about language as a whole, showing how it is generally used in speech and writing of various kinds' (Kübler and Aston 2010: 504). Baker (2010: 12) suggests that this 'could be seen as a prototypical corpus in that it is normally very large, consisting of millions of words, and texts collected from a wide range of sources representing many language contexts'. There are three generations of general corpora, the first of which is represented by the Brown family. The BROWN Corpus is a 1-million-word collection of written American English from 1961 (Kučera and Francis 1967). Its British counterpart, the London-Oslo/Bergen (LOB) Corpus is 1 million words of written texts also collected in 1961 (Johansson, Leech and Goodluck 1978). Both BROWN and LOB are otherwise known as synchronic corpora, as their texts stem from one period of time. Some years later, two new corpora joined this family: the Freiberg Brown Corpus of American English (FROWN), consisting of 1 million words from the 1990s (Hundt, Sand and Skandera 1999), and the Freiberg London-Oslo/Bergen (FLOB) Corpus of 1 million words of British English from the 1990s (Hundt, Sand and Siemund 1998). Another example of this first generation is the International Corpus of English (ICE), which includes a number of 1-million-word corpora collected from 1990–94 in countries where English is a first or official language (Nelson 1996).

The second generation of corpora grew in size and an example is the British National Corpus (BNC), a 100-million-word corpus of spoken and written English (Aston and Burnard 1998). The American National Corpus (ANC) is designed on the same principle

(Reppen and Ide 2004), but with two differences, namely that data from the ANC stems from 1990 onwards, whereas data in the BNC is from 1960–93, and there are newer text types in the ANC such as blogs and web pages (Reppen 2009). Another corpus based on the design of the BNC is the Turkish National Corpus (TNC) of 50 million words (Askan et al. 2012). Further examples of approximately 100-million-word corpora include the Corpus di Italiano Scritto (CORIS) (Rossini Favretti, Tamburini and De Santis 2004), the Corpus del Español (Davies 2002) and the Russian Reference Corpus (Sharoff 2004). The third generation of general corpora are even larger; for instance, the Bulgarian National Corpus contains 1.2 billion words (Koeva et al. 2012). Also, the Bank of English (BoE), which emerged as part of the COBUILD project (Sinclair 1987), contains 650 million words of spoken and written texts and is constantly being updated, making it a monitor corpus (Clear 1987), in that texts are continuously added to the corpus and changes can be tracked using software. Another example is the Corpus of Contemporary American English (COCA), the largest online freely available spoken and written corpus, at 450 million words collected since 1990 (Davies 2010).

These corpora have a number of applications. For example, they can be used to offer valuable information about how a language or a variety of languages can be used, or they can be used as a reference for comparison purposes. For instance, linguistic analyses have included the examination of collocation in BROWN (Kjellmer 1994), and modality in the Brown family (Degani 2009). Furthermore, different varieties of one language have been examined in ICE (Hundt and Gut 2012). Studies of a more sociolinguistic nature include exploring lexical change using BROWN and the ANC (Fengxiang 2012), taboo language in the BNC (McEnery and Xiao 2004) and gender differences in specialised corpora and the BNC (Schmid 2003; see Baker 2010 for more about corpora in sociolinguistics). Pragmatics has also been examined, for example the use of apologies in the BNC (Deutschmann 2003) and laughter in the BNC and other corpora (Partington 2006; see also Caines, McCarthy and O'Keeffe, Chapter 25 this volume). General corpora are also increasingly being used for lexicography (see Hanks 2009). Another application is in the field of language teaching and learning (see O'Keeffe, McCarthy and Carter 2007; Reppen 2009, 2010a). Using large corpora teachers can, for example, study specific linguistic items rather than using their intuition (Sinclair 1997), and students can use corpora for data-driven learning (Johns 1991; see also Warren, Chapter 24 this volume), for access to authentic language (Aston 1995) and as a source of reference (Chambers 2005). Large corpora can also support the creation of textbooks (McCarten 2010), or grammar books (Biber et al. 1999; Carter and McCarthy 2006; see also in this volume Caines, McCarthy and O'Keeffe, Chapter 25 on spoken corpora; Chambers, Chapter 26 on written corpora; and Motteram, Chapter 6 for courseware design using other digital resources).

Although the uses are plentiful, a major issue in corpus linguistics is the ability of users to interpret the findings (see O'Keeffe and Farr 2003). As general corpora are large, users must accustom themselves to working with an abundance of data, which requires skills in which the user may need training (see O'Keeffe and Farr 2003; Sinclair 2003). When comparing a smaller corpus with a general corpus, it must also be acknowledged that different sized corpora are not comparable, and therefore, in order to draw conclusions, the rule of thumb is to calculate figures in words per million. Also, the size of a corpus is important when considering the focus of the investigation, for example, while corpora of a million words are useful for grammatical co-occurrence patterns, they might not be useful for lexical studies (Reppen 2010a; see also Li, Chapter 33 this volume for details on the use of CALL for lexico-grammatical acquisition).

## Specialised corpora

In contrast to general corpora, a specialised corpus is more restricted and may be regarded as specialised if it involves any or all of the following criteria as outlined by Flowerdew (2004: 21):

1. it has been compiled for a specific purpose (e.g. to investigate a particular item;
2. it represents a particular context (e.g. setting, participants and communicative purpose);
3. it represents a genre (e.g. sales letters);
4. it includes a particular type of text/discourse (e.g. biology textbooks);
5. it represents a subject matter/topic (e.g. economics);
6. it represents a variety of English (e.g. learner English).

Corpora which have emerged so far and which can be classified as specialised emanate from various contexts such as:

- *Education*: the International Corpus of Learner English (ICLE; see Meunier, Chapter 27 this volume); the Michigan Corpus of Academic Spoken English (MICASE) (Simpson-Vlach and Leicher 2006); the British Academic Written English (BAWE) corpus (Nesi 2012); English as a Lingua Franca in Academic settings (ELFA) (Mauranen 2012); the Michigan Corpus of Upper-level Student Papers (MICUSP) (O'Donnell and Römer 2012).
- *Business*: the Cambridge and Nottingham Business English Corpus (CANBEC) (Handford 2010).
- *Law*: the Cambridge Corpus of Legal English (CCLE).
- *Professional English*: the Corpus of Spoken Professional American English (CSPAE) (Yaguchi, Iyieri and Okabe 2004).
- *Society*: the Corpus of London Teenage English (COLT) (Stenström, Andersen and Hasund 2002).
- *Internet*: the Internet has also been used as a specialised corpus (see Renouf 2002) and as a source for building specialised corpora (Hundt, Nesselhauf and Biewer 2009: 1–7; see also Kilgarriff 2001 and Kilgarriff and Grefenstette 2003 for more on the use of the Internet as a corpus). Online corpora such as the Enron Corpus and the Cambridge and Nottingham E-Language Corpus (CANELC) also exist.

Although specialised corpora are normally smaller than general corpora precisely because of their narrower focus (Lee 2010: 114), they have been criticised because of their size (Sinclair 2004). However, research has shown that they can yield reliable results when investigating high-frequency items and that a corpus does not always need to consist of millions of words and a large number of texts (Biber 1990). The message is clear that while small corpora are not suitable for all types of studies (Koester 2010: 77), they do have advantages over larger corpora. For instance, they are not decontextualised, and as a result they allow the researcher to explore a much closer link between the corpus and the contexts in which the texts are produced (O'Keeffe 2007; Koester 2010: 74). The size of the corpus means that each occurrence of a particular form can be explored, and not just a random sample, which is common when working with general corpora. They also provide insights into patterns of language use in particular settings, and as the corpus compiler is often the analyst, they usually have a high degree of familiarity with the context which assists the interpretation of the data, in a way that is not often possible when dealing with larger corpora (see Handford 2010; Koester 2010). However, it is worth noting that not all specialised corpora have to be small, and indeed as highlighted by O'Keeffe et al. (2007), a specialised corpus can be defined as large if it contains a million words or more. Handford (2010: 258) lists CANBEC as one such example; another is the 1.9-billion-word Corpus of Global Web-based English (GloWbE), compiled by Davies (2013).

In a language teaching and learning context (see Warren, Chapter 24 this volume), Tribble (2002) argues for the use of small specialised corpora to inform pedagogy (Johns 1991; Flowerdew 2004; Reppen 2010a). He claims that large corpora do not meet the needs of teachers and learners in ESP/EAP, for instance, as they either provide 'too much data across too large a spectrum or too little focused data to be directly helpful with EAP' (Tribble 2002: 132). Smaller corpora, on the other hand, yield more insights which are directly relevant for teaching and learning (Flowerdew 2004). Aston (1997) highlights that small specialised corpora are not only a valuable asset in their own right as a means of discovering the characteristics of a particular area of language but also useful in helping and training students to use bigger corpora more appropriately. Reppen (2010b) highlights that when used in a teaching and learning context, specialised corpora can help to identify unfamiliar/high-frequency words, provide concordance lines from which to develop class activities, identify word senses and practise inferencing strategies. Reppen shows how she used a small specialised corpus in her own teaching context by collecting a set of class papers from an elementary writing group. The writing was coded for three types of errors: noun morphology, verb morphology and subject/verb agreement. Reppen then used the corpus to generate a list of errors to inform instruction and as a source of classroom activities (see also Reppen, Chapter 29 this volume). The challenges, however, of using small corpora in the classroom have not gone unnoticed. Gavioli (2002), for example, highlights the practical difficulties of balancing the materials provided to students which, on the one hand, need to be limited and controlled for teaching, but on the other hand need to be plentiful in order to allow the students enough data to work on for the facilitation of confident linguistic hypotheses. She claims that particular teaching/learning needs may not always align with practical issues in an ESP context (see Flowerdew 2009 for a more critical account of corpora in ESP; Gavioli 2005).

## Parallel corpora

While a monolingual corpus contains one language, a multilingual corpus contains two or more languages, and the latter can be divided into two categories: parallel and comparable. Parallel corpora are designed based on the relationship of translation between texts, thus having an original group of texts and translations of those texts (Tognini-Bonelli and Sinclair 2006). A comparable corpus does not contain translations of texts, but rather texts collected in a number of languages and based on the same communicative function (Kenning 2010), much like the BACKBONE corpus discussed later. The first parallel corpus was the Canadian Hansard Corpus (Tognini-Bonelli and Sinclair 2006), which consists of government documents in English and Canadian French. One of the best known parallel corpora is the English-Norwegian Parallel Corpus (ENPC), containing original and translated texts in both languages (2.6 million words), therefore making it bidirectional (Johansson, Ebeling and Oksefjell 2002). The Oslo Multilingual Corpus (OMC) is an extension of the ENPC, including English, Norwegian, German, Finnish, Swedish, Dutch, French and Portuguese texts (OMC 2010). Based on a similar design, the English-Swedish Parallel Corpus (ESPC) consists of 2.8 million words of bidirectional English and Swedish texts (Altenberg, Aijmer and Svensson 2001). An online freely available parallel corpus is the Open Parallel Corpus (OPUS), which is a growing collection of translated texts from the Web (Tiedemann 2012).

One thing that sets parallel corpora aside from other corpora is that they have bilingual concordances, where all occurrences of a search word in both languages are found and presented alongside each other. This concordancer 'trawls through all the parts of a parallel corpus, retrieving not only all the occurrences of the search item in context, but also the sentences that contain the corresponding segments in the other language/languages' (Kenning 2010: 491). The applications of parallel corpora are varied, and Bowker and Pearson (2002) categorise their users into three domains. First, language teachers and learners can use parallel corpora as a dictionary which offers multiple examples of context, and to examine how words are translated across languages. Students can also analyse specific language features across languages, or identify how cultural references are dealt with during translation (Bowker and Pearson 2002).

The second group of users are translators and translation students. They can use parallel corpora for these same reasons, but also to examine what happens during a translation (Bowker and Pearson 2002), assisting with both practical and research-based translation (Kenning 2010). It has been suggested that 'each translator's dream is a resource which instantly provides reliable candidate translations, and this is what a parallel corpus ideally offers' (Kübler and Aston 2010: 510; see also Chapter 38 in this volume for other translation technologies). Baker (2000) examines individual translators' styles in the Translational English Corpus (TEC – 2 million words at the time of her analysis), and Xiao and Yue (2009) examined some translation universals in a 200,000-word sample of the Lancaster Corpus of Mandarin Chinese (LCMC) and the 1-million-word Contemporary Chinese Translated Fiction Corpus (CCTFC) (for more on parallel corpora for translation studies, see Véronis 2000 and Xiao and Yue 2009).

The third group of users are computational linguists, who can use parallel corpora to test alignment software and give further insights into machine translation (Bowker and Pearson 2002; see Caines and Buttery 2010 for more on training computers in NLP). Of course, lexicographers also use parallel corpora for bilingual lexicography, and contrastive linguists use them to describe a given language and explore the similarities and differences between languages (Kenning 2010).

Issues to consider with parallel corpora include the fact that one needs pairs of texts in two or more languages for the creation of a corpus, and multilingual texts are harder to find than monolingual ones. The Web helps in that many texts are now in electronic format; therefore the user does not have to scan the texts to be exploited for analysis. Texts, however, need to be preprocessed to prepare them for alignment, which is the creation of links between texts so they can be used for later investigations (see Bowker and Pearson 2002; Kenning 2010). Lastly, there are not a lot of publicly available parallel corpora because of the complexity in getting permission to use a text and its translation (Kübler and Aston 2010).

## Historical corpora

The earliest historical electronic resources emerged in the 1980s with the Dictionary of Old English database prepared in Toronto and the Augustan Prose Sample and the Century of Prose Corpus compiled at Cleveland State University (Rissanen 2000: 7). Since that time, corpus linguistics has continued to make its mark on the history of English through the growing number of historical corpora representing various periods, genres, dialects, registers and social strata of English (Kytö 2012). Claridge (2008: 242) defines a historical corpus as one which has been intentionally created to represent past stages of a language and/or to study language change. Developments in historical corpus linguistics have been loosely grouped into four categories (see Rissanen 2000: 8–13):

1   multipurpose: includes the widely known c. 1.5-million-word Helsinki Corpus (c. 730–1710) and the c. 1.7-million-word ARCHER corpus (c. 1650–1900) (Yáñez Bouza 2011;

Kytö and Pahta 2012), which together extend over several centuries and a wide range of genres.
2. Old and Middle English: general and author-based corpora, such as the c. 3.5-million-word Toronto Dictionary of Old English Corpus in Electronic Form, which consists of nearly all extant Old English writings (with the exception of some parallel manuscripts) (Healey 1999).
3. Middle and Modern English: genre and regional variety corpora, including the c. 2.6-million-word Corpus of Early English Correspondence (CEEC) (Nevalainen and Raumolin-Brunberg 1996) from 1417–1681, and the c. 1.5-million-word Corpus of Early English Medical Writing (CEEM) spanning 1375–1750 (Taavitsainen and Pahta 2010).
4. Renaissance and Twentieth-Century English: includes the Lampeter Corpus (see Claridge 2000; Kytö and Pahta 2012: 128–131).

While 'long and thin' corpora (Rissanen 2000: 10) such as the Helsinki Corpus have been the norm, advances in historical corpus linguistics have witnessed the emergence of much larger corpora such as the 400-million-word Corpus of Historical American English (COHA) (Davies 2012), which when added to Rissanen's (2000) list marks a period of movement in the approach taken to the compilation of historical corpora. Its online accessibility and availability means that it will have a considerable impact on research in the area of historical corpus linguistics and in some way provides an insight into its future.

The history of English has been revolutionised by corpus linguistics (Lee 2010: 113–114), and indeed Rissanen (2012) claims that if it had not been for corpus linguistics, evidence-based historical linguistics might not have survived, let alone experience the renaissance it did (Kytö 2012: 3). Its merits include the fact that corpus linguistics has provided researchers with the tools to collect, sort and analyse large quantities of data with speed and accuracy (Rissanen 2012) (see the earlier section on specialised corpora). Corpus methods have also helped to eliminate the idea of fragmentation which often occurs in historical linguistics and have facilitated the replicability and accuracy of linguistic results (see Kytö and Pahta 2012). However, the literature has also highlighted the challenges involved in historical corpus linguistics (see Claridge 2008). For example, the transference of text from handwriting or printing into computerised format presents an edited truth of the language used in the original, and means that the nature of the editorial process and involvement of researchers' time is crucial for the reliability of the corpus data. In terms of sampling, there is a clear imbalance of gender representation, with most texts being produced by men, as women did not have opportunities for formal education to the extent that men had up until the 1800s or later. Also, very few texts have been preserved from representatives of the less educated social classes (see Rissanen 2008). In addition, as corpora often span several centuries, the definition of genre for certain periods does not always hold true for others, and this gives rise to difficulties in corpus compilation, which require careful consideration (see Rissanen 2008). Therefore, like all other corpus linguists, scholars of historical corpus linguistics need to be especially aware of how the corpora have been compiled, how they can be used and what their limitations are.

In language teaching and learning contexts, scholars such as Curzan (2008) have discussed how historical corpus linguistics has been incorporated into pedagogy. Corpora such as COHA mean that students have immediate access to data which act as rich sources of linguistic evidence, and the time previously spent tracking down and collecting data has been considerably reduced. Students can pursue their own questions about language and linguistic change and engage more interactively and holistically than before with historical change across morphological, syntactic, semantic and orthographic levels as well as different varieties and registers (see also

Biber, Conrad and Reppen 1998). Brinton (2012) also highlights the potential for pragmatic and discourse-based analyses of the history of English (see Culpeper 2010). However, Rissanen (2008: 65, 2012) highlights the need to fully understand the language form studied and the main characteristics of the literary, political, social, geographical and cultural background from which the texts arise. Without this understanding, he claims, fatal misinterpretations of textual evidence may take place. A more recent shift in corpus linguistics is the development of multimodal corpora, outlined next.

## Multimodal corpora

A multimodal corpus includes 'transcripts that are aligned or synchronised with the original audio or visual recordings' (Lee 2010: 114). This type of corpus, while still in its infancy (Knight 2011), involves both textual and nontextual data. It has been acknowledged that one shortcoming of spoken corpora is that they lack visual representations by showing speech in textual format (Knight and Adolphs 2007; Knight and Tennent 2008), which the multimodal approach is attempting to tackle by depicting communication in its 'entire complexity' (Blache, Bertrand and Ferré 2009: 38). One example is the Nottingham Multimodal Corpus (NMMC), a 250,000-word corpus with recordings and transcriptions collected from single-speaker and dyadic conversations in an academic context (Knight et al. 2008). Another is the SACODEYL corpus, which includes transcribed interviews with British, German, French, Italian Spanish, Lithuanian and Romanian adolescents between 13 and 18 years of age (Hoffstaedter and Kohn 2009). Each language contains twenty to twenty-five video-recorded interviews, which have been transcribed and stored as corpora, and then thematically and linguistically annotated (Hoffstaedter and Kohn 2009). The annotated sections are time-stamped, so there is synchronisation between the transcripts and the accompanying audio files (Widmann, Kohn and Ziai 2011). A corpus based on the same premise is the BACKBONE corpus, which contains data collected from adults who speak regional varieties of languages, as well as lesser taught languages (British-English, Irish-English, German, French, Spanish, Turkish, Polish and manifestations of English as a lingua franca). The Santa Barbara Corpus of Spoken American English (249,000 words) can also be read online with the transcripts and audio files synchronised (for more multimodal corpora see Knight 2011).

Multimodal corpora move beyond the field of traditional corpus linguistics because they are 'potentially useful to many other fields in linguistics, including pragmatics, conversation analysis, discourse analysis, sociolinguistics, as well as language technologists working on speech recognition, audio (visual) file search technologies, and in some cases, natural language processing' (Haugh 2009: 76). For example, verbal and nonverbal behaviour can be examined (Knight and Tennent 2008); head, eye, hand and body movements can be analysed (Allwood 2009), as well as lexical, prosodic and gestural features (Allwood 2009; Blache et al. 2009; Knight 2011), thus facilitating a deeper understanding of context (Adolphs, Knight and Carter 2011). For instance, Knight and Adolphs (2007) studied head-nod behaviour and verbal backchannels on a subset of NMMC, and Dahlmann and Adolphs (2009) analysed the relationship between the multiword unit *I think* and pauses in the English Native Speaker Interview Corpus (ENSIC). As well as this, Allwood (2009) notes that multimodal corpora can be used to examine, and in turn improve, any kind of communicative behaviour such as presentation techniques, teaching-related communication and doctor-patient communication.

Shortcomings of multimodal corpora include the fact that they are not generally available (although SACODEYL and BACKBONE are), are many thousands of words in size (compared to the vast general corpora mentioned earlier), and some are not yet transcribed (Knight 2011).

Technical issues also need consideration; for example, the data needs to be collected and transcribed, which is much more time-consuming and expensive than what is involved in compiling other corpora. Furthermore, a timeline is required to align text with speech, power is needed for the algorithm to show gestures, and the storage required for the files is very large (Knight and Tennent 2008). Moreover gestures need to be coded, which is a complex process (Knight 2011; see also Blache et al. 2009 for more on annotation). Therefore, while some considerations are often similar to other types of corpus compilation such as what to record, how to record, storing recordings, transcribing recordings, storing/saving transcriptions, what should be analysed and how can it be done (Allwood 2009; see also Reppen, Chapter 29 this volume), for multimodal corpora, technical issues regarding recording, lighting, placement and type of equipment need further attention. However, this type of corpus is a significant move in corpus linguistics, and over time the limitations should be reduced (see Hauck, Galley and Warnecke, Chapter 5, and Tschichold and Schulze, Chapter 37 this volume for more multimodal technologies). The remainder of this chapter discusses the future implications of the types of corpora we have outlined.

## Future directions

Many types of corpora have emerged, and the trend looks set to continue largely because research within the corpus paradigm has proven so fruitful (Lee 2010: 107). The future therefore looks promising in terms of the kinds of innovation we can expect and how they might benefit pedagogical contexts. In this final section, we highlight some issues related to the future advancement of each of the corpus types:

1. General corpora should continue to grow and reach trillion-word size (Baker 2010: 12), and similar to the emergence of mega-corpora such as COCA they are expected to be more freely available. With the availability and diversity of texts online, it is likely that we will witness more contemporary text types being included, representing the emergence of digital communication, such as the Birmingham Blog Corpus (Kehoe and Gee 2012).
2. Specialised corpora require more attention to context and the markup of contextual features and the co-textual environment in order to facilitate the interpretation of smaller specialised datasets (see Flowerdew 2009: 411–412). Also, the need to continue to explore how specialised corpora can be used in pedagogy and how challenges can be overcome remains a valid future line of enquiry.
3. Parallel corpora need to address issues of representativeness. In their current state, they 'span relatively few genres (mainly fiction, parliamentary proceedings, technical manuals), [and] a limited set of languages' (Kenning 2010: 488). It is thought that a more representative spectrum would greatly enhance innovation and insight in the area of parallel corpora.
4. Historical corpora need more attention to synergy between resources, research agendas and collaboration across interdisciplinary borders (Kytö 2011: 443–444). Kytö lists three overarching categories for future directions: enhancing and adding to resources and methodologies for studying long-term and recent change; ensuring comparability and links across corpora, and other electronic resources and software; and increasing our knowledge of the sociohistorical and cultural context of corpus texts, with special reference to interdisciplinary considerations.
5. Multimodal corpora need to be larger, more representative and include a range of media via digital modes of communication. Knight (2011) highlights the need to improve technical devices and suggests that as more investigations are implemented, limitations such as coding gestures will be reduced.

This chapter has provided a brief overview of the main types of corpora which exist as an introduction for scholars who are new to corpora and corpus linguistics. The pedagogical applications may be examined more closely in other chapters in this volume which focus on specific corpus types (see Caines, McCarthy and O'Keeffe, Chapter 25, Chambers, Chapter 26, and Meunier Chapter 27).

## Further reading

Davies, M. (2012) 'The 400 million word Corpus of Historical American English (1810–2009)' in I. Hegedus and A. Fodor (eds) *English Historical Linguistics 2010: Selected Papers from the Sixteenth International Conference on English Historical Linguistics (ICEHL)*, Pecs, 23–27 August 2010: 231–262.

This chapter offers an overview of the 400-million-word COHA corpus of texts collected between 1810 and 2009 from a range of sources including nonfiction books, popular magazines, fiction and newspapers. The author describes how such a corpus can be used to research changes in American English on morphological, phraseological, lexical, syntactical and semantic levels.

Friginal, E. and Hardy, J. (2013) *Corpus-Based Sociolinguistics: A Guide for Students*, Abingdon, Oxon: Routledge.

This book explores the use of corpus-based tools in the study of sociolinguistics. It does so through three overarching themes, including an introduction to the use of corpus linguistics for the exploration of sociolinguistics (e.g. overviewing corpus-based tools, and corpus-based sociolinguistics), a compilation of corpus-based studies in this domain (e.g. gender, language variation and politeness) and examples of how to conduct corpus-based sociolinguistic research (e.g. Biber's Multidimensional Analysis).

Kipp, M., Martin, J.C., Paggio, P. and Heylen, D. (eds) (2009) *Multimodal Corpora*, Berlin: Springer.

A selection of state-of-the-art papers from the International Workshop on 'Multimodal Corpora: From Models of Natural Interaction to Systems and Applications', including texts on collecting, annotating and analysing multimodal corpora from a range of disciplines such as computational linguistics, artificial intelligence, psychology and human-computer interaction.

McEnery, T., Xiao, R. and Tono, Y. (2006) *Corpus-Based Language Studies*, London, UK: Routledge (and companion web source http://cw.routledge.com/textbooks/0415286239/resources/corpa.htm)

An excellent introduction to corpus-based language studies, offering an overview of corpus linguistics, and covering some of the main themes in corpus linguistics, including annotation, sampling, balance and representativeness, types of corpora and statistical information used in corpus analysis. The companion website offers a comprehensive survey of corpora and some resources and tools which the authors used in their case studies.

Xiao, R. and Yue, M. (2009) 'Using corpora in translation studies: The state of the art' in P. Baker (ed), *Contemporary Corpus Linguistics*, London, UK: Continuum: 237–261.

This chapter examines the use of corpora in the study of translation. The authors offer a case study comparing Chinese fiction with Chinese translations of English language fiction to explore the area of translation universals.

## References

Adolphs, S., Knight, D. and Carter, R. (2011) 'Capturing context for heterogeneous corpus analysis: Some first steps', *International Journal of Corpus Linguistics*, 16(3): 305–324.

Aksan, Y., Askan, M., Koltuksuz, A., Sezer, T., Mersinli, Ü., Demirhan, U. et al. (2012) 'Construction of the Turkish National Corpus (TNC)', in *Proceedings of the Eight International Conference on Language Resources and Evaluation (LREC 2012)*, İstanbul, Turkey (online), available: http://www.lrec-conf.org/proceedings/lrec2012/papers.html (accessed 20 Feb 2014).

Allwood, J. (2009) 'Multimodal corpora', in A. Lüdeling and M. Kytö (eds), *Corpus Linguistics. An International Handbook*, Berlin: Mouton de Gruyter: 207–225.

Altenberg, B., Aijmer, K. and Svensson, M. (2001) *The English-Swedish Parallel Corpus (ESPC) Manuel*, Sweden: Department of English, University of Lund and Department of English, University of Göteborg.

Aston, G. (1995) 'Corpora in language pedagogy: Matching theory and practice', in G. Cook and B. Seidlhofer (eds), *Principle and Practice in Applied Linguistics: Studies in Honour of H. G. Widdowson*, Oxford: Oxford University Press: 257–270.

Aston, G. (1997) 'Small and large corpora in language learning', in B. Lewandowska-Tomaszczyk and P. Melia (eds), *PALC 97: Practical Applications in Language Corpora*, Lodz: Lodz University Press: 51–62.

Aston, G. and Burnard, L. (1998) *The BNC Handbook*, Edinburgh: Edinburgh University Press.

Baker, M. (2000) 'Towards a methodology for investigating the style of a literary translator', *Target*, 12(2): 241–266.

Baker, P. (2010) *Sociolinguistics and Corpus Linguistics*, Edinburgh: Edinburgh University Press.

Biber, D. (1990) 'Methodological issues regarding corpus-based analyses of linguistic variation', *Literary and Linguistic Computing*, 5(4): 257–269.

Biber, D, Conrad, S. and Reppen, R. (1998) *Corpus Linguistics: Investigating Language Structure and Use*, Cambridge: Cambridge University Press.

Biber, D., Johannson, S., Leech, G., Conrad, S. and Finegan, E. (1999) *Longman Grammar of Spoken and Written English*, London, UK: Longman.

Blache, P., Bertrand, R. and Ferré, G. (2009) 'Creating and exploiting multimodal annotated corpora: The ToMA project', in M. Kipp, J.C. Martin, P. Paggio and D. Heylen (eds), *Multimodal Corpora*, Berlin: Springer: 38–53.

Bowker, L. and Pearson, J. (2002) *Working with Specialized Language. A Practical Guide to Using Corpora*, London, UK: Routledge.

Brinton, L.J. (2012) 'Historical pragmatics and corpus linguistics: Problems and strategies', in M. Kytö (ed), *English Corpus Linguistics: Crossing Paths (Language and Computers – Studies in Practical Linguistics 76)*, Amsterdam, Netherlands: Rodopi: 101–131.

Caines, A.P. and Buttery, P.J. (2010) 'You Talking to Me? A predictive model for zero-auxiliary constructions', in *Proceedings of the 2010 Workshop on NLP and Linguistics: Finding the Common Ground, ACL-2010*, Uppsala: Association for Computational Linguistics: 43–51.

Carter, R. and McCarthy, M. (2006) *The Cambridge Grammar of English*, Cambridge: Cambridge University Press.

Chambers, A. (2005) 'Integrating corpus consultation into language studies', *Language Learning and Technology*, 19(2): 111–125, [online], available: http://llt.msu.edu/vol9num2/chambers/default.html (accessed 25 Aug 2012).

Claridge, C. (2000) *Multi-Word Verbs in Early Modern English. A Corpus-Based Study*, Amsterdam: Rodopi.

Claridge, C. (2008) 'Historical corpora', in A. Lüdeling and M. Kytö (eds), *Corpus Linguistics: An International Handbook Vol. 1*, Berlin: Walter de Gruyter: 242–259.

Clear, J. (1987) 'Trawling the language: Monitor corpora', in M. Snell-Hornby (ed), *ZuriLEX Proceedings*, Tubingen: Francke: 383–389.

Culpeper, J. (2010) 'Historical pragmatics', in L. Cummings (ed), *The Pragmatics Encyclopedia*, London, UK: Routledge: 188–192.

Curzan, A. (2008) 'Historical corpus linguistics and evidence of change', in A. Lüdeling and M. Kytö (eds), *Corpus Linguistics: An International Handbook Vol. 1*, Berlin: Walter de Gruyter: 1091–1109.

Dahlmann, I. and Adolphs, S. (2009) 'Spoken corpus analysis: Multimodal approaches to language description' in P. Baker (ed), *Contemporary Corpus Linguistics*, London, UK: Continuum: 125–139.

Davies, M. (2002) *Corpus del Español: 100 Million Words, 1200s-1900s*, [online], available: http://www.crpusdelespanol.org

Davies, M. (2010) 'The Corpus of Contemporary American English as the first reliable monitor corpus of English', *Literary and Linguistic Computing*, 25(4): 447–465.

Davies, M. (2012) 'Expanding horizons in historical linguistics with the 400-million word Corpus of Historical American English', *Corpora*, 7: 121–157.

Davies, M. (2013) *Corpus of Global Web-Based English: 1.9 Billion Words from Speakers in 20 Countries*, available: http://corpus2.byu.edu/glowbe/

Degani, M. (2009) 'Re-analysing the semi-modal ought to: An investigation of its use in the LOB, FLOB, Brown and Frown corpora', *Language and Computers*, 69(1): 327–346.

Deutschmann, M. (2003) *Apologising in British English*, Umeå: Umeå University Press.

Fengxiang, F. (2012) 'A quantitative study on the lexical change of American English', *Journal of Quantitative Linguistics*, 19(3): 171–180.

Flowerdew, L. (2004) 'The argument for using English specialised corpora to understand academic and professional settings', in U. Connor and T. Upton (eds), *Discourse in the Professions: Perspectives from Corpus Linguistics*, Amsterdam, Netherlands: John Benjamins: 11–33.

Flowerdew, L. (2009) 'Applying corpus linguistics to pedagogy. A critical evaluation', *International Journal of Corpus Linguistics*, 14 (3): 393–417.

Gavioli, L. (2002) 'Some thoughts on the problem of representing ESP through small corpora', in B. Kettemann and G. Marko (eds), *Teaching and Learning by Doing Corpus Analysis*, Amsterdam, Netherlands: Rodopi: 293–303.

Gavioli, L. (2005) *Exploring Corpora for ESP*, Amsterdam, Netherlands: John Benjamins.

Handford, M. (2010) 'What can a corpus tell us about specialist genres?', in A. O'Keeffe and M. McCarthy (eds), *The Routledge Handbook of Corpus Linguistics*, London, UK: Routledge: 255–269.

Hanks, P. (2009) 'The impact of corpora on dictionaries', in P. Baker (ed), *Contemporary Corpus Linguistics*, London, UK: Continuum: 214–236.

Haugh, M. (2009) 'Designing a multimodal spoken component of the Australian National Corpus', in M. Haugh, K. Burridge, J. Mulder and P. Peters (eds), *Selected Proceedings of the 2008 HCSNet Workshop on Designing the Australian National Corpus*, Somerville, MA: Cascadilla Proceedings Project: 74–86.

Healey, A. (1999) 'The dictionary of old English corpus on the World Wide Web', *Medieval English Studies Newsletter*, 40: 2–10.

Hoffstaedter, P. and Kohn, K. (2009) 'Real language and relevant language learning activities: Insights from the SACODEYL project', in A. Kirchhofer and J. Schwarzkopf (eds), *The Workings of the Anglosphere. Contributions to the Study of British and US-American Cultures*, Trier: WVT.

Hundt, M. and Gut, U. (eds) (2012) *Mapping Unity and Diversity Worldwide: Corpus-Based Studies of New Englishes*, Amsterdam, Netherlands: John Benjamins.

Hundt, M., Nesselhauf, N. and Biewer, C. (eds) (2009) *Corpus Linguistics and the Web*. Amsterdam, Netherlands: Rodopi: 1–7.

Hundt, M., Sand, A. and Siemund, R. (1998) *Manual of Information to Accompany the Freiburg-LOB Corpus of British English ("FLOB")*, [online], available: http://www.hit.uib.no/icame/flob/index.htm (accessed 6 Jun 2013).

Hundt, M., Sand, A. and Skandera, P. (1999) *Manual of Information to Accompany the Freiburg-Brown Corpus of American English (Frown)*, [online], available: http://khnt.hit.uib.no/icame/manuals/frown/INDEX.HTM (accessed 6 Jun 2013).

Johansson, S., Ebeling, J. and Oksefjell, S. (2002) *The English-Norwegian Parallel Corpus Manual*, Oslo: Department of British and American Studies University of Oslo.

Johansson, S., Leech, G. and Goodluck, H. (1978), *Manual of Information to Accompany the Lancaster-Oslo/Bergen Corpus of British English, for Use with Digital Computers*, Oslo: University of Oslo.

Johns, T. (1991) 'Should you be persuaded. Two samples of data-driven learning materials', *English Language Research Journal*, 1–14.

Kehoe, A. and Gee, M. (2012) 'Reader comments as an aboutness indicator in online texts: Introducing the Birmingham Blog Corpus', *Studies in Variation, Contacts, and Change in English Vol. 12. Aspects of Corpus Linguistics: Compilation, Annotation and Analysis* [online], available: http://www.helsinki.fi/varieng/series/volumes/12/kehoe_gee/ (accessed 26 Feb 2014).

Kenning, M.M. (2010) 'What are parallel and comparable corpora and how can we use them?', in A. O'Keeffe and M. McCarthy (eds), *The Routledge Handbook of Corpus Linguistics*, London, UK: Routledge: 487–500.

Kilgarriff, A. (2001) 'Web as corpus', in P. Rayson, A. Wilson, T. McEnery, A. Hardie and S. Khoja (eds), *Proceedings of the Corpus Linguistics 2001 Conference*, Lancaster: UCREL: 342–44.

Kilgarriff, A. and Grefenstette, G. (2003) 'Introduction to the special issue on the web as corpus', *Computational Linguistics*, 29(3): 333–348.

Kjellmer, G. (1994) *A Dictionary of English Collocations Based on the Brown Corpus*, Oxford: Clarendon Press.

Koester, A. (2010) 'Building small specialised corpora', in A. O'Keeffe and M. McCarthy (eds), *The Routledge Handbook of Corpus Linguistics*, London, UK: Routledge: 66–79.

Koeva, S., Stoyanova, I., Leseva, S., Dimitrova, T., Dekova, R. and Tarpomanova, E. (2012) 'The Bulgarian National Corpus: Theory and practice in corpus design', *Journal of Language Modelling*, 1: 65–110.

Knight, D. (2011) 'The future of multimodal corpora', *RBLA, Belo Horizonte*, 11(2): 391–415.

Knight, D. and Adolphs, S. (2007) 'Pragmatics and corpus linguistics: A mutualistic entente', in J. Romero-Trillo (ed), *Corpus and Pragmatics*, Berlin: Mouton de Gruyter: 172–190.

Knight, D., Adolphs, S., Tennent, P. and Carter, R. (2008) 'The Nottingham Multi-Modal Corpus: A demonstration', Paper presented at the 6th *Language Resources and Evaluation Conference*, Palais des Congrés, Mansour Eddahbi, Marrakech, Morocco, May 2008.

Knight, D. and Tennent, P. (2008) 'Introducing DRS (The Digital Replay System): A tool for the future of Corpus Linguistic research and analysis', Paper presented at the 6th *Language Resources and Evaluation Conference*, Palais des Congrés, Mansour Eddahbi, Marrakech, Morocco, May 2008.

Kübler, N. and Aston, G. (2010) 'Using corpora in translation', in A. O'Keeffe and M. McCarthy (eds), *The Routledge Handbook of Corpus Linguistics*, London, UK: Routledge: 501–515.

Kučera, H. and Francis, W. (1967) *Computational Analysis of Present-day English*, Providence: Brown University Press.

Kytö, M. (2011) 'Corpora and historical linguistics', *Revista Brasileira de Linguistica Aplicada*, 11(2): 391–415.

Kytö, M. (2012) 'Introduction', in M. Kytö (ed), *English Corpus Linguistics: Crossing Paths (Language and Computers – Studies in Practical Linguistics 76)*, Amsterdam, Netherlands: Rodopi: 1–6.

Kytö, M. and Pahta, P. (2012) 'Evidence from historical corpora up to the twentieth century', in T. Nevalainen and E.C. Traugott (eds), *The Oxford Handbook of the History of English*, Oxford: Oxford University Press: 123–133.

Lee, D.Y.W. (2010) 'What corpora are available?', in A. O'Keeffe and M. McCarthy (eds), *The Routledge Handbook of Corpus Linguistics*, London, UK: Routledge: 107–121.

Mauranen, A. (2012) *Exploring ELF: Academic English Shaped by Non-Native Speakers*, Cambridge: Cambridge University Press.

McCarten, J. (2010) 'Corpus-informed course book design', in A. O'Keeffe and M. McCarthy (eds), *The Routledge Handbook of Corpus Linguistics*, London, UK: Routledge: 413–427.

McEnery, A. and Xiao, R. (2004) 'Swearing in modern British English: The case of *fuck* in the BNC', *Language and Literature*, 13(3): 235–268.

Nelson, G. (1996) 'The design of the corpus', in S. Greenbaum (ed), *Comparing English Worldwide: The International Corpus of English*, Oxford: Clarendon Press: 27–35.

Nesi, H. (2012) 'Laughter in university lectures', *Journal of English for Academic Purposes*, 11(2): 79–89.

Nevalainen, T, and Raumolin-Brunberg, H. (eds) (1996) *Sociolinguistics and Language History: Studies Based on the Corpus of Early English Correspondence*, Amsterdam, Netherlands: Rodopi.

O'Donnell, M. and Römer, U. (2012) 'From student hard drive to web corpus (part 2): The annotation and online distribution of MICUSP', *Corpora*, 7: 1–18.

O'Keeffe, A. (2007) 'The pragmatics of Corpus Linguistics', keynote paper presented at the fourth *Corpus Linguistics Conference* held at the University of Birmingham, Birmingham, July 2007.

O'Keeffe, A. and Farr, F. (2003) 'Using language corpora in initial teacher education: Pedagogic issues and practical applications', *TESOL Quarterly*, 37(3): 389–418.

O'Keeffe, A., McCarthy, M. and Carter, R. (2007) *From Corpus to Classroom. Language Use and Language Teaching*, Cambridge: Cambridge University Press.

OMC (2010) *Oslo Multilingual Corpus*, [online], available: http://www.hf.uio.no/ilos/english/services/omc/ (accessed 12 Jun 2013).

Partington, A. (2006) *The Linguistics of Laughter: A Corpus-Assisted Study of Laughter-Talk*, London, UK: Routledge.

Renouf, A. (2002) 'WebCorp: Providing a renewable data source for corpus linguists', in S. Granger and S. Petch-Tyson (eds), *Extending the scope of corpus-based research*, Amsterdam, Netherlands: Rodopi: 39–58.

Reppen, R. (2009) 'English language teaching and corpus linguistics: Lessons learned from the American National Corpus', in P. Baker (ed), *Contemporary Corpus Linguistics*, London, UK: Continuum: 204–213.

Reppen, R. (2010a) *Using Corpora in the Language Classroom*, Cambridge: Cambridge University Press.

Reppen, R. (2010b) 'Corpora in the classroom: Forging new paths', Paper presented at Annual TESOL Convention, Denver, CO.

Reppen, R. and Ide, N. (2004) 'The American National Corpus: Overall goals and the first release', *Journal of English Linguistics*, 32(2): 105–113.

Rissanen, M. (2000) 'The world of English historical corpora', *Journal of English Linguistics*, 28(1): 7–20.

Rissanen, M. (2008) 'Corpus linguistics and historical linguistics', in A. Lüdeling and M. Kytö (eds), *Corpus Linguistics: An International Handbook Vol. 1*, Berlin: Walter de Gruyter: 53–68.

Rissanen, M. (2012) 'Corpora and the study of the history of English', in M. Kytö (ed), *English Corpus Linguistics: Crossing Paths (Language and Computers – Studies in Practical Linguistics 76)*, Amsterdam: Rodopi: 197–220.

Rossini Favretti, R., Tamburini, F. and De Santis, C. (2004) 'A corpus of written Italian: A defined and a dynamic model', in A. Wilson, P. Rayson and T. McEnery (eds), *A Rainbow of Corpora: Corpus Linguistics and the Languages of the World*, Munich: Lincom-Europa: 27–38.

Schmid, H.J. (2003) 'Do men and women really live in different cultures? Evidence from the BNC', in A. Wilson, P. Rayson and T. McEnery (eds), *Corpus Linguistics by the Lune*, Frankfurt: Peter Lang: 185–221.

Sharoff, S. (2004) 'Methods and tools for development of the Russian Reference Corpus', in D. Archer, A. Wilson, and P. Rayson (eds), *Corpus Linguistics Around the World*, Amsterdam, Netherlands: Rodopi: 167–180.

Simpson-Vlach, R. and Leicher, S. (2006) *The MICASE Handbook: A Resource for Users of the Michigan Corpus of Academic Spoken English*, Ann Arbor: University of Michigan Press.
Sinclair, J. (ed) (1987) *Looking Up*, London, UK: HarperCollins.
Sinclair, J. (1997) 'Corpus evidence in language description', in A. Wichmann, S. Fligelstone, T. McEnery and G. Knowles (eds), *Teaching and Language Corpora*, London, UK: Longman: 27–39.
Sinclair, J. (2003) *Reading Concordances*, London, UK: Longman.
Sinclair, J. (2004) *Trust the Text: Language, Corpus and Discourse*, London, UK: Routledge.
Stenström, A-B, Andersen, G. and I.K. Hasund, (2002) *Trends in Teenage Talk*, Amsterdam, Netherlands: John Benjamins.
Taavitsainen, I. and Pahta, P. (eds) (2010) *Early Modern English Medical Texts. Corpus Description and Studies*, Amsterdam, Netherlands: John Benjamins.
Tiedemann, J. (2012) 'Parallel Data, Tools and Interfaces in OPUS', Paper presented at the 8th *International Conference on Language Resources and Evaluation* (LREC 2012), Istanbul, Turkey, 2012.
Tognini-Bonelli, E. and Sinclair, J. (2006) 'Corpora', in K. Brown (ed), *Encyclopedia of Language and Linguistics*, Amsterdam: Elsevier: 216–219.
Tribble, C. (2002) 'Corpora and corpus analysis: New windows on academic writing', in J. Flowerdew (ed), *Academic Discourse*, London, UK: Longman: 131–149.
Véronis, J. (ed) (2000) *Parallel Text Processing. Alignment and Use of Translation Corpora*, Amsterdam, Netherlands: Kluwer Academic Publishers.
Widmann, J., Kohn, K. and Ziai, R. (2011) 'The SACODEYL search tool: Exploiting corpora for language learning purposes', in A. Frankenberg Garcia, L. Flowerdew and G. Aston (eds), *New Trends in Corpora and Language Learning*, London, UK: Continuum: 167–180.
Xiao, R. and Yue, M. (2009) 'Using corpora in translation studies: The state of the art', in P. Baker (ed), *Contemporary Corpus Linguistics*, London, UK: Continuum: 237–261.
Yaguchi, M, Iyeiri, Y. and Okabe, H. (2004) 'Style and gender differences in formal contexts: An analysis of *sort of* and *kind of* appearing in the CSPAE', Paper presented at the 5th Annual Wenshan Conference on ELT, Literature, and Linguistics.
Yáñez-Bouza, N. 2011. 'ARCHER past and present (1990–2010)', *ICAME Journal*, 35: 205–236.

# Appendix 28A
# Websites

| Corpus Archives | | Details |
|---|---|---|
| Corpus BYU | http://corpus.byu.edu/ | Free online search facility (registration required) |
| Lextutor | http://www.lextutor.ca | Free |
| Linguistic Data Consortium (LDC) | http://www.ldc.upenn.edu/ | Membership fee |
| Oxford Text Archive | http://ota.ahds.ac.uk/ | Free |
| *General Corpora* | | |
| American National Corpus (ANC) | http://www.americannationalcorpus.org/ | Free |
| Bank of English (BoE)/ Wordbanks | http://www.mycobuild.com/about-collins-corpus.aspx  http://www.collinslanguage.com/content-solutions/wordbanks | Subscription fee |
| British National Corpus (BNC) | http://www.natcorp.ox.ac.uk/ | Free online search facility  Licence fee for corpus |
| BROWN Corpus | http://icame.uib.no/brown/bcm.html | Subscription fee or can be purchased with ICAME |
| Bulgarian National Corpus | http://ibl.bas.bg/en/BGNC_en.htm | Free online search facility |
| Corpus del Español | http://www.corpusdelespanol.org/ | Free online search facility |
| Corpus di Italiano Scritto (CORIS) | http://corpora.dslo.unibo.it/coris_eng.html | Free online search facility |
| Corpus of Contemporary American English (COCA) | http://corpus.byu.edu/coca/ | Free online search facility |
| Freiberg Brown Corpus of American English (FROWN) | http://khnt.hit.uib.no/icame/manuals/frown/ | Subscription fee or can be purchased with ICAME |
| Freiberg London-Oslo/Bergen Corpus (FLOB) | http://icame.uib.no/flob/ | Subscription fee or can be purchased with ICAME |
| International Corpus of English (ICE) | http://ice-corpora.net/ice/ | Some corpora are freely available for research purposes |
| London-Oslo/Bergen Corpus (LOB) | http://khnt.hit.uib.no/icame/manuals/lob/ | Subscription fee or can be purchased with ICAME |
| Russian Reference Corpus | http://bokrcorpora.narod.ru/index-en.html | Free online search facility of pilot version |
| Turkish National Corpus (TNC) | http://www.tnc.org.tr/index.php/en/ | Free online search facility (registration required) |

*(Continued)*

## Specialised Corpora

| | | |
|---|---|---|
| British Academic Written English (BAWE) | http://www2.warwick.ac.uk/fac/soc/al/research/collect/bawe/ | Available through the Oxford Text Archive |
| Cambridge and Nottingham Business English Corpus (CANBEC) | http://www.cambridge.org/gb/elt/catalogue/subject/custom/item3646597/Cambridge-English-Corpus-Business-English/?site_locale=en_GB | Not publicly available |
| Cambridge and Nottingham E-Language Corpus (CANELC) | http://www.ncl.ac.uk/linguistics/research/publication/178260 | Not publicly available |
| Cambridge Corpus of Legal English (CCLE) | http://www.cambridge.org/gb/elt/catalogue/subject/custom/item3646600/Cambridge-English-Corpus-Cambridge-Corpus-of-Legal-English/?site_locale=en_GB | Not publicly available |
| Corpus of London Teenage English (COLT) | http://www.hd.uib.no/colt/ | Licence fee or can be purchased with ICAME |
| Corpus of Spoken Professional American English (CSPAE) | http://www.athel.com/cspa.html | Licence fee |
| English as a Lingua Franca Corpus (ELFA) | http://www.helsinki.fi/englanti/elfa/ | Freely available once user agreement has been signed |
| Enron Email Corpus | https://www.cs.cmu.edu/~enron/ | Free |
| International Corpus of Learner English (ICLE) | http://www.uclouvain.be/en-cecl-icle.html | Licence fee |
| Michigan Corpus of Academic Spoken English (MICASE) | http://quod.lib.umich.edu/m/micase/ | Free online search facility |
| Michigan Corpus of Upper-level Student Papers (MICUSP) | http://micusp.elicorpora.info/ | Free online search facility |
| WebCorp | http://www.webcorp.org.uk/live/ | Free online search facility |

## Parallel Corpora

| | | |
|---|---|---|
| Canadian Hansard Corpus | http://www.ldc.upenn.edu/Catalog/catalogEntry.jsp?catalogId=LDC95T20 | Subscription fee |
| Contemporary Chinese Translated Fiction Corpus (CCTFC) | http://www.bfsu-corpus.org/static/cctfc/ | Free online search facility |
| English-Norwegian Parallel Corpus (ENPC) | http://www.hf.uio.no/ilos/english/services/omc/enpc/ | Not publicly available beyond creator institution |
| English-Swedish Parallel Corpus (ESPC) | http://www.sol.lu.se/engelska/corpus/corpus/espc.html | Not publicly available beyond creator institution |
| Lancaster Corpus of Mandarin Chinese (LCMC) | http://www.lancs.ac.uk/fass/projects/corpus/LCMC/ | Available through the Oxford Text Archive |

| | | |
|---|---|---|
| Open Parallel Corpus (OPUS) | http://opus.lingfil.uu.se/ | Free |
| Oslo Multilingual Corpus (OMC) | http://www.hf.uio.no/ilos/english/services/omc/ | Not publicly available beyond creator institution |
| Translational English Corpus (TEC) | http://ronaldo.cs.tcd.ie/tec2/jnlp/ | Free |

| *Historical Corpora* | | |
|---|---|---|
| ARCHER Corpus | http://www.alc.manchester.ac.uk/subjects/lel/research/projects/archer/ | Free online search facility once user agreement has been signed |
| Corpus of Early English Correspondence (CEEC) | http://www.helsinki.fi/varieng/domains/CEEC.html | Available through the Oxford Text Archive |
| Corpus of Historical American English (COHA) | http://corpus.byu.edu/coha/ | Free online search facility |
| Dictionary of Old English Corpus in Electronic Form | http://www.ota.ox.ac.uk/desc/2488 | Available through the Oxford Text Archive |
| Early English Medical Writing | http://www.helsinki.fi/varieng/CoRD/corpora/CEEM/EMEMTindex.html | CD-ROM by John Benjamins |
| Helsinki Corpus | http://www.helsinki.fi/varieng/CoRD/corpora/HelsinkiCorpus/ | Available through the Oxford Text Archive |
| Lampeter corpus | http://khnt.hit.uib.no/icame/manuals/LAMPETER/LAMPHOME.HTM | Available through the Oxford Text Archive |

| *Multimodal Corpora* | | |
|---|---|---|
| BACKBONE Corpus | http://webapps.ael.uni-tuebingen.de/backbone-search/faces/initialize.jsp | Free |
| Nottingham Multimodal Corpus (NMMC) | http://www.cs.nott.ac.uk/~axc/DReSS/LRECw08.pdf | Not publicly available beyond creator institution |
| SACODEYL Corpus | http://sacodeyl.inf.um.es/sacodeyl-search2/ | Free |
| Santa Barbara Corpus of Spoken American English | http://www.linguistics.ucsb.edu/research/santa-barbara-corpus | Free online search facility |

# 29
# Designing and building corpora for language learning

*Randi Reppen*

This chapter provides a brief overview of corpora and tools that are available for language learning and then provides specific information and guidelines for creating and using corpora for language learning. Key considerations for constructing specialised written and spoken corpora are provided. Useful teacher and learner tools for corpus analysis are presented along with example activities.

This chapter explores the advantages of and resources for building corpora for language learning along with the considerations involved in that task. Discussions of corpora often revolve around the aspect of size and how many millions of words are included in a corpus. This chapter focuses on the specialised use of corpora, and as such the notion of size is not a major consideration. Representativeness is the guiding principle; that is, whether the corpus reflects the range of language used in the context it is representing. Even in large corpus projects representativeness should be a guiding principle. This helps to assure that the language in the corpus represents the language domain that is being explored. Building corpora for language learning can enhance the resources available to students and teachers for practice and exploration. Since each classroom is composed of different learners, with different needs and language learning experiences and learning styles, creating a corpus of language for a specific classroom context can be a valuable resource for language teaching.

## Why build language learning corpora?

With all the other tasks that teachers juggle, the heading of this section asks a legitimate question: why build language learning corpora? Other questions worth asking (and answering) are: How can this be accomplished in an efficient manner? What resources already exist? How can corpora be used to enhance language learning? This chapter will address these questions and others related to designing and creating corpora for language learning. Previous chapters in this section have provided ideas and insights as to what a corpus is and how spoken or written corpora can be used to learn about language and language use, and some of the ways that corpora can be used to enhance language learning. In this chapter we will see specifically how to plan and create corpora for language learning and also some ways to use these resources to facilitate learning.

Before getting into the details of building corpora, let's first take a brief look at some of the existing online corpora that can be effectively used in language classes and as language learning resources. Some examples of corpora that represent a range of different contexts of language use include the British National Corpus (BNC; http://www.natcorp.ox.ac.uk/ or http://corpus.byu.edu/bnc/) and the Corpus of Contemporary American English (COCA; http://americancorpus.org). These corpora organise language by the context of use or register (e.g. newspapers, academic prose, fiction). This organisation provides resources that can be used by teachers and students to explore how language varies across different contexts of use (e.g. spoken vs. written, newspapers vs. academic; see Murphy and Riordan, Chapter 28 this volume) and to identify common patterns of use such as collocations.

In addition to these large corpora which represent a variety of contexts of language use but which are not primarily designed for pedagogical purposes, there are also corpus resources that have been designed with a pedagogical focus. A pedagogically focused companion to the COCA site is Word and Phrase (http://www.wordandphrase.info), where in addition to seeing contextualised frequency information users can input texts and compare their texts to academic texts or other contexts of use (e.g. spoken or newspapers). The site also highlights the type of vocabulary used in the text that was input as to the number and types of words from the general and academic word lists, thus giving teachers (and learners) information about the types of words being used.

Two other valuable free corpus resources that can be used for intermediate to advanced academic language instruction are MICASE (Michigan Corpus of Academic Spoken English; Simpson, Briggs, Ovens and Swales 2002) and MICUSP (Michigan Corpus of Upper-level Student Papers; Simpson-Vlach and Leicher 2006). These two corpora were created with language pedagogy in mind. They are designed to represent language use at an American university (the University of Michigan). Although only collected at the University of Michigan, MICASE is a searchable collection of spoken language events that are typical of spoken interactions at American universities (e.g. class lectures, study groups, office hours, interactions with university offices). The site includes filters that can be used to refine searches in order to make them maximally adaptable to a range of users. For example, a student interested in finding out about undergraduate biology lectures can specify this through the search filters. Or, perhaps the teacher is doing a unit on hedging; students can be guided to enter search terms that will identify hedging and then look at the contexts of where these occur. MICASE offers teachers and students a tremendous resource of readily available authentic academic spoken interactions from a variety of contexts of use, ranging from formal lectures to students interacting with each other. In addition to access to the corpus, the MICASE site also provides links to teacher resources and lessons that can be used or adapted for a particular classroom. The site also provides support for first time users through FAQs and online tutorials.

MICUSP, the other corpus resource representing language from the University of Michigan, is a collection of 829 papers written by upper-level students (not first- or second-year students) that received a grade of A or A+. Like MICASE, MICUSP can be searched as a general resource or by looking at specific aspects of academic student writing, such as abstracts or referencing. This corpus is a valuable resource that provides students with examples of discipline specific writing. MICUSP is particularly useful in this regard since it is often difficult to provide learners with academic writing produced by soon-to-be classmates, instead of the journal articles or newspaper language that are so often used as examples for learners. Both MICUSP and MICASE are available online through free user-friendly interfaces and allow teachers to provide students with examples of the language that is used in a university context.

A distinct advantage of these corpora for language learning contexts is that the language in these corpora is exactly the language that learners will be surrounded by in an American English university setting.

As valuable as these freely available corpora are, they may not address the specific needs of particular learners or of certain classroom contexts, so now we move on to the 'why' of creating corpora for our language classes. One reason is that a corpus can provide a valuable resource for informing instruction and for materials development. Classroom-specific corpora help teachers identify patterns of language that are typical of specific contexts of language use (e.g. informal conversation, lectures, introductions used in academic papers, disciplinary specific vocabulary) and bring these examples into the classroom. Using software programs that are described in the next section, teachers can easily identify structures that are problematic for students or identify vocabulary that would be beneficial to include, thus helping learners to fine-tune their language. Granted this is a much easier for written tasks, but it is also possible to collect and use spoken language to inform instruction. Ideally spoken language is transcribed and can then be explored using the same tools and software that are used with written texts (see Caines, McCarthy and O'Keeffe, Chapter 25 this volume).

In addition to having a snapshot of language as it is used in various contexts, a corpus can be a valuable resource in many ways such as providing learners with hands on opportunities to explore how language varies in different contexts of use or for different goals; exploring characteristics of language in certain tasks and/or disciplines; or becoming more autonomous language users. Some ideas for classroom use and materials development will be provided in a later section, but first we will look at some things to consider when building corpora for classroom use.

## What are the key considerations when designing/building language learning corpora?

In the previous section, the example corpora that were presented were already compiled and available online, each with a search interface that allowed the corpus to be explored. Those corpora are useful resources, but do not always fit our learners' or our instructional needs. In this section we will find out how to create corpora for use in our classrooms. Undertaking any corpus building task requires certain considerations (see Reppen 2010 and O'Keeffe, McCarthy and Carter 2007 for more details). The goal of building a corpus must be clear and purposeful. This is the most important consideration. One of the best ways to achieve this is through a series of questions:

- What do I hope to learn from this corpus? This will guide what is collected.
- What texts (spoken and/or written) will best suit my goals or best represent the slice of language I am representing? This will aid in identifying the texts to be collected.
- How will the corpus be used? This will help shape what is collected and the tools that may be needed.
- Who will use this corpus? Is it just for teacher use(s), or will students also use the corpus? This will inform the level of support and additional information provided.
- Am I building a corpus on my own or with colleagues? If multiple colleagues are contributing texts, then more developed guidelines are needed for file naming and corpus format conventions (these are described in the next section).

After thinking about these questions and using those answers to inform our corpus design, we are now ready to get to some specific details related to building a corpus for classroom use.

## Designing and building corpora

### Building a corpus from written language

A first step that shapes the collection of texts is to know the specific instructional goals and the expected uses and outcomes of the corpus. In a beginning course, this might consist of collecting class readings that will allow students to reinforce vocabulary and provide a means for recycling target vocabulary and a resource for exploring words in context. At an advanced level, students might be asked to bring texts that represent the disciplines that they will be studying. Then the teacher can assemble the texts into a class corpus that can be explored in various ways. In either case, whether the students are bringing in texts (in electronic format) or the teacher is collecting the texts, they will be in many different sources and formats such as Word files, PDFs or downloaded web pages. Each of these has formatting conventions that need to become transformed into a uniform format to interact with the software programs that will be used with these texts. But first, we will want to name the files in a systematic and meaningful manner.

Once texts have been collected, the texts need to be named in a manner that reflects the content of the file. For example, if a corpus of readings from different disciplines and levels are being collected, a text from a biology reading in a first-year class could have the filename BIOrXXy1. Each discipline being collected would be assigned a logical three-letter abbreviation (e.g. eng = engineering; chm = chemistry; egl = English). An *r* would always appear after the discipline label to indicate these are readings, as opposed to syllabi or lectures. XX would be used to number the text (e.g. BIOr01y1, BIOr02y1, etc.). If more than ninety-nine texts from a particular discipline are expected, then use three places. The final part of the filename is the academic year represented by the text (e.g. y1, y2 ... y5). This manner of file naming allows for easy sorting by discipline and/or by year, and if these are part of a corpus that contains more than just readings (e.g. syllabi, lectures) it also allows for sorting by task type or context of use. Of course, depending on the levels and designations used in particular programs any two- or three-character descriptors can be used to indicate level. Even though the file naming conventions should be as transparent as possible, it is strongly recommended that a key of the codes used (e.g. eng = engineering and egl = English) be created to avoid confusion later, and to serve as a resource for future users.

Now that we have consistent and descriptive filenames, the files will need to be converted to a format called plain text in order to be used with most corpus software programs. Converting files is a simple process. A search of the Web will quickly result in free programs (e.g. Word2txt or PDF2txt) that can be used to convert texts from various formats into plain text. These programs can be used to convert files one-by-one or in batches – that is groups of files in the same format (e.g. all the Word files or all the PDF files). If web pages are being downloaded, simply save these as plain text files so that there is no need to convert the files. Once the files are in text format, the programs listed later can be used to explore the files and develop materials.

### Building a corpus from spoken language

Collecting spoken language is a bit more involved than collecting written texts since the spoken events will need to be recorded, transferred to a computer and then keyed in, or transcribed. Digital recorders are not expensive, and most recorders will allow the user to capture and save sound files. It is convenient if the recorder has a USB port that can be plugged directly into the computer to facilitate file transfer from the recorder to the computer. After transferring the files from the recorder, the same file naming conventions described for written files apply to audio files. Before the audio files can be used, they require the additional step of being transcribed. That is, a person will listen to the audio file and create a text file by keying in the language. Prior to beginning the transcription, it is important to decide on certain conventions – for example, whether shortened forms such as *cuz* for *because* or *gonna* for *going to* will be transcribed as is or whether the full forms will be entered. It is also important to standardise the way shortened forms are spelled. For example, if *cuz* is chosen as the preferred spelling for the shortened form of *because,* then that must always be used and not variations such as *coz* or *cos*. There are no right or wrong choices, just the need for consistency. These decisions will be guided by how the files will be used. Will they be used to look at differences between formal and informal language (e.g. informal conversation vs. more formal interactions with a supervisor)? In that case, transcribing forms as they are (e.g. *gonna*, *cuz, wanna*), might be worthwhile to see how language varies (or does not) across different contexts (e.g. classmates interacting in group work vs. giving a class presentation). In some cases it is possible to get existing transcripts for certain spoken events. If these are used, it is important to listen to the audio files and read the transcripts to make certain that they are accurate and that the conventions that are being used in the other parts of the corpus are being followed in these already transcribed files.

Although the considerations described earlier may seem overwhelming when considered as a whole, it is not so overwhelming when taken in steps. For example, beginning with one class and only certain types of texts (e.g. readings or lectures) from that course can make the task manageable. Once the methods for collecting, organising and exploring the corpus have become familiar, then expand to collecting other types of tasks or courses. That will make the task of creating a corpus doable and more efficient as the corpus collection expands to include other types of class language and tasks.

## *Tools for analysis*

There are many resources for exploring a corpus. Some of the most common tools are concordancing programs such as AntConc, MonoConc and WordSmith. These programs can provide information about the texts in a corpus including word lists, frequency information of words in order from most to least frequent, in alpha order with frequency information, words that co-occur (e.g. clusters, n-grams), a key word or phrase along with its context (KWICs, or key words in context) and collocation information (what words co-occur with the target words). For example, if the word *however* was entered as a search term, a concordancing program would tell you how many times *however* occurred (frequency) and in how many texts (dispersion), helping the user to see if *however* was used many times only in one text or a few times in many texts. We can also see which words tend to occur with *however* and even provide a graphic display of where in the text(s) *however* occurred (see Figure 29.1).

In addition to information about how a word is distributed within texts and across the corpus, it is also easy to see a word or group of words in context. KWICs show the target word(s) in context, as in Figure 29.2, which shows *however* and the context in which it occurs. The amount of text shown on either side of the target word can be modified to provide more or less context. In addition, with a single click, the complete original source text can be displayed. Words that frequently occur with the target word are highlighted in a different colour, helping to identify common patterns of use.

All the programs mentioned (AntConc, MonoConc and WordSmith) will perform the functions described earlier. As with any software program, each has its strengths and features that make it more suitable for certain users. Spending time with trial versions to see which of these programs best meets your needs is strongly recommended. Of these three programs, AntConc is free, while MonoConc and WordSmith cost about £50 each.

# Designing and building corpora

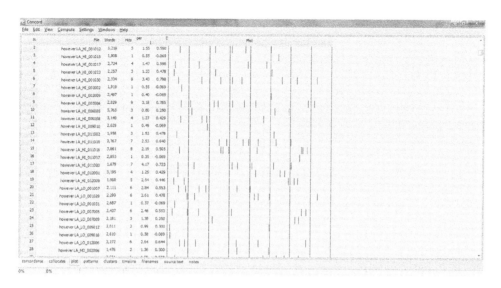

Figure 29.1  WordSmith 6.0 plot showing position of *however* in texts

Figure 29.2  Examples from the KWIC of *however* using WordSmith 6.0

## How can language learning corpora be applied in the classroom?

Now that the nuts and bolts of designing and building a corpus have been described along with the tools for exploring the corpus, we come to the last question, which is perhaps the most relevant for classroom purposes: how can language learning corpora provide resources to enhance instruction and materials development? The first most obvious and easiest use is in the area of vocabulary. Vocabulary is central to language learning, and having easy access to a resource for providing a variety of different vocabulary activities can be invaluable. Any of the programs described in the previous section can be used to create word lists along with frequency information. These lists can be used to identify patterns of vocabulary use across different written and/or spoken tasks. Learners can use KWICs of target vocabulary to practise discovering meaning from context, to see words that frequently go together or to fine-tune word senses. KWICs can be used to develop instructional activities ranging from gap fill to more contextualised language use across paragraphs or sections of text.

Moving away from a vocabulary focus, the plot function in any of the three software programs mentioned can be used to highlight patterns within and across different types of texts. For example, if students are writing empirical papers, the use of passive voice can be demonstrated by providing a model text and plotting the use of passive verbs. This provides a visual reinforcement of the pattern of using passive voice predominantly in the methods section of research writing. By then adding their texts, students can compare the use of passive voice in their writing with that of the model text.

Another example of a language learning activity is to identify written or spoken texts that exemplify instructional goals and then identify texts that do not exemplify the instructional goals (e.g. some papers that received failing grades and some that received A grades). Using corpus tools, learners can then look at the differences across the two groups of texts. Some example activities could include looking at vocabulary frequency and variety (using the word list function), focusing on particular grammatical forms or the use of transitions (using the KWIC function), comparing the distribution of certain structures such as linking or transition words (using the Plot function) across successful and unsuccessful texts.

The use of KWICs for identifying patterns of use or identifying word senses is another activity that is easily brought into the classroom through corpus resources. For this type of activity it is useful to identify some particular words or patterns that are being used in nonstandard ways and then have students look at a nonlearner corpus to see how the pattern differs from the one found in their writing or speaking. As an example of a word sense activity, consider if students are using the word *notorious* with a positive connotation when typically this word is used with a negative sense. Examples of 'notorious scientists' will not be common, while references to 'notorious criminals' will be. This type of hands-on discovery activity can be more powerful than simply having students look up words in a dictionary. This type of active engagement helps to promote learning. It also allows learners to realise that they can independently explore aspects of language use, and they may become motivated to explore corpora to become autonomous learners, able to increase their accuracy and proficiency through the use of corpus resources.

It can be useful to combine classroom specific corpora with online resources. Students can create a corpus of their own writing and compare aspects of their writing with writing produced in MICUSP, for example, or in discipline-specific classes. Students can compare reporting verbs used in their papers with reporting verbs found in the MICUSP corpus. Students can also use MICUSP to explore the language used to describe graphs and charts or explore how citations are used across different disciplines or in the specific disciplines that they are planning to study.

## What are the key issues in using language learning corpora?

The guiding principle in using corpora or corpus resources in a language learning context is to enhance learning. This can be accomplished through activities that raise learner awareness of the different contexts of language use and also through activities that promote learner autonomy. The simple existence of a corpus does not necessarily make it an appropriate tool for language learning. The questions that were provided at the beginning of this chapter continue to be relevant. The corpus being used must support the language learning goals. Obviously, the use of a corpus of academic writing is not going to work to create activities or raise learner awareness for features of spoken language, but neither will the use of a discipline-specific corpus be useful to provide information about a different discipline. So, selecting or creating corpora that represent the language learning goals is essential.

It is also important to remember not to overgeneralise from a specialised corpus created for classroom use to general language use or to other aspects of language use. A specialised classroom corpus is a valuable tool for informing language learning in the particular context for which it was created, and used appropriately it provides a powerful resource for materials and activity development for teachers and for hands-on activities for learners.

## Looking to the future

In just the last five years there has been a significant increase in the corpus resources available online, and this trend is likely to continue. In addition to increased availability of corpus resources, developments in technology have also changed how we can explore and examine language. The use of multimodal corpora and the types of tools for looking at spoken language will probably all improve in the next decade. These developments will allow for a more contextualised, robust picture of language use that can include gestures and intonation. Improvements such as these will provide welcome resources for teachers and their students. As more teachers and students begin to use corpora and corpus tools for instructional purposes, they will be able to provide feedback to corpus builders and software developers that should result in more user-friendly tools and resources for building and using corpora for language learning. This will allow the use of corpora for language learning to become more user-friendly and more efficient.

## Further readings

Compleat Lexical Tutor (http://www.lextutor.ca)
    In addition to access to various corpora and tools, this site allows you to input texts for vocabulary analysis based on the academic word list (AWL) and the General Service List. There are some great tools on this site that are worth exploring. Check out Text Lex Compare! The site also has many useful articles on corpora and language teaching and tests for assessing vocabulary.

Corpus.BYU.edu (http://corpus.byu.edu)
    This site links to the many free online corpora (e.g. COCA, TIME, COHA) that are searchable through a user-friendly interface, with lots of help features embedded into each function. The interface for the searches is the same regardless of the corpus. Users can search on words or groups of words, or use part-of-speech and wildcard searches. The results display can be in table or bar chart format, thus allowing users to decide which format is most appropriate. This site has one of the best interfaces with the BNC for word and phrase searches.

Corpus of Contemporary American English (COCA) (http://www.americancorpus.org)
    An online, searchable 450-million-word corpus of American English arranged by register, including newspapers, spoken language, fiction and academic texts. The texts in this corpus are from 1990 to the present. This site allows the user to also conduct searches by part of speech (POS). COCA can be a powerful tool for raising learner awareness of the differences between spoken and written language.

MICASE – Michigan Corpus of Academic Spoken English (http://quod.lib.umich.edu/m/micase)
    This free, online, searchable corpus of academic spoken language is a valuable resource. The online concordancer is user-friendly and has a number of search options. In addition to transcripts, the sound files are also available. The corpus is available for purchase for a modest fee (use from the website is free). There are links to lesson materials that have been prepared based on MICASE. There is also a free shareware program for transcription that can be downloaded.

Michigan Corpus Linguistics (http://www.elicorpora.info)
: This site links users to many free online valuable corpora and corpus resources. In addition to MICASE and MICUSP, there is also a corpus of Generation 1.5 writing and a corpus of conference presentations. Teachers can find clear instructions on how to use the site and also many activities for using the suite of corpora from this site along with premade lessons. Language researchers and students will also find useful materials from this well-designed site.

MICUSP – Michigan Corpus of Upper-Level Student Papers (http://micusp.elicorpora.info/)
: This free, online, searchable corpus of student papers from a variety of sixteen disciplines provides teachers and students with many useful resources. The searches can be designed to target specific disciplines, types of writing and/or parts of papers (e.g. conclusions, citations). The bar graph that displays results provides an easy-to-interpret visual.

Reppen, R. (2010) *Using Corpora in the Language Classroom*, Cambridge: Cambridge University Press.
: This user-friendly book includes detailed descriptions ranging from creating corpora to using available corpora and tools. The final chapter is a description of corpus activities from vocabulary to discourse for a variety of proficiency levels and across different language skills.

## References

AntConc. (2007–2013) *Anthony, Laurence Tokyo*, Japan: Waseda University, available: http://www.laurenceanthony.net/software/antconc/

Davies, M. (2008) *The Corpus of Contemporary American English (COCA): 400+ Million Words, 1990-Present*, available: http://www.americancorpus.org

O'Keeffe, A., McCarthy, M. and Carter, R. (2007) *From Corpus to Classroom*. Cambridge: Cambridge University Press.

Reppen, R. (2010) 'Building a corpus: What are the basics?', in A. O'Keeffe and M. McCarthy (eds), *The Routledge Handbook of Corpus Linguistics*, London, UK: Routledge: 31–38.

Simpson, R., Briggs, S.L., Ovens, J. and Swales, J.M. (2002) *The Michigan Corpus of Academic Spoken English*, Ann Arbor, MI: The Regents of the University of Michigan.

Simpson-Vlach, R. and Leicher, S. (2006) *The MICASE Handbook: A Resource for Users of the Michigan Corpus of Academic Spoken English*, Ann Arbor, MI: The University of Michigan Press.

WordSmith Tools (1996–2014) *Scott, Mike*, Oxford: Oxford University Press/Lexical Analysis Software Ltd., available: http://www.lexically.net/wordsmith/index.html

# Part V
# Gaming and language learning

# 30
# Metaphors for digital games and language learning

*Jonathon Reinhardt and Steven Thorne*

This chapter explores digital games and their relevance and usefulness to L2 learning and pedagogy for both researchers and educators. First, the chapter describes game genres and types and presents an overview of possible game experiences. It then discusses the familiar CALL metaphor of tool and tutor (Levy 1997), as well as the more recent metaphor of ecology, in application to digital gaming and illustrates each with reference to research and pedagogical implications. Then, it examines a potentially new CALL metaphor of 'game as method' by first examining several parallels between game design and L2 activity design parameters; these include goal-orientation, interaction or interactivity, feedback, context and motivation. Each of these parallels holds implications for developing and implementing 'gameful' L2 instruction. The chapter concludes with a critical evaluation of the game as method metaphor by examining and interfacing the concepts of digital games with L2 learning theories and pedagogical methodologies, and proposes that 'gamefulness' may be a better conceptualisation for the metaphor.

## Game as tutor, tool, ecology and method

Throughout much of the industrialised world, digital information and communication technologies, social media sites, and virtual and gaming environments are now widely integrated into educational, professional and recreational realms of everyday life activity. Online gaming, the topic of this chapter, was once considered a niche market colonised by unruly teens and young adults. This is no longer the case, the evidence for which can be found in the fact that the video game industry is larger than both the film and music industries in terms of annual revenue. The Entertainment Software Association notes that the average gamer is now 35 years of age, with a near-even split between women and men (45% and 55% respectively) (Entertainment Software Association 2015). The growing interest in digital games has been accompanied by a rapid proliferation in the types and genres of games being developed, and this has led to considerable attention to the use of games and game-informed pedagogy in general education and literacy contexts (Gee 2007b; Steinkuehler 2007; Squire 2008a) as well as among foreign and second language researchers and educators (Mawer and Stanley 2011; Reinders 2012; Thorne 2012; Sykes and Reinhardt 2013).

Teachers of second and foreign (L2) languages have considered the potential of digital games for pedagogy since the first video games were developed for personal computers. One of the earliest and most highly praised computer-assisted language learning (CALL) multimedia (videodisc) programs, *A la rencontre de Philippe* (Furstenberg and Malone 1993), used adventure and role-playing game mechanics to immerse players in a social drama context designed for meaningful language use and learning. In 1991, Hubbard noted the growing popularity of digital games and implored teachers to consider, before implementation, whether a game was truly a game and whether the quality of interaction with and around the game was linguistically rich enough to lead to desirable outcomes. Critics like Phillips (1987) had even discussed games as a paradigm for conceptualising CALL applications, as he saw features in many CALL programs that cultivated intrinsic motivation, incorporated elements of competition and had both constitutive and regulative rules. He ultimately rejected the paradigm, however, because he felt that games by definition had nonconsequential outcomes and were thus not truly authentic. Moreover, he argued that game-regulative language was limited in register and wider applicability. The CALL field instead embraced the metaphors of tutor and tool (e.g. Levy 1997), and more recently ecology (e.g. Lam and Kramsch 2003), to conceptualise the use of technology for language learning.

While their arguments are still cogent, neither Phillips nor Hubbard might have predicted the level of sophistication digital game design would reach in the next two decades, the affordances of the Internet for social interaction or the worldwide growth of digital gaming as diverse arrays of social and cultural practices. The language used in, around and about games has increased in quantity, quality and diversity, as game playing has become a truly global, interactive, multiplayer and often multilingual practice. As increasing numbers of L2 learners play digital games outside the classroom, and games are produced in an increasing variety of game genres and languages, it has become easier to imagine digital games as authentic, consequential and widely applicable L2 learning resources. L2 learning and pedagogy scholars have begun investigating the potential of games for language learning in depth (e.g. Thorne, Black and Sykes 2009; Cornillie, Thorne and Desmet 2012; Sykes and Reinhardt 2013), and an increasing number of L2 educators have started their own explorations in practice.

The mercurial growth in popularity of digital games has inspired a parallel and highly controversial discussion regarding the use of game mechanics to inform L2 materials, assessment, and curriculum development and implementation. Identified as 'gamification' (New Media Consortium Horizon Report 2013) by the corporate training and marketing industries, the new metaphor has captured the imagination of L2 educators, who – noting the fervour with which their students play digital games outside of class – wonder if they can tap into the educational and motivational features of digital games without actually bringing them into the classroom. The argument is that if the game design mechanics that teach and motivate players can be analysed and transferred to traditional 'analogue' L2 learning activities, learners might be as engaged in them as they are in digital gaming. Teaching then becomes 'game-informed', 'game-inspired' or 'gameful' – and game becomes a metaphor for method. Although savvy L2 educators have always had gameful teaching practices as part of their pedagogical repertoire, such as goal-orientation, interactivity, usable feedback, and importance of situated and meaningful contexts for language use, the new term provides new understandings to the potential benefits of games and gameful thinking for language learning. We will critically address the issue of gamification in a later section.

The purpose of this chapter is to explore digital games and their relevance and usefulness to L2 learning and pedagogy. As new technologies have emerged over the past few decades, the field of CALL has responded by developing frameworks that guide pedagogy (see e.g. Higgins

1983; Levy 1997; Warschauer and Healey 1998; Kern and Warschauer 2000; Bax 2003; Lam and Kramsch 2003; Meskill 2005; Blyth 2008). However, digital games have proven particularly challenging in this regard, in part because for many educators, as well as the general public, online gaming has yet to be considered an appropriate context for learning in the traditional sense (Thorne and Fischer 2012). With this acknowledgement, this chapter offers several entry points to the topic of online gaming for both researchers and educators. First, the chapter describes game genres and types and presents an overview of possible game experiences. It then discusses the familiar CALL metaphor of tool and tutor, as well as the more recent metaphor of ecology, in application to digital gaming and illustrates each with reference to research and pedagogical implications. Then, it examines a potentially new CALL metaphor of game as method by first examining several parallels between game design and L2 activity design parameters; these include goal orientation, interaction/interactivity, feedback, context and motivation. Games typically promote goal orientation just as learning tasks do: they afford particular interactions through intentioned designs; they provide players with feedback that is scaffolded, measured, and well-timed; they embed learning activity in meaningful and relevant contexts; and they motivate players by engaging them in a balance of reward and challenge. Each of these parallels holds implications for developing and implementing gameful L2 instruction. The chapter concludes with a critical evaluation of the game as method metaphor by examining and interfacing the concepts of digital games with L2 learning theories and pedagogical methodologies. Because the definition of game includes several entailments that make it problematic, we propose that gamefulness may be a better conceptualisation for the proposed new metaphor. Throughout, there is an attempt to locate the notion of gamefulness in instructed L2 settings and to underscore the importance of pedagogically aligning gameplay with additional materials and activities.

## Game genres and types, past and present

Attempts to taxonomise digital games according to genre are challenged by hybrid games that have come to outnumber 'pure' exemplars, a development compounded by the ongoing diversification of hardware platforms, connectivity features and player configurations. The earliest genres of video games, afforded by console, mainframe and arcade technologies, included shooter and sports games, like *Pong* (Atari 1972), as well as adventure and role-playing games inspired by science fiction and fantasy, like *Colossal Cave Adventure* (Crowther 1976). While consoles, PCs and handheld devices have been game platforms from the beginning, hardware has evolved from mainframes and arcade machines to web browsers and mobile devices that rely on broadband access, which has afforded even more diversification of game type and genre. Consoles were originally restricted to singleplayer and co-present multiplayer (usually dual) play off of a cartridge, but with broadband availability players can play with others at a distance and games can be downloaded from the Internet.

Traditional game genres include action, adventure, role play, strategy and simulation, each of which may offer affordances for language use. Action game behaviours usually entail quick reaction time, physical dexterity and eye-hand coordination, and traditionally involve shooting, driving and parcour-like acrobatics. Adventure game features include following progressive storylines, finding clues and solving puzzles, often enshrouded in narratives of mystery and discovery. Action and adventure features are often combined and realised as the 'action-adventure' genre. Role-playing games (RPGs) are typified by character customizability and completion of goal-oriented quests for rewards and experience points, and are sometimes split into 'Western' and 'Eastern' types. Western RPGs traditionally involve the development of a single avatar, while Eastern RPGs usually involve managing a team of avatars. Traditionally combined with the narrative features of adventure games, RPGs have also more recently been combined with sandbox or nonlinear open designs, where story narrative is less emphasised than character development. Strategy game behaviours include planning, exploration and resource management, and combat that does not require physical dexterity. Strategy designs can use real-time mechanics in which the game or other players react immediately to a player's actions, or turn-based mechanics, meaning the player completes a set of actions and then allows the game or other players to take their turns, which may involve forced wait time. Simulation behaviours are similar to strategy, but do not usually involve combat, and may instead focus on the management of a city, farm, business or daily life tasks or situations. Because simulation games do not have endgame or win states, some do not consider them games (Juul 2005).

Games in any of these genres may incorporate more or fewer affordances for language use, depending on how central language is in learning game rules, whether players are required to follow narratives in order to play and the extent to which player-to-player interaction is required for gameplay. Action game behaviours may not necessarily involve language use, though players may learn the language of strategy and tactics if playing with others. Still, action behaviours allow players to experientially engage in game activity, thus affording agency, and the real-time dynamics inherent to action mechanics may drive language use, and language learning, through the repeated association of specific language forms with specific kinds of events and actions. Adventure behaviours, because they are built around narrative mechanics, most obviously afford language use, particularly comprehension, and clues and puzzles can be linguistic in nature, although they are not necessarily so. Role-playing games, because they involve decision-making and developing a character, may afford identity play and completing quests usually demands language comprehension in the form of reading and understanding quest texts. Strategy and simulation games may involve language in comprehending game rules, which tend to be relatively complex and scaffolded for players, and turn-based or timed turn strategy behaviours may afford learners extra time for comprehension.

As social networking technologies have become increasingly accessible, casual social games have emerged that allow players to play with their networked friends. While traditional games that appeal to so-called hard-core players remain tied to consoles or PCs, the massively multiplayer online role-playing game (MMORPG) genre emerged when remote servers could host persistent game worlds accessible by players who did not know each other, which gave rise to new player affinity groups and in-game social formations (such as guilds and persistent online teams). In this way, improved broadband access and sophistication of technology continually lead to new affordances for hardware, software and player configurations, and ultimately new reconfigurations and recombinations of game genres and features. For example, the Xbox One (Microsoft 2013) and PlayStation 4 (Sony 2013) consoles require persistent online connectivity and allow cloud-based game storage. In addition, as tablet computers allow for more screen space, mobile games are increasingly including massively multiplayer features.

Hybridity also typifies the thematic content of games. As global gamer culture has become polylingual and transcultural, the gaming industry has internationalised. Game themes traditionally match genres, so that action games are often military or sports themed, while adventure games may draw on science fiction/fantasy themes like those found in Tolkien's *Lord of the Rings*, or the 16th-century Chinese epic *Journey to the West*. While it can be argued that games reflect the cultures of their developers and players to an extent (Cornelliussen and Rettberg 2008), developers play each others' games and draw on themes and narratives from mythologies and literatures all over the world. Developers with global marketing ambitions will often create games set in generic-looking settings with no location identifiers, and then localise them to appeal to particular markets – for example, games localised for Germany are sometimes rid of gore and violence to appeal to consumers. A recent analysis of the Wikipedia article on video game developers (2011) shows that 357 digital game development companies were in 33 different countries, with 60% in English-speaking countries. Most major games are published in the dominant languages of the developed world – Mandarin, Cantonese, English, Spanish, Portuguese, Japanese, French, German, Italian, Russian and Korean – and many games are formally and informally translated into other languages. Most games sold in North America are easily playable in French or Spanish, because of the Canadian and Latin American markets, and in Europe and Asia many games are playable in the languages of the region because of market distribution.

## Familiar metaphors for game-mediated L2 pedagogy

Since its inception in the late 1970s, the field of CALL has traditionally used functional metaphors as a means of conceptualising the pedagogical orientation of computer technologies. Levy (1997) explained that the metaphors of computer-as-tutor and computer-as-tool emerged out of conceptualisations of tutorial and nontutorial distinctions (Higgins 1983; Taylor 1990). Originally, tutorial CALL was meant to be used outside of the classroom, replacing or augmenting functions associated with a teacher. The metaphor had parallels in behaviourist theories of learning (Warschauer and Healey 1998; Kern and Warschauer 2000), which entailed mind-as-container and communication-as-conduit frames (Lakoff and Johnson 1980; Sfard 1998). Accordingly, tutorial CALL focused on the ability of the computer to provide repetitive input and targeted feedback, especially for grammar and vocabulary learning. Nontutorial CALL was simply an umbrella term for anything outside of grammatically oriented tutorial programs, such as uses of technology to communicate with others or a tool for expression or the creation and manipulation of information.

Stretching the tutor metaphor, Higgins (1983) made the interesting distinction between computer as magister (i.e. the drillmaster) and as pedagogue (i.e. the facilitator). His distinction reflected the newly emerging learning metaphors of cognitivism and constructivism, which emphasised the active role of the learner and aligned with communicative language teaching. The computer-as-tool metaphor then emerged from 'nontutorial CALL', first with constructivism, and then as reflective of the sociocultural theory–informed mediating role of technology (Salaberry 1999; Thorne and Payne 2005; Kern 2006; Thorne 2008a), correlating respectively with the cognitive and sociocognitive conceptualisations of L2 learning (Kern and Warschauer 2000; Blyth 2008). Lam and Kramsch (2003) note that conceptualisations for learning over the decades often reflected prevailing understandings of technology, so that focus on memory capacity in the '50s and '60s equated to behaviourism, processing power in the '70s and '80s to cognitive-constructivism, and communication and networking power in the '90s and '00s to social and ecological views of learning. As Lam and Kramsch (2003) describe, new metaphors of technology as ecology or social simulacrum have arisen that parallel the rise in social networking applications and align with new conceptualisations of literacies (see also Thorne 2013). This more recent ecological view accommodates the breakdown of traditional boundaries between places and times for learning, the role of the learner/user as both consumer and producer of knowledge and the distinctions between learning as work and learning as play.

### Games as L2 learning tutors

Digital games and game-mediated L2 learning environments can be understood with the traditional metaphors of tutor and tool, as well as with the new metaphor of ecology. As tutors, games can be seen as sources for linguistic input that are tirelessly capable of repetition when needed, meaningfully contextualised as part of event-driven scenarios, simulations and goal-directed sequences, and controlled by the player. Higgins's (1983) pedagogue metaphor is particularly appropriate, since a well-designed game provides its player with a sense of agency, even though game rules limit a player's activities. In other words, a game creator acts as 'guide on the side', as it were, by designing the game according to particular parameters, but the player makes choices and does the actual playing. Considering a digital game for tutorial purposes requires evaluation of the language use embedded in and required of the game.

The thematic content of some commercially available games corresponds with familiar L2 learning units, especially certain simulation, strategy, adventure and role-playing games, that create an engineered space which potentially 'integrates the many benefits of online gaming to produce . . . educationally related outcomes in simulated . . . interactional contexts' (Sykes 2008: 10–11). For example, *The Sims* series offers players hundreds of contextualised vocabulary items related to household items and daily life, while city, farming and restaurant management social network games provide playable and experiential contexts for their respective themes. Purushotma (2005) notes that a life simulation game like *The Sims* provides substantial exposure to thematic and topical vocabulary that correlates with early levels of L2 study. A related study by Miller and Hegelheimer (2006) illustrated that supplemental learning materials effectively reinforced game-enhanced learning tasks with *The Sims* (see also Ranalli 2008). DeHaan (2005) found that an L2 Japanese learner was able to learn sports vocabulary in a baseball action game through contextual clues and repetition, although deHaan also noted that the learner had trouble focusing on both rules and language because of time pressures while playing (see also deHaan, Reed and Kuwada 2010). Although they are few in number, digital games created for L2 learning are purposefully designed to correspond with familiar curriculum units that teach vocabulary, grammar and culture. For example, the game *Zon* (Zhao and Lai 2009) was developed as a quest-based multiplayer game for learning L2 Chinese; the game begins with a simulation of the Beijing airport, mimicking the experience of a student going abroad and the routine encounters one would expect to confront upon first entering a Chinese-speaking context.

Teachers might find some games too narrow in language register for broad applicability; for example, many games focus on the registers of strategy, tactic, planning and action. Still, even games with limited registers contextualise vocabulary comprehension for the very real purpose of gameplay, and so offer opportunities for contextualised language use. In this way, digital games might be understood as interactive texts, especially useful for reading development, and similar to uses of literature and film, such games are more effective as learning environments when supplemented with focused vocabulary, discussion and writing activities in classroom contexts.

## *Games as L2 learning tools and environments*

Digital games can also be understood as tools for L2 learning that lead to the development of communicative competence and its interactional and discourse correlates. As a tool, the computer mediates the construction or development of understanding through interaction with information and other users. From this perspective, a game as an L2 learning tool would provide the player with a means to interact with L2 discourses, users and communities. In a study of the 3D multiuser learning environment *Quest Atlantis*, Zheng, Young, Wagner and Brewer (2009) examined expert-learner interaction and the English language development of two adolescent Mandarin Chinese speakers. Data from quest logs, interviews and participant observation indicated that intercultural collaboration for quest completion resulted in the learning of various syntactic, semantic, pragmatic and discourse practices. Zheng et al. (2009) also described instances in which the learners co-constructed meaning at the discourse level and modified one another's cultural perspectives through tasks centred on a shared goal. In addition, Zheng et al. (2009) noted that since many of the tasks focused on the co-construction of cultural knowledge, the expert speaker and less experienced English user each took on the roles of learner and instructor. As a result, both interlocutors gained an increased appreciation for cultural differences. Zheng et al. (2009) suggested that similar developmental trajectories could occur through goal-directed activity in commercial gaming environments not specifically built for educational purposes (e.g. Thorne 2008b).

Researchers have examined L2 learning through games in contexts where players are using the L2 to interact with other players about the game. Much of this work has been descriptive and focused on L2 use as it relates to learning. For example, Piiranen-Marsh and Tainio (2009) examined how two Finnish players of *Final Fantasy X* learned English by anticipating, repeating and sometimes mocking in-game dialogue while playing together, in effect co-constructing collaborative learning episodes.

Using a game as a tool for L2 learning requires consideration of the quality and quantity of interaction afforded by the game, for example, whether it has a chat function, whether game activities require player-player interaction and whether that interaction is linguistic in nature. Multiplayer games most obviously afford interaction, but not all multiplayer games afford or require interaction to the same degree. For example, many social network-based games push players to 'neighbour' each other, but 'visiting' one another may not involve language use at all. Of all game types, MMORPGs seem to offer the most potential (Lai, Ni and Zhao 2012), as players in most MMORPG designs have to interact often and negotiate roles in order to play successfully. While many multiplayer games include highly specialised vocabulary that may be of limited use outside of gaming contexts, it is important to keep in mind that communicative engagement in a tool or use paradigm is primarily functional in nature, and goal-directed interactional and interpersonal meaning is paramount. From this perspective, L2 learning tasks in game settings have the potential to encourage interaction between players through, and about, the game content. If the game design does not require interaction, supplemental classroom or instructional tasks might be designed to promote or demand it (e.g. the work of Jeff Kuhn (2014) using the game *Minecraft* for university composition courses).

## *Games as L2 learning ecologies*

Technology-as-ecology might be considered a metaphor derivative of, and therefore subsumed under, technology-as-tool, since ecological systems are functionally defined. Indeed, metaphors should not be understood as exclusive of one another, but coexisting (Lam and Kramsch 2003); one might well argue that players learning from in-game content are using the game as a tool as well as a tutor. When addressing pedagogical applications, however, it is useful to consider how gameplay is part of a larger ecology of game-related texts and practices, that is, what have been termed paratexts (Apperley and Beavis 2011) or attendant discourses (Thorne, Black and Sykes 2009; Reinhardt and Sykes 2012). Understanding games as ecologies for L2 learning requires recognition of how technology has fundamentally shifted the traditional temporal, spatial and functional parameters of education. Gamers play games, and thus potentially learn, at any time, at any place, from anyone, in both productive and consumer roles, for entertainment as well as for more 'serious' purposes. From this perspective, game playing is an interconnected ecology of social-cultural texts and practices that have the potential to extend as well as transform traditional or 'transmission' notions of learning from teachers and textbooks.

Research on games as L2 learning ecologies has included studies of the linguistic features of paratexts (e.g. Thorne, Fischer and Lu 2012), communities of L2 gamers (e.g. Chik 2012), and mobile, place-based game design and implementation (e.g. Holden and Sykes 2011; Thorne 2013). Thorne et al. (2012) found that the texts and practices surrounding *World of Warcraft* (*WoW*), that is the in-game quests, online discussion boards, and online strategy guides, illustrated a great variety of linguistic registers, genres and functions (see also Steinkuehler and Duncan 2008). Multiplayer games may provide interactional opportunities for language use, competition and collaboration. Rama et al. (2012) showed that MMORPG gameplay can emphasise communicative competence and promote goal-oriented and collaborative interaction among novices and experts. In their study, an expert *World of Warcraft* player with beginning Spanish language skills was able to leverage his gaming expertise and learn Spanish more effectively than a more advanced Spanish learner with little gaming experience. Peterson (2012) examined the chat transcripts of a dozen EFL players of the MMORPG *Wonderland* and found evidence for the development of sociopragmatic competence and the establishment of joint intersubjectivity, as well as increased confidence and willingness to communicate. Zheng, Newgarden and Young (2012) showed that *WoW* players engage in a variety of communicative activities and that gameplay involves considerable affordance for values realising through co-action.

Holden and Sykes (2011) found that Spanish learners' awareness of the language ecologies in local neighbourhoods was transformed by playing a mobile game that had the learners solve a local mystery in Spanish. Because the game situated language use outside traditional educational boundaries, learners developed new perspectives on the purpose of learning Spanish, using mobile technology and playing digital games. Related research has also shown that digital game spaces afford informal, autonomous learning. For example, Chik (2012) showed that gamers in Hong Kong engage in English and Japanese language learning practices informally and autonomously, on their own and with other gamers, in order to play the latest games before they are translated into Cantonese. Learning practices involve reading and listening to in-game dialogues and instructions, interacting with other players, and reading and writing in online discussion forums. Thorne (2008b) and Thorne and Fischer (2012) provided evidence of informal and polylingual language use in MMO contexts by surveying players and examining discussion board exchanges about the use of online games for language learning. While players report language learning opportunities through gameplay, they are also conscious that the casual and fluent language use in games does not equate to formal prestige varieties and academic genres. In a study of younger school-age children playing recreational games at home, Sylvén and Sundqvist (2012) showed that the language proficiency of English learners was positively correlated to their gaming experiences, presumably as those learners had exposure to English in games outside of school.

As the aforementioned research recognises, games and gaming may not easily fit into traditional L2 educational structures, and treating games as mainly tutor or tool may not realise their full potential. This said, the ecological metaphor is congruent with the concept of digital multiliteracies (New London Group 1996; Knobel and Lankshear 2007; Thorne 2013), which claims that literacy development is multifarious, dynamic and complex. From a multiliteracies view, learning happens both in school and out of school, while working and playing, from teachers and from interaction with peers alike. Game playing can thus afford the development of multiliteracies – most obviously, what has been called 'game literacy' (Gee 2007b; Squire 2008b), or the critical awareness that game systems, dynamics and discourses are representative of reality (Bogost 2007), and that even nonplayful human activity like learning and working can be game-like, heterarchical and counter-hegemonic (Thomas and Brown 2009).

Game genres that would typically lend themselves to ecologically oriented 'learning in the wild' activities (Thorne 2010) would be relatively complex games with significantly active player communities such as massively multiplayer online games. The goal of game-as-ecology activities would be to develop game-mediated literacies through critical analysis and participation in mediated discourses about and around games as cultural texts and social practices (e.g. Squire 2008b; Alexander 2009; Lacasa, Martinez and Mendez 2010). To this end, and in addition to gameplay, players/students might design and describe avatars and game worlds, write fan fiction based on game narratives or storylines, analyse game dynamics and mechanics, make guides to gameplay, participate in game strategy forums, write game critiques and even design games themselves. From this perspective, gaming and games are ways to be in and to understand the world, and language is not learned only from or through games, but as constitutive of the ecology of the broader discourses surrounding games.

## A new metaphor for a familiar practice: Game as method

As discussed earlier, digital games can be conceptualised metaphorically as tutors, tools and ecologies for computer-assisted L2 pedagogy, both in the adaptation of commercial games to enhance L2 learning and in the design and implementation of game-based L2 learning environments (Reinhardt and Sykes 2012, 2014; Sykes and Reinhardt 2013). In addition, the concept of a game itself can be taken as a metaphor for learning activity. Learners can play digital games and participate in game-related social practices, and reciprocally, game elements can be incorporated into a learning activity, assessment procedure or curriculum, making the very lesson itself game-like. In this sense, the game informs, and even becomes, the pedagogical method, and the activity is 'gamified'.

The concept of gamification, or 'the integration of game elements, mechanics, and frameworks into non-game scenarios' (New Media Consortium 2013: 20), has taken the corporate training and marketing industries by storm, as proponents in those industries might put it. Perhaps because of these corporate origins, well-known games studies scholars have denounced gamification (Schell 2010; Bogost 2011), and sceptics have become understandably wary of applying it to broader educational contexts. However, many proponents (see e.g. Kapp 2012) argue that gamification should not be considered a slick and easy way to make learning fun. It is neither new, as the principles are familiar to experienced educators, nor simple, as it is more than just applying badges, points, levels and rewards, and gamification should certainly not be considered a facile panacea as technological innovations are often portrayed in education. Kapp defines gamification as 'a careful and considered application of game thinking to solving problems and encouraging learning using all the elements of games that are appropriate' (ibid.: 15–16). McGonigal (2011), for example, proposes the term 'gameful' in contrast to 'playful', as an adjective to describe the quality of having game-like elements, but not necessarily being a true game in the sense of focusing exclusively on ludic activity.

Much of the debate surrounding gamification revolves around terminology and the problematic definition of game, which is sometimes as much in the disposition of the players as in the rules that define it. For current purposes, the terms game-informed and gameful are preferred as adjectives that modify, but do not unrecognisably alter, the core activity of computer-assisted language learning and teaching. To understand the potential value of game-informed L2 pedagogy, it is useful to compare how games are designed with how languages are often taught. These parallels, presented in brief here but discussed at length in Sykes and Reinhardt (2013), are centred on goal orientation, interactivity, feedback provision, context of playing and learning, and motivation.

## Games promote goal-oriented behaviour

One of the defining characteristics of a game is that it demands goal-oriented behaviour from its players. If a player does not know the object of a game, one could argue he or she does not recognise it as a game, but could consider it open-ended play. Well-designed games afford goal orientation by providing challenges that are scaffolded and achievable, thus promoting measured risk planning and taking. Feedback (see later) is provided just when needed, at appropriate levels, and with meaningful, albeit often low-stakes, consequences. The goal-orientation systems constitutive of games thus relate a sense of agency and control to the player, even though mechanics put in place by the game's designer set the parameters of possible action.

Goals in games tend to focus on winning or reaching the next level and accumulating experience or other rewards that function as resources for continued play. Goals tend to vary by game genres, so that in action games, quick reaction time and physical finesse often define the goals, while in strategy and simulation games planning and tactics are required, although goals may be more open-ended. In adventure games, goals are progressive and more linear in nature, and in role-playing games, players usually are given quests, or sets of linked activities to complete that lead to particular rewards. Players may have multiple, simultaneous goals while playing, which well-designed games help manage.

In L2 teaching, goals are understood as a defining quality of a curriculum, unit or learning task. In task-based teaching and learning activity design, the goal is expressed as learning objectives, which implicate specific activities and outcomes that meet them. Tasks should be contextualised, relevant and learning-centred, and are ideally student-driven and thus motivating and effective (Van den Branden, Bygate and Norris 2009). In practice, however, learning goals are often driven by curriculum dictates and high-stakes testing, with secondary consideration given to the importance of learner orientation to them. Learners are sometimes given little agency, or the choices they are given are limited or inconsequential. The result is that learners can lose motivation and develop little autonomy or capacity to self-direct.

If L2 pedagogy were informed by game design principles, the goals of L2 pedagogical tasks would be primarily driven by learners, even while they are guided by instructors and curricular demands. In game design, player agency is promoted by scaffolding the goal-orientation process through provision of feedback regarding which goals are set, which can be set, and the progress a player is making towards reaching them. In game-informed L2 pedagogy, a learner would have constant and customizable access to his or her own goal progress. Learners would be aware of the purpose of a particular learning task and the expected outcomes, which they would have some agency in choosing. To a certain degree, learners would be able to customise task sequences and stakes, and consequences would be discernible and integrated (Salen and Zimmerman 2004), thus contributing to task authenticity and motivation.

## Games provide interactivity on multiple levels

Game design theorists Salen and Zimmerman (2004) argue that a good digital game is engaging and immersive because it is interactive in several different ways. It is cognitively interactive if it engages players cinematically through artful graphics, sounds, music and narratives. A game provides strong functional interactivity if it provides a well-designed interface that is intuitive and comprehensive while at the same time customizable and eventually invisible to the expert player. Unlike cinema and literature, a game is explicitly interactive, since it allows players to interact with elements in the game itself, and game outcomes are based on player choices. Finally, a well-designed game is highly interactive on a cultural level, meaning it has relation to cultural themes, texts and social practices outside the game itself.

Interaction is also posited to be beneficial, if not requisite, for language learning. Cognitively, processes of comprehension and development are thought to require interaction on intra-psychological and interpsychological (Lantolf and Thorne 2006; Gass and Mackey 2012), or social, levels. Social interaction is understood as foundational to language pedagogy and is at the heart of communicative language teaching (Savignon 1972). Effective language pedagogy also incorporates cultural interaction, as the development of intercultural competence (Byram 1998) becomes a key objective of modern language curricula.

The relationship between interaction and interactivity is a subtle point but one that is important in application to game-informed insights to L2 pedagogy. In games, interaction is an affordance, or a potential for action. In other words, designed interactivity affords interaction and interaction and play are inseparable. In L2 pedagogy, interaction is sometimes seen as a precondition for learning rather than inseparable from the learning that emerges from interactive conditions. To afford gameful L2 interaction and thus learning, interactivity would be designed into pedagogy on cognitive, functional, explicit and cultural levels. Cognitively interactive learning environments would be immersive and rich in sensory input. Learning activities would be functionally interactive and intuitively carried out without excessive explanation of directions or procedures. Designed interactivity would regularly offer choices to learners and have outcomes that are consequential and integrated with the next activities. Finally, culturally interactive learning environments would bridge familiar and local cultures with new and global conceptualisations, that is, they are transcultural in nature. Designed interactivity thus acts as an affordance for interaction and learning.

### *Games give feedback that is timely, individualised and instructional*

Well-designed games are especially good at giving feedback at just the right time, in just the right amount, at just the right level and in a way that encourages continued play. Feedback in game design can be a sound, a point, a message, a success or a failure state that results from a player action. When feedback is timely, it is obvious, and the player knows what action likely caused it. When feedback is individualised, it takes into consideration what feedback has already been given, and adjusts the quality and quantity according to the player's immediate need. In this way, feedback provided at the right time, of the right nature and in the right amount is likely within the player's zone of proximal development (Vygotsky 1978), and functions to scaffold the player's development. In other words, it is instructional rather than punitive, and is formative rather than summative.

Feedback in L2 instruction is frequently not immediate, and so learners are not always aware whether their performance is meeting goals. Although it is not always possible to provide timely feedback in L2 performance, gameful feedback provision would be as targeted as possible, so that learners would know when they were in fact being provided feedback, and for what aspects of their performance (e.g. fluency or accuracy). Game-informed feedback would also be gradated, so that overt and communicative mistakes were given more attention than less serious errors (Brown 2007). Some tests might be more customizable, so that learners were given some choice as to how much items were worth. Following game mechanics that reward persistence and repeated attempts at difficult tasks, a gameful approach to design of language learning environments would enable learners the opportunity to revisit their mistakes and gain rewards for fixing them.

### *Games provide meaningful contexts for play and learning*

A game has been defined as a set of rules contextualised by narratives that structure a coherent fictional world (Juul 2005). Through representation, narratives provide the means to learn the rules and play the game, but because games from similar genres have similar rules, players can transfer rule knowledge between games of similar genres even if their themes differ. Kapp (2012: 27) observes that game representations are models of real systems and concepts, abstracted to clarify cause-and-effect relationships. Game context can be understood as the context represented by the game narratives around the rules (i.e. the context-in-the-game of abstractions), as well as the cultural and situational context of where, when, and by whom the game is played (i.e. the context-of-the-game). A game developer creates a 'designed narrative' in a game, but a player creates a 'personal narrative' as he or she plays it, experiencing the design in a unique, agentful way (Neitzel 2005).

As a form of storytelling, game narratives play a key role in cultural transmission and participation, and these narrative schemata and framing help to situate cognition and learning. In most current approaches of L2 pedagogy, context is recognised as central to meaning and teachers strive to create meaningful contexts for L2 learning. Older L2 pedagogical approaches, for instance grammar-translation and audio-lingualism, however, sometimes focus on form to the exclusion of meaning, and grammatical competence is seen to contrast with communicative competence (Hymes 1972). The most widely accepted theories of second language acquisition posit that language is both form and meaning, and language learning happens by noticing form in conjunction with referential and functional-pragmatic value.

Language pedagogy informed by game design principles of situated goal-directed activity would recognise that just as a game rule has no function without designed narratives, language form has no meaning without narrative context. Just as a game is not a game until it is played, language is a mere abstraction until it is put to meaningful use. As Volosinov has remarked, it is 'solely through the utterance [communicative activity] that language makes contact with communication, is imbued with its vital power, and becomes a reality' (1973: 123; Thorne and Lantolf 2007).

## Games motivate through engagement

The final parallel to draw for game-informed L2 pedagogy is between conceptualisations of motivation in game design and learning theory. In game design theory, motivation is understood as emerging from the balance between challenge and reward or accomplishment. Game designers try to keep players engaged by providing challenges and rewards through goal and feedback systems targeted at, or just beyond, a player's level. Czikszentmihalyi (2008) identified this state as 'flow', or the sense of complete engagement and control in uncertain situations. If an activity is too challenging, the player is frustrated, but if it's too easy, the player is bored.

Motivation in learning is often conceptualised as prerequisite and determinative of learning success. Intrinsic motivation is often considered to be more desirable than extrinsic motivation, as the latter depends on external factors. In language learning, integrative orientation is seen as more indicative of long-term success, while instrumental orientation is more immediate and practical. Dörnyei (2001) offers a more nuanced account of motivation, and suggests that activity is initially motivated by processes of choice and selection, then followed through by executive functioning and constantly reassessed throughout.

Game-informed insights from motivation research to L2 learning acknowledge that flow states potentially optimise L2 learning (Egbert 2003), and that motivation is a process, or outcome, as much as it is a preexisting variable. Individualisation of learning activity would allow learners to find their own balance of challenge and reward. Recognising that extrinsic and intrinsic factors are fluid and not necessarily preconditional, gameful activities would have learners reflect on and revisit their motivations over time. Process models of motivation implicate providing choice and agency to students, and explicitly incorporating executive processes like planning, decision-making and critical evaluation into learning activities.

## A gameful future

In game-informed L2 pedagogy, instructors, activity designers and learners alike are more attuned to gameful thinking, or the awareness of game-like elements such as competition, exploration, narrative, mimesis, collaboration and representation that are part of everyday human life and interaction (Kapp 2012: 11). Game literacies add to gameful thinking the important element of application or competence, the ability to effectively understand and contribute to complex social-semiotic practices.

In this chapter, L2 pedagogical uses of digital games have been conceptualised with the traditional CALL metaphors of tutor and tool, as well as with the more recent metaphor of ecology. Games have traditionally been defined as representative, rule-based systems that are played for nonserious purposes. While the nonserious quality of games allows them to function as realms of mimesis and simulation, and thus are potentially effective for learning, these functions are in good part dependent on player disposition, and if the player knows the end goal is punitive (a grade or mark), the game may cease to be a game in her mind. This is the 'artificial unintelligence' that Phillips ascribed to games for CALL in 1987. A more nuanced interpretation of gamification for digitally mediated L2 pedagogy might be gamefulness as method, where the ontological entailments of game are not pivotal. As McGonigal notes (2011), the term gameful invokes creativity and collaboration while still retaining a serious quality, unlike 'playful'. Creativity, curiosity and collaboration are hallmark goals of L2 pedagogy, whether digitally mediated or not, and successful L2 instructors have long been practicing various versions of gamefulness as method. While gameful teaching is not entirely new, traditional and new metaphors may help us see the familiar in a new light, and thereby to reconceptualise pedagogical paradigms to more fully utilise and benefit from emerging technologies and social practices.

## Further reading

Gee, J. (2007a) *Good Video Games and Good Learning*, New York, NY: Peter Lang.
    This seminal volume describes the uses and benefits of online gaming environments from learning sciences and literacy development perspectives.
Reinders, H. (ed) (2012) *Digital Games in Language Teaching and Learning*, New York, NY: Palgrave Macmillan.
    This edited volume includes chapters exploring language learning through game play.
Reinhardt, J. and Sykes, J.M. (2014) 'Digital game activity in L2 teaching and learning', *Language Learning and Technology*, 18(2): 9–19.
    This special issue includes articles examining digital gaming and issues of autonomy, willingness to communicate, writing and micro-blogging.
Sykes, J. and Reinhardt, J. (2013) *Language at Play: Digital Games in Second and Foreign Language Teaching and Learning*, New York, NY: Pearson.
    This volume presents a comprehensive approach to understanding online gaming from a second language acquisition perspective and includes extensive discussion supporting the use of games in instructed L2 contexts.
Thorne, S.L., Cornillie, F. and Piet, D. (eds) (2012) 'Digital games for language learning: Challenges and opportunities', *ReCALL Journal*, 24(3): 243–256.
    This special issue of *ReCALL Journal* includes articles exploring various uses of commercial as well as L2 learning–designed game environments for language education.

## References

Alexander, J. (2009) 'Gaming, student literacies, and the composition classroom: Some possibilities for transformation', *College Composition and Communication*, 61(1): 35–63.
Apperley, T. and Beavis, C. (2011) 'Literacy into action: Digital games as action and text in the English and literacy classroom', *Pedagogies*, 5(2): 130–143.
Bax, S. (2003) 'CALL – Past, present and future', *System*, 31: 13–28.
Blyth, C. (2008) 'Research perspectives on online discourse and foreign language learning', in S. Magnan (ed), *Mediating Discourse Online*, Amsterdam: Johns Benjamins: 47–70.
Bogost, I. (2007) *Persuasive Games: The Expressive Power of Videogames*, Cambridge: MIT Press.
Bogost, I. (2011) 'Gamification is bullshit', *Atlantic Monthly*, 8 August 2011, published online at: http://www.theatlantic.com/technology/archive/2011/08/gamification-is-bullshit/243338/
Brown, D. (2007) *Principles of Language Learning and Teaching*, 5th edn, New York, NY: Pearson Longman.
Byram, M. (1998) *Teaching and Assessing Intercultural Communicative Competence*, New York, NY: Multilingual Matters.
Chik, A. (2012) 'Digital gameplay for autonomous language learning', in H. Reinders (ed), *Digital Games in Language Learning*, New York, NY: Palgrave Macmillan: 95–114.
Corneliussen, H.G. and Rettberg, J.W. (2011) *Digital Culture, Play, and Identity A World of Warcraft® Reader*, Cambridge, MA: MIT Press.
Cornillie, F., Thorne, S. and Desmet, P. (2012) 'Digital games for language learning: Challenges and opportunities', *ReCALL*, 24(3): 243–256.
Czikszentmihalyi, M. (2008) *Flow: The Psychology of Optimal Experience*, New York, NY: Harper.
deHaan, J. (2005) 'Acquisition of Japanese as a foreign language through a baseball video game', *Foreign Language Annals*, 38(2): 282–286.
deHaan, J., Reed, W.M. and Kuwada, K. (2010), 'The effect of interactivity with a music video game on second language vocabulary recall', *Language Learning and Technology*, 14(2): 74–94.
Dörnyei, Z. (2001) *Teaching and Researching Motivation*, London, UK: Longman.
Egbert, J. (2003) 'A study of flow theory in the foreign language classroom', *Modern Language Journal*, 87(4): 499–518.
Entertainment Software Association (2015) *Essential Facts About the Computer and Video Game Industry*, available: http://www.theesa.com/wp-content/uploads/2015/04/ESA-Essential-Facts-2015.pdf (accessed 17 Jun 2015).
Furstenberg, G. and Malone, S. (1993) *A la rencontre de Philippe*, New Haven, CT: Yale University Press.
Gass, S. and Mackey, A. (2012) *The Handbook of Second Language Acquisition*, New York, NY: Routledge.
Gee, J. (2007a) *Good Video Games and Good Learning*. New York, NY: Peter Lang.
Gee, J. (2007b) *What Video Games Have to Teach Us about Learning and Literacy*, 2nd edn, New York, NY: Palgrave Macmillan.
Higgins, J. (1983) 'Computer assisted language learning', *Language Teaching*, 16: 102–114.
Holden, C. and Sykes, J. (2011) 'Leveraging mobile games for place-based language learning', *International Journal of Game-based Learning*, 1(2): 1–18.
Hubbard, P. (1991) 'Evaluating computer games for language learning', *Simulation and Gaming*, 22: 220–223.
Hymes, D. (1972) 'On communicative competence', in J. Pride and J. Holmes (eds), *Sociolinguistics*, Harmondsworth, Middlesex: Penguin Education: 269–293.
Juul, J. (2005) *Half-Real: Video Games Between Real Rules and Fictional Worlds*, Cambridge, MA: MIT Press.
Kapp, K. (2012) *The Gamification of Learning and Instruction: Game-Based Methods and Strategies for Training and Education*, San Francisco, CA: Pfeiffer.
Kern, R. (2006) 'Perspectives on technology in learning and teaching languages', *TESOL Quarterly*, 40(1): 183–210.
Kern, R. and Warschauer, M. (2000) 'Theory and practice of network-based language teaching', in M. Warschauer and R. Kern (eds), *Network-Based Language Teaching: Concepts and Practice*, New York, NY: Cambridge University Press: 1–19.
Knobel, M. and Lankshear, C. (eds) (2007) *A New Literacies Sampler*, New York, NY: Peter Lang.
Kuhn, J. (2014) 'Journaling the Zombie Apocalypse: Minecraft in college composition', available: https://www.youtube.com/watch?v=ZpGRopPNWI4
Lacasa, P., Martínez, R. and Méndez, L. (2008) 'Developing new literacies using commercial videogames as educational tools', *Linguistics and Education*, 19: 85–106.

Lai, C., Ni, R. and Zhao, Y. (2012) 'Digital games and language learning', in M. Thomas, H. Reinders, and M. Warschauer (eds), *Contemporary Computer-Assisted Language Learning*, London, UK: Bloomsbury: 183–200.

Lakoff, G. and Johnson, M. (1980) *Metaphors We Live By*, Chicago, IL: University of Chicago Press.

Lam, W.S.E. and Kramsch, C. (2003) 'The ecology of an SLA community in computer-mediated environments', in J. Leather and J. van Dam (eds), *Ecology of Language Acquisition*, Dordrecht: Kluwer Publishers: 141–158.

Lantolf, J.P. and Thorne, S.L. (2006) *Sociocultural Theory and the Genesis of Second Language Development*, Oxford: Oxford University Press.

Levy, M. (1997) *Computer-Assisted Language Learning: Context and Conceptualization*, Oxford: Clarendon Press.

Mawer, K. and Stanley, G. (2011) *Digital Play: Computer Games and Language Aims*, Peaslake: Delta Publishing.

McGonigal, J. (2011) *Reality Is Broken: Why Games Make Us Better and How They Can Change the World*, New York, NY: Penguin.

Meskill, C. (2005) 'Metaphors that shape and guide CALL research', in J. Egbert and G.M. Petrie (eds), *CALL Research Perspectives*, Mahwah, NJ: Lawrence Erlbaum: 25–40.

Miller, M. and Hegelheimer, V. (2006) 'The SIMS meet ESL: Incorporating authentic computer simulation games into the language classroom', *Interactive Technology and Smart Education*, 4: 311–328.

Neitzel, B. (2005) 'Narrativity in computer games', in J. Raessens and J. Goldstein (eds), *Handbook of Computer Game Studies*, Cambridge, MA: MIT Press: 227–249.

New London Group (1996) 'A pedagogy of multiliteracies: designing social futures', *Harvard Educational Review*, 66: 60–92.

New Media Consortium (2013) 'NMC Horizon Report 2013: Higher education edition', available: http://www.nmc.org/pdf/2013-horizon-report-HE.pdf

Peterson, M. (2012) 'Learner interaction in a massively multiplayer online role playing game (MMORPG): A sociocultural discourse analysis', *ReCALL*, 24(3): 361–380.

Phillips, M. (1987) 'Potential paradigms and possible problems for CALL', *System*, 15: 275–287.

Piiranen-Marsh, A. and Tainio, L. (2009) 'Other-repetition as a resource for participation in the activity of playing a video game', *Modern Language Journal*, 93(2): 153–169.

Purushotma, R. (2005) 'You're not studying, you're just ...', *Language Learning and Technology*, 9(1): 80–96.

Rama, P., Black, R., van Es, E. and Warschauer, M. (2012) 'Affordances for second language learning in World of Warcraft', *ReCALL*, 24(3): 322–338.

Ranalli, J. (2008) 'Learning English with The Sims: Exploiting authentic computer simulation games for L2 learning', *Computer Assisted Language Learning*, 21(5): 441–455.

Reinders, H. (ed) (2012) *Digital Games in Language Teaching and Learning*, New York, NY: Palgrave Macmillan.

Reinhardt, J. and Sykes, J. (2012) 'Conceptualizing digital game-mediated L2 learning and pedagogy: game-enhanced and game-based research and practice', in H. Reinders (ed), *Digital Games in Language Learning and Teaching*, New York, NY: Palgrave Macmillan: 32–49.

Reinhardt, J. and Sykes, J.M. (2014) 'Digital game activity in L2 teaching and learning', *Language Learning and Technology*, 18(2): 9–19.

Salaberry, R. (1999) 'A commentary on Carol Chapelle's "CALL in the year 2000: Still in search of a paradigm"', *Language Learning and Technology*, 3(1): 104–107.

Salen, K. and Zimmerman, E. (2004) *Rules of Play: Game Design Fundamentals*, Cambridge, MA: MIT Press.

Savignon, S.J. (1972) *Communicative Competence: An Experiment in Foreign Language Teaching*, Philadelphia, PA: Center for Curriculum Development.

Schell, J. (2010) 'DICE 2010. Design outside the box', available: http://www.g4tv.com/videos/44277/dice-2010-design-outside-the-box-presentation

Sfard, A. (1998) 'On two metaphors for learning and the dangers of choosing just one', *Educational Researcher*, 27(2): 4–13.

Squire, K. (2008a) 'Open-ended video games: A model for developing learning for the interactive age', in K. Salen (ed), *The Ecology of Games: Connecting Youth, Games, and Learning*, Cambridge: MIT Press: 167–198.

Squire, K. (2008b) 'Video-game literacy: A literacy of expertise', in J. Coiro, C. Lankshear, M. Knobel and D. Leu (eds), *Handbook of Research on New Literacies*, Mahwah, NJ: Lawrence Erlbaum: 635–669.

Steinkuehler, C. (2007) 'Massively multiplayer online gaming as a constellation of literacy practices', *eLearning*, 4: 297–318.

Steinkuehler, C. and Duncan, S. (2008) 'Scientific habits of mind in virtual worlds', *Journal of Science Education and Technology*, 17: 530–529.

Sykes, J. (2008) *A Dynamic Approach to Social Interaction: Synthetic Immersive Environments and Spanish Pragmatics*, Unpublished doctoral dissertation, University of Minnesota, Minneapolis.

Sykes, J. and Reinhardt, J. (2013) *Language at Play: Digital Games in Second and Foreign Language Teaching and Learning*, New York, NY: Pearson.

Sylvén, L.K. and Sundqvist, P. (2012) 'Gaming as extramural English L2 learning and L2 proficiency among young learners', *ReCALL*, 24(3): 302–321.

Taylor, M. (1990) 'Simulations and adventure games in CALL', *Simulation and Gaming*, 21: 461–466.

Thomas Brown, J.S. (2009) 'Why virtual worlds can matter', *International Journal of Learning and Media*, 1(1): 37–49.

Thorne, S.L. (2008a) 'Mediating technologies and second language learning', in J. Coiro, M. Knobel, C. Lankshear and D. Leu (eds), *Handbook of Research on New Literacies*, Mahwah, NJ: Lawrence Erlbaum: 417–449.

Thorne, S.L. (2008b) 'Transcultural communication in open Internet environments and massively multiplayer online games', in S. Magnan (ed), *Mediating Discourse Online*, Amsterdam, Netherlands: John Benjamins: 305–327.

Thorne, S.L. (2010) 'The 'intercultural turn' and language learning in the crucible of new media', in F. Helm and S. Guth (eds), *Telecollaboration 2.0 for Language and Intercultural Learning*, Bern, Switzerland: Peter Lang: 139–164.

Thorne, S.L. (2012) 'Gaming writing: Supervernaculars, stylization, and semiotic remediation', in G. Kessler, A. Oskoz and I. Elola (eds), *Technology Across Writing Contexts and Tasks*, CALICO: San Marcos, TX: 297–316.

Thorne, S.L. (2013) 'Digital literacies', in M. Hawkins (ed), *Framing Languages and Literacies: Socially Situated Views and Perspectives*, New York, NY: Routledge: 192–218.

Thorne, S.L., Black, R. and Sykes, J. (2009) 'Second language use, socialization, and learning in Internet interest communities and online games', *Modern Language Journal*, 93: 802–821.

Thorne, S.L. and Fischer, I. (2012) 'Online gaming as sociable media', *ALSIC: Apprentissage des Langues et Systèmes d'Information et de Communication*, 15(1), available: http://alsic.revues.org/2450; DOI: 10.4000/alsic.2450

Thorne, S.L., Fischer, I. and Lu, X. (2012) 'The semiotic ecology and linguistic complexity of an online game world', *ReCALL*, 24(3): 279–301.

Thorne, S.L. and Lantolf, J. (2007) 'A linguistics of communicative activity', in S. Makoni and A. Pennycook (eds), *Disinventing and Reconstituting Languages*, Clevedon, UK: Multilingual Matters: 170–195.

Thorne, S.L. and Payne, S. (2005) 'Evolutionary trajectories, Internet-mediated expression, and language education', *CALICO Journal*, 22(3): 371–397.

Van den Branden, K., Bygate, M. and Norris, J. (2009) *Task-Based Language Teaching: A Reader*, Amsterdam, Netherlands: John Benjamins.

Volosinov, V.N. (1973) *Marxism and the Philosophy of Language*, Cambridge, MA: Harvard University Press.

Vygotsky, L.S. (1978) *Mind in Society: The Development of Higher Psychological Processes*, Cambridge, MA: Harvard University Press.

Warschauer, M. and Healey, D. (1998) 'Computers and language learning: An overview', *Language Teaching*, 31: 57–71.

Zhao, Y. and Lai, C. (2009) 'MMORPGs and foreign language education', in R.E. Ferdig (ed), *Handbook of Research on Effective Electronic Gaming in Education*, Hershey, PA: IGI Global: 402–421.

Zheng, D, Newgarden, K. and Young, M.F. (2012) 'Multimodal analysis of language learning in World of Warcraft play: Languaging as values-realizing', *ReCALL*, 24(3): 339–360.

Zheng, D., Young, M., Wagner, M. and Brewer, R. (2009) 'Negotiation for action: English language learning in game-based virtual worlds', *Modern Language Journal*, 93(4): 489–511.

# 31
# Mini-games for language learning

*Frederik Cornillie and Piet Desmet*

This chapter provides an introduction to mini-games for language learning and explores their utility in second and foreign language learning. From a theoretical perspective, mini-games merit attention for two reasons. First, in second language acquisition (SLA) venues, interest in the theoretical implications of practice has amplified in recent years (see e.g. DeKeyser 2007), and the investigation of mini-game-based practice using methodologies specific to the field of CALL (such as the automated logging of response times in learner performance) may likely yield novel insights into the development and nature of linguistic knowledge gained through practice, and into the roles of task conditions and consistent corrective feedback. Second, research on mini-games may shed light on the affordances of designed environments for sustaining learners' engagement in language practice, more specifically on the potential of narrative, nonlinguistic goals and positive feedback. Notwithstanding the theoretical justifiability of language learning mini-games, the empirical research is rather scant to date, and the current widespread support for communicative language pedagogies may seem to defy usage of mini-games in classrooms. This contribution is intended to form an accessible, yet comprehensive and interdisciplinary introduction into the concept and affordances of mini-games, and advocates (1) theory-grounded, evidence-based, and user-centred design of such games, (2) thorough evaluation for use in classrooms and (3) investigation within an architecture of human cognition which is known as skill acquisition theory in the SLA literature.

## What are mini-games for language learning, and how can they be positioned within the broader area of 'digital game-based language learning'?

We define *mini-games for language learning* as technology-based activities (1) that are intended to improve learners' mastery of specific linguistic constructions in a second or foreign language (L2), (2) which afford explicit, form-focused, bite-size, and typically fast-paced practice, (3) which offer immediate feedback on learners' responses and (4) that are goal-directed in the sense that learners pursue nonlinguistic goals in addition to practising their language skills. Such goal-direction may be supported – first, and more typically – by extrinsic mechanisms and reinforcement (such as points and rewarding systems), or – potentially in more interesting ways – goal-direction may be enabled by design attributes associated with gaming that have a more intrinsic appeal, such as story, game cores and positive failure feedback. In either case, non-linguistic goal-direction is intended to catalyse learner motivation and, consequently, to increase the time learners spend on L2 practice tasks. This definition is based on a comparative review of mini-games and on related literature in the fields of SLA and (educational) game design, and will be unpacked in the remainder of this section.

Mini-games have been around since the early days of research, development and practice in the field of computer-assisted language learning (CALL) (see e.g. Stevens 1984). Yet, two fairly current evolutions have spawned new potential for mini-games as effective tools for the development of skills in an L2: (1) the steep rise and democratisation of mobile technologies and the coinciding commercial success of games that are distributed through mobile devices; and (2) the renewed emphasis in SLA research on the dynamic interaction between explicit and implicit knowledge and the relevance of instructional strategies that focus learners' attention on formal aspects of language (e.g. Hulstijn 2002; Ellis 2005), including explicit instruction followed by systematic practice (see Gatbonton and Segalowitz 2005; Ranta and Lyster 2007). In the rest of this section, we will first position mini-games for language learning with respect to other types of games used in L2 teaching and learning (L2TL), and will then elaborate on the practical benefits and design attributes of mini-games.

## Situating mini-games within digital game-based language learning

Games are notoriously complex expressions of human creativity and culture, and often defy categorisation (see Reinhardt and Thorne, Chapter 30 this volume for more details on typologies of games). Nonetheless, a high-level typology may help to situate the many types of games with respect to one another. In the area of digital game-based language learning (DGBLL), such a typology can aid to comprehend the various approaches that are being taken to use games in order to support L2TL. Here, we distinguish between two dimensions that may frame mini-games in the area of DGBLL, namely their relation to situated avatar-based games and their primary design purpose.

### Relation to situated avatar-based games

A first dimension that helps to position mini-games within DGBLL is the relation of mini-games with what we will henceforth call *situated avatar-based games*. Situated avatar-based games typically figure large open worlds in which players have much freedom to explore and take action. They include storylines to give a sense of purpose to the player's actions, represent a personification of the player in the form of an avatar, and thus cast the player as a character in a story. Examples of the latter include game genres such as interactive fiction/text adventure games, and the more recent popular genre of massively multiplayer online role-playing games (MMORPGs), such as *World of Warcraft* (see Sundqvist, Chapter 32 this volume), in which many players collaborate and compete with each other simultaneously in a vast fictional (typically 3D) space. Mini-games, by contrast, are much more constrained, and come in formats such as puzzles, quizzes and arcade or dress-up activities. They usually feature simple gameplay and can be played in short amounts of time. For this reason, they are considered examples of 'casual games' (Mawer and Stanley 2011). Although the difference between mini-games and situated avatar-based games is not absolute, these game types may be distinguished from one another in terms of design attributes, complexity of the skills involved in playing, contextual characteristics and affordances for L2TL.

## Mini-games for language learning

First, on the level of design, the prefix 'mini-' implies that mini-games are constrained and are narrower in scope than situated avatar-based games. They lack the openness which typifies situated avatar-based games, and do not feature extensive storylines or a personification of the player. Further, mini-games can be embedded within a situated avatar-based game, and may influence how play of such a game evolves. A later section discusses the design attributes of mini-games in more detail.

Second, in comparison with a situated avatar-based game, a mini-game involves simple rules and is usually easy to operate. Hence, playing a mini-game requires only basic problem-solving and simple cognitive-motor skills, and mini-games are typically played in short bursts. Situated avatar-based games require more commitment from the player in terms of skill and time investment.

Further, mini-games differ from situated avatar-based games in terms of contextual features including the number of players simultaneously involved, required hardware, production costs and target audiences. Gameplay of mini-games typically involves only one player, whereas situated avatar-based games usually involve multiple players in competition or collaboration. On a technological plane, mini-games can be played on relatively low-end and low-cost devices such as mobile phones, whereas situated avatar-based games are developed using state-of-the-art 3D technologies and demand more advanced hardware configurations; yet, this gap in terms of required hardware seems to be narrowing, as computing power and screen real estate of mobile devices are ever increasing. Also, mini-games are produced on lower budgets than situated avatar-based games, as the development of both technology and content require less effort. Further, we may distinguish mini-games from situated avatar-based games in terms of target audiences. Popular wisdom has it that situated avatar-based games appeal mainly to (the stereotype of) the hard-core gamer. Arguably, mini-games have a wider target audience, and may also attract people that are less accustomed to gaming.

Finally, and most importantly, mini-games have different affordances for L2TL than situated avatar-based games. Because of their casual nature and more constrained scope, they appear to be particularly suitable for focused practice of enabling L2 skills (that is to say, knowledge of vocabulary, grammar, spelling or pronunciation). Situated avatar-based games, in general, make better candidates for more holistic practice of the four major L2 skills (reading, listening, speaking and writing) as well as for the development of intercultural and social skills. From the perspective of task-based language teaching (Ellis 2003), situated avatar-based games would seem useful for language practice with *tasks*, in which learners must use the L2 meaningfully and communicatively in an attempt to obtain a certain nonlinguistic (communicative) outcome. In contrast, mini-games appear similar to *exercises*, that is, pedagogical activities which do not result in a nonlinguistic outcome, but which are intended to help learners develop understanding of a specific linguistic aspect. Later in the chapter, we will expound on the affordances of mini-games from the perspective of SLA theory.

### *Primary design purpose*

A second dimension that helps to frame mini-games for L2 learning within DGBLL concerns the primary design purpose of a mini-game, in other words, how the designer of a particular game intended it to be used. The primary design purpose may be either to educate or to entertain. This relates to a subfield of CALL known as *tutorial CALL* (Hubbard and Bradin Siskin 2004), where computer-based activities were designed specifically with L2TL in mind. Tutorial CALL software includes content that is tailored for L2 learners, controls the learning process according to a set of preprogrammed rules, evaluates the learner's linguistic responses and gives automated corrective feedback. Tutorial CALL software has been contrasted with – and has of late been somewhat marginalised with respect to – software applications that were not designed with L2TL in mind (and thus lack specific linguistic-pedagogical features), but may nonetheless be repurposed for L2TL. Examples of the latter are email, wikis, voice over Internet protocol (VoIP) tools, and software for social networking.

This distinction also emerges in the area of DGBLL, and relates to whether a particular game that is being used in L2TL was specifically engineered for L2 learning and for supporting the L2 learning process, or whether it was primarily designed for entertainment purposes. In recent years, CALL researchers have developed different labels for this dichotomy. Cornillie, Thorne and Desmet (2012) built on terms from the (early) CALL literature and from the more general game-based learning literature, and proposed the labels *tutorial CALL games* and *(commercial) off-the-shelf games* to respectively refer to games that were specifically devised for the purpose of language teaching and learning, and to games that were designed for the purpose of entertainment. Reinhardt and Sykes (2012) put forward the terms *game-based learning* (working with educational and L2 learning purposed games) and *game-enhanced learning* (the use of vernacular games). Whatever the labels used, the major pedagogical differences between both types of games are that tutorial CALL games focus on power genres of L2 use (these are varieties of the L2 that are usually taught in classrooms and institutionalised curricula) and have linguistic-pedagogical assessment and support strategies (such as corrective feedback) built into the system. Playing off-the-shelf games, on the other hand, often involves the use of less canonical L2 registers – or sometimes does not even require use of the L2 – and because these games do not monitor the learner's speech or give linguistic support, their implementation in L2 classrooms more strongly demands pedagogical support from teachers or peers prior to, during or subsequent to play in order to raise learners' (meta-)linguistic awareness and perhaps speed up the L2 learning process.

To illustrate this distinction in the area of mini-games, we refer to a pedagogical implementation of an off-the-shelf mini-game devised by the authors of the teacher development book *Digital Play* (Mawer and Stanley 2011). The off-the-shelf game, called *Orbox*, requires the player to navigate a ship (by pressing the arrow keys) to a target in a 2D space without flying off into deep space. By itself, the game is not interesting for L2TL – it does not even involve language – but the language teacher can make the activity pedagogically useful by repurposing it for the L2 classroom, namely by creating an information gap between two learners, which necessitates their use of language. On the website that accompanies Mawer and Stanley's (2011) book (http://www.digitalplay.info/blog/2010/03/09/drilling-directions/), a lesson plan is given on how this game could be used for drilling the topic 'giving and understanding directions' in pairs, with one learner looking at the screen and giving directions, while the other player executes the directions on the keyboard without looking at the screen. While the game may provide 'implicit', game-embedded feedback if a learner gets any of the directions wrong, it gives neither feedback on linguistic form nor remediation, but the teacher may give such linguistic support on an as-needed basis.

A tutorial version of the topic 'drilling directions', then, could be a simulation of taxi driving. The learner first plays the driver and executes directions given by a virtual client (listening), and then plays the client who follows his preferred route visualised on the screen (speaking). If the learner experiences problems, the system provides corrective feedback, as well as a link to a list of useful phrases with target pronunciations (possibly accompanied by translations in the mother tongue). For each learner, the system keeps track of the number and type of mistakes per linguistic construction, and perhaps performs an error analysis, on the basis of which new routes can be generated (to be offered as remediation). Increasing time pressure, various routes from one point to another, and perhaps unexpected obstacles as the taxi is approaching its destination keep such

Mini-games for language learning

a game interesting. Finally, the system can provide corrective feedback adapted to the theme of the game: deviating from the route (e.g. pressing the left key or saying 'to the left' rather than pressing the right arrow key or saying 'to the right') would cost fuel, or perhaps clients.

Some language teaching innovators like Mawer and Stanley have advocated the implementation of off-the-shelf games in the L2 classroom rather than the use of tutorial CALL games, arguing that the latter are often not much fun and mostly feel like 'thinly disguised tests' (2011: 15). We share the critique that tutorial CALL games haven't lived up to expectations, and will argue further in this chapter that the key to making them successful is not to disguise language instruction and practice in elements of game design, but to make instruction at the same time explicit and purposeful/relevant for L2 learners.

## Four broad categories of games for L2TL

On the basis of these two dimensions, we can distinguish the following four broad categories of games to support L2 learning: mini-games designed for L2TL purposes; off-the-shelf mini-games; situated avatar-based games that were designed for L2TL, also called *synthetic immersive environments* (Sykes, Oskoz and Thorne 2008); and off-the-shelf situated avatar-based games. Table 31.1 provides examples for each of these categories.

When we use the term 'mini-games' in this chapter, we refer mainly to mini-games designed for L2 learning purposes (i.e. tutorial mini-games). In what follows, we will argue that such games offer unique practical benefits for classroom L2 teaching, as well as a number of affordances for the L2 learning process which may be theoretically justified (see later).

## Practical benefits of mini-games for L2 learning

The practical benefits of mini-games for L2 learning are threefold. First, in comparison with situated avatar-based games, mini-games may be cheaper alternatives for introducing gaming in L2 learning curricula. Game developers are working on methods to reduce the production and distribution costs of (immersive) situated avatar-based games, also with a view to making their technology more affordable for educational purposes (see e.g. Hollemeersch et al. 2010). Still, the implementation of such games in classrooms remains relatively expensive. Moreover, the development of immersive avatar-based games specifically for L2TL comes with serious design challenges. As a result, examples of such games that have been successfully adopted in a language training curriculum are few.

Second, because the content in off-the-shelf games is typically not adapted to or integrated in L2 teaching curricula, teachers may either be reluctant to using them in class, or may have a hard time selecting appropriate ones (for an excellent guide on pedagogically appropriate uses of off-the-shelf games in the language classroom, see Mawer and Stanley 2011). Mini-game

*Table 31.1* Examples of DGBLL according to two dimensions

|  | *Mini-games* | *Situated avatar-based games* |
| --- | --- | --- |
| Designed for L2TL (tutorial) | Johnny Grammar's Word Challenge (British Council); the *MindSnacks* series of apps | *Tactical Language and Culture Training System* (Johnson 2007) |
| Off-the-shelf | *Orbox* game (Mawer and Stanley 2011) | *World of Warcraft* |

technology may offer materials designers, teachers or even learners templates with which they can easily author content that is suitable for L2TL.

Third, in instructed L2 learning, teachers may have insufficient resources to pay close attention to learners' individual performance while they work with games and to provide individualised support, including timely, consistent feedback. One of the major benefits of tutorial mini-games for L2TL is that learner performance can be measured in automated ways and linguistic support can be tailored to individual needs.

## Design attributes of mini-games for L2 learning: Linguistic-pedagogical support and nonlinguistic goal-direction

The most typical characteristics of mini-games for L2 learning are that they can be completed in a short amount of time and require little problem-solving and cognitive-motor skill. However, when we inspect mini-games in closer detail, we quickly see that they often have very different features. In this section, we present an overview of key design attributes, based on an exploratory comparative analysis of mini-games for L2 learning, and give brief descriptions of these attributes. For more detailed discussion of these design attributes, as well as examples of and links to mini-games, we refer interested readers to a deck of slides that accompanies this chapter (https://goo.gl/EGDaIE). In addition and by way of examples within this chapter, please see Figures 31.1 and 31.2.

The design attributes of mini-games may be grouped into two sets, depending on their primary objective. A first set of attributes is primarily linguistic-pedagogical in nature (see Table 31.2). These attributes are intended to structure and support the L2 learning process while learners are interacting with mini-games.

A second set of design attributes includes typical design elements of games or *game attributes* (see Table 31.3). These attributes are all somehow related to how learners are engaged in

*Table 31.2* Linguistic-pedagogical attributes of mini-games

| Attribute | Description |
| --- | --- |
| Linguistic focus and learning aim | What the game focuses on from a linguistic point of view, and which enabling skills (knowledge of lexicon, spelling, grammar) and main skills (reading, writing, listening, speaking) are addressed. |
| Context and meaning focus | How the linguistic constructions are contextualised (decontextualised, contextualised at the level of the chunk or sentence, or as part of a story), and thus how the learner's attention is focused on meaning. |
| Response design | How the software constrains (the types of) responses that learners are allowed to give. Typically, mini-games have closed-response designs, with selected response measures such as multiple choice, but more open-response designs are also possible, such as typing or even speaking. |
| Item selection and sequencing | How particular items are selected and sequenced (and repeated) throughout practice. A popular sequencing technique in mini-games is the spaced repetition system designed by Leitner (1972), which repeats more often those items which the learner frequently answers incorrectly. |
| Learner control | To what extent the learner (rather than the system alone) may control aspects of practice, such as content or pace. |
| Assessment and feedback | How the game assesses performance and how it gives feedback ('knowledge of results' feedback, or more extensive linguistic explanation). |

Mini-games for language learning

He has __ enormous appetite.

*Figure 31.1* Mini-game *Article Wolf*, providing focused practice of English articles in the meaningful context of a story
Source: © Biscuit Software Ltd.

*Table 31.3* Game attributes of mini-games

| Attribute | Description |
| --- | --- |
| Excessive positive feedback and rewarding | Feedback in response to desirable behaviour that is often disproportionate to the action required from the user; also called *juicy* feedback (Juul 2010: 45). Examples are: points and excessive animations for single actions; badges, praise, etc. for longer-term performance. |
| Competition | Competition with oneself (personal best score), with artificially intelligent opponents, with other players, or between groups of players. Aggregation of highest scores on leaderboards. |
| Time pressure | Whether or not players need to compete with time while striving to complete objectives. |
| Fantasy | 'Make-believe environment, scenarios, or characters' (Bedwell, Pavlas, Heyne, Lazzara and Salas 2012: 4) that are inherent in the format of the game (not in its content). An example is representing response options as balloons to pop. This term traces back to Malone's (1981) pioneering work on instructional games, and is not to be confused with the genre of fantasy games. |
| Game core and nonlinguistic outcomes | The challenge that critically requires player involvement in the interaction (e.g. a language exercise linked to the fantasy of a fish in a leaking tank), and the nonlinguistic outcomes that come with resolution of the challenge (e.g. saving the fish). |
| Positive failure feedback | Communication of failure (i.e. corrective feedback) that supports the player's motivation, for instance through engaging and varied animations. Typically contingent upon the fantasy of the game (e.g. the fish goes to heaven). |
| Story | Elements of narrative included in the content (items) of the game. |

437

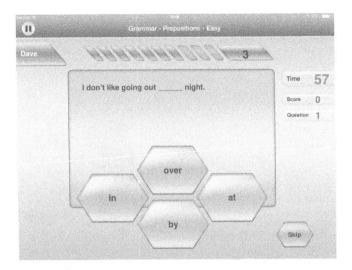

*Figure 31.2* Mini-game *Johnny Grammar's Word Challenge*, providing practice of vocabulary and grammar with time pressure

Source: © British Council.

achieving nonlinguistic goals, and hence are intended to increase the time learners spend on L2 practice.

We note two limitations of our typology. First, we note that the difference between these two types of attributes (linguistic-pedagogical and game attributes) is not absolute, and some attributes may belong to both categories. Second, we admit that there are more principled ways to identify design attributes than a comparative review of mini-games (see e.g. Bedwell et al. 2012 for a more rigid analysis of game attributes). However, we did not intend this typology to be exhaustive, and hope that it may be used as a first step towards a framework for designing and evaluating mini-games for the purpose of L2TL. We invite readers to challenge this framework and to build upon the ideas presented here.

When designing mini-games for L2 learning, it may be tempting to implement as many design attributes as possible. Yet, what will work best is likely to depend to a large extent on the learning context and on the individual characteristics of learners. We will revisit this in a later section.

## How can the use of mini-games in the language classroom be theoretically justified?

### Mini-games in L2 pedagogy: A revival of drilling in disguise?

If we look at mini-games from the perspective of L2 pedagogy, they seem closely related to what has long been known as *drilling*, a concept that is used more or less interchangeably with the terms *(drill and) practice, pattern practice, focused/systematic/controlled practice*, and *focus on forms* (for the confusing distinction between the latter term and the concept *focus on form*, see Long 2007: 121–123). In its broadest sense, 'drilling' refers to activities in an L2 that focus on specific linguistic constructions and that involve a great deal of repetition, feedback and often time pressure, with the goal of developing explicit knowledge about these constructions as well as skills in the L2 (DeKeyser 2007).

Three types of drills have been distinguished (DeKeyser 2007; Paulston and Bruder 1976): mechanical, meaningful and communicative. Mechanical drills, by way of their design, permit only one correct response and do not require that the learner comprehends the meaning of the sentence in order to succeed at the task. The textbook example is entirely decontextualised practice of verb conjugations. Next, there are meaningful drills, which also limit the range of responses fairly strictly, but demand that the learner comprehends the input on both a structural and a semantic level in order to succeed. Communicative drills, finally, require learners to draw on their own experiences and add new (unpredictable) information to the context provided by the teacher. In other words, in communicative drills, learners convey personal meaning. Further, irrespective of their type, drills can target comprehension skills or production skills, can be oral or written, and can focus on diverse formal aspects of the L2 (phonological, morphological, syntactic or lexical form). Thus, the term drilling has many facets, and covers a diverse range of activities for L2 practice.

However, drilling and related terms have come to be used most commonly in their most narrow sense, namely as mechanical practice activities that focus exclusively on grammar in listening and speaking tasks, and in which learners 'repeat sentences that are related only by the fact that they share some grammatical pattern' (Lightbown 2008: 27). As is well known, such spoken pattern drills were strongly encouraged by audiolingualism, a method of language teaching that was quite popular in the mid-20th century. Its main objective was to help L2 learners develop (spoken) communicative ability. It was deeply rooted in structural linguistics and behaviourism (Skinner 1957), and treated L2 learning as the result of a formation of habits, in which repetition and feedback played a significant role. Its main premise, then, was that if learners are engaged intensively in the habit of oral productive practice, they will acquire the skills that are implied in communicative competence. Hence, audiolingualism steered away from formal (grammar) instruction, but put oral pattern practice centre stage.

Since the communicative turn in language teaching methodology, the theoretical grounds of audiolingualism have been discredited, and empirical research has shown that the type of drilling that seems to have formed the flagship of the method (that is to say, mechanical drilling) is ineffective and sometimes even disadvantageous for the development of communicative L2 ability (for a detailed discussion see DeKeyser 1998; Wong and VanPatten 2003). Consequently, language teachers trained against the backdrop of communicative approaches usually eschew such drills, and by extension sometimes even meaningful and communicative drills. It remains open to investigation, however, whether drills of the latter two types are effective for L2 development.

Mini-games are similar to drills in a number of aspects: they focus on specific linguistic constructions, they involve a great deal of repetition and feedback, and there is a certain behaviourist ring to their reward mechanisms. Moreover, they are reminiscent of early CALL programs, many of which were faithful implementations of behaviourist principles (including reinforcement and punishment feedback). As a result of the apparent similarities between mini-games and drills, and of the narrow interpretation that drilling usually gets in L2 pedagogy, teachers may be sceptical about the utility of mini-games for L2 development. Such scepticism is probably justified for certain types and uses of mini-games. Yet, on the basis of current theory and empirical evidence in SLA, there is still support for many types and implementations of mini-games.

## *Mini-games in SLA theory: Perspectives from skill acquisition theory*

Theoretical support for the potential usefulness of mini-games comes from SLA theories that focus on *automaticity*, which we define here as the effortless and quick retrieval of linguistic constructions (particular items/instances and more complex grammatical schemata) from long-term memory, largely without conscious attention. Such theories tally well with mini-games, because they emphasise the role of continued and consistent practice, ideally accompanied by feedback, for the development of automaticity. Of the various theories that have been proposed (see DeKeyser 2001 for a review), we will zero in on skill acquisition theory (SAT; DeKeyser 1998, 2008), because it offers the greatest explanatory power for phenomena in L2 learning related to practice, as well as practical guidelines for the design and evaluation of mini-games for L2 practice.

SAT is a theory of L2 learning that is rooted in a more general theory of human cognition. Its main premise is that when becoming skilful at a certain task in the L2, learners move through a series of stages that differ with respect to (1) the effort with which learners perform the task and (2) the type of knowledge on which learners rely in order to perform the task. In the first stage of skill acquisition, learners develop *declarative knowledge* about something ('knowledge that'; also called *explicit knowledge*), such as the knowledge that countable nouns in English go with the quantifier *many*, or the knowledge that the concept [CAT] is expressed by the three-letter sequence *cat* which belongs to the semantic field [ANIMALS]. In the second stage, learners put this knowledge to use (e.g. *many cats*), which contributes to the building up of *procedural knowledge* ('knowledge how'; also called *implicit knowledge*). In the initial phase of proceduralisation, the retrieval and application of declarative knowledge is effortful, which shows in learners' behaviour: it is error-prone and slow. Yet, procedural knowledge develops quickly, and its advantage is that the information becomes available as a ready-made chunk in memory, which speeds up retrieval. The last stage of skill acquisition involves the fine-tuning of procedural knowledge. This results, over time and with much practice, in automatic, fluent and error-free performance of the particular skill, which is supposed to draw mainly on implicit knowledge (DeKeyser 1998, 2008).

Thus, the advantage of skill learning is that over time, the skill (e.g. applying the rules for quantifiers in English) becomes automatised, which frees up attentional resources for higher-order thinking in more complex tasks (e.g. delivering a formal talk on your company's annual revenues). The downside of the process is that automatisation is 'trapped' in a specific skill: it does not transfer well to other skills (DeKeyser 1997). In L2 development, the skill-specificity of automatisation explains the phenomenon that a good L2 writer is not necessarily a fluent L2 speaker, and that learners trained according to audiolingualism are not necessarily good at communication in the L2 – these learners are primarily trained in parroting form-form mappings rather than in conveying personal meaning. In order to promote transfer from one skill to another, SAT emphasises the importance of similar task conditions (e.g. comprehension vs. production, oral vs. written) as well as declarative knowledge. Such abstract knowledge may help to bridge the differences between different tasks. Therefore, it needs to be taught explicitly in the beginning of the acquisition process, and needs to be repeated when performing the skill (i.e. during proceduralisation and automatisation), for instance through meta-linguistic corrective feedback. SAT is known as a *strong-interface theory* of L2 learning: it posits that implicit/procedural and explicit/declarative knowledge are both relevant for L2 learning, and that explicit knowledge contributes to the development of implicit knowledge (see also Hulstijn 2002; Ellis 2005). Note that in SAT, declarative knowledge is important, but the theory also allows space for the incidental build-up of a procedural knowledge base without initial declarative knowledge (i.e. as the by-product of communication).

So, from the perspective of SAT, mini-games are promising. They offer opportunities for focused and continued practice of enabling skills, which is essential for the automatisation of knowledge. They can deliver individualised, consistent, and just-in-time feedback, possibly accompanied by meta-linguistic explanations. So, mini-games may constitute just those vital, highly focused, and potentially also motivating practice activities that SAT considers necessary for L2 development.

It is highly desirable, however, that mini-games move beyond the level of mechanical practice. There may be scope for mechanical mini-games in the initial stages of skill acquisition, namely in order to develop declarative knowledge. Yet, declarative knowledge is restricted: it is limited to form-meaning mappings out of context (e.g. in the case of explicit vocabulary learning: [CAT] = *cat*) and sometimes even to form-form mappings (e.g. *many* goes with countable nouns). Since the essence of L2 learning is about learning to communicate – that is, to produce form-meaning mappings that convey personal and situated meanings – instructional designers must come up with practice activities that force L2 learners to focus on the meaning of linguistic constructions, and that engage them in genuine communication. Meaningful and communicative practice supported by mini-games may, over time, help learners to develop knowledge that could transfer to their performance (accuracy, and possibly fluency) on complex, authentic language tasks. We will turn to the implications for practice and research in the final sections of this chapter.

## What are the key findings of empirical research on mini-games?

Empirical research on L2 learning with mini-games is scant. In this section, we highlight three key papers published through peer-reviewed venues that qualify as empirical studies on L2 learning with mini-games.

Stevens (1991) tracked first-year Arabic university students' problem-solving strategies in a computerised version of the popular game *Hangman*, which involved spelling practice of English words extracted from texts studied in their academic programme. Results show that students used strategies considered optimal for learning in half of the solved problems, compared to 92% of the solved problems in the case of ESL teachers, who were viewed as model learners. The authors did not investigate whether the different strategies used in the fairly mechanical practice tasks resulted in higher competence regarding orthographic combinations on complex transfer tasks subsequent to practice.

Stevens (1984) investigated the effect of learner control in computerised practice tasks on the development of knowledge about verb complements (gerund vs. infinitive). Control was operationalised as having or not having the opportunity to choose (by using game paddles) the constructions to practise with and to vary the order of their presentation. The participants were twenty-four learners of ESL. Development was measured as the difference between performance on pre- and posttests (of which the design is not documented in this paper). Although the differences were insignificant, the learners with control outperformed those who had practised the constructions in a predetermined choice and order. Interestingly, the former learners also spent less time solving the problems, as well as less time in the screen that contained explanation of the grammar rules. Stevens suggests that the learners who had control approached the sentences more out of a desire to explore their meaning than the other learners.

Strong empirical support for the usefulness of mini-games to further lexical development comes from Cobb and Horst (2011). Using the suite of mini-games shipped with the popular *My Word Coach* series designed for explicit vocabulary learning, the authors carried out an ecologically valid experiment with fifty young ESL learners in Canada. The various games focused both on form and on form-meaning connections. Growth was measured using a battery of pre- and posttests that targeted form recognition, meaning recognition, free production and speed of lexical access. Two months of game use resulted in huge gains in recognition vocabulary in comparison with normal vocabulary growth, increased speed of lexical access and more use of

English words in a storytelling task. The study shows that intensive practice with mini-games helped to develop knowledge both at the declarative level (larger recognition vocabulary) and at the procedural level (faster access to already known words), and that the practice effect transferred to the more complex skill of storytelling. From the perspective of skill acquisition theory, the latter result is particularly noteworthy, given the differences between the skill applied in practice (written comprehension) and the skill used in the follow-up storytelling task (spoken L2 production).

## What are the key considerations when designing or evaluating mini-games for use in language learning and teaching contexts?

When designing or evaluating mini-games for use in L2TL, we recommend the following five-step cycle: a 360-degree and user-centred needs analysis; the provision of explicit instruction prior to play; creation of a purposeful context for practice; meaning-focused practice with mini-games; and communicative follow-up activities with space for a wide range of corrective feedback types. This cycle may be repeated in order to improve the instructional design.

Start with a 360-degree needs analysis of the learning and teaching context, covering linguistic needs, nature of the linguistic constructions, and learners' individual differences and their culture. First, identify linguistic needs on the basis of learners themselves, taking into account the register of the L2 in which the learners will be most active in out-of-class contexts. For instance, it makes little sense to teach and practise the difference between *less* and *fewer* if your learners will never need to write a formal text in English. Next, for grammar practice in particular, select constructions on the basis of their linguistic characteristics. There is reason to focus on grammatical constructions that have wide scope (i.e. apply to many cases), that are reliable (in other words, have few exceptions) and that are simple; other patterns may be more easily acquired through implicit learning (DeKeyser 1998). Further, when selecting the games, consider a wide range of learner characteristics such as language aptitude ('Do learners have the necessary academic ability to work with grammatical concepts?'), age (younger learners may be more interested in repetitive games than older learners) and *achievement motivation* ('Are learners likely to be motivated by game attributes such as positive feedback, rewarding, or competition, or is a more intrinsic approach required?'). Finally, culture may play a role: language drills may be more readily accepted in some cultures than in others.

Next, any declarative knowledge that is likely to help proceduralisation and automatisation of the skill needs to be pretaught. Depriving learners of such declarative knowledge equals the bad practice of hiding instruction in the ludic enjoyment of mini-games. This will be ineffective, and may even make learners frustrated during practice. This does not imply that grammar ought to be taught deductively: learners may be more motivated when they work out rules by themselves before the teacher explains them (Ranta and Lyster 2007).

Then, set up a purposeful context for practice with mini-games, such as a (murder) mystery that needs to be solved. In the parlance of task-based language teaching, this will give learners nonlinguistic outcomes to pursue, while working towards realising language aims. What context is most powerful depends, again, on individual differences. However, in order to increase the chances that learners are engaged in meaningful rather than mechanical practice, an absolute requirement is that (the content of) practice with mini-games is embedded in authentic texts in the L2, such as a murder story. Progression in the mini-games could lead to the gradual unveiling of the mystery, which could both capture learners' interest and engage them in meaningful processing of the practice items.

Next comes focused practice with mini-games. The games may be varied, but need to generate opportunities for meaningful practice. Mechanical practice alone is not likely to result in better performance on more complex communicative tasks, so mini-games must be selected and designed that require learners to focus on the meaning of linguistic constructions, ideally with (semi-)open response designs. Communicative mini-games are highly desirable but can be challenging to design and develop, considering that learners may find typing cumbersome in games, and that human language technology (including automatic speech recognition) may not (yet) be sufficiently robust for handling learners' responses in (spoken) interaction. Further, the conditions of practice can be varied over time. Practice needs to start out without time pressure, with linguistically simple utterances and with little game element interactivity, so that learners have ample time and attention to apply and develop declarative knowledge. As learners improve, time pressure and the linguistic complexity of utterances could be increased, and additional game elements could be introduced in order to progressively increase cognitive demands during practice. Increasing the cognitive demands of practice steadily could both keep learners interested and provide fewer opportunities to spend attention on language form, which is considered a necessary step towards automatisation (Johnson 1994).

In order to realise transfer to other L2 skills, it is mandatory that practice is followed (and possibly also preceded; see Gatbonton and Segalowitz 2005) by activities with a more communicative focus. For instance, learners could role play as detectives in a murder case and report on their investigation, or play the suspects, using the linguistic constructions that were in focus during practice. Or, they could come up with alternative versions of the story, and rewrite (parts of) the text. Also at this point, teachers should not refrain from providing a wide range of corrective feedback types, on an as-needed basis and if necessary including meta-linguistic explanation, in order to help learners realise transfer through declarative knowledge.

## Suggestions for future research

In the investigation of the potential of mini-games for L2 development, a specific role for CALL research is to apply methodologies afforded by technology, such as logging and learner-centred adaptivity. Logging systems can provide fine-grained longitudinal measures of learners' response times and accuracy rates during practice, which are central in a SAT perspective. Further, through learner-centred adaptivity, the conditions of practice can be varied, such as time pressure, type of feedback or other game elements, which may yield information on how well specific skills are automatised, and at what point in the learning process such design attributes are best introduced or withdrawn. Reichle (2012) presents ideas on how proceduralisation of L2 skills may be coupled with gameplay mechanics. This could be done by requiring players to produce grammatical utterances in speech act types that are essential to a particular game context, such as questioning witnesses in a game set in a court of law, or casting spells in a wizardry game.

A second critical suggestion for research is to investigate transfer of learning. It would not be surprising to observe improvement of skills during focused practice, both in terms of increases in accuracy and in terms of faster response times. The critical question is whether the skill that is practised is relevant for learners' performance in communicative L2 tasks.

Finally, in line with a recommendation by DeKeyser that is now nearly two decades old (1998), we advocate longitudinal and fine-grained experimental research on skill acquisition with mini-games in ecologically valid research settings such as language classrooms and learners' homes. Given the little time there usually is for communicative L2 instruction, teachers are not likely to spend much time on focused practice with mini-games in classrooms, and may therefore choose to relegate practice to contexts outside of class. Consequently, the many design attributes of games supposedly associated with learner motivation may play a mediating role in their L2 development, as these could determine how much time learners spend on practice (see also Sundqvist, Chapter 32 this volume).

## Acknowledgements

This contribution was partly realised through interaction with the project *Games Online for Basic Language Learning*, funded with support from the European Commission (519136-LLP-2011-NL-KA2-KA2MP). This publication reflects the views only of the authors, and the Commission cannot be held responsible for any use which may be made of the information contained therein.

## Further reading

Gatbonton, E. and Segalowitz, N. (2005) 'Rethinking communicative language teaching: A focus on access to fluency', *The Canadian Modern Language Review/La Revue Canadienne Des Langues Vivantes*, 61(3): 325–353. doi:10.1353/cml.2005.0016.
  Gatbonton and Segalowitz introduce an instructional design model for focused practice known as Automatization in Communicative Contexts of Essential Speech Segments (ACCESS). The ACCESS model is noteworthy in that it weds communicative L2 teaching methodology with focused practice, rather than alternating between the two. The model leaves scope for mini-games in the 'language consolidation' phase, which is tightly integrated with communicative practice tasks.
Wong, W. and VanPatten, B. (2003) 'The evidence is IN: Drills are OUT', *Foreign Language Annals*, 36(3): 403–423 and also DeKeyser, R.M. (1998) 'Beyond focus on form. Cognitive perspectives on learning and practicing second language grammar', in C. Doughty and J. Williams (eds), *Focus on Form in Classroom Second Language Acquisition*, Cambridge: Cambridge University Press: 42–63.
  Readers interested in SLA research on focused practice are recommended to read the work of Wong and VanPatten (2003) and DeKeyser (1998). The former paper argues, on the basis of psycholinguistic research in SLA, that mechanical drills are unnecessary and even disadvantageous for L2 learning. DeKeyser's paper takes a broader perspective on focused practice by pointing at the potential relevance of meaningful and communicative drills, and discusses its history and utility in terms of skill acquisition theory.

## References

Bedwell, W.L., Pavlas, D., Heyne, K., Lazzara, E.H. and Salas, E. (2012) 'Toward a taxonomy linking game attributes to learning: An empirical study', *Simulation & Gaming*, 43(6): 729–760. doi:10.1177/1046878112439444
Cobb, T. and Horst, M. (2011) 'Does Word Coach coach words?', *CALICO Journal*, 28(3): 639–661.
Cornillie, F., Thorne, S.L. and Desmet, P. (2012) 'Digital games for language learning: From hype to insight?', *ReCALL*, 24(3): 243–256. doi:10.1017/S0958344012000134
DeKeyser, R.M. (1997) 'Beyond explicit rule learning: Automatizing second language morphosyntax', *Studies in Second Language Acquisition*, 19(2): 195–221.
DeKeyser, R.M. (1998) 'Beyond focus on form. Cognitive perspectives on learning and practicing second language grammar', in C. Doughty and J. Williams (eds), *Focus on Form in Classroom Second Language Acquisition*, Cambridge: Cambridge University Press: 42–63.
DeKeyser, R.M. (2001) 'Automaticity and automatization', in P. Robinson (ed), *Cognition and Second Language Instruction*, New York, NY: Cambridge University Press: 125–151.
DeKeyser, R.M. (2007) 'Introduction: Situating the concept of practice', in R.M. DeKeyser (ed), *Practice in a Second Language: Perspectives from Applied Linguistics and Cognitive Psychology*, New York, NY: Cambridge University Press: 1–18.
DeKeyser, R.M. (2008) 'Skill Acquisition Theory', in B. VanPatten and J. Williams (eds), *Theories in Second Language Acquisition*, New York, NY: Routledge: 97–114.

Ellis, N.C. (2005) 'At the interface: Dynamic interactions of explicit and implicit language knowledge', *Studies in Second Language Acquisition*, 27(20): 305–352.
Ellis, R. (2003) *Task-Based Language Learning and Teaching*, Oxford: Oxford University Press.
Gatbonton, E. and Segalowitz, N. (2005) 'Rethinking communicative language teaching: A focus on access to fluency', *The Canadian Modern Language Review/La Revue Canadienne Des Langues Vivantes*, 61(3): 325–353. doi:10.1353/cml.2005.0016
Hollemeersch, C.-F., Pieters, B., Demeulemeester, A., Cornillie, F., Van Semmertier, B., Mannens, E., et al. (2010) 'Infinitex: An interactive editing system for the production of large texture data sets', *Computers & Graphics*, 34(6): 643–654. doi:10.1016/j.cag.2010.09.012
Hubbard, P. and Bradin Siskin, C. (2004) 'Another look at tutorial CALL', *ReCALL*, 16(2): 448–461.
Hulstijn, J.H. (2002) 'Towards a unified account of the representation, processing and acquisition of second language knowledge', *Second Language Research*, 18(3): 193–223. doi:10.1191/0267658302sr207oa
Johnson, K. (1994) 'Teaching declarative and procedural knowledge', in M. Bygate, A. Tonkyn and E. Williams (eds), *Grammar and the Language Teacher*, Hemel Hempstead, UK: Prentice Hall: 121–131.
Johnson, W.L. (2007) 'Serious use of a serious game for language learning', in R. Luckin, K.R. Koedinger and J. Greer (eds), *Proceeding of the 2007 conference on Artificial Intelligence in Education: Building Technology Rich Learning Contexts That Work*, Amsterdam, The Netherlands: IOS Press:67–74.
Juul, J. (2010) *A Casual Revolution: Reinventing Video Games and Their Players*, Cambridge, MA: MIT Press.
Leitner, S. (1972) *So lernt man lernen. Angewandte Lernpsychologie – ein Weg zum Erfolg*, Freiburg im Breisgau: Verlag Herder.
Lightbown, P.M. (2008) 'Transfer appropriate processing as a model for classroom second language acquisition', in Z. Han (ed), *Understanding Second Language Process*, Clevedon, UK: Multilingual Matters: 27–44.
Long, M.H. (2007) *Problems in SLA*, Mahwah, NJ: Lawrence Erlbaum Associates.
Malone, T.W. (1981) 'Toward a theory of intrinsically motivating instruction', *Cognitive Science*, 5(4): 333–369.
Mawer, K. and Stanley, G. (2011) *Digital Play. Computer Games and Language Aims*, Peaslake: Delta Publishing.
Paulston, C.B. and Bruder, M.N. (1976) *Teaching English as a Second language: Techniques and Procedures*, Cambridge, MA: Winthrop.
Ranta, L. and Lyster, R. (2007) 'A cognitive approach to improving immersion students' oral language abilities: The Awareness-Practice-Feedback sequence', in R.M. DeKeyser (ed), *Practice in a Second Language: Perspectives from Applied Linguistics and Cognitive Psychology*, New York, NY: Cambridge University Press: 141–160.
Reichle, R.V. (2012) 'Sprites and rules: What ERPs and procedural memory can tell us about video games and language learning', in H. Reinders (ed), *Digital Games in Language Learning and Teaching*, Basingstoke: Palgrave Macmillan: 139–155.
Reinhardt, J. and Sykes, J.M. (2012) 'Conceptualizing digital game-mediated L2 learning and pedagogy: Game-enhanced and game-based research and practice', in H. Reinders (ed), *Digital Games in Language Learning and Teaching*, Basingstoke: Palgrave Macmillan: 32–49.
Skinner, B.F. (1957) *Verbal Behavior*, New York, NY: Appleton-Century-Crofts.
Stevens, V. (1984) 'Implications of research and theory concerning the influence of choice and control on the effectiveness of CALL', *CALICO Journal*, 2(1): 28–34.
Stevens, V. (1991) 'Computer HANGMAN: Pedagogically sound or a waste of time?', Revised version of a paper presented at the 24th TESOL Convention, San Francisco, California, USA, 6–10 March 1990. ERIC Document Reproduction Service.
Sykes, J.M., Oskoz, A. and Thorne, S.L. (2008) 'Web 2.0, synthetic immersive environments, and mobile resources for language education', *CALICO Journal*, 25(3): 528–546.
Wong, W. and VanPatten, B. (2003) 'The evidence is IN: Drills are OUT', *Foreign Language Annals*, 36(3): 403–423.

# 32
# Gaming and young language learners

*Pia Sundqvist*

This chapter examines digital gaming and young language learners. The focus is mainly on the relationship between playing digital games in English and learning English as a foreign or second (henceforth L2) language. *Young learners* are defined as children in primary school between the ages of 5 and 12 (cf. Ellis 2013). Whereas the starting age of formal L2 English instruction may vary between countries, due to the status of English as a global language many young learners already know some English when it is introduced in school, and playing digital games may very well be one reason why this is the case. It is well known that children tend to rely heavily on implicit learning mechanisms (Muñoz 2008; DeKeyser 2012), and it is thus possible that children pick up language through playing digital games. Teachers, then, need to be familiar with the world of their learners, perhaps more now than ever, because several studies have shown a relationship between digital gaming and aspects of L2 proficiency (see later). Thus, it is essential that we study the role of gaming for language learning not only among adult or teenage learners (see Reinhardt and Thorne, Chapter 30 this volume), but also among young learners.

The main aim of this chapter is to provide an overview of the role of gaming in L2 learning among children as well as to shed light upon the relevance of gaming research for L2 learning as a field of inquiry. The chapter opens with a brief section about pioneering work on gaming and language learning after which some key issues about gaming in- and out-of-school will be addressed, followed by a section devoted to the importance of various game genres for language learning, where different points of view are discussed. The next section addresses the question of the relevance of gender to the topic of gaming and language learning, before the chapter closes with a discussion of some pedagogical implications for the young language learner classroom.

## Pioneering work on gaming and language learning

With the development of the Internet and new media in the 1990s, access to authentic target language input was just a click away for L2 learners across the globe. Rapid technological advancement led to rapid growth also in the number of video games available on the market and some scholars in the field of applied linguistics and second language acquisition saw the potential of literacy and L2 development with the help of such games. One of them was James Paul Gee, whose seminal work (Gee 2003, 2007a, 2007b) paved the way for a number of subsequent studies. Among Gee's greatest contributions is his list of thirty-six general learning principles at play in video games. Through careful explanations and definitions of the principles, Gee provides useful concepts and tools for research on the relationship between digital gameplay and L2 proficiency/learning. Seven of his principles are briefly discussed in this chapter, since they have been frequently used in various studies. As regards terminology, Gee uses the term *video games* to cover games played on game consoles (e.g. PlayStation and Xbox) and those played on computers. In the present chapter I prefer the term *digital games*. This term has become increasingly common over the last few years and encompasses, in addition to the description of video games given a decade ago by Gee (2003), games played on tablets and smartphones, for example.

First, according to Gee (2007b), most aspects of a digital game environment are set up to encourage learners/players to be active and critical (Active, Critical Learning Principle). Further, learners/players can take risks while playing where real-world consequences are lowered ('Psychosocial Moratorium' Principle). Moreover, learners/players take on and play with various identities, for example, real-world, virtual and projective identities; there are several opportunities in a game to mediate on the relationship between new and old identities (Identity Principle). Furthermore, digital games offer opportunities for repeated practice that is not 'boring' (Gee 2007b: 223), making learners/players spend a great deal of time on task (Practice Principle). Learners/players also get to operate within but at the outer edge of their resources, and tasks come across as challenging but doable ('Regime of Competence' Principle). Another crucial learning principle has to do with the fact that learners/players are given explicit information 'both on demand and just in time, when the learner needs it or just at the point where the information can best be understood and used in practice' (Explicit Information On-Demand and Just-in-Time Principle; Gee 2007b: 226). Finally, learners/players constitute what Gee refers to as *affinity groups*; that is, groups that are bonded primarily through 'shared endeavors, goals, and practices and not shared race, gender, nation, ethnicity, or culture' (Affinity Group Principle; Gee 2007b: 227). These principles clearly illustrate various affordances of digital games (see Reinhardt and Thorne, Chapter 30 this volume) and, in addition, accord well with a sociocultural approach to second language learning (see e.g. Lantolf and Thorne 2006). That is, there is a belief that language learning takes place when novice learners (players) interact with more skilled learners (players) in a social context (the digital game); and more specifically, there is an interplay between L2 input, learners' (players') language output, and the feedback learners (players) receive on their spoken and/or written (game) production, all of which is conducive for L2 development (the Interaction Hypothesis; Long 1981). A detailed demonstration of such game interaction between two young L2 English learners, where one is a novice player and the other more experienced, can be found in Piirainen-Marsh and Tainio (2014).

Seminal work also grew out of the field of education and technology design. Noticing apparent differences linked to gender regarding digital gameplay, Kafai (1996) set out to investigate what digital games young American learners (aged 9 and 10, from mixed ethnic backgrounds) would design if they were allowed to create them themselves. She found that girls preferred less violence in their games compared to boys. Other differences between boys and girls had to do with game characters, worlds and genres. On the basis of Kafai's work, it is fair to say that most current commercial-off-the-shelf (COTS) games reflect boys' tastes more than girls'. Using a term from linguistics, Cassell and Jenkins (1998: 26) neatly sum up gender-related differences in relation to digital gameplay: 'boys' tastes constitute the *unmarked* option in the game world' (my italics); that is, the preferences of boys are privileged over those of girls – most

447

games are designed for and marketed to boys. Thus, with Kafai's important findings and this quotation as a backdrop, the role of gender in a chapter about gaming and young learners merits further attention (see also Hayes and Lee, Chapter 11 this volume).

## Gaming in and outside school: Key issues

To begin with, scant attention has been given to the relationship between digital gaming and L2 learning among young learners, regardless of whether we are talking about digital game-based learning (Prensky 2001) in schools or possible learning effects from gaming outside of school. For this reason alone, the relatively small number of young language learner studies that have been conducted become particularly valuable. Further, the games used in instructional, formal settings are generally educational games whereas those used in noninstructional, informal settings are COTS games, even though – of course – the reverse conditions may also apply (for the use of COTS games in school, see Van Eck 2009). In what follows, studies on both game types and settings are presented in order to shed light on key issues about gaming in and outside of school.

### *Empirical studies about digital gameplay and L2 learning*

Several empirical studies among university-level L2 learners have revealed a positive relationship between digital gameplay and various aspects of participants' L2 proficiency (see e.g. Cheung and Harrison 1992; Miller and Hegelheimer 2006; Ranalli 2008; Reinders and Wattana 2011; Peterson 2012; Rama et al. 2012), and similar findings have also been reported for secondary school learners (Kuppens 2010; Sundqvist 2011; European Commission 2012; Sundqvist 2013a). Results from studies targeting young learners are also by and large positive, as the rest of this section will show.

In a study among Dutch preliterate children, it was found that informal language contact in the home, for instance via television and digital games, correlated with better receptive vocabulary (Persson 2011). Similarly, in an interview study among Swedish preschoolers (aged 5 and 6), the children said that they learned foreign languages through the same types of activities (Sundqvist 2013b). As for educational games used in schools, in a study among Iranian 7-year-olds with no prior knowledge of English, an experimental group learned children's vocabulary (such as animal names) through a computer game (*SHAIEx*) and a control group via traditional teaching methods. After a teaching period of forty-five days, with three ninety-minute sessions of English per week, the experimental group scored significantly higher than the control group on a final vocabulary test, which included ten words (Aghlara and Hadidi Tamjid 2011). In a Canadian study, francophone L2 English learners aged 12–13 were instructed to play a suite of educational vocabulary training mini-games (see Cornillie and Desmet, Chapter 31 this volume), *Word Coach*, for Nintendo Wii or DS in school (Cobb and Horst 2011). The target words in *Word Coach* come from Nation and Beglar's (2007) Vocabulary Size Test. This test offers ten questions at each 1,000-word-family level up until level 14, and a test score reflects an estimation of a test taker's number of word families known at each level. The Vocabulary Size Test tests word recognition as opposed to word production; a test taker is supposed to match a target word in a short nondefining context (example: *soldier: He is a **soldier***) with one of four options (*person in a business, student, person who uses metal,* or *person in the army*). Based on data from one pretest and two posttests, the Canadian study revealed, for example, that two months' gaming coincided with one to two years' growth in the recognition of L2 vocabulary and that instances of code-switching were reduced, but also that the learners found the systematic reappearance of words rather boring.

Educational games in schools differ in comparison with COTS games in out-of-school settings. In a Turkish study investigating children between 10 and 14 years old playing COTS games in English at Internet cafés, it was found that gameplay promoted L2 learning, in particular with regard to vocabulary skills (Turgut and Irgin 2009). COTS games may of course also be played in domestic settings. In a Finnish study (Piirainen-Marsh and Tainio 2009), the researchers investigated two boys who played *Final Fantasy X* in their homes. These boys were of the same age as the children in the Turkish study. It was found that the Finnish boys imitated 'salient features of the game characters' talk'; there was a great deal of repetition and this practice was 'inextricably linked to learning' (Piirainen-Marsh and Tainio 2009: 166). Similarly, again based on data from the two boys, Piirainen-Marsh (2011) show how involvement in digital gameplay aligns well with the development of L2 interactional competence. There are more studies among young learners showing positive findings. For example, in a study among primary school children in Singapore – the youngest were 8 and the oldest 12 – it was concluded that the more time they had reported spending on playing digital games during weekdays, the more likely they were to fare better for English in school (Skoric, Lay Ching Teo and Lijie Neo 2009). Likewise, a Swedish study showed positive correlations between L2 English proficiency (comprehension and vocabulary) and COTS gameplay among 11- and 12-year-olds (Sylvén and Sundqvist 2012). Another Swedish study, this time among 10-year-olds, examined language-related computer use plus a number of other variables and revealed that, when nongamers, moderate gamers and frequent gamers were compared, *all* frequent gamers (a majority of whom were boys) were strongly motivated to learn English. Although many children in the other two groups were also motivated, those groups nevertheless contained larger proportions of less motivated learners (Sundqvist and Sylvén 2014). Finally, based on findings from Early Language Learning in Europe (ELLiE), a large-scale project among learners aged 10 and 11 in seven countries, Muñoz and Lindgren (2011) conclude that exposure to the target language through out-of-school activities was one very important factor for explaining the results on reading and listening comprehension; digital gameplay was one of the activities examined. In sum, recent studies reveal connections between young learners' involvement in digital gaming and various aspects of L2 proficiency, regardless of setting (i.e. in or outside school) or type of game played (i.e. educational or COTS, see earlier discussion).

## *Potential problems – intriguing issues*

A brief review of the results reported earlier in combination with the fact that *play* is central to child development (Huizinga 1938/1955) should make policy makers, language teachers and parents eager to introduce digital games as a tool for L2 learning also among primary school children, but as we know, that is not always the case. As regards in-school use of digital games for language learning, problems may arise in some countries, for instance where the curriculum conflicts with teachers' incorporation of games in the language classroom. In addition, there may also be countries or particular communities where parents would find the use of games for language learning controversial. Further, an incorporation of learners' out-of-school experiences can also be difficult in places where schools tend to focus more on social control than on learning (cf. Jenkins, Purushotma, Weigel, Clinton and Robison 2009). As for allowing young children to play digital games in their homes, over the years many parents have struggled with what to do and say about it, fearing for instance game addiction, negative psychological effects of violent games and lack of physical activity. However, parental attitudes towards gaming may also come across as positive, possibly because many parents today have backgrounds as gamers themselves.

## Different game genres – differing affordances for language learning

The gaming industry offers all kinds of games but there is little consensus on how to categorise games into different genres. However, for the purpose of analysis in L2 language research it is useful to categorise games – regardless of whether a study is quantitative or qualitative, or adopts a mixed-methods design. Three models that describe varying types of game categorisation are presented in this section: deHaan (2005), Kinzie and Joseph (2008), and Sundqvist (2013c) (a fourth model can be found in Kafai 1996). As shown in Chapter 30 (Reinhardt and Thorne, this volume), different games provide different affordances for language learning. For this reason among others, it can be relevant to see how particular games are categorised depending on what model is used. Two COTS games, *World of Warcraft* (*WoW*) and *The Sims*, are therefore used as examples to allow for comparisons of games as well as of categorisation models. Such systematic comparisons should make it possible to better understand which COTS games might be more beneficial to the development of young learners' L2 proficiency.

### Models for the categorisation of game genres in language research

In his model of game categorisation, deHaan (2005) divides COTS games into four genres: (1) sports, (2) virtual pet, (3) simulation and (4) role-playing and action/adventure games. He evaluates each category and argues that games classified into the first three genres are beneficial for language learning, while games classified into the fourth are not. Sports games, such as the *FIFA*, *NHL*, and *NBA* series, are said to allow for linguistic bootstrapping. In other words, L2 learners can use the language they know in decoding unknown language through constant exposure to and repetitions of, for example, lexical items, semantic context or grammar in a controlled environment. Furthermore, since gameplay is enjoyable, learners' affective filter is lowered and, as a consequence, possible barriers to learning are reduced. (The affective filter is a concept originally introduced by Krashen (1982) and it has to do with the influence of non-linguistic, affective factors on L2 learning, for example, anxiety, motivation and self-confidence.) Young L2 learners may benefit in particular from sports games, deHaan claims, since such games are rich in both aural and textual information and children can easily use the possibility of pausing a game while contemplating new target language input (such as unknown cardinal or ordinal numbers on the screen or expressions of various emotions in the commentaries). The repetition in these games is 'an integral part of their language teaching capabilities' (deHaan 2005: 231), and repetition is of course very important for beginning/young learners. Some of Gee's (2007b) learning principles mentioned earlier are clearly reflected in deHaan's arguments. For example, the repetitive parts of sports games deHaan brings up relate to the Practice Principle, and the possibility to pause a sports game whenever necessary connects with the Explicit Information On-Demand and Just-in-Time Principle.

In virtual pet games, the second genre, players care for their pet by feeding or exercising it regularly, for example. *Hamster Academy*, *Howrse*, and *Tamagotchi* are three typical examples. In contrast to sports games, where mainly receptive linguistic abilities are involved, deHaan (2005) points out that pet games test learners' productive abilities: the learner must take responsibility for his or her target language use because incorrect use may harm the pet (however, one might question how productive pet games really are in comparison with, for example, role-playing games). Pet games undoubtedly appeal to many primary school children, and they offer exposure to frequent target language vocabulary (*drink, eat, feed, jump, play, sleep*, etc.), which is exactly what young L2 learners need.

The third genre, simulation games, differs from the two previous genres in that, for the most part, a player/learner does not need to comprehend much of the language to start playing a simulation game. With the help of icons and drag-and-drop functions, the L2 learner may decode language at his or her own pace while being part of the reality which is simulated. *SimCity* and *FarmVille* are two examples; in the former, the player is supposed to found and develop a city while keeping the citizens happy and maintaining a stable budget; in the latter, the player manages a farm (raising livestock, ploughing land, etc.). Thanks to the frequent use of icons in simulation games, the cognitive load is not particularly heavy, making such games accessible to young L2 learners. More advanced learners may use simulation games to consciously practise particular aspects of language; one well-known example is Purushotma (2005), who used *The Sims* to teach himself German.

The fourth game genre in deHaan's (2005) model encompasses role-playing games (RPG) and action/adventure games, such as *Final Fantasy* (RPG) and the *Tomb Raider* and *Grand Theft Auto* (*GTA*) series (action/adventure). DeHaan does not treat RPGs and action/adventure games as two subgenres; instead he views them as rather similar types of games. Games in this genre are conversation heavy (textually and/or aurally) and include multiple forms of simultaneous on-screen information which make them less accessible for young learners. Thus, there is a linguistic threshold in these games, which deHaan puts as follows:

> Although a player may be very motivated to play and finish these epic games, a language learner may be much less enthusiastic about having to restart saved games, or play the entire game over again in order to listen again to a word or sentence not understood the first time the game is played.
>
> *(deHaan 2005: 234)*

Furthermore, deHaan highlights the fact that conversations in RPGs and adventure games often discuss people, places or actions that are not visible on the screen. This feature makes language difficult to decode and, therefore, L2 learners may become overwhelmed and lose interest in the game itself as well as in learning the language. However, it should be mentioned that other researchers have argued the opposite, namely that just because a player/learner is strongly motivated to make progress in a game, he or she is ready to spend a great deal of time on gameplay in order to decipher in-game language and thereby making it possible to continue playing (cf. Gee 2007b; Kuppens 2010; Sundqvist and Sylvén 2012; Sylvén and Sundqvist 2012). In addition, this fourth category covers a very broad variety of games, many of which, for instance, are not particularly 'conversation heavy'.

## Six activity modes

In comparison with deHaan (2005), Kinzie and Joseph (2008) present a conceptually different model of game categorisation. It is based on the results of a survey targeting educational game preferences among American middle school children. They suggest the use of six so-called activity modes to describe types of gameplay: (1) active, (2) explorative, (3) problem-solving, (4) strategic, (5) social and (6) creative play. COTS games are typically associated with active/performative play, they argue, but also with other modes. Shooter games, such as *Counter-Strike* and *Call of Duty*, typically offer the active mode, as do arcade-style (e.g. *GTA*) and some puzzle games (e.g. *Tetris*). Games where physical space and travel are simulated through the game and where previously played areas of the game can be revisited (e.g. *The Legend of Zelda* and *Metroid*) are connected with the explorative mode. As indicated by its name, problem-solving games are about solving problems or puzzles (e.g. *Bejeweled* and *Myst*). As regards games offering the strategic mode, emphasis is on manipulating resources over time to achieve a goal decided by either the players themselves or the game (e.g. *Age of Empires* and *Civilization*). One example of a game offering the social play mode is *Happy Farm*. Such games involve interaction between players and game characters, and also interaction and collaboration among players. Games characterised as offering the creative mode of play have to do with games in which players create, for example, a particular environment (e.g. a city in *SimCity*) or develop characters' looks or skills (e.g. *goSupermodel*). Thus, Kinzie and Joseph (2008) provide a model of game categorisation based on the modes of play; possible language learning from gaming is beyond the scope of their study. However, their model still constitutes a suitable theoretical framework in qualitative L2 learning research targeting young learners, since it provides useful game descriptions and was developed from data collected among children. It would be less suitable for quantitative studies, though. Many games would easily fit the descriptions of more than one mode/category – a game such as *WoW* would include all six (see later) – and it is difficult to see how it would be possible to incorporate overlapping modes/categories in a quantitative method of analysis. In the following section, a possible path is described for analysing games quantitatively in L2 research.

## *The Scale of Social Interaction Model*

On the basis of language learning potential, Sundqvist (2013c) takes yet another approach to game categorisation in her Scale of Social Interaction (SSI) Model. In order to avoid simultaneous categorisation along multiple axes, she proposes the use of one axis for game categorisation, namely the scale of the social interaction in the game. This scale is directly linked to the number of players involved in simultaneous gameplay: (1) singleplayer, (2) multiplayer and (3) massively multiplayer games. Singleplayer games are played on one's own (e.g. *Assassin's Creed 1*, *Horse Saga*, and *Super Mario Galaxy*), whereas multiplayer games involve a minimum of two players and commonly a maximum of around thirty (e.g. *Call of Duty*, *Counter-Strike*, and *League of Legends*). However, many singleplayer games also have a multiplayer mode (e.g. *Civilization Revolution*, *Forza Motor Sport* and *Halo*). As a rule of thumb, Sundqvist suggests that such games be classified as multiplayer games (for methodological details and a list of sixty categorised games, see Sundqvist 2013c). Massively multiplayer games (also known as massively multiplayer online games, or MMOs), involve as many as hundreds or thousands – or in the case of *EVE Online*, even tens of thousands – of players in simultaneous gameplay. The underlying hypothesis of the SSI Model is that the larger the scale of social interaction offered by the categories, the higher the chances of encountering co-players from various countries and, as a consequence, the need for a shared language (generally English) among the players. Involvement in authentic oral and written game interactions would then contribute to naturalistic L2 learning (Benson 2011). Thus, from the perspective of L2 learning, the SSI Model suggests that MMOs are more beneficial than multiplayer games which, in turn, are more beneficial than singleplayer games. According to Thorne, Black and Sykes (2009: 808), social virtual worlds and MMOs comprise 'the most socially and cognitively complex forms of interactive media currently available' (see also deHaan, Reed and Kuwada 2010), especially when players use their L2. Steinkuehler and Duncan (2008: 531) talk about such games fostering 'scientific habits of mind', that is, the ability to, for instance, use counterarguments, understand feedback, and build on others' ideas. However, with regard to the L2 proficiency skills needed in order to play MMOs and the cognitive demands of such games, MMOs are out of reach of most (but not all) primary school children.

*Table 32.1* Categorisation of *WoW* and *The Sims* according to three models

| Model | Game category | WoW | The Sims |
|---|---|---|---|
| deHaan (2005) | Sports | No | No |
|  | Virtual pet | No | No |
|  | Simulation | Yes | Yes |
|  | Role-playing and action/adventure | Yes | No |
| Kinzie and Joseph (2008) | Active | Yes | No |
|  | Explorative | Yes | No |
|  | Problem-solving | Yes | No |
|  | Strategic | Yes | Yes |
|  | Social | Yes | Yes |
|  | Creative | Yes | Yes |
| Sundqvist (2013c) | Singleplayer | No | Yes |
| 'The SSI Model' | Multiplayer | No | No |
|  | Massively multiplayer | Yes | No |

## Applying the three models to WoW and The Sims

In Table 32.1, *WoW* and *The Sims* are categorised according to each of the three models. Based on deHaan's (2005) conclusions, *WoW* and *The Sims* would be equally useful in terms of L2 learning, since both are categorised as simulation games. However, *WoW* is first and foremost an RPG and action/adventure game, and as such would not be particularly conducive to learning, according to deHaan. In Kinzie and Joseph's (2008) model, the two games come across as very different: whereas *WoW* offers all six modes of play, *The Sims* involves three. Also in the SSI Model (Sundqvist 2013c), the games come across as very different, since *WoW* is a massively multiplayer game and *The Sims* singleplayer. According to the SSI Model, *WoW* would be more beneficial for L2 learning than *The Sims*.

This comparison of *WoW* and *The Sims* reveals that digital game categorisation is no clear-cut case. Depending on what model is used, games are described in different ways and as such, different L2 effects are predicted. It could also be added that although the model by Kinzie and Joseph (2008) was developed from young learner survey data and for educational purposes, it was not specifically developed for the purpose of L2 research. Clearly, there is a great need for more studies on the relationship between types of COTS games and L2 learning and, moreover, what model(s) might be useful in such research. For studies targeting young L2 learners, of the three models presented here, the one by deHaan (2005) would probably be the most suitable. A major reason why this model would be preferred has to do with the fact that it encompasses all kinds of games, including games generally played by children. For studies on adolescent and adult language learners, any of the three models would work; which model to choose would ultimately depend on the focus of the research.

## How is gender relevant for gaming and language learning?

Findings about game preferences among boys and girls are similar to those among adult men and women, and if we believe there is a connection between game-playing habits and L2 learning, gender needs to be a variable in L2 research. This section first presents gender-related findings relevant to gaming in general and then gives an account of game-based studies among young learners in particular. With that as a backdrop, the relevance and consequences of using gender as a variable in future game-based L2 learning studies are briefly discussed.

## Gender-related differences in game-playing habits

Gender certainly cannot be ignored in game-related language research. Across the globe, we know that there are similar differences between how boys and girls choose to be involved in digital gameplay. Salonius-Pasternak and Gelfond (2005) summarise such findings from a psychological perspective and discuss potential benefits of gameplay. Among other things, they conclude that on average, boys play games more frequently and for longer periods of time than do girls. Moreover, boys and girls generally play different types of games and the main differences correspond to gender stereotypes. Whereas boys tend to play games that feature 'action, individual prowess, and winning through competition', girls are more likely to play games (often related to fashion or dating) that feature 'in-depth social interactions and character development through story telling' (Salonius-Pasternak and Gelfond 2005: 12). Kinzie and Joseph (2008) found that the largest between-gender differences appeared in preferences for active-mode games: the boys were much more likely to select this category than girls. The boys were also more likely to select games offering the strategic mode. In contrast, the creative and explorative modes of play appealed more to the girls than to the boys. In line with these conclusions, *The Sims* should be more appealing to girls than to boys and *WoW* more appealing to boys than to girls – and, indeed, that is the case (Gee and Hayes 2010; Jansz, Avis and Vosmeer 2010; Sundqvist and Sylvén 2012). Another difference between genders has to do with how game-playing sessions end: boys tend to stop playing either upon winning or losing, or when their avatar/character runs out of lives, whereas girls tend to stop when they get bored (Kafai 1998). As for educational digital games, Chu (2004) found that fifth-grade (that is, around the age of 11) boys tended to consider them boring, while the girls did not.

With regard to young learners and gendered play, an early comprehensive study found that children in kindergarten viewed the playing of digital games as more appropriate to boys than to girls (Wilder, Mackie and Cooper 1985). They also found that even among equally experienced computer users, in comparison with the boys, the girls underrated their ease of interaction and skills. Further, when computer interaction was unsuccessful, it was more likely to undermine the girls' confidence. Interestingly, the authors argue that this might indicate that computer interaction and its consequences can be different for boys and girls. Another American study involving 291 participants from kindergarten to sixth grade (approximately ages 4–5 to 12) revealed that most participants' computer use in the home consisted of playing digital games and, furthermore, software and Internet use tended to be gender-specific activities (Kafai and Sutton 1999). Whereas software designed specifically for boys has been very successful in terms of sales, software designed for girls has been less so, even though there are exceptions, for instance with the game *Barbie Fashion Designer*. This particular game, which targets girls from the age of 6, was used in a study aiming to reveal what makes girls play games (Subrahmanyam and Greenfield 1998). Similar to what has been described earlier, one conclusion was that girls like nonaggressive gaming activities which allow them to create fantasies set in familiar settings and using familiar characters.

## Gameplay and gender stereotypes

With these differences in mind, the fact that girls in general end up spending less time playing COTS games than boys may very well be due to gender-role stereotyping and lack of female characters in the majority of games currently on the market (cf. Kafai 1996; Beasley and Standley

2002; Mou and Peng 2008), sexism within some gaming contexts (Dietz 1998; Jansz and Martis 2003) or fear of facing harassment (Sarkeesian 2012). In short, many games simply do not appeal to either girls or women, which undoubtedly has implications for their game-playing habits as well as subsequent possible L2 acquisition. However, as stressed by Carr (2005: 465), female gaming worldwide is 'variable enough to suggest that gender is not a reliable predictor of gaming habits'.

With regard to facts about girls' lack of interest in digital games and lesser involvement in gameplay as compared with boys, it needs to be mentioned that research shows that girls as well as adult women tend to underreport information about their digital game-playing habits (Cooper, Hall and Huff 1990; Williams, Consalvo and Caplan 2009). Why this is the case can be explained by gender-role theory: since gaming has long been associated with masculine culture, it is 'not as socially appropriate' for females and, therefore, they underreport times for gaming (Williams et al. 2009: 706). Another explanation for gender-related differences is provided by Yee (2008: 88); based on online survey data from MMO players, he argues that men/boys and women/girls have 'very different social access points to online games and these determine quite frequently what each of them will play'. Thus, the potential connections between game-playing habits, gender, and L2 proficiency/learning are complex to investigate, but that is no reason for avoiding doing so.

## What are the pedagogical implications of gaming for language teaching?

The emerging picture of gaming among primary school children has clear pedagogical implications for language teaching. Most importantly, in order to bridge young learners' out-of-school experiences of encountering and/or using the L2 in COTS games and teachers' classroom teaching, teachers may need to raise their own awareness by acknowledging what is happening outside of class. Therefore, a first step for teachers may be to explicitly ask each learner about his or her game-playing habits (for ideas on how this can be done, see, e.g. Sylvén and Sundqvist 2012). Learner responses can then be used for tailoring individual as well as group instruction. For young L2 learners, a large proportion of the time spent studying is devoted to building vocabulary. Considering the fact that digital games appear to be particularly useful in L2 vocabulary acquisition, they constitute one of many learning paths to which teachers can direct their students, both for work in the classroom and in the home. Most likely, games would be especially motivating to and helpful for those who struggle with memorising words 'the old-school way' and those who learn more easily while using another identity (cf. Identity Principle). Other valuable game-based findings could be used to further inform language teaching practice, for instance that some (but not all) learners are likely to benefit a great deal from competitive L2 tasks in the classroom and that others (but not all) might do so from collaborative L2 work, only to give two examples.

Finally, digital games provide young learners with the opportunity to negotiate society's rules and roles; they also allow learners to experiment not only with language but also with, for example, aggression, in a safe setting: there are no consequences in the personal lives of the learner/gamer outside of the game. Using Gee's (2007b) terminology, this is the 'Psychosocial Moratorium' learning principle of digital gameplay. If the aim is to advance our understanding of the role of digital gameplay for young L2 learners, one fruitful way would be to initiate interdisciplinary projects (see e.g. suggestions by Neville 2010), since the answers are likely to be found beyond the scope of traditional second language acquisition studies. Main objectives could include examination of learner variation with regard to in-school and out-of-school digital gameplay, attitudes towards the L2, and L2 proficiency, and to take gender into account as a background variable. In particular, it would be important with projects focusing on the transition from primary to secondary school – a sadly underresearched area.

## Further reading

International Telecommunications Union http://www.itu.int/
    A site providing international statistics about, for example, Internet access and use.
Kafai, Y.B., Heeter, C., Denner, J. and Sun, J.Y. (eds) (2008) *Beyond Barbie® and Mortal Kombat: New Perspectives on Gender and Gaming*, Cambridge, MA: MIT Press.
    A book looking at how gender intersects with the broad context of digital games.
Reinders, H. (ed) (2012) *Digital Games in Language Learning and Teaching*, Basingstoke: Palgrave Macmillan.
    A volume bringing together current research into game-based language learning.
Thorne, S.L., Black, R.W. and Sykes, J.M. (2009) 'Second language use, socialization and learning in Internet interest communities and online gaming', *The Modern Language Journal*, 93(Focus Issue): 802–821.
    An article discussing L2 uses of technology and identity development through fan fiction and online games.

## References

Aghlara, L. and Hadidi Tamjid, N. (2011) 'The effect of digital games on Iranian children's vocabulary retention in foreign language acquisition', *Procedia – Social and Behavioral Sciences*, 29: 552–560.
Beasley, B. and Standley, T.C. (2002) 'Shirts vs. skins: Clothing as an indicator of gender role stereotyping in video games', *Mass Communication and Society*, 5(3): 279–293.
Benson, P. (2011) *Teaching and Researching Autonomy*, Harlow, UK: Pearson Education.
Carr, D. (2005) 'Context, gaming pleasures and gendered preferences', *Stimulation and Gaming*, 36(4): 464–482.
Cassell, J. and Jenkins, H. (1998) 'Chess for girls?: Feminism and computer games', in J. Cassell and H. Jenkins (eds), *From Barbie to Mortal Kombat: Gender and Computer Games*, Cambridge, MA: MIT Press: 1–32.
Cheung, A. and Harrison, C. (1992) 'Microcomputer adventure games and second language acquisition: A study of Hong Kong tertiary students', in M.C. Pennington and V. Stevens (eds), *Computers in Applied Linguistics*, Clevedon, UK: Multilingual Matters: 155–178.
Chu, K.C. (2004) 'Gender reactions to games for learning among fifth and eighth graders', Unpublished masters thesis, Michigan State University.
Cobb, T. and Horst, M. (2011) 'Does Word Coach coach words?', *CALICO Journal*, 28(3): 639–661.
Cooper, J., Hall, J. and Huff, C. (1990) 'Situational stress as a consequence of sex-stereotyped software', *Personality and Social Psychology Bulletin*, 16(3): 419–429.
deHaan, J. (2005) 'Learning language through video games: A theoretical framework, an evaluation of game genres and questions for future research', in S.P. Schaffer and M.L. Price (eds), *Interactive Convergence: Critical Issues in Multimedia*, Oxford: Interdisciplinary Press: 229–239.
deHaan, J., Reed, W.M. and Kuwada, K. (2010) 'The effects of interactivity with a music video game on second language vocabulary recall', *Language Learning and Technology*, 14(2): 74–94.
DeKeyser, R. (2012) 'Age effects in second language learning', in S. Gass and A. Mackey (eds), *The Routledge Handbook of Second Language Acquisition*, Abingdon: Routledge: 442–460.
Dietz, T.L. (1998) 'An examination of violence and gender role portrayals in video games: Implications for gender socialization and aggressive behavior', *Sex Roles*, 38(5/6): 425–442.
Ellis, G. (2013) "Young learners': clarifying our terms', *ELT Journal*, 65(1): 75–78.
European Commission (2012) 'First European Survey of Language Competences', Brussels: European Commission.
Gee, J.P. (2003) *What Video Games Have to Teach Us about Learning and Literacy*, New York, NY: Palgrave Macmillan.
Gee, J.P. (2007a) *Good Video Games + Good Learning: Collected Essays on Video Games, Learning and Literacy*, New York, NY: Peter Lang.
Gee, J.P. (2007b) *What Video Games Have to Teach Us About Learning and Literacy*. Revised and Updated edition, New York, NY: Palgrave Macmillan.
Gee, J.P. and Hayes, E.R. (2010) *Women and Gaming: The Sims and 21st Century Learning*, New York, NY: Palgrave Macmillan.
Huizinga, J. (1938/1955) *Homo Ludens: A Study of the Play-Element in Culture*, Boston, MA: The Beacon Press.

Jansz, J., Avis, C. and Vosmeer, M. (2010) 'Playing *The Sims 2*: An exploration of gender differences in players' motivations and patterns of play', *New Media & Society*, 12(2): 235–251.

Jansz, J. and Martis, R.G. (2003) 'The representation of gender and ethnicity in digital interactive games', in M. Copier and J. Raessens (eds), *Level Up: Digital Games Research Conference*, Utrecht: Utrecht University: 260–269.

Jenkins, H., Purushotma, R., Weigel, M., Clinton, K. and Robison, A.J. (2009) *Confronting the Challenges of Participatory Culture. Media Education for the 21st Century*, Cambridge, MA: The MIT Press.

Kafai, Y.B. (1996) 'Gender differences in children's constructions of video games', in P.M. Greenfield and R.R. Cocking (eds), *Interacting with Video*, Norwood, NJ: Ablex Publishing Corporation: 39–66.

Kafai, Y.B. (1998) 'Video game designs by girls and boys: Variability and consistency of gender differences', in J. Cassell and H. Jenkins (eds), *From Barbie to Mortal Kombat: Gender and Computer Games*, Cambridge, MA: MIT Press: 90–114.

Kafai, Y.B. and Sutton, S. (1999) 'Elementary school students' computer and Internet use at home: Current trends and issues', *Journal of Educational Computing Research*, 21(3): 345–362.

Kinzie, M.B. and Joseph, D.R.D. (2008) 'Gender differences in game activity preferences of middle school children: Implications for educational game design', *Educational Technology Research & Development*, 56(5/6): 643–663.

Krashen, S.D. (1982) *Principles and Practice in Second Language Acquisition*, Oxford: Pergamon.

Kuppens, A.H. (2010) 'Incidental foreign language acquisition from media exposure', *Learning, Media and Technology*, 35(1): 65–85.

Lantolf, J.P. and Thorne, S.L. (2006) *Sociocultural Theory and the Genesis of Second Language Development*, New York, NY: Oxford University Press.

Long, M.H. (1981) 'Input, interaction and second language acquisition', in H. Winitz (ed), *Native Language and Foreign Language Acquisition*, New York, NY: Annals of the New York Academy of Sciences: 259–278.

Miller, M. and Hegelheimer, V. (2006) 'The SIMs meet ESL. Incorporating authentic computer simulation games into the language classroom', *Interactive Technology & Smart Education*, 3(4): 311–328.

Mou, Y. and Peng, W. (2008) 'Gender and racial stereotypes in popular video games', in R. Ferdig (ed), *Handbook of Research on Effective Electronic Gaming in Education*, Hershey, PA: IGI Global: 922–937.

Muñoz, C. (2008) 'Symmetries and asymmetries of age effects in naturalistic and instructed L2 Learning', *Applied Linguistics*, 29(4): 578–596.

Muñoz, C. and Lindgren, E. (2011) 'Out-of-school factors – The home', in J. Enever (ed), *ELLiE: Early Language Learning in Europe*, London, UK: British Council: 103–124.

Nation, P. and Beglar, D. (2007) 'A vocabulary size test', *The Language Teacher*, 31(7): 9–13.

Neville, D.O. (2010) 'Structuring narrative in 3D digital game-based learning environments to support second language acquisition', *Foreign Language Annals*, 43(3): 446–469.

Persson, L. (2011) *Language Learning in the 21st Century: Foreign Language Acquisition Through Informal Language Contact at Home*, Paper presented at EUROSLA 21, Stockholm, 8–10 September 2011.

Peterson, M. (2012) 'Learner interaction in a massively multiplayer online role playing game (MMORPG): A sociocultural discourse analysis', *ReCALL*, 24(3): 361–380.

Piirainen-Marsh, A. (2011) 'Enacting interactional competence in gaming activities: Coproducing talk with virtual others', in J.K. Hall, J. Hellerman and S. Pekarek Doehler (eds), *L2 Interactional Competence and Development*, Bristol: Multilingual Matters: 19–44.

Piirainen-Marsh, A. and Tainio, L. (2009) 'Other-repetition as a resource for participation in the activity of playing a video game', *The Modern Language Journal*, 93(2): 153–169.

Piirainen-Marsh, A. and Tainio, L. (2014) 'Asymmetries of knowledge and epistemic change in social gaming interaction', *The Modern Language Journal*, 98(4): 1022–1038.

Prensky, M. (2001) *Digital Game-Based Learning*, St. Paul, MN: Paragon House.

Purushotma, R. (2005) 'You're not studying, you're just . . .', *Language Learning and Technology*, 9(1): 80–96.

Rama, P.S., Black, R.W., van Es, E. and Warschauer, M. (2012) 'Affordances for second language learning in *World of Warcraft*', *ReCALL*, 24(3): 322–338.

Ranalli, J. (2008) 'Learning English with *The Sims*: exploiting authentic computer simulation games for L2 learning', *Computer Assisted Language Learning*, 21(5): 441–455.

Reinders, H. and Wattana, S. (2011) 'Learn English or die: The effects of digital games on interaction and willingness to communicate in a foreign language', *Digital Culture and Education*, 3(1): 4–28.

Salonius-Pasternak, D.E. and Gelfond, H.S. (2005) 'The next level of research on electronic play: Potential benefits and contextual influences for children and adolescents', *Human Technology*, 1(1): 5–22.

Sarkeesian, A. (4 December 2012) 'The mirror', available: http://tedxwomen.org./speakers/anita-sarkeesian-2/ (accessed 18 Sept 2013).

Skoric, M.M., Lay Ching Teo, L. and Lijie Neo, R. (2009) 'Children and video games: Addiction, engagement, and scholastic achievement', *CyberPsychology & Behavior*, 12(5): 567–572.

Steinkuehler, C.A. and Duncan, S. (2008) 'Scientific habits of mind in virtual worlds', *Journal of Science Education and Technology*, 17(6): 530–543.

Subrahmanyam, K. and Greenfield, P.M. (1998) 'Computer games for girls: What makes them play?', in J. Cassell and H. Jenkins (eds), *From Barbie to Mortal Kombat: Gender and Computer Games*, Cambridge, MA: MIT Press: 46–71.

Sundqvist, P. (2011) 'A possible path to progress: Out-of-school English language learners in Sweden', in P. Benson and H. Reinders (eds), *Beyond the Language Classroom*, Basingstoke: Palgrave Macmillan: 106–118.

Sundqvist, P. (2013a) 'Categorization of digital games in English language learning studies: Introducing the SSI Model', in L. Bradley and S. Thouësny (eds), *20 years of EUROCALL: Learning from the Past, Looking to the Future. Proceedings of the 2013 EUROCALL Conference, Évora, Portugal*, Dublin/Voillans: © Research-publishing.net: 231–237.

Sundqvist, P. (2013b) *Elever i förskoleklass pratar språk: Ämnesdidaktiska konsekvenser för undervisning och lärarutbildning [Pre-school students talk about language: Subject-matter effects on teaching and teacher education]*, Paper presented at NOFA 4, Trondheim, Norway, 29–31 May 2013.

Sundqvist, P. (2013c) 'The SSI Model: Categorization of digital games in EFL studies', *European Journal of Applied Linguistics and TEFL*, 2(1): 89–104.

Sundqvist, P. and Sylvén, L.K. (2012) 'World of VocCraft: Computer games and Swedish learners' L2 vocabulary', in H. Reinders (ed), *Digital Games in Language Learning and Teaching*, Basingstoke: Palgrave Macmillan: 189–208.

Sundqvist, P. and Sylvén, L.K. (2014) 'Language-related computer use: Focus on young L2 English learners in Sweden', *ReCALL*, 26(1): 3–20.

Sylvén, L.K. and Sundqvist, P. (2012) 'Gaming as extramural English L2 learning and L2 proficiency among young learners', *ReCALL*, 24(3): 302–321.

Thorne, S.L., Black, R.W. and Sykes, J.M. (2009) 'Second language use, socialization and learning in Internet interest communities and online gaming', *The Modern Language Journal*, 93(Focus Issue): 802–821.

Turgut, Y. and Irgin, P. (2009) 'Young learners' language learning via computer games', *Procedia – Social and Behavioral Sciences*, 1(1): 760–764.

Van Eck, R. (2009) 'A guide to integrating COTS games into your classroom', in R.E. Ferdig (ed), *Handbook of Research on Effective Electronic Gaming in Education*, Hershey, PA: Information Science: 179–199.

Wilder, G., Mackie, D. and Cooper, J. (1985) 'Gender and computers: Two surveys of computer-related attitudes', *Sex Roles*, 23(3/4): 215–228.

Williams, D., Consalvo, M. and Caplan, S. (2009) 'Looking for gender: Gender roles and behaviors among online gamers', *Journal of Communication*, 59(4): 700–725.

Yee, N. (2008) 'Maps of digital desires: Exploring the typography of gender and play in online games', in Y.B. Kafai, C. Heeter, J. Denner, et al. (eds), *Beyond Barbie® & Mortal Kombat: New Perspectives on Gender and Gaming*, Cambridge, MA: MIT Press: 83–96.

# Part VI
# Purpose designed language learning resources

# 33
# CALL tools for lexico-grammatical acquisition

*Li Li*

Computer-assisted language learning (CALL) has been used for some time now in facilitating the acquisition of linguistic knowledge and the development of language skills. Much research has been carried out to investigate how technologies can improve the effectiveness of language learning, in particular in developing knowledge of lexis, although slightly less attention has been given to grammar. Situated in this context, the primary focus of this chapter is on CALL tools for lexico-grammatical acquisition. Vocabulary and grammar are very important language components as Wilkins (1972: 111–112) tells us, 'while without grammar very little can be conveyed, without vocabulary nothing can be conveyed'. This point illustrates why vocabulary and grammar are so central to English language teaching. For many language learners and teachers, vocabulary and grammar are the most important systems as they are viewed as a foundation for developing communicative skills. Many English language teachers and learners emphasise the importance of learning vocabulary and grammar, and devote much time to developing language knowledge in these areas. This is especially true for foreign language learners, as they normally study in an instructed environment which does not provide them with many opportunities to acquire the target language. In such a learning environment, teachers emphasise the importance of learning vocabulary and grammar for both academic and social purposes. Equally, students recognise the importance of vocabulary and grammar to their language learning.

In this chapter, I will focus on lexico-grammatical features of language learning to explore the potentials of technology and how technology applications can and should be used in promoting language learning. This chapter starts with an overview of the benefits of technology in language learning and the applications of technology in second language (L2) classrooms in improving lexical and grammatical knowledge. Then I will discuss principles of integrating CALL tools in these language areas and key issues from a research perspective. The chapter finishes with a future perspective in the development of CALL for lexico-grammatical acquisition.

## Benefits of CALL in lexico-grammatical acquisition

*How vocabulary and grammar are learnt*

The importance of technological applications in language acquisition is widely recognised and research in technology-supported language teaching discusses extensively the benefits of CALL in improving language knowledge and skills.

In order to understand how CALL benefits lexical and grammar acquisition, it is important to understand how language is learnt. *Lexis* 'refers to all the words in a language, the entire vocabulary of a language' (Barcroft, Sunderman and Schmitt 2011: 571). This includes individual words, collocations, and fixed and semi-fixed expressions and idioms such as *here and there*, *you know* and *happy hour*, which are taught and learnt as single lexical chunks because vocabulary learning frequently involves learning 'chunks' that are longer than individual words. Grammar concerns how words grammatically connect to each other to make sense. Both vocabulary and grammar are important elements of language learning. Swan and Walter (1984) claim that vocabulary acquisition is the largest and most important task facing the language learner. Lewis (1993: 89) went further to argue that 'lexis is the core or heart of language'. Grammar is an equally important component, especially in developing communicative competence (Canale and Swain 1980). In terms of how vocabulary and grammar are learnt and what approaches should be used to teach them, there is constant debate on whether they should be considered as separate or interrelated. In this chapter, the focus is not on this debate, therefore both views are considered in the applications of CALL.

There are different theoretical perspectives regarding how language is learnt. One predominant view of language learning is based on a sociocultural perspective of learning, which suggests that learning happens when learners participate in a social context and use language as both their cultural and mediational tool. In this process, the expert (teacher) provides the novice (learner) help to allow sufficient development; such help is termed *scaffolding*. Scaffolding is an important element of sociocultural theory and it is widely acknowledged that learners develop in their zone of proximal development (ZPD) because of the scaffolded help they receive. ZPD is where learning and development come together and is 'the distance between the actual developmental level as determined by independent problem solving and the level of potential development as determined through problem solving under adult guidance or in collaboration with more capable peers' (Vygotsky 1978: 86). In this process, language or other artefacts are used to mediate thoughts between the expert and novice; thus learning is mediated, first at the interpersonal level and then at the intrapersonal level. Language is viewed as a psychological tool, 'a means for engaging in social and cognitive activity' (Ahmed 1994: 158). Sociocultural perspectives highlight the interrelationship between language, interaction, learning and community to offer a holistic perspective of language learning (Ellis and Barkhuizen 2005).

Lexico-grammatical acquisition has received much attention from linguists, researchers and teachers, and it is widely accepted that it is necessary to teach these language components explicitly, especially where English is learnt in an instructed environment. In teaching and learning vocabulary, there are three important aspects of knowledge: form, meaning and use (Nation 2001). The form of a word refers to its pronunciation (spoken form), spelling (written form) and any word parts that make up this particular item (such as a prefix, root and suffix); meaning refers to what the word is about when people talk about it; and use involves the grammatical functions of the word or phrase, its collocations (a word or phrase that is often used with another word or phrase) and constraints on its use. The current trend of learning grammar is one that combines form, meaning and functions (Larsen-Freeman 1991). These three dimensions interact with each other and should be considered together in teaching. That is, learning grammar perhaps should not only focus on mastering the rules but also consider the meanings and function of these rules in communication where social factors are important. It is important to note that in both vocabulary and grammar teaching, the use and function of the language is emphasised and the context where language is used. This view is in line with a sociocultural perspective of language learning. However, vocabulary and grammar teaching and learning are also highly influenced by other theories, such as cognitive learning theory which emphasises the importance of cognitive level of knowledge acquisition through enhancing noticing on form and providing opportunities for practice.

Chapelle (2003: 56) takes the key concept of interaction (see also Reinhardt and Thorne, Chapter 30 this volume) and proposes three theoretical perspectives regarding technology use in language learning: interaction hypothesis, sociocultural theory and depth of processing theory. These different theoretical perspectives place different emphasis on how technology can facilitate language learning. Take a human-computer interaction as an example: the interaction hypothesis emphasises obtaining enhanced input; sociocultural theory advocates gaining help in using the language; and the depth of processing theory focuses on opportunities for increased attention to language. So, the focus of human-computer interaction can vary from different perspectives. From an interaction hypothesis perspective, technology can be used to obtain enhanced input through marking a grammatical form on the screen, modifying the difficulty level by providing images or adding elaborations to increase the potential for understanding. From a sociocultural theoretical perspective, language is closely related to the context it is used in. For example, technology can be used to create various situations where the target language (a particular word) is used. The interaction between a learner and the computer can prompt attention to language from the depth of processing theory perspective. Distinguished as they are, in practice CALL designers and teachers review, select and apply these theories in an integrated way and follow the principles of how language is learnt from a second language acquisition (SLA) perspective. Citing Kramsch (2000), Kern (2006: 187) observes, 'it is important to bear in mind that SLA is itself informed by a rich variety of theoretical frameworks and has consistently resisted a single overarching theory'.

## Benefits of CALL

Technology affordances in facilitating language learning have been widely recognised and acknowledged (see e.g. Li 2015). In general, positive attitudes towards using CALL in facilitating lexis and grammar are reported in various studies (e.g. Mahmoudi, Samad and Razak 2000; Can and Cagiltay 2006). Despite the different theories informing CALL and research approaches to it, it is possible to identify six important benefits of technology on language learning in relation to lexico-grammatical acquisition (the focus is placed on why technologies are effective and how they can contribute to a theory of language learning):

- technology can provide students with high-quality, authentic linguistic materials;
- technology can facilitate the acquisition of linguistic knowledge;
- technology can mediate learning through which learners appropriate new understandings;
- technology can provide students with individualised instruction;
- technology can provide students with immediate, accurate and individualised feedback;
- technology can increase student motivation and enhance engagement.

The remainder of this section will provide a detailed discussion of the claimed benefits.

## Technology can provide learners with high-quality, authentic linguistic materials

CALL can provide authentic language resources in instruction. CALL also provides a context for the study of language use. Many teachers and researchers believe language in context facilitates learning. For example, learners are able to see how vocabulary is used and collocates with other words, and how a grammar rule is used in various situations to achieve different communicative purposes (e.g. through corpus linguistics). This is one of the key elements of communicative language teaching. When experiencing language in real-life situations, learners will be able to apply the language skills they acquire in similar contexts. Many digital materials are developed to address the issue of contextualised materials and authenticity, especially with the availability of the Internet. Authenticity in language learning materials in particular has been receiving CALL material developers' and teachers' attention, especially since 1990 (Jung 2005).

Apart from authenticity, CALL also develops a variety of language resources. Learning materials from single text-based materials to multimodal materials have been developed, for example, audio, visual and multimedia materials. Chapelle and Jamieson illustrate this point:

> There are presentations of grammatical points ... (they might) include animation to make a point and practice exercises with feedback that allow students to test their understanding of the point. Perhaps because of their regular use of the Internet, students feel more engaged by interactive materials that provide feedback than they do with exercises in a workbook.
> *(Chapelle and Jamieson 2008: 7)*

The use of multimodal learning materials does not only help retain learners' attention but also improves the learning outcome (Silverman and Hines 2009).

## Technology can facilitate the acquisition of linguistic knowledge

CALL is believed to increase learners' linguistic knowledge. Multimedia presentations, including graphics and video clips, have a positive effect on vocabulary acquisition (e.g. Tsou, Wang and Li 2002; O'Hara and Pritchard 2008; Kim and Gilman 2008; Silverman and Hines 2009). In an experimental study, Nakata (2008) showed significant differences between students who learned words through lists and those who learned words through the use of computers; the study has demonstrated the superiority of computers over lists. Similarly, Tozcu and Coady (2004) conducted a case study to examine the outcomes in vocabulary acquisition when using interactive computer-based texts as opposed to traditional materials with fifty-six intermediate level students from various first language (L1) backgrounds. The study suggested that the experiment group who used a tutorial computer-assisted courseware outperformed the control group in vocabulary knowledge, reading comprehension, and reading speed. However, Proctor, Dalton and Grisham (2007) found no evidence of positive effect of a reading tutor (the Universal Literacy Environment) on vocabulary acquisition. Therefore, assumptions cannot be made that computers (technology) always enhance linguistic acquisition, and the realisation of technology affordances might be closely related to students' learning style, appetite, motivation and other factors (e.g. the length of intervention). From a cognitive perspective, 'noticing' is a necessary condition in successful SLA (Schmidt 1990), and research on SLA suggests that learners benefit from any assistance that helps them focus on a specific language form.

Research has shown that linguistic input increases when learners notice linguistic features, using techniques such as marking salience, modification or elaboration (Schmidt 1990).

Modification, making the input understandable to the learner through any means that 'gets at the meaning', for example, images, L2 dictionaries and L1 translation, enhances linguistic acquisition. As such, technology presents itself as a useful tool for modification to increase linguistic competence (Belz and Kinginger 2003). Gu (2003) found that strategies of directing attention and memorising words are the most helpful in vocabulary learning. CALL applications can be used to attract students' attention and help them memorise words. Tozcu and Coady (2004) investigated the effect of direct vocabulary learning using CALL on vocabulary knowledge, reading comprehension and speed of word recognition and found that a tutorial CALL programme (New Lexis) assisted learners to gain more highly frequent vocabulary; they concluded that computer-assisted vocabulary instruction increased not only vocabulary learning but also reading comprehension. Torlakovic and Deugo (2004) investigated whether CALL systems could be used for grammar teaching by conducting an experimental study. The result suggests that the experiment group outperformed the control group. In a Saudi context, Abu-Seileek and Rabab'ah (2007) conducted an experimental study to investigate the effectiveness of computer-assisted grammar instruction in teaching verb tenses. The results reveal significant differences between the groups in favour of the computer-based grammar instructional method, and more specifically the structure-guessing approach. Chenoweth and Murday (2003) also suggest that online grammar instruction resulted in high grammatical accuracy in writing. However, studies also show that technology does not necessarily facilitate grammar acquisition. For example, in exploring the benefit of participation in chat or discussion forums, Coniam and Wong (2004) and Zhang et al. (2007) revealed no positive evidence of CALL in grammar acquisition.

CALL software can help learners develop vocabulary learning strategies (Horst, Cobb and Nicolae 2005), which students might benefit from for their future learning. Like vocabulary, students and teachers can use a corpus to find examples of grammatical structure. Corpus analysis can be used as formal instruction or independent study. When students are introduced to the tools, they might be able to carry on using them in their future learning.

*Technology can mediate learning through which learners appropriate new understandings*

In enhancing linguistic knowledge, CALL also facilitates appropriate understanding of the language. For example, the use of videos, images and animations can help learners to understand abstract and difficult vocabulary. In some cases, the visual thesaurus can mediate the understanding of the relationship between words (e.g. synonyms and antonyms). Yoshii and Flaitz (2002) suggest that the more help learners receive (e.g. images, sounds and animations), the better vocabulary acquisition is. As such, online dictionaries and resources can be used in assisting vocabulary learning. CALL programmes (e.g. the use of shared screen, images, music and other artefacts) can be used as mediational tools to assist understanding.

*Technology can provide students with individualised instruction*

Chapelle (2007) made it clear that one of the criteria for good e-learning materials is learner fit, which means the materials must address the learners' needs and level. CALL can provide individualised interactive instruction containing carefully selected language materials. Students are individuals, and they have different learning styles and use different learning strategies which will influence both pace and approach to learning. CALL programmes can facilitate individualised learning to its maximum and help learners build their own learning profiles. Learners can access the materials at their pace and make progress at their level. Chapelle and Jamieson summarise this point:

> CALL materials allow learners to vary the amount of time they spend, the help they request, or the path they take through a learning activity. Because CALL can tailor instruction specifically to individual learners, CALL has a greater potential for good learner fit than do other materials (Chapelle 2001).
>
> *(Chapelle and Jamieson 2008: 7)*

### *Technology can provide students with immediate, accurate and individualised feedback*

Feedback on student language production is important for language learning. Ellis, Basturkmen and Loewen (2002: 430) conclude that 'there are strong theoretical reasons for claiming that the teacher's role in a communicative task should not be limited to that of communicative partner. The teacher also needs to pay attention to form'. By receiving feedback, learners are able to notice the gap between their knowledge and the correct linguistic form, such as grammar. Explicit feedback can also help students understand why their language production is correct or incorrect, which research suggests can lead to better grammar learning (Nagata 1993). Computer-assisted feedback can provide immediate, accurate, consistent and individualised feedback (Tsutsui 2004).

### *Technology can increase student motivation and enhance engagement*

Learner engagement is an important factor in learning a language. One of the widely acknowledged benefits of CALL is that it increases learner engagement (Braine 2004). CALL provides a nonthreatening and less restrictive language environment, which enables learners to take control of their learning process. Individualised and consistent CALL feedback reduces embarrassment and psychological anxiety (Torlakovic and Deugo 2004). Chenoweth and Murday (2003) also conclude that an online French programme engages learners better than the learning which occurs in a classroom. CALL promotes independent learning and develops autonomy and learning strategies because many CALL activities and materials are designed for students to conduct independent individual study. In this respect, CALL materials in a student-centred task-based classroom enable students to accomplish a task and to regulate it in an online classroom (Egbert 2005).

Technology can also engage learners with more interaction. Interaction lies at the heart of language learning. Interaction can be classified in the CALL context as 'interaction between people', 'interaction between a person and the computer' and 'interaction within a person's mind' (Chapelle 2003). CALL programmes and applications provide opportunities for students to interact with the technology, peers, teachers and even the wider community (e.g. through Web 2.0 technologies). By interacting with the computer, learners are more engaged in the process of acquiring vocabulary and grammar, noticing the differences and their own progress, using the computer as a tool to help their understanding and so on. CALL programmes and applications do not only provide opportunities for interaction and participation but also for communication and collaboration, which allow students to apply language they have learnt in real-life situations. In computer-mediated communication (CMC), where negotiation of meaning takes place, technology is particularly useful in enhancing SLA from an interactionist perspective (Yanguas 2010). Although the literature suggests that CMC is mainly used to promote fluency, it does have a positive effect on accuracy. For example, Pellettieri (2000) claims that text-based online chat may foster negotiation of meaning and form-focused interaction, thereby developing grammatical competence. In a more learner-centred learning environment where language is used as a social tool to co-construct knowledge through authentic tasks, technology can facilitate the natural use of language. In such a learning environment, computer technologies provide students with a context where they use language (vocabulary and grammar) to collaborate. This is especially true with Web 2.0 technology, for example, the use of blogs, wikis and other social networking and knowledge co-construction tools (see e.g. Zhang et al. 2007; Wong and Looi 2010; Lomicka and Lord, Chapter 18 this volume).

Technology can benefit language learning in many areas, and this overview is merely a snapshot of what technology can do. Of course, caution has to be taken here, as technology can have a negative impact on language learning if not used appropriately. In the next section, I will consider principles of using technology.

## Principles of integrating CALL tools

The principles of integrating CALL tools in lexico-grammatical teaching are based on empirical research in investigating CALL use in L2 classrooms and CALL material evaluation (Chapelle 2003). In evaluating effective CALL materials, Chapelle (2001, 2007) proposed a framework encompassing six criteria, including language learning potential (focus on form), meaning focus (focus on meaning of the language), learner fit, authenticity (how authentic the learning is in relation to real-life situations), positive impact (e.g. motivation, autonomy and engagement) and practicality (resources available).

There are strong reasons to consider these six criteria: first, we need to acknowledge that language is context-based and situation-oriented; second, there is need to have accurate complex and realistic language use; third, we need to consider learner differences and perceptions in language teaching and learning, and finally it is crucial to realise that the practical environment is important. Based on the six criteria outlined in the previous paragraph, it can be suggested that the use of CALL to achieve effective language learning may adhere to the following principles:

- Have a specific language learning feature as the target/purpose of the activity. In designing CALL activities and implementing CALL applications in teaching, teachers need to be aware of the specific linguistic outcome or purpose of that activity. The question the teacher needs to ask is, 'is it form, meaning or use that this is activity is about?'
- Understand SLA research and link it to the use of CALL materials and pedagogy. From an SLA perspective, teachers need to understand why and how technology could be used to assist vocabulary and grammar learning.
- Materials, activity and language learning focus in the specific context, bearing in mind the sociocultural and educational contexts. This principle includes the availability of technology, preparedness of teachers and learners in using technology (e.g. technology confidence and competence), curriculum and testing requirements.
- Specifically address learners' needs and level from both linguistic and cognitive perspectives. By considering the learners' needs, interests and levels, the full potential of CALL materials and applications may be realised.
- Link what students are learning (vocabulary and grammar) to the context in which they are used. Students need to see the relevance of what they learn in real-life situations. This could be done either by analysing real-life materials where a particular language item is used

(e.g. a TV series) or by giving students opportunities to use the learnt language to conduct an authentic task.
- Provide conditions to assist students to appropriate the language. Technology can be used as a mediational tool to facilitate conceptual understanding (either grammar structure or vocabulary). In terms of vocabulary, for example, an animation or visuals of 'ash cloud' can be used to assist learners understand not only the meaning of the word but the potential impact of it, which contributes to their deep understanding.
- Raise students' interests in engaging in learning. Learners' involvement and motivation plays a major role in successful learning. One of the affordances of technology is its positive impact on motivation, engagement and participation. Therefore, technology should be used to address the affective aspects of learning. For example, web-based learning instruction can produce authentic learning environments in which a task-based approach is employed to enable learners with more productive rather than passive roles in the process (Thomas and Reinders 2010).

Having considered the benefits and principles of using technology in language learning, I will outline some applications of technology in vocabulary and grammar teaching.

## Applications of CALL in lexico-grammatical acquisition in L2 classrooms

### Focus on vocabulary

Vocabulary learning follows two broad approaches: implicit learning and explicit learning. Implicit learning is acquisition of knowledge about the underlying structure of a complex stimulus environment by a process which takes place naturally, simply and without conscious operations (Ellis 1995: 107). Implicit learning is natural and meaning focused, and vocabulary and grammar can be acquired through meaning-focused, communicative activities such as reading and listening (Hulstijn 2003). On the contrary, explicit learning is 'any activity geared at committing lexical information to memory' (Hulstijn 2001: 271). It is the deliberate and intentional learning of vocabulary.

The earlier CALL programs typically included language learning activities, such as text reconstruction, gap-filling, speed-reading, simulation and vocabulary games. These programmes mainly focused on helping learners to remember the forms of vocabulary by providing them with different exercises and are strongly associated with explicit learning. The later programmes include the development of multimedia applications (Groot 2000) and the use of the Internet and Web 2.0 technologies. One common feature of these multimedia computer-assisted vocabulary application or network-based learning programmes is emphasising learning vocabulary in context and understanding meanings through various activities. Another important trend is they address learners' needs and learning styles through the use of multimodal materials and give learners as much freedom as possible to choose what to learn and how to learn. In the following paragraphs, I will provide some examples of popular tools in vocabulary teaching.

### Multimedia games

Multimedia packages with vocabulary learning activities are the most popular type in language learning. Vocabulary learning rates are reportedly higher in the computer-mediated situations than when using print materials (Laufer and Hill 2000). The use of visual texts improves learning, although the downside of using multimedia materials is that teachers need to spend more time on instruction (Kim and Gilman 2008). Many multimedia materials can be used to facilitate learning, and the most prevalent are educational games. Games are popular tools to enhance vocabulary learning. Interactive games can provide language learners with opportunities to practise language and have fun while learning. Because games are generally designed to reward and provide immediate feedback, learners can be motivated to achieve high scores. Games can also engage students with multimodal materials, including sound and visual animations. Digital games can offer opportunities for collaboration and interaction which might be difficult to achieve in other contexts (see Reinders 2012 and also Part V, this volume). Here I would like to illustrate this with three games:

### BBC WORDMASTER

http://www.bbc.co.uk/worldservice/learningenglish/flash/wordmaster/

This is an interactive game to test vocabulary skills. There are thousands of words to practise. The game gives the player a sentence with one word missing and the player needs to beat the clock to complete the sentence with the letters provided. This game can be used either for whole-class teaching or by individual learners outside of class. Activities like this could encourage participation and collaboration.

### ONLINE WORD GAME

http://www.vocabulary.co.il/

This is a vocabulary website with impressive Flash online word games. The vocabulary games include an online word search, an online crossword puzzle, and hangman online (it is called *HangMouse* here). This can be used for whole-class teaching or by individual learners outside of class, especially young learners to help with memorising words and understanding the meaning of the words and images that are used. This could also be used to help learners develop correct pronunciation.

### DECORATING

http://www.ur.se/sprk/engelska/inredning/

This interactive game helps learners to comprehend vocabulary by listening to *Roger's* requests and furnishing his room. This game is particularly suitable for beginner learners to practise vocabulary. The focus is not on memorising but on understanding. This could be used as a consolidation activity.

## Online dictionaries

Online (digital) dictionaries are becoming essential for language learning because of their advantages over the traditional dictionary:

- They are easy to access (as long as Internet access is available);
- They can be accessed and used by many learners at the same time;
- They include multimedia resources, meaning that learners can learn vocabulary by focusing on form, meaning and use at the same time;
- They are generally free;
- They include thesaurus tools.

**VISUWORDS ONLINE GRAPHICAL DICTIONARY**

http://www.visuwords.com/

Visuwords is a web-based visual dictionary and thesaurus tool which uses Princeton University's WordNet and a visualisation tool to build a visual network of words. Users can search for words to look up their meanings and associations with other words and concepts in a visual interface. The diagrams produced by Visuwords shows how words associate. This tool is especially useful for intermediate and adult learners since it requires analytical skills to identify the differences and similarities between words. This could be used as a self-study module to improve academic skills. The colour scheme used therein with the associations could be improved with more contrasting colours for visually challenged learners/users.

Some online dictionaries can also record personal search histories (e.g. *Ninja Words*) to help learners to build up an individualised word bank.

## Focus on grammar

Grammar teaching requires structured input, explicit instruction, production practice and feedback about correctness according to Ellis (2006). CALL can provide students with opportunities in all these aspects, promoting discourse-based approaches, explicit instruction and interaction.

## Websites

Web-based learning has become popular as a result of the access to Internet and flexible learning. Language teachers and CALL developers devote much attention and energy in putting language learning resources for students and teachers to use in language teaching. This is especially true for grammar.

**ENGLISHCLUB**

http://www.englishclub.com/grammar/index.htm

This website is full of English learning resources and strategies, including grammar. Web-based learning is especially useful for independent and individual learning. The website does not only help learners to understand grammar knowledge, but also to assess their own weakness and get immediate feedback. However, this requires students to have knowledge or awareness about their own learning styles and strategies, and ability to process information without assistance from the tutor. The immediate feedback could also have a negative impact on students as this might put off some learners.

Web-based mobile applications are an example of this kind of grammar teaching. Li and Hegelheimer (2013) developed and implemented a web-based mobile application, Grammar Clinic, for an ESL writing class. Drawing on insights from the interactionist approach to SLA, the Noticing Hypothesis, and mobile-assisted language learning (MALL), Grammar Clinic was designed as a series of outside-class grammar exercises in the form of sentence-level error identification and correction. It provides instant feedback for its exercises and includes a short grammar handbook. A total of fifteen common grammatical error types are identified and used in this application.

## Online forums

Computer-mediated communication is popular among L2 learners. The benefits of CMC are widely evidenced in the literature, and one striking affordance of CMC is to provide learners

## CALL tools for lexico-grammatical acquisition

with opportunities to use the target language in real-life situations. In terms of grammar acquisition, this could be used as an informal learning tool where learners can participate in online forum discussions on grammar usage and functions. By participating in online discussions, learners not only identify gaps in their knowledge of grammar, but they also share what they know to support other learners.

There are many online forums available worldwide. For example, English Club Grammar Help (http://www.englishclub.com/esl-forums/viewforum.php?f=199&sid=94b54e43007 fed1c8deb3546849df4e7) allows learners to introduce a new post, view a post and reply to a post as they wish. Other examples might include the use of social networking sites such as Facebook as a means of promoting class discussions around grammar problems. They have the advantage of providing online, immediate language support and promote a more dialogic approach to learning about grammar.

### Instant messaging

Instant messaging (IM) systems are normally installed on users' computers and the majority of this software is free (see e.g. Skype and Google Chat). They not only offer text-based communication but also audio and video chatting functionalities. Equally, such programmes are not limited to one-to-one communication, but may be extended to multiple users. In relation to vocabulary and grammar acquisition, IM could be used in synchronous tutorials or to offer instant feedback. Vsee is free software which enables videoconferencing and screen share that can be used for giving students instant corrective feedback in grammar. Eftekhari (2013) conducted an exploratory study of using this tool to provide students with instant feedback in one-to-one tutorials and found that students are likely to take up the correct form after receiving feedback. This tool (see Figure 33.1) allows the student and teacher to conduct a virtual face-to-face

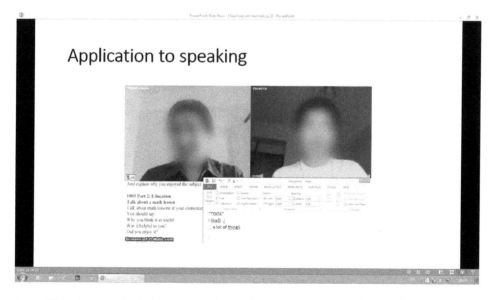

*Figure 33.1* A screenshot of Vsee used to provide immediate corrective feedback, with short transcription of included text

tutorial. When students are speaking, the tutor can provide both verbal and written corrective feedback, which will be available for students to view after the task is finished.

## A lexico-grammatical approach

Although vocabulary and grammar are often studied and researched as separate systems, it is difficult to separate them when considering language in use since words often cluster to form grammatical patterns. A lexico-grammatical perspective treats lexicon and grammar as two inherently connected parts of a single entity (Liu and Jiang 2009: 62). That is, when studying vocabulary, we do not only look at collocation (how likely words are to occur next to each other) but also colligation, which is how words go together in grammatical rather than lexical patterns (McCarthy, O'Keeffe and Walsh 2010). In this respect, corpus linguistics software is a useful tool to address the close lexical and grammatical connection which many words share. This type of software has two basic functions: concordancing and frequency counts showing how often a word is used (see Part IV of this volume).

The most basic and commonly used function of a corpus database is the key word in context (KWIC) feature which shows how a searched word is used in the corpus. For example, the verb *suggest* is searched using Corpus Concordance English (v.6.5) with AA Academic Abstracts that contain thesis and dissertation abstracts at master's and doctoral levels from universities in countries where English is the native language (174,000 words). The result shows how *suggest* is used for academic purposes (Figure 33.2). Clearly, *suggest* is followed by Nouns and Clauses (see the boxed examples 022 and 026). The concordance also indicates that *suggest* is used in a particular way in an academic context (see 028–033 and 040–044).

The main advantage of using corpus-based approaches in learning and teaching is that they provide opportunities for learners to access a large amount of natural language. Corpus linguistics presents a useful learning tool which promotes autonomy, individualised learning and authentic language materials. The use of corpora can help learners to understand relationships

*Figure 33.2* Concordance for *suggest*

between words, both lexical (collocation) and grammatical (colligation). For example, Carter and McCarthy (2006: 431) list the most common particles that we use and the verbs they usually collocate with (cited in McCarthy et al. 2010: 45):

- go/hang/knock/mess *about*
- forge/go/keep/move *ahead*
- come/go/get/take *off*
- break/come/go/put *out*.

Learners can be encouraged to find the most frequently used words and how they collocate with other words either individually or collaboratively. Corpus tools thus are used as study tools that enable learners to explore language patterns. The use of corpus tools can also help teachers to identify important or appropriate words students need to learn at a specific level or for a specific purpose. For example, students majoring in business will be able to identify the top 100 business words and see how they are used. In this respect, a corpus is also useful for looking at different registers of language – for example, we can compare how words are used in news reports, business documents and academic papers. We will also find that the grammar of words is different across registers. Corpus-based tasks can help learners with difficult aspects of vocabulary learning, for example, lexical chunks and idioms. Lexical chunks help the flow of the interaction and ensure speaker and listener understand each other in spoken discourse (McCarthy et al. 2010: 55) whereas the lack of knowledge of idioms can impede meaning. Lexical chunks and idioms are important for both fluency and accuracy, and the latter can be classified according to their grammar (McCarthy et al. 2010). A data-driven approach can be a useful way for studying both in context where learners are exposed to corpus data in the form of concordances. O'Keeffe, McCarthy and Carter (2007) suggest that the study of large corpora makes us question these conventional divisions and helps us see how grammar and lexis interpenetrate and overlap in all kinds of ways. There are many free corpora and students and learners can also build their own corpus.

## Key issues from research-based studies

Using technology to assist vocabulary and grammar acquisition involves more than just CALL materials. Li (2008, 2014) points out that teachers play an important role in integrating technology in language teaching because the teacher makes important pedagogical decisions in terms of what materials are used, how effective the materials are in prompting lexical and grammatical knowledge, how to maximise the benefits of technological tools and their own beliefs about the usefulness of technology in achieving pedagogical goals. Thus, the first and foremost question in mind is, how appropriate is technology in pedagogical considerations?

As discussed earlier, technology has many affordances and benefits in language learning. CALL tools and applications must be utilised with a clearly defined role. For example, Kim and Gilman (2008) point out that an effective way to improve learning English vocabulary is to offer graphics that illustrate what the vocabulary means; therefore, visual tools should be more encouraged for lexical acquisition. Technology does not only act as a linguistic-enhanced tool, but an affective tool (to motivate learners), a scaffolding tool and so on. In actual teaching, the question is whether technology can provide enhanced input, engage and motivate learners or facilitate understanding. Without considering the role of technology explicitly in an activity or task, it is hard to understand how and to what extent technology can assist learning. For example, Nakata (2008) found there were no significant differences between computers and cards in vocabulary learning, and thus in order to fully explore the potential of computers, linguistic outcome should not be the only measure of learning.

The last issue with using technology in teaching vocabulary and grammar or other aspects of language learning is that a clear learning outcome needs to be defined. This works as a basis for pedagogy and the role of technology. For example, in grammar teaching, if form is focused and expected as a learning product, then technological tools which can facilitate understanding grammar rules and provide exercises are considered appropriate. On the other hand, if function is more concerned, then a technological application which could provide students with real-life examples of language (e.g. videos and corpus) and context to use such a language is desired. Research suggests that technology is beneficial in vocabulary teaching and there is not enough evidence about how grammar acquisition improves with the assistance of technology; therefore, it is necessary to build evaluation (both judgemental and empirical) in CALL activities (Chapelle 2001, 2007).

## Future developments of CALL for lexico-grammatical acquisition

Developments in CMC have resulted in language changing, in particular in words and grammar. New words are created and new meanings are added to existing words. Grammar rules are changing too with the emergence of e-grammar, which varies according to contexts and technologies applied (Herring 2007). Grammar in CMC (especially text-based chat) is different from traditional spoken grammar in the way that it sometimes breaks or modifies grammar rules. This change in language and the development of technology in language change has created considerable speculation and a growing body of research. For language learning purposes, what is interesting is not only looking at the new meanings of words and accepting the modified rules and structure of utterances, but also developing an understanding and knowledge of how words collocate – existing weak and strong collocations might change. What is also interesting is to look at colligation: how words go together in grammatical rather than lexical patterns. In this line of inquiry, we can see the greater use of learner corpora, perhaps a corpus of CMC language (see Farr and Riordan 2015).

In the same way, CALL tools are developing more and more to include social and affective aspects. Therefore, the role of learners is becoming more central in using these tools, meaning CALL tools are developing more and more as learning tools rather than teaching tools. We can already see CALL tools moving in this direction, for example, web-based learning materials, dictionaries and games. This shift will enable learners to develop more communicative and sociolinguistic competences. Equally, new technology apps and tools are developing for language learning. This requires language teachers, researchers and CALL developers to further explore how these tools can be used to facilitate lexico-grammatical acquisition. One particular area is the use of web-based mobile applications in assisting learners to conduct independent and individualised learning. In summary, there are so many different ways that teachers can make use of technologies in facilitating lexical and grammar learning, and realising the full potential of technology relies on how teachers link their pedagogical goals to the affordances that technology can offer.

## Further reading

Chapelle, C.A. and Jamieson, J. (2008) *Tips for Teaching with CALL: Practical Approaches to Computer-Assisted Language Learning*, White Plains, NY: Pearson Education: chapters 1–2.
    This book is a professional reference with practical classroom approaches that is firmly grounded in CALL research. The chapters provide the reader with well-conceived and realistic approaches to

language instruction using examples in vocabulary and grammar learning. The chapters offer the reader an opportunity to link what the research says and what teachers can do in using CALL in facilitating lexis and grammar learning. The chapters include colour screenshots of authentic CALL software, along with descriptions, level information and notes. There are demonstration tips to show readers how to use various technology applications.

Nakata, T. (2012) 'Web-based lexical resources', in C. Chappelle (ed), *Encyclopedia of Applied Linguistics*, Oxford, UK: Wiley-Blackwell: 6166–6177.

This book chapter outlines web-based lexical resources for teachers, students and researchers. Detailed discussion is offered regarding online dictionaries, word lists, vocabulary tests and software, corpora and concordancers, vocabulary profilers, guides for teaching and learning and vocabulary quizzes. This chapter also provides researchers with bibliographies on vocabulary, online articles and lexical databases. It is a useful starting point for anyone who is interested in using the Internet in vocabulary teaching, learning and research.

## References

AbuSeileek, A.F. and Rabab'ah, G.A. (2007) 'The effect of computer-based grammar instruction on the acquisition of verb tenses in an EFL context', *The JALT CALL Journal*, 3(1–2): 59–80.

Ahmed, M.K. (1994) 'Speaking as cognitive regulation. A Vygotskian perspective on dialogic communication', in J.P. Lantolf and G. Appel (eds), *Vygotskian Approaches to Second Language Research*, Norwood, NJ: Ablex Publishing Corporation: 157–172.

Barcroft, J., Sunderman, G. and Schmitt, N. (2011) 'Lexis', in J. Simpson (ed), *The Routledge Handbook of Applied Linguistics*, London, UK: Routledge: 571–583.

Belz, J.A. and Kinginger, C. (2003) 'Discourse options and the development of pragmatic competence by classroom learners of German: The case of address forms', *Language Learning*, 53(4): 591–647.

Braine, G. (2004) 'Teaching second and foreign language writing on LANs', in S. Fotos and C. Browne (eds), Mahwah, NJ: Lawrence Erlbaum Associates: 93–107.

Can, G. and Cagiltay, K. (2006) 'Turkish prospective teachers' perceptions regarding the use of computer games with educational features', *Educational Technology & Society*, 9(1): 308–321.

Canale, M. and Swain, M. (1980) 'Theoretical bases of communicative approaches to second language teaching and testing', *Applied Linguistics*, 1(l): 1–47.

Carter, R.A. and McCarthy, M.J. (2006) *The Cambridge Grammar of English*, Cambridge: Cambridge University Press.

Chapelle, C. (2001) *Computer Applications in Second Language Acquisition: Foundations for Teaching, Testing, and Research*, Cambridge: Cambridge University Press.

Chapelle, C. (2003) *English Language Learning and Technology: Lectures on Applied Linguistics in the Age of Information and Communication Technology*, Amsterdam, Netherland: John Benjamins Publishing.

Chapelle, C. (2007) 'Challenges in evaluation of innovation: Observations from technology research', *Innovation in Language Learning and Teaching*, 1(1): 30–45.

Chapelle, C. and Jamieson, J. (2008) *Tips for Teaching with CALL: Practical Approaches to Computer-Assisted Language Learning*, White Plains, NY: Pearson Education.

Chenoweth, N.A. and Murday, K. (2003) 'Measuring student learning in an online French course', *CALICO Journal*, 20(2): 285–314.

Coniam, D. and R. Wong (2004) 'Internet relay chat as a tool in the autonomous development of ESL learners' English language ability: An exploratory study', *System*, 32(3): 321–335.

Eftekhari, S. (2013) 'Student's experience with technology-supported error correction for speaking in promoting accuracy and fluency in preparing in the IELTS', Unpublished MEd dissertation, University of Exeter.

Egbert, J.L. (2005) 'Conducting research on CALL' in J. Egbert and G. Petrie (eds), *CALL Research Perspectives*, Mahwah, NJ: Lawrence Erlbaum: 3-8.

Ellis, N.C. (1995) 'The psychology of foreign language vocabulary acquisition: Implications for CALL', *International Journal of Computer Assisted Language Learning*, 8(2–3): 103–128.

Ellis, R. (2006) 'Current issues in the teaching of grammar: An SLA perspective', *TESOL Quarterly*, 40(1): 83–107.

Ellis, R., Basturkmen, H. and Loewen, S. (2002) 'Learner uptake in communicative ESL lessons', *Language Learning*, 51(2): 281–318.

Ellis, R. and Barkhuizen, G. (2005) *Analyzing Learner Language*, Oxford, UK: Oxford University Press.
Farr, F. and Riordan, E. (2015) 'Tracing the reflective practice of student teachers in online modes', *ReCALL*, 27(1): 104–128.
Groot, P.J.M. (2000) 'Computer assisted second language vocabulary acquisition', *Language Learning & Technology*, 4(1): 60–81.
Gu, Y. (2003) 'Vocabulary learning in a second language: person, task, context and strategies', *TESL-EJ*, 7(2), available: http://www-writing.berkeley.edu/TESL-EJ/ej26/a4.html (accessed 10 Dec 2013).
Herring, S.C. (2007) 'A faceted classification scheme for computer-mediated discourse', *Language@Internet*, 4, article 1, available: http://www.languageatinternet.de/articles/2007/761 (accessed 17 Jan 2014).
Horst, M., Cobb, T. and Nicolae, I. (2005) 'Expanding academic vocabulary with an interactive on-line database', *Language Learning & Technology*, 9: 90–110.
Hulstijn, J.H. (2001) 'Intentional and incidental second language vocabulary learning: A reappraisal of elaboration, rehearsal and automaticity', in P. Robinson (ed), *Cognition and Second Language Instruction*, Cambridge: Cambridge University Press: 258–286.
Hulstijn, J.H. (2003) 'Incidental learning and intentional learning', in J. Doughty and M.L. Long (eds), *The Handbook of Second Language Acquisition*, Oxford: Blackwell Publishing Ltd.: 349–381.
Jung, U.O.H. (2005) 'CALL: Past, present and future – A bibliometric approach', *ReCALL*, 17(1): 4–17.
Kern, R. (2006) 'Perspectives on technology in learning and teaching languages', *TESOL Quarterly*, 40(1): 183–210.
Kim, D. and Gilman, D.A. (2008) 'Effects of text, audio, and graphic aids in multimedia instruction for vocabulary learning', *Educational Technology & Society*, 11(3): 114–126.
Kramsch, C. (2000) 'Second language acquisition, applied linguistics, and the teaching of foreign languages' *The Modern Language Journal*, 84: 311–326.
Larsen-Freeman, D. (1991) 'Teaching grammar', in M. Celce-Murcia (ed), *Teaching English as a Second or Foreign Language*, New York, NY: Newbury House: 279–296.
Laufer, B. and Hill, M. (2000) 'What lexical information do L2 learners select in a CALL dictionary and how does it affect word retention?', *Language Learning & Technology*, 3(2): 58–76.
Lewis, M. (1993) *The Lexical Approach*, Hove, UK: LTP.
Li, L. (2008) 'EFL teachers' beliefs about ICT integration in Chinese secondary schools', Unpublished doctoral thesis, Queen's University, Belfast.
Li, L. (2014) 'Understanding language teachers' practice with educational technology: A case from China', *System*, 46(1): 105–119.
Li, L. (2015) 'What's the use of technology? Insights from EFL classrooms in Chinese secondary schools', in C. Jenks and P. Seedhouse (eds), *International Perspectives on ELT Classroom Interaction*, Basingstoke: Palgrave: 168–187.
Li, Z. and Hegelheimer, V. (2013) 'Mobile-assisted grammar exercises: Effects on self-editing in L2 writing', *Language Learning & Technology*, 17(3): 135–156.
Liu, D. and Jiang, P. (2009) 'Using a Corpus-based lexicogrammatical approach to grammar instruction in EFL and ESL contexts', *The Modern Language Journal*, 93(1): 61–78.
Mahmoudi, E., Samad, A., & Razak, N. (2012) 'Attitude and students' performance in Computer Assisted English Language Learning (CAELL) for learning vocabulary', *Procedia – Social and Behavioral Sciences*, 66: 489–498.
McCarthy, M.J., O'Keeffe, A. and Walsh, S. (2010) *Vocabulary Matrix*, Boston, MA: Heinle-Cengage ELT.
Nagata, N. (1993) 'Intelligent computer feedback for second language instruction', *The Modern Language Journal*, 77(3): 330–339.
Nakata, T. (2008) 'English vocabulary learning with word lists, word cards and computers: Implications from cognitive psychology research for optimal spaced learning', *RECALL*, 20(1): 3–5.
Nation, I.S.P. (2001) *Learning Vocabulary in Another Language*, Cambridge: Cambridge University Press.
O'Hara, S. and Pritchard, R. (2008) 'Hypermedia authoring as a vehicle for vocabulary development in middle school English as a second language classrooms', *Clearing House: A Journal of Educational Strategies, Issues and Ideas*, 82(2): 60–65.
O'Keeffe, A., McCarthy, M. and Carter, R. (2007) *From Corpus to Classroom: Language Use and Language Teaching*, Cambridge: Cambridge University Press.
Pellettieri, J. (2000) 'Negotiation in cyberspace: The role of chatting in the development of grammatical competence', in M. Warschauer and R. Kern (eds), *Network Based Language Teaching: Concepts and Practice*, Cambridge: Cambridge University Press: 59–86.

Proctor, C.P., Dalton, B. and Grisham, D.L. (2007) 'Scaffolding English language learners and struggling readers in a universal literacy environment with embedded strategy instruction and vocabulary support', *Journal of Literacy Research*, 39(1): 71–93.

Reinders, H. (ed) (2012) *Digital Games in Language Learning and Teaching*, Basingstoke: Palgrave Macmillan.

Schmidt, R. (1990) 'The role of consciousness in second language learning', *Applied Linguistics*, 11: 129–158.

Silverman, R. and Hines, S. (2009) 'The effects of multimedia enhanced instruction on the vocabulary of English-language learners and non-English-language learners in pre-kindergarten through second grade', *Journal of Educational Psychology*, 101(2): 305–314.

Swan, M. and Walter, C. (1984) *The Cambridge English Course 1*, Cambridge: Cambridge University Press.

Thomas, M. and Reinders, H. (eds) (2010) *Task-Based Language Learning and Teaching with Technology*, London; New York, NY: Continuum.

Torlakovic, E. and Deugo, D (2004) 'Application of a CALL system in the acquisition of adverbs in English', *Computer Assisted Language Learning*, 17(2): 203–235.

Tozcu, A. and Coady, J. (2004) 'Successful learning of frequent vocabulary through CALL also benefits reading comprehension and speed', *Computer Assisted Language Learning*, 17(5): 473–495.

Tsou, W., Wang, W. and Li, H.-Y. (2002) 'How computers facilitate English foreign language learners acquire English abstract words', *Computers & Education*, 39(4): 415–428.

Tsutsui, M. (2004) 'Multimedia as a means to enhance feedback', *Computer Assisted Language Learning*, 17(3): 377–402.

Wilkins, D. (1972) *Linguistics in Language Teaching*, London, UK: Arnold.

Wong, L.-H. and Looi C.-K. (2010) 'Vocabulary learning by mobile-assisted authentic content creation and social meaning-making: Two case studies', *Journal of Computer Assisted Learning*, 26(5): 421–433.

Vygotsky, L.S. (1978) *Mind in Society: The Development of Higher Psychological Processes*, Cambridge, MA: Harvard University Press.

Yanguas, Í. (2010) 'Oral computer-mediated interaction between L2 learners: It's about time', *Language Learning & Technology*, 14(3):72–93.

Yoshii, M. and Flaitz, J. (2002) 'Second language incidental vocabulary retention: The effect of text and picture annotation types', *CALICO Journal*, 20(1): 33–58.

Zhang, T., Gao, T., Ring, G. and Zhang, W. (2007) 'Using online discussion forums to assist a traditional English class', *International Journal on E-Learning*, 6(4): 623–643.

# 34
# CALL tools for reading and writing

*Hsien-Chin Liou*

The popularity of new technologies and their related multiliteracies have permeated many areas of language learners' lives. Facebook, smartphones, and tablet PCs serve as communication and relationship building devices in addition to being learning tools. In this chapter, recent common views on how to learn and teach L2 reading and writing through technological enhancement are first discussed. Although using new technologies to enhance L2 literacy skills under traditional theoretical views hold and are still practised by language teachers, sociocultural perspectives and data-driven learning are recently on the rise, bringing up innovative design of various tasks and tools such as interactive online reading, collaborative writing, automatic writing evaluation, corpus-based learning and online glosses. Based on theoretical and pedagogical considerations, this chapter then illustrates how to apply current technologies to teach L2 literacy skills effectively using e-books, weblogs, wikis, Google Docs, corpus and concordance, mobile devices, automatic essay graders and other innovative program design, together with important considerations thereof. Then, CALL empirical evidence for teaching and learning L2 literacy skills is illuminated with a more prominent social practice orientation. Succinctly, both L2 acquisition factors like interaction, feedback and group dynamics in the L2 reading and writing processes, and technological design factors pose challenges when teachers design language tasks to enhance learners' literacy. Future perspectives on how to harness updated technologies to facilitate learning of L2 reading and writing skills and pave the way for learners' workplace competence and lifelong informal learning will be suggested.

Using Internet and computing technologies for the teaching of reading and writing skills has been popular ever since their potentials were explored by researchers and teachers who specialise in computer-assisted language learning (CALL). In this chapter, current applications of CALL for enhancing the literacy skills specifically for second language (L2) learners are addressed with theoretical underpinnings, recent application cases, important considerations for applications, crucial issues from research findings and future perspectives.

## Theoretical underpinnings

Grabe, an established second language reading specialist, draws upon ten instructional implications for traditional reading approaches based on prior reviews of reading theory, research and assessment:

(1) ensure fluency in word recognition; (2) emphasize the learning of vocabulary; (3) activate background knowledge; (4) ensure acquisition of linguistic knowledge and general comprehension; (5) teach recognition of text structures and discourse organization; (6) promote development of strategic readers rather than mechanical application of strategy checklists; (7) build reading fluency and rate; (8) promote extensive reading; (9) develop intrinsic motivation for reading; and (10) contribute to a coherent curriculum for student learning.

*(Grabe 2004: 44)*

When we apply these implications into CALL environments, not every one of these implications harnesses the potentials of computer technologies, nor can the computer instruct every aspect of the reading tasks to learners as well as teachers. However, CALL indeed gains from the second implication of emphasising vocabulary for reading, and the eighth one promoting extensive reading. In contrast, very limited L2 writing theories in traditional contexts have been formulated, and still fewer have been applied in CALL.

On the other hand, two major theoretical influences seem to impact heavily upon recent CALL development for L2 reading and writing: sociocultural theory and data-driven learning. Different from the cognitive camps, language professionals who advocate sociocultural theory (e.g. Warschauer 2005; Adela and Gutiérrez 2006; Compernolle and Williams 2013; Karlström and Lundin 2013) emphasise interaction as an essential element for L2 development. The human mind is mediated by various tools; as psychological tools and cultural artefacts, computers help internalise the target language by moving agency from the intrapersonal phase to the interpersonal phase via technology-mediated communication. The mediation can take place either through interacting with other human beings at a different place and time or with the online content designed in the system beforehand. Such mediated interaction facilitates learners' progress towards more advanced levels of their language proficiency through their 'zone of proximal development' (Vygotsky, 1978; Warschauer 2005: 42). Mainly for vocabulary acquisition and writing in CALL, data-driven learning (Johns 1991), unlike deductive rule-based or pattern-based lexico-grammatical teaching, relies on inductive ways of uptaking regular phenomena in the target language. Data-driven learning could provide L2 learners with prolific example sentences as language models. The most common CALL tool for data-driven learning may be a concordance program, or a concordancer, which, like a search engine, yields output from its input or corpora after the user gives a target word or phrase as the key (see Warren, Chapter 24 this volume). With speech as well as text for input, concordancers ideally can enhance all four language skills; however, given the state of the art and available concordancers being developed, that L2 learning of vocabulary and that of writing are the major two application types. New forms of CALL which apply concordancers or corpus-informed instruction tend to have strong effects because they develop effective teaching tools which encourage or enable deeper or more versatile data-driven learning, which may lead to higher level literacy attainment. Yoon's review (2011) of twelve studies on concordancing activities confirms that concordance use could assist L2 learners' linguistic aspects of writing once proper training is provided. As vocabulary is closely tied to learning of both reading and writing skills, data-driven learning which focuses on vocabulary learning is emphasised.

## Applying technologies for reading and writing

Earlier research indicates that specifically designed computer programs could help students' writing accuracy in their sentence-level production (Liou, Wang and Yeh 1992), even with stand-alone personal computers. As the World Wide Web became accessible to most language classes in the 1990s, web texts could be served as authentic input in order to enhance students' reading and vocabulary performance (Liou 1997). Recent CALL development for reading and writing can be shown from corpus-informed applications (see Part IV of this volume), online glosses, digital or interactive reading (interactive reading and e-book reading), collaborative writing and automatic writing evaluation.

## *Corpus-informed instruction or tools*

As one of the ambitious corpus projects (Liou et al. 2006), CANDLE (Corpus And Natural language processing for Digital Learning of English) developed an innovative web-based environment for English learning with advanced data-driven and statistical approaches (http://candle.cs.nthu.edu.tw). The EFL (English as a foreign language) CANDLE project integrated the expertise of computer scientists and applied linguists and developed various tools and English learning tasks. The project used various corpora, including a Chinese-English parallel corpus (Sinorama) and various natural language processing (NLP) tools to construct effective English learning tasks for intermediate learners with adaptive computational scaffolding. TOTALrecall (http://candle.cs.nthu.edu.tw/totalrecall/totalrecall/ totalrecall.aspx) and TANGO (http://candle.cs.nthu.edu.tw/collocation/webform2.aspx) were two concordance tools for learners derived from this project. Learning tasks included mainly reading (TextGrader; Huang and Liou 2007), intercultural competence (Liaw 2006), writing (Tseng and Liou 2006; Yeh, Liou and Li 2007) and vocabulary (Chan and Liou 2005). The two concordancers developed in CANDLE were mostly applied to the learning of vocabulary or writing because their output sentences provide authentic contextual supports for L2 learners. Liaw (2006) intended to use TOTALrecall as assistance for her learners to acquire more word knowledge for reading comprehension, but it turned out those college students took example sentences as materials for extensive reading. Designed as CALL tutorial modes by incorporating insights from corpus analyses, Tseng and Liou (2006) and Yeh et al. (2007) show teaching of synonymous adjectives and conjunctions online could be effective for college student-writers.

For academic writing specifically, the analysis of the textual or phrasal aspects of abstracts of RAs (research articles in scholarly journals) could be transformed into online teaching materials for EFL graduate students. Hsieh and Liou (2008) extended the results of abstract analysis to the development of online course content for the explicit teaching of abstract writing in the discipline of applied linguistics. Results from the comparison of patterns found in the corpora of fifty abstracts of RAs published in journals and fifty abstracts of papers given at conferences – written by novice, nonnative writers in a learner corpus – formed the core of the online course content, along with principles of L2 writing and CALL task design. A Concordancer for Academic wRitten English (CARE; http://candle.cs.nthu.edu.tw/care) and a synchronous peer review tool were incorporated into a Moodle-based course. The abstract-writing unit was then incorporated into an academic writing course in which the analysis of thirty-five graduate students' writing samples demonstrated some improvement in their writing. The study suggests that corpus-informed online instruction with learner corpus insights can enhance students' academic writing. Similar efforts are also illustrated in another project by Chang and Kuo (2011) within the discipline of computer science. Along this line with more automation efforts, Liou, Yang and Chang (2012) developed an automatic abstract writing system which features hints at the level of functional moves, key words or transitional words as suggestions while students are composing online.

## Online glosses for reading

For L2 or EFL readers, lack of enough vocabulary is often a major issue of reading difficulties. Dictionary use or application of word knowledge while reading has been investigated by some researchers (Liou 2000). Online glossary help has thus been a repeated topic for CALL when researchers desire to address learners' reading problems. The effects of online glosses as scaffolding were investigated concerning whether the gloss language is L1 or L2, and whether the gloss media include text only or multimodal items (audio, graphics or others). Taylor (2013: 75) summarises the benefits of online glosses with three points: '(1) the learners' attention is fully brought to the glossed item with CALL glossing, (2) it is faster and more flexible and (3) it gives the learner more control over the reading process'. Current popular forms of online glosses (or annotations) like Microsoft Office Translator show additional information when the user hovers over the target term with the cursor or clicks on it.

## Digital or interactive reading

Popular digital reading takes the form of e-book reading or interactive reading among participants. E-books and portable digital reading devices such as iPads, Kindles, or smartphone devices make online extensive reading accessible anytime and anywhere as L2 readers desire. Termed as interactive reading, Murphy (2010) through his online task design devised learner interaction through computer-mediated communication to go with a web-based multiple-choice reading comprehension exercise. Students in remote locations work in pairs, receive different reading feedback and interact with members in order to enhance text comprehension.

## Collaborative writing

Also termed computer supported collaborative writing (CSCW, cf. Grosbois, Chapter 19 this volume), collaborative work for L2 writing has been much encouraged due to the widespread use of Internet communication and the influence of the sociocultural theory. Wikis, weblogs, Moodle, Google Docs, Facebook and so on all have been applied to the design of collaborative writing tasks. The tasks can take the form of brainstorming for prewriting preparation, co-construction of one composition among pairs or group members, and peer reviews for postwriting textual improvement. Through collaboration, joint responsibility over the creation of the essays means that L2 students may be more receptive to peer suggestions and giving feedback reciprocally, an opportunity missed when they write alone. Not merely a cognitive act, collaborative writing encourages social interaction which is constructive to students' preparation for the future workplace, where they may be required to work together.

## Automated writing evaluation

Earlier efforts for computer programmes to provide assessment and feedback as writing evaluation were demonstrated in the development of grammar checking (Liou 1991). Recently, corpora and advanced computation algorithms enable more sophisticated systems to be accessible to language students such as MY Access![1] or Criterion.[2] Automated writing evaluation (AWE) software is designed to provide instant computer-generated scores for a submitted essay along with diagnostic feedback. Such software provides more writing practice for L2 learners and saves human graders' or teachers' time in rating and correcting errors in student essays.

However, the precision of AWE systems can vary with their use of corpora and processing capacities in the design against different detection levels of spelling, word form, sentence structure or organisation. They remain much less precise when content of the student writing is concerned, as current AWE systems are not designed to comprehend the text. Depending on their corpora and processing capacities, current AWE systems would generate more or less linguistic errors or false alarms, and their assessment of student text quality may fluctuate at least with topic, genre or rhetorical mode differences (see Shermis and Burstein 2013 and Chapelle, Cotos and Lee 2015 for comprehensive updated overviews).

## Important considerations

Echoing courseware design in Motteram's chapter (Chapter 6 this volume) dealing with online materials, the nature of tools or the devices, and principles of applications are emphasised when we consider how to apply technologies for L2 reading and writing in the classroom, be it traditional or online. To illustrate through different glossing systems as online materials, after a series of literature reviews Taylor (2013) offers suggestions for using online glosses effectively for language instruction. He suggests that an online first language (L1) glossed text can be adopted to enhance students' motivational and comprehension needs as well as acquiring lexical items used in context. However, if the instructional objective is: 'to provide the learner with the skill of deriving meaning from context, perhaps providing less CALL L1 glosses may be a more logical option, especially [for] more advanced learners' (Taylor 2013: 75). The match between kinds of learning materials and instructional goals has always guided CALL applications.

Online glosses, corpus tools, and mobile or handheld devices provide ever more exciting facilities for learning and teaching a second or foreign language in the field of CALL. To apply these devices to teaching L2 reading and writing, the nature of online tools or the devices themselves demonstrate a wide range of varieties and thus bring distinct learning effects. For instance, two common computer-mediated communication tools, asynchronous Google Docs and synchronous Google Chat are quite different concerning the affordances they provide for peer reviews in writing classes. Pai and Liou (2009) found that their learners preferred commenting in Google Docs since it permitted delayed response, which allowed them to think more critically about what to comment on. In addition, feedback generated from asynchronous comments versus synchronous chats did not seem to cause much difference on subsequent revision changes. Web-based history tracking provided by wikis promises a full record of how learners revise their essays through different stages in time and in space (if the wiki document is co-edited or constructed by more than one learner). By comparing the composing processes and products between individual writing and collaborative writing, Liou and Lee (2011) found that wiki-based collaborative writing tasks have offered students good opportunities to learn from each other and students believe such collaborative activities improved their writing. Compared with essays produced by individuals, the essays written by pairs tended to be longer and more accurate. Further, students working in pairs tended to spend much more time making revisions due to their selected collaborative pattern and a tendency to make more text-based changes. Meanwhile, it seems that students involved in pair work enjoyed and perhaps benefitted from such a collaborative process so they would desire to invest their time. The results of the comparison of collaboratively and individually written texts indicate that teachers who want to implement collaborative writing do not worry too much about the quality of collaboratively written texts. If students can engage in constant negotiation and regard such a collaborative task positively, they produce quality texts which meet teachers' writing objectives. Students' time allocation, participation and reflections on the learning experience all indicate that with the assistance of wikis, the collaborative writing task can be implemented successfully as an after-class assignment. At the same time, it affords students great opportunities to learn from each other not only concerning writing skills but also collaborative skills during the process.

Other than the roles played by materials and tools, principles of CALL applications and context of their use together are probably of paramount importance in determining the learning effects. Technological applications for language teaching is never neutral, as agents of learners and the teacher can make each learning context which interacts closely with CALL applications unique. Yoon (2008) and Chen and Cheng (2008) both emphasise the context of technology use interacting with learners' (and teachers') individual willingness and success in using specific technologies. However, language teachers play an essential role in making learning gains of CALL ensured and visible. For instance, in a blog-enhanced peer review project for EFL college students, it was found that the activities stimulated the learners' interest in improving their writing (Liou and Peng 2009): the students made more revision-oriented comments and had more success in revising their compositions. Thus, blogs could serve as a suitable platform for EFL writing instruction concerning giving opportunities for interaction. Yet, not all of the students felt confident about providing useful peer feedback. They argue that teacher training on how to guide students to give constructive feedback properly is essential to make computer-mediated peer review effective.

As part of the contextual factors in CALL implementation, teachers' CALL literacy, goals of instruction and learner characteristics may overwrite the capacity of a very powerful technological innovation. Chen and Cheng (2008) adopted a naturalistic classroom-based approach to explore the interaction between how an AWE program, MY Access!, was implemented differently in three EFL college writing classes. They aimed to understand students' perceptions on the effectiveness of using the automatic writing evaluation system in improving writing. Different outcomes were yielded from the three contexts where the teachers understood AWE distinctly as a potentially formative or summative evaluation tool: it was perceived more favourably when the program was used to facilitate students' early drafting, compared with giving a final grade for the completed student essay, and the revising process was followed by human feedback from both the teacher and peers during the later process. This study also reveals that without a teacher's assistance, the autonomous use of AWE could cause frustration to students and thus limit their learning of writing. With these inherent limitations, language teachers need to be critically aware that the adoption and implementation of AWE in their own classes require sound pedagogical designs and considerations for the learning of writing. Similarly, Lee, Cheung, Wong and Lee (2013) confirmed the aforementioned principle of application by giving both feedback from the AWE system and the teacher. They ran a writing workshop and adopted an AWE system under the design of both the system feedback and teacher feedback (i.e. blending the two learning modes). They suggest future needs to improve the system feedback on paragraph coherence, their workshop design and grading criteria. Some CALL tools applied in the same context may still yield different learning outcomes given learner characteristics. In a CALL peer review activity, Yang and Meng (2013) found that the less proficient students improved more during text revision than the more proficient students did after their online feedback training on error correction. The weaker students were better able to detect and correct both local errors (i.e. grammatical) and global errors (i.e. text development, organisation and style) in their own and peers' texts. Their texts improved as a result of receiving immediate feedback and having the opportunity to explicitly observe how their more proficient peers provided corrections and useful suggestions to peers and clarified writing problems for text improvement. The more proficient students did not trust their peers' suggestions as much and made corrections mainly on local errors.

In a word, CALL teachers, like other language teachers, need to play skilfully the balancing game of weighing tools, materials and contextual factors (instructional goal, teacher's preparation, learners' willingness to use the technology, etc.), when they adopt the technologies into their classroom of reading and writing, and become critically aware of how each element interacts with another in order to achieve instructional effectiveness.

## Important issues from research

In terms of issues from research-based studies on reading and writing in CALL, we need to be aware of three crucial dimensions, given the blooming of recent related research and ever-changing technological innovations: understanding the past literature through a longer span of observation of existing studies; designing a curriculum of both textual and multimodal expressions; and attending to how our L2 learners accommodate technologies in their daily lives as social practice. Access to literature synthesis or quantitative meta-analysis provides systematic examination on specific CALL topics where meta-analysis pools quantifiable learning gains across a range of quasi- or true experimental studies (Liou and Lin forthcoming). As one of the scholars who took a long-term interest in reviewing how online glosses are applied, Taylor (2013) has provided several comprehensive reviews using the method of quantitative meta-analyses. In 2006, Taylor analysed eighteen studies that compared the efficiency of traditional first language (L1) glosses with that of electronic L1 glosses in L2 reading. He concludes that providing learners with electronic glosses (e-glosses) had a large effect on understanding more text ($d = 1.09$, where $d$ is effect size) than those learners with paper-based glossing aids. With different numbers of studies, his meta-analytical studies consistently confirmed that e-glosses were better (Taylor 2009, 2013). Similarly but with a focus on differential gains for reading or vocabulary learning, Abraham (2008) surveyed eleven experimental studies in order to compare the effects of L2 learners' access to computer-mediated glosses (L1, or L1 and L2 together) to those without such access. The results showed that computer-mediated glosses had an overall medium effect ($m = 0.73$, another effect size measure) on their reading comprehension and a large positive effect ($m = 1.40$) on incidental vocabulary learning. That is, e-glosses demonstrated a larger learning effect on learning of vocabulary than of reading. Yun (2011) considered ten primary studies with thirty-five weighted mean effect sizes (overall, $d = 0.37$), by examining specific variables such as modes of glosses, test type, and language proficiency. Yun found that multiple hypertext glosses were more likely to yield an influence on beginning learners' L2 vocabulary acquisition. To sum up, a learner's learning background, type of skill or knowledge (reading or vocabulary), and type of e-glosses (in L1 or L2, textual or multimodal) can possibly impact on the final language learning gains.

With the widespread use of the Internet and multimedia, to be able to read and write in L2 properly requires not only technical mastery and textual literacy but also a new kind of multimodal expression. Hafner explains that multimodal expression is:

> a higher level of conceptual mastery, understanding how to engage in digital practices, which often involves using language in combination with other semiotic resources for communication, entering into relationships with new kinds of audiences, constructing new kinds of identities, and participating in new kinds of online spaces.
>
> *(Hafner 2013: 830)*

Evidently, the remix culture is here with digital natives, where remix is defined as creating 'new cultural artefacts by combining the digital texts of others available on the Internet (e.g. music, movies, news items, videos) in new and unexpected ways' (Hafner 2013: 831). Design is needed for learners to be able to express themselves via remix, and for language teachers to transform their curriculum. In a multimodal blogging project, Liou (2011) recruited twenty-five undergraduate students majoring in English from an EFL writing course. Various blog assignments were designed which encouraged peer review, collaborative writing and incorporation of multimedia. A case study approach with mixed quantitative and qualitative methods was applied. An evaluation questionnaire was designed to obtain the participants' perceptions on technology integration and task design. Specific cases of eight participants' online works were examined in detail to investigate their use of multimodal texts on the blog with semiotic awareness through transduction and transformation (Kress 2003, 2005). The experience of these EFL multimodal authors was found to be closely accompanied by their semiotic awareness, so they demonstrated wide blogging use with pictures and other media, besides text, to produce their writing for expressing messages to readers or viewers. Such awareness could be inherently equipped before they took the current writing course or through experimenting with various blogging assignments in this course. Synaesthesia, defined as the emergent creation of qualitatively new forms of meaning as a result of 'shifting' ideas across semiotic modes (Kress 2003: 36), is evident in various cases in this study. The roles peers played as commentators and contributors in collaborative writing pointed to beneficial learning. Blogging was useful in terms of self-reflections on their writing performance, motivating in a writing class, and facilitative when combined with peer reviews and multimodal representations (for graduate-level multimodal textual analyses, see Rowley-Jolivet 2012).

Digital literacy as a 21st-century skill has a great influence on not only how our learners acquire L2 reading and writing skills, but also on how they acquire digital literacy outside of the classroom in their informal learning (cf. Dudeney and Hockley, Chapter 8 this volume). Radical changes in the past decade due to technological advances on the Internet have had a tremendous impact on what people do with texts and their social practice using semiotic means. Barton and Potts (2013: 817) advocate the need for researchers to frame some central issues on language and language teaching – more often mediated by Internet technologies nowadays – such as 'access; accommodation, mediation, and negotiation; and linkages and expansion'. Larger social relations for L2 learners than fan fiction are required for socialisation in order to acquire the target literacy skills, for example access to professional communities. In other words, digital participation necessitates negotiation in order for learners to be accommodated into the target community for socialisation. To provide support for L2 learners with privileged practices in digital realms, 'pedagogical designs, co-presence of learners with a common first language, and large social relations' may be recommended as well (Barton and Potts 2013: 818). Further, Barton and Potts endorse the social practice orientation which incorporates knowledge of learners' practice in order to make informed classroom decisions about how and what to teach, at the same time building on what learners are already doing.

## Looking into the future

CALL teachers are continually looking for new technological options to enhance their teaching; often, they combine more than one tool or platform. Similarly, learners by themselves acquire the literacy of playing with several gadgets, or are taught to do so by teachers or peers in both the classroom and outside. Naturally, L2 learners, whether digital natives or immigrants, acquire multiliteracies in order to succeed or survive in school as well as in their future workplaces.

## Tool flexibility and combination

CALL designers or courseware developers face ever more exciting development options and challenging tasks to realise tools for future teachers and learners. To illustrate for L2 reading issues, earlier by Cobb (2007) and Huang and Liou (2007), moderate successes were achieved:

> by tackling two problems of natural texts: one is that new words are not naturally recycled often enough to make them memorable to learners; the other is that new words tend to occur in contexts that are difficult to understand.
>
> *(Horst 2007: 2)*

Cobb took a text modification approach by combining the use of a concordancer. Huang and Liou provided a solution for the insufficient recycling of new words in natural texts and the high unknown word densities through statistical corpus computation with word lists. More techniques in natural language processing and corpus computation are needed to advance research in this area. In terms of tool combination by users, it is commonly observed that our learners as digital natives often use various search engines such as Google to look for information they need, including terms or words they do not understand in the target language. Designers of concordancers advocate their usefulness for language learning. Inevitably, learners would apply either the new concordancer alone or the program plus other familiar search engines. Geluso (2013) tested the hypothesis that native speakers of English perceive learner-generated phrases to be more natural after nonnative learners have searched the phrases on Google and modified them in light of the frequency of search results. Nonnative speakers were found to perceive phrases that generated more results in Google searches to be more natural. In another study by Yeh, Liou and Yu (2007), MY Access! and a concordancer (TOTALrecall) were used together to help students' writing revision. In the future, more available tool options will provide more exciting facilities but also more challenges for CALL teachers and researchers to understand how the tool combination makes a difference on learning of reading and writing, and meanwhile how each of the tools respectively plays its role in the complex context.

## Informal versus formal learning

To find authentic discourse, to create authentic interactions, and to extend the audience for students are core triggers for the development of future L2 reading and writing skills. Meanwhile, to go beyond formal learning is a corollary for our learners who use technologies both inside and outside of the classroom; informal learning outside of the formal instruction provides opportunistic educational encounters when students are surfing on the Internet. With handheld devices increasingly available and affordable to learners of different levels worldwide, findings of a survey on informal learning for mobile users (Clough et al. 2013) indicate that different usage patterns revealed in various learner adaptations point to a better fit to their needs. Cox (2013: 85) advocates new strategies to 'take account of the eclectic nature of e-learning and the growing influence of informal learning'. To devise instructional strategies connecting formal and informal learning experiences is also recommended (Lai, Khaddage and Knezek 2013). Informal CALL (outside of the classroom or in the workplace) would become a challenging context for researchers to identify how and why lifelong learning of reading and writing takes place.

*Importance of multiliteracies*

Language teachers will soon tackle not only textual literacy for classroom learners, but also multiliteracies and multimodal expressions in order to prepare them for skills used in the next-generation workplace. The mastery of traditional literacy skills mainly using texts is needed, but a heavy demand may be placed on how our learners can command other media for their semiotic resources. In other words, design is indispensable for learners to be able to express themselves via remix, as well as for language teachers to transform their curriculum.

To conclude, this chapter has highlighted the more important current applications of technologies for L2 reading and writing. It has provided important considerations for L2 teachers to implement those applications in language instruction, and has raised crucial issues from research studies. In the future, both language teachers and learners will face ever more exciting innovative technological facilities as well as a more demanding workplace which requires new literacies, where reading and writing with technology plays a key role. All these challenges await in the field of CALL research.

## Acknowledgements

The chapter is partially funded by several National Science Council projects (NSC92–2524-S007–002, 99–2410-H035–059-MY3, 100–2511-S-007–005-MY3 and 102–2410-H-035–051-MY3). I would like to express my gratitude to a long-term collaborating colleague, Professor Jason S. Chang, and several colleagues both at National Tsing Hua University and at Feng Chia University, many research assistants, and participating students who have inspired this chapter and provided their kind help.

## Further reading

Chang, C.K. and Hsu, C.K. (2011) 'A mobile-assisted synchronously collaborative translation–annotation system for English as a foreign language (EFL) reading comprehension', *Computer Assisted Language Learning*, 24(2): 155–180.
   On the application of a mobile device concerning the differences of group sizes, Chang and Hsu found that the reading comprehension of junior college students who were grouped into twos, threes, and fours had significantly higher levels of comprehension than individual students, but those grouped into fives did not. Most of their students agreed that the system was easy to use and perceived the system positively.

Li, M. and Zhu, W. (2013) 'Patterns of computer-mediated interaction in small writing groups using wikis', *Computer Assisted Language Learning*, 26(1): 61–82.
   Influenced by the sociocultural theory and the view of 'collective scaffolding', Li and Zhu examined three collaborative writing groups of Chinese college students and, based on the wiki history data, found three patterns: 'collectively contributing/mutually supportive, authoritative/responsive, and dominant/withdrawn ... in terms of equality and mutuality' (p. 61). Students' perceptions supported the collectively contributing pattern concerning the learning opportunities provided.

Rowley-Jolivet, E. (2012) 'Oralising text slides in scientific conference presentations: A multimodal corpus analysis', in A. Boulton, S. Carter-Thomas and E. Rowley-Jolivet (eds), *Corpus-Informed Research and Learning in ESP Issues and Applications*, Amsterdam, Netherlands: John Benjamins Publishing Company: 137–165.
   Rowley-Jolivet innovatively drew upon oral data which came from spoken commentaries in scientific conference presentations (on video recording) and textual information on slides. Her analysis focused on grammar metaphor and three kinds of meta-functions: textual, ideational and interpersonal. Then, these language features of text slides and their equivalent spoken commentary in scientific conference presentations were compared and discussed.

## Notes

1 MY Access! Vantage Learning (https://www.myaccess.com/myaccess/do/log): A web-based writing system that returns feedback and a grade on submitted essays.
2 ETS Criterion Online Writing Evaluation Service (http://www.ets.org/criterion): A web-based instructor-led writing tool that helps students write and revise their essays. It gives them immediate diagnostic feedback and opportunities to practise writing on their own.

## References

Abraham, L.B. (2008) 'Computer-mediated glosses in second language reading comprehension and vocabulary learning: A meta-analysis', *Computer Assisted Language Learning*, 21(3): 199–226.
Adela, G.A. and Gutiérrez, G. (2006) 'Sociocultural theory and its application to CALL: A study of the computer and its relevance as a mediational tool in the process of collaborative activity', *ReCALL*, 18(2): 230–251.
Barton, D. and Potts, D. (2013) 'Language learning online as a social practice', *TESOL Quarterly*, 47(4): 815–820.
Chan, T.P. and Liou, H.C. (2005) 'Effects of web-based concordancing instruction on EFL students' learning of verb-noun collocations', *Computer Assisted Language Learning*, 18(3): 231–250.
Chang, C.F. and Kuo, C.H. (2011) 'A corpus-based approach to online materials *development* for writing research articles', *English for Specific Purposes*, 30(3): 222–234.
Chapelle, C.A., Cotos, E. and Lee, J. (2015) 'Validity arguments for diagnostic *assessment* using automated writing evaluation', *Language Testing*, OnlineFirst, Jan. 27.
Chen, C.E. and Cheng, W.E. (2008) 'Beyond the design of automated writing evaluation: pedagogical practices and perceived learning effectiveness in EFL writing classes', *Language Learning and Technology*, 12(2): 94–112.
Clough, G., Jones, A.C., McAndrew, J.P. and Scanlon, E. (2013) 'Informal learning with PDA and smartphones', *Journal of Computer Assisted Learning*, 24(5): 359–371.
Cobb, T. (2007) 'Computing the vocabulary demand of L2 reading', *Language Learning and Technology*, 11(3): 2–3.
Compernolle, R.A. and Williams, L. (2013) 'Sociocultural theory and second language pedagogy: Editorial', *Language Teaching Research*, 17(3): 277–281.
Cox, M.J. (2013) 'Formal to informal learning with IT: Research challenges and issues for e-learning', *Journal of Computer Assisted Learning*, 29(1): 85–105.
Geluso, J. (2013) 'Phraseology and frequency of occurrence on the web: native speakers' perceptions of Google-informed second language writing', *Computer Assisted Language Learning*, 26(2): 144–157.
Grabe, W. (2004) 'Research on teaching reading', *Annual Review of Applied Linguistics*, 24: 44–69.
Hafner, C.A. (2013) 'Digital composition in a second or foreign language', *TESOL Quarterly*, 47(4): 830–834.
Horst, M. (2007) 'From the special issue editor', *Language Learning and Technology*, 11(3): 2–3.
Hsieh, W.M. and Liou, H.C. (2008) 'A case study of corpus-informed online academic writing for EFL graduate students', *CALICO Journal*, 26(1): 28–47.
Huang, H.T. and Liou, H.C. (2007) 'Vocabulary learning in an automated graded reading program', *Language Learning & Technology*, 11(3): 64–82.
Johns, T. (1991) 'Should you be persuaded: Two examples of data-driven learning', in T. Johns and P. King (eds), Classroom Concordancing. *English Language Research Journal*, 4: 1–16.
Karlström, P. and Lundin, E. (2013) 'CALL in the zone of proximal development: Novelty effects and teacher guidance', *Computer Assisted Language Learning*, 26(5): 412–429.
Kress, G. (2003) *Literacy in the New Media Age*, London, UK: Routledge.
Kress, G. (2005) 'Gains and losses: New forms of texts, knowledge, and learning', *Computers and Composition*, 22: 5–22.
Lai, K.W., Khaddage, F. and Knezek, G. (2013) 'Blending student technology experiences in formal and informal learning', *Journal of Computer Assisted Learning*, 29(5): 414–425.
Lee, C., Cheung, W.K., Wong, K.C. and Lee, F.S. (2013) 'Immediate web-based essay critiquing system feedback and teacher follow-up feedback on young second language learners' writings: An experimental study in a Hong Kong secondary school', *Computer Assisted Language Learning*, 26(1): 39–60.

Liaw, M.L. (2006) 'E-learning and the development of intercultural competence', *Language Learning and Technology*, 10(3): 49–64.
Liou, H.C. (1991) 'Development of an English grammar checker: A progress report', *CALICO Journal*, 9(1): 57–70.
Liou, H.C. (1997) 'The impact of WWW texts on EFL learning', *Computer Assisted Language Learning*, 10(5): 455–478.
Liou, H.C. (2000) 'The electronic bilingual dictionary as a reading aid to EFL learners: Research findings and implications', *Computer Assisted Language Learning*, 13(4–5): 67–76.
Liou, H.C. (2011) 'Blogging, collaborative writing, and multimodal literacy in an EFL context', in M. Levy, et al. (eds), *WorldCALL: International Perspectives on Computer Assisted Language Learning*, New York, NY: Routledge: 3–18.
Liou, H.C., Chang, J.S., Chen, H.J., Lin, C.C., Liaw, M.L., Gao, Z.M., et al. (2006) 'Corpora processing and computational scaffolding for an innovative web-based English learning environment: The CANDLE project', *CALICO Journal*, 24(1): 77–95.
Liou, H.C. and Lee, S.L. (2011) 'How wiki-based writing influences college students' collaborative and individual composing products, processes, and learners' perceptions', *International Journal of Computer Assisted Language Learning and Teaching*, 1(1): 45–61.
Liou, H.C. and Lin, H.F. (forthcoming). 'A survey of CALL meta-analyses and transparency analysis' in Carol A. Chapelle and Shannon Sauro (eds), *The Handbook of Technology in Second Language Teaching and Learning*, Malden, MA: Wiley-Blackwell.
Liou, H.C. and Peng, C.Y. (2009) 'Training effects on computer-mediated peer review', *System*, 37(3): 514–525.
Liou, H.C., Wang, S.H. and Yeh, Y. (1992) 'Can grammatical CALL help EFL writing instruction?', *CALICO Journal*, 10(1): 23–44.
Liou, H.C., Yang, P.C. and Chang, J.S. (2012) 'Language supports for journal abstract writing across disciplines', *Journal of Computer Assisted Learning*, 28(4): 322–335.
Murphy, P. (2010) 'Web-based collaborative reading exercises for learners in remote locations: The effects of computer-mediated feedback and interaction via computer-mediated communication', *ReCALL*, 22(2): 112–134.
Pai, C.W. and Liou, H.C. 'Comparison of synchronous and asynchronous computer-mediated peer reviews of EFL college students', Paper presented at CALICO 2009, Arizona State University, March 2009.
Rowley-Jolivet, E. (2012) 'Oralising text slides in scientific conference presentations: A multimodal corpus analysis', in A. Boulton, S. Carter-Thomas and E. Rowley-Jolivet (eds), *Corpus-Informed Research and Learning in ESP Issues and Applications*, Amsterdam: John Benjamins Publishing Company: 137–165.
Shermis, M.D. and Burstein, J. (eds) (2013) *Handbook of Automated Essay Evaluation: Current Applications and New Directions*, New York, NY: Routledge.
Taylor, A.M. (2006) 'The effects of CALL versus traditional L1 glosses on L2 reading comprehension', *CALICO Journal*, 23(2): 309–318.
Taylor, A.M. (2009) 'CALL-based versus paper-based glosses: Is there a difference in reading comprehension?', *CALICO Journal*, 27(1): 147–160.
Taylor, A.M. (2013) 'CALL versus paper: In which context are L1 glosses more effective?', *CALICO Journal*, 30(1): 63–81.
Tseng, Y.C. and Liou, H.C. (2006) 'The effects of online conjunction materials on college EFL students' writing', *System*, 34(2): 270–283.
Vygotsky, L.S. (1978) *Mind in Society: The Development of Higher Psychological Processes*, Cambridge, MA: Harvard University Press.
Warschauer, M. (2005) 'Sociocultural perspectives on CALL', in J. Egbert and G.M. Petrie (eds), *CALL Research Perspectives*, Mahwah, NJ: Lawrence Erlbaum: 41–51.
Yang, Y.F. and Meng, W.T. (2013) 'The effects of online feedback training on students' text revision', *Language Learning and Technology*, 17(2): 220–238.
Yeh, Y., Liou, H.C. and Li, Y. (2007) 'Online synonym materials and concordancing for EFL college writing', *Computer Assisted Language Learning*, 20(2): 131–152.
Yeh, Y., Liou, H.C. and Yu, Y.T. (2007), 'The influence of computerized feedback and bilingual concordancing on EFL students' writing', *English Teaching and Learning*, 31(1): 117–160.

Yoon, H. (2008) 'More than a linguistic reference: The influence of corpus technology on L2 academic writing', *Language Learning and Technology*, 12(2): 31–48.

Yoon, H. (2011) 'Concordancing in L2 writing class: An overview of research and issues', *Journal of English for Academic Purpose*, 10: 130–139.

Yun, J. (2011) 'The effects of hypertext glosses on L2 vocabulary acquisition: A meta-analysis', *Computer Assisted Language Learning*, 24(1): 39–58.

# 35
# CALL tools for listening and speaking

*Úna Clancy and Liam Murray*

According to the law of causality, nothing happens in isolation. This is particularly perceptible when it comes to examining CALL and its impact on the TESOL classroom. In order to appreciate the rise of CALL as a pedagogical tool, with particular reference to its application to teaching listening and speaking skills, it is pragmatic to look at some of the fundamental – and occasionally overlooked – contributing factors which so deftly shaped its beginnings. As such, a number of key historical and social circumstances stand out and will be discussed, specifically in relation to the advent of digital acoustics and the long-term use of audio in language pedagogy. The primary focus of this chapter will be on the sounds of English; both listening and speaking arise together in natural communication and teaching contexts through their shared medium: sound. As listening and speaking skills are rarely employed in isolation, often used and therefore taught in tandem, they will be regarded here as integrated skills. The CALL tools selected for discussion are primarily those aimed at oral/aural integrated skills instruction. This chapter seeks to explore CALL resources which have the potential to provide authentic and sociolinguistically relevant learning opportunities for those who wish to communicate using the medium of global conversation: the English language.

## Changing soundscapes: Digital acoustics and TESOL

### The evolution of recorded sound

The sound of a voice singing *Au clair de la lune*, recorded by the little-known Édouard-Léon Scott de Martinville in 1860, is the earliest known recording of a human voice (Rosen 2008). 'The recordings were not intended for listening; the idea of audio playback had not been conceived' (ibid.). Although the recording device, the phonautograph, was relatively limited – capable only of recording sound waves *visually* (the name itself means 'to write speech') – it marks the beginning of an acoustic revolution brought about through the partnership of machine and sound.

This revolution, fuelled by the creative and innovative technological advances of the following century (e.g. the gramophone and vinyl records) was further intensified by the landmark invention of magnetic tape in 1928. This invention was the genesis of the subsequent development of a state-of-the-art recording process that converted sound signals, by way of a microphone, into electrical impulses and recorded them analogously along the tape, introducing for the first time the playback function.

Concurrently, the American engineer Dolby was developing an all-important noise reduction system, which would bring a jump in recording quality and audio fidelity. It was an improvement which arguably contributed to the worldwide commercial success of the tape cassette as a medium. It wasn't long before Philips released the first commercial compact cassette in 1964. Soon after, Sony launched the Walkman and so began a radical change in the listening habits of the world: recorded sound was now accessible and mobile.

## Recorded audio and foreign language learning

The new tape recording techniques, the introduction of Dolby's eponymous noise reduction system, and the subsequent commercialisation of the cassette not only transformed the music and film industries, but by causality the language learning environment of the time. 'The coincidental advent of the tape recorder created a fortuitous juncture of technology and pedagogy' (Stack 1971: 3). Up until this point the only way one could hear a certain language being spoken was to communicate in real time with a native/expert speaker (either face-to-face or by radio or telephone), or indeed make the journey to the place in which the target language was in use. Improvements in audio technology swiftly redefined these parameters, as evidenced by the rapid growth of foreign language laboratories throughout the sixties and seventies. 'Audio has face validity in foreign language instruction simply because much of language use is oral/aural' (Roby 2004: 529).

Tape cassettes were relatively cheap, and cassette players were smaller and lighter than the reel tape equipment that preceded them. Tape players also had the additional advantage of the playback function, allowing for learners to replay tape segments with relative ease. According to Osada (2004: 63), one of the biggest obstacles facing learners who listen in real time is that 'before we can sort out what we just heard, the speech disappears. What is worse, we cannot get the speech repeated'. Recorded audio and the playback function would neatly sidestep this problem and go on to become a powerful tool in easing the heavy cognitive load reported in the L2 listening process.

Hocking, one of the early champions of the pedagogical value of audio use in language teaching, contended that: 'sound brings language to life, and life to language' (in Huebener 1965: 140). Technology had introduced a robust way of bringing sound to life by way of a medium other than a live speaker. For the first time in history, audio could be manipulated as a *physical entity*: sound could now be saved, copied, edited, slowed down, speeded up, played back and so forth. This new technology afforded language learners the opportunity to hear accurate language models that 'never suffered fatigue' (Roby 2004: 530). It is a fact that can be deemed pivotal to the way foreign language listening and speaking skills were subsequently taught, learned and delivered.

One could say that the timing was particularly well-suited for the corresponding emergence of an audio-lingual method of language learning using tape-based systems. This pedagogical development had as much to do with the audio engineers who developed the magnetic tape as it did with those who were, at that time, advocating behaviourist theories of language learning. Arguably, this method could not have emerged were it not for the catalytic developments in acoustic transmissions that were revolutionising the day-to-day listening habits around the world. Nothing happens in isolation: both pedagogical theory and technology were developing in tandem, a symbiosis which continues to gain traction.

## From analogue to digital

In 2008 the haunting notes of a long since deceased individual singing *Au clair de la lune* were heard for the first time since their original recording. This was made possible thanks to the technological advances made in the interim, which allowed for the sound image, the phonautogram, to be 'converted from squiggles on paper to sound' (Rosen 2008). Nearly 150 years after the event, the sounds were extracted using high-resolution digital scans and optical imaging to capture the patterns of undulating lines containing the original sound data. These were then decoded and separated into sixteen tracks and compressed into a single corresponding digital audio file (see Scott de Martinville 1860).

The intriguing journey of this sound snippet serves as a succinct example highlighting the full extent of the technological advances in audio that have been made in little more than a century and a half. Listening to the sound of the old folk song today, one is reminded of the great feat of transcending analogue sound and stepping into a digital world; 'Listeners are now left to ponder the oddity of hearing a recording made before the idea of audio playback was even imagined' (Rosen 2008).

The 1980s saw the dawn of digital sound recording and digital audio. To understand the process of digital representation of sound, it is useful to think of the way in which film represents motion. A movie is made by viewing still images in a rapid sequence at a constant rate (known as frames per second). When these images are displayed in sequence at a uniform rate, it tricks the viewer into thinking they are seeing continuous motion, when in fact what they are seeing is a collection of a number of discrete images per second. Digital sound recording works in the same way: discrete samples of sound waves are stored and later reproduced at the same rate to create the illusion of a continuous sound wave. (See Cipriani and Giri 2013 for a thorough introduction to digital sound processing.)

Sound then, in its digital form, is nothing more than a vast collection of binary code (1s and 0s). This means that, as a digital medium, sound can be recorded, copied, edited, and played back with the greatest of ease and without the need for the bulky, often expensive, equipment once used in language laboratories. Today, mass storage allows computers to save and manipulate audio files quickly, easily, and above all cheaply. Digital sound has become a powerful resource in a world where listening and speaking skills provide the largest percentage (45% and 30% respectively) of our total communicative competence (Feyten 1991).

The advent of digital sound recording precipitated a move from an analogue soundscape to a digital one. This paradigm shift, coupled with the launch of the Web in the early 1990s, saw a medium emerge which would forever change the dynamic of the language labs of the 1960s: digital sound. This shift has not only revolutionised the way we hear and share language but also how we teach it. It has opened up a world of possible teaching tools, which we are still discovering: 'creating opportunities which are as exciting and as full of potential for language teachers and learners as anything seen in the 1960s' (Vanderplank 2010: 1).

## The digital language laboratory

Roby (2004) insightfully connects two significant historical events: in the same year as the computer was named the 'machine of the year' by *TIME Magazine* (Rosenblatt 1983), the Computer Assisted Learning and Instruction Consortium (CALICO) was founded (see Healey, Chapter 1 this volume for a discussion of CALL acronyms). Naturally the early language labs were almost exclusively focused on the 'sound' skills of listening and speaking (Roby 2004); however, the invention of the computer assisted in the emergence of audiovisual language resources. Today the language laboratory has morphed into what might now be called the digital language learning hub. The words *language, learning, media, resource* and *centre* have become interchangeable with facilities which offer expanded media avenues for language learning (Lawrason 1990). Lawrason also reported that 'fewer labs now seem to limit their learning technology to audio' (ibid.: 23). Roby echoes this: 'the lab of the 1980s was not to be limited to audio technology' (2004: 528). This still holds true today: the invention of the computer brought with it a way of converting real-world information into digital media, offering us ample possibilities and tools for language teaching via audio and visual 'bimodal presentation' (Vanderplank 2010: 16).

*The digital classroom*

The average TESOL classroom (naturally there are exceptions, namely in developing regions) is beginning to look more and more like a digital language hub: often well furnished with at least one PC or teacher laptop with audiovisual facilities. Students themselves often arrive to class fully equipped, most with smartphones in their pockets and more often with laptops and tablets as their primary 'slate and chalk'. The paperless classroom has all but arrived. The introduction of wireless broadband in most institutions has greatly improved the speed and quality of data transfer via computer, making a fully networked, connected classroom a reality. No longer do teachers need to 'book time' in the language lab; the classroom has become the lab.

## Pedagogical perspectives on oral/aural skills

*Listening and speaking: An integrated skill*

'In meaningful communication, people employ incremental language skills not in isolation but in tandem' (Hinkel 2006: 113). Take something as straightforward as a conversation: 'one needs to be able to speak and comprehend at the same time' (ibid.). Hinkel calls on language teachers to therefore address these skills simultaneously and states that aural skills readily lend themselves to the integrated teaching of oral skills. 'The simplest and most basic type of integrated teaching incorporates the skills in the same language medium, either spoken to include listening and speaking, or written to include reading and writing' (Hinkel 2010: 116). As such, in this chapter listening and speaking skills will not be discussed as two isolated entities but rather treated as 'integrated skills' (Hinkel 2006: 113), which arise together in natural communication and teaching contexts through their shared medium: sound.

*Early perspectives*

In their in-depth exploration of second language listening, Flowerdew and Miller (2005) neatly outline the listening goals of some of the most widely adopted pedagogical approaches in language teaching. Beginning with the grammar-translation approach, they note that in fact, there was no learning goal related to listening. As this approach was used mainly in the teaching of 'dead' languages such as Latin and ancient Greek, by default, there was never a focus on speaking skills. The goal was to access the messages of its literature; therefore, reading and writing skills were naturally the focus. They also concede that in the period of grammar-translation there was 'no means of electronic recording' (ibid.: 4). Not having such a medium would have naturally limited any efforts to introduce an oral/aural dimension to the teaching of these languages.

CALL tools for listening and speaking

*The emergence of the oral/aural focus*

The direct-method approach has been attributed to a reaction to the restrictive grammar-translation approach (Flowerdew and Miller 2005; Harmer 2007) and it is here that we begin to see the emergence of an aural/oral focus. Although the direct-method is often credited with being the first approach to truly focus on listening, 'there was no systematic attempt at teaching listening or at developing listening strategies in the learners' (Flowerdew and Miller 2005: 6). The authors acknowledge that while successive approaches often tested listening comprehension by using listening exercises together with the written text, the exercises unfortunately held 'little or no relevance to the outside world' (ibid.: 7).

*The 'mim-mem' approach*

Perhaps predictably, Flowerdew and Miller (2005) cite the US Defense Forces language programmes, which were established during and after World War II, as the beginning of the 'Army Method', commonly referred to as the audio-lingual method today. The outbreak of the war understandably heightened the need for those on the ground to be equipped to communicate with their allies and indeed their enemies. Given the practical requirement of oral language exchange for basic communicative interactions, reading and writing skills were simply not expected of the learner and therefore not taught explicitly (Hinkel 2010). Curiously, the authors do not mention the advent of electronic sound recording in their discussion of the method. Given what we know about the congruent audio technological advances, it would seem as important a factor in the emergence of a method which saw a shift in focus to learners' oral/aural skills, as the political circumstances of the time.

It is in their discussion of the audio-lingual approach that we see a language teaching method focused extensively on listening; however, the authors highlight that the aim was to manipulate structures rather than to develop listening skills (Flowerdew and Miller 2005). The approach became known as the 'mim-mem' method: its emphasis was on mimicking the language and memorising the dialogues. The development of listening skills, according to Mendelsohn, was left to chance: 'They'll pick it up by osmosis' (1998: 81). Learners were not being taught how to listen. It was an approach to linguistic development that viewed languages as 'ultimately finite entities and might be learned through *imitation* and *practice*' (Osada 2004: 54). Harmer (2007: 64) uses the following example of a typical stimulus/response drill:

TEACHER:   There's a cup on the table . . . repeat
STUDENTS:  There's a cup on the table
TEACHER:   Spoon
STUDENTS:  There's a spoon on the table
TEACHER:   Book
STUDENTS:  There's a book on the table
TEACHER:   On the chair
STUDENTS:  There's a book on the chair
etc.

*The true impact of technology on language pedagogy*

Roby (2004: 527) calls the 1970s and 1980s a 'period of malaise' for language laboratories. The reader may recall that this period was also witnessing a sharp criticism of the audio-lingual approach, which had up until then been the 'orthodoxy in the field' (ibid.). Its popularity as a teaching method had waned significantly. The decline of audiolingualism can perhaps been attributed to two contributing factors. The first was the well-documented Chomskyan (1959) rebuttal of 'behaviourism', which heralded a growing challenge to the long-serving theory of language as an expression of 'verbal behaviour' (Skinner 1957: 3). The second, less cited factor was the limitations of the technology in use: many language labs of the time were still using reel-to-reel systems. The ramifications of bulky, often unreliable audio equipment which furnished early language labs should not be overlooked. According to Taylor:

> when the expensive lab equipment of the 1950's and 60's began to break down, few teachers pressured administrators to keep the labs in good condition. Consequently, students who went to the lab found that [. . .] the equipment was broken [. . .] With fewer and fewer students using the lab, administrators could not allot money for lab repairs or new equipment.
>
> *(Taylor 1979: 229)*

Although many language teachers adopted the cassette player relatively quickly, it would take nearly two decades for Philips's invention to fully work its way into the lab. By that time, language labs had had their heyday and in many institutions had become nothing more than 'electronic graveyards' (Turner 1969: 1).

The audio-lingual method's fall from grace highlights two important issues: the 'Changing Winds and Shifting Sands' (Marckwardt 1972) of opinion about best practice in foreign language pedagogy and the limitation of early technology (Hanson-Smith 2003). Audio recording would eventually become a staple of the language classroom, but not before the language lab and its associated audio-lingual approach had fallen deeply out of favour with the TESOL community. It is not outside of the realm of possibility that this may have inadvertently, or even subconsciously, affected how language teachers viewed audio-based teaching tools for teaching aural skills. Perhaps by not wanting to associate with a 'failed' venture, the effect was that a whole range of potentially beneficial audio aids was left unexplored and listening skills was left to languish like Cinderella in the basement, outshone by its three more audacious sisters: reading, writing and speaking.

Prabhu's viewpoint on 'failed methods' may also be useful to reflect on here:

> When a method considered to be good has been implemented on a large scale and later thought not to have 'worked', an important part of the reason identified has been that teachers followed the method 'mechanically', with no sense of understanding or identification.
>
> *(Prabhu 1990: 172)*

A connection can be made between the language lab and CALL: although they are tools, not methods, they have both been subject to the type of mechanical use that Prabhu describes and therefore ultimately distrusted and even rejected by some. It is therefore imperative that TESOL teachers be able to identify and understand for themselves the teaching potentials offered by technology in order for them to be successfully incorporated as learning tools. We need to be careful to ensure that we are not to just 'mechanically' follow CALL trends but that we can identify their value in the TESOL context:

> If we're really serious about stimulating learning, then we should think in terms of something like a cognitive catalyst. Rather than just serving up digital content and assuming the

students will absorb it, we should be creating artefacts that function like enzymes for the intellectual digestive system ... thus moving us away from the current trend of privileging the 'object' over the 'learning'.

*(Feldstein 2006: para. 4)*

Prabhu (1990: 172) succinctly describes pedagogical intuition, or a teacher's beliefs about how learning actually happens and how their teaching supports this process, as a teacher's 'sense of plausibility'. That is to say all teachers have their own individual, sometimes subconscious, philosophy of how their students learn, and this in turn influences how they subsequently approach the task of teaching. It is when a teacher's sense of plausibility is engaged that 'the activity of teaching is productive', and this in turn will be reflected in an engaged and productive learning environment (ibid.). Accordingly it is only if teachers feel that certain CALL tools fall within their own 'sense of plausibly' that their use in the classroom will be productive. If this cannot be done in earnest, then CALL tools should be avoided as they will only result in mechanical teaching, which is not only undesirable but can be detrimental to the learner.

Looking at these pedagogical trends, it is clear that listening and speaking instruction has undergone an evolution. The 'listen and repeat' approach of the audio-lingual period gave way to the 'question and answer' comprehension approach (Vandergrift 2004) and now we have welcomed a more real-time approach, favouring communicative and collaborative learning. Communicative language teaching (CLT) places great value on teaching learners to communicate meaningfully through a target language. It is an approach 'based on the premise that what we do in the classroom should have real-life communicative value' (Flowerdew and Miller 2005: 12). The following sections of this chapter aim to highlight the potential that certain CALL tools have for providing learning opportunities which have the type of real-life communicative value TESOL classrooms seek to provide.

## How do we listen?

How native speakers and language learners listen is markedly different. There is an assumption that just because learners may be immersed in a linguistic soundscape that they are also listening. While this may be true for some, it may well be that most learners are *hearing* rather than listening to the ambient language. 'While hearing provides a basis for listening, it is only a precursor for it' (Rost 2011: 12). 'The natural ability to hear [...] is often mistaken for a fully developed skill that needs no further fine-tuning' (Flowerdew and Miller 2005: 21).

Rost describes listening 'as one of the crucial components of spoken language processing – there is no spoken language without listening' (Rost 2011: 1). Its relevance and pervasiveness in language however, he adds, does not necessarily make it 'knowable' (ibid.). He cites four main characteristics of listening that people tend to agree on (ibid.: 2–4). Listening is:

1   receptive (receiving what the speaker actually says)
2   constructive (constructing and representing meaning)
3   collaborative (negotiating meaning with the speaker and responding)
4   transformative (creating meaning through involvement, imagination and empathy).

He asserts that by considering listening in its broadest sense, we can in turn practice an 'informed teaching' of this skill (Rost 2011: 4).

*Language: Text or sound?*

Given that audio technology is a relatively new classroom tool, and that originally the aim of early language teaching was to read literature rather than communicate orally, it is somewhat understandable that many linguists (and teachers) have assumed a textual stance on language and perhaps lost sight of the fact that, in Bloomfield's words, 'writing is not language, but merely a way of talking about language by means of visible marks' (1933: 21). To put it another way, language is speech first, writing second. Therefore teaching the sounds of a language is distinct from teaching the script. While this might appear to some as a prima facie statement, predominantly research efforts have focused more on literacy skills development and perhaps overlooked the fact that empirical findings 'may not automatically transfer from reading to listening' (Osada 2004: 57–58). Although they both derive from the same linguistic system, 'they are linguistically different from each other' (ibid.: 59).

Nowhere has this point been made clearer than in the nascent field of corpus linguistics (see Part IV of this volume). The development of corpus linguistics, specifically spoken corpora analysis, has provided the TESOL community with rich data showing the distinct features found in naturally occurring spoken language: short bursts of speech, topic-comment structures and topic restatement, paratactic (additive linking) ordering, false starts, abandoned structures, ellipsis, fillers and so forth (McCarthy and Slade 2007; Roland et al. 2007). As Rost (2011) points out, these features have in the past been erroneously considered by some as signs of careless language use. Yet, it has now been firmly established that spoken and written language 'follow different realisation rules' (ibid.: 28).

Admittedly, there is now a widespread recognition that spoken language is central to competent communication, and as such should have as much a place in second language acquisition (SLA) pedagogy as written forms of language. It therefore follows that authentic examples of spoken English should be incorporated in TESOL instruction. Liu (2011: 2) identifies the grammar-translation method and communicative language teaching as 'the two major currents that run through our EFL courses. The first current focuses upon elements of accuracy in written work, while the second emphasizes fluency in speaking'. However, by only focusing on fluency, we are not adequately addressing the emerging oral/aural issues related to the global spread of English.

## The sociolinguistic effect on oral/aural pedagogy

As we have seen, there have been many advances made in both linguistic theory and technology, shaping the way we view, use and in turn, teach language. These new perspectives contribute to a certain dynamism, which Hinkel (2006: 109) calls the 'hallmark of TESOL's disciplinary maturation'. It is impossible to ignore the fact that we are experiencing a paradigm shift relating to the English language, its users, and its uses. Since the mid-90s the line between English as a foreign language (EFL) and English as a second language (ESL) has become blurred, and English as a lingua franca (ELF) is emerging as the leading use of the language (Jenkins 2015: 2–5).

*Global English*

Jenkins (2015) calculates that there are approximately seventy-five territories in the world today where English is spoken either as a first language or as an official second language. She gives a figure of just over 329 million L1 speakers (ibid.) and in 2003 Crystal conservatively estimated that there were 430 million L2 English speakers. Even then it was a figure well above the total number of L1 speakers of English and one which, according to Jenkins (2015), is likely to be steadily increasing. 'Approximately one in three of the world's population are now capable of communicating to a useful level in English' (Crystal 2012: 155). Nonnative to nonnative communication (as opposed to the traditional nonnative to native model) is now the leading interchange of the English language. According to Hinkel (2006), this has impacted greatly on perspectives of the way English, particularly its sound system, is taught. It follows that in order to teach oral and aural skills, we must be able to provide real, authentic input that reflects the reality of English use today.

## The sounds of English(es)

In the preface to *Pygmalion*, George Bernard Shaw wrote, 'no man can teach himself what [the English language] should sound like from reading it' (1916/2003: preface). The often quoted 'GHOTI = FISH' example is further testament to the widespread irregularities of English pronunciation in relation to its written representation. 'As any student of English can attest, written English is only an approximate representation of the spoken language' (Atkielski 2005: 1). The International Phonetic Alphabet (IPA) has long been used as a classroom tool to bridge the problems caused by the disparity of text-to-sound in English, based on the premise that 'the transcription can represent a precise, standard pronunciation, independent of the individual or regional accent of any teacher or audio recording' (ibid.). For centuries, phoneticians have used the IPA to describe one particular 'standard' British accent. Commonly known as Received Pronunciation (RP), it sometimes goes by other monikers: Public School Pronunciation, Educated Southern British English, the Queen's English, and the BBC Accent (Harrington et al. 2000; Roach 2004). And yet:

> the number of native speakers of this accent who originate in Ireland, Scotland and Wales is very small and probably diminishing, and it is therefore a misnomer to call it an accent of BRITISH English. It is an accent spoken by some English people.
> 
> *(Roach 2004: 239)*

By using such a narrow 'standard' pronunciation model, we run the risk of marginalising the largest group of speakers of English (not to mention the subtle imbuing of what is in essence a socially divisive element within TESOL pedagogy). Indeed 'an insistence on the superiority of established educational models is not in keeping with a democratic ideology on linguistic diversity' (Modiano 1999: 22).

## What's in an accent?

Sociolinguistic research has shown that 'social identities are transmitted and constructed simultaneously with linguistic content' (Hay and Drager 2007: 90). The TESOL community is becoming more aware that often a person's accent is 'inextricably bound up' with their social and individual identity (Seidlhofer 2001: 57–58). Indeed, Daniels (1995: 8) writes about the 'imaginary umbilical cord' connecting speakers to their mother tongue. He proposes that learners, perhaps unconsciously, avoid cutting the connection by retaining the sounds, rhythms and intonation of their mother tongue. Whatever the reason, sociolinguistic-minded TESOL teachers have begun to embrace the idea that in this international linguistic community of which we are a part, *all* speakers of English have an equal right to express their identity (be it regional or L1) by means of their accent. As Widdowson (1994: 385) reminds us, nobody owns English anymore: 'The very fact that English is an international language means that no nation can have custody over it'.

Listening and speaking skills are perhaps the first of the four skills to feel the inevitable knock-on effect in a long line of linguistic dominos that surround the process of learning a language that is shared by the majority of the world. The objective has now become to help learners to achieve a level of intelligibility based on 'realistic rather than idealistic language models' (Hinkel 2006: 116). It has also been suggested that learners be introduced to not just one, but a variety of L1 and L2 English accents, in order to strengthen their receptive repertoire and accommodation skills (Jenkins 2000). Thus, there is a current need for specific TESOL materials to practice skills that 'might allow us to project more pedagogically realistic and sociolinguistically relevant goals for ELT' (Matsumoto 2011: 110).

If there truly is 'a growing need [. . .] for international citizens to be able to understand not just standard British or American spoken English, but other varieties spoken around the world' (Flowerdew and Miller 2005: xi), the TESOL classroom must cater to this need. Instead of stressing a pronunciation model 'independent of the individual or regional accent' (Atkielski 2005: 1), we must begin to think how we can expose, rather than shelter, learners to a variety of English language listening experiences. Learners need to be able to 'tune into each other's accents' (Jenkins 2000: 96). One could argue that the task at hand is to heighten intercultural awareness in authentic communicative tasks and provide opportunities for enhancing learners' oral/aural skills in a world where most communicative interactions through English take place between nonnative speakers of English..

'Language varies. This observation is the cornerstone of sociolinguistic research' (Hay and Drager 2007: 90). What then of the IPA, a static model which in a recent estimate represents less than 2% of native English speakers' accents? (Robinson n.d.). Are we to continue to use this model to teach English pronunciation? Native-speaker imitation would seem to contradict the current CLT approach to teaching a language (Hinkel 2010). This is where CALL tools can be seen to hold a specific pedagogical advantage in the changing linguistic landscape. Web connection and digital sound allow for unprecedented access to the varied sounds of English: 'for foreign language educators it has never been an issue of whether to use audio technology; it has been a question of how' (Roby 2004: 529).

What we are now interested in are the sociolinguistic dimensions of listening and speaking skills, and it is here we can begin to explore how digital audio can been used to enhance a way of teaching that has 'shifted from targeting a nativelike accent to targeting intelligibility' (Hinkel 2006: 115). We now find ourselves in need of teaching materials which have the potential to not only teach the 'nuts and bolts' of the language but which also have the potential to expand learners' sociolinguistic understanding of the language – in other words, to sufficiently equip them with the appropriate skills to enter the current global English conversation.

## Purpose designed CALL tools for oral/aural skills

This section does not intend to engage in the 'digital native/immigrant' (Prensky 2001) discussion of learners/teachers. While undeniably a provocative if not slightly redundant debate (see Bennett, Maton and Kervin 2008; Benini and Murray 2014 for a critical review of the debate), it carries with it a risk of distracting from the task at hand, which is to provide examples of effective pedagogical tools which have the potential to fit with contemporary English language learners' needs. It seeks to look objectively at the way in which certain CALL tools can help today's English language learners and teachers, regardless of their position on the digital provenance spectrum, to enhance the listening and speaking skills currently required to communicate in what has become the medium of global conversation: the English language. The primary resources under discussion are: Voxopop, dictionary.com, and ClipFlair.

## Voxopop

Stollhans describes Voxopop as a 'voice based e-learning tool' (2015: 185). She writes that it is distinct from other online forums in that the exchange of ideas is 'done in oral instead of written form' and 'therefore seen as an opportunity to practice oral performances in the target language' (ibid.):

> Voxopop talkgroups are a fun, engaging and easy-to-use way to help students develop their speaking skills. They're a bit like message boards, but use *voice* rather than text and a have a specialised user interface. No longer confined to a physical classroom, teachers and students of oral skills can interact from home, or even from opposite sides of the planet. Anywhere. Anytime.
>
> *(Voxopop 2007)*

Stollhans (2015: 186) points out that while technology has permeated the majority of language classrooms, 'technology is hardly ever used to actively focus on productive skills'. Some of the advantages of the Voxopop platform are that it has been designed to function on minimal equipment (laptop or smartphone), and Stollhans attests to its user-friendly and self-explanatory nature. Stollhans's 2015 case study evaluated the use of the Voxopop tool for a university-based project which called for final-year students of German to record themselves speaking about an aspect of their year abroad and to discuss it in a Voxopop talkgroup. She states that it involved 'listening to other students' contributions online, understanding them and replying to them with another recording' (ibid.: 187).

The fact that the students could 'practice, listen back and re-record themselves before uploading their contributions' (Stollhans 2015: 185) was seen as highly beneficial in creating a low-pressured environment for learners to operate in. If subscribing to Krashen's affective filter hypothesis (1982), which holds that language acquisition is impeded by anxiety, which can create a barrier to the acquisition process (i.e. the learner's filter goes 'up' and the opportunity to acquire language is lost), one could view this low-pressured production period as conducive to 'lowering' any affective filters that may otherwise be in place.

If fluency emerges on its own and is something that cannot be taught (Krashen 1982), then the least language teachers can do is to provide learners with opportunities so that they can develop fluency on their own. Not only does Voxopop have the potential to provide engaging tasks that the learner can participate in and by doing so, develop their fluency, it also allows for exposure to a wide variety of L2 English accents. As not all TESOL classrooms can provide this kind of variety, this CALL tool is particularly significant as it has the potential provide learners with opportunities to exchange recordings with other L2 speakers from all over the world.

## Dictionary.com

The next CALL tool under discussion is the online dictionary. One could argue it to be the most fundamental of all purpose designed CALL tools and therefore merits a place in this discussion. The humble dictionary's transition from an analogue to a digital database has opened up the long-serving language tool much like a Swiss army knife. In particular, we now see the integration of digital audio data in most online dictionaries. The quick access to digital sound files provided by online dictionaries can be seen as a huge benefit to learners wishing to access information about the sounds of words, but also for teachers who can direct their students to the database without any real interruption to teaching pace. Although many online dictionaries now have integrated audio, for ease of purpose this discussion will centre around one open source online dictionary: dictionary.com (available at http://dictionary.reference.com).

With over 5.5 billion words searched annually and 95 million mobile app downloads, dictionary.com has established itself as one of the leading online English dictionaries. The following four apps offered by dictionary.com are particularly relevant for language learners:

1   Dictionary.com: free, available on both Apple and Android devices
2   Flashcards: free, available on both Apple and Android devices
3   Thesaurus REX: nominal charge, only available on Apple devices
4   Word Dynamo (vocabulary and games): nominal charge, only available on Apple devices.

Dictionary.com bases its content on the Random House Unabridged Dictionary. The preface to the 1966 edition states that the Random House Dictionary steers 'a linguistically sound middle course' between the 'lexicographer's Scylla and Charybdis: should the dictionary be an authoritarian guide to "correct" English or should it be so antiseptically free of comment that it may defeat the user by providing him with no guidance at all?' (Stein 1966: preface). The dictionary's careful navigation of 'having to chose between two evils' is particularly evident in its avoidance of narrow IPA transcription. Naturally, this 'middle course' was therefore inherited by dictionary.com.

The innovative presentation of pronunciation on dictionary.com is worth discussing. Whereas traditional dictionaries usually use only a narrow phonetic transcription using the standard IPA, dictionary.com offers its users some alternatives.

You can simply click on the audio icon and listen to the word as illustrated in Figure 35.1.

You can also toggle between the 'IPA' transcription and 'Spell' (a 'layperson's phonetic breakdown' of the word) options, shown in Figure 35.2.

By clicking the 'Syllables' button the word is automatically formatted to visually show the individual syllables, as in Figure 35.3.

*Figure 35.1* Common audio icon

*Figure 35.2* Common audio icon with IPA transcription and spell options

# CALL tools for listening and speaking

*Figure 35.3* Audio icon option showing individual syllables

This degree of flexibility ensures that learners with no prior knowledge of the IPA are not alienated, and those who are familiar with it are not limited to it but can equally avail themselves of the additional audio support. There is no limit to the amount of times a learner can listen to the audio – it is here that we can really appreciate the added value that the computer doesn't fatigue:

> It is difficult to imagine assigning a student to listen to and repeat a word or phrase 20 times, but the computer controls allow this kind of intensive, individualized, autonomous practice without the physical difficulties entailed in, say, audiotape.
>
> *(Hanson-Smith 2003: 26)*

Having easy access to this type of instant sound modelling is something that will undoubtedly change the way pronunciation is taught and learned in the TESOL environment.

## *ClipFlair*

The next specifically designed CALL resource to be discussed is ClipFlair, an online project launched in 2011 and funded by the European Commission:

> *ClipFlair* is a web platform for foreign language learning through interactive re-voicing and captioning of clips. The application gallery hosts easily accessible and shareable activities in 15 languages which can be used by teachers in their courses or carried out by learners independently.
>
> *(ClipFlair 2011)*

In their report on ClipFlair, Banos and Sokoli (2015) make clear that the effectiveness of audiovisual translation tasks to learn a foreign language have long been acknowledged. They draw on Talaván Zanón's (2013) review of the benefits of using audiovisual material in the foreign language classroom, citing variety, motivation and the exposure to authentic linguistic and cultural aspects in context as the main benefits of integrating audiovisual material in a language classroom.

They acknowledge that while audiovisual tools may be of great benefit to the language classroom, the task of learning to use the technology and of sourcing appropriate material to create class activities with clear methodological learning goals can often be 'daunting' for teachers (2015: 204). As a purpose designed language tool, ClipFlair aims to address this often-occurring problem by integrating a methodological framework in its design, and by providing materials and activities specifically chosen by ClipFlair project members.

According to its document on conceptual framework and pedagogical methodology, ClipFlair's platform design 'takes into account different proficiency levels of expertise in teachers and must be not only "learner-friendly" but also "teacher-friendly"' (Zabalbeascoa, Sokoli and Torres 2012: 45). As such, task authors were requested to provide 'necessary metadata such as the title of the activity, name of the author(s), keywords, aims, estimated time for completion of tasks, languages, level according to the Common European Framework (CEFR), skills acquired, mode of feedback to learners, etc.' (Banos and Sokoli 2015: 208). The idea is that a well-indexed database makes the task of sourcing appropriate material much easier for teachers. YouTube, for instance, has been described as 'a massive, heterogeneous, but for the most part accidental and disordered public archive' (Burgess and Green 2009: 88). ClipFlair, in contrast, claims to be a well-designed, well-ordered, easily accessible public audiovisual library where users can browse for specific, well-indexed resources for language teaching.

Banos and Sokoli report on a pilot study that lasted approximately one year and involved 37 tutors and 1,213 learners, who tested 84 language learning activities for 12 languages; English, Portuguese, Spanish, Arabic, Chinese, Catalan, Romanian, Polish, Basque, Irish, Estonian and Italian. Seventy percent of the *ClipFlair* activities were tested in class with a teacher acting as the mediator. They report that learners' feedback from the pilot showed 'more than 80% found the activities used interesting and useful for language learning, and reported that they would like to work on similar activities to learn foreign languages' (Banos and Sokoli 2015: 212).

The activities offered by ClipFlair have been organised into three categories (Banos and Sokoli 2015: 209):

1 repeat (rendering the verbal part of the clip as literally as possible)
2 rephrase (free rendering or noticeable rewording of the text)
3 react (producing a new communicative contribution in response to a previous one).

These activities certainly offer learners opportunities to practice the well-defined elements of listening that Rost (2011) highlights: receptive, constructive, collaborative and transformative. Within this framework, ClipFlair's approach to oral/aural activities can be seen as supporting an 'informed teaching' of the skills. The platform will be freely accessible until 2020.

## The future

'Every technological innovation used in CALL has arisen first in some other field and for some other purpose' (Hanson-Smith 2003: 21). While this chapter explored the emergence of electronic and digital audio and traced its beginnings to areas outside of language pedagogy, in terms of emerging purpose designed CALL tools, this statement no longer holds true. Of course, Voxopop, dictionary.com, and ClipFlair are not the only purpose designed digital resources available to support the development of oral and aural skills:

SpeakApps (available at http://www.speakapps.eu/) is an open-source platform promoting interactive applications to practice oral skills through its three pedagogically designed language learning tools: videochat, tandem and langblog.
Glogster (available at http://edu.glogster.com/) is an online learning platform that allows users to collect text, audio, video and images from both outside sources and the Glog media library, which has compiled digital 'learner-approved' content.
Mydocumenta (available at http://www.mydocumenta.com/) is another media platform which offers a similar multimedia resource for students interested in integrating audio-visual resources as a learning support.

There are also many resources available which, with a little imagination, can be quickly and easily repurposed so that they become not only 'cognitive catalysts' but useful in the context of improving oral/aural skills:

- Skype
- FaceTime
- WhatsApp (audio message service)
- QR (Quick Response) codes (linked to audio/video content)
- Digital Dictaphones.

One of the greatest obstacles that still remains in successfully implementing CALL material in today's TESOL classrooms is that often we forget that regardless of age, gender, digital heritage (of both teacher and learner) and so forth 'at every screen are two powerful information-processing capabilities, human and computer' (Tufte 1991: 89). If teachers today can begin to see the CALL resources currently available as an extension of their own teaching and incorporate them into their 'sense of plausibility' (Prabhu 1990: 172), that is to say their own pedagogical intuition, the risk of 'mechanical teaching' will be minimised.

The global position that English holds and the implications this brings have led to a search for materials and approaches that recognise what it means to be a learner in today's world. Perhaps one of the most obvious pedagogical advantages that CALL can offer today's learners and teachers interested in improving and promoting oral/aural skills is its ability to offer exposure to a variety of sounds of English. CALL tools are easily the best equipped to support the task of teaching oral/aural skills of a language which is evolving in both its form and use. It is a realisation which could see future (and existing) TESOL teachers embrace CALL as a vital tool in oral/aural skills instruction.

Should this global spread of English continue, it is not unlikely that the theme of language localisation will begin to emerge in TESOL. This would call for a withdrawal of a prescriptive presentation of English pronunciation and the adoption of a descriptive account to include accent variety. The tradition of using a prestige variety of English and setting learners the onerous goal of native accent approximation will no longer seem relevant or desirable. 'The chances of societies and academies successfully preserving a particular form of pronunciation against the influence of community and social changes are as unlikely as King Canute's attempts to defeat the tides' (Harrington, Palethorpe and Watson 2000: 927).

## Further reading

Jenkins, J. (2015) *Global Englishes: A Resource Book for Students*, 3rd edn, Abingdon, Oxon: Routledge.
    Jenkins provides a dynamic and well-researched treatment of some of the most contemporary issues currently surrounding the English language. *Global Englishes* covers topics ranging from historical and sociopolitical influences to sociolinguistic perspectives of English as a lingua franca, and the implications of the global spread of English. It contains key readings which explore current debates borne of these linguistic developments, making it ideal for those interested in researching this topic further.

Roby, W.B. (2004) 'Technology in the service of foreign language learning: The case of the language laboratory', in D. Jonassen (ed.), *Handbook on Research on Educational Communications and Technology*, Mahwah, NJ: Lawrence Erlbaum: 523–542.
    This is an interesting overview of the language lab, its history and its decline (primarily in the American context). Roby traces the trajectory of the language lab against a backdrop of historical, social and pedagogical movements. In doing so he invites the reader to examine the context within which this (somewhat controversial) resource emerged. He weaves perceptive connections among various historical events and advances in audio technology that coincided with the language lab's emergence. Thus Roby's article attempts to convey a 'bigger picture' to allow the reader to experience a broader view of the ways in which historical events and media advancements have shaped language pedagogy.

Rost, M. (2011) *Teaching and Researching: Listening*, Harlow, UK: Longman.
Of particular interest to those seeking to understand the linguistic, psycholinguistic and pragmatic processes that are involved in oral language perception. Rost provides a sound theoretical overview of the acoustic and psychoacoustic aspects of listening, which are often omitted in practical teaching guides. It is an impressive treatise of the subject, and although it includes recommended types of listening instruction, its value is in its nonexpert friendly elucidation on the more theoretical, often esoteric side of listening. It is an accessible body of work, making it an ideal read for anyone interested in the phenomenon of listening.

## Websites

ClipFlair (2011) *ClipFlair* [online], available: http://clipflair.net/ (accessed 20 May 2015).
Dictionary.com, LLC (2015) *Dictionary.com* [online], available: http://dictionary.reference.com/ (accessed 20 May 2015).
The British Library Board (n.d.) *The British Library* [online], available: http://www.bl.uk/ (accessed 20 May 2015).
Voxopop/Chinswing Pty Ltd (2007) *VOXOPOP* [online], available: http://www.voxopop.com/ (accessed 20 May 2015).

## References

Atkielski, A. (2005) 'Using phonetic transcription in class', [online], available: http://www.atkielski.com/ESLPublic/Phonetics%20%20Using%20Phonetic%20Transcription%20in%20Class.pdf (accessed 20 May 2015).
Banos, R. and Sokoli, S. (2015) 'Learning foreign languages with ClipFlair: Using captioning and revoicing activities to increase students' motivation', in K. Borthwick, E. Corradini and A. Dickens (eds), *10 Years of the LLAS E-Learning Symposium: Case Studies in Good Practice*, Dublin: Research-publishing.net: 203–213.
Benini, S. and Murray, L. (2014) 'Challenging Prensky's characterization of digital natives and digital immigrants in a real-world classroom setting', in J. Pettes Guikema and L. Williams (eds), *Digital Literacies in Foreign and Second Language Education*, CALICO Monograph Series, 12: 69–85.
Bennett, S., Maton, K. and Kervin, L. (2008) 'The 'digital natives' debate: A critical review of the evidence', *British Journal of Educational Technology*, 39(5): 775–786.
Bloomfield, L. (1933) *Language*, Chicago, IL: University of Chicago Press.
Burgess, J.E. and Green, J.B. (2009) *YouTube: Online Video and Participatory Culture*, Cambridge, UK: Polity Press.
Chomsky, N. (1959) 'A review of BF Skinner's *Verbal Behavior*', *Language*, 35(1): 26–58.
Cipriani, A. and Giri, M. (2013) *Electronic Music and Sound Design – Theory and Practice with Max and MSP*, ConTempoNet.
Crystal, D. (2003) *English as a Global Language*, Cambridge: Cambridge University Press.
Crystal, D. (2012) 'A global language' in P. Seargeant and J. Swann (eds), *English in the World. History, Diversity, Change*, Abingdon: Routledge.
Daniels, H. (1995) 'Psycholinguistic, psycho-affective and procedural factors in the acquisition of authentic L2 phonology', *Bologna '94 English Language Teaching, British Council Italy*, 77–82.
Feldstein, M. (2006) 'There's no such thing as a learning object', *eLearn Magazine* [online], 5(2), available: http://elearnmag.acm.org/archive.cfm?aid=1145672 (accessed 22 May 2015).
Feyten, C.M. (1991) 'The power of listening ability: An overlooked dimension in language acquisition', *The Modern Language Journal*, 75(2): 173–180.
Flowerdew, J. and Miller, L. (2005) *Second Language Listening: Theory and Practice*, Cambridge: Cambridge University Press.
Hanson-Smith, E. (2003) 'A brief history of CALL theory', *CATESOL Journal*, 15(1): 21–30.
Harmer, J. (2007) *The Practice of English Language Teaching*, New York, NY: Pearson Longman.
Harrington, J., Palethorpe, S. and Watson, C.I. (2000) 'Does the Queen speak the Queen's English?', *Nature*, 408(6815): 927–928.
Hay, J. and Drager, K. (2007) 'Sociophonetics', *Annual Review of Anthropology*, 36: 89–103.
Hinkel, E. (2006) 'Current perspectives on teaching the four skills', *TESOL Quarterly*, 40(1): 109–131.

Hinkel, E. (2010) 'Integrating the four skills: Current and historical perspectives' in R.B. Kaplan (ed), *Oxford Handbook in Applied Linguistics*, 2nd edn, Oxford: Oxford University Press: 110–126.
Huebener, T. (1965) *How to Teach Foreign Languages Effectively: Theodore Huebener*, New York, NY: New York University Press.
Jenkins, J. (2000) *The Phonology of English as an International Language*, Oxford: Oxford University Press.
Jenkins, J. (2015) *Global Englishes: A Resource Book for Students*, 3rd edn, Abingdon, Oxon: Routledge.
Krashen, S.D. (1982) *Principles and Practice in Second Language Acquisition*, Oxford: Pergamon.
Lawrason, R.E. (1991) 'The changing state of the language lab: Results of 1988 IALL Members Survey', *Language Laboratory*, 28: 21–30.
Liu, Q. (2011) 'On current conditions of pronunciation teaching and learning under occupation-related criterion', *English Language and Literature Studies*, 1(2): 2–7.
Marckwardt, A. (1972) 'Changing winds and shifting sands', *MST English Quarterly*, 21(3): 5.
Matsumoto, Y. (2011) 'Successful ELF communications and implications for ELT: Sequential analysis of ELF pronunciation negotiation strategies', *The Modern Language Journal*, 95(1): 97–114.
McCarthy, M. and Slade, D. (2007) 'Extending our understanding of spoken discourse' in C. Davison and J. Cummins (eds), *International Handbook of English Language Teaching*, New York, NY: Springer: 859–873.
Mendelsohn, D.J. (1998) 'Teaching listening', *Annual Review of Applied Linguistics*, 18: 81–101.
Modiano, M. (1999) 'International English in the global village', *English Today*, 15(2): 22–28.
Osada, N. (2004) 'Listening comprehension research: A brief review of the past thirty years', *Dialogue*, 3(1): 53–66.
Prabhu, N. (1990) 'There is no best method – Why?', *TESOL Quarterly*, 24(2): 161–176.
Prensky, M. (2001) 'Digital natives, digital immigrants part 1', *On the Horizon*, 9(5): 1–6.
Roach, P. (2004) 'British English: Received Pronunciation', *Journal of the International Phonetic Association*, 34(2): 239–245.
Robinson, J. (n.d.) Received Pronunciation [online] British Library, available: http://www.bl.uk/learning/langlit/sounds/find-out-more/received-pronunciation/ (accessed 20 May 2015).
Roby, W. B. (2004) 'Technology in the service of foreign language teaching: The case of the language laboratory', in D. H. Jonassen (ed), *Handbook of Research on Educational Communications and Technology*, 2nd edn, Mahwah, NJ: Lawrence Erlbaum: 523–541.
Roland, D., Dick, F. and Elman, J.L. (2007) 'Frequency of basic English grammatical structures: A corpus analysis', *Journal of Memory and Language*, 57(3): 348–379.
Rosen, J. (2008) 'Researchers play tune recorded before Edison', *The New York Times* [online], available: http://www.nytimes.com/2008/03/27/arts/27soun.html?_r=1& (accessed 20 May 2015).
Rosenblatt, R. (1983) 'A new world dawns', *TIME Magazine*, 121(1).
Rost, M. (2011) *Teaching and Researching: Listening*, Chicago, IL: Longman.
Scott de Martinville, É-L. (1860) Recorded source on *Wikipedia* [online], available: https://en.wikipedia.org/wiki/Édouard-Léon_Scott_de_Martinville (accessed 8 Jun 2015).
Seidlhofer, B. (2001) 'Pronunciation', in R. Carter and D. Nunan (eds), *The Cambridge Guide to Teaching English to Speakers of Other Languages*, Cambridge: Cambridge University Press.
Shaw, G.B. and Laurence, D.H. (1916/2003) *Pygmalion*, New York, NY: Penguin Adult.
Skinner, B.F. (1957) *Verbal Behavior*, Acton, MA: Copley Publishing Group.
Stack, E.M. (1971) *The Language Laboratory and Modern Language Teaching*, Oxford: Oxford University Press.
Stein, J.M. (ed) (1966) *Random House Dictionary of the English Language*, New York, NY: Random House.
Stollhans, S. (2015) 'The e-learning tool Voxopop and its benefits on oral skills: Activities for final year students of German' in K. Borthwick, E. Corradini and A. Dickens (eds), *10 Years of the LLAS E-Learning Symposium: Case Studies in Good Practice*, Dublin: Research-publishing.net: 185–192.
Talaván Zanón, N. (2013) *La subtitulación en el aprendizaje de lenguas extranjeras*. Barcelona: Octaedro.
Taylor, H.M. (1979) 'A viable ESL/EFL Language Lab', *TESOL Quarterly*, 13(2): 229–239.
Tufte, E.R. (1991) *Envisioning Information*, Cheshire, CT: Graphics Press.
Turner, E.D. (1969) *Correlation of Language Class and Language Laboratory. ERIC Focus Reports on the Teaching of Foreign Languages, no. 13*. New York, NY: American Council on the Teaching of Foreign Languages.
Vandergrift, L. (2004) '1. Listening to Learn or Learning to Listen?', *Annual Review of Applied Linguistics*, 24: 3–25.

Vanderplank, R. (2010) 'Déjà vu? A decade of research on language laboratories, television and video in language learning', *Language Teaching*, 43(01): 1–37.

Widdowson, H.G. (1994) 'The ownership of English', *TESOL Quarterly*, 28(2): 377–389.

Zabalbeascoa, P., Sokoli, S. and Torres, O. (2012) Conceptual Framework and Pedagogical Methodology [online], available: http://repositori.upf.edu/bitstream/handle/10230/22701/ClipFlair%20Conceptual Framework.pdf (accessed 20 May 2015).

# 36
# Multimodality and CALL

*Nicolas Guichon and Cathy Cohen*

This chapter explores the issues pertaining to multimodality, which has always been considered a defining characteristic of CALL (Chapelle 2009). The chapter begins by critically examining the various definitions of multimodality, especially in the field of second language acquisition and cognitive psychology, and explores the distinction between mode, modality and channel. With reference to specific studies conducted in the field, we then investigate the potential of multimodality for second language comprehension and interaction. These studies support the idea that learning may be enhanced when teachers and learners have access to diverse modes. We also raise the question of cognitive load, which is especially crucial when information available in different modalities has to be processed, potentially leading to the division of attention between several channels. To address the issue of multimodality in CALL, we take an overview of computer-mediated tasks and discuss the challenges identified by researchers. Because videoconferencing used for telecollaboration brings together different challenges posed by multimodality, we focus on what is at stake both for the teachers and the learners when they are interacting online with a desktop videoconferencing system. First, we explore the potential of multimodality for CALL. The last two sections are devoted to studying multimodality in CALL, first from the learners' perspective and the literacies that need to be developed, and then from the language teachers' point of view, especially with regard to training them for current and future mediated teaching.

## Introducing multimodality as a defining characteristic of CALL

Any learning activity is multimodal by nature: language teachers in their classrooms use different semiotic resources (their voices, their gestures, sentences they write on the board, various documents or artefacts) to expose learners to the second language (L2) and involve them in meaning-making activities. Yet, the advent of the Internet and other multimedia technologies, the possibilities they provide to crucially 'integrate imagery, voice, sound, written text, and other semiotic modes' (Nelson 2006: 57), and the consequent changes in communication modes and conventions (Royce 2006: 366) create learning opportunities and have incited CALL researchers to envisage multimodality in a new light. Several researchers consider multimodality as a defining characteristic of CALL (see for instance Chapelle 2009). Indeed, Kress and Van Leeuwen have underlined the fundamental role technology plays in the semiotic process 'through the kinds of meaning which it facilitates or favours, and through the differential access to the means of production and reception which it provides' (1996: 233).

We propose to define *mode* as the type of semiotic representation (textual, aural and visual) used to present information. Jewitt (2009: 22) underlines that considering something as a mode requires 'a shared cultural sense of a set of semiotic resources'. *Modality* corresponds to the semiotic realisation of one mode; for instance, the visual modality of videoconferencing is realised through the webcam image. Modalities are asynchronous when production occurs at a different moment from reception (as is the case when one participant writes a post on a blog and another participant reads it), whereas synchronicity corresponds to the simultaneity of production and reception, as is the case when two partners interact using videoconferencing. Multimodality makes sensory information accessible in diverse semiotic modes and offers the opportunity to produce, comprehend and exchange information simultaneously through different channels (Guichon and McLornan 2008). *Channels* are part of what Mayer calls 'the human information processing system' (2005: 31), which allows individuals to process information via two channels, combining or dissociating visual and/or pictorial channels and auditory and/or verbal channels. Finally, *media* (e.g. video clips) are the technological means of inscription and production that shape the ways any message is conveyed and accessed. Thus, we propose to distinguish static, dynamic and interactive media (see Table 36.1), as these different types of dissemination and access seem to have an impact on the way information can be presented and understood. For instance, the dynamic feature of a video clip requires a different cognitive treatment from a static medium which can be accessed at leisure, as we will show later in the chapter.

Table 36.1 provides three examples of learning media that will be used throughout this chapter in order to further our comprehension of multimodality and to investigate implications for language learning and teaching and for CALL design. The table also distinguishes between two types of temporality, whether the semiotic resources are proposed asynchronously or synchronously. For instance, an online dictionary is a static medium in that it provides written content that remains unchanged on a web page. The content of an online dictionary is realised through textual and visual modes and is processed via learner visual and verbal channels. In contrast, a videoconference-based exchange in L2 occurs synchronously; it is interactive in that participants construct meaning in conjunction with each other in a unique and (mostly) improvised manner via textual mode (the written chat), aural mode (the voice of the interlocutor through the microphone) and visual mode (the image conveyed by the webcam).

*Table 36.1* Modes and media in different temporalities

| Temporality of the medium | Asynchronous | | Synchronous |
|---|---|---|---|
| Nature of the medium | Static | Dynamic | Interactive |
| Examples of learning media | An online dictionary for children | A captioned video clip inserted in a learning environment | A conversation in L2 via a videoconferencing tool |
| Semiotic modes | Textual (written definitions) and visual (accompanying illustrations) | Textual (subtitles), aural (reporter's voice, interviews), visual (video images) | Textual (text chat), aural (interlocutors' voices), visual (interlocutors' images) |
| Channels | Visual/pictorial and/or auditory/verbal | | |

As appears clearly with these examples, several modes are generally combined to represent the meaning of a message; for instance, the meaning conveyed by a video clip is distributed across the video image, the voice of the journalist and the written information. Yet, as Jewitt (2009: 25) insists, 'the different aspects of meaning are carried in different ways by each of the modes in the ensemble. Any one mode in that ensemble is carrying a part of the message only: each mode is therefore partial in relation to the whole of the meaning'.

In sum, multimodality depends on (1) the variety of modes made available to present a piece of information and (2) the interactivity between the different modes, that is whether they are presented separately or are fully integrated. We contend that multimodality provides affordances for language learning, that is 'possibilities for action that yield opportunities for engagement and participation that can stimulate intersubjectivity, joint attention, and various kinds of linguistic commentary' (Van Lier 2004: 81). To present a document across several modes is, for instance, an affordance of multimedia. Knowledge about multimodality should then be of prime importance for CALL practitioners because they have the responsibility of choosing how to present and organise learning situations and thus need to know the potential and the limits of multimodality in order to maximise learning (Stockwell 2010). Without such knowledge, as Lamy cautions, we run the risk of 'missing out on explaining the nuances in the learning process' (2012: 121) and, as a result, may fail to take full advantage of the learning possibilities. Besides, the pervasiveness of multimodality in L2 learning entails developing new pedagogies that take into account the 'variety of text forms associated with information and multimedia technologies', as well as the 'proliferation of communication channels and media [which] supports and extends cultural and subcultural diversity' (New London Group 2000: 9).

## The potential of multimodality for CALL

In this section, we take a closer look at what is at stake with multimodality and how multimodal technologies may contribute to second language learning. It is important to emphasise that investigation in this domain is still in its infancy, resulting in 'a lack of research that examines the impact of th[e] combined use of tools on interaction and analyses multimodal communication in an online language classroom' (Hampel and Stickler 2012: 118–119).

Let us first consider certain key characteristics of multimodality. Kress and Van Leeuwen state that multimodality is:

> the use of several semiotic modes in the design of a semiotic product or event, together with the particular way in which these modes are combined – they may for instance reinforce each other [...], fulfil complementary roles [...] or be hierarchically ordered.
> *(Kress and Van Leeuwen 2001: 20)*

So, there may be redundancy or complementarity between the different modes. In the former case, the same information is repeated across several modes. For example, in an online dictionary, a lexical item can be provided in a textual mode (its graphic representation), an aural mode (its pronunciation) and a visual mode (a picture), thus creating a redundancy effect (see later) between the three semiotic representations. In the latter case, a complex piece of information, for instance a video clip inserted into a learning environment, can be conveyed by different modes, thus creating a multimodal text in which, at any given moment, one mode may carry one set of meanings (e.g. a clip showing images of monuments in Washington, DC, providing contextual elements) while another mode carries another set of meanings (a self-employed woman explaining how hard it is to raise a child in the US). Both modes give different but complementary information and provide learners with a 'rich multimodal learning experience' (Collentine 2009: 79).

Yet Kress and Van Leeuwen insist that visual and verbal media 'are not simply alternative means of representing the same thing' (1996: 76), but rather multimodality involves not only accessing information in different formats but also establishing interactivity between the various representations. Levine and Scollon (2004) consider multimodality to be a dynamic meaning-making process which is inseparable from the notion of interaction. Indeed, it is precisely the enriched interactional opportunities offered by the multimodal nature of technology-mediated environments which are thought to provide enhanced opportunities for second language learning. This will now be illustrated, considering first studies conducted with asynchronous static or dynamic media and then with synchronous interactive media.

Several studies carried out in static or dynamic media have shown that learning opportunities are enhanced when information is presented in more than one representational code. For example, Mayer and Anderson (1992) showed that learners were better able to understand how a bicycle pump worked when the information provided included both a written text and an animation, rather than a written text alone. Likewise, in a study investigating how multimedia annotations impact on the acquisition of second language vocabulary, Chun and Plass (1996) demonstrated that accompanying definitions by images fostered learning. So learners understand better when they are able to integrate visual and verbal representations because these are qualitatively different and are therefore complementary (Mayer 2005). Schnotz sheds further light on this question, insisting that having access to words and pictures may improve the potential for learning, but only on condition that 'the words and pictures are semantically related to each other (the coherence condition) and if they are presented closely together in space and time (the contiguity condition)' (2005: 60).

In the wake of the many telecollaborative projects that partner up learners from two different cultures and languages (cf. Guth and Helm 2010), there is a small but increasing number of studies which investigate how multimodality may foster language learning in synchronous interactive media (e.g. Blake 2005; Ciekanski and Chanier 2008; Hampel and Stickler 2012). We will next consider studies carried out in audiographic and then videoconferencing environments.

In a study conducted in an audiographic environment, which included voice and text chat and a shared word processing function, Blake (2005) posits that it was the complementarity of the voice and text chat modalities which favoured negotiation of meaning. Indeed, the tutor and learners made strategic use of the multimodality of the environment to further the interaction, with the tutor frequently reinforcing in the text chat what had been expressed in the voice chat, and the learner choosing the less face-threatening text chat over the voice chat to request linguistic assistance from the tutor. Ciekanski and Chanier (2008) highlight how working in a multimodal audiographic environment can encourage collaboration between learners. In their study, in which learners do a shared writing task, combining the audio and text modes is shown to enhance the learning process as participants focus on the writing process itself in order to make meaning.

In a videoconferencing environment which included linguistic (voice and text chat and a shared whiteboard), visual (icons, still and moving images) and gestural (via a webcam) elements, Hampel and Stickler (2012) show how teachers and learners combine the different modes which offer a wider range of possibilities to make meaning through a range of discourse functions (e.g. asking for clarification, requesting or providing lexical elements, agreeing and disagreeing, providing feedback). They observe that 'these functions are central for learning in all subjects, but they are particularly crucial in language learning where negotiation of meaning [...] has been shown to contribute to second language acquisition' (2012: 121).

The aforementioned studies also illustrate the benefits of synchronous interactive learning environments for accommodating individual differences and modal preferences. Individualising learning in this way supports interaction and increases the possibilities for language learning, as learners progressively develop strategies enabling them to take advantage of the different potentialities offered by the various modes, appropriate the tools at their disposal and adapt them to their own objectives.

So to sum up, the studies discussed in this section offer support to the idea that providing teachers and learners with diverse modes to make meaning may enhance language learning. The different modes available in synchronous interactive environments are interrelated and the learning opportunities offered will depend on how users choose to combine or dissociate the different modes. Hampel and Stickler argue that these media rich learning environments allow for 'a combination of different modes and multiple parallel representations' (2012: 134) and that this combination increases what Norris has referred to as 'modal density' (2004: 103), defined as the intricate interplay of different communication modes or the intensity of one particular mode used by a social actor. However, we are still some way off from understanding the complexity of multimodal perspectives (Jewitt 2011), and further empirical studies are clearly needed to identify the possibilities and limitations of multimodality for computer-assisted language learning (CALL).

## Issues raised by multimodality in CALL: Cognitive cost and polyfocality of attention

In this section, we will summarise findings from the field of cognitive psychology of which language educators need to be aware in order to have a better understanding of the challenges posed by multimodality to learners.

If multimodality is generally seen as a potential for language learning (see earlier), it nevertheless raises questions pertaining to the attention that is required from learners to process information provided in different modes. Not only is attention 'a resource of limited availability' (Wickens 1984: 15), but each channel (i.e. either visual/pictorial or auditory/verbal) involved in processing information is itself limited (Mayer 2005). When two modes are in competition, for instance a text accompanied by an oral message, the amount of time needed to switch between them is longer than the time required to process information within a single one. Besides, there is a cognitive bias, referred to as 'visual dominance', whereby humans generally prefer processing visual information (Wickens 1984: 253).

Cognitive psychologists have studied what multimodality involves in terms of cognition and have provided useful results for the field of CALL. Several effects have been identified. These are the modality effect, the split attention effect and the redundancy effect.

According to Sweller (2005), the *modality effect* occurs in conditions where multiple information sources are crucial for understanding and learning and where the visual information provided requires learners to divide their attention between them. In the domain of language learning, this effect was investigated by Guichon and McLornan (2008). The study assessed the treatment of the same document by intermediate level French learners of English but in different conditions (audio only, video only, video + subtitles in English, video + subtitles in French). Their findings showed that comprehension was enhanced when information was presented as richly as possible. However, it also provided evidence that when visual information was not directly related to the oral message (e.g. when images were unconnected to the reporter's oral comments), there appeared to be a cognitive overload. They further suggested that visual information which was not directly linked to the auditory information may distract learners' attention and create a split-attention effect. Thus, exposure to simultaneous but different information carries a cognitive cost which is sometimes too high for learners, creating processing difficulties (Moreno and Mayer 1999).

Sweller has underlined the *split attention effect* that may occur when individuals have to divide their attention 'between multiple sources of visual information [e.g. written text and pictures] that are all essential for understanding' (2005: 26). Mental integration of these multiple sources is required before comprehension and learning can take place, putting a substantial cognitive load on the processing capacities required to carry out this operation. Thus, reading an explicatory text while looking at the illustrations that accompany it may cause an overload of the visual channel and impinge on comprehension performances (Tricot 2007).

The *redundancy effect* (see Wickens 1984; Sweller 2005) is a somewhat different phenomenon and some researchers have noted its rather counterintuitive nature 'because most people think that the presentation of the same information, in a somewhat different way, will have a neutral or even positive effect on learning' (van Merriënboer and Kester 2005: 82). If the same piece of information is reiterated across several modes, when one source would be sufficient for comprehension and learning, there is redundancy between the different sources. Indeed, having to pay attention to several sources, in order to verify whether a given piece of information is identical, carries an unnecessary cognitive cost. Creating redundancy between two sources is only beneficial if learners have low prior knowledge of a notion. An example to illustrate this (see Table 36.1) is an online dictionary for children in which there is a word, such as *saxophone*, which is accompanied by a simple definition and an image showing the musical instrument. On the other hand, when learners have high prior knowledge, one source is sufficient to provide the required information for understanding. In the case of a text reiterated by an illustration, 'the eye wanders between the two sources [. . .], the learner loses time and mental effort with the search for redundant information' (Schnotz 2005: 63), and this has a negative impact on learning.

From all these results concerning the effects of multimodality on learning, the following elements can be underlined:

1. Providing information from different sources usually carries an extra cognitive load, but can nevertheless facilitate comprehension and learning. Yet, educators might want to be wary of providing seductive but irrelevant information, which might cause cognitive overload and end up interfering with learning (Clark and Feldon 2005). Furthermore, creating redundancy between several modes can be detrimental when learners have good prior knowledge of a notion.
2. Multimodality can have a scaffolding effect, for instance when subtitles are provided in a video clip. Yet, if subtitles facilitate comprehension (see Baltova 1999), they can also prove to be distracting in that they load on to reading skills and use a cue that would not be present in a real-life situation.
3. The cognitive treatment is different in a static medium, such as an online dictionary for children (see Table 36.1) in which learners have time to go from one source to the other, compared to dynamic or interactive media which puts more pressure on learners, obliging them to switch rapidly from one channel to another in a limited time and integrate the different pieces of information into a single representation. Thus, when possible, giving learners control over the delivery allows them to interrupt the flow of the input and thus avoid cognitive overload. This principle, that some researchers have called 'the self-pacing principle', posits that 'giving learners control over the pace of the instruction may facilitate elaboration and deep processing of information' (van Merriënboer and Kester 2005: 83).

Multimodal competence thus entails developing meta-cognitive strategies necessary for 'allocating, monitoring, coordinating, and adjusting [...] limited cognitive resources' (Mayer 2005: 36) when dealing with mediated learning situations.

4   As Ciekanski and Chanier (2008) have remarked, multimodality does not only concern the way a technology-mediated learning activity is presented but also refers to the dynamic process of meaning-making that is involved when learners have to deal with technology-mediated interactions. Thus, the dynamic character of computer-mediated communication (CMC) in language learning adds a new dimension to the allocation of attentional resources. In a web-mediated interaction, not only do learners have to pay attention to their interlocutors' multimodal messages (text chat, voice chat, webcam image), but they also have to divide their attention between several tasks (e.g. using the keyboard, checking the webcam image, accessing various documents) in what Scollon et al. have called the 'polyfocality of attention' (1999: 35). Jones goes as far as to say that polyfocality seems 'to be part of the very ethos of new communication technologies' (2004: 27). Thus, interacting online, for instance via videoconferencing, means that learners have to handle communication across several modes and switch quickly between the verbal and visual modes to participate fully in the exchange while they are engaged in simultaneous – and sometimes competing – tasks (Guichon, Bétrancourt and Prié 2012).

## Developing learners' multimodal competence

This section explores the question of new literacies that can be developed among learners to help them deal with mediated learning situations with appropriate competence. Erstad (2011) lists several key literacies which need to be developed by individuals working in digital environments. The following are particularly useful in the context of multimodal language learning situations:

- the ability to communicate using different meditational means;
- the ability to cooperate in net-based interactions;
- the ability to create different forms of information such as web pages.

Kress (2003) has proposed the concept of *multimodal competence*, and this has been further defined by the New Media Consortium as 'the ability to understand and use the power of images and sounds, to manipulate and transform digital media, to distribute them pervasively, and to easily adapt them to new forms' (2005: 2). Some authors have advocated the need to focus on *multimodal literacy* (Royce 2006; Fuchs, Hauck and Muller-Hartmann 2012), arguing that multimodality and its different semiotic realisations constitute a set of options from which a learner can choose in order to make meaning. For instance, Royce (2006) set up a digital storytelling project requiring learners of English to create multimedia narratives and integrate different multimodal elements (pictures, audio recordings, texts) for a writing composition class over several months. Nelson concludes that such projects, which incite learners to reflect upon the different possibilities of making meaning by combining different verbal and nonverbal means, could be useful in developing multimodal competence and multimodal literacy as defined earlier.

Experts working in the field have identified three types of skill that language learners need to acquire to work effectively in multimodal interactive situations. These are semio-pragmatic, psychocognitive and sociocultural skills.

With regard to *semio-pragmatic skills*, it is important for learners to go beyond their individual modal habits and preferences so that they can use two or more modes concurrently for meaning-making. Furthermore, they need to acquire a critical use of the different modes in order to 'familiarise themselves with the "grammar" of other modes such as the visual' (Hampel and Hauck 2006: 12). So, they will need to become skilled not just in switching linguistic codes, but also in switching semiotic modes. In addition, they need to acquire skills in a range of new codes, including online speech, writing and image (Fuchs et al. 2012).

Learners need to develop *psychocognitive skills* too. Indeed, working with unfamiliar tools in multimodal CMC language learning spaces may make strong affective demands on certain learners, potentially compromising the learning process. This can result in a lack of motivation, as well as computer or language anxiety and cognitive overload (Hampel and Hauck 2006; Fuchs et al. 2012).

Finally, it is important for learners to develop *sociocultural skills* in order to be able to deal with intercultural differences when communicating in virtual multimodal learning spaces (Fuchs et al. 2012). Hampel and Hauck emphasise the importance for learners to acquire intercultural awareness because 'modes, making meaning and communicating are influenced by cultural conventions' (2006: 13).

So how can teachers help to prepare learners to develop their multimodal competence? It is often assumed that today's users are able to apply their everyday knowledge of and familiarity with technology to multimodal CMC language learning situations. However, several recent studies (see Hubbard 2013) reveal this assumption to be imprecise for many learners who do in fact require targeted training to attain 'the level of readiness needed for effective use of technology in language learning tasks and activities' (Hubbard 2013: 166).

We make several recommendations concerning how language learners may be trained to function effectively in CMC environments, in order to acquire the necessary skills discussed earlier. First, to develop semio-pragmatic skills, it is advisable to allow learners to familiarise themselves with the different tools in the multimodal learning environment, by exchanging first in their L1 with their peers in less challenging and stressful conditions before starting to exchange in the L2 (Guth and Helm 2010). Familiarising the learners with the tools also includes sensitising them to the different affordances offered by CMC environments. Knowledge of these is crucial for the development of effective multimodal competence and should form an integral part of learner training. Besides, learners should be made aware that the structure of the multimodal digital learning environment will 'shape the affordances of the tool and mediate the interaction between participants' (Hampel and Stickler 2012: 133). So, for example, in an audiographic environment, not having access to the interlocutor's image (gestures, facial expressions, etc., via a webcam) which can enhance meaning-making may lead to increased anxiety in certain learners, affecting their participation and performance. Similarly, in a CMC environment which includes text chat, learners may behave differently when their written contributions are visible to all participants, from when they have the possibility of sending private messages, thereby modifying the interaction (Hampel and Stickler 2012).

Since the CMC learning environment is complex, it is important for learners to discover the various tools progressively, perhaps by adding a new mode at each step in order to allow learners to gain a critical understanding of the purpose of each mode and how several modes can be orchestrated (Guth and Helm 2010). For instance, it could be useful to point out to learners that, in a synchronous interactive mode, text chat can be used to ask for clarification or to comment on what somebody says, to avoid interrupting the flow of the online conversation in the voice chat (cf. Develotte, Guichon and Kern 2008). In addition, to help learners adapt to the multimodal environment, it could be helpful to allow them to mute one mode to the benefit of another, and then progressively learn to manage different sources and different channels concurrently.

Moreover, having a progressive introduction to new skills and knowledge should ease the affective demands made on learners by multimodal learning spaces, consequently reducing computer and language anxiety and cognitive overload. Organising collaborative group debriefing sessions in which learners share their experiences may be helpful too, not only to reduce affective demands, but also to promote reflective and critical thinking and reasoning (Hubbard 2004). Raising learners' awareness of their individual learning styles and strategies can contribute to their degree of success when working in CMC environments, with a particular emphasis on 'the metalinguistic and metacognitive side, to assist them in maximizing their use of this technology' (Hoven 2006: 251). Indeed, matching students' modal preference to the instructional modality has been shown to contribute to successful language learning (Plass, Chun, Mayer and Leutner 1998).

Mayer (2005), the cognitive psychologist (see earlier), has underlined the necessity of providing guidance in how to process the information presented – that is, determining what to pay attention to, how to organise it mentally and how to relate it to prior knowledge. The teacher acts then as a sort of cognitive guide who 'provides needed guidance to support the learner's cognitive processing' (Mayer 2005: 12). Fischer argues that CMC training 'entails not only guiding learners to make good pedagogical decisions to facilitate their learning, but also instructing them how to use technological resources in support of those pedagogical decisions' (2012: 28).

With regard to the development of sociocultural skills, Sadler encourages instructors to raise students' awareness of cultural conventions of CMC, including 'basic information about ways to hold the floor in synchronous communication and ways to ensure successful asynchronous collaboration', as well as 'a cross-cultural analysis of communication conventions for the participants' (2007: 26). In addition, familiarising learners with nonverbal elements of communication is crucial for enhancing their cultural sensitivity and awareness.

In sum, learners need to develop their multimodal competence by gaining a set of skills to work effectively in interactive language learning spaces. Acquiring these semio-pragmatic, psychocognitive and sociocultural skills requires training to enable learners to adapt progressively, so that they may benefit from the multimodality of the environment and maximise their learning possibilities.

## Teaching implications: Developing semio-pedagogical competence

Earlier in this chapter, we saw that the current digital era requires language learners to be equipped to manage static, dynamic and interactive technology-mediated situations, devise strategies to cope with cognitive load and make culturally aware use of multimodality in order to become 'multimodally competent' in meaning-making, be it in reception, production or interaction. In this concluding section, we will advocate the need to develop new teaching skills among language teachers in order to take into account the specificities of multimodality.

We propose to use the term *semio-pedagogical competence* (Develotte, Guichon and Vincent 2010; Guichon 2013) to refer to teachers' awareness of the semiotic affordances of media and modes and their subsequent ability to design appropriate technology-mediated tasks for language learning. This competence relates to the interfacing role of language teachers who have to learn to use the communication tools (forums, blogs, videoconferencing facilities, etc.) that are the most appropriate for the learning scenarios they propose, and to manage the ensuing interactions with the most adequate modes (textual, aural and/or visual communication, synchronous and/or asynchronous). Building on the previous sections of this chapter, Table 36.2 summarises the main characteristics of semio-pedagogical competence – media assessment, mode assessment and task design.

*Table 36.2* Semio-pedagogical competence

| | |
|---|---|
| **Media assessment** | the capacity to assess the affordances of each medium in terms of its potential for language learning |
| **Mode assessment** | the capacity to assess the cognitive demands of each mode on learners and to adjust them according to the pedagogical objectives |
| **Task design** | the capacity to design tasks that provide for:<br>– the processing of information either in one mode or in several modes<br>– learner control and progressive discovery<br>– culturally based use of multimodality |

As Jewitt has pointed out, 'understanding the semiotic affordances of medium and mode is one way of seeing how technologies shape the learner, and the learning environment, and what it is that is to be learned' (2004: 194). Just as language teachers have to become competent in assessing the level of complexity of documents to adjust their length or the guidance they provide, they also need to develop the overarching competence of knowing what medium or what combination of media will be appropriate for given pedagogical objectives.

In line with research in cognitive psychology (see earlier), language teachers also need to be aware of the cost of multimodality and polyfocality. Through the ambient discourses on digital natives, teachers are led to believe that learners who have always had computers in their environment and who participate regularly in online exchanges for social purposes are naturally equipped for language learning in CMC environments. Contrary to these misconceptions, teachers have to ensure that the modal density (Norris 2004) of each technology-mediated teaching situation they design does not exceed their learners' cognitive capacities while giving the learners the possibility to extend their multimodal competence (Hampel and Hauck 2006).

Following Tricot (2007), we can also recommend that teachers learn to assess the pertinence of any given technology-mediated situation and anticipate its learning cost by describing minutely the relationship between the media that are used, the mode(s) that will be harnessed by the learners and the expected learning outcomes. As Mayer has underlined, 'multimedia designs that are consistent with the way the human mind works are more effective in fostering learning than those that are not' (2005: 9).

Finally, in terms of task design, teachers should acquire the necessary skills to organise learner use of multimodality on the following continua:

- from one mode to a combination of modes;
- from static, to dynamic, to interactive media;
- from little to total control over the use of modes;
- from familiar to less familiar cultural codes.

Thus teachers adjust task design to the different parameters of multimedia and multimodality, learner needs and pedagogical objectives.

From our experience in teacher training, it appears crucial that teachers develop this semio-pedagogical competence through hands-on experience of multimodality as advocated by Lewis (2006). The latter engaged in a gradual discovery of an audiographic environment at the Open University (UK) and said several weeks were needed to overcome 'feelings of stress, bewilderment, and inadequacy' (2006: 595) before feeling 'at home with multimodality' (2006: 595). Another example of how such experiential teacher training is being provided is through an ongoing telecollaborative project between Irish undergraduate learners of French and student teachers enrolled in a master's degree in French as a foreign language in France. In this project the student teachers have to prepare and administer weekly forty-minute sessions via a desktop videoconferencing system over six weeks. The day after each online session, the student teachers analyse their own teaching performance in a group debriefing session led by a teacher trainer, using the multimodal traces of the interactions (composed of text chat messages and videos of both sets of participants) that have been stored on the system's server (Guichon 2013).

This technology-mediated situation combines four elements which are at the far end of the aforementioned continua: it combines several modes, is highly interactive, is controlled by the participants, and necessitates cultural awareness (e.g. understanding the different meanings attached to certain gestures across cultures). By engaging student teachers in such a technology-mediated situation, this telecollaboration project provides the opportunity to develop their semio-pedagogical competence. Indeed, student teachers have to adapt and develop their existing pedagogical competence to fit the demands of a situation where multimodality and its different components can be experienced. At the same time, the various pedagogical resources can be deployed progressively and, may then be reinvested in future offline or online teaching situations. If technical skills are not necessarily transferable from one teaching environment to another, we contend that critical semiotic awareness developed through this type of experiential teacher training programme can be valuable for dealing with multimodality in future language teaching situations.

This chapter has highlighted the centrality of multimodality for CALL. Although further research is clearly needed to identify the potential and limitations of multimodality for CALL, existing studies already suggest that giving learners access to a range of modes for meaning-making may enhance language learning. Yet, research has also shown that multimodality may pose cognitive challenges to L2 learners in terms of the attentional resources that are required to process multimodal information. Not only do learners need to acquire a certain number of skills to take full advantage of the multiple learning opportunities offered by the digital environments, but language teachers have to develop specific competences to harness multimodality and make the most of its potential for language learning.

## Further reading

Hampel, R. and Stickler, U. (2012) 'The use of videoconferencing to support multimodal interaction in an online language classroom', *ReCALL*, 24 (2): 116–137.
   This article focuses on how videoconferencing interactions are influenced by the affordances of the online environment. Analyses of written and spoken interactions reveal how multiple modes are used and combined by learners to make meaning. Furthermore, the study shows how teachers and learners gradually adapt to the multimodal environment, leading to the emergence of new interactional patterns.

Jewitt, C. (2011) 'The changing pedagogic landscape of subject English in UK classrooms', in K.L. O'Halloran and B.A. Smith (eds), *Multimodal Studies: Exploring Issues and Domains*, New York, NY: Routledge: 184–201.
   In this chapter, Jewitt explains how the pedagogical landscape of subject English classrooms in the UK is changing as a consequence of the use of technologies. Using the example of interactive whiteboards, Jewitt raises the question of an increasingly complex and rich semiotic classroom landscape that has an impact on the practices of interpreting information and making connections across the different modes and media at hand in the classroom.

## References

Baltova, I. (1999) 'Multisensory language teaching in a multidimensional curriculum: The use of authentic bimodal video in core French', *Canadian Modern Language Review*, 56(1): 32–48.

Blake, R. (2005) 'Bimodal CMC: The glue of learning at a distance', *CALICO Journal*, 22(3): 497–511.
Chapelle, C.A. (2009) 'The relationship between second language acquisition theory and computer-assisted language learning', *The Modern Language Journal*, 93(Focus Issue): 741–753.
Chun, D.M. and Plass, J.L. (1996) 'Effects of multimedia annotations on vocabulary acquisition', *The Modern Language Journal*, 80(2): 183–198.
Ciekanski, M. and Chanier, T. (2008) 'Developing online multimodal verbal communication to enhance the writing process in an audio-graphic conferencing environment', *ReCALL*, 20(2): 162–182.
Clark, R.E. and Feldon, D.F. (2005) 'Five common but questionable principles of multimedia learning' in R.E. Mayer (ed), *The Cambridge Handbook of Multimedia Learning*, Cambridge: Cambridge University Press: 97–115.
Collentine, K. (2009) 'Learner use of holistic language units in multimodal, task-based synchronous computer-mediated communication', *Language Learning and Technology*, 13(2): 68–87.
Develotte, C., Guichon, N. and Kern, R. (2008) '"Allo Berkeley ? Ici Lyon . . . Vous nous voyez bien ?", Étude d'un dispositif de formation en ligne synchrone franco-américain à travers les discours de ses usagers', *Alsic*, 11(2): 129–156.
Develotte, C., Guichon, N. and Vincent, C. (2010) 'The use of the webcam for teaching a foreign language in a desktop videoconferencing environment', *ReCALL*, 23(3): 293–312.
Erstad, O. (2011) 'Citizens navigating in literate worlds', in M. Thomas (ed), *Deconstructing Digital Natives. Young People, Technology and New Literacies*, New York, NY: Routledge: 99–118.
Fischer, R. (2012) 'Diversity in learner usage patterns', in G. Stockwell (ed), *Computer-Assisted Language Learning: Diversity in Research and Practice*, Cambridge: Cambridge University Press: 14–22.
Fuchs, C., Hauck, M. and Muller-Hartmann, A. (2012) 'Promoting learner autonomy through multiliteracy skills development in cross-institutional exchanges', *Language Learning and Technology*, 16(3): 82–102.
Guichon, N. (2013) 'Une approche sémio-didactique de l'activité de l'enseignant de langue en ligne: réflexions méthodologiques', *Education and Didactique*, 7(1): 101–116.
Guichon, N., Bétrancourt, M. and Prié, Y. (2012) 'Managing written and oral negative feedback in a synchronous online teaching situation', *Computer Assisted Language Learning*, 25(2): 181–197.
Guichon, N. and McLornan, S. (2008) 'The effects of multimodality on L2 learners: Implications for CALL resource design', *System*, 36(1): 85–93.
Guth, S. and Helm, F. (2010) *Telecollaboration 2.0: Language, Literacies and Intercultural Learning in the 21st Century*, New York, NY: Peter Lang Publishers.
Hampel, R. and Hauck, M. (2006) 'Computer-mediated language learning: Making meaning in multimodal virtual learning spaces', *The JALT CALL Journal*, 2(2): 3–18.
Hampel, R. and Stickler, U. (2012) 'The use of videoconferencing to support multimodal interaction in an online language classroom', *ReCALL*, 24(2): 116–137.
Hoven, D. (2006) 'Communicating and interacting: an exploration of the changing roles of media in CALL/CMC', *CALICO Journal*, 23(2): 233–256.
Hubbard, P. (2004) 'Learner training for effective use of CALL', in S. Fotos and C. Browne (eds), *Perspectives on CALL for Second Language Classrooms*, Mahwah, NJ: Lawrence Erlbaum: 45–68.
Hubbard, P. (2013) 'Making a case for learner training in technology enhanced language learning environments', *CALICO Journal*, 30(2): 163–178.
Jewitt, C. (2004) 'Multimodality and new communication', in P. Levine and R. Scollon (eds), *Discourse and Technology: Multimodal Discourse Analysis*, Washington DC: Georgetown University Press: 184–195.
Jewitt, C. (2009) *The Routledge Handbook of Multimodal Analysis*, London, UK: Routledge.
Jewitt, C. (2011) 'The changing pedagogic landscape of subject English in UK classrooms', in K.L. O'Halloran and B.A. Smith (eds), *Multimodal Studies: Exploring Issues and Domains*, New York, NY: Routledge: 184–201.
Jones, R.H. (2004) 'The problem of context in computer-mediated communication', in P. Levine and R. Scollon (eds), *Discourse and Technology: Multimodal Discourse Analysis*, Washington, DC: Georgetown University Press: 20–33.
Kress, G. (2003) *Literacy in the New Media Age*, London, UK: Routledge.
Kress, G. and Van Leeuwen, T. (1996) *Reading Images: The Grammar of Visual Design*, New York, NY: Routledge.
Kress, G., and Van Leeuwen, T. (2001) *Multimodal Discourse*, London, UK: Arnold.
Lamy, M.-N. (2012) 'Diversity in modalities', in G. Stockwell (ed), *Computer-Assisted Language Learning: Diversity in Research and Practice*, Cambridge: Cambridge University Press: 110–127.

Levine, P. and Scollon, R. (eds) (2004) *Discourse and Technology: Multimodal Discourse Analysis*, Washington, DC: Georgetown University Press.

Lewis, T. (2006) 'When teaching is learning: A personal account of learning to teach online', *CALICO Journal*, 23(3): 581–600.

Mayer, R.E. (2005) 'Introduction to multimedia learning', in R.E. Mayer (ed), *The Cambridge Handbook of Multimedia Learning*, Cambridge: Cambridge University Press: 1–17.

Mayer, R.E. and Anderson, R.B. (1992) 'The instructive animation: Helping students build connections between words and pictures in multimedia learning', *Journal of Educational Psychology*, 84: 444–452.

Moreno, R. and Mayer, R. (1999) 'Cognitive principles of multimedia learning: The role of modality and contiguity', *Journal of Educational Psychology*, 91: 358–368.

Nelson, M. (2006) 'Mode, meaning, and synaesthesia in multimedia L2 writing', *Language Learning and Technology*, 10(2): 56–76.

New London Group (2000) 'A pedagogy of multiliteracies: Designing social futures', in B. Cope and M. Kalantzis (eds), *Multiliteracies: Literacy Learning and the Design of Social Futures*, Melbourne: Macmillan: 9–37.

New Media Consortium (2005) 'A global imperative: The report of the 21st century literacy summit', available: http://www.nmc.org/pdf/Global_Imperative.pdf

Norris, S. (2004) 'Multimodal discourse analysis: A conceptual framework', in P. Levine and R. Scollon (eds), *Discourse and Technology: Multimodal Discourse Analysis*, Washington, DC: Georgetown University Press: 101–115.

Plass, J., Chun, D., Mayer, R. and Leutner, D. (1998) 'Supporting visual and verbal learning preferences in second-language multimedia learning environment', *Journal of Educational Psychology*, 90(1): 25–36.

Royce, T.D. (2006) 'Multimodal communicative competence in second language contexts', in T.D. Royce and W.L. Bowcher (eds), *New Directions in the Analysis of Multimodal Discourse*, Hillsdale, NJ: Lawrence Erlbaum Associates: 361–390.

Sadler, R. (2007) 'A cautionary tale of two cities', *CALICO Journal*, 25(1): 11–30.

Schnotz, W. (2005) 'An integrated model of text and picture comprehension', in R.E. Mayer (ed), *The Cambridge Handbook of Multimedia Learning*, Cambridge: Cambridge University Press: 49–69.

Scollon, R., Bhatia, V., Li, D. and Yung, V. (1999) 'Blurred genres and fuzzy identities in Hong Kong public discourse: Foundational ethnographic issues in the study of reading', *Applied Linguistics*, 20(1): 22–43.

Stockwell, G. (2010) 'Effects of multimodality in computer-mediated communication tasks', in M. Thomas and H. Reinders (eds), *Task-Based Language Learning and Teaching with Technology*, London, UK: Continuum: 83–104.

Sweller, J. (2005) 'Implications of cognitive load theory for multimedia learning', in R.E. Mayer (ed), *The Cambridge Handbook of Multimedia Learning*, Cambridge: Cambridge University Press: 19–30.

Tricot, A. (2007) *Apprentissages et documents numériques*, Paris: Editions Belin.

Van Lier, L. (2004) *The Ecology and Semiotics of Language Learning*, Dordrecht: Kluwer Academic.

van Merriënboer, J.J.G. and Kester, L. (2005) 'The four-component instructional design model: Multimedia principles in environments for complex learning', in R.E. Mayer (ed), *The Cambridge Handbook of Multimedia Learning*, Cambridge: Cambridge University Press: 71–93.

Wickens, C.D. (1984) *Engineering Psychology and Human Performance*, Columbus: Merrill Publishing Company.

# 37
# Intelligent CALL and written language

*Cornelia Tschichold and Mathias Schulze*

In this chapter, after a general introduction to Intelligent CALL, we discuss the provision of corrective feedback in Tutorial CALL, sketching the challenges in the research and development of computational parsers and grammars. These challenges are the main reason why very few ICALL systems have been put to wider pedagogical use, in spite of great advances in our understanding of the structure of language(s) and of the pedagogy of corrective feedback. The automatic evaluation and assessment of free-form learner texts paying attention to linguistic accuracy, rhetorical structures, textual complexity, and written fluency is at the centre of attention in the section on automatic writing evaluation. The section on reading and incidental vocabulary learning aids looks at the advantages of lexical glosses, or lookup information in electronic dictionaries, for reading material aimed at language learners. In the conclusion we reflect on the role of ICALL research in the context of general trends in CALL.

Calling some research and development in CALL 'intelligent' does not mean we are ascribing a particular quality to the results. Intelligent CALL (ICALL) is a 35-year-old field within predominantly tutorial CALL (Hubbard and Bradin-Siskin 2004; Heift and Schulze 2015, in press), which applies concepts, techniques, algorithms and technologies from artificial intelligence. Artificial intelligence (AI) is 'the science and engineering of making intelligent machines' (McCarthy 2007: n.p.). Most relevant to CALL is the AI research on natural language processing (NLP), user modelling, expert systems and intelligent tutoring systems (ITS).

NLP deals with both natural language understanding and natural language generation. In the former, written or spoken linguistic input is turned into a computational representation that captures phonological/graphological, grammatical, semantic and/or pragmatic features of the input. The latter is the reverse process: from a computational representation to written output. In ICALL, natural language understanding works with parsers and produces a formal linguistic representation of learner texts or their parts. Most ICALL systems focus on sentences and their parts. Based on this linguistic representation, the ICALL tool can provide corrective feedback and/or instructional guidance for the learner. Most research in ICALL between Nelson, Ward, Desch and Kaplow (1976) and the early 2000s was aimed at error detection in and correction of learner text and the provision of informative, meta-linguistic feedback for learners (see Heift and Schulze 2007 for an overview). More recently, ICALL has focused on texts written for learners using robust human language technologies such as lemmatisers (i.e. algorithms which remove inflectional endings to return the base form of a word), part-of-speech taggers and parsers to analyse and augment these texts with additional information that is made available and useful to language learners (Schulze and Heift 2013). The information (e.g. conjugational paradigms of verbs in a reading text and/or highlighted less salient word classes such as prepositions) focuses the learners' attention, helps them notice linguistic patterns by raising their language awareness and/or scaffolds their language use. In ICALL, natural language generation, the second approach in NLP, has always focused more on raising the students' language awareness. Such ICALL systems (Zock, Sabah and Alviset 1986; Bailin and Thomson 1988; Zock 1988, 1992) provide students with well-formed sentences to illustrate constructions in the L2.

Many NLP-based systems rely on linguistic information to parse or generate text (a parser grammar and a lexicon). This structure of linguistic rules and items – the knowledge of the system – can be described as the expert system that captures knowledge about a particular domain. In ICALL, they are used to model the learning domain, for example, aspects of the grammar of a language and parts of its lexicon. They are a rich source of structured (linguistic) knowledge that can guide and scaffold the students' learning processes. Learners can query this knowledge base and use it as a comprehensive reference tool in learner-computer interactions.

The representation of the student text, which is produced by the parser and contains detailed information about form and meaning of the student input as well as any deviations from the recorded items and rules, can be used to maintain a detailed record of the learners' grammatical knowledge as depicted in their texts. This is where the student model plays a role. A student model 'observes' the student's actions, maintains a data structure with this information, and infers beliefs about the student's knowledge based on these data. The record of this information over time, which is maintained in student profiles, provides the basis for inferring interrelated facets of the student's cognitive belief system about the learned language, that is, the construction of a student model (Self 1994). Information from the student model, in turn, provides some basis for the tailoring of learning sequences and contingent guidance.

Both the student model and the expert model are essential components of ITSs. Such systems are tutors in the sense of Levy's (1997, 2009) tutor-tool distinction in CALL. They are used in the teaching of various instructional settings and for various subjects and domains. Intelligent language tutoring systems (ILTSs) have been developed for the past thirty years for a wide range of first, second and additional languages as well as different proficiency levels (Heift and Schulze 2007). For instance, Robo-Sensei is a commercial ILTS for Japanese for all proficiency levels (Nagata 2009); Tagarela teaches beginner learners of Portuguese (Amaral and Meurers 2008, 2011), and E-Tutor is a comprehensive language learning environment for all proficiency levels of German (Heift 2010b).

ICALL systems that have been used in classrooms or for self-directed language learning are still rare, but the body of research studies is comparatively large. ICALL is a highly interdisciplinary field of research that draws on a number of disciplines in applied linguistics and computing (Matthews and Fox 1991; Matthews 1992a, 1992b, 1993) and publications are scattered. Two older printed ICALL bibliographies (Matthews 1992c; Bailin 1995) exist and so does an online list of bibliographies (http://www.noe-kaleidoscope.org/group/idill/Bibliography/IDILL%20 Bibliography/) in which entries go up to 2008. The monograph by Heift and Schulze (2007) provides a comprehensive overview of the main concepts and research questions in the field. Some of the shorter overviews are more recent (Gamper and Knapp 2002; Nerbonne 2003; Schulze 2008a; Schulze and Heift 2013). A number of edited and proceedings volumes and special issues contain collections of articles on ICALL (Bailin and Levin 1989; Bailin 1991; Swartz and Yazdani 1992; Thompson and Zähner 1992; Chanier 1994; Schulze, Hamel and Thompson 1999; Tokuda, Heift and Chen 2002; Heift and Schulze 2003; Maritxalar, Ezeiza and Schulze

2007; Schulze 2008b; Meurers 2009); particularly Holland, Kaplan and Sams (1995) provide a useful snapshot of important ICALL research at that time. The annual conferences of the Association for Computational Linguistics (ACL) include workshops on the building of educational applications, whose refereed papers are available through the ACL Anthology (http://aclweb.org/anthology/).

In our overview, we concentrate on three ways in which ICALL tools support the language learning process: corrective feedback on written texts, automatic writing evaluation and vocabulary learning.

## Corrective feedback on written text

Nagata (1996, 1998) concludes from her learner study that only CALL programmes that make use of the full potential of the computer, by providing immediate and informative feedback, will produce better learning results. Rooted in a similar conceptualisation, error detection and diagnosis resulting in corrective feedback – the so-called grammar-checking – were the main focus of research and development in ICALL (see Heift and Schulze 2007). Research findings on individualised feedback and the interaction of learners with computers gave a significant impetus to research in tutorial CALL (Heift and Schulze 2015, in press). Based on sophisticated NLP technologies, ICALL systems identify and diagnose errors in written learner input and then generate contextualised, contingent learner feedback. ICALL research has sought evidence that corrective feedback in CALL makes a difference in language development, and more specifically what kind of feedback makes a difference. Following Nagata's (1996) study, a number of researchers studied the value of corrective feedback (e.g. Heift 2001, 2004, 2010a; Pujola 2002; Rosa and Leow 2004; Bowles 2005), and the results generally support the claim that students benefit from the more explicit meta-linguistic feedback, that is, feedback about the appropriateness and well-formedness of the language used by students in the sentence or text segment. Although the usefulness and role of corrective feedback in second language development are still debated in applied linguistics, a consensus that the right corrective feedback at the right time contributes to learning and leads to improvement in language proficiency is emerging (see e.g. Russell Valezy and Spada 2006).

In the last three decades of the 20th century and in line with research in NLP, grammar-checking tools in ICALL used parsers that in turn relied on linguistic grammars. Very little research on statistical NLP was applied in ICALL; the work by Gamon and colleagues (Gamon et al. 2009; Gamon and Leacock 2010) is a notable exception; see also the next section on automatic writing evaluation. However, parsing learner texts poses huge challenges in the computational grammar and lexicon, in the linguistic and pedagogical processing of individual errors, and in the generation of corrective feedback. The computational grammar and lexicon need to cover the fragment of language the students are using in their language learning activities. The difficulty of writing a grammar and lexicon that provides a sufficient basis for the comprehensive and unambiguous analysis and interpretation of free textual input can be fathomed when one looks at the output of any popular online translation tool. Homogeneous inflected word forms and clitics, specific collocations, word order variations, and long-distance dependencies such as anaphors and separable prefixes in some languages still are challenges in a computational analysis. This is why many grammar checkers for foreign language learners never reached the coverage and robustness to be used in the classroom (Schulze 2001; L'Haire and Vandeventer Faltin 2003). ICALL systems that restricted the input students can provide by, for example, relying on sentence translation and build-a-sentence activities were more successful (Nagata 2009; Heift 2010b). On the other hand, the enormous research and development cost of a parser-based system targeted at a very limited set of language activities students could do did not lead to sustained and widespread use in language classrooms.

Of course, when it comes to processing learner texts, the challenge is not only to cover a certain range of lexical and grammatical constructions, but also to detect and diagnose constructions which deviate from the items and rules of the computational grammar. In other words, the purpose of an ICALL tool is to be able to handle linguistic errors in the text and to provide contingent corrective feedback. Since the number of possible utterances in any language is infinite and each can contain one or more errors, it is at best ineffective and often impossible to anticipate and record all student utterances any CALL system will ever have to handle. In a way this is the raison d'être for ICALL, because string-matching and regular-expression matching algorithms have to rely on the anticipation of student answers and errors.

In generative grammars that are used in ICALL parsers, such as those of Chomskyan provenance (Chomsky 1981; Cook and Newson 1996) and various phrase structure grammars (Pollard and Sag 1987, 1994), grammatical rules constrain which combinations of words are grammatically well-formed and can thus be processed. To enable the processing of sentences and constructions with errors, generally, two approaches exist: if the input cannot be parsed successfully with 'error-free' grammatical rules, the parser relies on a second grammar with so-called mal-rules. Every time such a rule for an erroneous stretch of text is triggered, the error location and category are recorded in the linguistic representation and feedback can be generated accordingly. Although mal-rules are robust, they also necessitate a certain level of error anticipation and this limits the coverage of the system. The second approach has often been called constraint relaxation (Dini and Malnati 1993; Menzel and Schröder 1998). Here a grammatical constraint such as subject-verb agreement is encoded as a preference in that the strictness of the agreement in person, gender and number is relaxed. If subject and verb do not agree in number, the system can then parse this segment and will simply note that subject and verb do not agree in number. Again this information is used to generate the relevant feedback for the student. An advantage is that error anticipation is hardly necessary in this approach. However, since parsers produce multiple results for longer sentences by finding ambiguities humans tend to overlook, the number of results grows exponentially with relaxed constraints (Vandeventer 2001). A simple sentence will suffice as an illustration: *He write her mother.* With relaxed grammatical constraints, both *He* and *her mother* can be seen as either subject or object; errors of agreement and word order will be noted accordingly; the lack of subject-verb agreement can be resolved by having the subject in the plural or the verb in third person; various missing verb arguments (e.g. the direct object) can be hallucinated and recorded as errors. And these are only some of the many possibilities.

This makes the pedagogical processing of individual errors by filtering out the most appropriate parse tree – a tree-like diagram that depicts the syntactic structure of a parsed sentence – so complex. In a language like German, where many verbs require a prepositional object and the preposition requires a case-marked noun phrase, what feedback does a student need who has selected the wrong preposition but case-marked the subsequent noun phrase as it should have been with the right preposition? Through the relaxed constraints, all these will be recorded as various errors in the many different parse trees. Similar problems occur in input with multiple errors in one sentence. Heift (2003) suggests that both linguistic and pedagogical algorithms need to be applied. Both algorithms use information from the parse of the sentence and the student model, which contains data about the student's prior language learning, linguistic performance over time, and inferences about their relevant knowledge states. Linguistically, the more probable parse trees will have to be selected; pedagogically, student errors that impact most on the correction processes in particular and language learning in general need to be presented first, one after the other.

Error correction and feedback on spelling, lexical choice, and grammar in a sentence is thus a complex endeavour. Evaluating and providing feedback and assistance on entire learner texts is even more challenging.

## Automated writing evaluation

Among the computer-based tools for language learners we increasingly find automated essay scoring software. These tools were originally developed with the aim of quick and cost-effective holistic scoring of relatively short texts written by native speakers (of English), and were not intended for texts written by language learners. Their history goes back to the 1960s when a program called PEG (Page Essay Grade) delivered a score based on features that can easily be measured such as essay length, and average word and sentence lengths (Shermis and Burstein 2003; Burstein 2009; Shermis 2014), features that were also used for readability indices common at the time. The aim of PEG was to arrive at the same holistic score as a group of human scorers would, and the system therefore needed to be trained on a large set of previously scored essays. These large sets of similar essays (argument essays all written to the same prompt) were available because the educational system of the US requires many high school leavers to write such essays as part of a nationwide test. Colleges use these essay grades as part of their admissions procedure. As a high-stakes exam component, these essays all need to be graded by two qualified raters. The grades used in this system are holistic and typically place each essay on a scale of 1 to 6. Where the two human raters disagree by more than a set margin, a third marker is consulted to adjudicate. A number of commercial systems that claim to produce scores that agree with human scorers approximately as well as human scorers agree with each other have been developed since, thus promising not only to speed up the grading process (one of the two human scorers is replaced by the automatic essay scoring system), but also to save considerable costs. The best-known among these are e-rater (by ETS), IntelliMetric (by Vantage), the Intelligent Essay Assessor (by Pearson), and PEG (now owned by Measurement Inc.). When the first automated essay scorers appeared on the market, essays normally had to be copied by professional typers before being entered into the grading engines, thus eating up some of the potential cost savings. Today, the technology used by the software has improved considerably, and together with the fact that computers are now commonplace and more and more students type rather than handwrite their essays, this cost-saving element is becoming more important. State-of-the-art automatic essay scoring systems have in fact been used since 1999 in the GMAT (Graduate Management Admissions Test) to replace one of the two human raters (Warschauer and Grimes 2008). It is likely that the use of such systems will become considerably more widespread in the near future, as the need for more writing in the educational system grows (Shermis 2014) and it becomes ever more common to type essays during exams. The growth of massive open online courses (MOOCs) is likely to provide another area of application for these systems (Balfour 2013).

Automatic essay scoring (AES) engines obviously do not read an essay in the same way a human reader would. Instead they attempt to replicate the scores given by human scorers as faithfully as possible. To achieve this, a large training set of (human-)scored essays is needed. The automatic scoring itself is achieved by a combination of three elements: a set of purely statistical measures, the results of shallow parsing and a semantics element that depends on the training set. The first group of measures, and the one that has been used the longest, consists of simple features including mean word length (in letters and/or syllables), mean sentence length, average number of sentences per paragraph and type-token ratio (TTR). The latter in particular often gives a good indication of the general quality of the text, but is rather heavily influenced by overall text length (Perelman 2014).

Employing a shallow parser makes another level of analysis possible. Shallow parsers determine the part-of-speech of each word (PoS tagging) and the main constituents of the sentence (noun phrases and verb phrases), but do not attempt to parse the sentence completely. The number and proportion of PoS tags can be analysed statistically as well. Parsing also allows some further calculations, such as counting the number of modifiers in each noun phrase or counting the number of words that come before the main verb. As averages, both these figures give an indication of the complexity of the sentences in the text.

Systems employing statistical measures and shallow parsing work best if used with a large training corpus. A set of several hundreds or even thousands of graded essays, all written to the same prompt and therefore containing a number of topic-specific vocabulary items, can be used to fine-tune the third element, the semantic engine at the heart of the system. The main semantics component of commercial scorers uses latent semantic analysis (Landauer, Foltz and Laham 1998) or a similar method. The human scores are analysed against the various elements of the software and the best fit is then used to predict the scores of the essays that need to be evaluated.

Such prompt-specific models (Ramineni and Williamson 2013) tend to achieve better overall results than the alternative generic models, which work without a specific content analysis. Generic models have the advantage of requiring smaller numbers of texts for calibration and thus allowing their use in contexts where no human grading has occurred yet (e.g. for quick feedback on drafts). In such cases, the training set can be used to arrive at the level of writing that can be expected in a particular school grade.

Shermis (2014) reports on a comparison of nine automatic scoring systems, mostly commercially available systems. Out of a pool of eight sets of up to almost 2,000 short essays (typically 300 words long) and free-form answers (typically 100 words long), the majority were made available to train the nine systems before the remainder were then used as a test set in the comparison. The results show that the best systems manage to successfully replicate human rating results, but also that there are a number of issues still to be resolved in terms of the validity of automatic scores.

The use of automatic essay scoring is controversial, of course (Balfour 2013; Deane 2013; Weigle 2013). The first aspect of these programs that users have to accept is the fact that they arrive at their results in a different way than humans do. Aeroplanes use different techniques to fly than birds do, so this is not a problem per se. More relevant in this context is the potential that students might learn to write in a style that the machine scores highly, and the fact that much of the scoring depends on the essay length and the exact comparisons made in evaluations (Perelman 2014). There are also doubts whether there are any positive effects on the quality of writing (Stevenson and Phakiti 2014).

Despite this origin in first language essay assessment, a number of these tools have been used and sometimes marketed for foreign language learning situations. In some cases, the engines have been repackaged as tools that provide local feedback and more formative feedback on the writing quality that goes beyond the summative feedback of a single digit score. Criterion, for example, uses the e-rater scoring engine. Li et al. (2014) report on a study where Criterion was used in an academic writing class for EFL students and conclude that such tools can serve a useful function as long as their limitations are clear. Lim and Kahng (2012) in their review of Criterion come to a similar conclusion. Coniam (2009) shows that BETSY, a program that is free for research purposes, reaches a good correlation with human raters, even if it does not become clear how the system achieves this.

If the emphasis is on feedback to the writer rather than overall scoring, the use of such tools is perhaps less controversial as this would have the primary aim of helping nonnative writers. Where automatic essay scoring has been used with learners, the positive outcomes tend to come from the grammar and word choice feedback (cf. Wang, Shang and Briody 2013, who used Vantage Learning's CorrectEnglish in Taiwan to good effect). For this level of feedback we need to remember that the target audience does not have native-speaker intuitions to fall back on when faced with a feedback message. The developers typically have the choice of tweaking the engine so as to improve the coverage (i.e. to catch more errors) but at the price of producing more so-called false positives (i.e. signalling an error where there is none). Because learners tend to put their faith into these programs even more than native speakers do, this is a dangerous strategy. Most developers have therefore opted for the more cautious and considerably more appropriate strategy of minimising false positives.

The results concerning higher-level aspects, that is, paragraph organisation, are less clear. Lee, Cheung, Wong and Lee (2009) found no statistically significant advantage of an experimental system based on latent semantic analysis for adult EFL writers, while Lee et al. (2013) call for more research into the specific needs by different age and proficiency groups, a call echoed in Li, Link and Hegelheimer (2015). The latter paper also shows that students need some support from their teachers to make good use of the feedback, but this has the advantage that teachers then feel they can leave some of the feedback duties to the program. One point of concern remains, however. The engines used for automatic essay scoring have been developed for use on argumentative essays, a genre which is perhaps not the most common task in the foreign language classroom, where many writing tasks involve longer prompts and different text types.

## Reading and incidental vocabulary learning aids

Comparing writing and reading from an ICALL perspective, their most important difference is that the focus on writing (as with corrective feedback) is predominantly on highlighting errors in learner texts (in addition to measuring the complexity and fluency of these texts), whereas in reading activities, the computer processes text that is almost error-free and augments it with additional information, as we will see shortly.

Extensive reading is generally considered to be a crucial tool to develop fluency for language learners who want to improve beyond the beginner stage. Since Krashen (1989), if not longer, reading is also thought to bring about incidental vocabulary acquisition, that is, a certain amount of vocabulary acquisition without this being a stated aim of the reading activity; and a good vocabulary size is needed to achieve fluency and comprehension when reading foreign language texts. Learners' level of reading comprehension and their vocabulary size correlate strongly and positively influence one another (Nation 2001; Grabe 2004; Webb and Chang 2015). Acquiring a sufficiently large amount of vocabulary is arguably the biggest task for the language learner, with estimates of around 3,000–5,000 word families at least being necessary to read authentic texts in English (Nation 2001, 2006; Schmitt and Schmitt 2014). Reading for pleasure and other extensive reading activities, for example for fluency, require all or almost all of the vocabulary to be known by the reader, but when involved in intensive reading and reading with the aim of developing the vocabulary, learners are thought to be able to deal with a slightly higher proportion of unknown words. Automatic recognition of individual words, particularly of high-frequency words, is necessary to ensure adequate top-down processing. This in turn facilitates good text comprehension. Encountering unknown words has the potential of interrupting this top-down process by the need for bottom-up processing of dealing with an individual lexical item.

When faced with an unknown word, readers can either ignore it, try to infer its meaning from the context and their linguistic knowledge, or they can decide to look it up in a dictionary.

In texts that have been prepared for learners, glosses can offer a further option. Glosses can make more texts accessible to learners and allow them to read texts with only minimal interruption. With more and more reading being done online or in electronic form, the option of electronic glossing on demand is becoming a more realistic option, including on mobile devices (Lee and Lee 2013), and has even been shown to be more effective than its equivalent paper version (Taylor 2013).

Hyperlinking any word in a text to an electronic dictionary is now quite easy, but glosses can also take a number of other forms, for example, a translational equivalent in the learner's first language, a single dictionary definition, a picture representation, an audio file or any combination of these. Research has shown that the combination of text with visual information is better for text comprehension and also for vocabulary acquisition than either format on its own (Chun and Plass 1996; Yoshii and Flaitz 2002; Plass et al. 2003; Yanguas 2009; Türk and Erçetin 2014), assuming a suitable picture can be found. Evidence in favour of multimodality also comes from the related area of video captioning (Montero Perez, Van Den Noortgate and Desmet 2013): language learners' comprehension and vocabulary uptake improves when videos have L2 captions.

Incidental vocabulary acquisition from glossed texts to some extent suffers from the fact that the learner's primary aim of text comprehension is helped best by keeping the interruptions that are necessary for looking up unknown words as short as possible, so as not to disrupt the flow of the text. For vocabulary acquisition, some engagement with the form and meaning of the unknown word is indispensable, however. Laufer and Rozovski-Roitblat (2011), for example, have shown that a certain amount of such focus on forms has benefits for vocabulary acquisition. Glossing provides faster access to a word's meaning than dictionary lookup, hence is advantageous for text comprehension (Chun 2001). If incidental vocabulary acquisition is a secondary aim, methods to get the learner to notice the word and focus on it for a short time should be helpful. Nagata (1999) tested this contrast when she compared glosses containing a translation with glosses containing two possible translations in a multiple-choice format. This very short mini-exercise proved to be beneficial for vocabulary acquisition. Huang and Lin (2014) report on a study where three glossing types were compared, two of them aimed at requiring a limited amount of extra mental effort. The best results for vocabulary learning were achieved where, of the three occurrences of the target word, the first and the third were glossed and the second required the learner to infer or retrieve the meaning in order to progress with the reading task.

Most studies on glosses report on relatively small-scale comparisons between different conditions, using materials prepared by the teacher or researcher. In these cases, the text in the glosses is written specifically for the reading passage and does not list the full dictionary entry with multiple meanings and other information not relevant for comprehension of the given text. Chun (2001) directly compared these two conditions: glosses written by the instructor and access to a bilingual dictionary entry. Learners preferred the glosses by the instructor and achieved better overall text comprehension, thus adding further weight to the strategy of keeping interruptions to a minimum while still ensuring that the reader understands the words.

While it is now technically possible to turn every word of an electronic text into a clickable link to a dictionary entry, this procedure does not provide custom-made or even context-sensitive glosses, that is, the type that is most helpful both for text comprehension and for vocabulary learning. However, tools such as QuickAssist (Wood 2011) that turn each word form in the text into a hyperlink automatically cut out the labour and time-intensive task of manual text glossing for instructors or material developers. QuickAssist circumvents the challenge of context-sensitive glosses by giving the learner/reader the choice of a lookup in a bilingual dictionary, for which the necessary base form of the word is automatically generated, letting the learner search for additional examples in the different texts and contexts of a tightly controlled corpus, and linking to the entries in the German Wikipedia for named entities and terminology. In addition, learners can look up the morphological paradigm of the search word. Such tools rely on robust NLP technologies, which are now available for a range of languages.

To conclude, we can now say that glossing electronic text for language learners is beneficial for the language learning process; however, there still remain a number of questions. The effectiveness of glosses for different learner groups, especially different proficiency levels, is not very clear yet. Linked to this may be the question whether there are text types that are more or less appropriate for glossing. Another area for research is the postreading exercise generation. But the central question for an ICALL approach to glossing is how NLP, or more specifically automatic word sense disambiguation, can be harnessed to produce glosses that are context-appropriate without the teacher having to enter all glosses manually.

As a small, highly specialised field of research, ICALL has made great strides computationally, linguistically and pedagogically in its almost forty years of existence. Computers became much faster and their storage capacity grew exponentially bigger; algorithms for storing and retrieving and for analysis and synthesis became more efficient and robust. This alleviated the challenges with computer processing times of the 1980s and 1990s. It facilitated the just-in-time parsing of linguistic input on a remote server, providing contingent feedback to learners in real time; the results of a dictionary lookup, for example, are presented almost instantaneously. Based on a vastly improved understanding of language(s), a number of robust NLP technologies such as part-of-speech taggers, lemmatisers, and spell-checkers have become available for a much wider group of languages, making their employment in ICALL systems possible. Again for a variety of languages, large corpora, tree banks and dictionaries have been created as open resources for researchers and developers and have been implemented in ICALL tools and systems. ICALL researchers have become increasingly aware of theories of second language development and advances in our understanding of language learning and have been able to apply these insights to innovative and functioning tutorial CALL systems.

Yet, ICALL systems are not in widespread use and the group of researchers in ICALL remains small. The main underlying reason for this is that the development of intelligent language tutoring systems is a complex and labour-intensive process that requires expertise in computational linguistics, software engineering, second language development and language pedagogy. This necessitates collaborative transdisciplinary research for which the human resources of one department or research centre are often not sufficient. Cross-university collaboration is frequently coupled to national or international project funding or happens in the context of PhD projects. Many of these projects have only a limited time span, preventing the sustainability of the research and development beyond a proof-of-theory prototype time and again. Due to the rapid advances in digital technologies, the success of many of these ICALL projects has also been hampered by the lack of widely accepted standards in important areas such as error categorisation and annotation, computational interfaces of NLP tools such as lexicons, taggers and parsers, and especially in ICALL specific domains such as parse tree filters and error priority queues (Heift 2003).

When it comes to error correction and feedback, ICALL research has to rely on empirical evidence about the role of practice in language learning and the efficacy of different forms of corrective feedback, for example; but discussions on these research topics in SLA research are ongoing and some findings have only been published relatively recently or are not yet conclusive. So in spite of the many contributions ICALL has made to advances in tutorial CALL and the promise of ICALL to help tutorial CALL realise its full potential, the vote is still out.

Therefore, current and future research in ICALL is exploring a number of avenues:

- In line with common trends in software engineering and NLP, modular (rather than monolithic) approaches are employed in the development of ICALL tools and systems. This enables researchers to implement existing NLP tools effectively and efficiently.
- Preference is given to the implementation of existing NLP tools that are known to be robust for a particular (set of) language(s) in contexts where a lot is known about the linguistic input, such as texts for learners versus texts from learners and tightly controlled linguistic input from learners. This applies in particular to the implementation of linguistic help tools for learners such as automatic glosses, but also to restriction of the search space through appropriate language activity design. For example, it is much easier to parse a sentence in a translation, dictation or build-a-sentence activity because all lexical items are known a priori.
- ICALL researchers pay increasingly more attention to current research in SLA (instead of relying on personal intuitions about and experiences in foreign-language learning). Processes such as language awareness and reflected linguistic practice can be well supported through ICALL tools: after part-of-speech tagging of an error-free reading text, less salient parts of speech such as prepositions can be highlighted to focus the learner's attention on form; lexical or grammatical constructions the learner wants to investigate further can be presented in a variety of appropriate textual contexts, retrieving such examples from very large corpora.
- ICALL researchers are acutely aware of the lack of commonly accepted standards in the field. Discussions about establishing and documenting robust error annotation schemes, part-of-speech classifications, corpus annotation and other relevant linguistic annotations as well as interface nomenclature for NLP tools are ongoing.

With recent advances in SLA, linguistics, and computation, all this might only mark the beginning of the contributions ICALL can make to language learning in technology-rich contexts.

## Further reading

Deane, P. (2013) 'On the relation between automated essay scoring and modern views of the writing construct', *Assessing Writing*, 18: 7–24.
   This paper appeared in a special issue of the journal on automatic essay scoring. It brings together the idea of a writing as a construct and the techniques used by e-rater, attempting to point to a middle road between rejection and uncritical adoption of these tools.

Heift, T. and Schulze, M. (2007) *Errors and Intelligence in CALL: Parsers and Pedagogues*, New York, NY: Routledge.
   In this book, the authors bring together the diverse literature on ICALL, sketching the developments in the field over the first thirty years. The theoretical and empirical concepts of (written) learner language are developed, and various parsing algorithms are discussed subsequently. Issues of student modelling and individualised or adaptive learning are central to later chapters. For anybody interested in ICALL, this is a good textbook to start with.

Hulstijn, J.H., Hollander, M. and Gredanus, T. (1996) 'Incidental vocabulary learning by advanced foreign students: The influence of marginal glosses, dictionary use, and reoccurrence of unknown words', *The Modern Language Journal*, 80(3): 327–339.
   The authors provide a very clear and readable overview of the contribution of glosses to vocabulary learning and show the need for follow-up exercises if any lasting vocabulary gains are to be achieved. The paper also includes specific recommendations for a CALL environment.

Li, J., Link, S. and Hegelheimer, V. (2015) 'Rethinking the role of automated writing evaluation (AWE) feedback in ESL writing instruction', *Journal of Second Language Writing*, 27: 1–18.

The authors present a mixed-methods study that investigated the effects a commercial AES system had on writing instruction and performance. The views of both instructors and students are described, and recommendations for the use of AES in the classroom are given.

## References

Amaral, L. and Meurers, W.D. (2008) 'From recording linguistic competence to supporting inferences about language acquisition in context", *Computer Assisted Language Learning*, 21(4): 323–338.

Amaral, L. and Meurers, W.D. (2011) 'On using intelligent computer-assisted language learning in real-life foreign language teaching and learning', *ReCALL*, 23(1): 4–24.

Bailin, A. (ed) (1991) *Special Issue of the CALICO Journal on ICALL* (Vol. 9 (1)).

Bailin, A. (1995) 'Intelligent computer-assisted language learning: A bibliography', *Computers and the Humanities*, 29(5): 375–387.

Bailin, A. and Levin, L.S. (eds) (1989) *Intelligent Computer-Assisted Language Instruction. Computers and the Humanities* (Special Issue) (Vol. 23 (1)).

Bailin, A. and Thomson, P. (1988) 'The use of natural language processing in computer-assisted language instruction', *Computers and the Humanities*, 22: 99–110.

Balfour, S.P. (2013) 'Assessing writing in MOOCs: Automated essay scoring and calibrated peer review', *Research & Practice in Assessment*, 8: 40–48.

Bowles, M. (2005) 'Effects of verbalization condition and type of feedback on L2 development in a CALL task', PhD dissertation, Georgetown University, Washington, DC.

Burstein, J. (2009) 'Opportunities for natural language processing research in education', in A. Gelbulkh (ed), *Springer Lecture Notes in Computer Science*, Heidelberg: Springer: 6–27.

Chanier, T. (1994) 'Special issue on language learning', *Journal of Artificial Intelligence in Education*, 5.

Chomsky, N. (1981) *Lectures on Government and Binding*, Dordrecht: Holland Foris.

Chun, D.M. (2001) 'L2 reading on the web: Strategies for accessing information in hypermedia', *Computer Assisted Language Learning*, 14(5): 367–403.

Chun, D.M. and Plass, J.L. (1996) 'Effects of multimedia annotations on vocabulary acquisition', *The Modern Language Journal*, 80(2): 183–198.

Coniam, D. (2009) 'Experimenting with a computer essay-scoring program based on ESL student writing scripts', *ReCALL*, 21(2): 259–279.

Cook, V. and Newson, M. (1996) *Chomsky's Universal Grammar. An Introduction*, 2nd ed. Oxford: Blackwell.

Deane, P. (2013) 'On the relation between automated essay scoring and modern views of the writing construct', *Assessing Writing*, 18: 7–24.

Dikli, S. (2006) 'An overview of automated scoring of essays', *The Journal of Technology, Learning, and Assessment*, 5(1): 4–35.

Dini, L. and Malnati, G. (1993) 'Weak constraints and preference rules', in P. Bennett and P. Paggio (eds), *Preference in Eurotra*, Luxembourg: Commission of the European Communities: 75–90.

Gamon, M. and Leacock, C. (2010) 'Search right and thou shalt find ... Using web queries for learner error detection', in *Proceedings of the NAACL HLT 2010 Fifth Workshop on Innovative Use of NLP for Building Educational Application*, Los Angeles: Association for Computational Linguistics: 37–44.

Gamon, M., Leacock, C., Brockett, C., Dolan, W.B., Gao, J., Belenko, D. and Klementiev, A. (2009) 'Using statistical techniques and web search to correct ESL errors', *CALICO Journal*, 26(3): 491–511.

Gamper, J. and Knapp, J. (2002) 'A review of Intelligent CALL systems', *Computer Assisted Language Learning*, 15(4): 329–342.

Grabe, W. (2004) 'Research on teaching reading', *Annual Review of Applied Linguistics*, 24: 44–68.

Guo, L., Crossley, S. and McNamara, D. (2013) 'Predicting human judgments of essay quality in both integrated and independent second language writing samples: A comparison study', *Assessing Writing*, 18: 218–238.

Heift, T. (2001) 'Error-specific and individualized feedback in a web-based language tutoring system: Do they read it?', *ReCALL*, 13(2): 129–142.

Heift, T. (2003) 'Multiple learner errors and meaningful feedback: A challenge for ICALL systems', *CALICO*, 20(3): 533–549.

Heift, T. (2004) 'Corrective feedback and learner uptake in CALL', *ReCall*, 16(2): 416–431.

Heift, T. (2010a) 'Prompting in CALL: A longitudinal study of learner uptake', *Modern Language Journal*, 94(2): 198–216.
Heift, T. (2010b) 'Developing an intelligent tutor', *CALICO Journal*, 27(3): 443–459.
Heift, T. and Schulze, M. (eds) (2003) 'Error analysis and error correction', *Special Issue of the CALICO Journal*, 20(3).
Heift, T. and Schulze, M. (2007) *Errors and Intelligence in CALL: Parsers and Pedagogues*, New York, NY: Routledge.
Heift, T. and Schulze, M. (2015) 'Research timeline: Tutorial CALL', *Language Teaching*, 48(4): 1–20.
Holland, V.M., Kaplan, J.D. and Sams, M.R. (eds) (1995) *Intelligent Language Tutors: Theory Shaping Technology*, Mahwah, NJ: Lawrence Erlbaum Associates.
Huang, L. L., and Lin, C. C. (2014) 'Three approaches to glossing and their effects on vocabulary learning', *System*, 44: 127–136.
Hubbard, P. and Bradin-Siskin, C. (2004) 'Another look at Tutorial CALL', *ReCALL*, 16(2): 448–461.
Krashen, S. (1989) 'We acquire vocabulary and spelling by reading: Additional evidence for the input hypothesis', *The Modern Language Journal*, 73(4): 440–464.
Landauer, T., Foltz, P. and Laham, D. (1998) 'An introduction to latent semantic analysis', *Discourse Processes*, 25(2–3): 259–284.
Laufer, B. and Rozovski-Roitblat, B. (2011) 'Incidental vocabulary acquisition: The effects of task type, word occurrence and their combination', *Language Teaching Research*, 15(4): 391–411.
Lee, C., Cheung, W.K.W., Wong, K.C.K. and Lee, F.S.L. (2009) 'Web-based essay critiquing system and EFL students' writing: A quantitative and qualitative investigation', *Computer Assisted Language Learning*, 22(1): 57–72.
Lee, C., Cheung, W.K.W., Wong, K.C.K. and Lee, F.S.L. (2013) 'Immediate web-based essay critiquing system feedback and teacher follow-up feedback on young second language learners' writings: An experimental study in a Hong Kong secondary school', *Computer Assisted Language Learning*, 26(1): 39–60.
Lee, H. and Lee, J.H. (2013) 'Implementing glossing in mobile-assisted language learning environments: Directions and outlook', *Language Learning & Technology*, 17(3): 6–22.
Levy, M. (1997) *Computer-Assisted Language Learning: Context and Conceptualisation*, Oxford, UK: Clarendon.
Levy, M. (2009) 'A tutor-tool framework', in P. Hubbard (ed), *Computer Assisted Language Learning: Critical Concepts in Linguistics* (Vol. I), New York, NY: Routledge: 45–78.
L'Haire, S. and Vandeventer Faltin, A. (2003) 'Error diagnosis in the FreeText project', *CALICO Journal*, 20(3): 481–496.
Li, J., Link, S. and Hegelheimer, V. (2015) 'Rethinking the role of automated writing evaluation (AWE) feedback in ESL writing instruction', *Journal of Second Language Writing*, 27: 1–18.
Li, Z., Link, S., Ma, H., Yang, H. and Hegelheimer, V. (2014) 'The role of automated writing evaluation holistic scores in the ESL classroom', *System*, 44: 66–78.
Lim, H. and Kahng, J. (2012) 'Review of criterion', *Language Learning & Technology*, 16(2): 38–45.
Maritxalar, M., Ezeiza, N. and Schulze, M. (eds) (2007) *Proceedings of the Workshop NLP for Educational Resources at the International Conference Recent Advances in Natural Language Programming 2007*, Borovets, Bulgaria: Bulgarian Academy of Sciences.
Matthews, C. (1992a) 'Fundamental questions in ICALL', in J. Thompson and C. Zähner (eds), *Proceedings of the ICALL Workshop, UMIST, September 1991*, Hull: University of Hull, CTI Centre for Modern Languages: 77–89.
Matthews, C. (1992b) 'Going AI. Foundations of ICALL', *CALL*, 5(1–2): 13–31.
Matthews, C. (1992c) *Intelligent CALL (ICALL) Bibliography*, Hull: CTI Centre for Modern Languages.
Matthews, C. (1993) 'Grammar frameworks in Intelligent CALL', *CALICO Journal*, 11(1): 5–27.
Matthews, C. and Fox, J. (1991) 'Foundations of ICALL. An overview of student modelling', in H. Savolainen and J. Telenius (eds), *Eurocall 1991. Conference on Computer Assisted Language Learning*, Helsinki: The Helsinki School of Economics and Business Administration: 163–170.
McCarthy, J. (2007) 'What is artificial intelligence?', available: http://www-formal.stanford.edu/jmc/whatisai/whatisai.html (17 Nov 2009).
Menzel, W. and Schröder, I. (1998) 'Constraint-based diagnosis for intelligent language tutoring systems', in *Proceedings of the IT&KNOWS Conference at IFIP'98 Congress*, Wien/Budapest: 484–497.
Meurers, W.D. (ed) (2009) 'Automatic analysis of learner language', *Special Issue of the CALICO Journal*, 26(3), San Marcos, TX: Calico.
Montero Perez, M., Van Den Noortgate, W. and Desmet, P. (2013) 'Captioned video for L2 listening and vocabulary learning: A meta-analysis', *System*, 41: 720–739.

Nagata, N. (1996) 'Computer vs. workbook instruction in second language acquisition', *CALICO Journal*, 14(1): 53–75.
Nagata, N. (1998) 'Input vs. output practice in educational software for second language acquisition', *Language Learning & Technology*, 1(2): 23–40.
Nagata, N. (1999) 'The effectiveness of computer-assisted interactive glosses', *Foreign Language Annals*, 32(4): 469–479.
Nagata, N. (2009) 'Robo-Sensei's NLP-based error detection and feedback generation', *CALICO Journal*, 26(3): 562–579.
Nation, I.S.P. (2001) *Learning Vocabulary in Another Language*, Cambridge: Cambridge University Press.
Nation, I.S.P. (2006) 'How large a vocabulary is needed for reading and listening?' *Canadian Modern Language Review*, 63(1): 59–82.
Nelson, G.E., Ward, J.R., Desch, S.H. and Kaplow, R. (1976) 'Two new strategies for computer-assisted language instruction (CALI)' *Foreign Language Annals*, 10: 28–37.
Nerbonne, J.A. (2003) 'Natural language processing in computer-assisted language learning', in R. Mitkov (ed), *The Oxford Handbook of Computational Linguistics*, Oxford: Oxford University Press: 670–698.
Perelman, L. (2014) 'When 'the state of the art' is counting words', *Assessing Writing*, 21: 104–111.
Plass, J., Chun, D.M., Mayer, R.E. and Leutner, D. (2003) 'Cognitive load in reading a foreign language text with multimedia aids and the influence of verbal and spatial abilities', *Computers in Human Behavior*, 19: 221–243.
Pollard, C.J. and Sag, I. (1994) *Head-Driven Phrase Structure Grammar*, Chicago, IL: University Press.
Pollard, C.J. and Sag, I.A. (1987) *Information-Based Syntax and Semantics*, Chicago, IL: University Press.
Pujola, J.-T. (2002) 'CALLing for help: Researching language learning strategies using help facilities in a web-based multimedia program', *ReCALL*, 14(2): 235–262.
Ramineni, C. and Williamson, D. (2013) 'Automated essay scoring: Psychometric guidelines and practices', *Assessing Writing*, 18: 25–39.
Rosa, E. and Leow, R. (2004) 'Computerized task-based exposure, explicitness and type of feedback on Spanish L2 development', *Modern Language Journal*, 88: 192–217.
Russell Valezy, J. and Spada, N. (2006) 'The effectiveness of corrective feedback for second language acquisition: A meta-analysis of the research', in J.M. Norris and L. Ortega (eds), *Synthesizing Research on Language Learning and Teaching*, Amsterdam: John Benjamins.
Schmitt, N. and Schmitt, D. (2014) 'A reassessment of frequency and vocabulary size in L2 vocabulary teaching', *Language Teaching*, 47(4): 484–503.
Schulze, M. (2001) 'Textana – Grammar and grammar-checking in parser-based CALL', PhD thesis, UMIST, Manchester.
Schulze, M. (2008a) 'AI in CALL: Artificially inflated or almost imminent?', *CALICO Journal*, 25(3): 510–527.
Schulze, M. (ed) (2008b) *Interfaces in Intelligent CALL. Special Issue of Computer Assisted Language Learning* (21.4), London, UK: Routledge.
Schulze, M., Hamel, M.-J. and Thompson, J. (eds) (1999) *Language Processing in CALL. ReCALL Special Publication (Proceedings of a One-Day Conference 'Natural Language Processing in Computer-Assisted Language Learning' Held at UMIST, 9 May 1998, Organised by the Centre of Computational Linguistics, UMIST, in Association with Eurocall)*, Hull: CTICML.
Schulze, M. and Heift, T. (2013) 'Intelligent CALL', in M. Thomas, H. Reinders and M. Warschauer (eds), *Contemporary Computer-Assisted Language Learning*, London; New York, NY: Continuum: 249–265.
Self, J.A. (1994) 'The role of student models in learning environments', *IEICE Transactions on Information and Systems*, 77(1): 8.
Shermis, M. (2014) 'State-of-the-art automated essay scoring: Competition, results, and future directions from a United States demonstration', *Assessing Writing*, 20: 53–76.
Shermis, M. and Burstein, J. (2003) *Automated Essay Scoring: A Cross-Disciplinary Perspective*, Mahwah, NJ: Lawrence Erlbaum Associates.
Stevenson, M. and Phakiti, A. (2014) 'The effects of computer-generated feedback on the quality of writing', *Assessing Writing*, 19: 52–65.
Swartz, M.L. and Yazdani, M. (1992) *Intelligent Tutoring Systems for Foreign Language Learning: The Bridge to International Communication* (Vol. 80), New York, NY: Springer Verlag.
Taylor, A. (2013) 'CALL versus paper: In which context are L1 glosses more effective?', *CALICO Journal*, 30(1): 63–81.

Thompson, J. and Zähner, C. (eds) (1992) *Proceedings of the ICALL Workshop, UMIST, September 1991*, Hull: University of Hull, CTI Centre for Modern Languages.

Tokuda, N., Heift, T. and Chen, L. (2002) *Special Issue on ICALL. Computer Assisted Language Learning*, 15(4).

Türk, E. and Erçetin, G. (2014) 'Effects of interactive versus simultaneous display of multimedia glosses on L2 reading comprehension and incidental vocabulary acquisition', *Computer Assisted Language Learning*, 27(1): 1–25.

Vandeventer, A. (2001) 'Creating a grammar checker for CALL by constraint relaxation: A feasibility study', *ReCALL*, 13(1): 110–120.

Wang, Y.-J., Shang, H.-F. and Briody, P. (2013) 'Exploring the impact of using automated writing evaluation in English as a foreign language university students' writing', *Computer Assisted Language Learning*, 26(3): 234–257.

Warschauer, M. and Grimes, D. (2008) 'Automated writing assessment in the classroom', *Pedagogies: An International Journal*, 3: 22–36.

Webb, S. and Chang, A.C.-S. (2015) 'How does prior word knowledge affect vocabulary learning progress in an extensive reading program?', *Studies in Second Language Acquisition*. doi:10.1017/S0272263114000606.

Weigle, S.C. (2013) 'English language learners and automated scoring of essays: Critical considerations', *Assessing Writing*, 18: 85–99.

Wood, P. (2011) 'Computer-assisted reading in German as a foreign language. Developing and testing an NLP-based application', *CALICO Journal*, 28(3): 662–676.

Yanguas, Í. (2009) 'Multimedia glosses and their effect on L2 text comprehension and vocabulary learning', *Language Learning & Technology*, 13(2): 48–67.

Yoshii, M. and Flaitz, J. (2002) 'Second language incidental vocabulary retention: The effect of text and picture annotation types', *CALICO Journal*, 20(1): 33–58.

Zock, M. (1988) 'Language learning as problem solving. Modeling logical aspects of inductive learning to generate sentences in French by man and machine', in *Proceedings of the Twelfth International Conference on Computational Linguistics* (Vol. 2), Budapest: John von Neumann Society for Computing Sciences: 806–811.

Zock, M. (1992) 'SWIM or Sink: The problem of communicating thought', in M.L. Swartz and M. Yazdani (eds), *Intelligent Tutoring Systems for Foreign Language Learning. The Bridge to International Communication*, Berlin: Springer: 235–247.

Zock, M., Sabah, G. and Alviset, C. (1986) 'From structure to process. Computer-assisted teaching of various strategies for generating pronoun constructions in French', in *Proceedings of the 11th Conference on Computational Linguistics*, Stroudsburg, PA: Association for Computational Linguistics: 566–569.

# 38
# Translation and technology
## The case of translation games for language learning

*Pierrette Bouillon, Cristiana Cervini and Manny Rayner*

Beginner language students cannot develop their productive skills without conversation practice, but it can be difficult for them to find partners. Below a certain level, the student is often so diffident about their minimal linguistic abilities that they feel it an unwarranted imposition to ask any native speaker to spend time practising with them. In these circumstances, a mechanical conversation partner equipped with speech recognition has obvious plausibility. Ideally, the conversation partner would be able to carry out a free conversation with the student, but systems of this kind are challenging to build. At the other extreme, a system which simply gives the student spoken examples to imitate is too limited; imitation gives no real practice in language production.

This chapter examines an intermediate strategy which has its roots in the work carried out at MIT by Seneff and her colleagues (Wang and Seneff 2007). Reusing technology initially developed in spoken language translation projects, the student is prompted with a source-language sentence, or some representation of it. Their spoken response is transformed into some kind of language-neutral form using speech recognition and machine translation methods, and compared with the corresponding language-neutral form for the prompt; the student is then given feedback about the correctness or otherwise of the match between the two language-neutral forms. The fact that multiple correct responses are in general possible gives the student the opportunity to practise production, but the system is still reasonably easy to develop. The chapter is largely organised around a case study using CALL-SLT, a multilingual web-enabled spoken translation game system under development at Geneva University since 2009. We describe initial evaluations, focusing on how the system works in practice, how it can be integrated into formal classroom teaching and what objective evidence there is that the speech recognition capabilities of the system help students acquire productive language skills.

### Spoken translation games: A compromise between simple repetition and automatic dialogue

Beginner language students cannot develop their productive skills without conversation practice, but it can be difficult for them to find anyone to talk to. Classroom teachers are stretched too thinly most of the time to be able to give the average student much attention. The first hurdle, often a difficult one, is thus to get to a point where live conversation practice with other people is a practical possibility.

Given that speech recognition has now become a well-established technology, it is natural to consider the idea of building mechanical conversation partners for beginner students, and numerous groups have explored different approaches in this direction. The most important practical problem involved in building such a system is that beginner students can have difficulties pronouncing the sounds of the L2, which makes it difficult for speech recognisers to understand what they are saying and respond appropriately; the more ambitious the range of language that the recogniser is intended to cover, the worse this problem becomes.

A popular but extreme response is to design the system so that the student, at each step, only has the option of repeating a specified sentence; this does indeed solve the recognition problem, but at the same time makes it impossible for the student to practise any skills except pronunciation. Here, we describe a compromise strategy, called a *spoken translation game*, which unites the technologies of *speech recognition* and *machine translation* (MT). Instead of being given an L2 sentence to imitate, the student is given an L1 sentence to translate orally; by making the translation request more indirect, they have the opportunity to practise both pronunciation and productive language skills.

The rest of the chapter is organised as follows. In the next section we give relevant background on speech recognition and discuss general issues that arise when it is integrated into a spoken translation game. We then describe initial work on translation games at MIT and introduce our main example, the CALL-SLT system developed at Geneva University. We next present results of two evaluations supporting the claim that systems of this kind are capable of improving students' use of language. In the final section we give suggestions for further reading.

## Speech recognition and translation

The central component of the spoken translation game is the speech recogniser. Ideally, it should recognise what the student *intends* to say, irrespective of how badly they pronounce it, in order to be able to give adequate feedback. This is sometimes difficult even for a human teacher. A reasonable compromise is to accept that the machine will only recognise speech which is reasonably well pronounced, and otherwise reject student utterances as incomprehensible; even this is, in general, well beyond the actual state of the art. We briefly outline the issues that arise.

Going back to first principles, a recogniser is a piece of software which takes speech as input and produces written text as output. It uses three main sources of information to do this: an acoustic model, a phonetic dictionary and a language model. The *acoustic model* defines correspondences between the phonemes of the language and their spoken realisations. These correspondences are extremely complicated; they depend both on the context (the same phoneme is pronounced differently depending on what comes before and after) and on the speaker (different speakers pronounce the same phoneme differently). It is not practically possible to write down the correspondences as rules. Instead, they have to be acquired, using machine learning methods, from large samples of recorded and annotated speech. This process is called 'training an acoustic model', and the nature of the acoustic model depends largely on the data used to train it. In particular, its success in understanding accents depends on whether examples of people speaking with those accents were included in the training data. For some kinds of speech recognition applications, in particular large-vocabulary dictation tools like Dragon Dictate, the acoustic model can be adapted to the individual speaker, to take account of their idiosyncratic preferences in pronouncing the different phonemes. This usually gives a substantial improvement in accuracy, but the associated complications in terms of creating and appropriately activating individual user profiles mean that this method is often hard to use in practice.

The *language model*, on the other hand, defines the relative probabilities of different possible sequences of words, whose possible realisations as sequences of phonemes are defined by the pronunciation dictionary; typically, a word will have more than one such realisation. Very roughly, the process of speech recognition works by having the acoustic model and pronunciation dictionary suggest different possible sequences of words based on the input speech signal; these are then filtered to pick out the ones that are most probable in terms of the language model. For example, in English it is far more likely that the words *stocks and* are followed by *bonds* than by *bombs* (anyone who doubts this is invited to look up both phrases on Google; the first gets about a hundred times as many hits as the second). A speech recogniser whose language model is aware of this fact, and which has got as far as guessing that the first two words of the input signal are *stocks and*, while the third is either *bonds* or *bombs*, will thus be inclined to choose the first alternative.

In general, the language model helps by constraining the space of choices that the recogniser needs to consider; the more tightly constrained this space is, the more accurate recognition will be. The degree to which the space can be constrained depends mainly on the complexity of the language (words and phrases) that the speech recogniser is required to be able to process. At one end of the scale, a recogniser designed to recognise free speech faces an extremely challenging task: it needs to consider tens or even hundreds of thousands of possible words, sometimes with only weak constraints on possible choices. For example, suppose a person introducing themselves says 'Hello, my name is ____'; even if we are sure that the last word is a name we already know, we often have trouble identifying it. At the other end of the scale, an answer to a yes/no question can be recognised very reliably; there are only two possibilities, which sound quite different from each other. In general, the accuracy of the recogniser will be inversely proportional to the number of possible alternatives allowed by the language model.

When constructing a speech recogniser for an application that will be used by beginner language students, the immediate problem is that they are unlikely to be able to pronounce many of the L2 sounds in a native-like way. An acoustic model trained on native speakers will thus have problems matching the sounds the students produce to the phonemes these sounds are intended to represent. A radical solution is to train the acoustic model on nonnative (L1) speech; for example, the Tactical Language and Culture Training System (TLCTS; Johnson 2007), which was used to give US servicemen with no previous experience of Arabic a crash course in the language prior to deployment in Iraq, used acoustic models trained on Americans, since the students were often incapable of producing reasonable approximations of native Arabic sounds. A solution of this kind is not only expensive to implement (a new set of acoustic models needs to be trained for each L1), but will also be considered unacceptable in many language-teaching contexts.

If it is not feasible to help the student by adjusting the acoustic model, the alternative is to exploit the language model and constrain the range of spoken input the system will need to recognise. Here, the simplest and most radical alternative is to ask the student at each turn to imitate a specified sentence (see Guichon and Cohen, Chapter 36 this volume); this cuts down the language model to the single sentence in question, reducing recognition to an alignment task. The advantage is that recognition can be made very accurate, to the point where detailed feedback can be given on phonological differences between the two versions of the sentence; the drawback is that the student, who is only imitating, has no opportunity to practise generative language, but only pronunciation.

# Translation and technology

The spoken translation game presented in this chapter is an alternative solution. It aims at constraining the student's language enough to allow accurate speech recognition, but still leaves the nature of their response sufficiently underspecified that they are forced to do more than merely imitate. The key components are the speech recogniser combined with a machine translation (MT) system. The most obvious way to build a system of this kind is to start with a speech recogniser for the L2 and an MT system which translates from the L2 to the L1. The system prompts the student with a sentence of the L1. They give a spoken response in the L2, and the MT system translates it back to the L1. If the translation is the same as the prompt, the machine accepts, otherwise it rejects.

The MT system is therefore the second main component of a spoken translation game: it verifies if what was recognised is a correct translation of the L1 sentence. A little experimentation with a commercial MT system like Google Translate, however, reveals problems. To start with, systems of this kind are not precise enough to produce perfect translations. Even more important, there are usually many ways for the student to respond with a phrase in the L2 which means the same as the L1 prompt, but the majority of them will not translate back to the prompt. One way to attack this problem is to use a rule-based interlingua MT approach. In contrast to statistical MT systems like Google Translate, a system of this kind starts by checking to see if the input sentence is syntactically correct, and if so represents its meaning in a language-neutral way (Jurafsky et al., Chapter 25).

With this approach, both the L1 prompt and a (syntactically correct) L2 response can be translated into the neutral form, called an interlingua, and then compared. The intention is that the interlingua should abstract away from the specific phrasing of the L1 and L2 sentences, so that many semantically equivalent sentences will map into the same interlingual form; for example, in a system designed to teach English, 'I'd like a coffee', 'Could I have a coffee?' and 'A coffee, please' might all map into the same interlingua, which abstracts away from the surface phrasing to express the essential information: the sentence is a request, and the thing being requested is a coffee.

In the next two sections, we look at two concrete examples of translation games developed at MIT and Geneva University, respectively.

## Initial work at MIT

The basic ideas of the speech translation game are already present in the system developed by Wang and Seneff (2007). Working within the context of the MIT spoken dialogue systems program, the authors reconfigured speech recognition and interlingua-based machine translation components previously used to build a bidirectional Mandarin-to-English speech translation system, and used them to construct an educational application designed to assist English-speaking students of Mandarin. The original speech translation application was designed for the domain of flight reservations; the translation game, in order to minimise the work involved used the same domain. The acoustic models used by the Mandarin speech recogniser were trained on speech from native speakers of Mandarin. The language models were originally trained on Mandarin translations of English flight reservation sentences automatically produced by the English-to-Mandarin machine translation system, and later augmented with data collected from user trials. The operation of the system is illustrated by the following dialogue (Wang and Seneff 2007):

    SYSTEM:   (*greet and prompt user*) Welcome! You are playing at level four. Okay, here's your first sentence to translate: 'The return date is Tuesday October 25'.
    USER:   (*translate with error*) fan3 hui2 ri4 qi1 shi4 si4 yue4 er4 shi2 wu3 hao4 xing1 qi1 er4.

539

SYSTEM: (*paraphrase in Chinese*) fan3 hui2 ri4 qi1 si4 yue4 er4 shi2 wu3 hao4 xing1 qi1 er4.
SYSTEM: (*paraphrase in English*) The return date is Tuesday April 25.
USER: (*repeat date*) shi2 yue4 er4 shi2 wu3 hao4.
SYSTEM: (*paraphrase in Chinese*) shi2 yue4 er4 shi2 wu3 hao4.
SYSTEM: (*paraphrase in English*) October 25.
SYSTEM: (*respond to user*) 'Great! You successfully translated the sentence in separate fragments. Let's move on to the next sentence: 'I need to fly to Hong Kong the day after tomorrow'.
USER: (*click on the help button*)
SYSTEM: (*repeat English prompt*) I need to fly to Hong Kong the day after tomorrow.
SYSTEM: (*offer example translation*) wo3 xu1 yao4 hou4 tian1 fei1 xiang1 gang3.
USER: (*imitate the translation*) wo3 xu1 yao4 hou4 tian1 fei1 xiang1 gang3.

...

SYSTEM: (*respond to user*) You translated nine out of ten sentences. You took on average 1.6 turns per sentence.
You have advanced to level five. Would you like to play another round?

In more detail, the architecture is as follows. At each turn, the system randomly selects an English sentence from a large corpus and presents it to the student. The student attempts to speak a Mandarin translation. Speech recognition and machine translation transform this into a list of key/value (KV) pairs, which in this system constitutes the language-neutral interlingua. The original English prompt is also transformed into KV form, and the two KV forms are compared, after which the system either accepts or rejects the response. If it rejects, the student has the option of trying to produce a phrase which corrects the erroneous part of their original response. They can also get help by requesting a written translation into Mandarin of the original English prompt.

The most challenging problems arise from the task of performing recognition on nonnative speech. The authors claim that both false positives and false negatives cause frustration to students, though false negatives are worse; students would be more disappointed by having the system reject responses they feel are right than by having it accept ones they believe are wrong. A simple strategy, which turns out to give a substantial reduction in false rejections without unduly inflating the false accept rate, is to set the speech recogniser to produce several different hypotheses for each student utterance ('n-best recognition'), and match the interlingua form produced by each hypothesis against the one produced by the reference. If any one of the resulting forms gives a match, the system counts the student's response as successful.

In later papers, Xu and Seneff (2008) briefly report a small user evaluation on five students, who used the system for a total of 615 utterances. All of the students gave 'positive opinions' and 'felt that use of the system was encouraging'. Xu and Seneff (2011) describe a dialogue-based application derived from the original translation game, which is also web-enabled using the Web-Accessible Multimodal Interfaces (WAMI) toolkit (Gruenstein, McGraw and Badr 2008) to enable remote access.

## CALL-SLT: A flexible multilingual platform for spoken translation games

CALL-SLT (Rayner et al. 2010) draws its basic inspiration from the MIT system, but has extended and modified the original design in several ways. Figure 38.1 illustrates the user

Translation and technology

*Figure 38.1* Screenshot of CALL-SLT interface for version used in experiments at University of Bologna

interface. The top row of buttons allows the user to choose the language-pair and the lesson (here 'Give your nationality'). The text on the right-hand side explains the content of the lesson in the L1 (Italian).

The student has received the prompt: DI' LA_TUA_NAZIONALITA : PORTOGHESE ('Say your nationality: Portuguese').

They have pressed the Help button to get assistance, and have been given three valid alternatives in the bottom pane, any of which they can listen to by pressing the associated microphone icon. They have clicked the first one and then initiated recognition to imitate it, getting the same result (the top pane) and a green bar showing that the system accepted their response.

We will refer to this example in the following discussion, which focuses on the differences between CALL-SLT and the original MIT system, in particular the strategies used for prompting, organisation of content, recognition and provision of online help.

## Form of prompts

The MIT system presents its examples directly from a collection of L1 sentences. CALL-SLT, in contrast, takes the interlingual form as primary, and converts it into a prompt which has the form of a speech act: here, instead of 'I am Portuguese', the prompt means 'Say your nationality: Portuguese'. The intent is that the student should be encouraged to formulate their response based on the meaning, rather than simply translating. The prompt is created from the interlingual form using a set of rules which the course constructor can easily adjust.

541

In other versions of the system (Figure 38.2), we have also experimented with the idea of using prompts which combine text with multimedia; for example, a prompt for a lesson focused on the task of ordering in a restaurant might start with a video file showing a cartoon waiter asking what the student wants to order, followed by a text prompt expressing the content 'ask for a steak' (Baur, Rayner and Tsourakis 2013; Rayner and Tsourakis 2013).

## Organisation of content

CALL-SLT organises content by collecting prompts into ordered sets called *lessons*; a lesson will typically contain twenty to fifty examples, grouped around a common theme. This can be syntactic (e.g. in French, requests with questions, future or conditional tense or nominal phrase; Bouillon et al. 2011), functional (talking about members of your family, ordering items in a restaurant; Bouillon et al. 2011; Rayner and Tsourakis 2013) or phonological

*Figure 38.2* Screenshot of multimodal version of CALL-SLT

(L2 sounds difficult for speakers of the L1, for example, English /θ/ for French-speakers; Jolidon 2013).

In the multimedia version of the system, it is also possible to link examples together into short dialogues using a simple XML-based scripting language; thus, for example, the prompt 'ask for a steak' can be followed by 'ask to have your steak rare' if the student's response is accepted and 'repeat: ask for a steak' if it is rejected.

## Recognition

From the point of view of software architecture, the largest differences between CALL-SLT and the MIT system are concerned with speech recognition. The MIT system creates language models by deriving them, using a statistical training method, from a set of training sentences. For the language model to be of adequate quality, experience shows that this set needs to be fairly large, containing at least thousands of examples. Collecting them is a time-consuming task, making it correspondingly difficult to port the application to new domains.

CALL-SLT adopts a different strategy, where a predefined reference grammar forms an integral part of the process of training the language model; the training examples which correspond mainly to the possible student answers essentially extract the relevant part of this grammar and use it as the model (Rayner, Bouillon and Hockey 2006). The key advantage of the grammar-based approach is that the training sets can be much smaller, making it correspondingly easier to write content for new domains.

The approach to recognition in terms of example-based construction of domain-specific grammars interacts well with the idea of splitting up content into lessons; by providing suitable annotations, the course developer can specify that they want specific language models created for given lessons or groups of lessons, with each language model constructed using only the relevant subset of examples. As explained earlier, this means that the coverage of the recogniser can be set to include only the grammar and vocabulary included in this subset and helps address a problem which many early users of the system pointed out: inexperienced students typically want a forgiving recogniser (they find it frustrating to be rejected all the time), while more accomplished students prefer recognition to be stricter, reducing the proportion of false positives. The student selects the level of 'strictness' they require from a scale containing alternatives ranging from least to most strict, and the system performs recognition using the most appropriate language model in the set of those that include the current lesson. This level can also be imposed by the teacher.

A noteworthy consequence of the grammar-based strategy is that recognition results are always sentences licensed by the grammar. It is hard to say whether this is a good or a bad thing. The language model helps correct unclear student pronunciation by biasing towards grammatically correct results, which makes the system more forgiving. The downside is that even clearly ungrammatical responses are sometimes corrected, so that the student gets no feedback on their mistake; a typical case is gender agreement errors in French.

## Online help and recognition feedback

CALL-SLT provides help and also gives recognition feedback on student answers.

*Help* is the set of possible written and spoken sentences corresponding to a given speech act (as shown in the box 'Je suis de nationalité portugaise' in Figure 38.1). In line with the basic idea of organising content around the interlingua, the system logs successful interactions by users whose profiles declare them as native speakers, saving the relevant sound files and associating them with the interlingua form for the current prompt. Each sound file is also tagged with the recognition result produced when it was recorded; since minor recognition errors (e.g. misrecognised articles) can still produce a valid match, these recognition results are reviewed and edited by the course designer. They can also specify restrictions on how help is presented, for example, requiring the student to attempt the example once or twice before they can access help examples.

If spoken help is available, the system plays the sound file while showing the associated transcription. If there are no sound files for the current prompt, it shows available text help. Since every prompt is ultimately derived from a written L2 sentence, it is always possible to show text help.

The *recognition feedback* is based on the result of the recognition. Its basic form is a simple choice between accepting (if the answer is a possible realisation of the speech act given the MT system) and rejecting (if it is not), communicated as a green or a red bar in the user interface. A refinement for rejected utterances is to attempt to point out incorrect portions of the user's response. Experimentation suggests that responses which differ substantially from the prompt are best presented as simple failures; since grammar-based recognition tries to force all student utterances into the space of grammatical sentences defined by the currently active language model, responses by the student which fall outside this space can often lead to bizarre recognition results that are only confusing if echoed back by the system.

In contrast, it is potentially useful to present details on a small mismatch, which is often caused by the student's misremembering or mispronouncing a single word or phrase. A possible strategy is to give fine-grained feedback only when the semantic difference between the interlingual representations of the prompt and the response consists of a single element. The version of this strategy which appears to work best exploits the help system; the system searches for the help example which displays the smallest difference against the current recognition result, then displays the recognition result with the differences highlighted in colour. The implicit assumption is that the student was trying to speak the selected help example, implying that there need to be help examples covering all common ways of responding. For the simple content that CALL-SLT is aimed at, this goal appears to be realistic. For some courses, the designer has entered all the help examples by hand; it is also possible to proceed more systematically, and implement a set of transformation rules which produce syntactic variants of all the help examples.

In the next section, we discuss evaluation and present two case studies performed using CALL-SLT.

## Evaluating spoken translation game systems

Although translation games have now begun to find their way into mainstream CALL systems (duolingo.com is a prominent example), there has been little work on evaluation. We list a few immediate questions:

1. *Integration.* Is it possible to integrate a system of this kind into an established language course?
2. *Teacher reaction.* What advantages and disadvantages do teachers perceive?
3. *Student reaction.* What motivates students to use the system?
4. *Value of online help.* Do the students benefit from access to online help?
5. *Value of speech recognition feedback.* Does recognition help the students learn?

Of these, questions 1–3 are essentially qualitative; it is reasonable to search for quantitative answers to questions 4 and 5. We summarise some results from studies carried out using two versions of CALL-SLT, which go at least some way towards providing initial answers. We now address the five questions in the context of a French-for-Italian-speakers version of the system, which was integrated into a Moodle-based e-learning platform at the University of Bologna, Italy. We then focus on the fifth question, and summarise an experiment carried out later using crowdsourced subjects recruited over the Web, in which one group used a normal version of CALL-SLT and a control group a version in which speech recognition capabilities had been disabled.

## *Evaluation at the University of Bologna*

The University of Bologna has a major European centre for language teaching (CLA, 'Centro Linguistico di Ateneo'), which evaluates 10,000–20,000 students per year. Many of the courses are organised according to principles of self-learning and blended learning and hosted on the popular Moodle platform (https://e-cla.unibo.it/bologna/?lang=en_utf8) (Cervini 2012). The first goal of the pilot study described here was to determine the practicability of integrating CALL-SLT content into an existing online course. The specific course chosen was aimed at Italian students of French who are at beginner or low-elementary level and studying French in blended mode learning or total self-learning. The French multimedia course for level A2 is structured into four modules, each of which offers a variety of self-corrective receptive exercises such as multiple-choice, fill-in, dictation, sentence reordering, listening comprehension, reading comprehension, drag and drop, category, and listen and repeat.

During the elaboration of the oral production exercises for the CALL-SLT system, efforts were made to merge the principles of the interactionist perspective and task-based language learning (Ellis 2003) with the rules of instructional design, in particular: provide rich input, encourage inductive chunk learning, provide feedback and respect learner syllabi/developmental processes. For example, the module 'Greetings and introductions' was linked to eight CALL-SLT lesson units. Each unit focused on a particular speech act ('Greetings', 'Give your age', 'Describe your family', etc.) and illustrated different ways of speaking, which correspond to different ways of conveying the same meaning provided in the student help. The eight units do not constitute a real dialog, but decompose it in different subtasks. For example, in the lesson 'Describe your family', a typical prompt might have the structure:

> Give your brother's name: Octavien

and possible responses would include both

> *Mon frère s'appelle Octavien* ('My brother is called Octavien')

and

> *Le nom de mon frère est Octavien* ('My brother's name is Octavien').

There will typically be ten to twenty examples in each unit. In this way, the student can learn different grammatical structures for the same speech act and practise the same structure many times with multiple examples; the details are presented in Bouillon, Cervini et al. (2011). Bouillon et al. (2012) describe an initial quantitative analysis using 1,065 recorded responses collected during use of the system by students during late 2011. The course teacher was asked to rate all the students' answers using a five-point scale, for the three criteria of lexical/grammatical correctness, phonetic adequacy and fluency; comparison with the system's accept/reject feedback showed reasonable correlation. Bouillon et al. (2012) evaluated the effectiveness of the help system by extracting pairs of responses where the same student was first rejected by the system without having listened to spoken help, then later was accepted after listening to it. The judge's average score for the second response did indeed turn out to be considerably higher.

In summary, these experiments give the following initial answers to questions 1–5:

1. *Integration.* It is straightforward to integrate a tool like CALL-SLT into an elementary online language course mainly focused on the improvement of receptive skill and to offer learners a repertoire of formulaic expressions (in the form of language acts, classified by topics) to be learned at their own speed and combined later in real scenarios.

2. *Teacher reaction.* Teachers perceive advantages and disadvantages. Among the advantages are the flexibility and adaptability of the system, which permits a certain freedom in the choice of the learning content (structuring of lessons, selection of examples, surface form of the linguistic acts and help examples to be provided). They also appreciate the fact that recorded speech can be recorded in a Word document, making it possible to listen to the students' spoken answers when it is convenient, to monitor their progress and evaluate their strengths and weaknesses. The 'recognition feedback' is still considered as unreliable compared to what they would get from a human teacher or a native speaker. Help would be more useful if it were progressive, showing words before complete sentences. It should also be automatic after a few attempts.

3. *Student reaction.* Qualitative evaluation (Bouillon et al. 2012; Cervini, Bouillon and Gasser 2013) gave encouraging results despite the still uncertain reliability of speech recognition. Most of the students assess CALL-SLT as 'very useful' or 'useful' for learning a foreign language and improving autonomous speaking skills. They say they would have liked to have had a richer variety of lessons available. Students subjectively perceive improvement in their fluency and pronunciation, and they appreciate being shown how to say the same thing in different ways. Feedback also suggested that students would like more exercises and more diversified lessons, which suggests the interest of combining the existing lessons with challenging ones where speech acts are presented in context.

4. *Value of online help.* As explained earlier, the quantitative results from Bouillon et al. (2012) show that the scores assigned by the course teacher to the student answers improve where the students listen to the help. This suggests that students benefit from using the online help, at least in the short term.

5. *Value of speech recognition feedback.* Very poor answers were reliably identified by the system; 90% of the answers annotated by the course teacher with the two lowest scores (on a scale of five) were also rejected by CALL-SLT.

## Crowdsourced Internet experiment

Although the aforementioned experiment arguably provides some support for the claim that the CALL-SLT system's speech recognition capabilities help students learn, the evidence cannot be considered direct. It would be more convincing to see a straightforward comparison, in which some students used the normal version of the system and a control group used a version where speech recognition was disabled. A demonstration that the first group performed significantly better would constitute a clear reason for believing that speech recognition is indeed important to a system like CALL-SLT.

Unfortunately, many well-known methodological problems arise if an experiment of this kind is attempted in a normal classroom environment. If all the students are randomly selected from a single homogenous group (e.g. the members of one or more classes), then it will soon become apparent that some students have an inferior version, negatively impacting their motivation. Since success in learning is highly connected to motivation, this will skew the result. Conversely, if the subjects are recruited from two different groups, which have no contact with each other (e.g. two distinct schools), there is the problem that a different result may only depend on the difference in quality between the two groups.

What is required, from this point of view, is a homogeneous group of students who have little or no contact with each other. The fact that CALL-SLT is deployed on the Web makes it feasible to find subjects by recruiting them from a large, geographically dispersed web forum, dividing these subjects randomly into two groups. The problem is that this methodological advantage comes at a high price. The students are no longer using the tool as part of a well-understood classroom learning program, and it is in general difficult to know much about their background or motivation.

With these caveats, we outline an experiment of this general kind, carried out in early 2013 using the Amazon Mechanical Turk (AMT) crowdsourcing site; full details are presented in Rayner and Tsourakis (2013). The version of CALL-SLT used was one configured for deployment on mobile Android devices in two subversions: one with full functionality, and one with recognition feedback disabled. Both versions echoed back the user's recorded voice after each response.

The content was an elementary French course designed for absolute beginners, which reused some of the content developed with the University of Bologna and introduced about eighty words of vocabulary and a dozen or so syntactic patterns. Text prompts were ported from Italian to English, and were also reconfigured to be in multimodal form, following the methods touched on in an earlier section here. The main content consisted of four lessons called 'About me', 'About my family', 'Restaurant' and 'Time and day'. There were also two lessons called 'Overview 1' and 'Overview 2', which consisted of a balanced selection of examples from the other lessons, and a lesson called 'Revision', which consisted of the union of the four main lessons.

Potential students were recruited though AMT, with a total of 130 people responding to the initial request. They were told that they would be given eight tasks over the course of eight days, one task per day; they would be paid $2 for each task – normal pay for AMT – and expected to work on it for twenty minutes. Each subject was assigned a given version of CALL-SLT at the beginning, either the normal one with recognition enabled (*Rec*) or one with recognition disabled (*No-rec*). Subjects were not able to see that other versions than their own existed.

The first task assigned was to install the app on a suitable Android device, following which the second (*Pre-test*) was to attempt Overview 1, which had the help function switched on, followed by Overview 2, where the help function was switched off. Tasks 3 to 6 were the four main lessons, Task 7 was Revision, and Task 8 was a repetition of *Pre-test*, which we called *Post-test*. The students were not told in advance that the pre- and posttests would be the same. There is an obvious methodological problem involved in repeating this content: on the other hand, the two tests were separated by more than a week, and the students had practised on many similar items in between. The advantage was that we could perform an item-by-item comparison, which did indeed prove useful.

After the Pre-test round, 50 of the original 130 entrants were left, representing the real students; 24 of these finished the course, equally divided between *Rec* and *No-rec*. At the end of the course, we evaluated student progress by first comparing performance on *Pre-test* and *Post-test*, and then comparing the resulting differences across *Rec* and *No-rec*. On a prompt-by-prompt comparison using the Wilcoxon signed-rank test, the *Rec* group turned out to be significantly better ($p < 0.02$) than the *No-rec* group; the cited paper gives details.

Needless to say, there are many aspects of both experiments described earlier that are methodologically less than satisfactory; taken together, though, they give some objective reasons to think that spoken translation game systems are capable of giving students more than systems which only support simple listening and repeating. This impression is supported by other experiments using CALL-SLT, and by subjective feedback received during postexperiment debriefing of subjects.

## Further reading

Readers interested in CALL systems of the general kind described here are best advised to consult the proceedings of the biannual workshop on Speech and Language Technology in Education (SLaTE); the recent ones are freely available on the Web. The original paper on spoken translation games is Wang and Seneff (2007), 'Automatic assessment of student translations for foreign language tutoring', in *Proceedings of NAACL/HLT 2007*, Rochester, NY. Another influential early paper, describing the TLCTS system, is Johnson (2007), 'Serious use of a serious game for language learning', in *Proceedings of the 2007 Conference on Artificial Intelligence in Education: Building Technology Rich Learning Contexts That Work*, IOS Press. More details on the CALL-SLT system are provided in Rayner, Tsourakis, Baur, Bouillon and Gerlach (2014), 'CALL-SLT: A Spoken CALL System based on grammar and speech recognition', *Linguistic Issues in Language Technology* 10(2). For background on speech and language processing in general, the standard text is Jurafsky, Martin, Kehler, Vander Linden and Ward (2000), *An Introduction to Natural Language Processing, Computational Linguistics, and Speech Recognition*, Prentice Hall.

## References

Baur, C., Rayner, E. and Tsourakis, N. (2013) 'A textbook-based serious game for practising spoken language', In *Proceedings of ICERI-2013*, Seville, Spain.

Bouillon, P., Cervini, C., Mandich, A., Rayner, M. and Tsourakis, N. (2011) 'Speech recognition for online language learning: Connecting CALL-SLT and DALIA', in *Proceedings of the International Conference on ICT for Language Learning*, Florence, Italy.

Bouillon, P., Gerlach, J., Baur, C., Cervini, C. and Gasser R.B. (2012) *Actes du 8ème Colloque Technologies de l'Information et de la Communication pour l'Enseignement*, Lyon, France: 206–211.

Bouillon, P., Rayner, M., Gerlach, J. and Estrella, P. (2011) 'Pour une interlangue utile en traduction automatique de la parole dans des domaines limités', *TAL (Traitement Automatique des Langues)*, 52: 1.

Bouillon, P., Rayner, M., Novellas, B., Starlander, M., Santaholma, M., Nakao, Y. et al. (2007) 'Une grammaire partagée multi-tâche pour le traitement de la parole: Application aux langues romanes', *TAL (Traitement Automatique des Langues)*, 47(3): 155–173.

Bouillon, P., Rayner, M., Tsourakis, N. and Zhang, Q. (2011) 'A student-centered evaluation of a web-based spoken translation game', in *Workshop on Speech and Language Technology in Education (SLaTE)*, Venice, Italy.

Cervini, C. (2012) 'Formation hybride et auto-apprentissage des langues étrangères au CILTA: vers un changement de paradigme par la révision du concept d'autonomie', Repères DoRiF n. juillet 2012 – *Le français dans le contexte plurilingue des Centres Linguistiques Universitaires italiens*, available: http://www.dorif.it/ezine/ezine_articles.php?id=14

Cervini, C., Bouillon, P. and Gasser, R. (2013) 'Jeu de traduction orale en ligne et apprentissage des langues', *Les Langues Modernes*, 4: 83–94.

Ellis, R. (2003) *Task-Based Language Learning and Teaching*, Oxford, UK: Oxford University Press.

Gruenstein, A., McGraw, I. and Badr, I. (2008) 'The WAMI toolkit for developing, deploying, and evaluating web-accessible multimodal interfaces', in *Proceedings of the 10th international conference on multimodal interfaces*, ACM: 141–148.

Johnson, W.L. (2007) 'Serious use of a serious game for language learning', in *Proceedings of the 2007 Conference on Artificial Intelligence in Education: Building Technology Rich Learning Contexts That Work*, IOS Press: 67–74.

Jolidon, A. (2013) 'Reconnaissance vocale et amélioration de la prononciation: élaboration et évaluation de leçons avec le logiciel CALL-SLT', masters thesis, University of Geneva, Faculté de Traduction et d'Interprétation.

Jurafsky, D., Martin, J.H., Kehler, A., Vander Linden, K. and Ward, N. (2000) *Speech and Language Processing: An Introduction to Natural Language Processing, Computational Linguistics, and Speech Recognition*, Upper Saddle River, NJ: Prentice Hall.

Rayner, M., Bouillon, P. and Hockey, B.A. (2006) *Putting Linguistics into Speech Recognition: The Regulus Grammar Compiler*, Chicago, IL: CSLI Press.

Rayner, M., Bouillon, P., Tsourakis, N., Gerlach, C., Georgescul, M., Nakao, Y. et al. (2010) 'A multilingual CALL game based on speech translation', in *Proceedings of LREC 2010*, Valletta, Malta.

Rayner, M. and Tsourakis, N. (2013) 'Methodological issues in evaluating a spoken CALL game: Can crowdsourcing help us perform controlled experiments?', in *Proceedings of the SLaTE Workshop*, Grenoble, France.

Tsourakis, N., Rayner, M. and Bouillon, P. (2011) 'Evaluation of a mobile language learning system using language-neutral prompts', in *Proceedings of Workshop on Speech and Language Technology in Education (SLaTE)*, Venice, Italy.

Wang, C. and Seneff, S. (2007) 'Automatic assessment of student translations for foreign language tutoring', in *Proceedings of NAACL/HLT 2007*, Rochester, NY.

Xu, Y. and Seneff, S. (2008) Mandarin learning using speech and language technologies: A translation game in the travel domain', in *Chinese Spoken Language Processing*, ISCSLP'08, 6th International Symposium on Spoken Language Processing, IEEE.

Xu, Y., and Seneff, S. (2011) 'A generic framework for building dialogue games for language learning: Application in the flight domain', in *Proceedings of Workshop on Speech and Language Technology in Education (SLaTE)*, Venice, Italy.

# Index

Page numbers in *italic* type indicate figures and tables.

AA Academic Abstracts 472
Abidin, M.J.Z. 19
ability level targeting 151–2
Abraham, L.B. 484
Abraham, R. 14
Abu-Seileek, A.F. 465
accents 499–500
accessibility 200, 219, 263–4
ACFTL *see* American Council of Teachers of Foreign Languages (ACTFL)
achievement motivation 442
ACL Anthology 524
acoustic model 537–8
acoustics, digital 491–4
acquisition approach to learning 129
action research (AR) 46
Active World 309
activities 95–8
activity theories 35, 44–6, 93
adaptation, theory 27
added value 131
ADDIE (Analysis-Design-Development-Implementation-Evaluation) 94, 134
Adler, R.P. 271
Adolphs, S. 350, 394
Advanced Research Projects Agency Network (ARPANET) 11, 15
advertising 17, 19
AES (automatic essay scoring) 526
affective filter hypothesis 501
affinity groups 35, 447
affordances 3, 17–18; environments and 231–2; evaluation 132; from games 417–18; and interaction 30; for language learning 35, 234, 450–3; media 72; of mini-games 433; and mobile devices 258, 301; multimodality 511; theory of 48–50
age and gender 160–72; background 160; and identity 160–1; learning and teaching implications 167–8; research 169; shift 160–1; theoretical perspectives 161–7

agency, creative 83
Ahmad, N. 19
AI (artificial intelligence) 380, 522
aids, writing 379–80
Aijmer, K. 351
*A la rencontre de Philippe* (game) 416
Alderson, J.C. 142
Alelo 182
Alevizou, P. 81–2
Alexopoulou, T. 381
algorithms 206, 395, 481, 525
Allan, R. 345
Allwood, J. 394
Allwright, D. *73*, 75
Amazon Mechanical Turk (AMT) 547
American Council of Teachers of Foreign Languages (ACTFL): guidelines 181; position paper 59–60; *Standards for Foreign Language Learning in the 21st Century* 59
American National Corpus (ANC) 349, 388–9
Analysis-Design-Development-Implementation-Evaluation (ADDIE) 94, 134
Andersen, O. 381
Anderson, R.B. 512
Anderson, T. 71, 76
annotations, corpus 377, 380–2
AntConc 408
anxiety, computer 149
Appel, C. 47
Appleby, R. 161
Apple IIe 14
applied linguistics 182, 274
apps 18–19, 89, 264, 502
AR (action research) 46
Archer, W. 71, 76
ARIS (Augmented Reality and Interactive Storytelling) 182
Army Method 495
Arnold, N. 76
ARPANET (Advanced Research Projects Agency Network) 11, 15

# Index

artefacts 94–5, 128, 130, 229
artificial intelligence (AI) 380, 522
assessment 380–2
Association for Computational Linguistics (ACL) 524
Aston, G. 366
'As We May Think' (Bush) 20–1
atheoretical CALL 26, 28
Atkins, S. 350
attendant discourses 421
*Au clair de la lune* (Scott de Martinville) 491, 493
audiographics 512
audiolingualism 439–40, 495
audiovisual material 503
Augmented Reality and Interactive Storytelling (ARIS) 182
Augustan Prose Sample 392
aural/oral focus 495
Austin, J. 174
Australia 117
Autobiography of Intercultural Encounters 181–2
automated writing evaluation (AWE) 481–4, 526–8
automatic essay scoring (AES) 526
automation 44, 131–2, 380–1, 383, 439–40, 442–3
autonomous learning 338
avatars 309, 418, 432–3, 435
AWE (automated writing evaluation) software 481–4

Babson Survey Research Group 256
BACKBONE 364, 391, 394
Bacon, S. 72–3
Baerentsen, K.B. 48
Baker, M. 392
Bakhtin, M. 48, 245
Bank of English (BoE) 389
Bannister, D. 287
Banos, R. 503–4
*Barbie Fashion Designer* 454
Baroni, M. 343
Barretta, A.G. 263
Barton, D. 485
Basanta, C. 340
Basharina, O. 27
BASIC 10, 14
Basturkmen, H. 466
Bates, A.W. 133
Bax, S. 13, 108–10, 116, 226, 228, 290, 297
BBC Active 212
BBC Micro 14
BBC *Wordmaster* 469
BBS (bulletin board system) 298
Becher, A. 46
Beck, M.B. 264
Beetham, H. 94
Beglar, D. 448; Vocabulary Size Test 448
behaviours 129, 418, 424, 496

Belshaw, D. 121–2
Belz, J. 366, 377–8
Bent, D. 225
Berners-Lee, Tim 11
'Best of …' (websites) (Ferlazzo) 212
BETSY 527
Bettsworth, B. 287
Biber, D. 351, 354
Bidjerano, T. 77
Birmingham University (UK) 340
Black, R.W. 35, 422, 452
Blake, R. 512
Blass, L.: *Grammar and Beyond* 379
Blattner, G. 259–60
blended learning 71, 90, 133
Blin, F. 2–3, 5, 47–8
blogging 95, 255, 269, 483, 485
Blyth, C. 256–7
BNC (British National Corpus) 337, 340, 342, 349, 388–9, 405
BoE (Bank of English) 389
Bolitho, R. 91, 94, 96–7
bookmarking sites 255
books, grammar 378–9
bootstrapping, linguistic 450
Boreham, N. 233
born digital 89–90
borrowing, theory 26
Bouillon, P. 5, 545–6
Boulton, A. 178, 344
boundaries, limitations and 197–209; background 197; definitions and examples 198–206; and the future 206–8
Bourdieu, P. 182
Bowker, L. 392
Bradin-Siskin, C. 18
Braun, S. 364, 378
Brazil 287
Brewer, R. 420
bridging activities 246
Brinton, L.J. 394
Briscoe, E.J. 381
British Council 10, 281, 285
British National Corpus (BNC) 337, 340, 342, 349, 388–9, 405
British Open University 71
broadband availability 417
Bronfenbrenner, U. 41–3, 46
Brown, J.D. 3, 141–2
Brown, J.S. 232–3, 271
Brown, K. 185
BROWN Corpus 367, 388–9
browsers 16
Brundtland Commission report 224
buffet, theory 28–9
Bulgarian National Corpus 389
bulletin board system (BBS) 298

551

# Index

Bunting, J. 354
Burbules, N.C. 200, 207
Burnard, L. 376
Bush, V. 20–1
Buttery, P. 350–2
Byram, M. 243
Byrne, R.: *Free Technology for Teachers* (blog) 212

CAI (computer-assisted instruction) 9, 12, 129
Caines, A. 4, 344, 351–2
Calero Alcaraz, J.M. 342
CALI (computer-assisted language instruction) 10
CALICO (Computer Assisted Learning and Instruction Consortium) 11, 493
*CALICO Journal* 35
California State University System 212
CALL *see* computer-assisted language learning (CALL)
CALL Bibliography (Jung) 18
CALL ecosystem model 234
'CALL in the Year 2000: Still in Search of Research Paradigms?' (Chapelle) 102
CALL-IS (Computer-Assisted Language Learning Interest Section) 215–16
Callister, T.A. 200, 207
*CALL Research Perspectives* (Egbert and Petrie) 102–4
CALL-SLT 536, 540–4
CALTs (computer-adaptive language tests) 141–2, 148, 157n2
Cambridge First Certificate in English (FCE) 381
Cambridge International Corpus (CIC) 378
Cambridge Learner Corpus (CLC) 378
Cameron, D. 163
Cameron, L. 274
Camstasia Studio 135
Canadian Hansard Corpus 391
CANBEC 391
CANDLE (Corpus And Natural language processing for Digital Learning of English) 480
Candlin, C.N. 340, 344
capability, creative 83
Cardini, A. 286
Cardoso, W. 287
CARE (Concordancer for Academic wRitten English) 480
CARLA (University of Minnesota's Center for Advanced Research on Language Acquisition) 205
Carr, D. 455
Carter, R.A. 350–2, 354, 370, 473; *English Grammar Today* 378
CASLA (computer applications in second language acquisition) 11
Cassell, J. 447–8
cassette players 492, 496
casual games 432

categorisations 76, 247, 450–3
CATs (computer-adaptive tests) 142
CAW (computer-assisted writing) 11
Caws, C. 3
Cazden, C.B. 270, 276–7
CCTFC (Contemporary Chinese Translated Fiction Corpus) 392
CDLTs (computer-delivered language tests) 141–2, 146–55
CEFR (Common European Framework of Reference) 181, 210, 219, 381, 503
CELL (computer-enhanced language learning) 11
Century of Prose Corpus 392
Cervini, C. 5, 545–6
CF (corrective feedback) 34, 107–8
Chabert, G. 302
Chalhoub-Deville, M. 142, 148
Chambers, A. 4, 108–10, 228, 338, 366, 368
Chang, C.-C. 301
Chang, C.F. 480
Chang, J.S. 480
Chang, K.-E. 298
Chang, W.L. 344
'Changing Winds and Shifting Sands' (Marckwardt) 496
Chanier, T. 512, 515
channels 510
Chao, C. 28
chaos systems and theories 41–2
Chapelle, C. 13–14, 27, 29, 40, 128–32, 142, 168, 463–7; 'CALL in the Year 2000: Still in Search of Research Paradigms?' 102; 'Interactionist SLA theory in CALL research' 104–5
Charles, M. 369
chat 11, 15, 203, 271–2
CHAT (cultural-historical activity theory) 44–6
cheating 149, 152
checklists 68, 90, 97, 130
Chen, C.E. 479, 483
Chen, H.I. 260, 479
Chen, H.J. 483
Cheng, W. 340–4
Cheng, W.E. 483
Chenoweth, N.A. 465–6
Cheung, W.K. 483, 528
children and gaming 446–58; affordances 450–3; background 446–8; and gender relevance 453–6; in schools 448–9
China 43, 204
Chinese keyboards 205
Chinnery, G.M. 18
Chomsky, N. 496, 525
Chow, G.S.-M. 227
Christie, B. 72
chronosystem model 47
chronotope 48
Chu, K.C. 454

552

Chun, D.M. 512, 517, 529
chunks 350, 462, 473
CIC (Cambridge International Corpus) 378
Ciekanski, M. 512, 515
CIF (Community Indicators Framework) 72, 81–4
citation practices 363
civic literacy 121–2
Clancy, U. 5
Clarebout, G. 27, 107–8
Claridge, C. 392
Clark, C. 259
classrooms: activities in 88–90, 95–8; DDL application in 339–41; digital 122–5, 494; discourse 382; face-to-face 90, 102; ideal 186; IWBs in 281–5; and language learning corpora 409–10; materials for 354; social networking tools in 260–3
CLC (Cambridge Learner Corpus) 378
Cleveland State University (US) 392
Clifford, Ray 1
CLIL (content and language integrated learning) 285
ClipFlair 503–4
cloud-based game storage 418
Cloudworks 81–2
CLT (communicative language teaching) 497
CMC *see* computer-mediated communication (CMC)
Coady, J. 464–5
Cobb, T. 441, 486
COBUILD 389
COCA (Corpus of Contemporary American English) 337, 340, 349, 365, 389, 405
code-switching 176–7
coding 118–19, 298
Coghlan, M. 215
cognitive: development 162, 243; linguistic theories 29; literacy 121; psychology 298–9, 513–15
Cognitive Presence 72
COHA (Corpus of Historical American English) 393
Cohen, C. 5
coherence 27
cohesion 82
CoI (Community of Inquiry) 71–2, 77, 80
collaboration 14, 17, 27, 46, 66, 258, 270, 284, 481–3, 512
collaborative online international learning (COIL) 242
collectives 232–3
colligations 472
collocations 178, 389, 405, 472
*Colossal Cave Adventure* 417
Colpaert, J. 28–9, 134–5
Comas-Quinn, A. 80
commercialisation 229
commercial-off-the-shelf (COTS) 447–8, 450
Common Core 212
Common European Framework (CEFR) 181, 210, 219, 381, 503

communication: drills 439; engagement 421; failed 249; goals 163; literacy 121; styles 180; synchronous 247
Communication Technologies Competency Standards for Teachers (ICT-CST) 57–8
communicative language teaching (CLT) 497
communities 81–4
communities of practice (CoPs) 30, 215–19, 232–3
Community Indicators Framework (CIF) 72, 81–4
Community of Inquiry (CoI) 71–2, 77, 80
competence: based instruction 57, 59; intercultural 181–3; multimodal 515; sociopragmatic 259
complexity theory (CT) 41–2, 46–7, 274–5, 277
complex systems 40–1
comprehensible output 271
computer-adaptive language tests (CALTs) 141–2, 148, 151, 157n2
computer-adaptive tests (CATs) 142
computer applications in second language acquisition (CASLA) 11
computer-assisted instruction (CAI) 9, 12, 129
computer-assisted language instruction (CALI) 10
Computer-Assisted Language Instruction Consortium (CALICO) 11
computer-assisted language learning (CALL) 3, 10–11, 14, 24–38; benefits of 463; ecosystem model 234; ergonomics 134; evaluation criteria for 168; games and 416, 431; ideal classroom for 186; Intelligent (ICALL) 522–35; interactionist theory for *105*; and mobile language learning 297–8; multimodality and 509–21; overview 24–5; in practice 32–4; research in 29–32; sources of 25–9; sustainable development in 223–38; teacher preparation for 61–5; tools 380, 461–77, 467–8, 478–508; trends in 34–6; *see also* ecological computer-assisted language learning (CALL) theories
Computer Assisted Learning and Instruction Consortium (CALICO) 493
computer-assisted writing (CAW) 11
computer-delivered language tests (CDLTs) 141–2, 146–55
computer-enhanced language learning (CELL) 11
computer-mediated communication (CMC) 1, 11, 17–18, 26, 72–3, 106–7, 180–1, 206, 242, 466–7, 515
'Computer-Mediated Discourse Analysis' (Herring) 76
computers 89–90; definition of 102; equipment 146–9; normalisation of 108–9; programming 119; roles for 12–13; as tools 269, 419; as tutor 71, 419; *see also* language testing and technology; microcomputers
computer supported collaborative writing (CSCW) 269–80; complexity of 274–5; defined 269–71; future of 276–7; learning and 271–5; and teacher education 275–6

553

Index

comScore 264
concepts, names for 9–12
Concordancer for Academic wRitten English (CARE) 480
concordancers 479, 486
concordances 338–40, 375, 391–2, 408, *472*
conduct, codes of 263
confident literacy 121
conflict 180
confluence 353
Coniam, D. 465, 527
CoNNECT (*Corpus of Native and Non-native EFL Classroom Teacher Talk*) 382–3
connections 18–19, 119–20, 277
Conole, G. 81–2, 92–4
Conrad, S. 378
Constantin de Chanay, H. 203
'Constructing Meaning with Computers' (*TESOL Journal*) 31
constructivism 27–8, 30–1, 96, 121, 298
*Contemporary CALL* 103
Contemporary Chinese Translated Fiction Corpus (CCTFC) 392
content and language integrated learning (CLIL) 285
content organisation 542–3
context: complications of 108–9; design 46–7, 275; game 425–6; of learning 163–4; mobile language learning 303–4; networked learning 71; social 165–8; socioaffective 273; standards in 66–8; technology 103
continuous assessment 152, 157n5
control experiment 441
conversations 176, 179–80, 351
CoPs (communities of practice) 216–17
copyright 117, 121, 123
Corbel, C. 141
CORIS (Corpus di Italiano Scritto) 389
Cornillie, F. 5, 27, 34, 107–8, 434
corpora for language learning 404–12; background 404–6; classroom applications for 409–11; designing and building 406–9; future for 411
Corpus And Natural language processing for Digital Learning of English (CANDLE) 480
Corpus Concordance English 472
Corpus del Español 389
Corpus di Italiano Scritto (CORIS) 389
Corpus of Contemporary American English (COCA) 337, 340, 349, 365, 389, 405
Corpus of Global Web-based English (GloWbE) 391
Corpus of Historical American English (COHA) 393
*Corpus of Native and Non-native EFL Classroom Teacher Talk* (CoNNECT) 382–3
corpus types 388–403; future directions 395–6; general 388–9; historical 392–4; linguistics 337;
multimodal 394–5; parallel 391–2; specialised 389–91; websites 401–3
CorrectEnglish (Vantage Learning) 528
corrective feedback (CF) 34, 107–8
COTS (commercial-off-the-shelf) 447–8, 450
Cotterill, J. 350
Council of Europe 181–2
course design 90–4
Coursera 213
co-writing 274, 276
Cox, M.J. 486
CPH (Critical Period Hypothesis) 162, 164
Crawley, E. 215
creative capability 82
Creative Commons 117, 123
creative literacy 121
Cresswell, A. 343
criteria, checklists of 90
*Criterion* 481, 527
critical literacy 121
Critical Period Hypothesis (CPH) 162, 164
critical theory of technology 198
Croker, R.A. 110–11
*Croquelandia* (game) 179
crowdsourced Internet experiment 546–8
crucibles of new media 242–3
Crystal, D. 118, 498–9
CSCW *see* computer supported collaborative writing (CSCW)
CT (complexity theory) 41–2, 46–7, 274–5, 277
Cultura 180, 245
cultural-historical activity theory (CHAT) 44–6
Cultural Identity in Academic Prose (KIAP) (Fløttum) 367–8
culture 165, 173–84, 205–6, 243; background 173; competence trends 181–3; exchanges online 179–81; incorporation of 174–7; Internet and target 177–9; language and 173–4; and literacy 120, 121; practices 103
Cummins, J. 185
curricula 116–17, 122, 225, 250, 290
Curry, N. 369–70
Curzan, A. 393
Cuth, S. 4
Cutrim Schmid, E. 4, 287
cyberbullying 19
Czikszentmihalyi, M. 426–7

Dabell, J. 377
Dahl, T. 367–8
Dahlman, A. 217
Dahlmann, I. 394
Dalton, B. 464
Danet, B. 204
Daniels, H. 499
Darhower, M. 31–2

database, corpus 472
data collection 111
data-driven learning (DDL) 337–47; advantages and disadvantages of 341–4; background 337; in classrooms 339–41; description 337–9; future developments in 344–5
data-driven learning (DDL), corpora and 335–412; background 337–47; designing and building 404–12; learners 376–87; spoken language 348–61; types and uses 388–403; written language 362–75
data gathering 153
Davies, B. 81, 83
Davies, G. 10
Davies, M. 391
DBR (design-based research) 101
De Bot, K. 41, 47
declarative knowledge 440
*Decorating* 469
deHaan, J. 420, 450–1, 453
DeKeyser, R.M. 443
de la Fuente, M.J. 298
de los Arcos, B. 80
Dembovskaya, S. 260
Desch, S.H. 522
design: features in virtual worlds 308–9; for language learning corpora 404–12; materials 288; of materials 303; of mini-games 433–5
design-based research (DBR) 101
designs: changing 120–2; in evaluation 138; evaluation compared to 128; evaluation issues in 131; for learning 94; mini-games 433–8, 442–3; research 110–11; for sustainability 233–4; tasks 275; test 151–3
Desmet, P. 5, 27, 107–8, 434
determinism, linguistic 174
Deugo, D. 465
developers of games 418–19
devices, digital 481
Deville, C. 148
deWaard, I. 42
DGBLL (digital game-based language learning) 432–5
dictionaries 343, 379–80, 469–70
dictionary.com 501–3
Dictionary of Old English 392
digital: communications 63–5; competences 117; divide 116, 205; games 42, 107, 446–9; natives 110, 116, 161; reading 481; technologies 88; tribalism 264; visitors 116
digital game-based language learning (DGBLL) 432–5
'Digital Games for Language Learning – Challenges and Opportunities' (*ReCALL* Special Issue) 34
digital literacies 11, 115–26, 485; background 115–16; description 116–17; in language

classrooms 122–5; and the language teacher 125–6; skills 117; taxonomy of 117–22
*Digital Play* (Mawer and Stanley) 434
Diigo group 216
Dikli, S. 151
Diniz, L. 354
Dirckinck-Holmfeld, L. 232
discourse 176, 350, 351
distance education 17
distant collaboration 270
Diversity University (DU MOO) 11
Divitini, M. 302
Dolby, R. 492
domain of teaching languages 217
domain-specific studies 350
Donato, R. 30, 34
Dooey, P. 142, 150
Dörnyei, Z. 426
Doughty, C.J. 33, 142, 168
Douglas, D. 142
drag-and-drop functions 451
drilling 438–9
DST (dynamic systems theory) 41–2, 46–7
dual coding theory 298–9
Ducate, L. 76
Dudeney, G. 3, 73, 117–19, 121–2
DU MOO (Diversity University) 11
Dunkel, P. 129
dynamic systems theory (DST) 41–2, 46–7

e-books 481, 526–8
ecological: approaches 258; games 421–3; metaphors 40, 200–2; research 256
ecological computer-assisted language learning (CALL) theories 39–54; affordances of 48–9; Bronfenbrenner's ecological systems theory 42–3; cultural-historical activity theory (CHAT) 44–6; definitions 39–41; dynamic systems theory (DST)/complexity theory (CT) 41–2; future of 50; studying 46–8; systems theories 39, 42–3, 46–8; technologies 200–2; toolkit 2, 39–41
Edmodo 97
education: distance 17; resources for 289; standards for 57–61; *see also* teacher education
EdWeb 212
EFL (English as a foreign language) 103, 446, 480, 498
Eftekhari, S. 471
Egbert, J. 3, 28, 33, 102–4, 103, 185–6; *CALL Research Perspectives* 102–4
e-glosses 484
EHEA (European Higher Education Area) 59, 66
ELDA (Evaluations and Language Resources Distribution Agency) 349
e-learning 92–3, 133, 223, 226, 234, 320, 465, 486

# Index

*E-learning* (OpenupEd.eu) 214
Electronic Village Online (EVO) 71–2, 215–16
ELF (English as a lingua franca) 498
ELFA (English as a Lingua Franca in Academic Settings) 350
e-literacy 73
ellipsis 351–2, 354–7
Ellis, N.C. 466, 470
Ellis, R.A. 90–1, 96–8, 132–3; 'Principles of Instructed Learning' 98
Elola, I. 271–3
ELT (English language teaching) 90, 92, 245
*ELT Journal* 358
engagement 363, 426–7
Engeström, Y. 30, 44, 45, 93, 233
English as a foreign language (EFL) 103, 446, 480, 498
English as a lingua franca (ELF) 498
English as a Lingua Franca in Academic Settings (ELFA) 350
English as a second language (ESL) 160, 498
*Englishclub* 470
English for Specific Purposes (ESP) 91–2
*English Grammar Today* (Carter) 378
English language teaching (ELT) 90, 92, 245
English Native Speaker Interview Corpus (ENSIC) 394
English-Norwegian Parallel Corpus (ENPC) 391
English Profile Project 357–8
English speakers 498–9
English-Swedish Parallel Corpus (ESPC) 391
ensemble, theory 27–8
Entertainment Software Association 415
environmental/ecological sustainability 223–4, 226, 234–5
EPA (US Environmental Protection Agency) 224–5
ephemerality 264
Erasmus experience 250
ergonomics 134, 136
errors 380–1, 530
Erstad, O. 515–17
ESL (English as a second language) 160, 498
ESP (English for Specific Purposes) 91–2
ESPC (English-Swedish Parallel Corpus) 391
essay scorers 526
eTandem 244–5
ethical standards 111
ethnographic studies 110, 129
E-Tutor 127, 134–6, 380, 523
eTwinning project 250
EuroCALL Conference (2008) 18
European Commission 250
European Diploma Supplement 250
European Higher Education Area (EHEA) 59, 66
EV (Electronic Village) 215–16

evaluations 90, 127–40; automated writing 481–2, 526–8; background 127–31; case studies analysis 133–7; changes in 131–3; future directions 137–8; of spoken translation game systems 544–8
Evaluations and Language Resources Distribution Agency (ELDA) 349
Evison, J.M. 350
EVO (Electronic Village Online) 71–2, 216
exosystems 42
expansive learning theories 44–6
experiential modelling 75, 80, 250
Explicit Information On-Demand 450
exploratory practice 75, 80, 250
extrinsic feedback 133

Facebook 19, 96–8, 259–60, 264
face-to-face (FtF) 106–7; classrooms 90, 102; interactions 133; learning 242, 260; theories 27
failed communication 249
Falsetti, J. 15
familiarity with computers 149
fan sites 179
*FarmVille* 19, 451
Farr, F. 354, 358
FCE (Cambridge First Certificate in English) 381
feedback 62–5, 466; corrective (CF) 34, 107–8; error correction and 530–1; *versus* evaluation 131–2; extrinsic 133; from games 424–5; online 45; peer 483; recognition 543–4; on tests 155; on texts 524–6
FeedBlitz (email service) 212
Feenberg, A. 198
Felix, U. 102, 129–30, 136
feminists 164, 168–9
Ferlazzo, L.: 'Best of . . .' (websites) 212
Fernández-Garcia, M. 26, 31–2
film transcripts 340
*Final Fantasy X* 421, 449
Finland 117
Fiori, M. 259–60
first generation activity theory 44
Firth, A. 40
Fischer, I. 422
Fischer, R.A. 136, 517
Flagship Media Library 178
Flaitz, J. 465
flaming 15, 19
FL (foreign language) context 282
FLOB (Freiberg London-Oslo/Bergen) Corpus 388
Fløttum, K.: Cultural Identity in Academic Prose (KIAP) 367–8
flow 426
Flower, L.S. 269
Flowerdew, L. 371, 390, 391, 494–5
flow theory 34, 107
fluency 162, 164, 501

focus on form 283
folksonomies 119
foreign language (FL) context 282
Forman, E.A. 270
Fortescue, S. 13
forums 17, 178–9
forums, online 470–1
4-Component Instructional Design Model 34, 108
FrancoToile 127, 134–6
Frau-Meigs, D. 277
free online courses 213–14
*Free Technology for Teachers* (blog) (Byrne) 212
Freiberg Brown Corpus of American English (FROWN) 388
Freiberg London-Oslo/Bergen (FLOB) Corpus 388
Friedberg, A. 200
FROWN (Freiberg Brown Corpus of American English) 388
FtF *see* face-to-face (FtF)
Fullan, M. 232
Futuresource 282

Gabrielatos, C. 341
Galley, R. 2, 81–2, 83
game-based learning (GBL) 34, 107, 163, 433–5
gamefulness 417, 423
games 435; 2D virtual 308; activity 451–2; avatar-based 107, 432–3; casual 432; categories of 452–3; choosing 168; cloud-based storage for 418; development of 107; digital 42, 107; as ecologies 421–3; educational 182, 449; gender and 453–5; genres 417–19, 450–3; interactivity in 424–5; language learning 35, 107; literacy 422; mini 431–45; motivation from 426–7; multimedia 468–9; reality 182; sport 450; translation 536–49; tutorial 434
gamification 108, 416, 423
gaming 19, 34, 415–58; bridging activities for 277; children and 446–58; description 415–30; literacy 118; mini-games 431–45; online 179; and young learners 446–58
Gamon, M. 524
Gao, T. 465
Gao, Z.M. 340
Garrett, N. 205
Garrison, D.R. 71–2, 76, 82
Gass, S.M. 27, 271
Gavioli, L. 391
Gay, G. 46–7
GBL (game-based learning) 34, 107, 433–5
Gee, J.P. 42, 447, 450, 455
GEG (Google Educator Groups) 218
Gelfond, H.S. 454
Geluso, J. 486
gender 163–6, 389, 447–8, 453–5; *see also* age and gender

general corpora 388–9
generalisations 163
Geneva University 537
genres 205–6, 362, 368, 447; game 417–19, 450–3
German language learning 106
Germany 343
'GHOTI = FISH' example 499
Gibson, J.J. 48
Gilman, D.A. 473
Gilquin, G. 339
Glisan, E.W. 59
global English 498–9
globalisation 197, 210, 242
Glogster 74–5, 78, 504
glossaries 481–2, 529
GloWbE (Corpus of Global Web-based English) 391
GMAT (Graduate Management Admissions Test) 526
goal-oriented actions 44–5, 47, 424
goals 117; games and 424; for students 219; for technology use 186–7
Godwin-Jones, R. 3, 18–19
Goodyear, P. 132–3
Google 486
Google Chat 482
Google Classroom 218
Google Docs 20, 482
Google Educator Groups (GEG) 218
Google tools 18
Google Translate 89, 539
Gopher protocol 15
governments 18, 291
Grabe, W. 269–70, 478–9
Graduate Management Admissions Test (GMAT) 526
Grahl, B. 255
grammar 174, 351–4, 378–9, 461–3, 465
*Grammar and Beyond* (Blass, Iannuzzi, Savage and Reppen) 379
*Grammar Clinic* (Li and Hegelheimer) 470
grammar-translation approach 494
Granger, S. 339, 366, 376, 378, 379
Greaves, C. 340
Gregg, K. 104
Grisham, D.L. 464
Grosbois, M. 4
Gross, S. 154
groups 35, 78, 447
Gruba, P. 141, 259
Guichon, N. 5, 513–14
Gunawardena, C.N. 72
Guth, S. 3–4, 243–4
Gutierrez-Colon Plana, M. 302

Hadjistassou, S. 45
Hafner, C.A. 340, 484
Hampel, R. 168, 512–13, 516

557

# Index

Handford, M. 391
handheld devices 486
Handley, Z. 160
*Hangman* 441
Hanks, J. 73, 75
Hanson-Smith, E. 3, 5, 28
Hardman, F. 286
hardware 95, 417
Haring-Smith, T. 270
Harklau, L. 275
Harre, R. 81, 83
Harrison, R. 259
Harvey, K. 350
hashtags 264–5
Hauck, M. 2, 516
Hayes, E. 3, 42
Hayes, J.R. 269
HCI (human-computer interaction) 46
Healey, D. 2, 31, 211
Hegelheimer, V. 142, 420, 470, 527–8; *Grammar Clinic* 470
Heift, T. 3, 380, 523–4
Heigham, J. 110–11
Helm, F. 3–4, 243–4
help, online 543–4
Helsinki Corpus 393
Hémard, D. 131–2
Hembrooke, H. 46–7
Henri, F. 270
Herring, S.C. 204; 'Computer-mediated discourse analysis' 76
heterochrony principle 47
hierarchies 79–80, 82
Higgins, J. 10, 12–13, 419–20
Higgins, S. 286
Hinkel, E. 494, 498–9
Hirvela, A. 343
historical corpora 392–4
Hocking 492
Hockly, N. 3, 117–19, 121–2
Holden, C. 422
Holland, V.M. 524
Holman, W.J. Jr. 120
homogeneity 378
Hong Kong 340, 343–4, 422
Hong Kong Engineering Corpus 337
Horst, M. 441
Hoven, D. 73
Hruska, B.L. 165
Hsieh, W.M. 480
Hsien-Chin, L. 366
Hsu, L. 301
HTTP protocol 16
Hu, W.-C. 104
Huang, H.T. 486
Huang, L.L. 298–9, 529
Hubbard, P. 2, 26–7, 39–40, 102, 110, 128–9, 210, 302–3, 416

Huh, K. 104
human-computer interaction (HCI) 46
human learning theory 29
Hunter College (US) 309
Hutchinson, A. 287
hybridity 418–19
Hyde, J.S.K. 163
Hyland, K. 276, 362–3, 369, 370
hyperconnectivity 118
hyperlinking 529
hypertext literacy 118, 122–3

IA (interaction account) 29–30
IALTs (Internet-adaptive language testing) 148–54
Iannuzzi, S.: *Grammar and Beyond* 379
IATEFL (International Association of Teachers of English as a Foreign Language) 12, 215
IBLT (Internet-based language testing) 146, 149, 152, 154
ICALL (Intelligent CALL) 11, 20, 132, 522–35
ICE (International Corpus of English) 340, 349, 388–9
ICFLE (Internet-mediated intercultural foreign language education) 242
icons 451
ICT (information and communications technologies) 11, 200, 233
ICT4LT (Information and Communications Technology for Language Teachers) 11, 200
ICT-CST (Communication Technologies Competency Standards for Teachers) 57–8
*ICT for Primary Education* (University of London) 213
identities 243; language learning and digital technologies 167; online 78; and social networking 258, 260; *see also* age and gender
ILTSs (intelligent language tutoring systems) 523
IM (instant messaging) 471
images 117–18, 123, 264
immersion programmes 162
implementing telecollaboration 246–9
India 204
individuality 152, 157n6, 161–2
informal language contact 448
information: digital literacies for 119; pull and push 18; revolution 17; searching for 123–4; sharing and mobile devices 18–19
information and communications technologies (ICT) 11, 200, 233
Information and Communications Technology for Language Teachers (ICT4LT) 11, 200
informed consent for research 111
innovation, technological 66, 69
Innovative Technologies for Engaging Classrooms (iTEC) 289
input 29, 257, 377
Instagram 264
instantiation, theory 26–7

instant messaging (IM) 471–2
institutional models 3, 234
instructed language learning 91
instructional systems design (ISD) 94, 134
instructors *see* teachers
integration, cultural 176
Intelligent CALL (ICALL) 11, 20, 132, 380, 522–35
intelligent language tutoring systems (ILTSs) 523
intelligent tutoring systems (ITS) 522
Intelligent Web-based Interactive Language Learning (IWiLL) 380
INTENT project 250
interaction 258, 466; hypothesis 242, 257, 298; and IWBs 286; mediated 479; multimodality and 512; participant 72, 77–9; perspectives 463; reading 481
interaction account (IA) 29–30
'Interactionist SLA theory in CALL research' (Chapelle) 104–5
Interactive Technologies in Language Teaching (iTILT) project 289
interactive whiteboards (IWBs) 115, 198–9, 281–95; background 281; in classrooms 281–2; future of 289–92; justification for 282–5; and learning outcomes 285–8; and teacher support 288–9
Interactive Whiteboards in Vocational Education and Training (SmartVET) 289
interactivity in games 424–5
intercultural: activities 45, 90, 94, 97; communications 205–6, 246; contact 179; literacy 120
intercultural communicative competence (ICC) 241–3
interdependence 248
interface 200
International Association of Teachers of English as a Foreign Language (IATEFL) 12, 215
International Corpus of English (ICE) 340, 349, 388–9
internationalisation 249–51
International Phonetic Alphabet (IPA) 499–500
International Society for Technology in Education (ISTE) 210, 219
International Society for Technology in Education/National Educational Technology Standards (ISTE/NETS) 57–9, 68
Internet: commercial sites 17; connections to foreign cultures 177–9; history of 11; impact of 15–16; and language learning 197, 320; multilingualism on the 204; and older learners 89; research reviews 18; telecollaboration and 241–2; use 464; *see also* Web, the
Internet-adaptive language testing (IALTs) 148–54
Internet-based language testing (IBLT) 146, 149, 152, 154
Internet-mediated intercultural foreign language education (ICFLE) 242

Internet Relay Chat (IRC) 11, 15
interplay 271–2
intersubjectivity 32
intrinsic feedback 133
intuitive efficiency 131
IPA (International Phonetic Alphabet) 499–500
iPods 298
IRC (Internet Relay Chat) 11, 15
IRT (item response theory) 142, 148
ISD (instructional systems design) 134
Iskold, L. 260
ISTE (International Society for Technology in Education) 210, 219
ISTE/NETS (International Society for Technology in Education/National Educational Technology Standards) 57–9, 68
iTEC (Innovative Technologies for Engaging Classrooms) 289
item response theory (IRT) 142, 148
iTILT (Interactive Technologies in Language Teaching) project 289
ITS (intelligent tutoring systems) 522
Ivy, T. 96
IWBs *see* interactive whiteboards (IWBs)
IWiLL (Intelligent Web-based Interactive Language Learning) 380

Jalkanen, J. 3, 233–4
Jamieson, J. 142, 464
Japan 94, 203, 204
Jenkins, H. 447–8
Jenkins, J. 498–9
Jewitt, C. 286, 510–11, 518
Jo, J. 366
Johns, T. 4, 338–9, 340, 344, 365, 371
Johnson, E.S. 46, 128
Johnson, K.A. 161
Johnston, B. 161
joint activity systems 46
Jolly, D. 91, 94, 96, 97
Jones, C. 13, 232
Jones, G. 371
Jones, L.C. 27, 111
Jones, N. 148–9
Jones, R.H. 515
Joseph, D.R.D. 450–4
*Journal of Computer-Mediated Communication* 11
Jung, O. 18
Just-in-Time Principle 450

Kabilan, M.K. 19
Kafai, Y.B. 447–8
Kahng, J. 527
kaleidoscope analogy 200, 202
*kana* characters 205
Kaplan, J.D. 524
Kaplan, R.B. 269–70
Kaplow, R. 522

559

Index

Kapp, K. 423, 426
Kárpáti, A. 18, 258, 269
Kauppinen, M. 233
Kehrwald, B. 71–3, 76, 83
Kelsey, K.D. 276
Kennedy, C. 226–7, 234, 302, 366, 368
Keogh, B. 377
Kern, R. 3, 463
Kessler, G. 2, 66–8, 210, 273, 275
keyboards, computer 204–5
keywords in context (KWICs) 178, 408
KIAP (Cultural Identity in Academic Prose) (Fløttum) 367–8
kibbitzers 340
Kilgariff, A. 343
Kim, D. 473
Kingston University (UK) 225
Kinn, T. 367–8
Kinzie, M.B. 450–4
Kirschner, P. 48
Klimanova, L. 260
Klinghammer, S.J. 31
Knight, D. 394, 395
Knobel, M. 243
knowledge 440
knowledge base 89
Koehler, M.J. 122
Koester, A. 350
Komatsu, S. 258
Kosem, I. 364
Kramsch, C. 177, 180, 182–3, 206, 207, 419, 463
Krashen, S.D. 451, 501, 528
Kress, G. 510–12, 515
Krishnamurthy, R. 364
Kukulska-Hulme, A. 18
Kuo, C.H. 480
KWICs (keywords in context) 178, 408–9, 472
Kwon, E. 382
Kytö, M. 395

L2 see second and foreign language (L2)
labeling 119
Laborda, G. 142
Lam, W.S.E. 166–7, 169, 419
Lamy, M.-N. 511
Lan, J. 298
Lancaster Corpus of Mandarin Chinese (LCMC) 392
language: acquisition 162; affordances 48–9; crossings 177; ecological perspective on 40; laboratory 493–4; literacy 117–19; mediation and 30; model 538; pedagogy 135; as a psychological tool 462; in social context theory 29; teaching 33
Language Institute at the University of Wisconsin–Madison 205
language learning 9–23; background 9–11; corpora design for 404–12; course design for 90–2; future of 20–1; Internet impact on 15–18; names associated with 9–12; and roles of learners and teachers 12–15; the social Web and 18–19
*Language Learning* 104
*Language Learning & Technology* journal 35
languages, nonalphabetic 205
*Language Teaching* 358
*Language Teaching Research* 358
language testing and technology 141–59; acronyms 142, 157n1; approaches to 141–6; background 141; benefits in 150–5; changing views on 155; drawbacks in 146–50; future of 155–6
languaging 89
Lankshear, M. 243
Lantolf, J.P. 30, 137, 257; 'SLA Theory Building: Letting All the Flowers Bloom!' 104
Lapkin, S. 257
large spoken corpora 349
Larsen-Freeman, D. 41, 274
Laufer, B. 529
Lawrason, R.E. 494
LCMC (Lancaster Corpus of Mandarin Chinese) 392
LCR (learner corpus research) 378
LCTLs (less commonly taught languages) 205
Leaky, J. 130, 136
Leander, K.M. 169
learner corpora 376–87; for annotation, assessment and rating 380–2; background 376; for grammar books 378–9; need for 376–8; understanding 382–3; and writing aids 379–80
learner corpus research (LCR) 378
Learner Presence 77
learners: access to technology of 115; behavior 384n1; and DDL 338–9, 341–2; of English 182; evaluating 136–7; and KWICs use 410; motivation 466–77; and multimodal competence development 515–17; older 89; preparation of 35, 339; roles of 14, 15; and social media 96–8; and technology 110; training for 133, 303; unsophisticated queries of 342–3; young 446–58; see also students
learning: approaches to 129, 243; autonomous 197, 338; blended and online 71; collaborative 258; constructive approaches to 298; context of 163–4; data-driven 389; designing for 94; digital game-based 448; environments and tools for 231–2; implications for 167–8; informal *versus* formal 486; interaction 30, 107; intercultural turn in 241; mediation and 30; with mobile devices 103, 302–4; and peer/self-evaluation 132; primary school 163; process of 79; sociocultural perspective 462; strategies for 366; task-based 96; transfer of 443; variations in 162; vocabulary 227; workplace 233; *see also* online learning, research in
Learning2gether 218

learning management system (LMS) 198–9, 248, 298
Learning Technology Special Interest Group (LTSIG) 12, 215
*Learning to Teach Online* (University of New South Wales) 213
Leblay, C. 275–6
Lee, C. 483, 528
Lee, D. 366
Lee, F.S. 483, 528
Lee, H.G. 3
Lee, L. 273
Lee, M. 48
Lee, S.L. 482
Lee, Y.N. 167
Leech, G. 350, 351, 377
Lehtonen, M. 224, 234
Lemke, J. 39, 47
*Lemonade Stand* simulation programme 10
*Le Monde* 366
Leonardo projects 225
Leontiev, A.N. 30, 44
Lepi, K. 256
Leppänen, S. 204
less commonly taught languages (LCTLs) 205
Levine, P. 512
Levy, M. 2–3, 27–9, 31–2, 34, 39–40, 92, 102, 105, 128, 226–7, 234, 302, 419, 523
Lewis, M. 462
Lewis, T. 518
lexical development research 441–2
lexical frequency studies 350–1
lexical variation (LV) ratio 382
lexico-grammatical acquisition CALL tools 461–77; background 461; benefits of 462–7; classrooms applications of 468–73; future developments for 474; integration principles 467–8; research into 473–4
lexicography 379–80, 389
Lexinote 227
Lextutor 364–9, 366
Li, L. 5, 470; *Grammar Clinic* 470
Li, Z. 527–8
Liaw, M.L. 480
Lifelong Learning Programme 225, 228
Lim, H. 527
Lin, C.-C. 298–9, 529
Lin, H. 276
Lindgren, E. 449
LINDSEI (Louvain International Database of Spoken English Interlanguage) 350
Lindström, B. 232
Linehan, C. 81, 83
Linguistic Data Consortium (University of Pennsylvania) 349
linguistic-pedagogical attributes of mini-games *436*
linguistics: corpus 337; *see also* applied linguistics
linguists, computational 392
Link, S. 527–8

Liou, H.C. 5, 14, 480, 482, 485–6
listening 301, 354
listening and speaking CALL tools 491–508; designs for 500–5; digital acoustics and TESOL 491–4; perspectives on 494–8; sociolinguistic effect 498–500
*List of Wikipedias* index 204
literacies 243, 276; conceptualisations of 419, 427; creative 121; critical 121; digital 11, 115–26, 485; hypertext 118, 122–3; multimodal 515; new media 117; online 241; texting 117–18, 122
Liu, M. 256–7, 259
Livemocha 227, 259
LMS (learning management system) 198–9, 248
LOB (London-Oslo/Bergen) Corpus 367, 388
Loewen, S. 466
logging systems 443
Lomicka, L. 4, 260
*London Adventure* simulation programme 10
London-Oslo/Bergen (LOB) Corpus 388
Long, M.H. 25, 33, 92, 168, 257
Longman Active Study Dictionary 379
Longman Spoken American Corpus 349
Lord, G. 4
Louvain International Database of Spoken English Interlanguage (LINDSEI) 350
LTSIG (Learning Technology Special Interest Group) 12, 215
Lundgren-Cayrol, K. 270
Lundin, R.W. 276
LV (lexical variation) ratio 382
*Lyceum* distance language 34

Ma, Q. 302
Macaro, E. 160
machine translation (MT) 206, 537, 539
McBride, K. 259
McCarten, J. 344–5
McCarthy, J. 81, 83
McCarthy, M. 4, 344, 349–54, 370, 473
McCormick, D. 30
McDonell, W. 30
McGee, I. 343
McGonigal, J. 423, 426
McLornan, S. 513–14
McLuhan, M. 198–206
Macmillan English Dictionary for Advanced Learners (MEDAL) 379, 384n1
macro literacy 120–2
macrosystems 42
magister roles 12–14, 419
magnetic tape 492
mailing lists 17
Malinowski, D. 3
MALL (mobile-assisted language learning) 35, 264
Malone, T.W. 437
Marckwardt, A.: 'Changing Winds and Shifting Sands' 496

# Index

Mardomingo, R. 80
Marinova-Todd, S.H. 162
Mark, G. 354
Marsden, E. 25
Marshall, D.B. 162
Martin, C. 367
Martín, M.E.R. 340
Martínez-Arbelaiz, A. 26, 31–2
Marton, F. 89
massively multiplayer online (MMO) games 34–5, 42, 452
massively multiplayer online role-playing games (MMORPGs) 19, 418, 421–2, 432
massive open online courses (MOOCs) 42, 132, 211, 213–14, 526
Master of Arts in Teaching English to Speakers of Other Languages (MATESOL) 210
materials: audiovisual 503; availability of 286; classroom 354; DDL learning 344; design 288, 303; management 63, 88; pedagogical 205
materials design flow chart *92*
materials development 88–100; background 88; changes in classrooms and learners on 88–9; for course design 90–2; and digital technologies 89–90; and the digital world 92–4; multimedia 197; overview 90–2; tools for 94–8
material-semiotic artefacts 47–8
MATESOL (Master of Arts in Teaching English to Speakers of Other Languages) 210
Mawer, K. 434–5; *Digital Play* 434
Maycock, L. 148–9
Mayer, R.E. 510, 512, 517–18
meaning, negotiating 242
meaning-focused activity 96
MEDAL (Macmillan English Dictionary for Advanced Learners) 379, 384n1
media: affordances of the 72; sharing 255; and skills development 63–5; social 11, 19, 63, 95–6, 101, 255
mediation 30, 44
mediums 203
Medlock, B. 381
memes 120, 124–5
'memex' 20
Mendelsohn, D.J. 495
Meng, W.T. 483
*Mentira* (game) 182
mentoring 217
Mercer, S. 274
MERLOT (Multimedia Educational Resource for Learning and Teaching Online) 212, 218
Meskill, C. 102, 111
mesosystems 42
metadata 376–7
meta-linguistic considerations 179
method, games as 423
methodology, research 76, 110–11, 341

Meunier, F. 4, 377
Meurers, D.K. 377, 380–1
Miceli, T. 366, 368
Michigan Corpus of Academic Spoken English (MICASE) 337, 340–1, 405–6
Michigan Corpus of Upper-level Student Papers (MICUSP) 405–6
microblogging 174, 255
microcomputers 10, 12, 15–16
Microsoft Office Translator 481
microsystems 42
Miller, L. 494–5
Miller, M. 420
Mills, N. 258, 260
'mim-mem' method 495
mind maps 97
mini-games 431–45; background 431–8; designing or evaluating 442–3; future research for 443–4; in language classroom 438–41; research on 441–2
miscollocations 380
miscommunication 180
Mishra, P. 122
MIT 539–40, 543
Mitchell, K. 259
Mitchell, R. 25
Mitra, S. 215
MMO (massively multiplayer online) games 34–5, 42, 452
MMORPGs (massively multiplayer online role-playing games) 19, 418, 421–2, 432
mobile: apps 89; background 296; considerations for 303–4; devices 18–20, 182, 264, 302–4; learning 103, 258, 296–307; literacy 118; phone usage 116; research outcomes into 300–2; technology 288–91; theories in 296–300; tools 89–90
mobile-assisted language learning (MALL) 35
mobility 18–19
modality 389, 513–14
MonoConc 408
monolingual collocation dictionaries 343
monolingual corpora 369
MOO (multiuser object orientated domain) 308–9
MOOCs (massive open online courses) 42, 132, 211, 213–14, 526
*MOOCs Directory* 214
MOOs (Multi-User, Object-Oriented dimension) 11, 15
MOOssiggang 309
Morgan, B. 161
Morgan, C. 233
Morgan, T. 71–2, 81, 83
Mosaic web browser 11, 16
Moss, G. 286
motivation 77–8, 131, 339, 466–77; achievement 442; games and 426–7; and user profiles 259

562

Motteram, G. 2–3, 94, 97, 162–3, 482
MT (machine translation) 537, 539
MUDs (Multi-User Dungeons) 11
multilingualism 204, 367–71
multiliteracies 243, 487
multimedia 17–18, 117–18; games 468–9; literacy 118, 122–3; presentations 464; resources 285
Multimedia Educational Resource for Learning and Teaching Online (MERLOT) 212, 218
multimodality 509–21; cognitive costs of 513–15; and competence development 515–17; corpora 345, 394–5; defining 509–11; expression 484; potential of 511–13; and teaching implications 517–19
multiplayer games 19, 421, 452
Multi-User, Object-Oriented (MOOs) dimension 11, 15
Multi-User Dungeons (MUDs) 11
multiuser object orientated domain (MOO) 308–9
MundoHispano 15–16, 309
Muñoz, C. 449
Murday, K. 465–6
Murphy, B. 4
Murphy, P. 481
Murray, L. 5
Musser, J. 277
*MY Access!* 481, 483, 486
Mydocumenta 504
Myles, F. 25
*My Word Coach* 441

Nagata, N. 524, 529
Nah, K.C. 298, 302
Nakata, T. 464, 473–4
names, importance of 9–12
narratives, game 426
Nation, P. 448; Vocabulary Size Test 448
National Council of Less Commonly Taught Languages 205
National Educational Technology Standards (NETS) 57
National Literacy and Numeracy strategies 291
native speakers 49, 134, 174, 176–9, 244
natural language processing (NLP) 61, 132, 380–2, 522
naturally occurring language 338
Naylor, S. 377
NBLT (network-based language teaching) 241
needs analysis 91–2
negotiation of meaning (NoM) 29, 106
Nelson, G.E. 522
Nelson, M. 515
Nesi, H. 364, 371
'Net generation' 116
netiquette 15, 121
NETS (National Educational Technology Standards) 57

network-based language teaching (NBLT) 241
networks 71, 120, 124, 217
Neuman, W. 31
neurodevelopment 162
Newgarden, K. 34–5, 422
New Labour government (UK) 282
new media 117, 241–2, 242–3
New Media Consortium 515
news, social 255
Nicaise, E. 382
NLP (natural language processing) 61, 132, 380–2, 522
NMMC (Nottingham Multimodal Corpus) 394
NNS (nonnative speakers) 366
Nokelainen, P. 131
NoM (negotiation of meaning) 29, 106
nonalphabetic languages 205
nonnative speakers (NNS) 366
nonnative teacher talk 382–3
nontechnocentric research 129
nonwords 350
normalisation 108–9, 116, 226, 228
Norris, S. 513
Norton, B. 168
Norway 302
Norwich Institute for Language Education 212
noticing 285, 298, 464
Nottingham Multimodal Corpus (NMMC) 394

objects 44
Ochs, E. 164
Ockey, G.J. 142
O'Dowd, R. 180, 249, 273
OERs (open educational resources) 289
off-task discussion 32
off-the-shelf games 434–5
OIE (online intercultural exchange) 242
O'Keeffe, A. 344, 349–50, 354, 358, 473
Oller, J. 26, 28
OMC (Oslo Multilingual Corpus) 391
Onat-Stelma, Z. 94, 162–3
'One Tablet per Child' projects 115
online: connectivity 418; culture exchanges 179–81; help 543–4; language learning 205–6; learning communities 181–4; literacies 242; safety 120, 124
online intercultural exchange (OIE) 242
online learning, research in 71–87; background 71–2; findings and discussion 77–84; methodology 75–6; Social Presence in 72–3; training module for 73–5
online word game 469
open educational resources (OERs) 289
Open Office 17
Open Parallel Corpus (OPUS) 391
open source resources 17, 89
Open University (UK) 34, 518–19

# Index

OpenupEd.eu (*E-learning*) 214
operations 44
OPUS (Open Parallel Corpus) 391
Orbox 434
O'Reilly, T. 277
O'Reilly Radar Team 277
organisational structures 233–4
Orland-Barak, L. 46
Ortega, L. 275
Osada, N. 492
Oskoz, A. 271–3
Oslo Multilingual Corpus (OMC) 391
O'Sullivan, Í. 339, 363, 366, 368
output hypotheses 257, 271
Owston, R. 233
*Oxford Hachette French-English Dictionary* 371

Page Essay Grade (PEG) 526
Pai, C.W. 482
Paivio, A. 298
P&P (pen and paper) tests 148–50, 152–5
Paolillo, J. 205
parallel corpora 391–2
paratexts 421
participation 72–3, 74, 77–9, 81–2, 120
partners, language 179–80
patterns 41, 201–2; and corpora 410; and gender differences 163; of participation 74, 77–9; in textbooks 176
Pavlenko, A. 137, 168
Pearson, J. 392
Pearson Education 256
pedagogy 20, 63–4, 68, 110, 131, 135; approaches to 168, 212; and corpora design 405; developments in 228–9, 232–3; gaming and 455; impediments to 259; IWBs and 285–8; learner corpora and 376–87; magister roles and 12–14; materials for 178, 205; metaphors for game-mediated L2 419–23; mini-games in 438–9; practices 260; and spoken language corpora 348–61; technology networks for 215–19; training for 303; usability of 131; and written language corpora 362–75
peer evaluations 45, 132, 483
peer-mediation 275
peer scaffolding 273
PEG (Page Essay Grade) 526
Pegrum, M. 73, 78, 83, 117–19, 121–2
Pellettieri, J. 467
Pemberton, L. 269
pen and paper (P&P) tests 148–50, 152–5
Peng, J.-E. 42
Perez, L.: *Something To Do on Tuesday* 13
Pérez-Paredes, P. 342
personalisation 119–20
personal learning environments (PLEs) 211–13
personal learning networks (PLNs) 120, 214–19

personal literacy 120, 124
Petersen, S.A. 302
Peterson, M. 4, 422
pet games 450
Petrie, G.M. 102–4, 103; *CALL Research Perspectives* 102–4
Peuronen, S. 204
Philips 492
Phillips, D.C. 30
Phillips, M. 416, 426–7, 496
Phillips, N.C. 169
phonautogram 493
phonautograph 491
photos 265
phraseology 340
Piirainen-Marsh, A. 421, 447
Pim, C. 97, 162–3
pinyin 205
Piper, A. 14
PL (Programmed Learning) 12
planning 246–8
Plass, J. 27, 512
PLATO (Programmed Logic for Automated Teaching Operations) 9–10, 13–15
play and child development 449
PlayStation 4 (Sony 2013) 418
PLEs (personal learning environments) 211–13
PLNs (personal learning networks) 120, 214–19
podcasts 95
polyfocality 513–15, 518
*Pong* 417
Poore, M. 95
pop-up ads 19
portfolios 181–2
positioning 81, 83
Potts, D. 485
power tests 153
Pöyhönen, S. 233
Prabhu, N. 496–7
Practice Principle 450
practitioners 75
pragmatism 177, 179, 350, 353, 389
praxis, collaborative 217
Prensky, M. 110, 115–16
primary school learning 163
principles, digital games 447
'Principles of Instructed Learning' (Ellis) 98
print literacy 117
privacy 263
problem-solving, research into 441
procedural knowledge 440
process, hierarchy *versus* 79–80
Proctor, C.P. 464
productive language samples 153–4
productivity 234
professional associations 215–19
professional development 289

profiles, user 259
Programmed Learning (PL) 12
Programmed Logic for Automated Teaching Operations (PLATO) 9–10, 13–15
programmes, for teacher preparation 61–2
Project Gutenberg 17
projecting 73, 83–4
pronunciation 499, 502–3
proofreading 344
prosody 383
prosumers 118
psychocognitive skills 516
psycholinguistics 29, 256–7
'Psychosocial Moratorium' Principle 455
Purushotma, R. 420, 451
push and pull mechanisms 18, 212, 227
push aspect of mobile learning 302
pushed output 271
*Pygmalion* (Shaw) 499

Quah, J. 102, 111
*Quest Atlantis* 420
questionnaires 245
QuickAssist 529
QWERTY keyboard 204–5

Rabab'ah, G.A. 465
Rama, P.S. 35, 422
Random House Unabridged Dictionary 502
Raspberry Pi 119
rating 380–2
Rayner, M. 5, 547
Rayson, P. 350
REAder-specific Practice (REAP) 178
reading and writing, CALL tools for 478–90; background 478–90; considerations 482–4; future of 485–7; research issues 484–5; technologies for 479–82; theory 479
*ReCALL* 18, 107; 'Digital Games for Language Learning – Challenges and Opportunities' 34
Received Pronunciation (RP) 499
recogniser software 537
recognition feedback 543–4
recording technology 349
record keeping 62
redundancy effect 514
reference 337–8, 388–9
refinement, theory 28–9
Reichle, R.V. 443
Reinhardt, J. 5, 246, 257, 260, 277, 423, 434
relativity, linguistic 174
reliability 149–50, 175, 177–8
remix 121, 124–5, 485
remote scoring 153–4
rephrasing strategies 383
*Report of the World Commission on Environment and Development* (United Nations) 224

Reppen, R. 5, 354, 371, 391; *Grammar and Beyond* 379
research 101–12, 258; age and gender 168–9; background 111–12; on benefits of CALL 463; on children and digital gameplay 448–9; complementary options to 104; contributions through 111–12; and DDL 337–42; design and methods 109–11; and development 107; evaluation 128; exemplars 106–9; ICALL 529–31; on mini-games 441–2; multimodality 511–13; reading and writing 102–3, 484–5; reviews 18; social networking 256–60; student selection for 110; theories 31–2, 103–6; understanding 101–3; written corpora 362–3
Ring, G. 465
Riordan, E. 4
Rissanen, M. 391, 393, 394
Ritter, M. 180, 249
Robertson, I. 226
Robinson, J. 263–4
Robo-Sensei 523
Roby, W.B. 493–5
Rodriguez, J. 263
Roever, C. 147
role-playing games (RPGs) 418–19, 451
Romeo, K. 303
Römer, U. 343, 345, 353–4
Rost, M. 497, 503
Rourke, L. 76
Rowling, J.K. 340
Royce, T.D. 515
Rozovski-Roitblat, B. 529
RP (Received Pronunciation) 499
RPGs (role-playing games) 418–19, 451
Rühlemann, C. 351
Ruiz-Madrid, M.N. 378
Rundell, M. 379
Rushkoff, D. 119
Russian Reference Corpus 389

SACODEYL (System Aided Compilation and Open Distribution of European Youth Language) 358, 364, 394
Sadler, R. 517
Salaberry, R. 102
Salamoura A. 381
Salen, K. 424
Säljö, R. 89
Salmon, G. 74
Salonius-Pasternak, D.E. 454
Sampson, D.G. 304
Sams, M.R. 524
Sánchez-Tornel, M. 342
Sangrà, A. 133
Sansone, M. 116
Santa Barbara Corpus of Spoken American English (SBCSAE) 349, 394

Sapir, E. 173–4
Sapir-Whorf hypothesis 173–4
Sargeant, H. 287
SAT (skill acquisition theory) 439–41
Savage, A.: *Grammar and Beyond* 379
*savoirs* 243
Sayers, D. 185
scaffolding 424–5, 462
Scale of Social Interaction (SSI) Model 452
Schäfer, L. 380
Schieffelin, B. 164
SchMOOze University 15–16, 309
Schnotz, W. 512
Schrock, K. 212
Schulze, M. 5, 42, 523–4
SCMC (synchronous computer-mediated communication) 106
Scollon, R. 512, 515
scoring, test 151, 153–4, 157n3
Scott de Martinville, É.-L.: *Au clair de la lune* 491
screencasts 212
screen sharing 471–2
SCT *see* sociocultural theory
search 119, 339
Searle, J. 174
second and foreign language (L2) 18, 212; classroom 43; conceptualisations of 419; evaluation and 133–5; and gaming 416–23; learners 35; self-repair in 106; and social networking 256–62; sustainabilty and 227; theoretical approaches to 256–8
second generation activity theory 44
second language acquisition (SLA) 25–30, 101; computer supported collaborative writing and 274–5; ecology metaphor in 40; and game-based learning 34, 431–2; mini-games in 339–441; oral/aural issues and 498; theories 242, 271, 297–8, 463
Second Life 48–9, 89, 309
security issues 149
Seidlhofer, B. 378
Selber, S. 136
self-destructing apps 264
self-determination theory 34, 108
self-directed language learning 178
self-evaluation 132–3
self-organised learning environments (SOLEs) 215
self-repair 106, 111
Selinker, L. 271
semio-pragmatic skills 515–16
semiotic budget 49
SEN (special educational needs) 285
Seneff, S. 536, 539–40
server problems 203
sex *see* gender
Sha, G.Q. 343

*Shaping the Way We Teach English* (US Department of State and the University of Oregon) 213
sharing 120
Sharma, P. 4
Sharples, M. 269
Shaw, G.B.: *Pygmalion* 499
Shea, P. 77
Shermis, M. 527
Short, J. 72
*SimCity* 451
*Sims, The* 420, 450–1, 453–4
simulations 10, 19, 420
Sinclair, J.McH. 339, 344
Sinclair Spectrum 14
single activity systems 45
singleplayer games 452
SITES-M2 study 233
situated avatar-based games 432–3, 435
situated learning 30
skill acquisition theory (SAT) 439–41
skills: computer programming 119; DDL and improved 339; development 17, 71–3, 79–80; learning 440; listening and speaking 354, 494; psychocognitive 516; semio-pragmatic 515–16; sociocultural 516; technical 20, 63–5; 21st century 3, 115–17; writing 343
Skype 20, 89, 203
SLA *see* second language acquisition
slacktivism 122
Slaouti, D. 94, 162–3
'SLA Theory Building: Letting All the Flowers Bloom!' (Lantolf) 104
smaller spoken corpora 349–50
smartphones 95
SMART Technologies 281
SmartVET (Interactive Whiteboards in Vocational Education and Training) 289
Smith, B. 27, 106–7, 111
Smith, F. 286
Smith, S. 339
Snapchat 264
Snow, C.F. 162
Soares, D.A. 287
social interaction 425
socially situated identities 166–7
social media 11, 19, 63, 95–6, 101, 255
social mediators 44
social networking (SN) 119, 179, 255–68; approaches to 256–8; background 255–6; considerations when using 263–4; future of 264–5; and gaming 418; research-based studies on 258–60; sites (SNS) 256–8, *261*; tools 260–3
Social Presence (SP) 71–4, 76, 78–9, 84
social relationships 164
social Web *see* Web 2.0
socioaffective context 273
socioconstructivist paradigm 271

sociocultural: approaches 257–8; information 178; issues 177; perspectives 161, 462; research 256; skills 516
sociocultural theory (SCT) 30, 35, 40, 83, 93, 133, 243, 298, 479
sociolinguistics 174, 176–7, 389, 498–500
sociopragmatic studies 260
software 102, 408, 454, 472, 481–2; automated writing 526–8; development 135, 290; evaluation 129; programmes 13, 60–1
Sokoli, S. 503–4
SOLEs (self-organised learning environments) 215
Soliya Connect Programme 181
*Something to Do on Tuesday* (Perez and Taylor) 13
Sony 492
sound recording 491–5
SP (Social Presence) 71–4, 76, 78–9, 84
Spain 117
spatial resources 48
SpeakApps 228–31, 234, 504
speaking and listening CALL tools *see* listening and speaking CALL tools
speaking skills 354
special educational needs (SEN) 285
specialists 64
specialized corpora 390–1
speech recognition and translation 537–9
speech to text 20
split attention effect 513–14
spoken language corpora 348–61; background 348; case studies 354–7; defined 348–50; future of 357–8; research into 350–4
spoken translation game 537
spoof websites 123–4
sport games 450
Squire, K. 298
Sripicharn, P. 339–40
SSI (Scale of Social Interaction) Model 452
*Standards for Foreign Language Learning in the 21st Century* (American Council of Teachers of Foreign Languages (ACTFL)) 59
Stanley, G. 97, 215, 434–5; *Digital Play* 434
Stannard, R. 212
*Star Trek* 20
Statista.com 264
stereotypes 167–8, 181, 454–5
Stevens, V. 217–19, 218, 441
Stevenson, J. 154
Stevenson, M.P. 256–7, 259
Stickler, U. 512–13
Stockwell, G. 4, 27, 28–9, 31–2, 34, 102, 128, 227, 302
Stollhans, S. 501
strategic training 303
strong-interface theory 440
students: codes of conduct for 263; and corpora use 392–4; and IWBs 285–6; mobile devices use by 258, 301–2; mobility of 250; and research projects 110; and speech recognition systems 537; and technology expertise 211; *see also* learners
subjects 44
Sun, C.S. 344
Sundqvist, P. 5, 422, 450, 452–3
Sung, Y.-T. 298
support, social 217
Sussex, R. 298
sustainability 223–38; designs for 233–4; environmental/ecological 223–4, 226, 234–5; second and foreign language (L2) 227
Swain, M. 89, 257, 271
Swales, J.M. 362, 366–7
Swan, K. 72, 462
Sweller, J. 513–14
Sykes, J. 422–3, 434, 452
Sylven, L.K. 422
symbolic competence 183
synaesthesia 485
synchronicity 247, 388, 510, 513
synchronous computer-mediated communication (SCMC) 106
synthesis, theory 27–8
synthetic immersive environments 435
System Aided Compilation and Open Distribution of European Youth Language (SACODEYL) 358, 364
system feedback, automated 131–2
systems theories 228–9

Taalas, P. 3, 233–4
taboo languages 389
Tactical Language and Culture Training System (TLCTS) 538
Tagarela, 523
tagging literacy 119
Tahtinen, S. 217
Tainio, L. 421, 447
Taiwan 298
TALL (technology-assisted learning) 11
Tanaka, H. 227
tandem learning sites 17
Tang, E. 382
TANGO 480
Tao, H. 353
target language (TL) cultures 308–9
Tarnanen, M. 233
task-based language teaching (TBLT) 33
task-based learning 96
tasks: DDL 339, 344; design 275; for mobile learning 303; telecollaborative 247–8
taxonomies 13, 117, 342–3
Taylor, A.M. 481, 482, 484
Taylor, H.M. 496
Taylor, K.H. 169

# Index

Taylor, M.: *Something To Do on Tuesday* 13
TBLT (task-based language teaching) 33
teacher education 210–22; background 210; and computer supported collaborative writing 275–6; and MOOCs 213–14; problems in 210–11; professional associations for 214–19; self-help for 211–13; standards for 219–20
teacher preparation, standards for 57–70; contextualised examples for 66–8; establishing standards 65–6; future directions of 68–9; overview 57–61; technology and 61–5
teachers 61–2; codes of context for 263; and computer use 10, 392; and DDL 338–9, 342; development 288–9, 382; and digital literacies 125; ESL 182; evaluation and 132–3; and learner identities 167–8; and materials development 95; and new technologies 198–9; nonnative 382–3; and parallel corpora use 392; perceptions of 163; power erosion of 17; roles of 13–15; self-help for 211–13; sense of plausibility 497; and skills promotion 97–8; on social networking 258–9; telecollaboration and 246–8; training for 122, 133, 290, 344
Teachers of English to Speakers of Other Languages (TESOL) 12, 65–8, 215–16, 219–20, 491–508
Teacher Training Videos (TTV) 212
teaching: grammar and vocabulary 462–3; implications for 167–8; mechanical 497, 505; semio-pedagogical competence development 517–19; vocabulary 473–4; and written corpora 362–3
Teaching Channel, The 212
TeachingEnglish site (BBC) 212
Teaching Presence 72, 83
teamwork 270–1
TEC (Translational English Corpus) 392
technical training 303
technocratic perspective 200
technologies 9; access to 115; comfort with 116; definitions of 198; examples of *201*; literacy in 118–19; predictions for future of 20–1; relational view of 200; transmission (pull) 18
Technology, Pedagogic and Content Knowledge (TPACK) 122
technology-assisted learning (TALL) 11
technology-enhanced language learning (TELL) 12
Technology Standards Task Force (TESOL) 12
technology-varied contexts 3
technophobes 132–3
TEI (Text Encoding Initiative) 376
telecollaboration 27, 46, 66, 180–1, 206, 241–54, 366; background 241; challenges of 248–9; frameworks for 241–4; models of 244–6; normalisation of 249–51; planning and implementing 246–8

*Telecollaboration in Foreign Language Learning* (Warschauer) 242
TELL (technology-enhanced language learning) 11, 12
Tempus projects 225
terminology 9–12, 117
TESOL *see* Teachers of English to Speakers of Other Languages
TESOL–Electronic Village Online (EVO): *Tutoring with Web 2.0 Tools* 71
*TESOL Journal*: 'Constructing Meaning with Computers' 31
TESOL Standards 66–8, 210
testing *see* language testing and technology
textbooks 176, 178
Text Encoding Initiative (TEI) 376
texting literacy 117–18, 122
text reduction 264–5
texts, limitations of 206–7
theories: ensemble 2; perspectives 161–7, 463; pluralism 104; role of 103–6; technological 256–7
Thewissen, J. 381
third generation activity theory 44
Thomas, D. 232–3
Thomas, M. 259
Thomas, S. 277
Thorne, S.L. 5, 180, 206, 246, 277, 422, 434, 452
Thurstun, J. 344
*TIME Magazine* 493
TLCTS (Tactical Language and Culture Training System) 538
TL (target language) cultures 308–9
TNC (Turkish National Corpus) 389
Tognini-Bonelli, E. 338
Tomlinson, B. 90, 94
tools: for analysis 408–9; CALL 380, 467–8, 478–508; for collaboration 217; communication 484; corpus 473, 480; courseware development 94–8; design for mobile language learning 303–4; development *130*; evaluation of 129, 134–6; flexibility and combination 486; games as 420–1; learning 128, 231–2; lexico-grammatical acquisition 461–77; for listening and speaking CALL 491–508; online text location 178; social networking 255–8, 260–3, 265; social web 258; Web 212
topical relevance 378
Torlakovic, E. 465
TOTALrecall 480
Tottie, G. 351
Touchstone series 354, 371
Tozcu, A. 464–5
TPACK (Technology, Pedagogic and Content Knowledge) 122
training 133, 303
trait perspectives 163–4

Translational English Corpus (TEC) 392
translations 89, 392, 536–49
transliteracy 277
Traynor, B. 217
trends 34–6
Trettvik, J. 48
Tribble, C. 364, 371, 391
Tricot, A. 518
Tschichold, C. 5
Tseng, Y.C. 480
Tsourakis, N. 547
TTV (Teacher Training Videos) 212
Turkish National Corpus (TNC) 389
turn-construction 353
tutorial CALL 433–4
tutoring 1, 73–5, 419
*Tutoring with Web 2.0 Tools* (TESOL–Electronic Village Online (EVO)) 71
tutors, games as learning 419–20
21st century skills 3, 115–16
type-token ratio (TTR) 526

UNESCO ICT-CST 58, 68
UNESCO ICT Standards for Teachers 11
UNICollaboration platform 250–1
United Kingdom (UK) 117, 119, 282–3
United Nations: *Report of the World Commission on Environment and Development* 224
United States (US) 59, 117, 204, 302
University of Bologna 545–6
University of Illinois 9
University of London: *ICT for Primary Education* 213
University of Maryland 211
University of Michigan 405–96
University of Minnesota's Center for Advanced Research on Language Acquisition (CARLA) 205
University of Missouri–St. Louis 309
University of New South Wales: *Learning to Teach Online* 213
University of Oregon 211; *Shaping the Way We Teach English* 213–14
University of Pennsylvania (Linguistic Data Consortium) 349
US Defense Forces 495
US Department of State: *Shaping the Way We Teach English* 213–14
US Environmental Protection Agency (EPA) 224–5

validity, test 150, 471–2
value of research 111–12
Vanderbilt University (US) 225
van Es, E. 35, 422
van Hazebrouck, S. 287
Van Leeuwen, T. 510–12
van Lier, L. 39, 40, 43, 48, 258
Van Rooy, B. 380

Vantage Learning (CorrectEnglish) 528
Varghese, M. 161
Varonis, E. 27
Vásquez, C. 102
Vassar College (US) 309
verbal abilities 163
verbal behaviour 496
video: captioning 529; conferencing 89, 97, 198–9, 203, 471; documents 134; games 415, 447
Vienna-Oxford International Corpus of English (VOICE) 350
Viewpoint series 354
virtual learning environments (VLEs) 89, 121
Virtual Software Library (VSL) 216
virtual worlds 48, 101, 308–19; background 308; and benefits in CALL 309–10; design features 308–9; future direction of 317–18; research findings on use of 310–15; and research issues 315–17
visual dominance 513
visual media literacy 118
*Visuwords Online Graphical Dictionary* 40
VKontakte 260
VLEs (virtual learning environments) 89, 121
vocabulary 227, 301, 409–10, 461–3, 465, 468, 473–4, 529
Vocabulary Size Test (Nation and Beglar) 448
vocalisations 351
VOICE (Vienna-Oxford International Corpus of English) 350
Volosinov, V.N. 426
Voxopop 501
Vsee (software) 471–2
VSL (Virtual Software Library) 216
Vyatkina, N. 366, 377–8
Vygotsky, L. 29, 30, 44, 133, 243, 256

Wagner, J. 40
Wagner, M. 420
Walkman 492
Walsh, S. 382
Walter, C. 160, 462
WAMI (Web-Accessible Multimodal Interfaces) 540
Wang, C. 539
Wang, L. 302
Wang, S. 102
Ward, J.R. 522
Ware, P. 66, 249, 273
Warnecke, S. 2
Warren, M. 4, 340, 343–4
Warschauer, M. 13, 35, 168, 200, 422; *Telecollaboration in Foreign Language Learning* 242
Web, the: commercialisation of 17; as corpus 343; emergence of 16–17; materials development and 95–6; the social 18–19; *see also* Internet

569

# Index

Web 2.0 12, 18–19, 20; development 277; tools 269; tutoring with 73–5
Web-Accessible Multimodal Interfaces (WAMI) 540
web conferences 215
Webcorp 343
Webheads in Action 215, 217–19
webinars 212
websites 19, 123–4, 401–3, 469–70
Wenger, E. 217
Wen-Ming, H. 366
West, R. 92
Westbrook, K. 4
White, C. 28
White, L. 377
White, P. 298
Whorf, R, 173–4
Whyte, S. 287
Wible, D. 380
Widdowson, H.G. 499–500
widgets 274
Wikipedia 204, 271
wikis 95–6, 269, 482
Wilkins, D. 461
Williams, E. 72
willingness to communicate (WTC) 43
Willis, J. 364
Wilson, A. 350
Wittgenstein, L. 200
*Wonderland* 422
Wong, K.C. 483, 528
Wong, R. 465
Word and Phrase 405
wordandphrase.info 365
*Word Coach* 448
Word Lens 89
word lists 350, 410, 464
word processors 13–14, 20
WordSmith 408–9
workplace learning 233
*World of Warcraft (WoW)* 19, 34–5, 42, 179, 422, 432, 450, 453–4
worlds 309
World Wide Web 11, 480
writable web 269

writing: academic 362–3; assessment testing 148; CALL tools for reading and 478–90; collaborative 481–3; descriptive 96–7; process of 275–6; skills 343, 364–7; teaching of 371; *see also* computer supported collaborative writing (CSCW)
written language corpora 362–75; background 362; and the classroom 364–7; defining 363–4; integration challenges 371, 375; in a multilingual context 367–71; from research to teaching 362–3
WTC (willingness to communicate) 43

Xbox One (Microsoft 2013) 418
Xiao, R. 392

Yang, D. 185–6
Yang, H. 527
Yang, P.C. 480
Yang, Y.F. 483
Yannakoudakis, H. 381
Yee, N. 455
Yeh, Y. 480, 486
Yoon, H. 343, 366, 479, 483
Yoshii, M. 465
Young, M.F. 34–5, 420, 422
young learners *see* children and gaming
YouTube 18, 178, 503
Yu, Y.T. 486
Yue, M. 392
Yun, J. 484
Yutdhana, S. 108

Zander, V. 257, 260
Zanón, T. 503
Zervas, P. 304
Zhang, T. 465
Zhang, W. 465
Zheng, D. 34–5, 420–2
Zimmerman, E. 424
*Zon* 420
zone of proximal development (ZPD) 462
Zourou, K. 277
ZPD (zone of proximal development) 462

Milton Keynes UK
Ingram Content Group UK Ltd.
UKHW031955060324
438929UK00018B/660